THE GROUNDBREAKERS!

THERE IS A FIRST TIME FOR EVERYTHING:

1,804 answers to first time happenings in Major League Baseball that you were curious to know

Richard L. Chilton

MINDSTIR MEDIA

Published by Mindstir Media
1931 Woodbury Ave. #182 | Portsmouth, New Hampshire 03801 | USA
1.800.767.0531 | www.mindstirmedia.com

Printed in the United States of America

ISBN-13: 978-0-9889595-3-8

Library of Congress Control Number: 2013932163

WHO NOT ONLY LOVES THE GAME OF BASEBALL as it's played, but is also captivated by its romance and history? I hope to bring within these pages some of that to light for not just the casual fan, or the committed fan, but for the baseball junkie that lies within many of you, as it does with me.

As you enter these pages you will be pleased, and surprised at who you find, for within them you will discover players, managers, umpires, teams, and executives that have broken new ground in the history of baseball. Those that have broken new ground by being the first on their team, the first in their league, or the first in the long history of major league baseball, to have accomplished a particular feat. We call these people and situations, "Groundbreakers". You will find the questions challenging, and they will stimulate the curiosity of you and your friends; and you will find many of the answers surprising.

There may be more information in "Groundbreakers" than you planned on, or needed, but I have always believed that if you truly enjoyed baseball you wanted to know not just a one or two word answer to your question, but the story behind the answer, taking you to the moment of its happening, and bringing the event more clearly into focus.

You may, at rare times, find a conflict as to the exact number or date used in this book, and therein lies a reason to wonder. It may be because accurate records can sometimes become distorted in the keeping of official statistics, as we have found, especially in baseball's earlier years. You can be assured that concentrated efforts were made, to check, recheck, and at times to check once again to provide accuracy to its contents.

Sit back, and in your mind recall the smell of the newly mown field, and hear the crack of the bat, and the roar of the fans, as this book takes you back when some event happened for the first time in major league history, and you may have been there! So "**LET'S PLAY BALL!**"

DEDICATION

This book is dedicated to my mother and father who,
back in the 1930's, introduced me to this wonderful
game by taking me to weekday afternoon games,
Ladies' Day and weekend doubleheaders.

I would be remiss if I didn't include my membership in
The Society for American Baseball Research (SABR) for
their wonderful efforts to keep my historical curiosity alive,
active, accurate and up-to-date by their continuing education.

THE LINEUP CARD

1. Who was the winning pitcher in the first National League game?

The first National League game was played on April 22, 1876 between the Boston Red Stockings (Braves), and the Philadelphia Athletics down at Philadelphia's Jefferson Street Grounds, before a crowd of about 3,000 fans - a sloppy game endured with twenty errors committed by both sides. Boston scored twice in the top of the 9th inning to come away with a 6-5 win, and the diminutive, 5'9" 140 pound Boston right-hander, Joe Borden, notched the first victory of the new major league.

2. Who was the first pitcher to throw a no-hitter in National League history?

George Washington "Grin" Bradley, a right-hander with the St. Louis Brown Stockings, threw the first major league no-hitter when he defeated the Hartford Dark Blues, and their Irish-born right-hander, Tommy Bond, 2-0, on July 15, 1876. Hartford was glad to see "Grin" move on as this was the third shutout by him in the three-game series.

3. Who was the first pitcher to hit over 200 batters in his career?

No, it wasn't southpaw Mitch "The Wild Thing" Williams, because of his nickname, who only hit 52 batters and threw 44 wild pitches in his eleven-year career. Rather we have to go back a century when Gus "Cannonball" Weyhing was terrorizing batters with his out-of-control pitches.

"Cannonball" pitched his first game for the Philadelphia Athletics on May 2, 1887, and by the time his rookie season was over he had led the league in hit batsman with 37, and had fired 49 wild pitches, but he did win 26 games.

The following season his wildness continued as he led the league for the second time in hitting batters, raising it to 42, and also led the league in wild pitches with 56, but, here again, he was a winning pitcher with 28 wins.

Gus went on to play for ten teams in his 14-season career, and racked up his 200th hit batsman in 1894 with the Philadelphia Phillies, and finished his career, on August 21, 1901, in his only game with the Cincinnati Reds, a complete 9-inning effort that he lost, giving up just 3 earned runs, but yes, he did hit two batters that day to bring his career hit batsman record to 277, to go along with his 240 wild pitches, but he did win 264 games while dropping 232 with a 3.88 Era.

4. Who was the first African-American pitcher in major league history to toss a no-hitter?

On May 12, 1955, in Wrigley Field, "Toothpick Sam" Jones of the Chicago Cubs became the first African-American pitcher to pitch a no-hitter when he defeated the Pittsburgh Pirates 4-0. There were some anxious moments in the top of the 9th inning when Jones walked the bases loaded, and then proceeded to strike out SS Dick Groat looking, RF Roberto Clemente swinging, and LF Frank Thomas looking, to preserve the shutout and the no-hitter.

5. Who was the first African-American pitcher in major league history to lose a game in which his opposing pitcher pitched a no-hitter?

The tables were turned on "Toothpick Sam" Jones on April 28, 1961, when he was on the losing side of the no-hitter pitched by 40-year old Warren Spahn, for his 290th win, and 52nd shutout, as Hank Aaron drove in the only Milwaukee Braves run of the game for a 1-0 win over the San Francisco Giants.

6. Who was the first pitcher to make at least 25 starts a season over 20 consecutive seasons?

We have to give the consistency award for being ready to toe the rubber on a regular basis to right-hander Greg "The Professor" Maddux who began his career on September 2, 1986, with the Chicago Cubs, and from 1987 through the 2006 season, with the Cubs and the Braves, and then with Los Angeles Dodgers, started the game out in Dodger Stadium on Sunday, August 13th against the San Francisco Giants right-hander Jason Schmidt, and these two aces dueled for 8 scoreless innings before each gave way to a reliever, and the Dodgers pulled out a 1-0 win in ten innings, but giving the title of being the first pitcher to start 25 games or more for 20 consecutive seasons to "The Professor."

7. Who was the first pitcher to pitch a 5-inning no-hitter?

After the New York Giants took the opener of a doubleheader, 8-2, against the St. Louis Cardinals, on September 14, 1903, rookie right-hander Leon "Red" Ames, starting his 17-year career, pitched a 5-inning no-hitter, striking out 7, before the game was called because of darkness brought on by an impending storm. It was one of two games Ames won that year, going 2-0.

8. Who was the first pitcher to win over 100 games as a relief pitcher?

Although his professional career was interrupted while in the minor leagues by World War II, where he won the Purple Heart in action during the Battle of the Bulge, Hoyt Wilhelm was drafted in 1948 by the New York Giants after two successful years, winning 20-games each year in the North Carolina State League. He stayed in their farm system until 1952, when, at the age of 28, the Giants brought him up to try his knuckleball talents coming from the bullpen. He made his major league debut with the Giants on April 18, 1952 as a relief pitcher, completing his rookie year by setting a then-record National League high of 71 relief appearances, recording league bests with a 2.43 Era, a .833 winning percentage, and 15 relief wins, for a 15-3 record. In addition he is widely known for hitting the only home run in his 21-year career in his first major league at bat on April 23, 1952.

On February 26, 1957 he was traded to the St. Louis Cardinals for outfielder Whitey Lockman. On September 21st he was put on waivers and selected by the Cleveland Indians.

After being waived to the Cleveland Indians by the St. Louis Cardinals, with 363 consecutive relief appearances, Tribe manager Bobby Bragan gave him six starts before waiving him to the Baltimore Orioles. There, in his ninth major league start, facing the New York Yankees on a drizzly September 20, 1958 day he pitched a no-hitter.

In 1958 he went to Baltimore on waivers. Sent off to the Chicago White Sox, in a multi-player trade involving shortstop Luis Aparicio, on January 14, 1963, he ended the 1967 season passing the 100 wins in relief level with 106. He later set a major league record for pitchers, in 1968, by playing in 319 games without an error.

Relief was where it was for Hoyt, he concluded his 21-year career with the Los Angeles Dodgers on July 10, 1972 with a record 124 wins in relief, 143 wins overall to become the first relief pitcher to record over 100 wins, and, along with his 227 saves, to be the first relief pitcher, in 1985, to enter Cooperstown.

9. There have been five pitchers who have had their no-hitters broken up with two outs in the 9th inning by a home run; who was the first to suffer this chance for fame?

Rick Wise, while pitching for the Boston Red Sox on July 2, 1975, had two out in the bottom of the 9th inning of the first game of a doubleheader at County Stadium, when Milwaukee's George Scott clouted a two-run home run to make it 6-2, and Danny Darwin followed with a solo shot as Wise won the opener 6-3, and became the first to lose immortality by a final batters' home run.

10. Who was the first pitcher to give up a home run to Roger Maris in 1961 launching him to his record 61 that season?

Paul Foytack, the Detroit Tigers right-hander, surrendered Maris's first home run of the 1961 season on April 26th in Detroit.

11. Who was the first relief specialist in major league history?

That would be Fred "Firpo" Marberry, the Washington Senators right-hander. In 1924, his second season in the nation's capitol, he led the league in games with 50, and in games saved with 15, and followed that up in 1925 with 15 games saved, and in 1926, again leading the league for the third consecutive year with 22 saved. In his 14-year career he led the league in saves five times, for a career total of 101 to be acknowledged as the first relief specialist in major league history.

12. Who was the first American League African-American pitcher to win 20 games in a season?

Jim "Mudcat" Grant, who came up on April 17, 1958 with Cleveland, and pitched well for his first seven years with the Indians, before moving over to the Minnesota Twins, where, in 1965, he had his finest season, leading the American League in wins with a 21-7 record, completing fourteen games, including six shutouts, to become the first African American pitcher in the American League to break the 20-wins plateau.

13. Who was the first pitcher to win the coveted Cy Young Award in both the American and National Leagues?

Right-hander Gaylord Perry of the San Francisco Giants came in second in the Cy Young Award voting in 1970 after leading the league in wins with 23, complete games with 41, and innings pitched with 328.2. Traded to Cleveland on November 29, 1971, Perry had another fine year winning the American League Cy Young Award with his league leading 24 wins, losing 16, and 29 complete games, while posting a 1.92 Era. After being traded to the Texas Rangers on June 13, 1975, and spending three years there, he moved on to the San Diego Padres on January 25, 1978, and that season, at age 39, won his second Cy Young Award with a 21-6, 2.73 Era to become the first pitcher to capture the Cy Young Award in both leagues.

14. Who was the first major league pitcher to strike out four consecutive batters in one inning?

Ed "Cannonball" Crane, the New York Giants right-hander, on his way to a one-hit, 1-0 win over the Chicago Colts (Cubs), was the first pitcher to strike out four consecutive batters in one inning when he set down four Colts, the first one reaching first on a dropped third strike, in the 5th inning of a game on October 4, 1888.

15. Who was the first pitcher with 300 career saves to come on in relief of a pitcher with 300 career wins?

On Monday, April 8, 1991 Nolan Ryan, with the Texas Rangers, started a game in which Goose Gossage, with 300 career saves, came on in relief in the 8th inning of a 5-4 loss to the Milwaukee Brewers.

16. Who was the first modern day pitcher to pitch a pair of complete game victories, and throw more than 18 innings that day?

It was a tall order for the right-handed Detroit rookie, "Kickapoo Ed" Summers when he took the mound at Bennett Park on Friday, September 25, 1908, He started and pitched a complete game against the Philadelphia Athletics winning, 7-2.

He then turned around and started the second game of the double-header and got locked up in a scoreless duel through nine innings, and kept pitching through the 10th inning when his teammates finally pushed across a run, and "Kickapoo" had won his second game with a two-hit shutout, 1-0. That made him a "Groundbreaker" by being the first to pitch two complete game victories covering over 18 innings in one day.

17. In the modern era of baseball who threw the first nine-inning no-hitter?

On July 12, 1900 Cincinnati Reds' southpaw, Frank "Noodles" Hahn, pitched a nine-inning no-hitter, the first in the modern era, defeating the Philadelphia Phillies, 4-0, in Crosley Field. Hahn gave up five walks, but struck out seven.

18. Who was the first pitcher to pitch in over 100 games in a single season?

Mike Marshall, the Los Angeles Dodgers right-hander, set a new major league record in 1974. He became the first pitcher to pitch in over 100 games when he pitched in 106 games, covering 208 innings, saving a league leading 21 games, and compiling a 15-12 record, all in relief.

19. Who was the first relief pitcher to save 40 or more games in a season?

Dan Quisenberry, the Kansas City Royals right-hander, made his major league debut on July 8, 1979 as a relief pitcher, and in the following season led the American League in games with 75, games finished with 68 and saves with 33. In 1983 "Quiz" appeared in a league leading 69 games, finishing 62 and saving 45. That effort made him the first relief pitcher to save over 40 or more games in a season.

20. Who was the first pitcher to record his last major league win by throwing one pitch for a triple play?

Ken Ash knew how to go out on a winning note. The Cincinnati Reds' right-hander, with a heretofore unimpressive four-year career record of 6-8 with a 4.96 Era was called upon to come on in relief of right-hander Larry Benton in the top of the 6th[th] inning at Redland Field on Sunday, July 27, 1930, with Cincinnati down by a run a 3-2 to "Marse Joe" McCarthy's Chicago Cubs only to find the bases loaded, and no one out, and first baseman Charlie Grimm at the plate. Ash, known for a nasty curveball that got him ground ball outs, fired his first pitch, and Grimm slammed into a 4-5-2-3-5 triple play to end the inning. In the bottom half of the inning Evar Swanson pinch-hit for Ash, and the Reds came back to score four runs and take a 6-3 lead. Right-hander Ray "Jockey" Kolp came on to pitch the last three innings to get the save.

Ash, by throwing just one pitch, retired the side and won his last major league game. His final mound appearance was on September 26, 1930 and his final season showed a fine 2-0 record, half of those wins coming on one pitch.

21. Who was the first pitcher to strike out the side on nine pitches?

Forty pitchers in major league baseball have thrown nine-pitch, three-strikeout half-innings. In fact three have done it more than once.

The first to do it was right-hander John Clarkson of the Boston Beaneaters of the National League in the 3rd inning, on June 4, 1889, as he set down centerfielder Jim Fogarty, right fielder Sam Thompson, and first baseman Sid Farrar in the 3rd inning in his 4-2 win over the Philadelphia Quakers (Phillies).

22. **Who was the first pitcher, in the modern era, to retire the side by striking out three batters on nine pitches?**

Southpaw George Edward "Rube" Waddell, on July 1, 1902, wins his first game for the Philadelphia Athletics, after having pitched for the Chicago Orphans in the National League, in 1901. He shutout the Baltimore Orioles, 2-0, on two hits, pitching to only 27 batters, for the two base runners had been erased by the strong arm of catcher Ossee Schreckengost.

In the 3rd inning he struck out shortstop Billy Gilbert, utility 2B "Handsome Harry" Howell, and RHP Jack Cronin on nine pitches, and he didn't stop there for he struck out that same trio of batters again in the 6th and 9th innings, but on more than nine pitches.

23. **Who was the first pitcher to win the Cy Young Award while losing more games than he won?**

Right-hander Eric Gagne of the Los Angeles Dodgers made his debut on September 7, 1999 starting five games, finishing none in 30 innings of work that gave him a 1-1 record in his rookie season.

In 2002 he was converted into a reliever and maintained that role up to, and including, the 2003 season where his final stats that season showed a 2-3 won-lost record, finishing 67 games, and saving 55, to lead the league in those two categories, and having a very low 1.20 Era, which was good enough to be named the first pitcher to win a Cy Young Award with a losing record.

24. Who was the first pitcher to pitch in 1,000 games in his career?

Throwing the knuckle ball as Hoyt Wilhelm did no doubt added to his ability to maintain some arm strength in his later year in the major leagues. That said, for he who pitched for the Giants, Cardinals, Indians, Orioles, White Sox, Angels Braves, Cubs, and Dodgers in his 21-year career, that knuckle ball made it possible for him to pitch in 1,070 games in his major league career, far surpassing any challenger that quickly comes to mind.

25. Who was the first pitcher to start over 800 major league games?

That record is safely held by Denton "Cy" Young who started 815 games in his career from 1890 to 1911. Nolan Ryan at 773, and Don Sutton at 756 just were not born sooner to be challengers.

26. Who was the first, and only, pitcher to have over 100 shutouts in his

major league career?

No one comes close to Walter "Big Train" Johnson when it comes to shutouts as he recorded 110 in his 21-year career with the Washington Senators from 1907 to 1927.

27. Who was the first pitcher to record over 100 wins after the age of 40?

Some say "Life begins at 40," but Phil Niekro must have believed that life just continues on after 40, and so does winning games. He didn't let age stand in his way as he was the first to win over 100 games, after four decades, by winning 121 games before hanging up his cleats at the youthful age of 42 with a 318-274 record.

28. Who was the first pitcher to win 19 consecutive games?

Richard "Rube" Marquard, the southpaw of the New York Giants, won 19 consecutive games beginning with Opening Day in 1912. He was the first player to have such a lengthy consecutive game-winning streak.

29. Who was the first modern day National League pitcher to start over 600 games in his major league career?

The great Milwaukee Braves southpaw, Warren Spahn, stepped on the rubber on Friday, August 23, 1963 out in Dodger Stadium, against the Los Angeles Dodgers, before a crowd of 36,013, to start the 601 game of his career to be the first pitcher to exceed the 600-start mark, surpassing fellow Hall of Fame member, Grover Cleveland Alexander, who had previously held the record of 600. Spahnie closed down Los Angeles with an easy 6-1 win.

30. In these days of shuffling pitchers into a game, who was the first, and only, pitcher to have pitched 50 complete games in a season?

Right-hander Amos Rusie, "The Hoosier Thunderbolt", of the New York Giants, led the National League in a few categories in 1893, games (56), games started (52), complete games (50), innings pitched (482), hits (451), walks (218), strikeouts (208), shutouts (4), Era (2.78) that went along with his 29-18 won-lost record. Those 50 complete games don't look, at this writing, to be ever challenged.

31. Who was the first modern day pitcher to win 40 games in a single season?

One has to go way back to 1904 when "Happy Jack" Chesbro, the right-hander with the New York Highlanders (Yankees), took most every pitching honor that season by leading the American League in wins (41), games (55), games started (51), complete games (48), innings pitched (454.2), and batters faced (1720) and a winning percentage of .774.

For all that glory came despair when in the last game of the 1904 season, before 30,000 fans in New York, on October 10th, when in the top of the 9th, with the score tied, 2-2, and Boston catcher Lou Criger on third, Chesbro has a spitball get away from him for a wild pitch and Criger comes across to score the winning run, and the pennant clincher, as Bill Dinneen shuts down the Highlanders in the bottom of the 9th. To this day no one has exceeded "Happy Jack" and his 40 wins in a single season.

32. Who was the first modern day pitcher to win the Triple Crown of pitching, leading his league in wins, strikeouts, and Era.

In 1901, the man for whom the Cy Young Award was named, for pitching excellence, Denton True "Cy" Young, while pitching for the Boston Americans (Red Sox), created the Triple Crown by leading the newly formed American League in wins with 33 (with 5 shutouts), in strikeouts with 158, while posting an excellent 1.62 Era to earn the crown.

33. Who was the first pitcher to start, complete, and win both games of a doubleheader on the same day?

We will go back a long way for this one for it was on September 9, 1876 that the Hartford Dark Blues right-hander "Curveball" Candy Cummings pitched a morning game against Cincinnati in the inaugural season of the National League and had an easy 14-4 win.

Coming back in the afternoon game he again put down the Reds 8-4, to be the first pitcher to pitch two complete winning games on the same day, and it signaled for the first time that two games were played in the same day in major league history.

34. Who was the first modern day pitcher to pitch, and also win, two games on the same day?

Though Candy Cummings was inducted into the Hall of Fame, not because of his active career record of two seasons, and a 21-22 pitching record, but because he laid claim to being the person who invented the curveball, which doubters have had a bit of a trouble disproving. Nevertheless he was the first to have pitched, and won, both ends of a doubleheader.

Moving on to the modern era the New York Giants had a right-hander by the name of Joe McGinnity, who also has an address at Cooperstown, who on August 1, 1903, asked manager John McGraw if he could pitch both ends of the upcoming doubleheader with the Boston Braves.

It seemed that the Giants had fallen into a dreadful slump of winning just two of their last 13 games and needed a lift that McGinnity thought he could give.

McGraw gave him the go-ahead and McGinnity went out and pitched a complete nine-inning game setting down the Braves with six hits and winning 4-1.

Back he came for the second game and duplicated his former effort, allowing just six hits and winning 5-2.

McGinnity pulled this amazing feat three times that month on August 8th against the Brooklyn Dodgers, and on the 31st against the Philadelphia Phillies. He was the first pitcher to pitch and win three doubleheaders in one month.

Yes, this is the same Joe McGinnity who was quickly dubbed "Iron Man Joe" for this and similar efforts during his ten-year, 247 wins and 2.64 Era career. He wasn't called "Iron Man" for nothing.

35. Who was the first, and only, pitcher to pitch two shutouts in one day?

A manager couldn't ask for more out of his pitcher than skipper Frank Chance got out of "Big Ed" Reulbach on Saturday, September 26, 1908. With the Cubs fighting the Giants for the top spot in the National League, the Chicago right-hander went into Brooklyn and pitched a five-hit shutout in the morning game, beating Dodger right-hander Irvin "Kaiser" Wilhelm, 5-0.

Coming back in the afternoon game Reulbach was even more effective, allowing just three hits and a walk as he defeated Brooklyn southpaw Jim Pastorius, 3-0 in just one hour and twelve minutes, to become the first pitcher ever to pitch two shutouts in one day.

36. Who was the first modern day pitcher to win over 20 games for a last place team?

Southpaw Frank "Noodles" Hahn made his pitching debut on April 18, 1899 for the Cincinnati Reds and had an outstanding freshman year pitching 309 innings, having a 23-8, 2.68 Era record and leading the National

League in strikeouts with 145.

In 1901 Cincinnati wound up in last place with a sad record of 52 wins and 87 losses. That didn't stop Noodles from having another of his four career twenty-game seasons by leading the National League in innings pitched with 375.1, in strikeouts with 239, and complete games with 41. He also won 22 games which was 42.3% of his team's victories, the same number of wins as his three other starting teammates combined.

37. Who was the first pitcher to pick up two victories in relief in the same day?

On September 10, 1902 the Philadelphia Athletics southpaw George "Rube" Waddell came on in relief, before a crowd of 17,291, and pitched eight innings of relief as the A's went on to defeat the Baltimore Orioles 9-5.

Rube came back to pitch two more innings of relief in the nightcap and picked up his second win of the day, 5-4, to become the first relief pitcher to pick up a pair of wins in the same day.

38. Who was the first, and only, pitcher to strike out ten batters in a row?

Tom Seaver, the ace right-hander of the New York Mets, finished off his 2-1 win over the San Diego Padres on April 22, 1970 by striking out the last ten Padres in succession to become the first pitcher to strike out ten batters in a row.

It started by striking out Padres leftfielder Al Ferrara for the third out in the top of the 6th inning and continued on through the 7th, 8th, and 9th innings when he again struck out Ferrara for the third out of the game, and the 10th consecutive strike out in a row

39. Who was the first pitcher to have his perfect game broken up with two outs in the 9th inning?

George "Hooks" Wiltse, the New York Giant southpaw, saw his perfect game disappear on July 4, 1908, when, after retiring 26 Philadelphia Phillies in a row, with two outs in the 9th inning, he hit his opposing pitcher, George McQuillan, on a 1-and-2 pitch. On the prior pitch home plate umpire Charles Rigler had called it a ball, which appeared to be strike three, much to the dismay of "Hooks", and Giant fans who thought it a third strike, giving Wiltse his perfect game.

"Hooks" went on to pitch a hitless 10th inning and came away with a 1-0 no-hit victory when Art Devlin singled and scored on two Phillies' errors in the bottom of the 10th.

Rigler later admitted he had blown the strike three call and spent years supplying Wiltse with cigars to make up for that blown call.

40. Who was the first pitcher to give up a home run to Hank Aaron?

Vic Raschi, the St. Louis Cardinals right-hander, on Friday, April 23, 1954, became the first of a great many to give up a home run to Hank Aaron on his road to 755 career round-trippers. It came in the 6th inning, at Busch Stadium, a one out, solo home run, as the Milwaukee Braves went on to a 7-5 win.

41. Who was the first pitcher to give up a home run to Willie Mays?

Southpaw Warren Spahn of the Boston Braves, both future Hall of Fame residents, not only gave up Willie's first major league hit, on Monday, May 28, 1951, but also the first of Willie's 660 career home runs, when he hit a screamer into the left field stands of the Polo Grounds in the 1st inning for the Giants only run as Spahn and the Braves came away with a 4-1 win.

42. Who was first pitcher to win the Cy Young Award?

Don Newcombe, the Brooklyn Dodgers right-hander, in the sole selection for the newly established Cy Young Award, won it in 1956 with a 27-7, 3.06 Era which went along with his selection as the National League's Most Valuable Player Award, as he helped lead the Dodgers into the Fall Classic.

43. Who was the first American League pitcher to win the Cy Young Award?

In the third year of awarding the Cy Young Award "Bullet Bob" Turley, the New York Yankees right-hander, was the first American League pitcher to win the award based on his 21-7, 2.97 Era, in which he led his league in complete games with 19, and bases on balls with 128.

44. Who was the first 40-year old pitcher to have as his battery mate, a catcher who, too, was over 40 years old?

If you will go back to October 4, 1913 you will find that Washington manager, and right-hander, Clark "The Old Fox" Griffith, took the mound at age 43 for one inning in an end of the season "fun" game in which eight pitchers were used, five in the 9th inning, against the Boston Red Sox, while his older battery mate, coach John (Jack) Ryan, at age 44, handled his pitches. Washington won out 10-9, defeating Fred "Spitball" Anderson who went the distance.

45. Who was the first pitcher to give up a home run to Barry Bonds?

If you go back to Wednesday, June 4, 1986, you will see that outfielder Barry Bonds went 4-for-5, and hit his first major league home run, a solo shot in the 5th inning, off right-hander Craig McMurtry of the Atlanta Braves, as Pittsburgh cruised to a 12-3 win over Atlanta.

46. Who was the first pitcher to strike out as many batters in a game as his age?

Robert William Feller, better known as "Rapid Robert" began his major league career with the Cleveland Indians on July 19, 1936 at age 17, right out of Van Meter High School in Van Meter, Iowa.

He started eight games, finished five, pitched 62 innings, struck out 76 batters and had a 5-3 record.

It didn't take Feller long to show off his flaming fastball having struck out 15 and 10 batters in a game during the season leading up to Sunday, September 13, 1936 at League Park.

On that day against the Philadelphia Athletics Feller gave up two runs on two hits and struck out 17 batters over the course of nine innings to set down Philadelphia 5-2. He struck out everyone in the lineup at least once, second baseman Hugh Luby three times, and five others twice on the way to his 17 strike outs which made him the first pitcher to strike out as many batters as years he had been alive.

47. Who was the first, and only, pitcher to win a game against every team in both the American and National Leagues?

Alois "Al" Leiter who made his pitching debut, at age 21, in Yankee Stadium, on Tuesday, September 15, 1987, with the New York Yankees, and went on to pitch for the Blue Jays, the Marlins, and Mets finishing off his 19 major league seasons on October 2, 2005 back with the Yankees.

During his career the southpaw from Toms River, New Jersey pitched and won a World Series game with Toronto, in 1993, against the Philadelphia Phillies in Game One at the SkyDome in Toronto. In 1997 he started Game 3 of the World Series for the Florida Marlins against the Cleveland Indians, with no decision. He started Game 1 for the New York Mets in the 2000 World Series against the Yankees without a decision in a game that went 12 innings. He came back in Game 5 taking the loss as the Yankees scored two in the top of the 9th to win 4-2.

Then on Tuesday, April 30, 2002, out in Bank One Ballpark, Leiter, then with the New York Mets, allowed just three hits as he defeated the Arizona Diamondbacks, 10-1, to become the first pitcher to defeat every team in both the American League and the National League.

Over the course of his long career, Leiter won 162 games, beating every team in the major leagues at least once, to be the first, and only, pitcher to be able to say that he defeated all 30 major league teams.

48. Who was the first American League pitcher to throw two no-hitters in a single season?

Allie "Superchief" Reynolds, the Yankees right-hander, a five-time All-Star, no-hit the Cleveland Indians on July 12th, 1951, winning 1-0, and came back on September 28th to duplicate his earlier feat, this time the Boston Red Sox were the victims, 8-0.

49. Who was the first pitcher to pitch to three brothers in consecutive order in the same game?

This unusual event happened on Tuesday, September 10, 1963 at the Polo Grounds, in New York, when San Francisco Giants manager, Alvin Dark, down 3-0, in the top of the 8th inning, sent the three Alou brothers up to face the right-hander Carlton Willey of the New York Mets.

Jesus Alou pinch-hit for SS Jose Pagan and grounded out to shortstop Al Moran. Matty Alou pinch-hit for the pitcher, Bob Garibaldi, and struck out. That brought up the leadoff hitter, and third brother, RF Felipe who bounced back to Willey who tossed to 1B Tim Harkness to retire the side, and made Willey a "Groundbreaker" by being the first pitcher in major league history to retire three brothers in order and the 14,945 at the game can attest to it.

The Giants went on to lose, 4-2, with Willie McCovey's 38th, and Orlando Cepeda's 29th home runs, accounting for the Giants scoring.

50. Who was the first pitcher to pitch five shutouts against one team in one season?

Larry Jaster, the St. Louis Cardinals' southpaw, shutout the Los Angeles Dodgers on five mound appearances; April 25th, July 3rd, July 29th, August 19th, and September 28th in 1966. He hurled three at Dodger Stadium and two at Busch Stadium.

51. Who was the first, and only, pitcher to pitch a complete game of twenty or more innings, and not issue a walk?

One might say that Charles "Babe" Adams, the Pittsburgh Pirates right-hander, had things well under control in the July 17, 1914 game in Forbes Field against New York Giants southpaw Richard "Rube" Marquard.

Adams was known for his excellent location control, and his career average of 1.29 walks per nine innings was the second lowest in 20th century history.

In a game which resembled more of a marathon than a nine inning game, Adams was locked in a 1-1 pitching duel with Marquard through 20 innings, and although he had given up base hits, his usual excellent control had not deserted him as he had not allowed a player to walk.

In the top of the 21st inning, with the score tied, 1-1, "Laughing Larry" Doyle, the Giants second baseman, hit a two-run home run which gave Rube, and the Giants a 3-1 win.

What makes this story so unusual is not just the length of the game, and that both pitchers went the distance, but the fact that Babe Adams pitched the entire game, giving up 12 hits, without issuing one walk, the longest non-walk game in major league history. Marquard gave up 15, hits along with only two walks.

In today's game going nine is a reason for joy, can't imagine going 21 to ever be broken, especially by two pitchers.

52. Who was the first, and only, pitcher to ever finish up a game by striking out the entire batting order in the 7th, 8th, and 9th innings?

Tom Seaver, the ace right-hander of the New York Mets, struck out the final nine San Diego Padres, 19 in total, in winning a 2-1 two hitter on April 22, 1970.

53. Who was the first ambidextrous pitcher in major league history?

One has to go all the way back to Tuesday, July 18, 1882 when the ambidextrous Tony "The Apollo of the Box" Mullane, born in Cork, Ireland, took the mound for the Louisville Eclipse at Union Park, Baltimore, against the Orioles.

Starting off the 4th inning Mullane pitched left-handed against Baltimore's left-handed batters, and switched to pitching right-handed to Baltimore's right-handed batters.

The strategy worked pretty well until there were two outs in the 9th inning when first baseman Charlie Householder unloaded his only home run of the season which beat Mullane 9-8.

Almost eleven years to the day, on July 14, 1893, with Mullane now with Baltimore, he pitched the 9th inning left-handed, and the Chicago White Stockings (Cubs) found that to be to their liking as they added three more runs and went on to defeat Mullane with a 10-2 win.

Let the record show that "The Apollo of the Box" was the first pitcher to be able to go both ways.

54. Who was the first, and only, 20th century pitcher to pitch in a major league game throwing both left-handed and right-handed?

Greg Harris, with the Montreal Expos on September 28, 1995, pitching in relief against the Cincinnati Reds in the 9th inning that day, retired Reggie Sanders on a ground ball, pitching right-handed. With manager Felipe Alou's permission, Harris switched to being a southpaw, and walked Hal Morris, and got Eddie Taubensee to ground out.

Going back to being a right-hander Harris got Bret Boone to ground out to retire the side as Cincinnati went on to win 9-7.

The six-fingered glove Harris used for his ambidextrous exercise was sent off to be exhibited at the Hall of Fame.

55. Who was the first African-American pitcher to be a 20-game winner in the major leagues?

Don Newcombe, the hard-throwing Brooklyn Dodgers right-hander, became the first when he went 20-9 in 1951.

56. Who was the first pitcher to lose a complete game no hitter?

It was on a Thursday, April 23, 1964, down in Colt Stadium, before a meager crowd of 5,426, where Houston right-hander Ken Johnson was locked in scoreless tie with Cincinnati Reds southpaw Joe Nuxhall.

Going into the top of the 9th inning Joe Nuxhall grounded out to Bob Aspromonte at third, bringing up Pete Rose who bounced weakly back to Johnson, but his throw to 1B Pete Runnells went wild sending Rose to second on the error.

He moved over to third as Reds' 3B Chico Ruiz grounded out to Aspromonte. Next up was CF Vida Pinson who hit a ground ball to 2B Nellie Fox who misplayed it for an error as Rose crossed the plate for the only run. Frank Robinson then flied out to left to end the inning. Nuxhall closed down the Colt .45's in the 9th to take the win, 1-0. Johnson took the loss to become the first pitcher to pitch a complete game no-hitter and lose.

57. Who was the first, and only, pitcher to win 20 or more games and bat over .400 in the same season?

It was the Hall of Fame right-hander, Walter "The Big Train" Johnson, who had a 20-7, 3.07 Era on the mound and batted .433, going 42 for 97 at the plate, including two home runs and 20 runs batted in for the Washington Senators in 1925.

58. Who was the first pitcher to pitch a no-hitter in his first major league start?

When this right-hander made his pitching debut on April 18, 1953 with the St. Louis Browns, after being traded by the Syracuse Chiefs of the International League, for Paris-born right-hander Harry Makowsky, a.k.a. "Duke" Markell, and $35,000, no one paid particular mind, and rightly so.

Alva Lee "Bobo" Holloman didn't have inspiring credentials, but neither did Markell. Bobo spent the 1953 season appearing in 22 games, starting 10 and finishing one with a very unimpressive 5.23 Era.

Why am I telling you this? Everyone has their "15 minutes of fame" and that is what Bobo had on May 6, 1953, just a couple of weeks after his major league debut, when he faced the Philadelphia Athletics in Sportsman's Park, St. Louis.

In his 5th mound appearance, and his first major league starting assignment, Bobo came through with a 6-0 no-hitter beating A's southpaw Morrie Martin, 6-0.

Bobo not only shone on the mound, but contributed to the Browns' offense by driving home three runs on a pair of singles, the only hits of his brief career. I say brief for by July 19th Bobo will be out of the major leagues, with a career record of 3-7, and an Era of 5.23 over 65.1 innings.

Bobo can still lay claim to three distinctions, the fewest wins by a pitcher who has pitched a no-hitter, and the first to pitch one in his first major league start, and the only pitcher to have one out of every three career wins be a no-hitter.

59. **Who threw the first and only, Opening Day no-hitter in major league history?**

Bob Feller, the fireball right-hander of the Cleveland Indians, threw an Opening Day no-hitter on April 16, 1940 against the Chicago White Sox in their home field of Comiskey Park, Chicago, and winning 1-0.

That event led to a most unusual, and to date never duplicated, statistic that showed the entire White Sox team having the same batting average after the game, as before it 000.

60. **Who was the first American League pitcher to pitch and lose a complete game no-hitter?**

Andy Hawkins, the New York Yankees right-hander, on Sunday, July 1, 1990, had the terrible misfortune of pitching a no-hitter against the Chicago White Sox, but came up on the losing end of a 4-0 score.

With two out in a scoreless game in the bottom of the 8th, out in Comiskey Park, the Yankees' third baseman, Mike Blowers, misplayed right fielder Sammy Sosa's routine ground ball for an error. Sosa then stole second base, and Hawkins proceeded to walk shortstop Ozzie Guillen, and then centerfielder Lance Johnson to load the bases. That's when leftfielder Jim Leyritz dropped third baseman Robin Ventura's fly ball, and right fielder Jesse Barfield did the same when he lost DH Ivan Calderon's fly ball in the sun, allowing four runs to score. Leftfielder Dan Pasqua ended the inning by hitting a pop fly to shortstop Alvaro Espinoza.

The 8th inning line score showed four runs, no hits, three errors and two walks. The Yankees went down in the 9th, and with the White Sox ahead they didn't have to bat in the 9th and came away with a 4-0 win. The Pale Hose, with right-hander Barry Jones in relief, won the game, and Hawkins, before a crowd of 30,642, lost his bid for immortality.

61. **Who was the first pitcher in major league history to win the Triple Crown?**

The first of 15 different National League pitchers to have won the difficult acclamation of being a Triple Crown winner was Ireland-born Tommy Bond, of the Boston Red Caps, in 1877, when he won 40 games, struck out 170 batters and had a 2.11 Era.

62. **Who was the first modern day pitcher to pitch a perfect game?**

Denton True "Cy" Young, of the Boston Americans, was the first modern day pitcher to not allow a runner to get on base, recording a perfect game on May 5, 1904 when, at the Huntington Avenue Baseball Grounds, he shutout the Philadelphia Athletics, 3-0

63. Who were the first pitchers to tie for the Triple Crown Award?

It was a pair of Hall of Fame pitchers in 1905 that created the first tie for the Triple Crown Award

In the National League right-hander Christy Mathewson of the New York Giants went 31-9, struck out 206 batters, led the league in shutouts as well with 8, and posted a 1.28 Era.

Over in the American League southpaw Rube Waddell of the Philadelphia Athletics had a 27-10 record, struck out 287 batters, and compiled 1.48 Era.

64. Who was the first pitcher to win the coveted Triple Crown Award without winning twenty games?

The first time in history that a pitcher managed to capture the Triple Crown Award without being a 20-game winner happened in the American League, in 2006, when southpaw Johan Santana of the Minnesota Twins took the award with 19 wins, 6 losses, 245 strikeouts and a 2.77 Era.

65. Who was the first, and only, National League pitcher to win the prestigious Triple Crown Award while winning less than twenty games?

In 2007, just a year after Johan Santana broke the ice on under 20-game winners capturing the Triple Crown, right-hander Jake Peavy, while pitching for the San Diego Padres, did just that by winning 19 games, losing 6, striking out 240 batters, and posting a 2.54 Era

66. Who was the first pitcher to strike out over 2,000 batters in both leagues?

When it comes to strike outs the name Nolan Ryan quickly comes to mind. "The Ryan Express" struck out 2,359 National League batters and 3,355 American League batters in his 27-year career.

67. Who was the first pitcher to strike out Willie Mays?

The first of Willie Mays' strikeouts in his 22-season career happened in his first major league at bat, after being brought up from the Minneapolis Millers on May 25, 1951, when right-hander Emory "Bubba" Church of the Philadelphia Phillies gave Willie his "welcome to the big leagues" introduction as he slipped a called strike three past him. It didn't figure into the game as the Giants went on to an 8-5 win.

68. Who was the first pitcher to lead his league in strikeouts for two consecutive years, each year with a different team?

Right-hander Early Wynn (don't you love that name for a pitcher?), made his major league debut on September 13, 1939 with the Washington Senators, and went on for 23 colorful seasons with the Senators, Indians, and the White Sox before finishing out his career, 24 years to the day, on September 13, 1963 with the Cleveland Indians, where he pitched, and won, his 300th major league victory.

During the course of his career, where he acknowledged he would brush back his mother if she crowded the plate, "Gus" as was his nickname, struck out an American League best 184 batters while with Cleveland in 1957.

During the off season Wynn was traded on December 4, 1957 to the Chicago White Sox where he continued his fanning ability by sending a league-leading 179 junior circuit batters back to the dugout mumbling. With that effort Wynn became the first pitcher to lead his league in strikeouts for two consecutive years. "Gus" went on to establish residency in Cooperstown, moving in the summer of 1972.

69. Who was the first, and only, pitcher to win back-to-back Most Valuable Player Awards?

Southpaw "Prince Hal" Newhouser of the Detroit Tigers was the first, and only, pitcher to win consecutive MVP Awards when he won in 1944 with a record of 29-9, and a league leading strikeout total of 187, and a 2.22 Era. He came right back in 1945 with a 25-9, 212 strikeouts, 29 complete games, 1.81 Era season; tops in the American League, to be the first and only pitcher to do it in back-to-back years.

He came in second to Ted Williams in the balloting in 1946, when he had a 26-9, 1.94 Era, with 275 strikeouts

70. Who was the first pitcher to strike out over 300 batters in a season?

Hall of Fame southpaw George "Rube" Waddell, struck out a league leading 302 batters, pitched 34 complete games, with a 21-16, 2.44 Era record for the Philadelphia Athletics in 1903, becoming the first to go over 300 K's in a season.

71. Who were the first two defending Cy Young Award pitchers to face each other in a regular season game?

On August 28, 1989, southpaw Frank "Sweet Music" Viola, of the New York Mets, having won the 1988 American League Cy Young Award with the Minnesota Twins with a 24-7 record, out-pitched Orel "Bulldog" Hershiser, the 1988 National League Cy Young Award winner, who had a 23-8 record with the Los Angeles Dodgers, 1-0, in a regular season match up of defending Cy Young winners. It was the first time in major league history that two defending Cy Young Award winners faced each other.

72. Who was the first modern day pitcher to strike out four batters in one inning?

There is some controversy over who was the first pitcher to strike out four batters in one inning, with some saying it was "Hooks" Wiltse in 1906, and others claim that the newspaper account in the Brooklyn Eagle, describing southpaw Guy "Doc" White's effort as the first, being the correct version.

On July 21, 1902, in Brooklyn, the Superbas walloped the Philadelphia Phillies, 10-1, racking "Doc" White, who went on to lose 20 games that year, for 14 hits. Doc, however, will remember the 5th inning well, not for the four runs racked up by the Superbas, but for the four batters he struck out in that inning to finally get back to the dugout.

Shortstop "Bad Bill" Dahlen, and third baseman Charlie Irwin, both struck out. Then second baseman Ed Wheeler, flailing at a bad pitch, for strike three, had a reprise as the ball skipped through catcher Charlie "Red" Dooin's hands, going back to the fence, and Wheeler ended up on first. After Brooklyn's pitcher, Frank Kitson, singled, White retired the side by striking out leftfielder Jimmy Sheckard, giving "Doc" the distinction of being the first modern day pitcher to have to strike out four batters to get out of an inning.

73. Who was the first modern day pitcher to strike out seven batters in two consecutive innings?

We mentioned in the previous item, #72, about the erroneous claim that New York Giant southpaw George "Hooks" Wiltse was the first to strike out four batters in one inning. Well, there can be no confusion as to who was the first to strike out seven consecutive batters in two innings.

On May 15, 1906, in the 4th inning of a game against the Cincinnati

Reds, "Hooks" struck out the side, then in the 5th he struck out the leadoff hitter, third baseman Jim Delahanty, but when catcher Roger Bresnahan dropped strike three Delahanty went on to first. So "Hooks" proceeded to strike out the next three batters, giving him four for the inning, and seven over the course of the 4th and 5th innings, a major league record to this day.

74. Who was the first pitcher to strike out four batters in one inning twice in the same season?

On May 12, 1999 Chuck Finley, pitching 8 innings, and Troy Percival in the 9th, pitch a combined 3-hit, shutout for the Anaheim Angels 1-0 win over the New York Yankees. Finley struck out 11 Yankees including four in the 3rd inning, and became the 33rd pitcher in major league history to have a four- fanned frame. Showing his May effort was no fluke the 6'6" southpaw goes up against the Tigers of the Motor City, on August 15th, defeating Detroit, 10-2, and in the process strikes out four, to start the game in the 1st inning, and then became the first pitcher to strike out four batters twice in the same season.

75. Continuing on with that theme, who was the first pitcher to strike out four batters in one inning on three different occasions?

If the name Chuck Finley comes to the forefront don't be surprised for the lanky lefty added a third team to his list when, on April 16, 2000, while with the Cleveland Indians, he defeated the Texas Rangers, 2-1, setting down four batters on strikes in the 3rd inning.

76. Who was the first major league pitcher to pitch a no-hitter and then come back to be a major league umpire?

Back on September 27, 1905, "Big Bill" Dinneen, the Boston Americans' right-hander, pitched a 2-0 no-hitter against the Chicago White Sox in the first of two games. The White Sox took it out on Boston in the nightcap by blasting the Americans 15-1

After his retirement from playing on August 26, 1909, and after a 12-year career with the Washington Senators, and the Boston Braves, in the National League, and the Boston Red Sox and St. Louis Browns in the American League, Dinneen went on to become a highly regarded major league umpire from 1909 to 1937. He was the first to pitch a no-hitter and umpire one as well.

77. Who was the first pitcher to pitch a no-hitter for a National League team and, upon retirement, take up a second career as a National

League umpire?

The pitcher who kept his no-hitter and his umpiring career entirely in the senior circuit was the right-hander known as "The Arkansas Humming Bird", Lon Warnecke of the St. Louis Cardinals.

He fired his no-hitter in the second game of a doubleheader against the defending World Series champion Cincinnati Reds, on August 30, 1941, winning his 15th game of the season, 2-0, and having only three balls hit to the outfield.

He was sold to the Chicago Cubs in 1942 and saw limited playing time, before going into the Army from 1944-45.

Upon his return he played in nine games for the Cubs before his retirement as a player from Chicago on September 29, 1945. Warnecke took up umpiring in the Pacific Coast League from 1946 to 1948 and moved to the National League in 1949 where he stayed until 1955.

78. Who was the first pitcher to pitch a nine-inning game without the aid of an assist?

No assist needed here may have been the comment given by Cleveland Indians right-hander, Steve Gromek, when he retired the last New York Yankees batter in the first game of a double-header on July 4, 1945 out in Cleveland Stadium for a 4-2 win.

It seems Gromek induced the Yankee batters to keep the ball in the air, with the exception of two ground balls down to first baseman Mickey Rocco who scooped them up unassisted for the out.

The outs were recorded by 8 fly balls to LF Jeff Heath, 4 to CF Felix Mackiewicz, and 3 to RF Paul O'Dea. The infield had a popup to 3B Al Cihocki, 2 to 2B Dutch Meyer, 1 to SS Lou Boudreau, 2 foul popups to catcher Frankie Hayes, and 4 strikeouts for Gromek, and the two balls that Rocco took care of without help.

There you have it, 27 outs recorded with not one assist to aid the effort.

79. Who was the first reliever to win the Cy Young Award?

In 1974, Mike Marshall, the Los Angeles Dodgers right-hander, won the Cy Young Award with a 15-12 record, and a 2.42 Era, after leading the league in games played with 106, games finished with 83, and in saves with 21, having pitched 208.1 innings. With that record he became the first reliever to win the coveted award.

80. Who was the first reliever to win the National League's Most Valuable Player Award?

Casimir James Konstanty, better known as Jim, was a right-handed relief ace of the 1950 "Whiz Kids" Philadelphia Phillies who won the National League pennant, under Eddie Sawyer, beating out Brooklyn by two games.

As a large part of their success, Jim led the league in games with 74, games finished with 62, and saves with 22, and had a 16-7 won-lost record with a 2.66 Era to win the MVP Award.

81. Who was the first American League reliever to win the Cy Young Award?

Albert Walter Lyle, my friends call me "Sparky", the New York Yankees southpaw, became the first American League reliever to win the Cy Young Award when, in 1977, he led the league in game appearances with 72, and in games finished with 60, while compiling a 13-5 , 2,17 Era with 68 strikeouts in 137 innings pitched.

82. Who was the pitcher to be credited with the win in the first major league game played?

Joseph Emley Borden, born on May 9, 1854, in Jacobstown New Jersey, made his professional pitching debut on July 24, 1875 for the Philadelphia White Stockings, a National Association team. In his abbreviated tenure with the team, he was 2-4, both wins being shutouts, and the one on July 28, 1875 was the first no-hitter in professional baseball history. Since the National Association was not considered a major league team he is not credited with the first major league no-hitter.

When the National Association folded in 1875, Joe Borden signed a three-year contract with the Boston Red Caps, who had joined the newly formed National League for the 1876 season.

On April 22, 1876 the diminutive, 5'9" 140 lb., right-hander took the mound in the first National League (Major League) game played, down in Athletic Park, Philadelphia, and pitched the entire game as the Red Caps defeated the Athletics, 6-5, and Borden went down in history as being the first pitcher to win a major league game.

On July 15, 1876, at age 22, Borden pitched his last major league game, with the Red Caps, and was released after one year of his three-year $2,000 contract, and ended his career with a 13-16 won-lost, 2.56 Era record, and 43 strikeouts.

83. **Who was the first pitcher to strike out 21 batters, a major league record, in an extra-inning game?**

Tom Cheney, the Washington Senators' right-hander, struck out 21 Baltimore Orioles, on September 12, 1962, in a 16-inning effort, at Memorial Stadium, winning the game 2-1 on Bud Zipfel's 16th inning home run off right-hander Dick Hall.

84. **Who was the first pitcher to hit two home runs in two games in the same season?**

Jack Harshman, a southpaw swinging, and throwing pitcher, and first baseman, made his major league debut with the New York Giants on September 16, 1948 as a first baseman and played twelve games there before New York switched him to the mound where he pitched in two games in 1952 before being purchased, as a pitcher, by the Chicago White Sox on September19, 1953.

Spending five seasons with the Pale Hose they traded him in a multi-player deal to the Baltimore Orioles on December 3, 1957.

During the course of his 34 games on the mound for the Orioles in 1958, Harshman, always a decent hitter for a pitcher, blasted a pair of home runs in two different games during the course of that season, and had six in total, to be the only pitcher to hit two homers twice in a game in one season.

85. **Who was the first pitcher to win three Cy Young Awards?**

Sanford "Sandy" Koufax, born Sanford Braun, in Brooklyn, New York, was signed by the Brooklyn Dodgers as an amateur free agent on December 14, 1954, and what a gem he was.

He made his pitching debut with the Dodgers, at the age of 19, on June 24, 1955. Slow to develop, winning just nine games while in Flatbush, all of the talent was there for this hard throwing southpaw to be a star, and it began when the Dodgers moved out to Los Angeles in 1958.

In 1961 his flame-throwing ability surfaced when he led the National League in strikeouts with 269 to go along with an 18-13 record. In 1962 Koufax captured the earned run title with a 2.54 Era, and was an All-Star for the second time.

In 1963 the Cy Young Award was his with a brilliant 25-5, 1.88 Era, eleven shutouts, and he crossed the 300-strikeout threshold with 306, all league-leading numbers.

Winning the National League Era title five consecutive seasons, 1962-66, he captured his second Cy Young in 1965 with a 26-8, won-lost record, and 27 complete games over 335.2 innings, striking out 382 batters!

Proving he wasn't going to stand on ceremony, Koufax went out in 1966, and won his second consecutive, and third Cy Young Award, each of them by unanimous votes, with a 27-9, 1.73 Era, 27 complete games, five shut-outs, and fanning 317 batters in 323 innings pitched.

Sadly for baseball, October 2, 1966 was his final game; he retired on a winning season and spectacular career; 3 Cy Young Awards, 3 Triple Crowns, one MVP, 6 All-Star selections, four no-hitters, a perfect game, and the Hall of Fame awaited him on his first ballot induction in 1972 as the youngest player ever inducted into Cooperstown.

86. Who was the first pitcher to be credited with the first officially recognized "save" in major league history?

On Opening Day, April 7, 1969, the Los Angeles Dodgers right-hander Bill Singer, came on in relief of Don Drysdale, who had given up two first-pitch, first inning home runs to the Cincinnati Reds' Pete Rose and Bobby Tolan, and went on to pitch three scoreless innings, allowing no hits, walk-ing only one, and striking out one in his relief stint, as the Dodgers came back to defeat Cincinnati 3-2, and Singer went into the record books as being the first pitcher credited with a save.

87. Who were the first two pitchers to throw back-to-back no-hitters in the same ballpark on consecutive days?

This bizarre and "never could happen" experience happened, and it did so in Candlestick Park, San Francisco. On September 17, 1968, Gaylord Perry of the San Francisco Giants threw a no-hitter defeating St. Louis Cardinal right-hander Bob Gibson, 1-0, on Ron Hunt's solo home run.

On the following day, September 18th, sixteen hours after Perry pitched his no-hitter, Ray Washburn, the Cardinal right-hander decided it was his time for equal glory and pitched a no-hitter, with the help of run-scoring base hits by Mike Shannon and Curt Flood, winning 2-0.

The champagne must have flowed like water over those two days around San Francisco Bay. The first time two pitchers pitched consecutive no-hit-ters in the same ballpark, on consecutive days.

88. Who was the first, and only, pitcher to pitch four no-hitters in four consecutive years?

We mentioned earlier about the exploits of Sandy Koufax, and his credentials for greatness continue. He is the first pitcher to pitch no-hitters in four consecutive years, and he started by pitching a no-hitter for the Los Angeles Dodgers against the New York Mets, winning 5-0, on June 30, 1962. His second came on May 11, 1963, against the San Francisco Giants, winning 8-0, followed by his third against the Philadelphia Phillies, down in Shibe Park, on June 4, 1964, winning 3-0.

If that wasn't enough in the credentials department, he topped those three off on September 9, 1965, out in Dodger Stadium, before a crowd of 29,139, by pitching a perfect game, against the Chicago Cubs, winning 1-0.

In that game he defeated southpaw Bob Hendley who gave up just one hit, one walk, and one unearned run to set a record for the fewest number of hits allowed to both teams in a nine inning game.

89. Who was the first pitcher to strike out 19 batters in a nine inning game?

Steve "Lefty" Carlton, of the St. Louis Cardinals, must have created gale force winds by the actions of the New York Mets batters out in Busch Stadium, on September 15, 1969, when he set a major league record by striking out 19 New York Mets, but he still lost thanks to a pair of two-run home runs by Ron Swoboda, 4-3.

90. Who was the first, and only, pitcher to pitch three shutouts within four days against the same team?

This probably will come as no surprise since Walter "The Big Train" Johnson of the Washington Senators, pitched 113 shutouts during his 21-year career, to find out that three of those occurred over the course of a four-day trip to New York. Because Washington manager Joe Cantillon's mound staff was decimated by illness to themselves or their families only three pitchers made the trip up from Washington over this Labor Day weekend.

Johnson went to the mound on September 4th, and 5th, and shutout the New York Highlanders (Yankees) in both games, and then came back again on the 7th to pitch his third shutout, this a two-hit, no walk, 4-0 victory over Jack Chesbro.

Over the course of those three games Johnson allowed just 12 hits, walked only one, and struck out 12. Having three shutouts over four days kind of gives a new meaning to Labor Day.

91. Who was the only pitcher, in his 19-year career, to have never yielded a grand slam home run?

Right-hander Jim "Pancakes" Palmer of the Baltimore Orioles, elected to the Hall of Fame in 1990, and a winner of 268 regular season games, 3,948 innings pitched, gave up a career total of 303 home runs, but never one with the bases loaded.

92. Whose was the first, and only, starting rotation to have each of their four starting pitchers lose 20 or more games, not only in a season, but in back-to-back seasons?

This dubious honor goes to the four pitchers of the Boston Beaneaters rotation in 1905 who posted the following records, Irv Young, 20-21; Vic Willis, 12-29; Chick Fraser, 14-22; and Kaiser Wilhelm, 3-22.

In 1906 the Beaneaters tried to revamp their mound staff for better results. Here is a look at their success; Irv Young, a holdover from the past year went 16-25; and he was joined by a trio of new arms who went as follows: Vive Lindaman, 12-23; Jeff Pfeffer, 13-22; and Gus Dorner, 8-25.

Is it any wonder they came in seventh in their eight team National League division in 1905, and dead last, 67 games out of first place in 1906?

93. Who was the first pitcher to strike out the side on nine pitches in both the National League and the American League?

On April 19, 1968 Nolan Ryan, of the New York Mets, struck out three Los Angeles Dodgers in the 1st inning; Wes Parker, Zoilo Versalles, and Willie Davis, throwing just nine pitches.

Ryan also struck out all three batters in the 3rd inning, Claude Osteen, Wes Parker, and Zoilo Versalles, on his way to an 11 strikeout day, but losing 3-2 to Claude Osteen.

Moving over to the American League Ryan, now with the Anaheim Angels, on July 9, 1972, struck out three Boston Red Sox in the top of the 3rd inning on nine pitches; Sonny Siebert, Tommy Harper, and Doug Griffin on his way to a 16 strikeout, one hit, shutout of the Red Sox, 3-0. He then became the first pitcher in major league history to strike out the side on nine pitches in both leagues.

94. Who was the first, and only, pitcher in major league history to have over 200 wins and 150 saves?

Right-hander John Smoltz was drafted by the Detroit Tigers, and signed with them on September 22, 1985. On August 12, 1987 he was traded to the Atlanta Braves where he made his major league debut with them on July 23, 1988, spending twenty years with Atlanta, and having a 210-155 record, as well as 154 saves, leading the league in saves, with 55, in 2002.

On January 12, 2009 he signed on with the Boston Red Sox as a free agent, having a 2-5, no save record. He was released by the Red Sox on August 17, 2009, and signed with the St. Louis Cardinals two days later, having a 1-3 record, again with no saves. On November 5, 2009 the Cardinals granted him free agency, and Smoltz's 21-year career record, at this writing, shows 213 wins, 155 losses, a 3.33 Era and 154 saves. This makes him the first pitcher to record over 200 wins and 150 saves.

95. Who was the first, and only, pitcher to pitch a perfect game for 12 innings and lose, 1-0?

On May 26, 1959, in one of the most memorable games in history, Harvey Haddix, the Pittsburgh Pirate southpaw, retired the first 36 Milwaukee Braves batters through the 12th inning.

In the 13th inning second baseman Felix Mantilla reached first on third baseman Don Hoak's error, thereby ending any thoughts of a perfect game. Mantilla was then sacrificed to second. Hank Aaron was intentionally walked, and Joe Adcock followed with a home run into right centerfield, but it was reduced to just a double as Aaron, seeing the home run, left the playing field, and Adcock then passed Aaron on the bases with both Adcock and Aaron then being called out as Mantilla scored the winning run, and Haddix was tagged with a 1-0 loss.

Haddix became the 9th pitcher, at that time, to lose a no-hitter in extra innings.

Lew Burdette, who pitched all 13 innings, scattered 12 hits for his 8th win.

96. Who was the first pitcher to have over 3,000 strikeouts and have less than 1,000 walks in his career?

Hall of Fame, (1991), right-hander Ferguson Jenkins, made his major league debut with the Philadelphia Phillies on September 10, 1965, and went on to play with the Chicago Cubs, Texas Rangers, and Boston Red

Sox in his 284-226 won-lost, 19-year career. During his 4,500.2 innings pitched Jenkins struck out 3,192 batters, but just walked 997, to be the first pitcher to strike out over 3,000 batters while allowing 997 to get a free pass.

97. Who was the first pitcher to win a World Series Most Valuable Player Award, a Cy Young Award, and pitch a no-hitter?

That accomplished pitcher was Kansas City Royals right-hander Bret Saberhagen. He was the 1985 World Series MVP for his two wins against the St. Louis Cardinals, allowing only twelve Cardinal base runners in those two wins.

That same year, 1985, he won the American League Cy Young Award with a 20-6, 2.87 Era, and repeated that honor in 1989 with a 23-6, 2.16 Era, not only leading the American League in wins, but in complete games with 12, and innings pitched with 262.1.

To top all that off, Saberhagen, on August 26, 1991, pitched a no-hitter against the Chicago White Sox, winning 7-0 at Kansas City.

98. Who was the first pitcher to pitch a no-hitter in both the National League and the American League?

Back on September 18, 1897, Cy Young, pitching for the Cleveland Spiders in the National League, pitched a no-hit to the Cincinnati Reds, winning 6-0 in the first game of a doubleheader.

After the American League was established Young found himself hurling for the Boston Americans and, on May 5, 1904, he bettered his 1897 effort by pitching a 3-0 perfect game over the Philadelphia Athletics to be the first to no-hit two teams in the two major leagues.

99. Who was the first pitcher to pitch a no-hitter, and to help his own cause, by also hitting a home run?

Wes Ferrell, the Cleveland Indians ace right-hander, who could also handle a bat, had a big day on Wednesday, April 29, 1931 out in League Park II, against the St. Louis Browns. Ferrell not only no-hit the Browns, but struck out 8, allowed three walks, and faced just 29 batters. He made sure he had runs to support himself as he had a double, and a two-run home run off Browns' right-hander "Sad Sam" Gray, and drove in four runs as he went on to a 9-0 win over St. Louis, and became the first pitcher to hit a home run in the same game in which he pitched a no-hitter.

100. Who was the first pitcher to pitch a no-hitter in both the American and National Leagues in the modern era?

While we have spoken about Cy Young in a previous item we now turn our attention to what is considered the modern era, and see that the distinction of being the first to pitch a no-hitter in each league in the 20th century goes to Hall of Fame right-hander Jim Bunning.

He pitched his first no-hitter, while with the Detroit Tigers, against the Boston Red Sox, winning 3-0, in the first game of a double header on July 20, 1958.

Coming over to the Philadelphia Phillies in a five player trade on December 5, 1963, he took his first no-hitter to a higher level on Sunday, June 21, 1964, again in the first game of a doubleheader, at Shea Stadium, against the New York Mets, this one coming on Father's Day. To celebrate the day Bunning pitched a perfect game, striking out ten Mets on the way to a 6-0 victory, to make him the first in the 20th century to no-hit a team in each league, and make it special with a Fathers' Day perfect game in his second attempt.

101. Who was the first African-American to pitch a no-hitter?

Right-hander Earl Wilson of the Boston Red Sox, celebrated his first major league shut out in grand fashion on June 26, 1962 as he pitched a no-hitter against the Los Angeles Angels, winning 2-0, and put a special stamp on it by hitting a home run off the losing southpaw, Robert "Bo" Belinsky, who was probably still basking in the glory of the no-hitter he had just pitched against Baltimore on May 5th.

102. Who was the first, and only, pitcher to win a Cy Young Award while pitching for two different teams, in two different leagues, in the same season?

Rick Sutcliffe started the 1964 season pitching for the Cleveland Indians. His 4-5 won-lost record and 5.13 Era, may have prompted the Tribe to trade him to the Chicago Cubs on June 13th.

When he joined the Cubs the Windy City air must have had a positive effect on him for his record jumped to 16-1, with a 2.69 Era.

His trade to the National League led the Cubs to the NL East Division title, and that along with his stellar record made him the choice for the Cy Young Award.

103. **Who was the first pitcher to pitch a no-hitter, and not strike out a single batter?**

You have to go way back to August 30, 1912 when the diminutive southpaw, Earl Hamilton, of the St. Louis Browns no-hit the Detroit Tigers, winning 5-1, while allowing two walks and recording nary a strike out.

104. **Who was the first southpaw to win 300 major leagues games?**

That honor goes to "Gettysburg Eddie" Plank of the Philadelphia Athletics, who ended his 16-year major league career with a 305-183 record. Plank spent the 1915 season with the St. Louis Terriers of the Federal League where he had a 21-11 record which isn't counted here as part of his major league record. Subtracting those decisions "Gettysburg Eddie" shows up with a 305-183 career won-lost record with a 2.37 Era over 4,227.1 innings.

105. **Who was the first pitcher to retire right after pitching, and winning, 20 games for the first time in his 18-year career?**

That decision to hang up his cleats was one made by right-hander Mike "Moose" Mussina, who retired after pitching 18 seasons, 10 with the Baltimore Orioles, twice winning 19 games with them in 1995 and again in 1996, and having a 147-81 record.

After being granted free agency by the Orioles on October 27, 2000, Mussina signed on with the New York Yankees on December 7, 2000.

The five-time All-Star pitched for New York for 8 seasons having a 123-72 record, with twenty of those victories coming in his final season when he had a 20-9 record in 2008.

106. **Who was the first pitcher, to have pitched in both leagues, for 17 seasons, winning over 200 games, yet never won 20 games in a season?**

The right-hander who won many, just not twenty, in a season, was Milt "Gimpy" Pappas (born Pappastediodis) who made his pitching debut with the Baltimore Orioles on August 10, 1957, and stayed with them for nine seasons, winning 110 games before being traded over to Cincinnati on December 9, 1965 in a multi-player trade, one of whom was future Hall of Famer, Frank Robinson.

Spending three seasons in the "Queen City of the West", with the Reds, he won 30 games before moving on in another multi-player trade, on June

11, 1968, to the Atlanta Braves, where he stayed three years, winning 18 more games, before being purchased by the Chicago Cubs on June 23, 1970.

It was here that he had the most success, other than in Baltimore when, during his four-year stay in the "Windy City" he came the closest to being a 20-game winner by winning 17 games in both 1971 and '72, and the last of his 51 major league victories, ending his mound career on September 18, 1973 with 99 National League wins to go with his 110 American League wins for a career 209-164, 3.40 Era., record over 17 seasons.

107. Who was the first pitcher to win the Cy Young Award without recording a twenty-win season?

This Fresno, California native was signed by the New York Mets to an amateur free agent contract on April 3, 1966, and Tom Seaver made his major league debut with the Mets on April 13, 1967. With going 16-13 with a 2.76 Era in his freshman year, and earning a spot on his first of ten All-Star teams made him an easy selection for the Rookie-of-Year Award.

In 1969 he won his first Cy Young Award with a 25-7, 2.21 Era record. In 1973 "Tom Terrific" won his second Cy Young with a 19-10, NL best 2.08 Era. and 18 complete games, and with 251 strike outs it was a strong enough showing for him to win the award, yet be the first pitcher to win it without winning 20 games.

Proving to the selection committee that he would be back, he captured his third Cy Young Award in 1975 with a 22-9, 2.38 Era and again leading the National League in strike outs with 243.

When Seaver finished his 20-season career, on September 19, 1986, with the Boston Red Sox, his Hall of Fame credentials showed a 311-205, 2.86 Era. record, with 3,640 strikeouts, 61 shutouts, and 231 complete games, over 4,783 innings.

108. Who was the first, and only, pitcher to lead his league in victories five years in a row?

This pitcher not only led his league in victories five years in a row, he led the major leagues by being the southpaw with the most wins in a career, 363.

Warren Spahn, the lithe lefty with the high kick, who was signed as an amateur free agent with the Boston Bees in 1940, made his major league pitching debut on April 19, 1942. Appearing in four games, starting two, over a 15.2 inning span, he gave up 10 earned runs on 15 hits and walked 11.

Now baseball fans know that was not the Spahnie we all know, and have come to appreciate. Returning from World War II where he was highly decorated, he quickly became the mainstay of the Braves staff going 21-10 in 1947, 21-14 in 1949, 21-17 in 1950, and 22-14 in '51.

He continued to roll up 20-game victories, having 13 during his 21-year career, and from 1957 through 1961, he led the National League in victories with 21, 22, 21, 21, 21 wins to become the first, any only, pitcher to lead his league in victories five consecutive years on his way to a Hall of Fame career that showed 363-245 won-lost, 3.09 Era, record with 2,583 strike outs, 382 complete games including 63 shut outs.

109. Who was the first, and only, pitcher to lead his league in winning percentage three years in a row?

"Big Ed" Reulbach made his pitching debut on May 16, 1905 with the Chicago Cubs, spending the first 9 of his 12 major league seasons with them showing an impressive 136-65, .677 winning percentage.

During his stay in the "Windy City" the right-hander, in his second season, 1906, had an exceptional, league leading, 19-4, .826 winning percentage, and followed that in 1907 with a 17-4, .810, and came back in 1908 to lead again with a 24-7, .774 to make him the first, and only pitcher to lead his league in winning percentage three consecutive years.

"Big Ed" continued his winning percentage abilities ending his career on July 13, 1917 with the Boston Braves, and showing his 12-year National League career record of 161-96, a .626 winning percentage, and a 2.29 Era.

110. Who was the first, and only, pitcher to lead both the American and National Leagues in strikeouts three or more years in a row?

In 1992, the towering 6'10" southpaw, Randy "Big Unit" Johnson, was the strikeout king with the Seattle Mariners in the American League when he led the league with 241 strikeouts. He followed that in 1993 with a league leading 308, and again in 1994 by fanning 204, and finished off his four-year run in 1995 with 294 strikeouts.

On December 10, 1998 Johnson signed on as a free agent with the Arizona Diamondbacks and continued his strikeout mastery. In 1999 the Arizona southpaw fanned 364 National League batters, and followed that in

2000 with a 347- strikeout season.

In 2001 his strikeout   dominance continued when he struck out 372 batters. He finished off his four-year strikeout string by fanning 334 in 2002. Johnson is the first, and only, pitcher to have a league leading four-year strikeout string in both leagues.

111. Who was the first pitcher to record three putouts in the same inning?

This happened before a very small crowd of 1,100 fans at Fenway Park, Boston, on Thursday, September 26, 1940. In the 4th inning of a game against the Washington Senators the Boston Red Sox right-hander Jim Bagby Jr. set the major league record by being the first pitcher to make all three putouts in an inning. Two other pitchers would follow: Bob Heffner of the Red Sox on June 28, 1963, and Rick Reuschel of the Chicago Cubs on April 25, 1975.

Washington went on to win with three straight hits in the 9th inning, including the game winner by Cecil Travis, 6-5.

112. Who was the first, and only, pitcher to give up two grand slam home runs in the same inning, to the same player?

Los Angeles Dodgers right-hander, Chan Ho Park, not only had the dubious distinction of giving up two grand slam home runs in the same inning, on April 23, 1999, but to the same player, third baseman Fernando Tatis of the St. Louis Cardinals, in the 3rd inning of a 12-5 romp by the Redbirds over the Dodgers.

113. Who was the first pitcher to win a night game at Ebbets Field?

The answer to this goes far beyond a "W" in the "win" column. The first night game played at Ebbets Field, Brooklyn, was played on Wednesday, June 15, 1938 between the Brooklyn Dodgers and the Cincinnati Reds. This game, and the date, became historic for on that night, before 38,748 fans, Cincinnati southpaw, Johnny "The Dutch Master" Vander Meer, pitched his unprecedented second consecutive no-hit game, defeating the Dodgers, under the lights, 6-0.

Just four days earlier, on June 11th, "The Dutch Master" had mastered the Boston Braves with his first no-hitter, 3-0, in Cincinnati.

114. Who was the first pitcher to record back-to-back 300-strikeout

seasons?

This fire-balling right-hander not only had a 300-strikeout season in 1972, having 329 with the California Angels, but came back in 1973 to fan 383.

Nolan Ryan took it a step further when he went over 300 strikeouts again when a league leading 367 batters went down on strikes in 1974, making it three consecutive years of 300 strikeouts.

In fact, he exceeded the 300-strikeout level five out of six seasons from 1972-1977, and during his 27-year career the "Ryan Express" racked up six 300-strikeout seasons giving him the all-time record total of 5,714.

115. Who was the first pitcher to <u>twice</u> lead his league in wins, earned run average, and strikeouts?

There have been some great names who have accomplished this difficult task, but the one who was the first to do it was the great Christy Mathewson of the New York Giants, in 1905, when he went 31-8, with a 1.27 Era, and struck out 206.

He came back to do it again in 1908 when he had a 37-11 won-lost record, struck out 259 batters, and posted a 1.43 Era.

He took those impressive credentials a step further when he also led the National League in innings pitched, 390.2, shutouts,12, games played 56, games started, 44, games completed, 34, and in saves, 5.

Some of those other fellows who came along later to also do it, now called the Triple Crown, were Walter Johnson, Grover Cleveland Alexander, Lefty Grove, Sandy Koufax, and Roger Clemens.

But "Matty" remains to this day, the very first to do it, twice.

116. Who was the first, and only, pitcher to come on in relief and get the next 27 outs without allowing a base hit, walk, or hit batsman?

This very bizarre, memorable, and historic happening began on June 23, 1917, in Fenway Park, Boston, when southpaw Babe Ruth took the mound for the Red Sox in the first game of a doubleheader against the Washington Senators.

"The Babe" walked the first batter, second baseman Ray Morgan, and after every pitch complained to home plate umpire, Brick Owens, about his lack of ability to recognize the strike zone. Babe's control was not sharp, but his temper and tongue were. When Morgan went on down to first Ruth charged off the mound, and promptly planted a right to Owens' jaw, and was immediately ejected.

Red Sox manager Jack Barry quickly yelled to the bullpen to get someone up and ready to relieve the departing Babe. In came the big, 6'4" 220 pound right-hander, Ernie Shore, as his battery mate, Sam Agnew, took over behind the plate for Babe's catcher Chester "Pinch" Thomas. Ray Morgan decided to steal second against Agnew, not a good idea, as Sam gunned him down for the first out.

Shore went on to retire the next 26 batters he faced and went into the record books as pitching a perfect game, retiring all 27 men without a hit, walk, error, or hit batsman, thanks to Ruth's arm putting Morgan on, and Agnew's arm taking him away.

Agnew also added to the cause with a 3 for 3 day at the plate while Shore cruised to a 4-0 win, in relief.

The Babe came away with a fine of $100 and a suspension of ten days.

117. Who was the first pitcher to strike out over 200 batters in nine consecutive seasons?

George Thomas Seaver, known as "Tom Terrific" by his many New York Mets fans, made his major league debut with the Mets on April 13, 1967 and began his consecutive, over 200 strikeouts per season record the following season.

In the 1968 season he struck out 205 batters, and his next eight seasons showed 208, 283, 289, 249, 251, 201, 243, and 235 batters going down on strikes, just missing by four, with 196 in the 10th season when split assignments after being traded to the Cincinnati Reds in the 1977. He came right back in 1978 with 226 strikeouts, giving him nine consecutive, and ten out of eleven seasons crossing the 200-plus strikeout mark; quite a record.

118. Who was the first pitcher to strike out Ted Williams and also give up his first base hit?

This two-part question can be answered with a one person answer, Charles "Red" Ruffing, then a New York Yankee, and a former Boston Red Sox right-hander, was the first pitcher to strike out the "Splendid Splinter."

It happened on Opening Day, April 20, 1939, before a crowd of 30, 278 at Yankee Stadium, when Williams made his major league debut, striking out the first two times he faced Ruffing before coming back in the game to rifle a double for his first major league base hit.

In what could be deemed an historic day, for not only was it the debut of the great Ted Williams, but it was the only game that featured both Williams, and Yankee first baseman, Lou Gehrig.

Ruffing bested Robert Moses "Lefty" Grove that day, winning 2-0. It was only the second Opening Day shutout pitched by a Yankee up to that time.

Another interesting sidelight was the fact that the third base umpire was George Pipgras, who was the Yankees' starting pitcher on Opening Day in 1929 against the Boston Red Sox. His opponent on that day was Red Ruffing.

119. Who was the first modern day pitcher to be suspended by Major League Baseball for throwing a spitball?

It happened on Thursday, July 20, 1944, when Nelson Potter, the St. Louis Browns right-hander, took the mound against fellow right-hander, Hank Borowy of the New York Yankees at Sportsman's Park before a crowd of 13,093.

The Yankees' third base coach, Art Fletcher, watched Potter and noted he was bringing his fingers to his mouth.

The same criticism had been directed at Borowy by the hometown fans.

Warned by home plate umpire Cal Hubbard in the previous inning, Potter was again caught going to his mouth with his fingers, and was immediately ejected from the game in the 5th inning. The Browns went on to a 7-3 win as Denny Galehouse came on for the win, and George Caster the save.

On July 22nd American League President Will Harridge suspended Potter for ten days for allegedly "putting an illegal substance on the ball."

That alleged spitball, and the following suspension, may have cost Potter his only chance as a 20-game winner in his twelve-year career, as he ended that season with a 19-7 record, as he led the Browns to their only pennant that season.

120. Who was the first modern day pitcher to win 30 games in three consecutive seasons?

It should come as no surprise to learn that the first modern day pitcher to win 30 games in three consecutive seasons was "Matty", formally known as Christy Mathewson, the Hall of Fame right-hander of the New York Giants. In 1903, his fourth year in the big leagues, he went 30-13. He continued on with a 33-12 record in 1904, and repeated in 1905 with a 31-8 record, giving him 94 wins in that three-year period. In addition he also led the National League in strikeouts over those three years with 267, 212, and 206.

121. Who was the first pitcher to win 100 or more games in both the American and National Leagues?

If one thinks of winning pitchers, no matter the league, how can one forget the winningest pitcher in baseball history, Cy Young. During his 22-year career, which started in 1890, he won 241 games for the Cleveland Spiders of the National League, 45 for the St. Louis Cardinals, and 4 finishing out his career in 1911 with the Boston Rustlers (Braves).

In the American League he won 29 games with the Cleveland Naps (Indians), and 192 with the Boston Red Sox. This gave him 221 American League victories and 290 National League wins for his 511 career total.

122. Who was the first pitcher to win 25 or more games in a season in both the American and National Leagues?

You will have to go all the way back to 1901 when "Wild Bill" Donovan, the Brooklyn Superbas right-hander, not only led the National League in wins with 25, but in games pitched with 45, as well as in walks allowed with 152. One might presume that the latter figure helped him acquire his nickname; not so. He had already been given that nickname due to his explosive temper and erratic control. He once walked nine consecutive batters in the minors and 69 batters in 88 innings as a rookie with Washington in 1898.

Over in the American League, in 1907, with the Detroit Tigers, Donovan had another stellar year with a 25-4 record, and a league best .862 winning percentage.

123. Who was the first pitcher to pitch no-hit games in his first two full seasons in the major leagues?

The pitcher who started off his career on such a high note was Kansas City Royals right-hander Steve Busby. He no-hit Detroit, 3-0, on April 27, 1973 while winning 16 games that season

He came back the following year to not only win 22 games, but to no-hit the Milwaukee Brewers, 2-0, on June 19, 1974, retiring the last 24 batters.

In his next start his hot hand continued as he retired the first nine batters to establish an American League record of 33 straight batters retired.

124. Who was the first, and only, pitcher to win the Cy Young Award while pitching for a last place and a first place team?

From last place to first place was the history of Steve "Lefty" Carlton, as he pitched brilliantly for the Philadelphia Phillies. A winner of four Cy Young Awards, in 1972, '77, '80 and '82, it must have been frustrating in 1972 when although he won the award by leading the National League in wins, 27-10, games started with 41, complete games 30, innings pitched 346.1, in hits given up 257, and strikeouts with 310, his team ended up in last place in the National League East with a 59-97 record and he won almost half of those himself.

In 1977 his efforts weren't wasted as Carlton again led the league in wins with 23-10, to win the Cy Young Award, and his Phillies rose up to win the National League East title with an impressive 101-61 record.

His 329 career wins was more than enough for his easy election into the Hall of Fame in 1994.

125. Who was the first pair of right-handers to win the Cy Young Award?

The Cy Young Award was first given in 1956, but was awarded to only one player in major league baseball, until 1968 when Bob Gibson of the St. Louis Cardinals, with his 22-9 and amazingly miniscule 1.12 Era won it for the National League, and Denny McLain's 31-6, 1.96 Era won it in the American League. They each won their respective league's MVP Award that year as well.

126. Who was the first pair of southpaws, in the same season, to win the Cy Young Award in each league?

The first southpaws to win the Cy Young Award in their league in the same season didn't occur until Steve Carlton, then with the Philadelphia Phillies, won it with a league leading 23-10 record, and Albert "Sparky" Lyle joined him over in the American League with a league-leading 72 games saved for the New York Yankees in 1977.

127. Who were the first two Cy Young Award winners to be involved in a trade by the same team in the same day?

No way, you say? Oh yes, and it happened on Wednesday, December 16,

2009 when a four-club, nine-player trade was made in which the Philadelphia Phillies received 32-year old Roy Halladay, a 2003 Cy Young Award winner, from the Toronto Blue Jays, sending them three minor leaguers, and in turn sent Cliff Lee, to the Seattle Mariners for three prospects.

Toronto then flipped one of the prospects, outfielder Michael Taylor to the Oakland Athletics for a minor league third baseman, Brett Wallace.

This four-team trade was the first to involve Cy Young Award winners going to, and going from, one team, the Philadelphia Phillies, on the same day.

128. Who was the first pitcher in major league history to strike out 4,000 batters?

On July 11, 1985, right-hander Nolan Ryan of the Houston Astros, in the 6th inning of a game against the New York Mets, struck out outfielder Danny Heep, one of his 11 strikeouts in his seven innings on the mound, for his 4,000th career strikeout, as Houston won out 4-3 in 12 innings.

129. Who was the first southpaw in major league history to record 4,000 strikeouts?

It wasn't a good outing, but it was an historic one, for the newly acquired San Francisco Giant southpaw Steve Carlton on Tuesday, August 5, 1986, at Candlestick Park, when "Lefty" gave up seven runs in 3.2 innings against the Cincinnati Reds, but he did record his 4,000th career strikeout, when he struck out centerfielder Eric Davis, in the top of the 4th to become the second pitcher, and the first lefthander in history to reach that level.

130. Who was the first pitcher to lose a perfect game on a 3-2 count for ball four to the 27th batter he faced?

This is one of those games that are almost as famous for what didn't happen as for what did happen. It was on September 2, 1972, and right-hander Milt Pappas, of the Chicago Cubs, was breezing along with a perfect game going into the 9th inning, ahead, 8-0, against the San Diego Padres.

With two out, lefty-swinging outfielder Larry Stahl was sent up to pinch-hit. He worked the count to 3-2 and on the next pitch by Pappas plate umpire Bruce Froemming called it ball four, and Pappas had lost his perfect game. The next batter, utility infielder Garry Jestadt, was easily retired, and Pappas had his no-hitter, but lost perfection.

131. Who was the first pitcher to give up four consecutive home runs?

That dubious "honor" fell upon the right shoulder of Paul Foytack, at Cleveland Stadium, on Wednesday, July 31, 1963, who had recently joined the Los Angeles Angels from the Detroit Tigers. The deluge of round-trippers began in the 6th inning with the bottom of the Cleveland Indians' order, when #8 batter, Woody Held, hit his two-out solo home run. He was followed by pitcher Pedro Ramos, who hit his second home run of the day, then leftfielder Tito Francona added a third, with rookie shortstop Larry Brown following with the fourth consecutive solo home run, his first as a major league leaguer. Cleveland went on to a 9-5 win in the second game of a doubleheader.

132. Who was the first pitcher to give up a home run to Babe Ruth?

There was to be, as you well know, many other pitchers to follow, but on May 6, 1915, in the 3rd inning of a game at the Polo Grounds, Babe Ruth, pitching for the Boston Red Sox, clouts his first major league home run off New York Yankees right-hander Jack Warhop.

The Babe had two other hits that day, but four Red Sox errors were too much to overcome, and Ruth lost in the 13th inning, 4-3, to right-hander Edwin "Cy" Pieh.

133. Who was the first pitcher to give up a home run to Babe Ruth after he came over to the National League?

When Babe Ruth came over to the National League, after 21 years in the American, on February 26, 1935, he signed on as a free agent with the Boston Braves at the age of 40.

In his first National League game, on April 16, 1935, playing left field in Braves Field before an estimated crowd of 25,000, the largest crowd in their history, he faced the New York Giants outstanding southpaw Carl Hubbell. The Babe had a good day, going 2 for 4, striking out twice, but driving in three runs, including his 509th career home run, and his first National League home run, a 430-foot shot, and made a shoestring catch to take the Braves to a 4-2 win, one of only 38 they would win all season.

134. Who was the first pitcher to strikeout 100 or more batters twenty seasons in a row?

Initially this is a bit of a surprise, for this pitcher never won a season strikeout title. Upon reflection it falls into place as right-hander Don Sutton, who made his debut with the Los Angeles Dodgers on April 14, 1966, struck out 209 batters in his rookie year, and went on to exceed the century mark in strikeouts for 21 consecutive years, with five teams, from 1966-86, missing by one, with 99 in 1987, and pitching his final game, back with the Dodgers, on August 9, 1988.

Over his 23-year Hall of Fame career Sutton struck out a total of 3,574 regular season batters, and 61 in the post season.

135. Who was the first pitcher to win 20 games, and also hit .300 for a last place team?

Ned Garver, the St. Louis Browns right-hander, did just about all he could to help his ball club in 1951 when he pitched in 33 games, started 30, completed 24 to lead the American League, and had a 20-12, 3.73 Era. over 246 innings.

When he picked up his bat, Garver often batted in the 6th position, where he produced 29 hits, six doubles, a triple and a home run, driving in 9 runs and scoring 8 times with a .305 batting average. His home run came against the Chicago White Sox breaking a 4-4 tie for a late season win. He was named to the All-Star team that season and came in second, to New York Yankees catcher, Yogi Berra, for the Most Valuable Player Award. All for a team which came in last in the American League with a 52-102 record, but it did make him a "Groundbreaker."

136. Who was the first National League pitcher to win 20 games, and twice hit .300 in the same season?

Bring on that old hard throwing Brooklyn right-hander Burleigh "Ol' Stubblebeard" Grimes who went 23-11, with a 2.22 Era. while batting .306 with 16 runs batted in during the 1920 season.

He repeated that pitching and batting prowess in 1928, while with the Pittsburgh Pirates, when he led the league in wins (25), games (48), games started (37), completed games (28), shutouts (4), and innings pitched (330.1), to go long with a 2.99 Era.

His bat made a noise that year as well when he batted .321 with eight doubles, one triple, and 16 runs batted in. He just missed a third time, when with Brooklyn, in 1924, he had a 22-13 season, but just missed .300 with a .298 average.

137. Who was the first pitcher to come on in relief and pitch four scoreless innings, and also hit two 3-run home runs, the only

home runs in his three-year major league career?

When a pitcher is called upon in relief the manager expects him to shut down the opposition long enough to allow his team to win, or a chance to get back in the ball game.

That's exactly what Detroit right-hander Werner "Babe" Birrer did for Frank "The Yankee Killer" Lary, who had faced two batters in the top of the 6th inning at Briggs Stadium, with the Tigers holding on to a slim 5-4 lead against the Baltimore Orioles on July 19, 1955.

Birrer took it up a notch as he went on to shutout the Orioles over the next four innings, but had his bat give added insurance toward the victory. In the bottom of the 6th, after catcher Frank House, and second baseman Fred Hatfield singled, Birrer took right-hander George Zuverink downtown with a three-run home run to make it 8-4.

Then in the 8th inning Charlie Maxwell doubled, Frank House singled him to third, which set the stage for southpaw Art Schallock, who had come on in relief for Baltimore, to face Babe Birrer. Babe wasted no time as he hopped on Schallock's pitch and blasted his second three-run home run of the game to vault the Tigers to a 12-4 victory, giving Lary the win, Birrer his only home runs and runs batted in for his career and, of course, the save.

138. Who was the first pitcher to hurl a no-hitter in his first start for his new team after being traded?

The Philadelphia Phillies probably should have waited to give their right-hander, Don Cardwell, another start before trading him to the Chicago Cubs on May 13, 1960, along with first baseman Ed Bouchee for Tony Taylor and Cal Neeman.

Cardwell made his first start for the Cubbies, at Wrigley Field, just two days later, on May 15, 1960, and went into the record books by pitching a no-hitter against the St. Louis Cardinals, winning 4-0. It was the first no-hit game against the Cardinals since 1919.

139. Who was the first American League pitcher to pitch 18 scoreless innings in one game?

That very long day belonged to "Kickapoo Ed" Summers, a right-hander who made his major league debut with the Detroit Tigers on April 16, 1908. He had a fine freshman season going 24-12 with a 1.64 Era over 301 innings.

Those innings in 1908 may not have prepared him for the task he took on at Bennett Park, Detroit on July 16, 1909. Summers took the mound that day against a 30-year old rookie southpaw named Bill "Dolly" Gray of the Washington Nationals, who lasted through eight innings, allowing just one hit, before leaving due to an injury.

In came right-hander Bob Groom to replace Gray and continue the scoreless battle with "Kickapoo." The pitching battle continued with Summers going the full 18 innings, giving up seven hits, walking two, one intentionally, and struck out 10, in whitewashing Washington in the longest scoreless game in American League history.

Summers spent his entire five-year career with Detroit, finishing up on June 1, 1912 with a 68-45, 2.42 Era, pitching 9 shutouts over 999 innings, but none more earned than the one on July 16th.

140. Who was the first pitcher to win 30 games in a season, have over 300 career victories, and over 3,000 strikeouts?

It was not too difficult to come up with "The Big Train," Walter Johnson, on this one. Over his 21-year career, spanning from his debut on August 2, 1907 with the Washington Senators till his final game, with that same Washington ball club on September 30, 1927, this legendary pitcher won 33 games in 1912, and a league best 36 in 1913. During those other years he was a 20-game winner ten times, and he went on to roll up 417 wins, second all-time to Cy Young, 110 shutouts, no one has had more, and 3,509 strikeouts, tops at the time of his retirement. He was an original Hall of Fame inductee in 1936.

141. Who was the first pitcher to win the Cy Young Award and pitch in the World Series in the same season?

Big Don Newcombe, the Brooklyn Dodgers right-hander, had quite a year for himself in 1956 when he won the National League Cy Young Award with a 27-7, 3.06 Era, and also captured the Most Valuable Player Award that year as well. He started Game 2 of the World Series, against the New York Yankees, at Ebbets Field on Friday, October 5, 1956, before 36,217 fans, and became the first pitcher to capture both the Cy Young, and the NL MVP, and start a World Series game in the same season. Those honors didn't faze the Yankees as they picked up six hits and six runs before "Newk" gave way to Ed Roebuck, who finished off the 2nd inning, and gave the mound assignment over to right-hander Don "The Weasel" Bessent, who went the remaining seven innings for the win as Brooklyn came back for a 13-8 win. Newcombe came back to start the seventh game, losing to right-hander Johnny Kucks, 9-0.

142. Who was the first pitcher to pitch over 1,000 innings without surrendering a home run?

If a player was stepping into the batter's box looking to hit a really long ball he shouldn't be looking to "Twilight Ed" Killian, the Detroit Tigers southpaw, to serve it up.

Killian, who started his pitching career on August 25, 1903 with the Cleveland Naps (Indians), allowed a single home run in his rookie year. After that if a batter wanted to take "Twilight Ed" downtown they would have to hail a cab. Traded to Detroit in January 1904, he continued his stinginess, and gave up zero home runs in 1904-06.

Killian had pitched 1,001 innings before letting Philadelphia Athletics right fielder, Ralph "Socks" Seybold run around the bases unimpeded as "Socks" hit a home run in the bottom of the 8th inning on August 7, 1907, hanging a 4-2 loss on "Twilight Ed".

Killian, a 20-game winner in 1905 and 1907, hadn't given up a home run since he was with Cleveland on September 19, 1903, his rookie year, when Boston Pilgrims (Red Sox) shortstop Freddy Parent hit walk off home run in the bottom of the 9th inning for a 6-5 victory.

Killian was regarded as the toughest pitcher to hit a homer off in big league history giving up just nine in 1,598.1 innings over his eight-year career.

Adding to his accomplishments was the fact that he won both games of a doubleheader against the Boston Red Sox to clinch the 1907 American League pennant for Detroit.

143. Who was the first pitcher to win 15 games in relief in one season?

Casimir Jim Konstanty came into the major leagues on June 18, 1944 with the Cincinnati Reds, and was traded to the Boston Braves on April 18, 1946. On June 13th he was purchased by Toronto of the International League before moving on to the Phillies in 1948.

It wasn't until his 5th major league season, with the Phillies, that he had a breakout season when his slider and changeup made him a dominant force in the 1950 "Whiz Kids" race for the pennant.

In that pennant year Konstanty, used exclusively as a reliever, led the National League in games with 74, games finished with 62, and in saves with 22. Konstanty also did something no other relief pitcher had ever done; his 16-7 won-lost record was the first time a reliever had won 15 games in one season. It was also the first and only time he made the All-Star team, and also was named the 1950 MVP of the National League.

Much to the surprise of many, Konstanty was named the starting pitcher in Game 1 of 1950 World Series facing New York Yankee right-hander, Vic "The Springfield Rifle" Raschi. In a well-pitched game, Konstanty gave up a run in the 4th on a double by Bobby Brown, and two long fly ball outs, in 8 innings of work, while Raschi fired a two-hit shutout winning 1-0.

144. Who was the first American League pitcher to win 15 games in relief in one season?

In 1963, Dick "The Monster" Radatz, the flame-throwing right-hander of the Boston Red Sox, made 66 relief appearances, saving 25 games, and having a 15-6. 1.97 Era.

That was the first time a reliever won 15 games in one season, that is, until the following year, 1964, when Radatz won 16 games, all in relief, going 16-9 in 79 games, finishing 67, and saving a league best 29.

145. Who was the first pitcher, in the 20th century, by his overpowering pitching performance that season, have the league lower the pitching mound by five inches to better accommodate the hitters?

Yes, it was Bob "Hoot" Gibson, the hard-throwing right-hander of the St. Louis Cardinals. In 1968 he had a 22-9 record with an incredible 1.12 Era allowing, at one point, just two earned runs in 92 straight innings of pitching.

Along with his league-leading 268 strikeouts, he set a modern day record of 13 shutouts that led to a re-evaluation of the height of the pitching mound whereby they lowered it by five inches for the 1969 season.

In 1969 the reduction in the height of the mound didn't seem to bother Gibson who went on to have another successful season with his 20-13, 2.18 Era, striking out 269 batters, and leading the league in complete games with 28, over 314 innings.

146. Who was the first pitcher to lose 20 games for a pennant

winning team?

Losing 20 games in a season was not foreign to "Wabash George" Mullin, the Detroit Tiger right-hander. He had gone 21-21 in 1905 while leading the American League in games started (41), completed games (35), innings pitched (347.2), hits allowed (303), and in walks with 138.

In 1907, when the Tigers won the pennant, Mullin went 20-20, with a 2.59 Era, to become the first pitcher to lose 20 games while his team went to the World Series

Yes, "Wabash George" did pitch in the Big Fall Show, in Games 2 and 5, losing both, as the Cubs swept the Series.

147. Who was the first pitcher to have had a 300-strikeout season come on in relief of another pitcher who also had recorded a 300-strikeout season?

This unusual happenstance started on the evening of July 18, 2001 when Curt Schilling took the mound for the Arizona Diamondbacks out in San Diego against the Padres.

After Schilling had thrown two perfect hitless innings the game was suddenly interrupted when an explosion occurred in the left field light tower causing the game to be suspended.

The game is resumed the following evening, July 19th, and the new Diamondbacks' pitcher, who came on to take over the pitching duties for Arizona, in relief of Schilling, was southpaw Randy Johnson.

"The Big Unit" proceeded to give up just a lone 8th inning single to Padres backstop Wiki Gonzalez, striking out 16 Padres in his seven innings of relief for Schilling, and in so doing, broke the major league mark of Walter Johnson, (no relation), set on July 25, 1913.

In addition to setting the record for strikeouts in a game by a reliever, the "Big Unit" also set the National League reliever mark with seven consecutive strikeouts, just one shy of the major league record set by Ron Davis of the Yankees, on May 4, 1981.

So there you have it, one 300-strikeout pitcher relieving another 300-strikeout pitcher, for the first time in history, with those two combining for a one-hit, 3-0, shutout of the Padres. In retrospect you can now say that during their careers both pitchers, one a right-hander, one a southpaw, went on to exceed 3,000 strikeouts in their careers.

148. Who was the first American League pitcher to win 20-games with three different teams?

It all started for Roger "The Rocket" Clemens in his third year, after his debut with the Boston Red Sox on May 15, 1984, when he led the American League with a 24-4, 2.48 Era. in 1986. He followed that up in 1987 with a 20-9, seven-shutout season. He came back in 1990 with his third 20-game season for Boston with a 21-6, 1.93 Era.

On December 13, 1996, as a free agent, he signed with the Toronto Blue Jays and gave them an immediate 20-game winner by going 21-7, with a 2.05 Era in his first season north of the border. He repeated in 1998 with a 20-6, 2.65 record.

After only two seasons with Toronto he was traded by the Blue Jays to the Yankees for three players on February 18, 1999.

His pinstripe career lasted five years, and his only 20-game season with them was in 2001 when he went 20-3 with a 3.51 Era. completing his three-team twenty-game career on September 16, 2007.

149. Who was the first, and only, pitcher to win the Cy Young Award in three different decades, with three different teams?

This pitcher has won the Cy Young Award six times so it comes as no surprise to learn that Roger "The Rocket" Clemens, the Boston Red Sox right-hander, won the award in 1986 with a 24-4 record, and repeated the following year with a 20-9 season.

He won it again, in the next decade, in 1991 while with Boston with an 18-10, league leading 2.62 Era. record.

He won it for the 2nd and 3rd time in the 90's while with the Toronto Blue Jays having a league-leading 21-7, 2.05 Era in 1997, repeating in 1998, again with a league-leading 20-6, 2.65 Era. record.

That covered two decades and now moving on to 2001, with the New York Yankees, Clemens had a 20-3, 3.51 Era. to capture his 6th career Cy Young Award, winning it with his third team, in his third decade.

150. Who was the first pitcher to hit three batters in the first inning of post-season game?

Of all times for it to happen it came before a crowd of 49,131 at Oriole Park, Camden Yards, in the 1st inning of Game 2 of the American League Championship Series between Baltimore and the Cleveland Indians on

October 9, 1997.

Southpaw Jimmy Key started for Baltimore and obviously hadn't found his groove yet. Although the first batter leftfielder Bip Roberts struck out, shortstop Omar Vizquel was hit by a Key pitch. Manny Ramirez followed with a home run into deep center field, and third baseman Matt Williams singled to left, and then stole second while Key was hitting DH David Justice with a pitch. Catcher Sandy Alomar grounded out moving the runners up. Key then plunked his third batter of the inning, second baseman Tony Fernandez, with a pitch, followed by first baseman Kevin Seitzer, no doubt looking to not be the fourth to catch a pitch on his body, struck out. The Indians came away with a 5-4 win and Jimmy, no doubt, was looking for the Key to his control knob.

151. Who was the first southpaw to strike out 20 batters in a game?

When Randy Johnson took the mound against the Cincinnati Reds on May 8, 2001, he was throwing more heat than the desert Arizona sun as he fanned 20 Reds' batters in his first 9 innings of work. Since the game was tied going into extra innings the strikeout total doesn't match Roger Clemens', or Kerry Wood's total, accomplished in a nine-inning game.

Although the Reds picked up a pair of runs in the top of the 11th it wasn't quite enough as Arizona came back with three in their half of the 11th to pull out 4-3 win.

"The Big Unit" still goes down as the first southpaw to strike out twenty batters in a game.

152. Who was the first pitcher to literally use his head to drive in the winning run in an extra-inning game?

Bizarre, hard to believe, you're putting me on. No, it really did happen on Sunday, September 6, 2009, down in Turner Field, Atlanta, when the Cincinnati Reds played an extra-inning game against the Atlanta Braves.

In the top of the 12th inning, with the score tied at 2-2, the Braves rookie right-hander Kenshin Kawakami, who had come on in relief of Australian right-hander, Pete Moylan, in the top of the 11th, walked Reds' first baseman Joey Votto. Second baseman Brandon Phillips flied out to deep centerfield. Scott Rolen lined a single to left with Votto going to third on the play. Right fielder Wladimir Balentien then walked sending Rolen to second, and loading the bases.

Up comes pitcher Micah Owings, and with a 0-1 count, Kawakami unleashed a wild pitch that struck Ownings in the head sending him sprawled on the ground, as Votto crossed the plate with the third and deciding run.

Pitcher Bronson Arroyo then came in to pinch run for Ownings, who was credited with a run driven in on the play. Catcher Corky Miller then sent a deep sacrifice fly to center, scoring Rolen, who had advanced to third on the beaning, with an insurance run.

Shortstop Paul Janish then grounded into a fielder's choice at second to end the inning. Cincinnati went on to a 4-2 win, and Micah Ownings became the first pitcher to drive in the deciding run with his head.

153. Who was the first National League pitcher to have a higher season batting average than the National League home run leader?

This is an oddity, but true, that many do not realize. In 1982 southpaw Steve Carlton of the Philadelphia Phillies won the Cy Young Award with a 23-11, 19 complete games, 6 shutouts year, and had a .218 batting average, and striking out just 13 times in 109 plate appearances.

In the same season, 1982, Dave "Sky King" Kingman, playing first base for the New York Mets, led the National League in home runs with 37, with 535 at bats, striking out a league high of 156 times and compiled a .204 batting average. So there you have it, a Cy Young Award winner having a higher batting average than the home run leader.

154. Who was the first pitcher to pitch his first complete game, after over 40 starts, and have it be a perfect game?

On Sunday, May 9, 2010 out in Oakland-Alameda Stadium Athletics southpaw Dallas Braden's day was more than complete as he faced the last of the 27 Tampa Bay Rays' batters on his way to his first complete game, and a perfect game, as he threw 109 pitches, fanning six batters, and pleasing the hometown crowd of 12,228 as he came away with a 4-0 win, to become the first to make his first complete game perfect.

155. Who was the first pitcher to win the Cy Young Award in his second season in the major leagues?

Tim Lincecum, the right-hander of the San Francisco Giants was drafted in the first round of the 2006 amateur draft, and signed on June 30th that year. He made his major league debut on May 6, 2007 with the

Giants and had a 7-5, 4.00 Era. record as a freshman.

In his sophomore season, 2008, he blossomed into a very effective pitcher with an 18-5, 2.62 Era., a league leading .783 winning percentage, as well as a league's best 265 strikeouts. This was enough for him to be voted to the All-Star squad, and earn him the coveted Cy Young Award.

Just to prove the baseball world they were correct about his 2008 abilities he came back in 2009 to win another All-Star berth and back-to-back Cy Young Awards with his 15-7, 2.48 Era., and again lead the National League in strikeouts with 261, complete games with 4, and shutouts with 2, all for a team that gave him minimal run support throughout the season.

156. Who was the first pitcher to pitch nine innings of no-hit ball twice in one season, winning the first one, and then losing the second?

This unusual sequence of events happened to Cincinnati Reds' right-hander Jim Maloney when on August 19, 1965 he no-hit the Chicago Cubs, at Wrigley Field, over ten innings in the first game of a doubleheader, winning it when Leo Cardenas homered in the 10th for the Reds' victory.

It was retribution for an earlier loss in the year when Maloney lost a 1-0 game in eleven innings, after holding the New York Mets hitless for ten innings, before right fielder Johnny Lewis hit a home run to lead off the 11th inning.

157. Who was the first pitcher to have his perfect game broken up in the 9th inning by a pinch-hitter who hit his only home run of the year, and the final one of his career?

Some sympathy is certainly in order for right-hander Brian Holman of the Seattle Mariners when, on April 20, 1990, he was cruising along on his way to a perfect game, retiring 26 batters in a row, when the Oakland A's sent up southpaw swinging Ken Phelps, an eleven-year DH, and first baseman, to pinch hit with two out in the 9th.

On Holman's first pitch to Phelps he hit a solo shot for his only home run of the year, and the final one of his career.

Holman fanned Rickey Henderson for the final out, but lost his perfect game, no-hitter, and shutout all on one pitch. Holman and his Mariners did come away with a 6-1 victory.

158. Who was the first pitcher to retire over 40 batters in a row?

Right-hander Jim Barr of the San Francisco Giants began to establish that mark in his second major league season when on August 23, 1972 Barr retired the last 21 Pittsburgh Pirates he faced.

Then coming back on August 29th he then retired the first 20 St. Louis Cardinals he faced before outfielder Bernie Carbo doubled with two outs in the 7th inning. His 41 consecutive batters being retired streak came to an end with Barr finishing the game and coming away with a 3-hit shutout.

An interesting sidelight to that amazing record was that Barr struck out only three batters during that streak and depended upon his fielders to convert the other 38 batters into outs during the streak.

159. Who was the first pitcher to save over 30 games, but pitch in less than 40 innings?

In 1994 right-handed relief pitcher Lee Arthur Smith, of the Baltimore Orioles, must have believed in expending minimum effort to get the job done. At least that is what his record shows.

Smith was called into 41 games that season, closing out 39, and recording a league leading 33 saves, but he only pitched 38.1 innings in doing so. His 1-4 record aside, he is the first relief pitcher to have over 30 saves in less than 39 innings pitched.

160. Who was the first closer in major league history to have two 50-save seasons?

This Canadian-born right-hander of the Los Angeles Dodgers made his major league debut on September 7, 1999, but didn't record his first save until the 2002 season when Eric Gagne had 52. Proving that was no fluke he came back in 2003 to lead the National League in games finished with 67, and games saved with 55 to become the first closer to have back-to-back 50+ save seasons.

When Gagne pitched in his last game, on September 25, 2008, with the Milwaukee Brewers, his ten-year record showed 187 career saves.

161. Who was the first pitcher to close out a season with a perfect game?

Just as Bob Feller opened the season with a gem, Mike Witt, the 6'7" right-hander of the California Angels, closed his out with a more brilliant gem. It was on the final day of the regular season, September 30, 1984, that Witt took the mound against the Texas Rangers, and threw just 97 pitches, winning 1-0, striking out 10, and allowing no one to get on base for the first perfect game thrown by an Angel in their history, and the first since Cleveland right-hander, Len Barker pitched one on May 15, 1981, defeating the Toronto Blue Jays, 3-0.

162. Who was the first pitcher to pitch a complete nine-inning game with less than 60 pitches?

There's no proof that Charley "Red" Barrett, the Boston Braves' right-hander, had a heavy date the night of August 10, 1944, but he sure pitched like he did.

Barrett went up against the Cincinnati Reds right-hander Bucky Walters at Crosley Field, and after giving up two singles, and never being behind on a batter in his 58 pitches, the fewest ever in a 9-inning game, he came away with a 2-0 win in the fastest night game ever played; 1 hour, 15 minutes, and he did it in under 60 pitches.

163. Who were the first National Basketball Association players to face each other on the mound in a major league game?

It was Boston versus Chicago, but it was played on a diamond, not the hardwood. It was 6'8" right-hander Gene Conley of the Red Sox against 6'6" right-hander Dave DeBusschere of the White Sox, at Fenway Park. If one let his mind wander it may have come up with the Celtics versus the Knicks. That was for another game in another league. This was on Saturday, April 27, 1963, in what one could call the battle of the Soxes. Conley, who started, pitched to four batters in the 5th inning before being relieved by Jack Lamabe. DeBusschere came on in relief of starter Ray Herbert to get the last two outs in the 4th for Chicago. Boston went into a full-court press and came away with a 9-5 victory.

164. Who was the first, and only, pitcher to pickoff three base runners in one inning?

This rarity happened on Wednesday night, August 24, 1983, in the top of the 10th inning down in Memorial Stadium, Baltimore. With the score tied at 3-3 the Toronto Blue Jays' DH Cliff Johnson hit a go-ahead solo home run off Oriole right-hander Tim Stoddard. When right-fielder Barry Bonnell followed with a single to center, southpaw Felix "Tippy" Martinez came in to relieve Stoddard.

"Tippy's" first move was to first base where he picked off Bonnell for the first out. Martinez then walked pinch-hitter Dave Collins, and then promptly picked him off for out #2. First baseman Willie Upshaw followed with a single, but didn't stay on first long for "Tippy" picked him off as well to be the first and probably only pitcher, to come on in relief, and complete a trio of pickoffs in one inning.

Lenn Sakata, normally an infielder, had been shifted from second base to be the catcher in the 10th inning, a move the Blue Jays' base runners thought they could take advantage of, but were not counting on "Tippy's" prowess with his pickoff move. Sakata's bat came into play in the bottom of the 10th as he followed Cal Ripken's solo home run with a three-run home run of his own to win the battle of the birds, with the Orioles besting the Blue Jays 7-4.

165. Who was the first pitcher to lose 48 games in his freshman season?

This is hard to fathom, but as Casey Stengel used to say, "You can look it up." When right-hander John Francis Coleman, not to be confused with the many other Colemans that had toed the rubber, made his pitching debut with the Philadelphia Quakers of the National League on May 1, 1883 he never envisioned immediately going into the record books as a 20-year old.

He led the National League that year in four categories, in earned runs, giving up 291, in home runs allowed with 17, in hits allowed with 772, and the reason for this entry, in losses, going 12-48 with a 4.87 Era. , all in 65 games and 61 starts.

Poor John Francis, he went 5-17 in 1884 before being released in August only to be signed as a free agent by the Philadelphia Athletics on August 23, 1884. His four-year career there resulted into a 6-7 won-lost record. He pitched his final game on July 18, 1890 with the Pittsburgh Alleghenys, going 0-2 for the year, and 23-72 career-wise on the mound. During that career he did play some infield and outfield positions where his bat got him a .257 career batting average, but nothing could shake that 48 game loss in his rookie year.

166. Who was the first pitcher to lose all 16 games in which he received a decision?

Somewhere along the line some break should have come his way, but Minnesota Twins right-hander Terry Felton, couldn't seem to get one. Drafted in the second round of the amateur draft in 1986 Felton made his pitching debut, and only appearance of the season, on September 28, 1979 with Minnesota.

In 1980 he appeared in five games, started four, gave up 20 hits, two home runs, walked nine in 17.2 innings of work, which translated into an

0-3, 7.13 Era.

Coming back in 1981 he appeared in one game, pitched 1.1 innings, giving up four hits, two walks, and a home run, resulting in 6 earned runs and a horrendous 40.50 earned run average, but without a win or loss.

With the Twins exercising patience, and Felton showing resolve he came back in 1982 pitching in 48 games, 6 as a starter, and finishing 20 as a reliever over 117.1 innings. He gave up 18 home runs, 99 base hits, walked 76 batters which gave him a 4.99 earned run average and a woeful 0-13 won lost record. His final major league appearance was on September 28, 1982, exactly three years from his debut, and 16 losses later.

167. Who was the first pitcher to give up 11 base hits in one inning?

Look no further than Philadelphia Phillies right-hander Reggie Grabowski who had that humiliating experience on Saturday, August 4, 1934, down in Baker Bowl, before a crowd of 16,000, in the second game of a double-header against the New York Giants.

In the 9th inning Grabowski came on to pitch, with the Phillies down 10-4, and faced 15 batters, gave up 11 runs, 10 earned, 11 hits, 10 of which were singles, with eleven runs scoring in the inning as the Giants roll to a 21-4 win. Now for the topper, Grabowski doesn't take the loss, southpaw Roy "Snipe" Hansen does, one of 12 he will have that season. He started, went one third of an inning, and gave up three hits, one walk, and four earned runs in the five batters he faced. The Phillies never tied or went ahead so he took the loss.

168. Who was the first 40-year old pitcher to pitch a perfect game?

It wasn't long ago, just back on May 18, 2004, when Arizona Diamondbacks' southpaw Randy Johnson, at age 40 years, 256 days, gave 23,381 fans, that night at Turner Field, Atlanta, an historic thrill to see the first 40-year old pitcher in major league history shut down 27 Atlanta batters in a row, on 117 pitches, as "The Big Unit" became the first pitcher over 40 to pitch a perfect game, and the 17th pitcher, at any age, to pitch perfectly.

169. Who was the first National League pitcher to pitch a no-hitter after the age of 40?

It was a snowy, 38 degree night in Milwaukee County Stadium on April 28, 1961, before a chilled crowd of 8,518 of the faithful that came out to see that great, high-kicking, Braves' southpaw Warren Spahn, who had recently celebrated his 40th birthday just five day before, take the mound, and shut down the San Francisco Giants without a hit, walking two, and striking out 5, to beat right-hander "Toothpick Sam" Jones, 1-0, for his 52nd shutout, and 290th career win, to become the first National League, and southpaw pitcher over the age of 40, to pitch a no-hitter.

170. Who was the first relief pitcher to record 500 saves?

Trevor Hoffman, the right-handed relief pitcher, who developed a devastating change-up, made his major league debut with the Florida Marlins on April 6, 1993, and recorded the first two of his to be 500 saves with them.

On June 24, 1993 he was traded in a five-player exchange to the San Diego Padres where he played 16 seasons.

On June 6, 2007 Hoffman came on in the 9th inning, at PETCO Park, in relief against the Los Angeles Dodgers. With the Padres ahead 5-2 Hoffman gave up a lead-off double to Nomar Garciaparra, got two ground outs and then blew a fastball past catcher Russell Martin for a called strike three to nail down a 5-2 win for the Padres, and record his 500th career save, making him the first relief pitcher in history to reach that plateau.

171. Who was the first, and only, major league pitcher to cause the death of a batter by hitting him in the head with a pitched ball?

This first and only, tragedy will be one hopefully never repeated. It took place on August 16, 1920 at the Polo Grounds in New York.

In the top of the 5th inning Ray Chapman, 29, a very popular nine-year veteran Cleveland shortstop, who had been married the previous year, was planning on retiring after the season, was the lead-off batter.

Facing the right-handed batter was New York Yankee right-hander Carl "Sub" Mays, a surly, unpopular pitcher, and known for his unusual submarine motion when delivering a pitch. Chapman, batting .303 at the time, was known for crowding the plate, and when Mays delivered his 1-1 pitch, a fast spitball that came in high and inside, Chapman froze at the plate and failed to get out of the way of the submarine pitch and was struck in the head, breaking his cranium. With batting helmets not coming into use till 1971, the unprotected Chapman went down with blood rushing from his ear and remained motionless on the ground for several minutes. The ball rolled out toward Mays who retrieved it, thinking it had come from Chapman's bat, and threw to first. The stricken shortstop struggled to his feet, momentarily, with teammates' assistance, before collapsing again, and was carried from the field and taken by ambulance to St. Lawrence Hospital where he died the following morning from a 3 ½ inch depressed fracture of his skull.

When play resumed pinch-runner Harry Lunte was sent in to replace Chapman at first base, and was a force out on the next play. The Indians, who were ahead 3-0 at the time of the beaning, went on to beat the Yankees 4-3.

Joe Sewell, one of three Sewell brothers to play in the majors, replaced Chapman at shortstop and remained for a 14-year career, entering the Hall of Fame in 1977.

Chapman's wife, Kathleen, who was pregnant at the time of Chapman's death with a daughter, committed suicide in 1928.

172. Who was the first, and only, pitcher to win 24 consecutive games?

You have heard of 20-game winners, they can happen every season, but a 24-consecutive game winner?

Now that has happened only once so far, and "King Carl" or "The Meal Ticket" as Carl Hubbell, the Hall of Fame New York Giants southpaw, with the wicked screwball, was also called, won 253 games in his 16-year career, but no one has come close to his record that began on July 17, 1936 when, with a 10-6 record on that date, he went on a streak of 16 consecutive wins through the end of that season, then opened up the 1937 season with 8 more consecutive wins to establish the major league record of 24 consecutive wins.

His 26 victories, .813 winning percentage, and 2.31 Era. in 1936 led the National League. Then in 1937 he had 22 wins, .733 winning percentage, and 159 strikeouts led the NL again.

173. Who was the first, of the five pitchers, to have struck out 340 or more batters in a season?

George "Rube" Waddell, the Philadelphia Athletics southpaw, was the first of the five pitchers in history to strike out over 340 batters in a season when, in 1904, Rube fanned 349 in that season to lead the American League on his way to a 25-19, 1.62 Era. season.

The others were Bob Feller with 348 in 1946, Sandy Koufax with 382 in 1965, Nolan Ryan with 383 in 1973 and 367 in 1974, and Randy Johnson with 364 in 1999, 347 in 2000, and 372 in 2001.

174. Who was the first pitcher to win more than twenty games in fifteen or more seasons?

It should come as no surprise to learn that the same pitcher to win 20 or more games more than 15 times in his career was Denton True "Cy" Young, who recorded five 30-win seasons, and eleven 20-win seasons during his 22-year, 511-win career in the National and American Leagues.

175. Who was the first pitcher to give up over 500 home runs?

Robin Roberts made his pitching debut on June 18, 1948 with the Philadelphia Phillies. During his 19 seasons in the major leagues with Philadelphia, Baltimore, Houston and the Chicago Cubs, the Hall of Fame right-hander gave up a total of 402 home runs in his 14 years with the Phillies, and 103 with the three other clubs over the course of his 4,688.2 innings pitched in both leagues.

176. Who was the first pitcher to start over 600 games?

You have to take yourself back to the 19th century, when right-hander James "Pud" Galvin, "The Little Steam Engine," was pitching for the Pittsburgh Alleghenys (Pirates).

During the 1890 season Galvin was closing in on 600 starting assignments. Then in his 15th start that season "The Little Steam Engine" eclipsed the 600 mark to become the first pitcher to start that many games. When his 15 career seasons finally ended, on August 2, 1892, the diminutive 5'8" Pud's arm had thrown the first and last pitch to start a game, for the 688th and last time

177. Who was the first pitcher to pitch a no-hitter in his first major league start?

We have to go back to the 19th century, to the last game of the 1891 season on October 4th. On that day rookie southpaw Ted Breitenstein of the St. Louis Browns, after making his debut on April 28, 1891, and appearing in five games in a relief role, started his first major league game on this date against the Louisville Colonels. And was he ever a success. He set down Louisville without a hit, though he walked one, but faced just the minimum 27 batters in his 8-0 win.

178. Who threw the very first pitch in major league history?

Lon Knight, who was born Alonzo Letti, having been born of Italian immigrant parents, anglicized his name as a teenager, and the 23-year old right-hander was on the mound for the Philadelphia Athletics, and threw the very first major league pitch on April 22, 1876 against the Boston Red Stockings at Philadelphia's Jefferson Street Grounds in the first National League game played. The Red Stockings won the game, 6-5, in ten innings, with right-hander Joe Borden, as mentioned earlier in this section, getting the first major league win in history.

Interestingly all other scheduled Opening Day games were rained out that day, putting both Knight and Borden in the record books.

179. Who was the first pitcher to pitch a perfect game?

The first "Perfect Game Pitcher" was John Lee Richmond, the Worcester Ruby Legs 23-year old southpaw, who pitched the first perfect game in professional history when, on June 12, 1880, at the Agricultural County Fair Grounds in Worcester, he shut down the Cleveland Blues, allowing no one to reach base, winning 1-0.

He almost lost his chance for immortality when right fielder Lon Knight, (remember him as a pitcher for Philadelphia and throwing out the first pitch in major league history) saved the day when he threw out Cleveland's first baseman, Bill Phillips, at first base recording a rare 9-3 putout.

180. Who was the first pitcher to pitch two no-hit games in the same season?

In his first full season in the major leagues southpaw Johnny Vander Meer of the Cincinnati Reds stepped on the mound on June 11, 1938 against right-hander "Deacon Danny" MacFayden and the Boston Braves, and while giving up three walks, and striking out four, he shut down the Braves without a hit, winning 3-0, with no Braves player going beyond first base.

On June 15th, now on the mound for the very first night game in Ebbets Field, against right-hander Max Butcher of the Brooklyn Dodgers, Vander Meer wasn't quite as sharp as he was four days earlier, but sharp enough, although he walked eight, and struck out seven, and had a scare in the bottom of the 9th by walking the bases full, he ended it by getting Leo Durocher to pop up, and his second consecutive no-hitter of the year went into the record books as the Reds rolled to a 6-0 win.

There have been five pitchers who have pitched a pair of no-hitters in the same season: Johnny Vander Meer, June 11th and June 15th, 1938; New York Yankees Allie Reynolds, July 12th and September 28th, 1951; Virgil

Trucks of Detroit on May 15th and August 25th, 1952; Nolan Ryan with the California Angels on May 15th and July 15th, 1973; and Roy Halladay of the Phillies on May 29th and October 6th, 2010.

181. Who was the first pitcher to give up a home run to Mickey Mantle?

Randy Gumpert, the Chicago White Sox right-hander, surrendered the first home run to Mantle, a one out, 450-foot two-run blast into the seats at Comiskey Park, in the 6th inning on Tuesday, May 1, 1951, before a crowd of 14,776.

182. Who was the first pitcher to win only five games all season, while losing 19, yet did not give up a run in any of those five victories?

This happening was the result of Detroit Tigers' right-hander Virgil "Fire" Trucks unusual season in 1952 in which he won only five games all season, losing 19, but three of them were shutouts, and the other two were no-hitters, the first on May 15, 1952, beating the Washington Senators, 1-0. The second no-hitter came on August 25, 1952 when he defeated the Yankees, 1-0.

It looked like Trucks, in order to win, had to be flawless.

183. Who was the first pitcher to give up 50 home runs in one season?

Bert Blyleven, the strong-armed right-hander of the Minnesota Twins, wasn't unknown for having batters take him downtown on more than one occasion, and the 1986 season proved that when he gave up the gopher ball on 50 different occasions in 36 games over 271.2 innings to be the first pitcher to allow 50 batters to circle the bases unimpeded in one season.

Over his 22-year career he gave up 430 home runs in 692 games over 4,970 innings, and had a 287-250 career record making him a resident of Cooperstown in 2011.

184. Who was the first pitcher to pitch over 70 complete games in a season?

They may have called right-hander William Henry White, "Will" or "Whoop-La", but "Iron Arm" could have fit him more aptly.

In 1879 with the Cincinnati Reds, Will "Whoop-La" White led the National League in games with 76, in starts with 75, and in completed games with 75, while hurling 680 innings, to be the first to reach that level of complete games in a season, and showed a very impressive 43-31, 1.99 Era. that year.

185. Who was the first pitcher to pitch 187 consecutive complete games?

After reading about Will "Whoop-La" White we now ask the question as to who went to even greater heights of not needing relief once on the mound. That is until Chicago Cubs right-hander, Jack Taylor, came upon the scene, and started his consecutive complete game streak of games on June 20, 1901.

The streak reached 187 games on Thursday, August 9, 1906, in Brooklyn, when Taylor finished off the Superbas, by defeating them, 5-3.

It came to an end after 187 games, when in the 3rd inning, on Monday, August 13th, Brooklyn got to Taylor in the 3rd inning, and right-hander Orval Overall had to come on in relief, and took the Cubs to an 11-3 win. This "Groundbreaker" should not ever be challenged on that record.

186. Who was the first, and only, pitcher to come on in relief to throw one pitch to get a triple play, and end the inning?

There was no better, nor quicker, way to get out of a jam than what St. Louis Cardinals southpaw "Wee Willie" Sherdel accomplished on Wednesday, July 30, 1924 down in Baker Bowl, Philadelphia.

Right-hander Leo Dickerman had started for the Redbirds, but had run into trouble in the bottom of the 2nd after having given up four runs, and five hits. Sherdel was called in by manager Branch Rickey to relieve Leo, and found Phillies' catcher Jimmie Wilson on second, and pitcher Jimmy Ring on first with none out, and pinch-hitter Johnny Mokan at the plate.

Wee Willie's first pitch to Mokan was a softly hit bunt in the air to 1B "Sunny Jim" Bottomley for the initial out. Bottomley then threw over to second base to Jimmy Cooney to catch Wilson off the bag for the second out. Cooney relayed the ball to second baseman Rogers Hornsby, who was covering first base, retiring Jimmy Ring, who was trying to scramble back, for the third out. Three outs on one pitch in relief. Sherdel went on to finish the game, giving up four additional runs for a 9-8 victory.

187. Who was the first pitcher to ever win a game without throwing a pitch?

Can't happen you say? Oh, but some say it did, to Chicago White Sox southpaw Nick Altrock. There are those who say it is legend, but I just had to put it in here, after much empty research to confirm the date and the team here is the story.

In 1906 Altrock, with an excellent curveball and changeup and noted for his excellent pickoff moves was called into a game in the 9th inning, with the Sox down by a run, with two outs, and the bases loaded, and picked off the runner on first with his first move, to retire the side.

The Pale Hose came back in the bottom of the 9th to score two runs, and gave the Altrock the win to be the first pitcher to win a game without throwing a pitch.

Whether Altrock's effort was the first there, have been similar instances, but I just like to believe in this story about the colorful, zany southpaw.

188. Who was the first pitcher to have his glove taken away from him while on the mound pitching in a game?

This unusual event happened on April 16, 1928 when Boston Braves right-hander Charlie Robertson was detected, by Brooklyn Robins captain Max Carey, of doing odd things with the ball while it was in Charlie's glove. He complained to the umpire, Charley Moran, who took the glove away from Robertson and made him use a new glove. It didn't affect old Charlie for he went on to knock the Robins off their perch by winning 3-2. It was a first time that a pitcher had been relieved, not of his person, but of his glove while on the mound.

189. Who was the first relief pitcher to lead his league in earned run average?

In 1952 a right-hander by the name of Hoyt Wilhelm joined the New York Giants and had a sparkling rookie year with a 15-3 record along with 11 saves as he led the National League in games with 71, and in earned run average with 2.43, giving up 43 earned runs in 159.1 innings.

With that effort he became the first reliever to lead his league in Era.

190. Who was the first relief pitcher to have saved over 200 games in his career?

That honor also goes to Hoyt Wilhelm who during his 21-year career on the mound with eight teams pitched 2,254.1 innings in 1,070 games, and saved 227, to become the first pitcher to exceed the 200-save mark in major league baseball.

191. Who was the first modern day National League pitcher to record

all three putouts in an inning?

It happened out in Wrigley Field on Friday, April 25, 1975, when Chicago Cubs right-hander Rickey "Rick" Reuschel went to the mound in the top of the 3rd inning against the St. Louis Cardinals and had the first batter, catcher Ted Simmons, bounce back to him and Rick met him on the baseline for the first out. 1B Keith Hernandez bounced a grounder to 1B Pete LaCock who flipped to Reuschel for the out at first. 3B Ken Reitz did the same thing by grounding to LaCock who flipped to "Big Daddy" for his third putout of the inning, making him a "Groundbreaker."

192. Who was the first pitcher to retire 34 consecutive batters in one game?

On September 24, 1919 Boston Red Sox right hander Waite "Schoolboy" Hoyt faced the New Yankees at the Polo Grounds and retired them in order in the first.

The 2nd inning was to be different as the Yankees erupted for three straight singles to score the opening run. Hoyt settled down and retired the last three Yankees to end the inning.

Over the next ten innings Hoyt was perfect as no Yankee reached base. Fortunately teammate Babe Ruth came to Hoyt's aid by smashing a gigantic home run over the right field roof to knot the game at 1-1.

With the score tied at 1-1 Hoyt retired the first batter in the 13th inning, giving him thirty-four consecutive batters retired.

That didn't last however, as Yankee 1B Wally Pipp tripled deep to the wall in centerfield and 2B Del Pratt brought him home with a fly ball to Ruth.

Hoyt lost his game 2-1 but the record shows him as a "Groundbreaker" by being the first pitcher to retire 34 consecutive batters in a single game.

193. Who was the first American League pitcher to throw two complete 9-inning game victories in the same day?

Let's go back to July 1, 1905 when Chicago White Sox right-hander Frank "Yip" Owen went up against the St. Louis Browns.

He set the Brownies down in the first game, 3-2, and came back to pitch the second game, another classic nine inning complete game, to shutout St. Louis 2-0, to become the first American League pitcher to pitch two complete game wins in the same day.

194. Who was the first pitcher to pitch a no-hitter and yet never came to bat?

This hard to believe fact came to pass on April 27, 1973, when right-hander Steve Busby, after appearing in only five games since his debut on September 8, 1972 with the Kansas City Royals, went to the mound at Tiger Stadium, against Detroit, before a crowd of 16,345, and pitched a 3-0, no-hitter.

What was different, and the reason for Busby not batting, was the inauguration of the designated hitter rule that had an additional player bat in place of the pitcher in all future American League games. That day Steve Hovley, a .286 hitter, was the DH and he went 1-4 on the day.

195. Who was the first pitcher, and father, to pitch a no-hitter on Father's Day?

On Sunday, June 21, 1964 Jim Bunning, the ace right-hander of the Philadelphia Phillies, took the mound in the 2nd game of a doubleheader at Shea Stadium.

It was Fathers' Day, and Bunning gave something to his children they will long remember. He pitched a no-hitter, and defeated the New York Mets, 6-0, to become the first father to pitch a no-hitter on his day.

196. Who was the first pitcher to pitch a no-hitter as his last major league win?

Just how bizarre is this story? Joe Cowley was a right-handed pitcher who made his major league debut with the Atlanta Braves on April 13, 1982, and stayed with them for a year. He signed a free agent contract with the Yankees on November 22, 1983, and after two seasons was traded to the Chicago White Sox on December 12, 1985.

There, on September 19, 1986 he pitched a less than classic no-hitter against the California Angels, walking seven, and allowing a sacrifice fly, which provided the only run in his 7-1 no-hitter.

That would be a memorable day for Joe, for it would be his 33rd and last major league win, after 21 losses, for he was traded to the Philadelphia Phillies and concluded his five season career, going 0-4 for Philadelphia and ending up with a 33-25 record.

But Joe has the distinction of being the first pitcher to bow out of the major leagues with a no-hitter as his last victory.

197. Who were the first pitchers to match no-hitters on the same day?

As unusual as it is to have a no-hitter, what are the odds of having one in each league on the same day?

Well, it happened on Friday, June 29, 1990 at the SkyDome in Toronto, where right-hander Dave Stewart of the Oakland Athletics no-hit the Blue Jays, 5-0.

Over in the National League, Los Angeles Dodgers southpaw Fernando Valenzuela shut down the St, Louis Cardinals without a hit, winning 6-0, to complete the twin no-hitters on the same day; never before, never since. It was a true "Groundbreaker" moment.

198. Who was the first pitcher to pitch a no-hitter and not strikeout a batter?

As unusual as this is it happened on September 4, 1923 when New York Yankees right-hander "Sad Sam" Jones, turned in a classic no-hitter, walking only one, but, not striking out a single batter to elevate him to being the first pitcher to throw a no-hitter, but fail to fan a batter.

199. Who was the first pitcher to win 20 games with an earned run average over 5.00?

Leave it up to old Bobo to come up with numbers like that. Buck New-som, one of baseball's more colorful players, led the American League in seven different categories while pitching for the St. Louis Browns in 1938. He led in games started with 40, complete games with 31, innings pitched with 329.2, batters faced with 1,475, hits with 334, home runs with 30, and earned runs with 186 which led to his 5.08 Era. that went along with his 20-16 won-lost record.

200. Who was the first pitcher to be a victim of losing a game to a no-hitter, and then come back in the same season to win a game by pitching a no-hitter?

On Saturday, May 11, 1963, at Dodger Stadium Los Angeles, southpaw Sandy Koufax no-hit the San Francisco Giants, 8-0, with the Giants ace right-hander Juan Marichal taking the loss.

Then a month later, on Saturday, June 15th, Juan Marichal pitched a 1-0 gem, no-hitting the Houston Colts at Candlestick Park, and became the first pitcher to be beaten by a no-hitter, and then come back to win by pitching a no-hitter all in the space of a month.

201. **Who was the first pitcher to pitch a regular season inter-league perfect game?**

It was "Yogi Berra Day" on Sunday, July 18, 1999 at Yankee Stadium when right-hander David Cone took the mound against the visiting Montreal Expos in an inter-league game.

Cone faced 27 consecutive batters and set each one down in order, striking out 10 along the way, to be the first pitcher to pitch a no-hitter/perfect game in interleague play.

202. **Who was the first pitcher in modern major league history to pitch a shutout, and hit a home run in his first major league game?**

On Thursday, August 23, 2001, Colorado Rockies rookie right-hander Jason Jennings got the call to make his major league debut by starting the game against the New York Mets at Shea Stadium.

And what an impressive debut it was, as Jennings shutout the Mets, 10-0, on five hits, walked four, and struck out eight. He added to the Rockies run production by going 3-5, with two runs batted in, including hitting his first home run, a shot to right field in the 9th inning off right-hander Donne Wall

203. **Who was the first pitcher to be credited with pitching in a game without ever throwing a pitch?**

This unusual happening occurred at the Houston Astrodome on Monday, September 15, 1971 when in the top of the 9th inning, with the Astros down 4-1 to the Atlanta Braves, Astros manager, Harry "The Hat" Walker, called upon the 21-year old right-hander Larry Yount, who happened to be brother of Robin Yount, to make his major league debut. Yount was announced and made his way to the mound and after throwing a warm up pitch felt a sharp pain in his pitching elbow and had to stop throwing, and left the game, never to play again.

Right-hander Jim "Sting" Ray had to come on to relieve Yount who had been officially announced, and thus received credit for appearing in the game, but never threw a pitch to a batter.

204. **Who was the first pitcher to have his no-hitter broken up after nine innings?**

On Thursday, May 9, 1901, right-hander Earl "Crossfire" Moore, who had made his debut with the Cleveland Blues a couple of weeks earlier, on April 25, 1901, was rolling along with a no-hitter against the Chicago White Sox through nine innings. "Crossfire" "miss-fired" in the 10th as he gave up a leadoff single, plus another hit, and ended up losing the game 4-2.

205. Who was the first National League pitcher to have his no-hitter broken up after nine innings?

On that Saturday afternoon of June 11, 1904, Bob Wicker, the Chicago Cubs right-hander, was breezing along, after nine innings at the Polo Grounds with a no-hitter against the New York Giants.

In the 10th inning, with one out Wicker gave up a single, his only hit of the game, and lost his no-hitter, but he did come away with a 1-0, shutout over the men of McGraw.

206. Who was the first and only pitcher to no-hit the same team twice in his career?

On October 2, 1908, at League Park, a pitcher's battle ensued as the Cleveland Naps Adrian "Addie" Joss, a.k.a. "The Human Hairpin", toed the rubber against "Big Ed" Walsh, the Chicago White Sox right-hander. It took Addie just 74 pitches to set down 27 White Sox batters in a row and come away with a perfect game win, 1-0.

Let's not overlook "Big Ed", who struck out 15 Naps, gave up just four hits, with the only run coming on a passed ball by catcher Ossee Schreckengost in what many have called one of baseball's finest pitching performances.

Moving ahead to April 20, 1910 and Addie was again facing the Chicago White Sox, and showed them no more respect than he did two years earlier as he pitched a no-hitter against the Pale Hose to become the first, and only, pitcher to no-hit the same team twice in his career.

207. Who was the first pitcher to lead the league in both walks allowed, and games won in the same season?

You can look at "Grasshopper Jim" Whitney for the answer as the Boston Beaneaters right-hander made his major league debut on May 2, 1881, and proceeded to lead the National League that season by allowing 90 walks, and in games won with 31. He didn't stop being a leader there as he also led in games pitched with 66, games started with 63, innings pitched with 552.1, wild pitches with 46, batters faced with 2,301 and hits allowed, with 548, and games lost with 33.

He certainly made his presence known in enough categories in his rookie year.

208. Who was the first pitcher to lose 300 games?

Most everyone knows who won the most games -- Cy Young with 511 -- but did you know that Young was the first, and only, pitcher to lose over 300 games as he took the loss 316 times in his career.

209. Who was the first pitcher to make 1,000 appearances in a game for the same team?

When New York Yankees famed right-handed closer, Mariano "Mo" Rivera, was called in to close out the Toronto Blue Jays in a non-save situation in the 9th inning at the Yankee Stadium on Wednesday, May 25, 2011 it marked his 1,000 appearance on the mound in pinstripes which made him a "Groundbreaker" by becoming the first pitcher in major league history to pitch in that many games for the same team.

Rivera, who was born in Panama City, Panama, first thought of himself as a shortstop, but made his pitching debut with the Yankees on May 23, 1995, appearing in 19 games that season, starting 10, completing 2, with no saves. Moving to a permanent relief role the following season his 17-career, to date, shows a won-lost record of 75-55, recording 527 saves over the course of 1,171 innings, and makes him the 15th pitcher to register over 1,000 games in his career, but the first with a single team.

210. Who was the first American League pitcher to pitch a no-hitter in a night game?

It was a Wednesday evening at Briggs Stadium, on June 30, 1948, with 49,761 fans on hand, who saw Bob Lemon, the Cleveland Indians right-hander set down the Detroit Tigers, 2-0, without a hit for his 11th win of the season, and the first ever no-hitter to be pitched at night.

211. Who was the first modern day pitcher to have over 200 major league wins, but never won 20 games in a major league season?

Right-hander Joannes Pajkos was born on July 1, 1883 in Stefurov, Austria-Hungary, and made his major league debut with the New York Highlanders on April 15, 1909 under the name of Jack Quinn.

After spending three years in the American League with New York he went to the Boston Braves in 1913, before jumping to the Federal League with the Baltimore Terrapins just prior to the 1914 season.

1918 found him joining the Chicago White Sox for that season before returning to the Yankees where he stayed until being traded in December 1921 to the Boston Red Sox. He spent four years with the Red Sox, went on to spend six years with the Philadelphia Athletics, then over to the National League with two years in Brooklyn, and his 21st and final major league season with Cincinnati.

His career record shows 212-182 in both the AL and NL, but no twenty-game seasons. He did, however, win 26 games with the Terrapins of the Federal League in 1914, but also lost 22 games with them in 1915. Those two years don't have any bearing on Quinn being the first pitcher to exceed 200 major league victories without enjoying a single twenty-win season.

212. Who was the first pitcher to strike out over 2,000 batters for two different teams?

Randy Johnson made his major league debut with the Montreal Expos on September 15, 1988, remaining with them until he was traded to the Seattle Mariners on May 25, 1989.

During his ten years with Seattle, (1989-1998), "The Big Unit" disposed of 2,162 batters on strikes. Moving to Houston, where he appeared in just 11 games before being traded to the Arizona Diamondbacks on July 31, 1998, he went about striking out National League batters with equal frequency. During his 8-year stay in Arizona, (1999-2004, 2007-2008), 2,077 batters were victims of his fastball making Johnson the first pitcher to record over 2,000 strikeouts for two different teams.

By the time "The Big Unit" hung up his spikes after 22 seasons, pitching for six teams, he had 2,545 American League strikeouts, and 2,330 National League strikeouts.

213. Who was the first pitcher to have a 20-win season for both the New York Mets and New York Yankees?

The first pitcher to win 20 games in one season for both New York teams was right-hander David Cone who had a 20-3 season for the Mets in 1988, and when he went cross-town to the Yankees he had a 20-7 season in 1998 in the Bronx.

214. Who was the first pitcher to strike out four batters, and hit a home run in the same inning?

The second game of the doubleheader at Wrigley Field before 36,797 Cubs fans on Monday, September 2, 2002 couldn't have been better. First they saw Chicago destroy the Milwaukee Brewers 17-4 as Kerry Wood cruised to his 10th win, but what happened in the 4th inning was a first in major league history.

With the Cubs holding a 9-0 lead going into the top of the 4th inning, with one out, Woods struck out SS Bill Hall swinging, but as the ball got past Hundley he threw wildly past 1B Fred McGriff and Hall ended up on third base. Then Wood struck out RF Ryan Thompson swinging, and did the same to catcher Paul Bako, bringing up the Brewers southpaw pitcher, Andrew Lorraine, and got him, like the previous three batters, swinging at his delivery.

Going into the bottom of the 4th , after SS Alex Gonzalez homered, Todd Hundley walked bringing up Wood, who deposited Andrew Lorraine's pitch into the left-centerfield stands for a two-run home run, scoring Hundley. Sammy Sosa followed with a two-run home run, and after the inning was over Wood had a 14-run lead as Chicago went on to wrap up a 17-4 win, with Kerry Wood being the first pitcher to strike out four batters, and hit a home run in the same inning; truly a "Groundbreaker" achievement.

215. Who was the first pitcher to lead the league in wins and losses in the same season?

On May 2, 1881 right-hander James "Grasshopper Jim" Whitney made his major league debut with the Boston Beaneaters, and must have made some sort of an impression for he went on to lead the league in games started with 63, and games completed with 57, and in innings pitched with 552.1, but with his 2.48 Era. he still came away with a league leading 31 wins and 33 losses to be the first pitcher to be a league leader in both those categories in the same season.

I also must mention that "Grasshopper Jim" also led in hits with 548, walks with 90, and wild pitches with 46 that season.

During his ten-year career Whitney had a 191-204 record and a 2.97 Era.

216. Who was the first modern day pitcher to lead the league in wins

and losses in the same season?

We just have to go back to the 1979 season to find Hall of Fame, 318-game winner, Phil "Knucksie" Niekro, who broke in with the Milwaukee Braves on April 15, 1964, and now with the Atlanta Braves, filling that category when the right-hander led the National League in wins and losses with a 21-20 record over a league-leading 342 innings, with a 3.39 Era.

He also led in games started with 44, complete games with 23, hits (311), walks (113), batters hit by a pitch (11), and batters faced (1,436).

217. Who were the first modern-day 300-game winners to start a game against each other?

On Saturday, June 28, 1986, out in Anaheim Stadium, 43,385 fans were treated to being the first to see two 300-game winners face off against each other as right-hander Don Sutton of the California Angels took the mound against fellow right-hander Phil Niekro of the Cleveland Indians.

In the top of the 7th inning Sutton gave up a solo home run to Cleveland leadoff batter RF Cory Snyder to tie the game at 3-3. In the bottom of the 7th with one out Niekro gave up two singles and a walk to load the bases, and that brought in right-hander John Butcher who got Jack Howell, pinch-hitting for catcher Bob Boone, to hit into an inning-ending double play and send the game tied into the 8th

In the top of the 8th right-hander Doug Corbett replaced Sutton and both Hall of Fame 300-game winners were finished for the day.

The box score showed Neikro going 6.1 innings, allowing 10 hits and 3 earned runs, fanning 4. Sutton's ledger showed 7 innings, 7 hits and also 3 earned runs while striking out 6.

The Angels came up with a 6-run rally in the bottom of the 8th to go on and take a 9-3 win with neither Cooperstown resident getting the win or taking the loss.

218. Who was the first pitcher to win over 200 games, and finish his career with an Era. over 4.00?

Southpaw Earl Whitehill made his major league debut on September 15, 1923 with the Detroit Tigers. In 1926 he led the American League in earned runs allowed with 112.

On December 14, 1932 he was traded to the Washington Senators and there had his first and only 20-win season registering a 22-8 mark in 1933.

In 1935 Whitehill again led the American League in earned runs allowed, with 133. In December 1936 he was traded to the Cleveland Indians where he played for the 1937-38 seasons before finishing his 17-year career on September 30, 1939 with the Chicago Cubs showing a career record of 218 wins, against 185 losses and a 4.36 Era. to become the first pitcher to exceed 200 wins and an over 4.00 Era.

219. Who was the first pitcher to lose 27 consecutive decisions, where a decision was had?

On August 5, 1991, right-hander Anthony Young made his major league debut with the New York Mets. He struggled over the next two years winning just four games, but his consecutive losing streak began after two victories, one in St. Louis and the other in Montreal, on Wednesday, May 6, 1992, at Riverfront Stadium, when he went six innings, giving up five runs on six hits, in a 5-3 loss to Cincinnati southpaw Greg Swindell.

The losing streak ran for fourteen consecutive games in 1992, and carried over for thirteen more, concluding with his 27th consecutive loss on Saturday, July 24, 1993 against the Dodgers in Los Angeles.

The good news happened, and the streak was broken, when Young defeated the Florida Marlins, 5-4, at Shea Stadium on July 28th for his only win of the season.

We should keep one important fact in mind -- that Young was pitching for a Met team that was far from a winning team, with a 59-103 record, that even Young's 3.77 Era wasn't going to get a lot of support.

220. Who was the first one-eyed major league pitcher?

We have to go back to August 30, 1886 when right-hander Bill Irwin made his debut with the Cincinnati Red Stockings with only having one eye. Unfortunately his career ended after one season with his record showing two games started, two finished, with a 5.82 Era. that resulted in a career 0-2 record.

If we move to the modern day era we find right-hander Henry "Hi" Jasper making his major league debut with the Chicago White Sox on April 19, 1914, and playing two seasons with them, one with the St. Louis Cardinals, and his fourth and final season with the Cleveland Indians, and showing a 10-12, 3.48 Era. career record.

The third and final pitcher to pitch in the big leagues without vision in both eyes was Tom "Lefty" Sunkel, who debuted with the Cardinals on

August 26, 1937, pitched there two years, then on to the New York Giants for three years before finishing up with the Brooklyn Dodgers on September 29, 1944 with a 9-15, 4.34 Era. record.

221. Who was the first pitcher to throw ten shutouts in a season when he won less than 20 games?

It must have seemed that if he didn't pitch a shutout he didn't have too good a chance of coming away with a win, or that's the way "Big Ed" Walsh must have seen his 1906 season with the Chicago White Sox. He led the league in shutouts with 10, but could rack up just 17 wins against 13 losses, even with his miniscule 1.88 Era. He did finish off his 14-year career with 195 wins, against 126 losses, but with a spectacular 1.82.

222. Who was the first, and only, modern day pitcher to throw more than 15 shutouts in a season?

It will not come as much of a surprise to learn that in the 1916 season Grover Cleveland "Old Pete" Alexander, the Philadelphia Phillies Hall of Fame right-hander, led the league in many categories including shutouts with 16, complete games with 38, innings pitched with 389, wins with 33, and an Era. of 1.55, making him the first pitcher to exceed 15 whitewashes in a season.

223. Who was the first American League pitcher to pitch his first major league shutout, and then follow that with a no-hitter in his next start?

On Wednesday, June 29, 1983, before a crowd of 33,627 at the Yankee Stadium, southpaw Dave Righetti pitched his first major league shutout setting down the Baltimore Orioles on five hits, facing only 32 batters, on his way to a 7-0 win.

In his next start, on Monday, July 4, 1983, Righetti treated the 41,077 at Yankee Stadium to not only another shutout, but a no-hitter, as he set down the Boston Red Sox 4-0, walking four but facing just 29 batters.

It was the first no-hitter by a Yankee southpaw since George Mogridge on April 24, 1917, when he did it up in Fenway Park beating the Red Sox, 2-1.

224. **Who was the first pitcher to start over 30 games, complete over 20, win more than 25, and not record a single shutout in 255.1 innings pitched?**

Look no further than Leslie "Bullet Joe" Bush the right-hander of the 1922 New York Yankees who started 30 games completed 20, had a 26-7, 3.31 Era. record, but couldn't come up with a shutout in 255.1 innings pitched.

225. **Who was the first, and only, pitcher to win and lose 20 or more games in a season yet have an Era. under 2.00?**

Chicago White Sox right-hander, Jim "Death Valley" Scott, after being purchased from Wichita in the Western Association for $2,000, made his major league debut against the St. Louis Browns on a frigid Chicago afternoon on April 25, 1909. The 19-year old shut out the Browns, striking out 6, and in the process picked up his first big league base hit.

In 1913 Scott did something that has yet to be repeated, he won 20 games, lost a league-leading 21, but had a miniscule 1.90 Era. over 312.1 innings, to be first to post 20 wins and losses, yet keep his earned run average under 2.00. Losing more than winning wasn't uncommon for "Death Valley" Jim for his 9-year career with the weak-hitting Pale Hose showed 107-114, but with a respectable 2.30 Era. over 1,892 innings.

226. **Who was the first pitcher to start 6 consecutive games without recording a strikeout?**

On August 23, 1983 the Detroit Tigers purchased right-hander Glenn Abbott from the Seattle Mariners for $100,000. He started a game for Detroit on September 25th, and from that date on to July 21, 1984, he started six consecutive games, pitching two complete games, but did not record one strikeout. On August 14, 1984 Detroit gave him his release. In his 20 games, while with the Tigers, Abbott had a total of 19 strikeouts.

227. **Who was the first, of only two pitchers, in major league history, to give up 7 runs in the 1st inning and come back to win the ballgame?**

It doesn't get much more difficult than this, so much so that it took over 100 years for it to happen again. It first came about in Chicago when the St. Louis Cardinals were playing the Chicago Orphans (Cubs) on Saturday, September 29, 1900.

Cardinals' right-hander, Jack "Red" Powell, started for the Redbirds; and the Orphans teed off on him quickly, getting seven runs in the 1st inning.

Powell then slammed the door shut and those were all the runs Chicago got as the Cardinals chipped away to pick up ten runs of their own to erase that 1st. inning nightmare, and win 10-7.

You no doubt wonder when it happened for only the second time in ML history. Well, it was just a few years ago, when on Sunday, May 14, 2006, Chicago White Sox southpaw Mark Buehrle went up against the Minnesota Twins at the Hubert H. Humphrey Metrodome. Actually the game didn't start off well for Twins right-hander Carlos Silva in the top of the 1st when he gave up a leadoff single to LF Scott Podsednik, and followed that by hitting 2B Tadahito Iguchi with a pitch to put two men on, with two outs, and set the stage for RF Jermaine Dye to hammer one of Silva's' pitches for a 3-run home run.

With a 3-run lead White Sox southpaw starter Mark Buehrle, got off to an even worse start by having the Twins have their way with him by racking up 7 runs, on 7 hits, along with two errors, one by Buehrle who was off the mark on a bad throw looking for a force out at second, and another by SS Juan Uribe.

With that said, Buehrle went on to pitch six scoreless innings, giving up a total of 7 runs on 12 hits, along with two walks, before being relieved by right-hander Cliff Politte in the 7th inning, after catcher Mike Redmond hit ground-rule double to left-center field.

Politte, along with southpaw Neal Cotts, and closer, right-hander Bobby Jenks, slammed the door on the Twins with three innings of no-hit ball as Mark Buehrle came away with his fourth win, 9-7, but even more historically became only the second pitcher in major league history to win a game after giving up seven runs in the 1st inning, and 21,796 were witness to this once in a hundred year happening.

228. Who was the first pitcher to win 100 games, and strike out 1,000 batters in both the American and National Leagues?

Jim Bunning made his major league debut as a 23-year old right-hander with the Detroit Tigers on July 20, 1955. He stayed 9 years with Detroit, winning 118 games, including a no-hitter at Fenway Park, on July 20, 1958, beating the Red Sox 3-0. During his stay in the Motor City he struck out 1,406 batters before being traded, on December 5, 1963, along with catcher Gus Triandos, to the Philadelphia Phillies, for Don Demeter and Jack Hamilton. There with the Phillies he won an additional 89 games and 1,197 strikeouts in his 6-year stay there, including a perfect game against the New York Mets at Shea Stadium on Father's Day, June 21, 1964, winning 6-0.

He was traded to Pittsburgh on December 15, 1967 and after two years, after winning 14 games with them, was traded to the Los Angeles Dodgers where he won 3 games before being released on October 29, 1969, and went back to the Phillies where he finished his 22-year career with 106 wins and 1,449 strikeouts in the National League to become the first pitcher to exceed 100 wins, and 1,000 strikeouts in both leagues.

229. Who was the first pitcher to give up a clean base hit off the outfield wall, but be credited with a no-hitter?

This unusual turnabout from an excellent pitching performance, to a historic one, happened down in Shibe Park, on Friday afternoon, September 7, 1923, when Boston Red Sox right-hander Howard "Bob" Ehmke served up a pitch to Philadelphia Athletics right-handed pitcher William Jennings Bryan "Slim" Harriss. "Slim" hammered a double off the outfield wall for the first and only hit of the game given up by Ehmke.

Unfortunately "Slim" was so enamored with his hitting prowess that he failed to touch first base, and umpire Red Ormsby called Harriss out by that slim margin of his foot not touching the bag, and Ehmke went on not giving up a hit for the rest of the game to complete his no-hitter, facing just 28 batters, as he walked 1B Joe Hauser, preventing a "perfect" outing.

230. Who was the first pitcher in Major League history to win at least 15 games in 17 consecutive seasons?

This 20-year-old right-hander made his pitching debut with the Chicago Cubs on September 2, 1986, and the name of Greg Maddux became a household name for excellence and class throughout his 23-season career that came to an end on September 27, 2008 with the Los Angeles Dodgers.

In 1988 he won 18 games, and for the next 17 consecutive seasons, through 2004, with the Atlanta Braves and the Cubs, he never won less than 15 games to become the first pitcher in history to run up such a successful winning streak.

Over his long and successful career with the Braves, Cubs, Padres, and Dodgers, the soon-to-be Hall of Fame candidate, had a 355-227, 3.16 Era. record.

231. Who was the first relief pitcher to have 600 saves?

He started as a shortstop-third baseman in the minors, but was encouraged to switch to the mound and right-hander Trevor Hoffman made his big league debut there for the Florida Marlins on April 6, 1993. He picked up his first save on April 29, 1993 as the Florida Marlins defeated the Atlanta Braves. Four years later, on April 13, 1997, with the San Diego Padres, he recorded his 100th save against the Philadelphia Phillies.

He climbed higher on the saves list on September 24, 2006, when he came in for the Padres as they defeated the Pittsburgh Pirates for his 479th save which passed Lee Smith, the Montreal Expos right-hander, as the all-time saves leader.

Then on September 7, 2010, Hoffman was called in with his theme song, "Hells Bells" playing in the background, to preserve a 4-2 victory for the Milwaukee Brewers over the St. Louis Cardinals. That he did, for his 9th save of the season, and the 600th in his long and successful career, and establish a new figure for oncoming relievers to shoot for.

232. Who was the first National League reliever to save 50 games in a season?

On September 27, 1993, southpaw Randy Myers came on in relief to record his 50th save of the season, as the Chicago Cubs went on to beat the Los Angeles Dodgers, 7-3. Myers would end the season with 53 saves to lead the senior circuit, and become the first to reach the 50-mark in one season in NL history.

233. Who was the first pitcher to take the mound for a dozen teams?

If you are looking for an expert in the art of packing a suitcase you might look in the direction of right-hander Mike "The Nomad" Morgan who made his major league debut with the Oakland Athletics on June 11, 1978, and stayed two years before beginning his wandering ways throughout both leagues by joining, in this order, the Yankees, Blue Jays, Mariners, Orioles, Dodgers, Cubs, Cardinals, Reds, Twins, Rangers, and finally, in his 22nd season, the Arizona Diamondbacks, where he pitched his final major league game on September 2, 2002.

Over his peregrinating pitching performances for twelve teams, seven in the American League and five in the National, in four different decades, 1978-2002, his record showed 141-186, .423 Era., and no doubt a well-worn suitcase.

234. Who was the first, and only, pitcher to win the Triple Crown four times, three times in a row, and for two different teams?

There will be no eyebrows raised in disbelief when I say that this Hall of Fame right-hander can lay claim to all three of the above first times in baseball history.

I am talking about Grover Cleveland "Old Pete" Alexander who in 1915, while pitching for the Philadelphia Phillies, had a 31-10, record with 241 strikeouts, 12 shutouts, and a minuscule Era. of 1.22 to capture the pitching Triple Crown. He came back in 1916 to have a 33-12, 167 strikeouts, and 16 shutouts to go along with his 1.55 Era. Still on a roll "Old Pete" duplicated those past two seasons by winning the Triple Crown, in 1917, for a third time with the Phillies, with a 30-13 record, with 201 strikeouts, 8 shutouts and a 1.83 Era.

The 1918 season saw "Old Pete" wearing a Chicago Cubs uniform as he, and catcher "Reindeer Bill" Killfer, were traded on December 11th for catcher Bill "Pickles" Dillhoefer, right-hander Mike Prendergast, and $55,000.

It wasn't until the 1920 season, with Chicago, that Alexander once again captured the Triple Crown as he recorded a 27-14, 173 strikeout, 7 shutout season to go along with his 1.91 Era.to make him the first, and only, pitcher to win that Crown four times, three times in succession, and with two different ball clubs.

235. Who was the first, and only, pitcher to pitch a no-hitter on his birthday?

When "Wabash George" Mullin celebrated a holiday, and his birthday, he did it in grand fashion. Mullin was born on the 4th of July in 1880, so a celebration was always in order.

Three weeks before this day in 1912 the Detroit Tigers had asked waivers on their right-hander, but Mullin gave the Tigers reason to re-think that decision for on Thursday, July 4th, in the second game of a doubleheader at Navin Field, Detroit, he went up against the St. Louis Browns, on his 32nd birthday, and pitched a 7-0 no-hitter and helped to insure the win, and the celebration, by getting three hits and driving in two runs.

236. Who was the first pitcher to pitch over 7,000 innings?

Denton True "Cy" Young made his debut with the Cleveland Spiders on August 6, 1890 and the 23-year old right-hander went on to pitch for 22 seasons, racking up 511 wins, losing 316, over the course of 7,356 innings, before pitching his final innings on October 6, 1911 with the Boston Rustlers, to be the first to reach that high plateau.

237. Who was the first 200-game winner to retire after winning 20 games in his final season?

To pitch your final game, at age 36, with 210 wins over 14 seasons was the decision made by Chicago White Sox right-hander Eddie "Knuckles" Cicotte when he took the mound for the last time on September 26, 1920. He wound up his career with his third 20-win season, having led the American League in 1917 and 1919 with 28 and 29 wins, to be the first 200-win pitcher to wrap up his career with another 20-win season.

238. Who was the first pitcher to lose two complete games in one day?

Southpaw Dave Anderson started the 1890 season with the Philadelphia Athletics, but finished the season with the Pittsburgh Alleghenys (Pirates). There, in a triple-header, played on Monday, September 1, 1890, he pitched two complete games, losing the first game 10-9, and the second game, 3-2, to the Brooklyn Bridegrooms (Dodgers) to be the first pitcher to lose two complete games in one day.

239. Who was the first pitcher to throw a no-hitter on the road?

Buffalo Bisons Hall of Fame right-hander Jim "Pud" Galvin defeated the Worcester Ruby Legs, 1-0, on Friday, August 20, 1880, at the Worcester Agricultural County Fair Grounds. That was one of his 361 career victories.

240. Who was the first pitcher to have his first major league complete game be a perfect game?

On Saturday, April 21, 2012, before 22,472, out in Safeco Field, right-hander Phil Humber of the Chicago White Sox led the Pale Hose to a 4-0 victory over the Seattle Mariners. It was the third perfect game in White Sox history. Charles Robertson did it on April 30th, 1922, when he defeated the Detroit Tigers, 2-0, and Mark Buehrle shut down Tampa Bay, 5-0, on July 23, 2009.

Humber fell behind 3-0 to CF Michael Saunders leading off the 9th, but came back to strike him out. Pinch-hitter John Jaso then flied out, and a second pinch-hitter, Brendan Ryan took a checked swing and missed at a full-count pitch that came in low and outside, with the ball getting away from catcher A.J. Pierzynski. Ryan, not sure of umpire Brian Runge's call hesitated long enough for Pierzynski to retrieve the ball and fire it to Paul Konerko at first for the final out.

Humber struck out nine and threw 96 pitches in his first career complete game. A perfect one!

241. Who was the first National League pitcher to pitch a perfect game?

Jim Bunning of the Philadelphia Phillies, pitched a perfect game against the New York Mets at Shea Stadium on Father's Day, Sunday, June 21, 1964, as the former Detroit Tigers right-hander defeated the Mets before their home crowd, 6-0.

242. Who was the first pitcher to strikeout over 200 batters in a season where he had a losing record?

"Long Tom" Hughes, the Chicago Orphans (Cubs) right-hander became the first of 41 pitchers to strikeout over 200 batters, and come up with a losing record, when in the 1901 season he fanned 225, over 308.1 innings, having a 3.24 Era., but walking 115 and giving up 309 hits which no doubt led to his losing record of 10-23.

243. Who threw the first no-hitter in New York Mets history?

It was an historic night in Citi Field on Friday June 1, 2012 when 27,069 fans were witness to what millions of fans had been denied over the course of 8,019 Mets games heretofore.

Southpaw Johan Santana, with the crowd on its feet watched Santana, having come back from arm surgery, strike out St. Louis Cardinals third baseman David Freeze, with a classic change-up at 9:48 PM to become the first pitcher in Mets history to pitch a no-hitter.

Thanks had to go to leftfielder Mike Baxter who, in the 7th inning,. made an unbelievable catch off catcher Yadier Molina's line drive as he leaped up, extended his left hand and caught the ball in the webbing of his glove as he crashed into the wall, to save a base hit.

Santana came away with an 8-0 win, facing 32 batters, throwing 57 balls and 77 strikes as he erased the 50-year jinx that has dogged the Mets staff.

244. Who pitched the first perfect game in New York/San Francisco Giants history?

Speaking about overcoming a jinx the Giants, whether they be on the east coast or the west coast, have had outstanding pitchers since they played their first game on May 1, 1883 as the New York Gothams. Some have pitched no-hitters, but none a perfect game until Wednesday, June 13, 2012 when right-hander Matt Cain faced the Houston Astros at AT&T Park, before a home crowd of 42,298, and set down the visitors, 10-0, without a man getting on base, fanning 14 to tie the perfect game record of Sandy Koufax against the Chicago Cubs on September 9, 1965.

It was the 22nd perfect game in major league history as Cain was the beneficiary of two outstanding catches by his corner outfielders to preserve his perfect game.

In the 6th inning left fielder Melky Cabrera took a base hit from Chris Snyder by making a leaping catch off the wall. In the 7th inning right fielder Gregor Blanco ran into deep right-center to make a diving catch on the warning track off the bat of Jordan Schafer to insure Cain of going into the 9th inning where he had Juan Castro hit a ground ball to third for the 27th, and final out to make Matt Cain the first player in Giants history to pitch a perfect game.

His 125 pitches where the most ever thrown in a perfect game, 86 of them for strikes, and in the 9th inning his fastball was clocked at 90 mph.

245. Who was the first pitcher to start and complete all of his twenty games in a season?

One of the most liked and respected pitchers of his era Theodore Amar Lyons, affectionately called "Sunday Teddy," because his manager, Jimmy Dykes, always wanted him to start one of the two games of the Sunday doubleheader, made his debut with the Chicago White Sox on July 2, 1923. In his 20th year and at age 41, right-hander Ted Lyons started and completed all twenty games that season going 14-6, with a superb 2.10 Era. over his 180.1 innings pitched.

After service in the Marine Corps Lyons pitched his final game, at age 46, on Sunday, May 19, 1946, at Comiskey Park, pitching all nine innings, for his 28th consecutive complete game, but losing to the Washington Senators, 4-3.

His 21-year career, topped off by his Hall of Fame induction in 1955, showed a 260-230, 3.67 Era.record.

246. Who was the first, and only, pitcher to strike out the side on 9 pitches twice in the same season?

It shouldn't come as a big surprise to learn that Lefty Grove, who struck out 2,266 batters in his 17-year career with the Philadelphia Athletics and

Boston Red Sox, turned in two "immaculate" innings in the same season. The first time he struck out the side on nine pitches came in the 2nd inning, on August 23, 1928; in a 3-1 Athletics win, when Eddie Morgan, Luther Harvel, and Martin Autry of the Cleveland Indians went down on strikes with minimal effort by the Philadelphia Athletics southpaw.

Proving he could do it again he went into the 7th inning against the Chicago White Sox on September 27, 1928, and set down Moe Berg, Tommy Thomas, and Johnny Mostil on nine pitches in his 5-3 win over the Pale Hose, to become the first and only pitcher to have two immaculate innings in the same season.

B. SWINGING THE LUMBER

1. Who was the first batter to come to the plate in the first National League game?

George Wright, a future resident of Cooperstown, and an outstanding hitter and shortstop for the Boston Red Stockings, was the first batter to come to the plate against the Philadelphia Athletics, and grounded out to short at the Jefferson Street Grounds in the National League's inaugural game in Philadelphia on Saturday, April 22, 1876.

2. What player had the first base hit in National League history?

On April 22, 1876 centerfielder James Henry "Orator Jim" O'Rourke, of the Boston Red Stockings (Braves) is credited with having the first base hit, a single, in National League history.

3. Who was the player to get the first *extra* base hit in National League history?

The first two-bagger in NL history was hit by outfielder-third baseman "Long Levi" Meyerle of the Philadelphia Athletics. He also was the first to hit a triple when he hit the first three-bagger on April 24, 1876.

Meyerle started off the new major league in-s fast fashion as he was also the first person to receive a base on balls.

4. Who drove in the first run in National League history?

Jack Manning, the right-fielder of the Boston Red Stockings (Braves), drove in the National Leagues' first run in Boston's 6-5 win over the Athletics down in Philadelphia on Saturday, April 22, 1876.

5. Who hit the first National League home run?

On May 2, 1876 second baseman Ross Barnes, of the Chicago White Stockings (Cubs), hit the first National League home run, an inside-the-park shot, off Cincinnati Red Legs right-hander, William "Cherokee" Fisher at Avenue Grounds, Cincinnati. It was Barnes' only home run of the year, but he did capture the batting title with a .429 average. That was one of six home runs poor "Cherokee" gave up that season when he went 4-20 with a 3.02 Era.

6. Who was the first player to get 5 long hits in one game?

On July 9, 1885 centerfielder George Gore of the Chicago White Stockings faced the ace of the Providence Grays staff, right-hander Charles "Old Hoss" Radbourn. He hit Radbourn for three doubles and two triples to be the first player in major league history to have five long hits in one game.

7. Who was the first designated hitter in the National League?

On Thursday, June 12, 1997, the first major league interleague game was played down in The Ballpark in Arlington, when the Texas Rangers hosted the San Francisco Giants. The first player to come to bat as the designated hitter in that first ever regular season faceoff between the American League and National League was Glenallen Hill of the Giants, who fouled out to first baseman Will Clark in the top of the 2nd inning. The Giants went on to win 4-3.

8. Who was the first player to get a base hit in an interleague game?

San Francisco centerfielder Darryl Hamilton had the first interleague base hit when he singled to right field off Texas Rangers southpaw Darren Oliver to open up the game on June 12, 1997.

9. Who hit the first home run in interleague play?

San Francisco Giants right fielder Stan Javier hit a solo home run in the 3rd inning off southpaw Darren Oliver of the Texas Rangers on June 12, 1997, as the Giants went on to win, 4-3.

10. Who was the first, and only, batter to come to the plate three times in one inning, and face a different pitcher with each plate appearance?

On July 4, 1948, before a crowd of 24,363 at Fenway Park, the Boston Red Sox exploded for 14 runs in the 7th inning against the Philadelphia Athletics, on their way to a 19-5 victory. Ted Williams came to the plate three times in the inning to face right-handers Carl Scheib, Charlie "Bubba" Harris, and Bill McCahan, who retired Williams for the last out of the inning.

11. Who was the first player to hit four home runs in a single game, and strikeout seven times in a doubleheader in the same season?

A popular outfielder with the Cleveland Indians and Chicago White Sox, Pat Seerey was known for hitting the long ball, as he did on July 18, 1948, when after being traded to the White Sox, he hit four home runs in an 11-inning game against the Philadelphia Athletics in Shibe Park; two off right-hander Carl Scheib, one off right-hander Bob Savage, and the game winner off southpaw Lou Brissie, giving the White Sox a 12-11 win.

Pat, was a dead low-ball hitter, but had a blind spot for pitches that were high and inside which led to more than his share of strikeouts as witnessed by his striking out seven times in a doubleheader on Saturday, July 24, 1948, four times in the first game, and three times in the second game, on the road against the New York Yankees at the Stadium.

12. Who was the first player to ever be signed strictly for the purpose of being a designated hitter?

Hall of Famer Orlando Cepeda was signed by the Boston Red Sox on January 18, 1973 to become their DH. He batted .289 in 550 at bats while hitting 20 home runs and driving in 86 runs.

13. Who was the first player to hit three home runs in one game in both the American and National Leagues?

On May 21, 1930 Babe Ruth, the New York Yankees right-fielder, hit three consecutive home runs off Philadelphia Athletics right-hander Jack Quinn in the first game of a doubleheader.

When "the Babe" moved over to the National League, with the Boston Braves, he hit three home runs against the Pittsburgh Pirates on May 25, 1935; the first came off right-hander Red Lucas, and the next two off right-hander Guy "The Mississippi Mudcat" Bush.

That made him the first player to hit three home runs in both leagues, and the only two times Ruth had a three-homer game.

14. Of the twelve players who have hit two grand slam home runs in the same game, who was the first to do it?

This New York Yankee second baseman established more than one "first" on May 24, 1936, when "Poosh 'Em Up" Tony Lazzeri went on a hitting rampage against the Philadelphia Athletics down in Shibe Park on that Sunday afternoon before a crowd of 8,000.

He started it off in the 2nd inning when he hit a grand slam home run off Athletics right-hander George Turbeville. He followed that with his second grand slam home run in the 5th inning off right-hander Herman Fink. Not to show partiality he hit a solo home run off southpaw Woody Upchurch in the 7th inning, and also squeezed in a triple, along with a walk, and a strikeout, in his five official times at bat for a total of eleven runs batted in, (a new American League record), and 15 total bases for the game, as the Yankees banged out 19 hits in their 25-2 massacre of Connie Mack's nine.

15. Who was the first, and only, player to hit two grand slam home runs in the same inning?

This St. Louis Cardinals third baseman waited till the 3rd inning of the game against the Los Angeles Dodgers, on Friday, April 23, 1999, out in Dodger Stadium, before a crowd of 46,687, to make his bat explode. With the Cardinals down 2-0, RF Darren Bragg led off the top of the inning with a single to right. Dodgers' right-hander Chan Ho Park then hit SS Edgar Renteria with a pitch. 1B Mark McGwire then singled to right field to load the bases, and set the stage for Fernando Tatis, who crushed Park's pitch to deep left field scoring Bragg, Renteria, McGwire and himself, to make it 4-2.

That's just half the story. After CF J.D. Drew grounded out catcher Eli Marrero also took Park downtown with his home run deep down the left field line for the 5th Cardinals run.

Placido Polanco came in to pinch-hit for 2B David Howard and walked. Park then walked LF Joe McEwing, bringing up RHP Jose Jimenez who laid down a bunt, moving the runners up, and reached first safely on a fielder's choice. Bragg, up for the second time, reached first on an error with Polanco scoring. Renteria followed with a single to right with McEwing scoring. McGwire flied out to right field leaving the bases loaded for Tatis. He wasted no time in emptying them by taking Chan Ho Park deep for his second grand slam home run, scoring Jimenez, Bragg, Renteria, along with himself to be the first, and only, player in history to hit two grand slam home runs in the same inning, and off the same pitcher.

That was all for Park, as southpaw Carlos Perez came on to hopefully curb the merry-go-around on the bases, and St. Louis went on, after their 11-run 3rd inning to a 12-5 win with Jose Jimenez recording his second win of the year.

16. Who was the first, and only, player to win a batting title with having less than 100 hits?

Third baseman Bill Madlock of the Pittsburgh Pirates, in the 1981 strike-shortened season, had 95 hits in 279 at-bats for a .341 batting average, and captured the batting title in just 82 games.

17. Sixteen batters have hit four home runs in one game, fourteen since the 20th century. Who was the first batter to hit four consecutive

home runs in one game?

We have to go back to the 19th century when on Wednesday, May 30, 1894, in the second game of a doubleheader against the Cincinnati Reds, at Boston's Congress Street Grounds, when the Beaneaters second baseman Bobby "Link" Lowe hit two home runs in the 3rd inning, and followed that with two more in his next two at bats off the same Cincinnati Reds right-hander, Elton "Icebox" Chamberlain, all over the 250-foot left field wall of the Congress Street Grounds, as the Beaneaters blasted the Reds, 20-11. Lowe also added a single to give him 17 total bases for the game.

18. Who was the first player to hit a home run completely out of the original Polo Grounds?

The first home of the New York Giants before the familiar horseshoe shaped stadium was built in 1889 was located at 110th Street and 6th Avenue in Manhattan and was used as a polo field. During that time, on Saturday, September 11, 1886, the Giants played the Boston Beaneaters and faced the brilliant future Hall of Fame right-hander, Charles "Old Hoss" Radbourn, who served up one of first baseman Roger Connor's seven home runs that season, but this one cleared all obstacles, and went completely out of the Polo Grounds making Connor, a future Hall of Famer himself, the first to ever have that distinction.

19. Who, of the 23 players who have hit the first major league pitch they saw for a home run, was the first in the modern day era to do it?

In his very first at bat in the major leagues, on May 7, 1922, Pittsburgh Pirates outfielder Walter Mueller faced the Hall of Fame right-hander Grover "Pete" Alexander, then with the Chicago Cubs. On the first pitch delivered to him Mueller crashed a home run to be the first player to hit a home run on the first pitch he saw. Pittsburgh went on to an 11-5 win over Pete and the Cubs. The Muellers were known in the baseball world, as Walter had a brother Clarence "Heinie" Mueller, who had an eleven year career as an outfielder, and a son, Don, a right fielder, who played twelve years, ten with the New York Giants.

20. Who was the first, of only three modern day players, to have hit 14 home runs over a period of 15 games?

Albert Belle, the Cleveland Indians leftfielder, known for his ability to crush the ball for doubles and home runs began a home run streak on Thursday, August 31, 1995, when he hit a 10th inning two-run home run off Toronto Blue Jays right-hander Jimmy Rogers to give the Tribe a 6-4 win at Jacobs Field.

He continued hammering home runs the next day, and when his streak ended, on Saturday, September 23rd, after hitting his 46th home run of the season, off Kansas City Royals right-hander Mark Gubicza, and his 14th in that 15 game stretch he became the first player to display that continued home run power over such an abbreviated period.

21. Who was the first pitcher to hit three triples in a single game?

Right-hander Jouett Meekin of the New York Giants pitched the first game of a doubleheader out in Cleveland on Wednesday, July 4, 1894, and set down the Spiders (Indians) on six hits, 4-3. His bat was also active that day as Meekin became a "Groundbreaker" by being the first pitcher to bang out three triples in one game.

22. Who was the first player to have over 700 at-bats in a single season?

The 1980 season was a significant one for Willie Wilson, the Kansas City Royals leftfielder. He came away with a .326 batting average and led the American League in five categories including the first player to have over 700 official at bats with 705.

He also led the league in plate appearances with 745, in runs with 133, base hits, 230, and triples with 15. Interestingly he never again came close to those plate appearances nor at bats during the rest of his 19-year career.

23. Who was the first American League player to have two triples in the same inning?

Until July 13, 1946 there had been nine batters who had hit two triples in the same inning of a game. None had been in the American League. On that date Al "Zeke" Zarilla, the centerfielder with the St. Louis Browns, legged out two triples in the 4th inning against the Philadelphia Athletics, as the Browns rolled to an 11-4 win, before 5,336 fans down in Shibe Park. This was just the second time in modern day baseball history that this had occurred.

24. Who was the first player to hit the first pitch for a home run to start the season?

On the opening day of the 1986 season, before a crowd of 51,437, at Tiger Stadium, on April 7th, Boston Red Sox right fielder Dwight Evans stepped to the plate as the first batter to start the season in the top of the

1st inning. Facing him was Detroit right-hander, Jack Morris. Evans, liking what he saw, hit the first pitch for a home run to deep left-center field, to be the first player to start the season in such a manner.

25. Who were the first three batters to hit home runs to start a game?

One might say that the San Diego Padres outfield came to play on Monday, April 13, 1987, at Jack Murphy Stadium, and San Francisco Giants right-hander Roger Mason wasn't quite ready for what was about to happen.

The Giants got off to a fast start when 1B Will Clark doubled, and LF Jeffrey Leonard brought him home with a two-run home run in the top of the 1st inning off Andy Hawkins. CF Marvell Wynne opened up the bottom of the 1st inning for San Diego by crushing a 0-2 pitch deep down the right field line for a home run off Mason.

Then RF Tony Gwynn brought the 48,686 faithful to their feet when he followed with a home run to make it, 2-2. LF John Kruk also got the message, and crushed a ball deep into left-center field for the third consecutive home run of the game. After nine pitches Mason, who had a 2-0 lead, was down 3-2. The Giants went on to win 13-6, but the three Padres went into the record books as the first trio to start off their game with consecutive home runs.

26. Who was the first player to pinch-hit a home run in his first major league at-bat?

Of the 23 players who have accomplished this, the very first to do it was rookie outfielder Eddie "Pepper" Morgan of the St. Louis Cardinals. Coming up to pinch-hit in the 7th inning, on Tuesday, April 14, 1936, he hit the first pitch he saw off right-hander Lon "The Arkansas Humming Bird" Warneke of the Chicago Cubs, into the seats of Sportsman's Park for a two-run home run. It wasn't enough as Chicago came away with a 12-7 win.

It had to be a cause for celebration for Morgan for it would be the only home run he would hit in his two-year, 39 at-bat career. The following season Morgan ended up with Brooklyn.

27. Who was the first pitcher to be hit by a thrown pitch twice, and by a line drive once in the same game?

It seemed like no place was safe for Willard Schmidt, the Cincinnati Reds right-hander. He came to bat in the bottom of the 3rd inning of a game on Sunday, April 26, 1959, in Crosley Field, and faced Milwaukee Braves right-hander Lou Burdette who promptly plunked Schmidt with a pitch.

With the Reds batting around in this 6-run inning Schmidt again came to bat, this time facing right-handed reliever Bob Rush, and he gave Schmidt the same treatment by plunking him as well.

When Schmidt went back on the mound in the 4th inning, ahead 6-3, but probably still smarting by being hit twice in the previous inning by pitched balls, he had a new experience when Johnny Logan hit a line drive right back at Schmidt, and the ball struck him on the right hand and literally knocked him out of the game, with right-hander Orlando Pena having to come in to take over the mound duties.

Some solace came Schmidt's way as his Reds outlasted the Braves 11-10.

28. Who was the first batter to pinch-hit an extra inning grand slam home run in another hemisphere?

Benny Agbayani, the New York Mets leftfielder, waited until March 30, 2000 to become the first player to pinch-hit a grand slam home run in another hemisphere when he unloaded off southpaw Danny Young of the Chicago Cubs in the 11th inning as the New York Mets defeated the Cubs, 5-1, in the second game of the regular season, played in the Tokyo Dome, Japan.

29. Who was the first player, of the fourteen who have collected 40 or more doubles in one season, to do it in both the American and National Leagues?

"Big Ed" Delahanty, who played all the infield positions, as well as left field in his 16 major league seasons, had 40 or more doubles four times with the Philadelphia Phillies before moving over to the American League with Washington where he led the league with 43 in 1902.

30. Who was the first player in major league history to have four sacrifice bunts in a single game, and six in the doubleheader?

This unusual happening occurred in a doubleheader at Ebbets Field on Saturday, August 15, 1914, when the Brooklyn Robins hosted the Philadelphia Phillies.

Left-handed hitting Robins' first baseman, Jacob "Jake" Daubert, playing with a very bad foot, hindering his ability to run, used his bat control ability to lay down four sacrifice bunts in the first game, won by Brooklyn, 8-4.

In the second game Jake again had two more sacrifice bunts to give him a record six in the doubleheader as the Robins swept the Phillies by winning 13-5.

This display of bat control wasn't unusual for Jake for he holds the National League for career sacrifices with 329.

31. Who hit the first grand slam home run in National League history?

It happened up in Albany, New York, on September 10, 1881, when first baseman Roger Connor of the Troy Trojans hit what was then called the "ultimate" grand slam.

It came with Troy down 7-4 with two out in the bottom of the 9th inning, and the bases loaded, when southpaw Lee Richmond of the Worcester Brown Stockings served up the historic pitch, and the Trojans won the game 8-7.

32. Who was the first player to hit a grand slam home run from both sides of the plate in the same game?

They could call him ambidextrous or multidimensional for what Boston Red Sox third baseman Bill Mueller did on Tuesday, July 29, 2003 down in The Ballpark in Arlington against the Texas Rangers.

Mueller, batting 8th in the order, unleashed his batting machine by hitting a solo home run to right field in the top of the 3rd inning off right-hander R.A. Dickey.

Coming up in the 7th inning, with one out, and now batting from the right side, he unloaded a grand slam home run to left field off southpaw Aaron Fultz, driving in David Ortiz, Kevin Millar and Trot Nixon before him.

Mueller, with two outs, came back up in the 8th inning, and this time batting from the left side, again found the bases loaded, and promptly emptied them by driving a Jay Powell pitch deep into right-centerfield, scoring Gabe Kapler, Millar, and Nixon to put the Red Sox up, 14-4.

The Red Sox went on to win 14-7, and the 24,632 in attendance saw history made as Mueller became the first player to hit grand slam home runs from both sides of the plate in the same game. His day consisted of having three home runs, using both sides of the plate, two grand slams and nine runs batted in. Not bad for a #8 batter.

33. Who was the first American League player to hit a home run in his first major league at bat?

Luke Stuart, a second baseman for the St. Louis Browns, hit a home run, as a pinch-hitter, in his first major league at bat, on Monday, August 8, 1921. It came off Walter Johnson of the Washington Senators, down in Griffith Stadium, in the top of the 9th inning, with no outs and one runner aboard. It had no impact on the game as Washington rolled to a 16-5 win. It was Luke's only base hit in his very brief three-game, three at-bat major league career, but it made him a "Groundbreaker."

34. Who was the first modern day National League player to hit a home run in his first major league at-bat?

Southpaw swinging Johnny Bates, an outfielder making his major league debut with the Boston Beaneaters (Braves) on Thursday, April 12, 1906, at Washington Park, Brooklyn, connected for a home run in the 2nd inning off right-hander Harry "Rocks" McIntire of the Brooklyn Superbas (Dodgers) to be the first modern day National Leaguer to hit a home run in his first at-bat, as Boston's southpaw Irv "Young Cy" Young hurled a one hit, 2-0 win.

35. Who was the first, and only, player to have hit four doubles in a nine-inning game, twice in the same season?

On Sunday, August 29, 1999 right-fielder Albert Belle of the Baltimore Orioles went 4-5, at Tiger Stadium, batting in three runs, as he hit doubles off Detroit's Masao Kida, Matt Anderson, C. J. Nitkowski, and Nelson Cruz.

He came back on September 23, 1999, in the second game of a double-header, at Camden Yards against the Oakland Athletics, and again went 4-5, driving in three runs with three doubles off Omar Olivares, and another off Jimmy Haynes, helping the Orioles to a 12-4 win over Oakland.

36. Who was the first American League player to have five extra base hits in a game?

It was a Sunday afternoon at Fenway Park on July 14, 1946, and short-stop Lou Boudreau had brought his Cleveland Indians in to play Joe Cronin's Red Sox in a double header before 31,581 fans.

In the opening game Lou took it upon himself to get his team off to a good start, when he smashed a three-run home run off Red Sox right-hander, Joe "Burrhead" Dobson, in a four-run 1st inning. He went on to have himself a 5-for-5 game by adding four doubles to his round-tripper giving him 4 runs batted in, and 3 scored, but his twelve total bases weren't enough as Ted Williams went 4-for-5 with three home runs, and driving in 8 runs, as the Tribe bowed to Boston 11-10. Boudreau remains in the record books as being the first American League player to have five extra base hits in a nine-inning game.

37. Who were the first players in major league history to hit back-to-back inside-the-park home runs?

It was one of those delightful Sunday doubleheaders that used to be played back a few years ago. The setting was the Polo Grounds on June 23, 1946, and the New York Giants hosted the Chicago Cubs. In the 4th inning of the first game New York Giants right-hander Nate Andrews served up a fat pitch to Cubs leftfielder Marv Rickert which he deposited deep inside the cavernous confines of the Polo Grounds, which after having been chased down found Rickert crossing home plate with the first of two inside-the-park home runs. First baseman Eddie Waitkus followed in the batting order, and took a page out Rickert's book, and followed with an inside the park home run of his own. This made these two Cubbies the first players in modern major league history to hit consecutive back-to-back inside-the park home runs. Those were just two of the ten runs the Cubbies would score on their way to a 15-10 loss to the boys from Coogan's Bluff.

38. Who was the first player to hit a home run from both sides of the plate in the same game?

Never referred to for its originality by Chicago newspapers, on Friday, June 25, 1937, before a meager crowd of 6,294, at Wrigley Field, Chicago, Cubs left fielder Augie Galan came up in the 4th inning and batting lefty, hit a two-run home run off Brooklyn Robins right-hander "Fat Freddie" Fitzsimmons with shortstop Billy Jurges aboard.

When Galan came up to the plate in the 8th inning there was Billy Jurges again on base, and he now faced southpaw Ralph "Lefty" Birkofer. Batting from the right side this time, Galan again homered, propelling the Cubs to an 11-2 win, and he became the first player to hit a home run from both sides of the plate in the same game.

39. Who was the first player to hit 40 or more home runs in both the American and National Leagues?

When Darrell Evans, first baseman for the Detroit Tigers, hit his 40th home run of the season on October 2, 1985, off Toronto Blue Jays' right-hander Dave Stieb in the 6th inning to deep centerfield at Tiger Stadium, he became the first player in major league history to have 40 or more home runs in each league. He had previously hit 41 home runs in 1973 while playing for the Atlanta Braves.

40. Who was the first, and only, player to hit into a triple play in his last major league at bat?

It couldn't have been more embarrassing to come to the plate in your final major league at bat and proceed to hit into a triple play. Just ask Joe Pignatano of the New York Mets, who did just that in his last at bat on September 30, 1962.

Going into the top of the 8th inning on a dreary, damp day at Wrigley Field, in the last game of the season, the New York Mets were trailing the Chicago Cubs, 5-1. Sammy Drake led off the inning coming up as a pinch-hitter for right-hander Craig Anderson, and singled to center field off righty Bob Buhl.

Richie Ashburn followed with a single to right sending Drake to second. Up came Pignatano, and with the runners going, swung late on a fast ball and looped a soft liner over the diamond toward second. Cubs 2B Ken Hubbs made a diving catch, flipped the ball to 1B Ernie Banks to double off Ashburn, who then fired his throw to SS Andre Rodgers at second to retire Drake for the third out to complete the triple play. Interestingly none of the Mets involved in that play ever played in the major leagues again.

41. Who was the very first designated hitter in major league baseball, and what was his team?

When the American League decided to establish the designated hitter role in baseball the National League, in its traditional posture, declined to do the same.

On opening day, April 6, 1973, New York Yankees manager, Ralph Houk, inserted Ron Blomberg, heretofore a journeyman outfielder and first baseman, for the New York Yankees, as a designated hitter batting in the sixth position in the batting order. He became the first designated hitter in major league baseball when he stepped to the plate against RHP Luis Tiant of the Boston Red Sox, before an opening day crowd of 32,882 at Fenway Park.

Blomberg, although batting sixth in the order, came to the plate in the top of the 1st inning with the bases full, and walked on four pitches in his first at bat, bringing in RF Matty Alou with the first run for the Yankees in their three-run first inning and moving CF Bobby Murcer to third and 3B Graig Nettles to second.

Blomberg got an infield single in the top of the 3rd, and ended his day going 1-3, with that walk credited as the first run batted in by a DH.

Tiant settled down and went all nine innings as Boston went on to hammer the Yankees, and Mel Stottlemyre, 15-5 to open their season with a win.

42. Who was the first player to hit for the cycle in major league history?

Charles "Curry" Foley, born in Milltown, Ireland, was a left-handed pitcher, right-fielder, and first baseman, who made his major league debut on May 13, 1879 with the Boston Red Caps. In 1881 he moved to the Buffalo Bisons, and it was with them on May 25, 1882, that he was a big part in the 20-1 drubbing the Bisons gave Cleveland Blues as he became the first major league player to hit for the cycle.

43. Who were the first American League, and first National League players to hit for the cycle on the same day?

On September 17, 1920, LF Bobby Veach of the Detroit Tigers hit for the cycle by going 6-for-6 against the Boston Red Sox. On that very same afternoon, over in the National League, LF George Burns of the New York Giants hit for the cycle when he went 5-for-5 against the Pittsburgh Pirates.

44. Who was the first player to reach his 3,000th base hit by hitting a triple?

On September 16, 1996, Paul Molitor, the designated hitter for the Minnesota Twins, before a crowd of 16,843 out in Kauffman Stadium, became the first batter to collect a triple for his 3,000th career base hit when, in the top of the 5th inning, he connected off Kansas City Royals rookie southpaw, Jose Rosado, who went on to be credited with a 6-5 win.

45. Who was the first pinch-hitter in major league history?

On August 10, 1889 Michael "Smiling Mickey" Welch, a pitcher by trade, with the New York Giants, struck out when batting for a teammate pitcher, RHP Hank O'Day, as he became the first pinch-hitter in major league history.

It wasn't until 1892 when the rule to allow a pinch-hitter to bat in a non-injury situation was instituted. The first pinch-hitter to bat after that rule began has been credited to either "Princeton Charlie" Reilly of the Phillies on April 29, 1892, and/or "Dirty Jack" Doyle of the Cleveland Spiders on May 14th or June 7th in 1892.

46. Who was the first player to bat in seven runs off the same pitcher in the same inning?

In September 23, 1890, first baseman Ed "Jumbo" Cartwright of the St. Louis Browns hit a grand slam home run in the 3rd inning, and came back in the same inning to hit a three-run home run, all off rookie Ed Green of the Philadelphia Athletics. St Louis scored eleven runs in that inning on the way to winning an abbreviated seven-inning game, called because of darkness, 21-2.

Southpaw George Nicol got credit for a less than 9-inning no hitter, although he did walk nine batters in the game.

47. Who was the first pinch-hitter in major league history to get a base hit?

On May 14, 1892 Tom "Tido" Daly, a switch-hitting second baseman-catcher with the Brooklyn Bridegrooms, came in to pinch-hit in the 9th inning for the ill Hub Collins, and came through with the first pinch-hit a home run to tie the game!

He followed that with a single in the 10th to drive in another run, but it wasn't enough as Boston won 8-7.

48. Who was the first player to hit a home run in his first major league at bat?

The first player to hit a home run in his first major league at bat happened on Tuesday, September 10, 1895 when Joe Harrington, the Boston Beaneaters (Braves) second baseman, hit a home run, the first of three in his two-year career, against the St. Louis Browns in Boston's South End Grounds, in his initial plate appearance in the major leagues.

49. Who was the first major leaguer to have at least 200 base hits in a season?

"Big Sam" Thompson, the Hall of Fame right fielder with the Detroit Wolverines, led the National League when he banged out 203 hits in 1887, while also leading the league with a .372 batting average.

He also led the league in 1893 with 222 hits, and had 211 hits in 1895 with the Philadelphia Phillies.

50. Who was the first player to drive in over 600 runs in both the American and National League?

Frank Robinson, who patrolled the outfield, and held down first base for 21 seasons made his debut with the Cincinnati Reds on April 17, 1956. After ten years with the Reds, and driving in 1,009 runs he was traded to the Baltimore Orioles where he drove in another 545, before coming back to the National League and picking up another 59 with the Los Angeles Dodgers. Then it was on to California in the junior circuit where he added 160 more ribbies, and finished out with Cleveland, and those additional 39 runs driven in for the Tribe gave him 744 in the American League to go with the 1,068 from his 11 years in the National League to make him the first player to drive over 600 teammates across the plate in both leagues.

51. Who was the first player in major league history to hit for the natural cycle?

First we will identify a natural cycle. It is where a player hits for the cycle in the precise order of a single, followed by a double, followed by a triple, and then consummating in a home run.

There have been thirteen players who have hit for a natural cycle, and 28 year-old rookie leftfielder Bill Collins, who made his debut on April 14, 1910 with the Boston Braves, had a big day on October 6, 1910 when he became the first major league player to hit for a natural cycle as the Braves demolished the Philadelphia Phillies, 20-7.

52. Who was the first, and only, player in major league history to hit for a natural cycle, and conclude it with a grand slam home run?

It was a slugfest down in Shibe Park on that Friday, June 3, 1932, when the New York Yankees defeated the Philadelphia Athletics, 20-13.

Right in the middle of all that slugging emerged Yankees 2B "Poosh'Em Up" Tony Lazzeri who had single, then a double, followed by a triple, and completed the natural cycle by hitting a grand slam home run in the top of the 9th inning off right-hander Eddie Rommel.

Lazzeri is one of 14 major league players to hit for the natural cycle, and the only one to complete it with a grand slam.

53. Who was the first and only, pitcher to hit two grand slam home runs in the same game?

We've all heard of "power pitchers", but not in the "swinging the lumber" sense.

That wasn't the case on July 3, 1966 however, when Tony Cloninger, the right-handed pitcher of the Atlanta Braves, became the first National League player, and first pitcher to have a pair of grand slam home runs in the same game.

Cloninger started it off in the top of the 1st inning at Candlestick Park, when he came to bat, already ahead 3-0 on catcher Joe Torre's three-run home run, to find the bases loaded with two outs, and facing RHP Bob Priddy who had come in to replace San Francisco Giants starter, southpaw Joe Gibbon.

Cloninger, seeing a "Priddy pitch," sent it soaring into the left-centerfield stands for a grand slam home run, scoring 2B Frank Bolling, SS Woody Woodward, and 3B Denis Menke ahead of him to put Atlanta up 7-0.

Cloninger came up in the 4th inning, again with two outs, and again with the bases loaded, but with the Braves now ahead 9-0. On the mound was Giants southpaw Ray Sadecki and he gave him the same treatment he had given Priddy, and sent a Sadecki pitch into the right field seats for his second grand slam of the game, driving in Torre, Bolling, Menke, and himself to put the Braves up 13-0.

They went on to an easy 17-3 win.

A crowd of 27,002 Giants fans went home disappointed over the rout, but they were witness to the first two grand slams in one game by one National League player, and the first in major league history by a pitcher, who also established a new record for pitchers by driving in 9 runs in the game.

54. Who was the first, and only, pitcher to hit a grand slam home run in both the American and National League?

Lynwood "Schoolboy" Rowe, the Detroit Tigers right-hander, was known as a good hitter, and had a career .263 career batting average with 18 home runs. Included in those stats was a grand slam home run with Detroit on July 22, 1939, off Philadelphia Athletics right-hander Nelson Potter in the 2nd inning, as Detroit squeaked out an 11-10 win.

When moving over to the National League with the Philadelphia Phillies, he came up as a pinch-hitter on May 2, 1943, in the 6th inning and hit another grand slam, this off right-hander Alva "Beartracks" Javery, as the Phils had to go 12 innings to beat the Braves 6-5; the only pitcher to hit a slammer in both leagues.

55. Who was the first player to hit a grand slam home run in both leagues in the same season?

Leftfielder Greg Vaughn of the Milwaukee Brewers hit a grand slam home run off right-hander Jeff McCurry of the Detroit Tigers on July, 16, 1996. Moving over to the National League, after being traded by the Brewers on July 31st to the San Diego Padres, he faced right-hander Derek Wallace of the New Mets on August 16th and emptied the bases with a grand slam home run, to make him the first player to have a slam in both leagues in the same season.

56. In the modern era of baseball who was the first Triple Crown winner?

Napoleon "Larry" Lajoie, who made his major league debut on August 12, 1896 with the Philadelphia Phillies as a first baseman, went on to become a Hall of Fame resident due to not only his bat, but his excellent ability at second base where he played 2,035 games there over his 19 seasons.

In 1901, now established as a second baseman, he led the National in League eight categories; batting with .426, slugging with .463, base hits with 232, runs scored with 145, runs driven in with 125, doubles with 48, and home runs with 14. With those credentials he was a shoo-in to be the first player to win what is now known as the Triple Crown.

57. Who was the first player drive in four runs in a game in which he went hitless?

Yes, it did happen, there was no scorecard typo. It was Wednesday evening September 20, 2000 out in Coors Field. There 36,088 witnesses saw the Colorado Rockies right-handed hitting catcher, Ben Petrick, pull off a feat that was hard to believe.

Coming up in the bottom of the 2nd inning, and facing San Diego Padres right-hander Adam Eaton, and the Rockies behind 6-0, he found Todd Hollandsworth on third base with one out, and grounded out to shortstop

Neifi Perez at short, scoring Hollandsworth.

In the bottom of the 4th, with Colorado now behind, 11-2, Hollandsworth doubled to right field. Butch Huskey then grounded out to second baseman Damian Jackson with Hollandsworth moving over to third. That set the stage for Petrick to drive in his second run, which he did with a sacrifice fly to Juan Pierre in centerfield, scoring Hollandsworth.

Behind 14-4 in the bottom of the 6th, Petrick grounded out to short.

In the 8th inning San Diego had extended their lead to 15-5. Hollandsworth doubled to left field, and Huskey moved him up to third by flying out to center, Right-hander Earl "Buddy" Carlyle then got Petrick to ground out to second as Hollandsworth scored.

Now moving to the 9th, and Colorado now down 15-9, right-hander Heathcliff Slocumb was on the mound, and an error by 2B Damian Jackson put Todd Walker on first.

Hollandsworth then walked, as did Huskey to load the bases. Who should come up but Petrick, hitless so far, but with three runs batted in, and drew a walk from Slocumb which scored Walker from third for Petrick's fourth run batted. Trevor Hoffman came in to relieve Slocumb and got a double play scoring the Rockies 11th run as the Padres came away with a wild 15-11 win, and Petrick came away being able to say that he drove in four runs without managing a base hit.

58. Who was the first batter to hit 60 or more home runs in a single season?

George Herman "Babe" Ruth, on September 30, 1927, crushed his 60th home run of the season, off Washington Senators southpaw Tom Zachary, at the Yankee Stadium, for a newly established single season home run record.

59. Who was the first player to drive in over 100 runs in a single season while playing for two different teams that year?

Hall of Fame leftfielder Leon "Goose" Goslin drove in 38 runs in 47 games with the Washington Senators, before being traded to the St. Louis Browns for General Crowder and Heinie Manush on June 13, 1930.

Finishing out the season with the Browns, Goslin drove in 100 runs in his final 101 games in St. Louis to finish the season with 138.

60. Who was the first American League player to collect 200 hits in a

single season while playing for two different teams?

Leftfielder Julius "Moose" Solters played nine seasons in the American League. In 1935 he played in 24 games for the Boston Red Sox, and had 19 base hits.

On May 27, 1935 Moose was traded by the Red Sox, along with cash, to the St. Louis Browns for Ski Melillo. In his 127 games with the Browns Solters banged out 182 hits to give him 201 hits for the season playing for two different teams.

61. Who was the first, and only, player to be the first batter to bat in the opening of two new ballparks in the same season?

Two new ballparks were opened in the 2001 season, and Cincinnati Reds shortstop Barry Larkin was front and center for both of them. He was the first batter to come to the plate at Miller Park, Milwaukee, on April 6, 2001, and then repeated that performance as he was the first batter at the opening of PNC Park, Pittsburgh, on April 9, 2001.

62. Who was the first player to lead his league in batting and in strikeouts in the same season?

Babe Ruth, with all his hitting prowess, was not immune from going down on strikes, as the 1924 season demonstrated. Ruth, playing the outfield for the New York Yankees, led the American League in over five categories that season including the batting title with .378, and also in strikeouts with 81.

63. Who was the first, and only, American League player to lead his league in hits and walks in the same season?

Hall of Fame left fielder, and later in his career as a first baseman, Carl Yastrzemski, of the Boston Red Sox, led the American League in batting with a 321 average in 1963, and also in base hits with 183, in doubles with 40, and in walks with 95, to be the first to lead in base hits and walks in the same season.

64. Who was the first catcher to have over 300 career home runs?

"Yogi" Berra of the New York Yankees, exceeded the 300 career home run mark during the 1960 season, and went on to complete his 19-year major league career in 1965 with the New York Mets with 358 home runs.

65. Who was the first player to hit 30 or more home runs for 5 different teams?

Southpaw swinging Fred "Crime Dog" McGriff, first baseman-designated hitter, made his major league debut on May 17, 1986 with the Toronto Blue Jays, and had his first 30-homer season with them in 1988, with 34. He followed that up by leading the American League with 36 in 1989, and came back with 35 in 1990.

He began making his peregrinations in 1991 when he was traded over the winter to the San Diego Padres where he hit 31 round-trippers, and came back in '92 to lead the senior circuit with them hitting 35. In 1993 he again hit over 30 home runs, but not with the same team, as he had 18 with the Padres and 19 with the Atlanta Braves. Staying in Atlanta he drove 34 out of the park in 1994. The 1999 season found "Crime Dog" down in Tampa with the Devil Rays where he smoked 32 home runs.

Moving once again, in 2001, after hitting 19 home runs with Tampa he went north finishing the season with 12 with the Chicago Cubs. Then on Sunday, September 21, 2002 and still playing in the Windy City he came up with two outs in the first inning in PNC Park in Pittsburgh and hit a pitch by Pirate right-hander Kris Benson into the left centerfield seats for his 30th home run of the season to become the first player to hit over 30 home runs in a season for five different teams. For his career McGriff ended up with 493 home runs in his 19 seasons.

66. Who was the first player in the senior circuit to hit a pair of triples, and a pair of home runs in the same game?

The "Say Hey Kid," Willie Mays, the San Francisco Giants centerfielder, had quite a day for himself on Tuesday, May 13, 1958, against the Los Angeles Dodgers out in the Los Angeles Memorial Coliseum.

Willie went 5-for-5 including two triples and two home runs, a stolen base, and drove in four runs, as the Giants pounded out 26 hits on their way to a 16-9 romp over the Dodgers.

67. Who was the first American League player to have 140 or more RBIs in back-to-back-to back seasons?

When it came to knocking in runs no one was more productive over a six year span than "The Bambino." Babe Ruth started his streak with the 1926 season when he was the reason that he, and his teammates, crossed home plate 145 times.

It didn't stop there as Ruth followed that up in 1927 with 164, and again in 1928 with 142. He continued this habit of chasing base runners home for the next three years with 154, 153, and 163 to not only close out who was first, but who was foremost.

68. Who was the first player to hit 50 doubles and 50 home runs in the same season?

For Albert Belle, the leftfielder of the Cleveland Indians, 1995 was a 50-50 year; not just mediocre, but productive, as he became the first player to hit 50 home runs and 52 doubles in a season.

69. Who was the first player to hit 400 home runs and have 3,000 hits?

Stan "the Man" Musial, the pride of Donora, Pennsylvania, and the Hall of Fame outfielder and first baseman with the St. Louis Cardinals for his entire 22-year distinguished career, played his final game in a Redbird uniform on September 29, 1963. When he reflected back on those 22 seasons he saw that he was the first player to hit over 400 home runs (475), and have over 3,000 base hits (3,630).

An interestingly sidelight to his batting ability was that he had 1,815 hits at home, and an equal number on the road.

70. Who was the first modern day player to get seven base hits in his seven at bats in one game?

Cesar "Cocoa" Gutierrez, the Detroit Tigers shortstop, had quite a day at the plate in the second game of a doubleheader on June 21, 1970 at Cleveland Stadium against the Cleveland Indians. Wearing #7 on his uniform he clubbed 6 singles and a double in 7 at bats to put him in the record books of being the first to go 7-for-7 in a game, as the Tigers nipped the Tribe, 9-8.

71. Who is the first, and only, player to win batting titles in three different decades?

George Howard Brett, better known to his Kansas City Royals teammates and fans as "Mullet," made his major league debut at third base as a 20-year old on August 2, 1973 with the Kansas City Royals. He quickly became a hitting machine as he hit .282 in his first full season, and went on to hit over .300 in eleven of his 21 seasons, one of the many attributes that propelled him into the Hall of Fame.

He won his first American League batting title in 1976 with a .333 batting average, as well as leading the league in at bats (645), hits (215) and triples (14).

Showing that the 1976 season wasn't a fluke he came back in 1980, after narrowly missing a chance at .400, to again capture the batting title with a .390 batting average.

Now playing in his third decade, in 1990, he added his third batting title with a .329 average to make him the first player to win a batting title in three different decades. When "Mullet" ended his career on October 3, 1993, he had amassed 317 home runs, 3,154 hits, 1,583 runs scored, 1,595 driven in, and a .305 batting average. Cooperstown gave him residency in 1999.

72. Who was the first, and only, player in major league history to have 35 home runs, 100 runs batted in, and score 100 runs in 11 consecutive seasons?

Alex Rodriguez, commonly known as A-Rod, made his major league debut on July 8, 1994, as a shortstop with the Seattle Mariners, and showed off his hitting ability early on, in 1996, when he won the American League batting championship with a .358 average.

He continued his production at the plate, and began his historic offensive surge in 1998 when he hit 42 home runs, drove in 124 runs, scored 123 for the Mariners.

From 1998, and through his years with the Texas Rangers, and on with the New York Yankees, A-Rod maintained that pace of exceeding those marks in those three categories through the 2008 season. The streak may have ended then, but his accomplishment stands as being the first and only player to put up such an offensive record for eleven consecutive seasons.

73. Who was the first player, from a last place team, to win a batting title?

"Laughing Larry" Doyle, the second baseman with the last place New York Giants, won the batting title in 1915 with a .320 average, while leading the league in hits with 189 and doubles with 40.

74. Who was the first player to hit three home runs in a game three different times in the same season?

Hitting home runs was commonplace for Chicago Cubs right fielder Sammy Sosa, but not hitting three in a game three times in a season. That is what Sosa did beginning on August 9, 2001, at Wrigley Field, when he hit a solo shot off Colorado Rockies lefthander Mike Hampton in the 3rd inning, followed that with another solo shot off Hampton in the bottom of the 5th, and finished off with a solo home run off southpaw reliever Gabe White in the 7th. All for naught as Colorado went on to win 14-5.

Sosa put on a repeat performance, again at Wrigley Field, against the Milwaukee Brewers on August 22nd. This time Sosa didn't wait, for he hit a two-run home run off right-handed starter Makoto "Mac" Suzuki in the bottom of the 1st inning. He followed that up in the 5th with a three-run home run off right-hander John "Rocky" Coppinger. In the bottom of the 6th he again faced Coppinger, and again took him downtown, to right-centerfield, for his third home run of the game. The Cubs rolled to an easy 16-3 win.

The scene shifted to Enron Field on Sunday, September 23rd for a meeting with the Houston Astros. The venue changed, but not the result, when Sosa came up in the top of the 1st inning and blasted his 58th home run, a two-run shot off starter Tim Redding. Coming up again against Redding, to start the 4th inning, Sosa unleashed his second homer of the day off the right-hander, a solo shot to tie the game at 3-3.

In the 6th inning, with the score tied at 4, Sosa hit a leadoff home run to complete his third three-home run game of the season, and stands alone in that department. It wasn't enough, however, as the Astros won 7-6.

75. Who was the first player to hit three home runs in a game, six times in his career?

Although St. Louis Cardinals first baseman Johnny Mize didn't hit three home runs in a game three times in a season, as Sammy Sosa did, he hit three in a game twice in 1938, on July 13th, and July 20th.

In 1940 he again hit three in a game twice, on May 13th and September 18th.

On April 24, 1947, while with the New York Giants, Mize hit three home runs in a game, and did it for the sixth and final time on September 15, 1950, while finishing out his 15-year career with the New York Yankees.

Those six three-run home run games made Mize the first player to have half a dozen games in which he hit three home runs.

76. Who was the first player to hit a walk-off home run on Opening Day?

On Tuesday, April 19, 1949, New York Yankee right fielder Tommy Henrich came up to bat in the bottom of the 9th inning at Yankee Stadium, before a crowd of 40,075, with the score tied at 2-2, and hit a pitch by Washington Senators right-hander Sid Hudson into the right field stands for a walk-off home run giving the Yankees a 3-2 victory.

77. Who was the first player to hit a home run in his final major league at bat?

Right-hander Ed Scott of the Cleveland Indians knew how to bow out of major league baseball with a bang. That bang came from his bat as he hit a solo home run in the top of the 10th inning off Milwaukee Brewers right-hander Bill Reidy, on August 3, 1901, to give himself a complete game win, 8-7, in the last game he would play in the big leagues. It would be the second and final home run of his two-year pitching career.

78. Who was the first player to pitch, and hit for the cycle in the same game?

Jimmy "Pony" Ryan of the Chicago White Stockings started the game on Saturday, July 28, 1888 against the Detroit Wolverines in the outfield. In his first at bat he singled, and as an explosion of base hits began "Pony" was called on to switch his talents to the mound, and came on and pitched seven innings of relief, and during the course of the game, which ended up with a 21-17 Chicago win thanks partly to the bat of Ryan who ended up with that single, along with two triples, a double, and a home run to make him a "Groundbreaker."

79. Who was the first player to have 3,000 major league hits?

He has been called by some "baseball's first superstar", and as you read on you will understand why. He made his debut on May 6, 1871 with the Rockford Forest Citys, and after 27 seasons, 22 with the Chicago White Stockings (later the Colts, now the Cubs) he played 7 positions, primarily at first base.

In 1893, with the Colts, he picked up his 1,000th base hit. Then on July 18, 1897 he lined a single off rookie right-hander "Smiling George" Blackburn of the Baltimore Orioles in the 4th inning to become the first player to reach that hallowed plateau and collect 3,000 hits, in major league history as the Colts defeated Baltimore, 6-3. That player was first baseman Adrian

"Cap" Anson, of the Chicago Colts (Cubs).

Anson completed his 22-year career, with Chicago on October 3, 1897, with 3,012 career base hits, 1,880 runs batted in, and a .331 average giving him entrance to the Hall of Fame in 1939.

80. Fourteen players have driven in six runs in one inning, but who was the first, and only, player to drive in eight?

Fernando Tatis, the St. Louis Cardinals third baseman, rose above those previous fourteen players when, in an 11-run 3rd inning, in a game against the Los Angeles Dodgers, on May 23, 1999, he faced Chan Ho Park twice, and both times hit a grand slam home run off the right hander, and in so doing became the first player to drive in eight runs in one inning, a mark that seems unlikely to be surpassed.

Park brought a dubious distinction upon himself by being the first pitcher in the 20th century to give up two grand slam home runs in one inning.

81. Who was the first batter to be hit by a pitch twice in the same inning, but not be awarded first base?

They say a walk is as good as a hit, and so is a hit batsman, but not in the case of Baltimore Orioles third baseman John McGraw. Even though all three experiences get you on base that effort was denied "Mugsy" on July 18, 1897 by home plate umpire Jim McDonald in the 8th inning of a game against the Chicago Colts (Cubs).

It seems on two pitches delivered to the plate by Colts right-hander, Clark "The Old Fox," Griffith, McGraw was plunked by both of them. McDonald told McGraw to stay right up at bat for in the umpire's mind McGraw had purposely stepped in front of both of them. All Mugsy got out of that at bat was a couple of bruises on his 5'7" frame.

82. Who was the first player, in the American League, to be awarded the Triple Crown and win the Most Valuable Player Award in the same season?

Jimmie "Double X" Foxx of the Philadelphia Athletics, led the American League in home runs with 48, runs batted in with 163, and batting average with .356 in 1933 to be the first in the junior circuit to capture the coveted Triple Crown and win the Most Valuable Player Award in the same season.

83. Who was the first player to strikeout 200 times in a single season?

Mark "The Sheriff" Reynolds, the Arizona Diamondbacks third baseman-first baseman, known for his power hitting ability and for his weakness by going down on strikes, made his major league debut on May 16, 2007.

In 2008, his second year in the big leagues, Reynolds entered the record books on September 25th when the St. Louis Cardinals right-hander Joel Pineiro got him on a checked-swing for Reynolds 200th strikeout of the season, becoming the first player to whiff 200 times in a season. He exceeded that mark by the end of the season when he finished with 204. In so doing he led the major leagues with a 33.3% strikeout percentage.

Who knows where his future lies in this department for he led the National League in strikeouts with 223 in 2009, and 211 in 2010.

84. Who was the first full-time position player, in major league history, to finish the season with a lower batting average than his strikeout total?

This power hitter with an impressive 121 home runs and 346 runs driven in during his four-year National League career had the penchant for hitting the long ball or making pitchers look good by fanning. I am speaking of Mark Reynolds of the Arizona Diamondbacks who finished the 2010 season with a .198 batting average and a league-leading 211 strikeouts. That made him the first full-time position player to have a lower batting average than the number of his strikeouts.

85. Who was the first batter to face the New York Mets starting pitcher, right-hander "Fat Jack" Fisher, on opening day at Shea Stadium, April 17, 1964?

Dick Schofield, the shortstop of the Pittsburgh Pirates, was the leadoff hitter on that day popped out to 2B Larry Burright to record the first out in the stadium's history.

86. Who was the first player to hit over 100 home runs for two teams in the American League and another in the National League?

Jim Thome, the burly left-handed hitter, made his debut as a third baseman for the Cleveland Indians on September 4, 1991, and hit 337 home runs during his 13-year stay with the Tribe. Then on to the Phillies for four years at first base where he hit 101 home runs, and then over to the Chicago White Sox for four more seasons as a designated hitter where he racked up an additional 134 homers, making Thome a "Groundbreaker" by hitting over 100 homers for three different teams.

87. Who was the first pitcher to start a game as a designated hitter?

On Saturday, June 11, 1988, New York Yankees manager, Billy Martin, turned to a veteran National League right-hander, Richard "Rick" Rhoden, formerly a pitcher with the Pittsburgh Pirates, who was in his second year in pinstripes, to start the game as the DH.

Martin put the career .238 hitter batting in the 7th spot in the order. Coming up in the bottom of the 3rd inning, batting against Baltimore southpaw Jeff Ballard, he grounded to third. In his second at bat he drove in a run with a sacrifice fly to right field, scoring CF Jay Buhner, which tied the game at 3-3.

His DH day ended there as Jose Cruz pinch- hit for him in the 5th inning and grounded out to Billy Ripken at second. The Yankees went on to win 8-6 with John Candelaria besting Ballard.

88. Who was the first designated hitter to win a batting title?

DH Edgar Martinez of the Seattle Mariners won the batting title in 1995 when he hit .356, and led the American League in doubles with 52, and runs scored with 121.

89. Who was the first designated hitter to win a Gold Glove Award?

You probably did a double take when reading this question. How could that be? This was no misprint; unbelievable as it seems, it happened when Rafael Palmeiro won the American League Gold Glove Award at first base in 1999 while with the Texas Rangers. He had played in only 28 games at first base, no doubt quite admirably, while appearing in 135 games as a DH that season.

90. Who was the first designated hitter to win the home run title?

David "Big Papi" Ortiz, of the Boston Red Sox, won the home run crown when he belted 54 home runs for the Red Sox in 2006.

91. Who was the first batter in the first major league night game?

Major league baseball went under the lights for the first time on Friday evening, May 24, 1935, before a celebratory crowd of 20,422, when the Cincinnati Reds hosted the Philadelphia Phillies at Crosley Field.

The Phillies second baseman, Lou Chiozza, was the first batter to step up to the plate to face Reds right-hander Paul Derringer. Chiozza was also the first out as he grounded out to shortstop Billy Myers.

92. Who was the first catcher to lead the major leagues in triples?

You have heard him as an analyst on many major league games, but before that Tim McCarver, who made his major league debut as a 17-year old catcher with the St. Louis Cardinals on September 10, 1959, and played 21 seasons in the big leagues, predominantly with the Redbirds, and the Phillies, led the National League in triples with 13 in 1966, to become the first catcher to ever lead his league in triples.

A few years later, in 1972, Carlton Fisk, the Boston Red Sox catcher, was the first in the American League to lead his league in three-baggers with 9.

93. Who was the first pitcher to hit a home run in every National League park?

One baseball's great left-handed pitchers, Warren Spahn, who had 363 career victories, could also handle a bat when the long ball was needed. That was proven when on Monday, August 15, 1955, out in Busch Stadium, Spahn came up in the 8th inning, and hit a two-out solo home run off Cards' right-hander Mel Wright. That was his third homer of the year and made Spahn the first pitcher in history to hit a home run in every National League Park. The Milwaukee Braves went on win 12-1 with Spahn going 3-for-5, with a triple as well and three runs batted in. Spahn's 21-year career showed 35 home runs.

94. Who was the first, and only, player to hit three triples in one game two different times, for two different teams, in the same season?

The British-born third baseman/shortstop of the St. Louis Cardinals, Dave Brain, had three triples in a game at Pittsburgh on May 29, 1905 leading the Redbirds to a 6-3 win over the Pirates.

On August 8, 1905 Brain, now playing for the Pittsburgh Pirates, and what he did three months earlier to his new team he did to the visiting Boston Braves as he led the Pirates to a 5-4, 10th inning win to become the first and only player in major league history to have three triples in two different games for two different teams in the same season. He ended that season with eleven three-baggers.

95. Who was the first player to hit two home runs in one inning?

The first player to hit two home runs in one inning happened in the 8th inning, on June 10, 1880, when Charley Jones, the Boston Red Caps leftfielder, hit two in that inning against the Buffalo Bisons right-hander Tom Poorman, in a 19-3 rout in Boston's South End Grounds, to be the first in major league history to do so. It was two of Charlie's 5 home runs that season.

96. Who was the first player in American League history to hit two home runs in the same inning?

Two home runs in the same inning, by the same player, occurred in Sportsman's Park, on Monday, August 7, 1922, when St. Louis Browns centerfielder Ken Williams came up in the 6th inning and hit a two-run home run off southpaw George Mogridge of the Washington Senators. Coming back up again in the 9-run, 6th inning he, this time, faced right-hander Eric Erickson, again with one on, and hit his second two-run home run in the inning.

97. Who was the first player to hit a grand slam home run in each game of a doubleheader?

Third baseman Robin Ventura was a big part of the New York Mets doubleheader sweep of the Milwaukee Brewers at Shea Stadium on Thursday, May 20, 1999, when he came up to the plate in the bottom of the 1st inning of the first game and found 1B John Olerud, catcher Mike Piazza, and 2B Edgardo Alfonso filling the bases with two outs.

He hit southpaw Jim Abbott's pitch on a line to deep right field to drive in the Mets first four runs of the game with his grand slam home run.

The Mets went on to win the first game 11-10 in what no one would consider a pitcher's battle. In the nightcap the 19,542, predominantly Met fans, were treated to an historic moment when Robin Ventura came up in the 4th inning and found the bases F.O.M. (full of Mets), and facing southpaw Horacio Estrada. He quickly relieved him of having to check the runners as Ventura cleared the bases with a shot deep down the right field line for his second grand slam of the day, scoring RF Roger Cedeno, Edgardo Alfonzo, and John Olerud, to give the Mets a 9-0 lead which they would take to the 9th inning for a 10-1 victory. The fans went home, not only seeing a Mets sweep on the day, but seeing the first player to hit a grand slam home run in both games of a doubleheader.

98. Who was the first, and only, player to hit a grand slam home run in one game, and achieve the Golden Sombrero in a game the next day?

This unusual achievement happened to Travis Hafner, the Cleveland Indians designated hitter, on May 7, 2007, at Camden Yards. He hit a grand slam home run to right-center field, with two outs in the 8th inning, off Baltimore southpaw Jamie Walker, as the Indians won "a laugher," 10-1.

The next day, May 8th, the Indians were out in Angel Stadium of Anaheim before 41,731, and Hafner came to bat in the top of the 1st inning and struck out swinging at a wild pitch by Angels' right-hander Ervin Santana. He came up against Santana in the 3rd and again went down swinging for his second strikeout. Facing Santana in the 5th, he looked at a third strike, to go down for the third time. In the 7th inning, with Cleveland ahead 3-1, Hafner again saw Santana on the mound, and the Angels right-hander again sent Hafner back to the bench, mumbling, after striking him out for the fourth time. Having four strikeouts in a game by one player is called "the Golden Sombrero."

Whether Hafner accepted the Golden Sombrero or not means nothing. He won it thanks to Ervin Santana, who also won the game, 5-1.

99. Who was the first African-American to hit for the cycle in the major leagues?

It was on August 29, 1948, out in Sportsman's Park, in the first game of a doubleheader against the St. Louis Cardinals, when Brooklyn Dodgers 2B Jackie Robinson started on his way to his cycle, when he hit a 1st inning no-out, two-run home run off Cardinals southpaw Harry "The Cat" Brecheen.

He finished it off against five other Redbird pitchers with a single, double, and a triple, going 4-fo-6, and driving in two runs, scoring three, and stole a base as the Dodgers took the first game 12-7.

100. Who was the first player to hit for the cycle in both the American and National Leagues?

Bob Watson could hit anywhere, in either league. He proved that on June 24, 1977 when with the Houston Astros, down in the Astrodome, he hit a single, double, triple, and a home run off San Francisco Giants southpaw Bob Knepper taking the Astros to a 6-5 victory.

Over in the American League with the Boston Red Sox, down in Baltimore's Memorial Stadium, on September 15, 1979, he singled to right, driving in a run, off Orioles right-hander Dennis Martinez in the top of the 2nd inning, doubled to left in the 4th off Dennis Martinez, tripled to right in the 8th off southpaw Felix "Tippy" Martinez, and finished off the natural cycle with a one-out, two-run home run in the 9th off right-hander Don Stanhouse, to lead the Red Sox to a 10-2 win.

Watson was a "Groundbreaker" by being the first to hit for the cycle in both leagues.

101. Who was the first, and only, player-manager to win the Triple Crown?

Rogers Hornsby was named the manager of the St. Louis Cardinals on May 30, 1925, and went on to win the Triple Crown that year with a .403 batting average, 39 home runs and 143 runs driven in. The following year the 30-year old skipper-second baseman took the Cardinals to the World Series where they defeated the New York Yankees in seven games for the World Championship.

102. Who was the only player to lead the league in triples with three different teams?

The speedy Brett Butler made his major league debut with the Atlanta Braves on August 20, 1981, and went on to lead the National League in triples with 13 while with the Braves in 1983.

Moving over to the American League, on October 21, 1983, after being traded to Cleveland, the fleet-footed centerfielder again won the league title in triples, with 14 in 1986.

Back in the National League, now with the Los Angeles Dodgers, Butler again led the league in triples with 9 in 1994 to become the first player to lead the league in triples for three different teams, and in two different leagues.

103. Who was the first player to hit home runs from both sides of the plate in consecutive games?

"Steady Eddie" Murray, who made his major league debut with the Baltimore Orioles on April 7, 1977, certainly was no stranger to belting the ball out of the park, having done it 504 times in his 21 seasons in both leagues. But "Steady Eddie" became a "Groundbreaker" during the month of May 1987.

On May 8th he hit a home run from each side of the plate in Comiskey Park, against the Chicago White Sox. In the top of the 4th inning Murray stroked a solo home run off White Sox right-hander Jose DeLeon. He came back in the 9th inning, with the Orioles behind, 6-5, and with two outs hit a game-winning two-run blast off southpaw Ray Searage, scoring Cal Ripken for 7-6 Orioles win.

Staying in the groove Murray duplicated that home run feat the following day, on Saturday, May 9th, by hitting another pair of home runs again, one from each side of the plate. It started in the top of the 4th inning when Murray hit a two-out, two-run home run off southpaw Joel McKeon, scoring Cal Ripken and giving the Orioles a 7-6 lead. With two homeruns preceding Murray's trip to the plate in the 6th "Steady Eddie" took right-hander Bob James downtown to give Baltimore a 10-6 lead, and an eventual 15-6 win.

Murray became the first batter to hit home runs from both sides if the plate in two consecutive games, making him a true "Groundbreaker".

104. Who was the first player to win the league home run title in ten or more seasons?

This shouldn't come as a surprise when you learn that Babe Ruth was the first to win the home run title more than ten times. He captured the title with the Boston Red Sox six times, in 1918-1919, 1920-21, 23-24. When he moved to the New York Yankees he also won the title six times, from 1926 to 1931 for a total of 12 titles in all.

105. Who was the first player to hit three grand slam home runs in the same month?

Rudy York, made his major league debut as a catcher with the Detroit Tigers on August 22, 1934, and moved between there and first base for most of his career with Detroit, the Red Sox, Athletics and White Sox. Wherever he played the strong right-handed hitter was always a threat for the long ball, and displayed that in May 1938 when he hit a grand slam home run, at Briggs Stadium off Washington's right-hander Joe "Blackie" Kohlman in the 6th inning, on May 16th.

He followed that with one, again at Briggs Stadium, on May 22nd in the 1st inning off Boston Red Sox right-hander "Black Jack" Wilson, and ended the month with his third Briggs Stadium grand slam, on May 30th, and again in the 1ˢᵗ inning, this off Howard "Lefty" Mills of the St. Louis Browns, making York the first in history to have three grand slams in one month.

106. Who was the first player to hit five grand slam home runs in the same season?

Hall of Fame shortstop Ernie "Mr. Cub" Banks could always hit the long ball, proven by his 512 career round-trippers with the Chicago Cubs.

In 1955 Banks made the most of his long-ball chances when he connected for five grand slams. Of the 44 home runs he hit that season, to be the first to reach that level.

107. Who was the first modern day player to hit a grand slam home run in his first major league game?

When you hear the name "Bonds" you think of either the father, Bobby, or the son, Barry, for they were both prolific home run hitters. This time we are referring to Bobby, the father, who holds the unique distinction of being the first modern day (post 1900) player to hit a grand slam home run in his first major league game when, at Candlestick Park, on June 25, 1968, the San Francisco Giants right fielder came up to the plate in the 6ᵗʰ inning, in his third major league at bat, and with one out, found the bases loaded.

He promptly emptied them with a grand slam home run to deep left field off Los Angeles Dodgers' right-hander John Purdin to be a "Groundbreaker" for having a grand slam in a player's initial game.

108. Who was the first modern day player to drive in 10 or more runs in a single game?

When the St. Louis Cardinals first baseman, "Sunny Jim" Bottomley, came into Ebbets Field, Brooklyn on September 16, 1924, to play the Robins he never dreamed of the type of game he would have, no one would.

He was slotted in the cleanup position, and that's what he did. He started his hitting rampage in the 1ˢᵗ inning by hitting a two-run single off Robins' starter, right-hander Welton "Rube" Ehrhardt. In the 2ⁿᵈ he doubled home his third run, and followed that with a 4ᵗʰ inning grand slam off right-hander Art Decatur. "Sunny Jim" came back in the 6ᵗʰ and walloped a two-run home run off Decatur. In the 7ᵗʰ he hit a two-run single, this off southpaw Gomer "Tex" Wilson, And a run scoring single in the 9ᵗʰ to give southpaw "Wee Willie" Sherdel and the Cardinals an easy 17-3 win.

Bottomley's contribution for the day showed three singles, a double, and two home runs adding up to 6 hits in 6 at bats, three runs scored, while driving in 12 "Sunny Jim" was certainly sunny when he took off his cleats that day after being responsible for driving in 12 of the 17 runs racked up that day, and Bottomley had the first double-digit RBI day in modern history.

No player, until another Redbird, Mark Whiten, on September 7, 1993, has touched that record, but eleven others have since reached double digits in a single game.

109. Who was the first player to take the 3,000-hit club to the next level by reaching 4,000 career base hits?

The choices here are quite small, and when you look back in history the first and foremost player to reach this level would by Tyrus Raymond Cobb, a.k.a. "The Georgia Peach," who made his major league debut on August 30, 1905 as an 18-year old outfielder with the Detroit Tigers. Respected by many, and equally hated, his style of baseball brought intensity to the game, that just a few emulated in future years.

Cobb picked up his 4,000[th] base hit while playing right field with the Philadelphia Athletics in a game on Monday, July 18, 1927, at Navin Field, when he hit one of right-hander Sam Gibson's pitches that glanced off right-fielder Harry Heilmann's glove for a double, and Cobb's 4,000[th] career base hit was in the record books.

Detroit, and Gibson, went on to defeat Philadelphia's Lefty Grove that day, 5-3.

Cobb led the American League in base hits eight times, going over the 200-hit mark nine times and leading the league in stolen bases six times.

In his 22 seasons with Detroit, and his remaining two with the Philadelphia Athletics, Cobb, the speedy, aggressive, centerfielder came away from baseball in his final game on September 11, 1928, with 4,189 base hits, 897 stolen bases, and 1,938 runs driven in, to go along with a career batting average of .366, and an average of 224 base hits for his 24 seasons. Like him, or not, he got the job done.

Pete Rose, on Friday, April 13, 1984, and playing left field for the Montreal Expos, in Stade Olympique, in a 5-1 victory over the Philadelphia Phillies, doubled to right field in the bottom of the 4th, off southpaw Jerry

Koosman, to join Cobb as the only members of the exclusive 4,000-hit club.

110. Who was the first player, not to have the most hits in his career, but to have the most singles in his career?

The answer here is to turn the spotlight back on Ty Cobb, who not only had the most base hits, but not necessarily being noted as an extra base hitter, although he did have 1,136, amassing 3,053 singles in his 24-season career.

111. Who was the first American League player to win the batting title without hitting a home run in that season?

Hall of Fame second baseman, and then first baseman, Rod Carew, who made his major league debut as a 21-year old second baseman with the Minnesota Twins on April 11, 1967, showed his ability to make contact with the ball, and that was clearly demonstrated in 1969, when he batted .322 in his third season to capture the American League batting title.

Then in 1972 he again won the batting crown with a .318 average as he collected 170 base hits, including 21 doubles, 6 triples, and drove in 51 runs, but failed to bat himself in as he did not hit a single home run in his 535 at bats.

He became the first batting champion to go without a four bagger in the entire season.

112. Who was the first player to hit 200 home runs for two different teams in the same league?

Jimmie "Double X" Foxx hit 302 home runs in his 11 years with the Philadelphia Athletics, and then moving over to the Boston Red Sox for 7 years, hit another 222.

When he briefly moved over to the National League, in 1942, he added ten more with the Cubs and Phillies to complete his career total at 534.

113. Who was the first player to hit 200 home runs with a team in each league?

Mark "Big Mac" McGwire made his major league debut as a 22-year old third baseman for the Oakland Athletics on August 22, 1986. Moving between third, first, and the outfield he settled in at first base. During his twelve-year career in Oakland he hammered out 363 home runs.

On July 31, 1997 he was traded to the St. Louis Cardinals for three journeyman players, bringing his big bat, and settling in at first base where he played from 1997-2001.

During his five years in the Mound City McGwire twice led the National League in home runs, with 70 in 1998, and 65 in 1999, and when he played his final game on October 7, 2001 his home run numbers with the Cardinals showed 220 round trippers to make him the first player to have over 200 home runs for a team in each league.

114. Who was the first pitcher, in the modern era, to hit three successive home runs in a single game?

Right-hander Jim "Abba Dabba" Tobin was purchased by the Pittsburgh Pirates from the New York Yankees on April 14, 1937, and made his pitching debut on April 30, 1937 with the Pirates. He stayed with them until December 6, 1939 when he was traded to the Boston Bees (Braves) for right-hander "Tobacco Chewin' Johnny" Lanning.

It was here, at Braves Field, on Wednesday, May 13, 1942 that Tobin faced Chicago Cubs right-hander Jake Mooty in the 5th inning, and parked a solo home run. Coming up in the 7th he took another of Jake's pitches downtown for his second solo homer of the day. Right-hander Hi Bithorn replaced Mooty for the 8th inning, and Tobin gave him the same treatment with his bat by blasting a two-run home run to insure a 6-5 win for Tobin, and a place in the "Groundbreakers Club" by being the first pitcher to hit three successive home runs in one game.

Tobin wasn't a stranger to the long ball as he hit six home runs that season and had 17 in his nine-year career.

115. Who was the first, and only, player to have his first, and only, home run of his career be a bases loaded inside-the-park home run?

The scene was the cavernous confines of the Polo Grounds on Wednesday, April 27, 1949, when the lefty swinging New York Giants reserve outfielder, Pete Milne, was called up to pinch-hit by Giants skipper, Leo Durocher, with two outs, and the bases loaded in the 7th inning.

On the mound was Brooklyn Dodgers rookie right-hander Ezra "Pat" McGlothlin, who had come in to relieve right-hander Clarence "Bud" Podbielan.

Milne promptly greeted McGlothlin with a deep fly ball to the spacious Polo Grounds outfield, clearing the bases, and sending the Giants to an

11-8 victory over their hated borough rivals.

When Milne crossed the plate with that 11th run he became the first, and only, player to have his first, last, and only major league home run be a game-winning bases loaded, pinch-hit grand slam!

116. Who was the first, and only, player to hit home runs for four different teams in each four divisions in the same season?

Dave "Sky King" Kingman was drafted in the first round in 1970 by the San Francisco Giants, and made his debut on July 30, 1971. He played the outfield and some infield, but was kept around for his long ball hitting. On February 28, 1975 he was purchased by the New York Mets from the Giants for $150,000, and that started the travel adventures of Sky King.

Over his seven-team, 16-year career none was so odd, and more difficult to equal than his 1977 season.

In that year Kingman hit 9 home runs for the New York Mets in the National League Eastern Division, 11 home runs in 56 games for the San Diego Padres in the Western Division.

Over in the American League he hit 2 home runs in 24 at bats for the California Angels in the Western Division, then moving on to the Yankees he hit 4 home runs for them in 8 games in the AL Eastern Division, all done in just the 1977 season.

117. Who was the first player to hit 100 or more home runs for three different American League teams?

Reggie "Mr. October" Jackson, a moniker given him by the New York media, made his major league debut on June 9, 1967, as an outfielder with the Kansas City Athletics, but made his name as a solid, long ball hitting right fielder with the Oakland Athletics from 1968, when the team moved from Kansas City to Oakland, till 1975, hitting 269 home runs for the Athletics in his ten years with them.

In 1976 he was traded to the Baltimore Orioles where he played for one year before being granted free agency where he then moved over to the Yankees from 1977-81, contributing 144 home runs in his five years in New York.

It was back to the west coast in 1982, signing as a free agent with the California Angels, where he spent from 1982-86, and added to his 563 career home runs by hitting 123 home runs, to make him the first player to hit 100 or more home runs for three different teams.

118. Who was the first player to hit four home runs and then lose the game?

July 13, 1896 should have been a day of celebration for "Big Ed" Delahanty, the leftfielder of the Philadelphia Phillies out in West Side Park, Chicago. He had a big day at the plate hitting four inside-the-park home runs off Chicago Colts right-hander Adonis Terry, but it wasn't quite enough as the Colts came away with a 9-8 win. "Big Ed" led the National League that year with 13 homers and 126 runs batted in, and interestingly Terry gave up four of his season's six home runs, over 235.2 innings, in those nine innings that day.

119. Who was the first player to drive in over 100 runs in three successive seasons with three different teams?

Outfielder-first baseman Joe Carter was no stranger to driving runners in while driving pitchers crazy. Carter who drove in 100 runs in ten of his 16 seasons, could do it in any uniform as he demonstrated by driving in 105 Cleveland teammates in 1989, followed that in 1990 by sending 115 San Diego Padres across the plate, and continuing on in 1991 with Toronto by being responsible for 108 Blue Jays coming home to roost; that's three different teams, three successive seasons of 100 runs driven in.

120. Who was the first player to lead the league in base hits for three different teams?

Just look to Paul "The Ignitor" Molitor for that answer, for after his initial major league game on April 7, 1978 with the Milwaukee Brewers, this second baseman, third baseman, designated hitter showed the American League he could hit. In 1982 he had his first 200-hit season with 201. In 1991 this 1B-DH led the junior circuit by banging out 216 hits with the Brewers, and also leading the league in runs with 133, and triples with 13. In 1993, and now with the Toronto Blue Jays, Molitor led the American League in base hits once again, with 211. His third and final time he led the American League happened up in Minnesota when he had 225 base hits for the Twins, making him the first to lead the league in base hits for three different teams. "The Ignitor" lit up the fans with his 2,281 hits over his 21-season career, posting a .306 batting average.

121. Who was the first pitcher to hit a grand slam home run in his first

major league at bat?

"Frosty Bill" Duggleby, a right-handed pitcher for the Philadelphia Phillies, made his major league mound debut on Thursday, April 21, 1898 against the New York Giants.

Coming up in the 2nd Inning for his first major league at bat, he found the bases filled, and promptly unloaded them with a grand slam home run off southpaw Cy Seymour, and then coasted on to a 13-4 win to become the first pitcher to start off his batting career with a grand slam home run, and with that went on to become a member of the "Groundbreakers".

122. Who was the first player to hit a grand slam home run, not only in his first major league at bat, but on the first pitch he ever saw?

Right-handed hitting rookie third baseman Kevin Kouzmanoff made his major league debut on September 2, 2006 as a designated hitter for the Cleveland Indians, in a fashion never seen before in baseball history.

Before an evening crowd of 40, 222, at Ameriquest Field, Texas Rangers' RHP Edinson Volquez gave up a lead-off solo home run in the top of the 1st inning to CF Grady Sizemore. Things got worse for Volquez after that with a single to LF Jason Michaels, a two-out walk to RF Casey Blake, and another to SS Jhonny Peralta that loaded the bases for the rookie Kouzmanoff, coming up for his very first major league at bat.

The rookie took Volquez's first pitch to him, deep to center field for a grand slam home run, scoring Michaels, Blake, and Peralta, and giving the Indians an immediate 5-0 lead. That blow put Kouzmanoff in the record books as being the first player to hit the first pitch he saw in the big leagues for a grand slam home run, and, of course, made him an immediate member of the "Groundbreakers Club." Just for the record it gave the Indians a 6-5 win, and Cleveland southpaw Cliff Lee his 11th victory of the year.

123. Who was the first pitcher to have five two-homer games?

Wes Ferrell was a fine right-handed pitcher, winning 193 career games, and was known for wielding a good bat. He made his major league debut on September 9, 1927 with the Cleveland Indians up at Fenway Park, pitching an inning of relief against the Red Sox.

He didn't hit his first home run until 1929, but then got in the groove and had a two-homer game with the Indians in 1931, hitting nine home runs that year and driving in 30 runs.

He kept up his hitting when he was traded to the Boston Red Sox on May 25, 1934 in a multi-player deal. Once in Boston Ferrell added four more two-homer games from 1934-36. His homer production in Beantown showed 7 in 1935, and 5 in '36.

After his final game, at age 36, on May 6, 1941, with the Brooklyn Dodgers, Ferrell showed a career record of 38 home runs and 208 runs driven in. That is an impressive record for a pitcher, and the first to have five two-homer games in his career.

124. Who was the first, and only, player to have hit a home run in every inning, 1 through 16 in his career?

Willie Howard Mays, the "Say Hey Kid" is the only player in history to have hit a home run in every inning from the first through the sixteenth.

125. Who was the first player to hit 30 or more home runs in a season ten times, but never reached 500 career home runs?

"The Iron Horse", Lou Gehrig, the New York Yankees Hall of Fame first baseman, made his major league debut on June 15, 1923, after being signed as a free agent on April 23rd. During his 17-year stellar career he won many batting titles, for runs driven in, runs scored, hits, and home runs. He hit 30 or more home runs in 1927, 29, and 30-37, and averaged 37 home runs per season, but in the final total fell short by seven home runs of reaching the coveted 500 level.

126. Who was the first modern-era player to bat over .400 for a season?

Napoleon "Nap" Lajoie, the 26-year old second baseman for the Philadelphia Athletics, had a monstrous year in 1901 when he led the American League in runs with 145, hits with 232, doubles with 48, home runs with 14, and runs driven in with 125, and also to be the first batter to have a season batting average over .400, when he led the league, here as well, with .426.

Lajoie is considered one of the finest batters in the dead ball era, his .426 average remains today as a league record.

127. Who was the first, and only, player to get a base hit in three games in one day?

It happened on October 2, 1920, only because on that day the last scheduled triple-header in major league history was played. The venue was Forbes Field, Pittsburgh, and the Pirates played host to the Cincinnati Reds.

The Pirates dropped the first game 13-4, with Pirates third baseman Clyde "Pooch" Barnhart, going 2-for-4, with a single and a double.

In the second game the Reds prevailed again, downing the Pirates, 7-3, with Barnhart picking up a double, and driving in a run in four trips.

Now we come to the historic part of this Saturday afternoon, when the third game was played, but only for six innings before home plate umpire, Pete Harrison, and first base umpire, Hank O'Day, called the third game after 1:01, because of darkness, not unusual considering these guys were working three games for 24 innings, and the Pirates salvaged this game 6-0, on the right arm, and four-hit pitching, of "Jughandle Johnny" Morrison.

Weren't we originally talking about "Pooch" Barnhart? We were, and he didn't disappoint us as "Pooch" picked up a single in his third game of the day to become the first, and only, player to have one or more base hits in each of three games in one day.

128. Who was the first player-manager to pinch-hit a grand slam home run in an extra-inning game?

We'll take you out to Wrigley Field, Chicago, to the first game of a Sunday double-header, on September 13, 1931, between the Boston Braves and the hometown Cubs. Going into the bottom of the 11th inning, after the Braves had tied the score in the 9th at 7-7, the Cubbies found themselves with the bases loaded and two outs, and needing a run.

Rogers "Rajah" Hornsby, one of baseball's greatest hitters, looked down the bench for a pinch-hitter and found himself to be the most qualified. The player-manager, batting .331 at the time, inserted himself in the lineup, and facing Braves right-hander Bruce Cunningham. The "Rajah" proceeded to end the game with the first ever extra inning pinch-hit home run, taking the Cubs to an 11-7 victory.

Empowered by that dramatic win the Chicago fans were treated to a second game win, as well, as right-hander Guy Bush, "The Mississippi Mudcat", pitched a one-hit, 8-1, win.

129. Who was the first switch-hitter to win the batting title in his league?

Mickey Mantle, "The Commerce Comet", burst upon the American League as a 19-year-old switch-hitting outfielder with the New York Yankees on April 17, 1951.

His hitting ability couldn't be denied and he proved it more than once, ten times hitting .300 or better, in his 18-season career.

He broke new ground in 1956 when he won the American League batting title, his only one, when he hit an impressive .353 to become the first switch-hitter to win the AL batting crown. "The Mick" finished his Hall of Fame career on September 28, 1968 with 536 home runs and a .298 batting average.

130. Who was the first player to come to bat in the first American League game?

On April 24, 1901, the first game in American League history was played in Chicago, the only one that day, because three rainouts in other venues gave the White Stockings the honor of being the host to the Cleveland Blues (Indians) in South Side Park.

Oliver "Ollie" Pickering, the speedy centerfielder for Cleveland, claims to be the very first American League batter, when he led off in that first game. Chicago went on to win that first official American League game, 8-2.

Ollie started off his career in the new league well by batting .309, stealing 36 bases, and scoring 102 runs.

Later on the Chicago Tribune shortened the name "White Stockings" to "White Sox" to better accommodate limited headline printing space and the name remained.

131. Who was the first switch-hitter to collect over 500 career home runs?

New York Yankee centerfielder, Mickey Mantle, was the first switch-hitter to have over 500 career home runs when he finished his 18-year career in 1968 with 536.

132. Who was the first player to hit a home run from both sides of the plate in the same inning?

Cleveland Indians second baseman, Carlos Baerga, was the first major league player to hit a home run from both sides of the plate in the same inning.

It started off in the 7th inning on Thursday, April 8, 1993, at Cleveland Stadium, in a game against the New York Yankees, when Alvaro Espinosa, a pinch-hitter for third baseman Jeff Treadway, lined a single to right field off southpaw Steve Howe. Carlos Baerga, with no outs, drove him home with a two-run home run to deep left-center field.

Later, in this eight-hit, nine-run inning, Espinosa came to bat again and drilled a three-run home run off Steve Farr who had come on in relief of Howe.

That brought up Baerga once again. Switching to the other side of the plate against the right-hander, Baerga lined a solo home run to deep right-center to become a "Groundbreaker" by being the first player to hit a home run from both sides of the plate in the same inning, as the Indians rolled to a 15-5 win.

133. Who was the first National League player to hit a home run from both sides of the plate in the same inning?

Mark Bellhorn, the Chicago Cubs first baseman, took a page out of Carlos Baerga's book to just be only the second player in major league history to hit two home runs in one inning, each from the opposite side of the plate.

It was on Thursday, August 29, 2002, at Miller Park when the Cubs visited the Milwaukee Brewers. Switch-hitting first baseman Mark Bellhorn came to bat in the top of the 4th inning, with none out, and SS Alex Gonzalez on first via a walk, and hit southpaw Andrew Lorraine's pitch into the left-centerfield stands for a two-run home run to give the Cubs a 2-0 lead to start off a 10-run inning.

The Cubs batted around, and Bellhorn was up for his second at bat of the inning, and this time faced right-handed reliever Jose Cabrera, He took Cabrera downtown with his second homer of the inning, a three-run shot, to centerfield, scoring RF Angel Echevarria, and LF Moises Alou ahead of him to make Bellhorn the first National Leaguer, and the second ever to hit two home runs in one inning, each from the opposite side of the plate. 3B Bill Mueller finished off the seven-hit, ten-run inning with a solo home run as The Cubs went on, before a crowd of 29,324, to win a 13-10 slugfest.

134. Who was the first, and only, player to hit a grand slam home run in the first and second innings of a game?

"Diamond Jim" Gentile, a power-hitting first baseman, made his debut with the Brooklyn Dodgers on September 10, 1957, and went with them to Los Angeles the following year. Moving to the Baltimore Orioles in 1960, he moved into the record books with them on May 9, 1961, when out in

Metropolitan Stadium, in a game against the Minnesota Twins, he came up in the top of the 1st inning to find that right-hander Pedro Ramos had walked RF Whitey Herzog, CF Jackie Brandt had doubled him to third, and 3B Brooks Robinson had walked to load the bases. Gentile jumped on Pedro's pitch and sent it deep into centerfield for a grand slam home run.

In the top of the 2nd inning Ramos gave a single to the O's RHP Chuck Estrada, and walked Whitey Herzog, before right-hander Paul Giel came on in relief. Brandt drove in Estrada on Giel's two-base throwing error. Robinson was walked to load the bases for Gentile. He treated Giel the same way he did Ramos by blasting a grand slam home run into the deep right field seats for his second grand slam in two innings, and his 8th run batted in, to send the Orioles to a 9-0 lead in the top of the 2nd inning.

Gentile became a "Groundbreaker" by being the first to hit grand slam home runs in the first two innings of a game, and in successive at bats. The Orioles coasted on to a 13-5 win.

135. Who was the first Designated Hitter to hit a home run?

Friday, April 6, 1973 was opening day at the Oakland-Alameda Coliseum, and the crowd of 38, 207 were eager to start a new season. The Minnesota Twins had come in to play the Athletics, and face right-hander Jim "Catfish" Hunter.

DH Tony Oliva didn't wait long to get the Twins off to a good start in the new season. He came up in the top of the 1st inning to find 2B Rod Carew on second base with one out. He ended Hunter's pre-mature shut-out by blasting a two-run home run into the right field stands.

The Twins, getting off to a fast five-run start after two innings, went on to an 8-4 win for Minnesota right-hander Bert Blyleven, and Oliva became the first DH to hit a ball out of the yard.

136. Who was the first player to have 100 hits from each side of the plate in the same season?

In 1979 Gary Templeton, the St. Louis Cardinals shortstop, led the National League in base hits, with 211, but more importantly he was the first player in history to have 100 or more hits from each side of the plate, having hit 111 batting left-handed, and an even 100 batting right-handed during that season. He never approached 200 hits again in his 16-year career.

137. Who was the first American League player to have 100 base hits

from each side of the plate in one season?

Just a year after Gary Templeton became the first in baseball history to have 100 base hits from both sides of the plate in 1979, along came the Kansas City Royals outfielder, Willie Wilson, who played all three outfield positions in 1980, as he became the first in the AL to do it when he had 130 hits left-handed, and an even 100 right-handed.

138. Who was the first American League player to have 400 home runs and 3,000 hits?

It didn't take leftfielder Carl Yastrzemski long, after making his major league debut on April 11, 1961, with the Boston Red Sox, for him to rise to the top of the American League elite.

In 1967 he led the American League in runs (112), hits (189) home runs (44), runs batted in (121), and batting average (326) which made him an easy selection as that year's Triple Crown winner and MVP.

Continuing his accumulation of hits and home runs, on Wednesday, September 12, 1979, at Fenway Park, Yastrzemski lined a single in the 8th inning off New York Yankees right-hander Jim Beattie for his 3,000th base hit.

When added to his 400th home run which he hit on July 24th at Fenway, off Oakland Athletics right-hander, Mike Morgan, in a 7-3 Red Sox win, it made him the first American League player to reach that plateau. Boston went on to a 9-2 win that day to make Yaz's day complete.

When he played his final game for the Red Sox, on October 2, 1983, his career statistics showed 452 home runs and 3,419 base hits for a .285 batting average.

139. Who was the first player to win the Triple Crown in the National League?

Rogers "Rajah" Hornsby, the Hall of Fame second baseman, began his career with the St. Louis Cardinals on September 10, 1915, and is considered to be the greatest right-handed hitter in baseball history.

It is a tough claim to dispute when you review his 23-season career with five teams in both leagues, and his career batting average of .358.

In 1922 he batted .401, hit 42 home runs, and drove in 152 runs to become the first player to win the National League Triple Crown. That year was not necessarily unusual, for from 1920 through 1925 he batted

.370, .397, 401, .384, .424, .403, and had 20 seasons batting over .300, and three over .400.

140. Who had the first extra-base hit, and then the first home run in American League history?

Erve "Dutch" Beck, who made his debut with the Brooklyn Superbas in 1899 at second base, moved to the Cleveland Blues (Indians) for the 1901 season and on opening day, Wednesday, April 24, 1901, in a game against the Chicago White Stockings, doubled for the first extra-base hit in the American League history.

The following day Beck came back to hit the first home run in American League history, off Chicago's rookie southpaw, John "Buckshot" Skopec, but the Blues went on to lose, 7-3. Beck had six homers that season before moving over to the Cincinnati Reds before the 1902 season. "Dutch" played his final game, back in the American League, with the Detroit Tigers, on September 27, 1902.

141. Who was the first player to hit four doubles on the opening day of the season?

We are going to take you way back to April 24, 1901, when before a crowd of 10,023, on opening day for the American League, Detroit Tigers first baseman Frank "Pop" Dillon, swinging from the left side, ripped four doubles, including two in the 9th inning, the last off Milwaukee Brewers right-handed reliever Bert Husting, to give Detroit a 14-13 win over the Brewers.

142. Who was the first batter to hit for the cycle twice in the same season?

Floyd "Babe" Herman the Brooklyn Robins (Dodgers) right-fielder was known as a bit of a flake, but also as a fine hitter. He proved the latter part in 1931 when he hit for the cycle on May 18th to help Brooklyn defeat Cincinnati 14-4.

Proving his batting ability, he again hit for the cycle on July 24th out in Pittsburgh, but it wasn't enough as the Robins bowed to the Pirates, 8-7, but Babe became a "Groundbreaker" by being the first to hit for the cycle twice in the same season.

143. Who was the first player to pinch hit for Babe Ruth?

Babe Ruth made his major league debut on the mound for the Boston

Red Sox on Saturday, July 11, 1914, against the Cleveland Naps (Indians) at Fenway Park.

He struck out in his first at bat, but hung in there until the 7th inning when with the score tied 3-3 Red Sox skipper, Bill Carrigan called on George "Duffy" Lewis to come in and pinch-hit for Ruth and the leftfielder came through with a single, and later came around to score the fourth run, giving Babe a 4-3 win as southpaw "Dutch" Leonard came on in relief and struck out four of the six batters he faced to preserve the win for the Babe.

Just for the record, Ruth went 2-1, with one complete game, and a 3.91 Era. over 23 innings in his rookie year.

144. Who was the first player to hit three extra-inning grand slam home runs?

When it comes to hitting extra-inning grand slams Carlos Lee takes a back seat to no one. "El Caballo", as he was known to his teammates, hit his first on Friday, June 8, 2001, at Comiskey Park, when the White Sox left-fielder came to bat in the 10th inning in a game tied, 3-3, with their cross-town rivals the Chicago Cubs, to find the bases loaded and two outs, and emptied the bases with a grand slam home run to left field off right-hander Courtney Duncan to give the Pale Hose a 4-3 win.

Now with the Houston Astros, before a crowd of 42,537, at Minute Maid Park on Thursday, June 28, 2007, the Colorado Rockies scored a run in the top of the 11th inning to move ahead 5-4. In the Astros half of the inning Lee is up again with the bases loaded and two outs, and facing south-paw Brian Fuentes who serves up a pitch that Lee sends deep to left field for a game-winning grand slam home run to give the Astros a come-from-behind 8-5 win.

We now move to Coors Field on Wednesday, June 9, 2010, and Houston is again involved in an extra-inning game, tied 2-2 with the Rockies. Up comes Lee, again with the bases loaded, in the top of the 10th and quickly empties them with a grand slam home run to left field off right-hander Matt Belisle for a 6-2 Astros win.

"El Caballo" can now lay claim to be the first player to have three extra-inning grand slams in his career.

145. Who was the first player to hit over 60 home runs in a single season?

Ever since Babe Ruth reached the 60 home run level in 1927 baseball has awaited the emergence of a player who would surpass that mark. It came on October 1, 1961 when, before 23,154 fans at Yankee Stadium, Yankees centerfielder Roger Maris came up in the 4th inning, with one out, and faced Boston Red Sox RHP Tracy Stallard.

Maris, swinging from the left side, sent Stallard's pitch into the lower right field stands for Maris' 61st home run of the season, and the 240th Yankees home run of the year.

That was the only run needed as the Yankees, behind RHP Bill Stafford, defeated the Red Sox, 1-0.

146. Who was the first modern day batter to be hit by 50 pitches in a single season?

Ron Hunt, the Montreal Expos second baseman, was hit by a pitch thrown by Chicago Cubs right-hander Milt Pappas's in a game at Jarry Park, on September 29, 1971, for the 50th time in that season.

147. Who was the first player to hit 30 or more home runs in a season, and have more intentional walks than homers?

Willie "Stretch" McCovey, made his major league debut on July 30, 1959, as a 21-year old first baseman with the San Francisco Giants. His tremendous power was quickly apparent and throughout his career he was always a threat to break open a game with a home run. Most teams would pitch him carefully, and in some cases they would rather walk him than give him a pitch to hit.

That certainly was the case in 1970 when Willie had 39 home runs, and led the National League in walks with 137, 40 of them intentional. Willie was a "Groundbreaker" when it came to intentional walks over unintentional home runs. Interestingly, a year earlier, in 1969, he led the league in home runs with 45, and in intentional walks with 45. Over his 22-year career "Stretch" hit 521 home runs, was walked 1,345 times, with 260 intentional.

148. Who was the first player to have 500 home runs, and collect 3,000 base hits?

This was a close race for being the first player to have both 500 home runs and 3,000 base hits.

Henry "Hammerin' Hank" Aaron made his major league debut at the age of 20 as an outfielder for the Milwaukee Braves on April 13, 1954. Though not physically imposing at 6' 180 pounds, Aaron could hit with the best of them. He led the National League in home runs and runs driven in four times, and took two batting titles, in 1956 and 1959.

His absence of any serious injury allowed him to play 23 seasons, and in 3,298 games, which propelled him to the second game of a doubleheader in Crosley Field, Cincinnati, on May 17, 1970. In the first inning of the nightcap Aaron, who had collected 569 home runs, and 2,999 base hits, found 2B Felix Millan on second, due to an error by 3B Tony Perez, and drove him home with a single off Reds' right-hander Wayne Simpson, with the first run of the game, and the 3,000th base hit of Aaron's career.

In the 3rd inning, with one out, and Millan again on base, Aaron hit his 570th career home run, off Simpson. It wasn't quite enough as Cincinnati went on to take the nightcap from Atlanta, in the bottom of the 15th inning, on a single by southpaw reliever Don Gullett which drove in SS Dave Concepcion with the winning run, 7-6.

With that 1st inning single, coupled with his already 569 home runs, Aaron became a "Groundbreaker" by being the first player to have 500 home runs and 3,000 base hits, and the 33,217 in attendance were witnesses to history.

We mentioned that it was a close race to be first in both categories and this is how it played out. On Saturday, July 18, 1970, out in Candlestick Park, the San Francisco Giants hosted the Montreal Expos before a crowd of 28,879. In the bottom of 2nd inning Willie Mays came to bat having 620 home runs, and needing one more base hit to join Hank Aaron.

Expos right-hander Mike Wegener served up the historic pitch which Willie lined for a single to centerfield, and these two Hall of Fame players had established a very distinguished club, in a matter of 63 days.

As of this writing the club has doubled its membership with the addition of Eddie Murray and Rafael Palmeiro.

149. Who was the first player in major league history to hit home runs in his first two major league at bats?

It was a quiet day in Fenway Park when the St. Louis Browns came in to play the Boston Red Sox on Friday, September 14, 1951, but history would be made before a meager crowd of 5,466. The Red Sox would explode with five runs in the bottom of the 1st inning off right-hander Fred Sanford to take a 5-0 lead.

The historical part starts in the 2nd inning and the first major league at bat for rookie leftfielder Bob Nieman as he faced Boston southpaw Mickey

McDermott. With one out Nieman walloped a solo home run into the left field stands for his first big league home run. Coming back up in the 3rd inning Nieman liked the way McDermott threw, and deposited a two-out, two-run home run into the same left field stands, scoring CF Ken Wood to close the Red Sox lead to 7-4.

His first two major league at bats translated into two home runs and three runs batted in, nice job rookie.

150. Who was the first American League player to hit a home run in his first major league at bat?

Centerfielder Earl "The Earl of Snohomish" Averill (I love that sobriquet) made his major league debut on opening day, Tuesday, April 16, 1929, as a mature rookie, at age 27, as the opening day centerfielder for the Cleveland Indians at League Park, Cleveland.

The first pitcher he faced in the big leagues was Detroit Tigers southpaw Earl Whitehill. In the bottom of the 1st inning, and showing no awe or respect for the seven-year veteran, Averill put his pitch into the seats for a solo home run, the first by any American League player in his first at bat in the major leagues.

151. Who was the first major league player to hit four home runs in a doubleheader?

It took Earl Averill until his second season to make home run headlines again when on, Wednesday, September 17, 1930, at League Park in Cleveland, against the Washington Senators, in the first game of a doubleheader, the Cleveland centerfielder stroked his 15th home run, a grand slam in the 3rd inning off Senators right-hander Irving "Bump" Hadley.

Averill came back in the 5th inning and did the same thing, this time a two-run home run off "Bump," In the 6th inning he paid no respect to the reliever Fred "Firpo" Marberry for he took the right-hander downtown for a two-run home run, Averill's third of the game, giving him 8 runs batted in of the 13 Cleveland had in downing Washington, 13-7.

In the nightcap Averill kept his hitting stroke sharp and blasted his 18th home run of the year, with two-on and no-out in the 1st inning off southpaw Lloyd "Gimpy" Brown. That Wednesday afternoon effort made "The Earl of Snohomish" a "Groundbreaker" for the second time by being the first major league player to hit four home runs in a doubleheader.

152. Who was the first National League player to hit 500 career

home runs?

This entry has to be a favorite of mine for one of my two favorite ball-players I loved to watch as young boy in the Polo Grounds was Melvin Thomas Ott, the New York Giants right-fielder, and the Giants manager at the time of his historic home run.

It was a quiet summer afternoon on Wednesday, August 1, 1945 when 19,318 fans showed up at the Polo Grounds in New York to see the Giants take on the Boston Braves. A quick three runs in the bottom of the 1st put the Giants up 3-2.

In the 3rd inning when Mel Ott came to the plate he faced the portly Braves right-hander, Johnny Hutchings, and hit a solo home run into the right field stands, called "Ottville" by the Polo Grounds faithful, for his 500th major league home run to become the first National League player, and third major leaguer to reach that plateau. Ott hit 323 of his 511 career home runs into the "Ottville" portion of the Polo Grounds.

153. Who was the first National League player to hit four home runs in consecutive at bats?

Philadelphia Phillies third baseman Mike Schmidt hit four consecutive home runs at Wrigley Field, on April 17, 1976, against the Chicago Cubs in a wild, and woolly, 18-16 Philadelphia win in ten innings.

His first came against RHP Mike Garman, the next two off RHP Rick Reuschel, and his fourth off Rick's brother, Paul, a two-run shot in the 10th inning to win the ballgame.

154. Who was the first player to hit 30 home runs for four teams?

Jose Canseco, known as "The Chemist", was a Cuban-born outfielder, and a designated hitter, performing far better in the second assignment than the first.

He made his major league debut on September 2, 1985 as a 20-year old outfielder with the Oakland Athletics, and displayed his home run hitting prowess from the start. He hit thirty or more home runs five times with Oakland, leading the league twice with 42 in 1988, and 44 in 1991.

Moving on to the Texas Rangers he again surpassed the 30 mark in 1994 with 31. In 1998 with the Toronto Blue Jays he hit 46. On July 4, 1999 he hit his 30th home run for the Tampa Bay Devil Rays, and finished that season with 34, to become the first player to hit 30 or more home runs with four different teams.

155. Who was the first player to collect two base hits in one inning, twice in the same game?

It was Monday, June 22, 1925, at Sportsman's Park, St. Louis, and the Pittsburgh Pirates centerfielder, Max "Scoops" Carey, was about to make history. It began in the first inning when the Pirates leadoff batter, the switch-hitting Carey, singled, and as the Pirates batted around in that 8-run first inning leadoff batter Carey was up again, and singled again off the Cardinals right-hander Flint Rhem.

Coming back up in the 8th inning for the second time in a 10-run Pirate outburst, Carey again lashed out with two more singles, these off right-hander Johnny "Stud" Stuart as "Scoops" went 4-5, and was hit by a pitch twice, as "Deacon Bill" McKechnie's Pirates rolled to a 24-6 laugher.

Carey became a "Groundbreaker" that day by being the first player to have two hits in an inning twice in one game.

156. Who was the first, at age 47, and the oldest, player to hit a major league home run?

"Father Time", in the person of Julio Franco of the New York Mets, came to bat on April 20, 2006 in the 8th inning, at Petco Park, as a pinch-hitter, with one out, and hit a two-run blast into the right field stands, off San Diego Padres right-hander Scott Linebrink, to make him the oldest player in major league history, at 47 years, 240 days, to hit a home run.

He eclipsed the former record of Jack Quinn of the Philadelphia Athletics, set in 1930, who had a round-tripper at age 46 and 357 days. Franco continued to set the standard when, as a first baseman, he hit another home run on Saturday, September 30th that year, at Robert F. Kennedy Stadium, off Nationals' right-hander Beltran Perez in the 1st inning, with a two-on and two-outs shot to deep right-center field, in a 13-0 rout of the Washington Nationals, and after his 48th birthday!

157. Who was the first player to hit a home run in his first at-bat of the season in his first three seasons?

When Kazuo "Kaz" Matsui, a second baseman-shortstop for the New York Mets, hit an inside-the park solo home run in the 3rd inning off right-hander Jake Peavy in a game against the San Diego Padres, at Petco Park, on April 20, 2006, he became the first player in major league history to homer in his first at-bat of the season in each of his first three seasons.

It started on April 6, 2004, before an opening day crowd of 49,460 at Turner Field, Atlanta, when Matsui led off the opening day by hitting a solo home run in the top of the 1st inning off Braves right-hander Russ Ortiz.

The following year at the opening of the season at the Great American Ball Park in Cincinnati on April 4, 2005, Matsui came up in the top of the 1st inning with one out, and put the Mets on top with a solo home run to right field off right-hander Paul Wilson.

When Matsui did it on April 20, 2006, for the third year in a row, he became a "Groundbreaker" by being the first to hit a home run in his first at-bat of the season in his first three seasons.

158. Who was the first National League player to hit a home run on Opening Day in his first three at-bats of the season?

The 1994 season opened up perfectly, in a personal way, for Chicago Cubs CF Karl "Tuffy" Rhodes. Leading off the bottom of the 1st inning, before a crowd of 38,413, on April 4th, at Wrigley Field, Rhodes hit a home run off New York Mets starting right-hander Dwight "Doc" Gooden.

Coming back up in the 3rd inning, with two outs, Rhodes again stroked a Gooden pitch into deep left-center field for his second solo home run of the game tying the score at 2-2.

Rhodes led off the bottom of the 5th, again facing Gooden, and for the third successive at bat blasted a Gooden pitch for another solo home run into the same spot as before, left-centerfield to be the first in the senior circuit to have three consecutive round trippers on opening day and become a "Groundbreaker."

Gooden shook off the power display by "Tuffy", and had the prescription for victory as he hung on to defeat Mike Morgan and the Cubbies, 12-8.

159. Who was the first player to break the season home run mark of 61 set by Roger Maris in 1961?

The mark has been broken on more than one occasion, by more than one player, but St. Louis Cardinals first baseman, Mark "Big Mac" McGwire, was the first player to exceed 61 home runs, when in the 4th inning of a game at Busch Stadium, before 43,688 excited fans on Tuesday evening, September 8, 1998, he hit a two-out pitch off Chicago Cubs right-hander Steve Trachsel for a solo home run, at 8:18 Central Daylight Time, deep down the left field line, for his 62nd of the season to make him the first to break Roger Maris' 61 home runs record.

160. Who was the first player, with at least 100 base hits, to have more runs driven in than hits?

This bizarre happening occurred in the 1999 season when Mark "Big Mac" McGwire, the St. Louis Cardinals first baseman, led the National League in home runs with 65, and in runs batted in with 147, and did it with just 145 base hits. Now that's a first.

161. Who was the first player to hit at least 50 home runs in a season in four different seasons?

Although it has been done by another, Babe Ruth set the stage when he had 54 home runs in 1920, his first season with the Yankees, and followed that up with 59 in 1921, 60 in 1927, and 54 in 1928.

162. Who was the first National League player to hit at least 50 home runs in a season, and do it four different times?

Although Babe Ruth set the stage, a St. Louis Cardinals first baseman by the name of Mark McGwire introduced it to the senior circuit.

He started it with Oakland in 1996 with 52 home runs. Then he replicated that when he moved to the National League, during the season, in a trade for three players on July 31, 1997, leaving 34 home runs in Oakland, and adding 24 with St. Louis to give him 58 for the season. He continued his personal homer derby in 1998 by hitting 70, and added to his string by hitting 65 in 1999, to become the first National Leaguer to hit over 50 home runs four times during his career.

163. Who was the first player to retire after 22 seasons in the big leagues with the same number of base hits at home as on the road?

This is a great bit of trivia, and it belongs to Stan "the Man" Musial, of the St. Louis Cardinals. When he played his final game on September 29, 1963, before a Sportsman's Park crowd of 27, 576, he stroked a single off Cincinnati Reds right-hander Jim Maloney in the bottom of the 6th inning to close out his historical career showing that he had 1,815 hits at home, and 1,815 hits on the road. With all his other accomplishments it is an honor to have him be a "Groundbreaker" by being the first player to be so exact in his distribution of base hits throughout his career.

164. Who was the first modern day ballplayer to have three base hits in

the same inning?

Does the name Gene Stephens ring a bell? It was this reserve Boston Red Sox outfielder, who played understudy to Ted Williams, who had his chance on Thursday, June 18, 1953, at Fenway Park, and made the most of it.

Coming up to bat in the 7th inning, with the Red Sox ahead 5-3, Stephens, playing leftfield, faced Tigers right-hander Steve Gromek, and after catcher Sammy White singled to center Stephens followed with a single to right field sending White to third. Stephens then stole second. CF Tom Umphlett then singled to left scoring White and Stephens.

Eight batters later and coming up for the second time in this unbelievable 17-run inning, Stephens faced right-hander Dick "Legs" Weik, who had come on in relief of Gromek, and deposited a double to centerfield, scoring RHP Ellis "Old Folks" Kinder and Sammy White.

Now the score is 20-3, and up comes Stephens for the third time in the inning, this time facing right-hander Earl "Irish" Harrist, and continues his dis-respect for Detroit pitching by lining a single to right field scoring Kinder with the 21st run of the game, and sending White to third.

When the inning was over the Red Sox had a 22-3 lead and it took no imagination to find the Red Sox in a laugher, 23-3.

The game was over, but Gene Stephens became a "Groundbreaker:" by being the first and only player to have three hits in one inning.

The pity was that only 3,108 were in attendance to see this historical moment.

165. Who was the first player to go 7-for-7 in a regular nine inning game?

Rennie Stennett, the Pittsburgh Pirates second baseman, set a major league record by being the first player to have seven hits, a double, triple and five singles, in seven at-bats in a game at Wrigley Field on September 16, 1975 against the Chicago Cubs. Pirates southpaw, John Candelaria, was the easy winner by pitching a, would you believe 22-0 shutout.

166. Who was the first player to come to bat on television in a major league game?

Billy Werber, the Cincinnati Reds third baseman, was the leadoff batter, in the first game of a doubleheader, facing Brooklyn Dodgers right-hander

Luke "Hot Potato" Hamlin, in the 1st inning of the first televised major league game, played on Saturday, August 26, 1939, at Ebbets Field.

Cincinnati won the first game, 5-2, behind Reds right-hander William "Bucky" Walters. The Dodgers took the nightcap 6-1, with right-hander Hugh Casey getting the win.

The game was broadcast on experimental station W2XBS, which later became WNBC in New York. Radio announcer Red Barber described the game as it was filmed with two cameras, one camera on Barber, and the other was behind the plate. One receiving set was located in the press box, and a second at Rockefeller Center where crowds watched.

167. Who was the first player in a major league game to hit a home run in three different countries?

With the arrival of the Toronto Blue Jays and the Montreal Expos as major league franchises there have been many players who have homered in both of their ballparks. The player who holds the distinction of being the first to hit a home run in three different countries is centerfielder Steve Finley of the San Diego Padres who, on August 16, 1996, hit a two-run home run into deep right field, scoring 1B Wally Joyner, in the bottom of the 1st inning off New York Mets right-hander Robert Person, in a game played at the Estadio de Beisbol in Monterrey, Mexico; the first major league game played outside the United States or Canada. The Padres came away winning that 15-10 slugfest, with southpaw Fernando Valenzuela, credited with the win.

168. Who was the first modern day major league player to have a 200-hit season, and yet bat under .300 for that season?

Jo-Jo Moore, sometimes referred to as "The Gause Ghost", played left field for 12 years with the New York Giants, and had 201 hits in 155 games in 1935 for a .295 batting average.

A .300-hitter five times, he played his final game on September 21, 1941, with a career batting average of .298.

169. Who was the first modern day player (post 1900) to hit four home runs in a single game?

Lou Gehrig, the New York Yankee first baseman, hit home runs in four consecutive at bats in a game on Friday, June 3, 1932 down in Shibe Park against the Philadelphia Athletics. The first three were hit off right-hander George "Moose" Earnshaw, in the 1st inning a two-run shot, a solo home run in the 4th, another solo home run in the 5th inning, and in the 7th inning he hit a solo home run off right-hander Roy "Popeye" Mahaffey.

Gehrig ended his day going 4-for-6 with 6 runs driven in. The game saw a total of 33 runs and 36 hits in a 20-13 slugfest won by New York.

170. Who was the first player to have ten or more 200-hit seasons?

The field narrows down quickly when you consider that a prolific hitter with years of service must come into play. Players like George Sisler who had six, Paul Waner who had eight, and Ty Cobb, who had nine seasons, come to mind, but the first to have ten 200-hit seasons was infielder-out-fielder Pete Rose who made his major league debut on April 8, 1963 with the Cincinnati Reds, and played 24 seasons, 19 with the Reds, five with the Phillies, and 95 games with the Montreal Expos. In five of those 200-hit seasons Rose led the National League in base hits on his way toward being the all-time hits leader with 4,256.

There is a player out there who could top Rose's number shortly, and his name will come up just ahead.

171. Who is the first player to have ten consecutive 200-hit seasons?

Pete Rose may have been the first player to have ten 200-hit seasons, but even "Charlie Hustle" can't come close to the record that Seattle Mariners right fielder Ichiro Suzuki has put up.

This native of Kasugai, Japan, made his major league debut on April 2, 2001, at age 27, and pitchers in the American League are still trying to find a way to keep his bat silent, and him off the base paths.

He led the league in his freshman season when the southpaw swinging rookie had 242 hits. Proving that season was no fluke he has had over 200 base hits in the first ten years he has been in the major leagues, leading all batters in base hits seven times, the last five in a row, at this writing. When you are talking about "Groundbreakers" Ichiro has to be right up there in the forefront.

172. Who was the first player to hit over 100 career home runs?

Harry Duffield Stowe, who played under the name of Harry Stovey, played 14 years primarily in the outfield, and some at first base, with Worcester, Philadelphia, Boston, in the Players League and the National League, Baltimore, and Brooklyn. Beside being known for his great running speed and strong arm, he led his league in home runs six times and was in the top ten in home runs in 11 of his 14 years.

He had his greatest home run year in 1889 when he clubbed 19.

Upon his retirement, on July 29, 1893, Stovey had 509 stolen bases, and 122 career home runs to make him the first player to exceed the century mark in home runs.

173. Who was the first modern day player to win four consecutive major league batting titles?

Napoleon "Nap" Lajoie, playing at both first and second base during his 21 seasons led the American League in batting with a .426 average in 1901 with the Philadelphia Athletics. On April 21, 1902 he was granted free agency, and signed with the Cleveland Bronchos on May 31st. There he batted .378, and again led the American League. Following up on that he again led the league, with Cleveland, in 1903 with a .344 average. He continued adding on to his batting titles in 1904 with a .376 average to make it four consecutive titles.

Before Nap finished up his career he captured his 5th batting title in 1910 with a .384 average. His last two seasons saw him back with Philadelphia where he played his final game on August 26, 1916, amassing 3,242 base hits for a .338 career average, and his ticket to the Hall of Fame came in 1937.

174. Who was the first, of five players, in major league history to be intentionally walked with the bases loaded?

That ultimate compliment was bestowed for the first time in major league history upon Philadelphia Athletics second baseman Napoleon "Nap" Lajoie.

It happened in the top of the 9th inning on May 23, 1901 in Comiskey Park. Lajoie came up to the plate with the bases loaded, and his team down 11-7 to the Chicago White Sox.

With Lajoie, a career .300 hitter, and off to a fast start White Sox skipper Clark Griffith, and a fine right-handed pitcher, inserted himself on the mound and proceeded to throw four wide pitches walking in the eighth run.

The crisis was not yet over, however, as the bases remained loaded and up came two power hitters, right fielder Ralph "Socks" Seybold, followed by first baseman Harry "Jasper" Davis, and part-time catcher Morgan Murphy. Griffith got all three with infield outs and came away with an 11-9 win.

175. Who was the first, and only, pitcher to hit two home runs in the game in which he pitched a no-hitter?

That unique distinction went to right-hander Rick Wise of the Philadelphia Phillies when he no-hit the Cincinnati Reds, winning 4-0, in Riverfront Stadium on Wednesday, June 23, 1971.

When Wise went from the mound to the batter's box in the top of the 5th inning, with one out, he found RF Roger Freed on second having doubled to right field.

Wise quickly took Cincinnati southpaw Ross Grimsley downtown with a two-run home run to left field. Leading off the 8th inning, and holding a 3-0 lead, Wise showed no favoritism, and crushed a solo home run into the left field stands off right-hander Clay Carroll to become a "Groundbreaker", and go into the record books as being the first, and only, pitcher to throw a no-hit game, and help his own cause with two home runs as well.

176. Who was the first, and only, player to pinch-hit for Ted Williams?

On Tuesday, September 20, 1960, down in Memorial Stadium, neither the Baltimore Orioles nor the Boston Red Sox players had yet to break a sweat when in the top of the 1st inning, LF Ted Williams, came to the plate against Orioles right-hander Hal "Skinny" Brown with CF Willie Tasby on first.

Williams took a cut at Brown's pitch and lined a foul off ball off his foot, causing great pain, and forcing the injured Williams to the bench. Boston manager, Pinky Higgins, looked down the dugout and told Carroll Hardy, a reserve outfielder to go in and hit for the Splendid Splinter.

Unfortunately Hardy didn't come close to what a healthy Williams might have done. He lined one of Brown's pitches right back to him who in turn, threw to 1B Jim Gentile to double up Willie Tasby. The Orioles came away with a 4-3 win that day.

177. Who was the first player to pinch-hit for a pair of sluggers, both Roger Maris and Ted Williams?

Interestingly, Carroll Hardy, while with the Cleveland Indians in 1958, pinch-hit for Roger Maris in the 11th inning of the first game of a double header at Cleveland Stadium on May 18, 1958, and hit his first major league home run, with two on, and one out, off Chicago White southpaw

Billy Pierce to win the game for the Tribe 7-3.

Two years later, on September 20, 1960, Hardy, then with the Boston Red Sox was called upon to pinch-hit in the 1ˢᵗ inning for Hall of Famer Ted Williams, and wasn't quite as successful. He hit a liner back to Baltimore right-hander, Hal "Skinny" Brown, who threw to first to complete a double play.

178. Who was the first pitcher to go through an entire season, winning twenty games and never striking out?

Right-hander Johnny Sain, made his major league debut with the Boston Braves on April 24, 1942, and spent over six years with them before moving on to the American League with the Yankees in 1951, finishing out his career with the Kansas City Athletics on July 15, 1955.

The season we are talking about happened in 1946 when Sain went 20-14, and led the league in complete games with 24, and did not walk or struck out the entire season, coming to bat 94 times and having a .298 batting average that season.

179. Who was the first player to hit a walk-off grand slam home run in American League history?

When you think of American League home run hitters your thoughts quickly turn to Babe Ruth, and rightly so for he was the first American League player to hit a walk-off grand slam home run when he hit it in the 10ᵗʰ inning off Chicago White Sox right-hander George "Sarge" Connally, who had come on in relief of Urban "Red" Faber, on Thursday September 24, 1925 in Yankee Stadium, before a crowd of only 1,000. It gave the Yankees, and their southpaw "Big Ben" Shields, who went the entire 10 innings, a 6-5 win over the Pale Hose.

180. Who was the first modern day player to hit inside-the-park grand slam home runs in consecutive games on consecutive days?

Samuel James Tilden "Jimmy" Sheckard, was a southpaw swinging left fielder who made his major league debut with the Brooklyn Bridegrooms on September 14, 1897, and had one of his greatest seasons in 1901 with the renamed Brooklyn Superbas, when he batted .353, with 11 home runs and 104 runs driven in, and led the National League with 19 triples.

Those accomplishments were embellished, however, by his hitting an inside-the-park grand slam home run off Cincinnati Reds right-hander Archie "Lumbago" Stimmel at League Park on September 23ʳᵈ as the

Superbas rolled to a 25-6 win, with the help of two home runs, one a grand slam by Joe Kelly.

Sheckard's bat didn't cool off overnight for he came back the following day, on Tuesday, September 24th, and duplicated yesterday by hitting another inside-the-park grand slam home run to become the first player to hit inside-the-park grand slam home runs in consecutive games on consecutive days as Brooklyn pounded Cincinnati 16-2 and gave right-hander Frank Kitson, who had his only homer of the year, in that game, an easy victory.

181. Who was the first player, of the 25 who have hit 500 career home runs, to hit his 500th as a pinch-hitter?

On Friday, April 17, 2009, Gary Sheffield of the New York Mets, led off the bottom of the 7th inning as a pinch-hitter for RHP Sean Green, and on a full count, hit a line drive solo home run into the deep left field stands at the new Citi Field, off Milwaukee Brewers' southpaw reliever Mitch Stetter for Sheffield's 500th career home run, tying the game at 4-4.

The Mets, before 36,436, went on to win with a run in the bottom of the 9th, 5-4.

182. Who was the first player to start out his major league career with three consecutive 200-hit seasons?

Lloyd "Little Poison" Waner, the Pittsburgh Pirates centerfielder, banged out 223 base hits in his freshman year in 1927. He came back in the next two years with 221 base hits in 1928, and followed that with 234 hits in his third season in 1929.

No telling how long that streak would have continued, for in 1930 "Little Poison" was stricken with appendicitis, after 68 games, picking up just 94 hits, and missed the remainder of the season. He came back strongly in 1931, and went on to lead the National League in hits with 214.

183. Who was the first American League player to start his major league career by leading the league, in base hits, having over 200, and batting over .320 in his first three years?

Johnny Pesky, the Boston Red Sox shortstop, born John Paveskovich, started his major league career on April 14, 1942, and ended his freshman season by leading the American League in base hits with 205, while batting .331.

He entered military service in 1943, where he spent the next three years, until he returned to the Boston infield in 1946 and led the American League again in base hits with 208, while batting .335. He repeated the base hit title in 1947 with 207 and batted .324, giving him three consecutive playing years leading the American League in base hits, having over 200 each year to go along with his over .320 batting average.

184. With twenty-five players having hit 500 career home runs, the latest on April 17, 2009, who was the first to reach this exalted level?

It won't come as a surprise to anyone that George Herman "Babe" Ruth was the first player to hit 500 career home runs. It happened on Sunday, August 11, 1929, when, in the 2nd inning, with the bases empty, he crushed Indians' right-hander Willis Hudlin's pitch out of League Park, Cleveland, which landed on Lexington Avenue, for his 30th home run of the season, and the 500th of his career, but Cleveland went on to win 6-5.

Babe asked Mr. Jake Geiser, a detective friend, to see if he could retrieve the ball. Finding it in the possession of a young boy, Geiser retrieved the baseball, and gave it to the Babe who then autographed it, and gave, two baseballs to the young boy along with a twenty dollar bill.

185. Many fans know that Joe DiMaggio holds the consecutive game hitting streak with his 56-game streak in 1941. Who was the first player to have a 40-game consecutive hitting streak?

Tyrus Raymond Cobb, "The Georgia Peach", while with the Detroit Tigers in 1911, was the first to have a hit in 40 consecutive games. That was just the forerunner to his season where he led the American League in hits (248), doubles (47), triples (24), runs scored (147), runs driven in (127), stolen bases (83), and in batting with a .420 average.

186. Who was the first player to hit 40 or more home runs in a season, but drive in less than 100 runs in that season?

That unusual feat was credited to "The Duke of Flatbush," Edwin "Duke" Snider, the left-handed power hitting centerfielder of the Brooklyn Dodgers, who must have wondered where all the base runners were when he came to bat during the 1957 season when the "Duke" hit 40 home runs, he batted in only 92.

187. Who was the first National League player to hit a home run before

the age of 20, and after the age of 40?

That example of power at any age goes to Daniel "Rusty" Staub, who when he broke in with the Houston .45's on April 9, 1963 at first base, he had a home run while still at the tender age of 19, in fact he had six that year.

In 1985, at the age of 41, and completing his 23-season career, now with the New York Mets, he hit one home run, his 292nd career round-tripper.

"Le Grand Orange" joined quite a hitter, from many years earlier, in the American League, "The Georgia Peach" who accomplished the same feat, at age 18 in 1905 with Detroit, and then at 41, with the Philadelphia Athletics in 1928.

188. Who was the first, and only, player to appear in 500 major league games for four different teams, and collect 500 hits for each of those teams?

The man who got around, and played and produced when there, was the previously mentioned, Daniel "Rusty" Staub, a right-fielder, first baseman, and designated hitter during his 23-year career.

He started that career on April 9, 1963 with the Houston Colt .45's, and played six seasons in Houston, both as the Colt .45's and Astros, appearing in 833 games, and collecting 792 hits. He was traded to the Montreal Expos on January 22, 1969 and spent four years in Canada, playing in 518 games, and where the fans applied the sobriquet "Le Grand Orange" to the red-headed favorite.

After banging out 531 hits for the Expos they traded him on April 5, 1972 to the New York Mets, which proved to be his longest stay, nine years, 942 games and 709 hits later, Rusty packed his bags, at age 32, and moved to the American League when he was traded to the Detroit Tigers on December 12, 1975. His four years, and 549 games in the Motor City, produced 582 hits, and on July 20, 1979 Detroit sent him packing back to the Expos. On March 31, 1980 off he went to the Texas Rangers for a brief stay of 109 games, then back to the Mets where he played his final game on October 6, 1985.

His two leagues, four teams, 500 games and 500 hits with each, sets Rusty apart as the first to be that productive wherever he played.

189. Who was the first switch-hitter to win a Triple Crown?

Mickey Mantle, the switch-hitting centerfielder of the New York Yankees, not only won the batting title in 1956 with a .353 batting average, he also won the home run title with 52, and the runs batted in title with 130, which then made him the winner of the prestigious Triple Crown Award.

On top of that he led the American League in runs scored with 132, and slugging average with .705 which made him a shoo-in for the Most Valuable Player Award, as well, that year.

190. Who was the first player to play an entire season, with over 600 at bats, and not hit into a double play?

August "Augie" Galan came up to the big leagues on April 29, 1934 as a 22-year-old infielder with the Chicago Cubs, but was moved to the outfield the following year where he batted .314 in 646 at bats, led the league in runs scored with 133, and stolen bases with 22 in his 154 games. Not once in those 646 official at bats, did Galan hit into a double play.

He did, however, on Sunday, April 21, 1935, in a game tied 4-4 against the Cincinnati Reds, hit into a triple play, in the bottom of the 11th inning, with Reds 1B Jim Bottomley and 2B Alex Kampouris pulling it off to end the inning. The Reds went on to pick up four runs in the top of the 12th to come away with an 8-4 win as Reds' right-hander Paul Derringer got the decision over right-hander Clay Bryant.

191. Who was the first, and only, batter to ever pinch-hit for Ty Cobb?

Just the fact that this player not only pinch-hit for Ty Cobb, but was told to do so by the "Georgia Peach" himself, who was the player-manager of the Detroit Tigers at the time, is certainly newsworthy and historic.

It was on Friday, May 5, 1922 that the Detroit Tigers found themselves down in the bottom of the 9th inning, 6-0, to southpaw Bill "Beverly" Bayne of the St. Louis Browns who was cruising along with a one-hitter at Navin Field, Detroit.

When Larry Woodall, pinch-hitting for second baseman Danny Clark, picked up the second hit of the game off Bayne, Cobb, who was 0-3 that day, was next up. He looked down the bench and asked who could get a base hit. Rookie leftfielder Bob "Fats" Fothergill volunteered, and the portly outfielder, who became a very good hitter, replaced Cobb at the plate, but was unsuccessful.

Woodall later scored the lone run when RF Harry Heilmann hit a sacrifice fly, and Bayne came away with a two-hit victory, 6-1, before 7,000 disappointed fans. Detroit may have lost the game, but those fans saw something no one else had seen, a pinch-hitter for Ty Cobb.

Just a word about "Fats" Fothergill who may have been unsuccessful on that May afternoon, but the leftfielder of rotund proportions made his major league debut with the Detroit Tigers on April 18, 1922, just two weeks prior to his pinch-hitting assignment for Cobb. He went on after nine years in Detroit, to the Chicago White Sox for three seasons before playing his final season, and game on July 5, 1933 with the Boston Red Sox.

From 1926 to 1929 he was considered one of the most feared hitters in baseball finishing in the top ten in slugging during those four straight years. He holds the Detroit team record for the most pinch-hits in a season with 19 in 1929 His lifetime batting average was an impressive .325, and he hit over .300 in his first eight seasons and in 9 of his 12 seasons. Cobb's confidence on May 5th certainly was not misplaced.

192. Who was the first, and only, player to hit 50 or more home runs in a season ten years apart?

Willie Howard Mays was 24 years old when he led the National League in triples with 13, and in home runs with 51 with the New York Giants in 1955.

He came back ten years later, at age 34, to crush 52 home runs in 1965 with the San Francisco Giants.

193. Who was the first player to win the home run title in both the American and National Leagues during his career?

This native of Wahoo, Nebraska was naturally nicknamed "Wahoo Sam" Crawford. He made his major league debut on September 10, 1899 in the outfield with the Cincinnati Reds. Back in 1901, in his third year with the Reds, this right-fielder batted .330 and hit an astounding, for that era, 16 home runs to capture the National League home run title.

Jumping over to the Detroit Tigers in the American League before the start of 1903 season, "Wahoo Sam" continued to put up impressive numbers, especially when it came to hitting triples. In 1908 Sam led the American League in home runs with 7, while batting .311.

That 1908 season made Sam the first player to win the home run title in both leagues. Let's not forget he also won the runs batted in title three times with the Tigers as well. When he played his final game on September 16, 1917 with Detroit, he had 97 career home runs, and he held the American League career record for home runs with 70.

194. Who was the first player to lead both the American and National Leagues in triples?

In his rookie year of 1899 Jimmy "Buttons" Williams, the Pittsburgh Pirates 22-year old third baseman hit 27 triples to lead the National League. Before the 1901 season, "Buttons" jumped from the Pirates, over to the American League, to play second base with the Baltimore Orioles, where he led that league in triples with 21. He duplicated that effort the following year banging out another 21 triples in 1902 to lead the American League again.

The master of hitting triples has to be "Wahoo Sam" Crawford who missed out by being the first to lead both leagues in triples by a year when he led the National League in triples with 22 in 1902 while with Cincinnati. He then led the American League, with Detroit, in 1903 with 25. Crawford continued hitting three-baggers by winning the title in 1910 with 19, 1913 with 23, 1914 with 26, and 1915 with 19, winding up his career with 312 triples, first on the all-time list.

195. Who was the first American League player to hit a pinch-hit home run in his first major league at bat?

This one has an unusual twist. The first American League player to hit a pinch-hit home run in his first major league at bat was better suited for the gridiron than the baseball diamond. We're talking about Duke University All-American football star, Clarence "Ace" Parker, of the Philadelphia Athletics.

Coming up to pinch-hit in the 9th inning of a laugher played in Fenway Park on Friday, April 30, 1937, his Athletics were behind 15-3 to the Red Sox, and he was facing Boston right-hander Wes Ferrell. Parker hit a two-run home run to narrow the deficit to 15-5, and he entered the record books as being the first player to pinch-hit a home run in his first big league at bat.

There's more to the story. Parker's baseball career was an abbreviated one as the shortstop went on to hit just two home runs that season and compiled a two-year career batting average of .179.

Later in the year, on November 21, 1937, that same Ace Parker scored two touchdowns for the NFL Brooklyn Dodgers against the Pittsburgh Steelers, and eventually ended up in the National Football League's Hall of Fame in Canton, Ohio.

196. Who was the first player to hit a home run in each of the 32 baseball parks?

The way Frank Robinson, then with the California Angels on Wednesday, September 19, 1973, hit home runs during his 21-year-two-league career, it was not surprising that on this day, in the second game of a doubleheader against the Texas Rangers, at Arlington Stadium, that he, who had 586 in his career wouldn't add Arlington Stadium, to be the first player to have connected for a home run in 32 different major league baseball parks. The victim was southpaw Charlie Hudson, who after allowing a single to RF Richie Scheinblum, in the top of the 1st inning, followed that by delivering a one-out home run ball to DH Frank Robinson, his 27th of the year, which sailed into the left field stands.

197. Who was the first player to hit four triples in one game?

Shortstop George Strief of the Philadelphia Athletics had a big day at bat on June 25, 1885 when he hit four triples and a double against the Brooklyn Grays. His added double made him the first to have five extra-base hits in a game. His hits were not enough that day as Philadelphia fell by the football score of 21-14. "Scrappy" Bill Joyce third baseman for the New York Giants, who has been miscredited as the first to hit four triples did it in 1897.

198. Who was the first player to have scored a walk-off inside-the-park grand slam home run?

This essay should maybe be called a "run off," rather than a "walk off" home run. This unusual incident happened on July 25, 1956 in Forbes Field after the Chicago Cubs had rallied in the top of the 8th inning with a 7-run outburst to take a 7-4 lead over the Pittsburgh Pirates. With Cubs right-hander Omar "Turk" Lown loading the bases with Pirates, in came Jim "Professor" Brosnan to face future Hall of Famer Roberto Clemente, who promptly hit the first pitch high and far off the left field light tower.

With the ball still in play, and everyone running, Clemente circled the bases and scored with an inside-the-park "walk off" home run to win the game for Pittsburgh, 8-7.

199. Who was the first player to get a base hit for two different teams in two different cities on the same day?

On August 4, 1982 the New York Mets outfielder, Joel Youngblood, found himself in centerfield at Wrigley Field for an afternoon game against future Hall of Fame right-hander Ferguson Jenkins of the Chicago Cubs. Youngblood went 1-for-2, with a two-run single in the top of the third inning to help the Mets to a 7-4 win.

At the conclusion of the game he was notified that he has just been traded to the Montreal Expos for southpaw Tom Gorman. He packed his bags and immediately flew to Philadelphia where his new team had a night game with the Phillies at Veterans Stadium.

He arrived in time to be inserted into the lineup in the 6th inning in right field, replacing Jerry White, and put in the second slot in the batting order. In the top of the 7th inning he faced his second future Hall of Fame pitcher, southpaw Steve Carlton, and banged out an infield single. The Phillies went on to win, 5-4, but Youngblood became the first player in major league history to have played, and picked up a base hit, for two different teams, in two different cities in the same day. Just to add a little more unusualness to the story he also played in a day game and a night game, and picked up his hits against two future Hall of Fame residents, Jenkins and Carlton, a right-hander and a lefty, all on Wednesday, August 4th.

200. Who was the first American League pitcher to hit a grand slam home run since the Designated Hitter rule went into effect?

The pitcher who broke the ice in grand slam home runs since the designated hitter rule went into effect occurred in the top of the 2nd inning of an inter-league game against the Seattle Mariners on Monday, June 23, 2008, at Shea Stadium, New York. Mets southpaw ace Johan Santana, after giving up a single to 3B Adrian Beltre, a single to catcher Jeff Clement, and an error by 3B David Wright on CF Willie Bloomquist's ground ball loaded the bases for Mariners' RHP "King Felix" Hernandez. Santana served up a fat pitch to Hernandez who promptly drove a long fly ball to deep right-center field for a grand slam home run, scoring Beltrie, Clement, and Bloomquist before him with the fourth run of the inning, putting the Mariners on the road to a 5-2 win.

201. Who was the first player to hit a home run in his first and last, regular season major league at bat?

This is a bit bizarre, but true none the less. Paul Gillespie, a reserve catcher for the Chicago Cubs, came up to the big leagues during World War II and in his first major league at bat, on Friday, September 11, 1942, against the New York Giants, at the Polo Grounds, hit his first major league home run, a solo shot, in the 2nd inning, off Giants' right-hander Harry Feldman.

Playing in just five games that year, and just nine games in 1944, he did play in 75 games in 1945, and on Saturday, September 29, 1945, in his final regular season at bat in the major leagues, out in Forbes Field, he hit a two-run home run in the 4th inning off Pittsburgh Pirates right-hander Truett "Rip" Sewell as the Cubs, behind their right-hander Hy Vandenberg, went on to win the nightcap of the doubleheader, 5-0.

Gillespie then became the first player to hit a home run in his first and last regular season major league at bat.

With the Chicago Cubs playing the Detroit Tigers in the World Series that year, Gillespie did play in three games for Chicago, going hitless in six at bats.

Only one other player in major league history duplicated Gillespie's home run experience, John Miller, a reserve infielder-outfielder, who hit a home run in his first at bat, while with the New York Yankees on September 11, 1966, and then in his last at bat on September 27, 1969, with the Los Angeles Dodgers.

The only two home runs in his 61 major league at bats.

202. Who was the first batter to hit over .400 yet failed to win the batting title?

The year was 1911 and the competition was fierce for the American League batting title. "Shoeless Joe" Jackson batted .408, with 233 hits, 71 for extra bases, and scored 126 runs. Not a bad season by anyone's standards.

Unfortunately, Ty Cobb batted .420, with 248 hits, 79 for extra bases, and scored 147 runs. All other statistics aside .408 doesn't beat .420, and "Shoeless Joe" became the first player to exceed the .400 season average and fail to take the batting title.

Jackson went on to have the third highest career batting average in baseball history when he hung up his cleats on September 27, 1920 with a .356 career batting average.

203. Who was the first shortstop to lead his league in home runs?

Back in 1958 Ernie "Mr. Cub" Banks had quite a year. With his 47 home runs, and 129 runs batted in, he led the National League in both categories, and became the first senior circuit shortstop to capture the home run title.

204. Who were the first teammates to each hit their 300th career home run off the same pitcher in the same game?

This coincidence happened on Monday, April 13, 2009 out in Comerica Park before a crowd of 21,850. The victim of this historic event was Detroit Tigers right-hander Zach Miner.

We go to the top of a scoreless 2nd inning when Chicago White Sox right fielder Jermaine Dye led off the inning by hammering his 300th career home run, a solo shot to deep left-center field. Next up was 1B Paul Konerko who followed Dye's blast with a solo home run for his 300th career home run, as well, to join his teammate as the first to celebrate this impressive level of "swinging the lumber" together.

205. Who was the first batter to have twelve consecutive base hits?

With a great run Michael "Pinky" Higgins, the third baseman of the Boston Red Sox, ran off a hitting streak of twelve consecutive base hits that started on the first game of a Sunday doubleheader on June 19, 1938, at Comiskey Park, with a late game single off White Sox right-hander "Silent John" Whitehead.

In the second game of the doubleheader, against White Sox right-hander Bill "Bullfrog" Dietrich, "Pinky" went 3-for-3 with a walk. On Tuesday, June 21st Boston was at Briggs Stadium, Detroit, for another doubleheader. In the first game Higgins went 4-for-4, with a walk, against Detroit's fine curveball right-hander Tommy Bridges.

In the second game that day Higgins again went 4-for-4, this time rocking Tigers right-hander Alfred "Roxie" Lawson for four singles, giving him 12 consecutive base hits, accomplished over fourteen plate appearances, with those two bases on balls sandwiched between them, and "Pinky' Higgins became the first player in major league history to have twelve consecutive base hits.

206. Who was the first player to hit 50 or more home runs in four consecutive seasons?

During this period in major league history baseballs were flying off the bats of a selected few players. Names like Barry Bonds, Mark McGwire, and Sammy Sosa set, and shattered, home run records.

Over their careers Bonds hit 40 or more home runs five times, McGwire hit 50 or more home runs four times, but it was Sammy Sosa who hit 50 or more home runs four years in succession, with 66 in 1998, 63 in 1999, 50 in 2000, and 64 in 2001.

207. Who was the first player to appear in all 162 games as a designated hitter?

On December 12, 1975 the Detroit Tigers made a trade with the New York Mets for outfielder Rusty Staub. Using his powerful bat Staub was switched to the designated hitter position in 1976, and stayed in that role through the 1978 season when he played in every one of the 162 games played that year by the Detroit Tigers. No other player can make that claim.

208. Who were the first modern day players to hit .400 in their league in the same season?

These three players were no strangers to atmospheric batting averages as the 1922 season showed. Rogers Hornsby of the St. Louis Cardinals represented the National League with a .401 batting average.

Over in the American League, Ty Cobb, with the Detroit Tigers, also batted .401.

The overall leader was St. Louis Browns first baseman, George Sisler, who led everyone with his .420 batting average.

Cobb and Hornsby hit over .400 three times. Cobb in 1911, '12, and '22; Hornsby in 1922, '24, and '25. Sisler did it twice, in 1920 and 1922.

209. Who was the first player to win the batting championship in both the American and National Leagues?

"Big Ed" Delahanty was one of five brothers to have played in the major leagues. He was far more successful playing baseball than his siblings as he won the National League batting title while with the Philadelphia Phillies in 1899 with a .410 average, his third .400 year.

In 1902, now with the Washington Nationals in the American League, he won the batting title with a .376 average, to lay claim to being the first to lead each league for the batting title.

210. Who was the first National League player to win two or more batting titles while compiling a career batting average under .300?

In his third full major league season with the Los Angeles Dodgers, in 1962, leftfielder Tommy Davis led the National League not only in batting with a .346 average, but in hits with 230, and runs batted in with 153. He repeated that batting title in 1963 when he batted .326, but with four more years of batting .300, he ended up his 18-year career with a .294 career batting average.

211. Who was the first player to hit a home run off two 300-game winners in the same game?

This could be an interesting answer given the fact that two 300-game winning pitchers, and an eight-year veteran player, could meet up in a potential historic moment.

The batter came up with over 200 career home runs, and when he met up, while playing for the New York Yankees, in a game on Friday, April 24, 1987, at Cleveland Stadium, Rickey Henderson faced Cleveland Indians right-hander Phil Niekro, a 300-game winner, in the top of the 8th inning with no outs, and being behind, 4-1, promptly drove a solo home run into the stands.

Coming up in the top of the 9th, and now behind 4-3, he faced a second 300-game winner, Steve "Lefty" Carlton, with one on, and two outs, and Rickey did the same to him with a two-run home run to put the Yankees ahead 5-4. The Indians came up with two in the bottom of the 9th to pull out a squeaker, 6-5.

That put Rickey, "The Man of Steal" into the "Groundbreakers" as the first player in history to hit home runs off two 300-game winners in the same game, and I might add, in consecutive innings.

212. Who was the first batter to become the 3,000th strikeout victim of two Hall of Fame pitchers?

I am not sure that Cesar Geronimo, the Cincinnati Reds outfielder, will willingly offer up his two experiences at the hands, or should I say, arms of

Nolan Ryan in a game with the Houston Astros on July 4th, 1980, nor with Bob Gibson of the St. Louis Cardinals, when he faced that other power pitcher on July 17, 1974. Cesar was the victim of each of those pitchers' 3,000 career strikeouts

213. Who was the first player to drive in 100 runs in a season playing for two teams?

There are over thirty players that can lay claim to driving in over 100 runs while playing for two teams in the same season, but you have to go back to 1902 when first baseman Charlie "Piano Legs" Hickman had 16 runs batted in during his 28-game stay with the Boston Somersets (Red Sox), before moving over to the Cleveland Blues (Indians) where he drove in an additional 94 runs in 102 games to give him 110 ribbies on the season.

214. Who was the first batting champion to be traded even up for a home run champion?

This most unusual trade happened back on April 17, 1960 when the Detroit Tigers' right fielder, Harvey Kuenn, the American League batting champion the previous season, having had a .363 average, and who also led the league in hits with 198, and doubles with 42, was traded, even up, for the Cleveland Indians right-fielder, Rocky Colavito who tied for the American League home run championship with Washington Senators' slugger Harmon Killebrew in 1959 with 42.

Kuenn stayed but a year with Cleveland before being sent to the San Francisco Giants for southpaw Johnny Antonelli and OF Willie Kirkland. Colavito stayed four years with Detroit before moving on to the Kansas City Athletics for a year. Neither player ever led their league again in any category.

215. Who was the first player to hit three home runs in back-to back innings, and on his birthday?

OK, I have to admit this is really stretching things a bit, but it really did happen. You can look it up. There is nothing like celebrating your birthday in grand fashion, like having a big day with the bat if you are the Boston Red Sox shortstop. We're speaking of Nomar Garciaparra who did it up royally at Fenway Park, on Tuesday, July 23, 2002, his 29th birthday, by being the first player to hit three home runs in back-to-back innings on your birthday.

It started in the 3rd inning of the second game of a doubleheader against the Tampa Bay Devil Rays (now called Rays), when Nomar hit a two-run home run to left field, off Rays right-hander Tanyon Sturtz, scoring 2B Lou Meloni.

Nomar came back in that 10-run inning to again homer, this time off rookie reliever Brandon Backe, and followed up with a grand slam in the 4th inning off that same Backe, to lead his Red Sox to a lopsided 22-4 win over Tampa Bay. What better present to give oneself than a day at the ballpark where you have three home runs, one a grand slam, drive in eight runs, have 32,729 faithful fans applaud your efforts, and your birthday, as your team rolls to an easy victory.

216. Who was the first player in major league history to hit a single, double and a triple in the same inning?

It was a day to remember for the 34,764 fans who packed Fenway Park on Friday, June 27, 2003 as the Boston Red Sox played host to the Florida Marlins. Florida opened up the game with a run in top of the 1st, but after that it was all Boston as they came back with a 14-run barrage in their half of the 1st.

Led by centerfielder Johnny Damon, who opened the inning with a double to right field off right-hander Carl Pavano, he followed that with a triple to right off southpaw Michael Tejera, scoring 3B Bill Mueller and catcher Jason Varitek. In his third at bat of the inning with the score 13-1, he singled to left field off the Marlins right-hander Allen Levrault, scoring RF Trot Nixon with the 14th run of the inning as the Red Sox rolled to a 25-8 win as Johnny Damon became a "Groundbreaker" by being the first to have a single, double and a triple in the same inning, three quarters of the way to a cycle.

217. Who was the first designated hitter to hit over 40 home runs in a season?

David "Big Papi" Ortiz, made his major league debut with the Minnesota Twins on September 2, 1997 as a 21-year old first baseman, but has spent most of his career as a designated hitter. He signed on with the Boston Red Sox as a free agent on January 22, 2003, and has added tremendous left-handed power to the Sox. In the 2004 season "Big Papi" hit 41 home runs, followed by 47 in 2005 to be the first DH to hit over 40 home runs in a season.

He took it a step further in the 2006 season by being the first DH to hit 50 home runs when he led the American League in home runs with 54.

218. **Who was the first player to pinch-hit a grand slam home run in American League history?**

One has to go back to that afternoon of September 24, 1916 when Marty Kavanagh, a utility player for the Cleveland Indians, came up to pinch-hit with the bases loaded in the 5th inning of a game against Boston Red Sox southpaw Hubert "Dutch" Leonard.

Kavanagh slammed a hard ground ball over third base that continued to roll down the line until it met and rolled under a screen in deep left field, and couldn't be retrieved until after Kavanagh and those ahead of him had crossed the plate to bring the Indians to a 5-3 victory over the first place Red Sox.

Leonard gave up just four base hits in the game, but all for extra bases.

Kavanagh's home run was the only one he hit that year, but he did go on to lead the American League in pinch-hit at-bats with 46.

219. **Who was the first player to lead the American League in base hits, and then move to the National League and in the following year lead that league in base hits?**

It happened when centerfielder Lance "One Dog" Johnson left the American League with the Chicago White Sox in 1995 after leading the league in base hits with 186, and then moved over to the National League when he signed on with the New York Mets as a free agent on December 14, 1995.

In 1996 he duplicated his hit title of the previous season by leading the National League in base hits with 227, to be the first to lead both leagues in base hits.

220. **Who was the first player to collect 200 singles in a season?**

Ichiro Suzuki, the centerfielder of the Seattle Mariners, should be voted the president of the swinging singles club for the 225 singles that he hit in 2004, as part of the 262 league leading base hits he collected that season.

221. **Who was the first player to hit .300 with at least 30 home runs and drive in over 100 runs in his first two seasons?**

That feat belongs to "Prince Albert" Pujols, the stellar outfielder and first baseman of the St. Louis Cardinals, when in his freshman season he batted .329, had 37 home runs, and batted in 130 runs in 2001.

The sophomore jinx meant nothing to Pujols who came back to bat .314, had 34 home runs, and drove in 127 runs in 2002, to be the first to put up such awesome numbers in his first two seasons.

In 2003 he escalated those numbers by hitting 43 home runs, with 124 runs batted in, and led the league in batting with a .359 batting average.

222. Who was the first player to drive in 100 runs in each of his first ten years in the major leagues?

"Bucketfoot Al" Simmons, made his major league debut on April 15, 1924, as an outfielder with the Philadelphia Athletics, and promptly displayed his great batting ability by driving in 102 runs in his rookie year. He stayed in that hitting groove by driving in over 100 runs in his first eleven consecutive years, highlighting that streak in 1929, by leading the American League with 157 runs driven across the plate.

223. Who was the first catcher to hit 40 doubles in a season?

Catchers aren't known for being fleet afoot so hitting 40 doubles in a season is noteworthy. That thought didn't apply to Gordon "Mickey" Cochrane, catching for the Detroit Tigers in 1930, when he banged out 42 doubles to put his bat and legs together to drive in 85 runs and bat .357 that season.

Since "Mickey" led the way by being first to hit 40 doubles there have been a half dozen others to have hit 40 or more as well.

224. Who was the first player to win what is now called, "The Triple Crown"?

They didn't have a name for it back in Paul Hines' time, but as major league baseball became more mature in its never-ending statistical analysis Hines duly deserves to be mentioned here. Hines was the Providence Grays centerfielder when he led the National League in 1878 in batting with a .358 average, in home runs with 4, and in runs batted in with 50, in his 62 games played that year, which by today's standards would make him the first recipient of the Triple Crown.

Proving that the previous year was no fluke Hines came back to win the batting title in 1879 with a .357 average, and led the league in hits with 146, and still had a very respectable 52 runs batted in.

225. Who was the first player over the age of 40 to hit a grand slam

home run?

There was still power in the bat of Adrian "Cap" Anson when this aged ballplayer, on August 1, 1894, playing for the National League Chicago White Stockings (Cubs) in a game against the St. Louis Brown Stockings (Cardinals), at the age of 42 years, 3 months, went 5-for-7, including a grand slam home run as Chicago went on a tear, walloping St. Louis, 26-8.

Anson was known more as a line drive singles hitter, having 2,614 of them, which when added to his 582 doubles, 142 triples, and 97 home runs, added up to his impressive 3,435 career base hits, making him an easy selection for the Hall of Fame where he became a resident in 1939.

226. Who was the first batter to hit into a triple play?

This will take you way back in time, to May 13, 1876, to be accurate. On that date the New York Mutuals were the visitors at the Hartford Ball Club Grounds facing the Hartford Dark Blues in a National League game. In the 5th inning Dick Higham, the Hartford Dark Blues right-fielder, came to bat with the bases loaded. Centerfielder Jack Remsen was on first, second baseman "Black Jack" Burdock was on second, and the catcher Doug Allison was leading off third.

The runners were moving with the pitch as Higham hit a hard line drive at the Mutuals second baseman, Bill Craver, who then threw to first baseman Joe "Old Reliable" Start to double up Jack Remsen for the second out. Start quickly relayed the ball back to Craver, catching Burdock trying to return to the bag, to complete the first triple play in Major League (National League) history.

227. Who was the first player to have 250 hits and not lead his league in base hits?

When a player has a season of 250 base hits he can be pretty sure to lead the league in that category. Not so in 1930 when Chuck Klein, the Philadelphia Phillies right-fielder, had a very fine season when he led the National League in doubles with 59, and in runs scored with 158, to go along with his 250 base hits.

When the last game was played New York Giants first baseman "Memphis Bill" Terry had racked up a league-leading 254 base hits, capturing the batting title as well, with a .401 batting average.

228. Who was the first switch-hitter to win a home run title?

This first baseman made his major league debut on April 18, 1931, as a 27-year old first baseman with the St Louis Cardinals. James "Ripper" Collins didn't display his home run abilities until 1924 when he won the National League home run title with 35 home runs which made him the first switch-hitter to win a home run title.

229. Who was the first player to hit 40 or more doubles for seven consecutive seasons?

They called him "Ducky" or "Muscles," but maybe they should have called Joe Medwick, the St. Louis Cardinals leftfielder, if you'll pardon the pun, "Double Ducky" for his penchant and ability to hit the ball for two-bases with great frequency.

That thought was borne out by him being the first player to hit 40 or more doubles from his first full year with the Cardinals in 1933 on through 1939. During that run, Medwick, also known for his bulging biceps, hence the additional sobriquet "Muscles", led the National League in two-baggers with 64, 56, and 47 in 1936,'37, and '38.

His 17-year career with the Cardinals, Dodgers, Giants, and Braves, along with his career .324 batting average, was stellar enough to have this Gas House Gang member be inducted into Cooperstown in 1968.

230. Who was the first batter to personally break up five no-hit games?

He was a big hit, but not in the way you might imagine. Just ask Barry Moore, Dave McNally, Mike Cuellar, Dick Bosman and Catfish Hunter about "Pepito."

It seems that Cesar "Pepito" Tovar broke up more no-hitters than any batter in major league history. He started it off on April 30, 1967, in the second game of a doubleheader down in D.C. Stadium, when his 6th inning single was the lone Minnesota Twins hit off Washington Senators' south-paw Barry Moore.

On May 15, 1969, at Metropolitan Stadium, Baltimore southpaw Dave McNally saw his bid for a no-hitter go down the drain by one swing of Pepito's bat, a one-out single in the bottom of the 9th inning. Three months later, on Sunday, August 10, 1969, at Memorial Stadium, Tovar's 9th inning single to left field, off Baltimore Orioles southpaw Mike Cuellar, not only broke up his no-hit bid at the last moment, but also put an end to a consec-utive streak of 35 batters that Cuellar had retired over the course of his last two games. The right handed hitting "Pepito" really liked those southpaws.

Now we go to RFK Stadium on Thursday, August 13th, 1970, and Tovar is facing right-hander Dick Bosman of the Washington Senators, in the top of the 1st inning, and lays down a bunt single that rolls along the third base line, and becomes the Twins' only hit of the game, as Bosman squeezes out a 1-0 one-hitter, and the pesky "Pepito" once again spoiled a pitcher's bid for baseball immortality.

Tovar's fifth and final breakup came down in Arlington Stadium against Jim "Catfish" Hunter, on May 31, 1975 when the Yankee right-hander saw his no-hit bid go by the boards as that "Tovar guy" does it again, this time as the designated hitter for the Texas Rangers, when he singled to centerfield, with two out in the bottom of the 6th inning, for the Rangers lone hit of the game.

Cesar Tovar who made his major league debut on April 12, 1965 with the Minnesota Twins as an infielder-outfielder went on to also play with the Phillies, Texas Rangers, Oakland Athletics, and ended his twelve year career on September 22, 1968 with the Yankees, showed a career batting average of .278, and 1,546 base hits, five of which will long be remembered by those five pitchers who must have sent a celebratory farewell present to "Pepito" knowing he was out of their hair for good.

231. Who was the first pitcher to hit two home runs in one game?

The Philadelphia Athletics were playing the Boston Americans on May 8, 1906, and their roster was depleted by injuries so Connie Mack inserted Charles "Chief" Bender, his right-handed pitcher, who had 16 wins the previous season, and had a home run in his last game on May 5th, into left field in the 6th inning. The Chief responded well to his new role and hit two inside-the-park home runs off Boston southpaw Jesse Tannehill helping the A's to a 11-4 win and making him the first pitcher to hit two home runs in the same game.

232. Who were the first two pinch-hitters, from opposite teams, to each have a grand slam home run in the same game?

It was a Sunday afternoon, May 26, 1929, at the Polo Grounds, where the New York Giants played host to the Boston Braves before a crowd of 35,000. Going into the bottom of the 6th inning with the score tied, 2-2, Giants skipper John McGraw sent up the right-handed hitting infielder Pat Crawford to pinch-hit with the bases loaded. Crawford justified McGraw's decision by belting a grand slam home run off Braves right-hander Harry "Socks" Seibold as the Giants respond with a nine-run inning.

In the top of the 7th inning the Braves find themselves down 11-2, but are able to load the bases, and not to be outdone, their skipper Judge Fuchs sent up the right-handed hitting infielder Les Bell, to pinch-hit off the third Giants pitcher of the day, the Giants "Meal Ticket", Carl Hubbell, in his only relief appearance of the year. Bell laced into one of Hub's pitches and drove it into the left field stands for a bases-clearing grand slam home run to narrow the Polo Grounders' lead to 11-8. The Giants picked up four more runs in their half of the 7th and held on for a 15-8 win.

When the fans exited that game, under Coogan's Bluff, they could say that for the first time in history they saw two pinch-hitters, from opposing teams, hit grand slam home runs in successive innings of the same game.

233. Who was the first player to drive in a run in 17 consecutive games?

Oscar Ray Grimes, "Bummer" to his teammates, made his major league debut on September 24, 1920 with the Boston Red Sox at first base, but after playing that initial game moved over to the Chicago Cubs, and on June 27, 1922 went on a hitting tear that saw him drive in at least one run in the next 16 games. On July 23rd Grimes hit a home run in the Cubs 4-1 win over the Brooklyn Dodgers giving him a run batted in for the 17th consecutive game. His streak would be broken on July 25th against the Boston Braves, but he would end his season with 99 runs driven in, and a .354 batting average.

His major league career lasted only six seasons as he played his final game on August 12, 1926 with the Philadelphia Phillies, and he ended it with a career .329 batting average. His brother Roy, and his son Oscar, both played in the majors.

234. Who was the first batter to hit three grand slam home runs in a season four times?

With the power that Jimmie "Double X" Foxx displayed during his 20-year, 534 home run, career it isn't surprising that he won this "Groundbreaker" title.

It started in 1932 and he repeated it in 1934 when he hit three grand slams in those years with the Philadelphia Athletics. When he joined the Boston Red Sox in 1936, he did it with them in 1939 and 1940, making him the first to hit three grand slams in four different years.

235. Who was the first player to hit two inside-the-park home runs in the same game in both the American and National Leagues?

Roger "The Duke of Tralee" Bresnahan was an outfielder, but more notably known as a catcher, made his debut on August 27, 1897 with the Washington Senators, interestingly as a pitcher, but played a few positions, including third base for the Baltimore Orioles, when on Friday, May 30, 1902, in Oriole Park, in the first game of a doubleheader, he hit two inside-the-park home runs to help the Orioles to a 12-4 win over the Cleveland Bronchos (Indians).

On Monday, June 6, 1904, and now with the New York Giants, and playing each of the infield positions, and the outfield, had his second game of hitting two inside-the-park home runs when he did it in the Polo Grounds against the Pittsburgh Pirates in a 15-2 win to become the first player to hit two of them in the same game in each league.

236. Who was the first modern day National League player to hit two home runs in the same inning?

It was that portly outfielder, Hack Wilson, who had led the National League in home runs four times, had two of them in the 3rd inning for the New York Giants in the second game of a doubleheader sweep by the Giants on July 1, 1925 at Baker Bowl as New York went on to a 16-7 win over the Philadelphia Phillies. Wilson's first was a two-run home run, with one out, off southpaw Clarence Mitchell; the second in that 9-run inning, was a three-run home run, with two outs off right-hander Jack Knight.

237. Who was the first player to strikeout over 1,000 times?

As with many batting records, Babe Ruth is part of this one, as he was the first player to pass the 1,000-strikeout plateau when he did it during the 1930 season. When Babe played his last game, with the Boston Braves, in the first game of a doubleheader against the Philadelphia Phillies, in Baker Bowl, on May 30, 1935, his career strikeout total was 1,330.

238. Who was the first batter to strikeout 1,500 times in his career?

When Mickey Mantle made his first appearance upon the major league scene in the outfield with the New York Yankees on April 17, 1951, he was labeled a "can't miss" and his pundits were correct for "The Commerce Comet" could hit, hit for power, run and field.

His four home run championships, and his 1956 runs batted in title attest to that, as do his three MVP Awards. But that "can't miss" claim has to be re-examined, for "The Mick", with all his mighty home run blasts, missed enough to lead the American League in strikeouts five times, and saw him conclude his 1966 season with exactly 1,500 strikeouts. His two additional years, which ended with his final game on September 28, 1968, added another 210 to make him the first batter to fan over 1,500 times.

239. Who was the first player to win two Triple Crowns?

Rogers Hornsby, the St. Louis Cardinals second baseman, and one of the great all-time hitters, having batted over .400 in 1922, '24, and '25 and missing a fourth consecutive season by hitting .384 in 1923, won the prestigious Triple Crown in 1922 with 42 home runs, 152 runs batted in, while posting a .401 batting average.

In 1925 Hornsby again won the Triple Crown by posting 39 home runs, 143 runs driven in, and a .403 batting average, making him the first player to capture that title twice. He was also the MVP in the National League in 1925, and 1929.

240. Who was the first American League batter to twice capture the Triple Crown?

Often called one of the greatest left-handed hitters to ever play the game, "The Splendid Splinter" Ted Williams, in his third year in the big leagues, 1941, batted .406. His first Triple Crown came in the following year when he had 36 home runs, drove in 137 runs, and batted .356.

He repeated that honor when, in 1947, he again led the American League in all three categories by having 32 home runs, driving in 114 runs, and batting .343. His league leading 162 walks certainly inhibited his ability to hit more homers and drive in more runs. Williams also won the MVP Award twice, in 1946 and 1949.

241. Who was the first batter to have over 50 home runs in consecutive years?

We are shaving this closely as St. Louis Cardinals first baseman Mark McGwire was the first, when in 1996 he hit 52 home runs and came back in 1997 to hit 58. He also hit over 60 in 1970 when he blasted 70! Coming back in 1999 he dropped to 65.

Taking a look at the other guy, the right fielder of the Chicago Cubs, Sammy Sosa, he too exceeded 50 when he had 66 in 1998 and 63 in 1999 to make him the first to have 60 back-to-back years. But hold on for in those two years McGwire had 70 and 65 to tie Sosa for first over 60, and be the first over 70.

To take even a step further Sosa had four consecutive years of hitting 50 or more home runs when he had 66 in 1998, 63 in 1999, 50 in 2000, and 64 in 2001.

Those two alleged steroid sluggers sure did put on a home run derby show for the fans.

242. Who was the first, and only, player to win the batting title in his first two major league seasons?

Right-fielder Tony Oliva of the Minnesota Twins made his major league debut in a game on September 9, 1962, but qualified as a rookie when he captured the American League batting crown in his first full season in 1964 when he led the league with 217 hits and a .323 batting average.

He came back the following year to win the batting title once again with a .321 average while also leading the league in hits with 185.

243. Who was the first player to hit a walk-off home run in his major league debut?

September 9, 1971 will long be remembered by California Angels second baseman Billy Parker. It was on this day that Parker came up in the bottom of the 12th inning with the score tied at 2-2, and with two out, hit a solo home run off right-hander Floyd Weaver to defeat the Milwaukee Brewers, and give Eddie Fisher his 10th win of the year. Parker went into the "Groundbreakers" record books as the first player to hit a walk-off home run in his major league debut.

244. Who was the first player to hit pinch-hit home runs in three consecutive at bats?

Look out west to the Los Angeles Dodgers' Lee Lacy for this one. On May 2, 1978 Lacy pinch-hit for the pitcher, Terry Forster, in the 9th inning at Wrigley Field and hit a two-run home run off Cubs right-hander, Rick Reuschel to send the game into extra innings where the Cubbies scored a run in the 10th to win 5-4.

On May 6th out in Three Rivers Stadium, Lacy was called on again to pinch-hit, this time for CF Glenn Burke, and hit a 9th inning solo home run off John Candelaria as the Pirates went on to a 3-2 win.

His record-setting third pinch-hit home run came on May 17th in Dodger Stadium when Lacy pinch-hit for 2B Davey Lopes and hammered a solo home run in the 8th inning off Pirate southpaw Will McEnaney as the Dodgers rolled to an easy 10-1 win.

245. Who was first player to hit a home run completely out of a minor league stadium in a major league game?

In 1956 the Brooklyn Dodgers played some of their "home" games at Roosevelt Stadium, in Jersey City, New Jersey, which happened to be the former home of the New York Giants farm club, the Jersey City Giants.

On August 15th of that year the New York Giants were hosted by the Dodgers in a night game where 26,385 conflicting loyalties were most apparent. It was a battle between the big right-hander, Don Newcombe, for Brooklyn, and the stylish southpaw Johnny Antonelli for the Giants.

In this pitchers' battle the only run scored was a tremendous 4th inning blast off a Newcombe pitch by the Giants' Willie Mays as his home run totally cleared the outfield wall of the Stadium and sailed into the darkness of night as the "Say Hey Kid" became the first major leaguer to hit a home run out of a minor league park in a major league game.

Antonelli went on to pitch a two-hit shutout, striking out 11 for a 1-0 win.

246. Who was the first player to exceed 260 base hits in a season?

It took place at Safeco Field on October 2, 2004 when the Mariners' right-fielder Ichiro Suzuki, before a crowd of 45,817, lined a single to center field in the bottom of the 5th inning off Texas Rangers southpaw Kenny "The Gambler" Rogers for his 260th base hit of the season, to be the first player to reach that plateau. Rogers recorded his 18th win as Texas went on to win 10-4.

247. Who was the first catcher to ever win a National League batting title?

Eugene "Bubbles" Hargrave made his major league debut with the Chicago Cubs as a catcher on September 18, 1913, and moved on to the Cincinnati Reds in 1921 where he batted over .300 from 1922-27, and became the first catcher to lead the National League in batting when he hit .353 in 1926.

Playing his 12th and final season, with the Yankees, "Bubbles" finished his playing days on September 6, 1930 with a .310 career batting average.

248. Who was the first position player to be the victim of going hitless

in three different "perfect" games?

During his 18-year career infielder Alfredo Griffin played in 1,962 games, but three of them must have stood out perfectly clear.

On May 15, 1981, while with the Toronto Blues Jays, the switch-hitter went 0-2 against Len Barker when the Cleveland right-hander pitched his 3-0 perfect game.

Then on September 16, 1988 Griffin went 0-3 against the Cincinnati Reds southpaw, Tom Browning, when he pitched his 1-0 perfect game against the Los Angeles Dodgers.

While still playing shortstop with the Dodgers on July 28, 1991, Dennis "El Presidente" Martinez, the Expos right-hander, set down Griffin three times on his way to his 2-0 perfect game performance.

Alfredo Griffin joins the ranks of the "Groundbreakers" by being the first player to be the victim of, and participant in, three perfect games.

249. Who was the first, and only, player in major league history to hit three bases-empty home runs in a game where they became the only runs scored by either team in the whole game?

This oddity occurred in the second game of a doubleheader on August 27, 1951 at Philadelphia when Phillies catcher, Del Wilber walloped three bases-empty home runs off Cincinnati Reds southpaw Ken Raffensberger as the Phillies southpaw Ken Johnson shut out the Reds, 3-0.

250. Who was the first player to hit for the cycle on opening day?

Gerald "Gee" Walker, an outfielder who made his major league debut with the Detroit Tigers on April 14, 1931, was playing right field against the Cleveland Indians on Tuesday, April 20, 1937, before an opening day crowd of 38,200 at Navin Field, Detroit.

He came to the plate in the 2nd inning and hit a solo home run off Indians right-hander Mel Harder. That started him on his "cycle day" as he followed with a triple, double, and a single to go 4-4, scoring twice, with a run batted in, and was a big part in the Tigers 4-3 win.

That day he also became a "Groundbreaker" by hitting for the cycle in reverse.

251. Who was the first, and only, player in major league history to collect at least one base hit, and drive in one run in his team's first ten games?

Talk about being productive from opening day on Florida Marlins third baseman Jorge Cantu, when he doubled and drove in a run on Thursday, April 15, 2010, off Cincinnati Reds right-hander Aaron Harang, he became the first player to have a base hit and a run driven in for the first ten games of the Marlins' season.

252. Who was the first shortstop to hit 30 home runs in a season?

Right-handed hitting Vern "Junior" Stephens, of the Boston Red Sox, became the first shortstop to exceed the 30 home run total for a season when he hit 39 in 1949. He led the American League in runs batted in with 159 that season to go along with his .290 batting average.

253. Who was the first player to strikeout more than 100 times, while walking less than 10 times in a season?

That "swing rather than take" attitude made Florida Marlins catcher Miguel Olivo a "Groundbreaker" in the 2006 season when the righty swinger fanned 103 times while walking just 9 times. Guess the signal from the bench was it was okay to pitch to him with runners on base.

254. Who was the first player to hit a dozen inside-the-park home runs in a single season?

It was "Wahoo Sam" Crawford, the right-fielder of the Cincinnati Reds, who was the first player to hit twelve inside-the-park home runs in a single season when he led the National League in home runs with 16 in 1901.

255. Who was the first player to hit the first inside-the-park home run in two different stadiums in the same season?

Philadelphia Phillies shortstop Jimmy Rollins hit the first inside-the-park home run at Citizens Bank Park on June 20, 2004 off southpaw Dennys Reyes of the Kansas City Royals in the 2nd inning with two on as the Phillies went on to win 8-2.

When out at Petco Park, San Diego, on August 4th, Rollins hit his second in the 4th inning, a solo shot to right field, off the Padres right-hander Adam Eaton, in a 7-5 win to become the first to do it in two different parks in the same season and become a "Groundbreaker".

256. Who was the first player to have a walk-off base hit on consecutive

home game opening days?

On Friday, April 9, 1976, down in Arlington Stadium, Texas Rangers' shortstop, Toby Harrah, ended the Rangers home opener with a ringing walk-off single to left field in the 11th inning off Minnesota Twins right-hander, Bill Campbell, scoring catcher Jim Sundberg for a 2-1 Texas victory.

On Monday, April 11, 1977, in the next Texas Rangers home opener, down in Arlington, Toby Harrah (now playing third base) came up in the bottom of the 10th inning with the score tied at 2-2 with the Cleveland Indians, and crushed an inside-the-park solo home run off Cleveland southpaw Dave LaRoche for a 3-2 win. This, unlike the one in 1976, was more of a run-off home run, but as the jargon goes let's give a big Harrah to Toby for being the first player to have back-to-back "walk-off" base hits on consecutive home opening games of his team.

257. Who was the first player to hit a grand slam home run on opening day?

The first grand slam home run to be hit on opening day was crushed by New York Giants first baseman, Bill Terry, on April 12, 1927 in the 5th inning at Philadelphia off Phillies right-hander Hal Carlson. The Giants went on to roll to a 15-7 victory.

258. Who was the first player to pinch-hit for two future Hall of Fame players?

Carroll Hardy, a reserve outfielder, had an interesting career as a pinch-hitter. On May 18, 1958, which happened to be his 25th birthday, he came up in the 11th inning of a 4-4 tie to pinch-hit for Cleveland outfielder Roger Maris, and the rookie hit a three-run home run off Chicago White Sox southpaw, Billy Pierce.

But back to the Hall of Famers. On September 20, 1960, while with the Red Sox, down in Memorial Stadium, Baltimore, Hardy was called on to pinch-hit for Ted Williams, who was forced to leave the game in the 1st inning after fouling a pitch off his foot. CF Willie Tasby was on first with one out as Hardy faced Orioles right-hander Hal "Skinny" Brown, and promptly lined his pitch back at him and Skinny turned it into a double play. Baltimore went on to a 4-3 win.

Hardy was called upon to pinch-hit on May 31, 1961 for another left-fielder, Ted Williams's replacement, rookie Carl Yazstremski. It was in the bottom of the 8th inning, and Boston was down 7-4 to the Yankees, when

Hardy led off with a bunt single down the third base line off Luis Arroyo, and later scored when Frank Malzone singled to center. It wasn't enough as the Yankees went on to win 7-6. Hardy still can say that he was the first player to pinch-hit for two Hall of Fame players.

Hardy also played in the National Football League with the San Francisco 49ers during the 1955 season, catching 12 passes (four for touchdowns), and was the MVP of the Hula Bowl that year -- a Hardy man and a handy man to have around a ball club.

259. Who was the first player to win the Triple Crown?

"Sir Hugh" Duffy, the right-handed hitting outfielder for the Boston Beaneaters, won the Triple Crown in 1894, before it was so designated, when he had 18 home runs, drove in 145 runs, while batting .440.

260. Who was the first player to hit two home runs in an extra-inning game?

This rarity happened on a Wednesday afternoon on September 29, 1943 when the St, Louis Browns shortstop, Vern Stephens, came up in the top of the 11th inning in a tie ballgame, at Fenway Park, and faced Boston Red Sox right-hander Cecil "Tex" Hughson, and deposited a solo home run to put the Brownies ahead, 3-2.

In the bottom of the 11th the Red Sox pushed across a tying run, and the game went into the 13th inning, when Stephens hit his second extra inning home run, a solo shot, to give the Browns a 4-3 win over Boston.

261. Who was the first pitcher to hit two home runs in one game, twice in one season?

Wes Ferrell, an excellent pitcher and a very good pinch- hitter, was 14-5 on the mound in 1934, but at the plate Ferrell hit two home runs good for four runs, in his 7-3 win over the St. Louis Browns on July 13, 1934. He came back on August 22nd against the Chicago White Sox, to hit an 8th inning home run to tie the game, and then came back in the 10th to hit a two-out game ending home run for a 3-2 Boston victory over the Pale Hose.

With that effort Ferrell entered the "Groundbreakers Club" as being the first pitcher to hit two home runs in a game, twice in the same season.

262. Who hit the first walk-off grand slam home run in major

league history?

It was on September 10, 1881, in Albany, New York, when the south-paw swinging first baseman of the Troy Trojans, Roger Connor, came to the plate in the bottom of the 9th inning, with the bases loaded, and two outs, and down 7-4, to southpaw Lee Richmond and the Worcester Ruby Legs.

Roger crushed a Richmond pitch deep into the outfield clearing the bases and came home with the first walk-off home run in major league, (National League) history to give the Trojans, and their right-hander Mickey Welch, an 8-7 victory.

263. Who was the first player to hit his 500th career home run and his 550th career home run in the same season?

It is not surprising to learn that the southpaw swinging leftfielder of the San Francisco Giants, Barry Bonds, hit his 6th home run of the season, and 500th in his career, an 8th inning, two-run blast deep into right field at Pac Bell Park, on Tuesday, April 17, 2001, off right-handed reliever Terry Adams of the Los Angeles Dodgers, as the Giants came away with a 3-2 win.

On Monday, August 27, 2001, Bonds hit a solo shot to deep right-center, in the 5th inning at Shea Stadium, off the New York Mets right-handed starter, Kevin Appier, for his 56th of the season and the 550th of his career, as San Francisco scored a 6-5 victory over the Mets.

264. Who were the first pair of teammates to hit three triples each in the same game?

On June 14, 1876 outfielder George Hall, and infielder Ezra Sutton of the Philadelphia Athletics, went on a hitting binge that saw Sutton hit three triples in the game against the Cincinnati Reds and Hall, not only have three triples as well, but a home run to top it off as these two right-handed hitters led Philadelphia to a 20-5 win over the Cincinnati.

265. Who was the first player to hit two game-winning pinch-hit grand slam home runs in one season?

Let' take you down to Veterans Stadium, Philadelphia on April 30, 1978, where 31,101 fans saw their Phillies come into the bottom of the 5th inning in a 4-4 tie with the San Diego Padres.

Southpaw Randy Jones then allowed a run to make it 5-4, and walked

LF Greg Luzinski bringing in southpaw Bob Shirley in relief. Shirley gave an intentional walk to CF Gary Maddox, and then walked 2B Jim Morrison to load the bases, which brought up Davey Johnson to pinch-hit for Randy Lerch. Johnson promptly emptied the bases with a grand slam home run to centerfield, putting the Phillies up 9-4. That helped take the Phillies, thanks to Johnson's grand slam, to an easy 11-4 victory.

Now we take you back again to Veterans Stadium on June 3rd where a Saturday crowd of 31,442 saw the Phillies and the Los Angeles Dodgers locked in a 4-4 tie going into the bottom of the 9th inning. Southpaw Terry Forster was on the mound for Los Angeles and opened the inning by giving up a single to CF Gary Maddox. In a pick-off attempt that went wild it allowed Maddox to scamper to third. That brought up LF Greg Luzinski who was intentionally passed. Manager Danny Ozark then sent up Jerry Martin to pinch-hit for 3B Richie Hebner, and he too was given a free pass to load the bases. That again set the stage for Davey Johnson who was sent up to pinch-hit for 1B Jay Johnstone.

Johnson duplicated his earlier clutch hitting by blasting a walk off grand slam home run scoring Maddox, Luzinski, and Martin before him to give the Phillies a 5-1 win. That blast made Johnson a "Groundbreaker" by being the first to pinch-hit two grand slam home runs in the same season.

266. Who was the first National League player to ground into three double plays in an Opening Day game?

You can bet that Albert Pujols, the St. Louis Cardinals first baseman, and arguably the best player at this time in baseball, would have happily pushed this opening day of the 2011 season off if he knew what was about to happen to him. Playing in Busch Stadium, on Thursday, March 31st, before a hometown crowd of 46,368, Pujols took the collar, going 0-5. That was bad enough looking ahead to what was coming. He was retired on a foul pop-up in the bottom of the 1st and everything went downhill after that.

San Diego right-hander Tim Stauffer got him to hit into a ground ball double play in bottom of the 3rd, again in the 5th, but then in the 10th with right-hander Pat Neshek on the mound, and the score tied at 3-3, he got Pujols, with a runner on first, to bang into his third double play of the game, as the Padres won it with two runs in the top of the 11th, 5-3. That great hitter suffered his worse opening day, but became a "Groundbreaker" the hard way.

267. **Who were the first teammates to ever hit three home runs each in the same game?**

It happened on Tuesday, September 25, 2001, at Bank One Ballpark, when RF Jeromy Burnitz and 1B Richie Sexson of the Milwaukee Brewers twice hit back-to-back home runs, in the 4th and 6th innings, with each having a total of three as Burnitz hit one in the 2nd, and Sexson in the 9th in the Brewers 9-4 victory over the Arizona Diamondbacks.

268. **Who was the first player to lead the league in base hits for five consecutive seasons?**

Ichiro Suzuki, the southpaw swinging right-fielder of the Seattle Mariners, began his major league career on April 2, 2001, and this hitting-machine finished his freshman season by leading the American League that year with 242 base hits.

He didn't stop there, and during the next ten seasons banged out over 200 hits each year, including being the league leader seven times, and from 2006 through 2010 he was the league leader in hits for five consecutive seasons.

He not only was the first player to lead the league for five consecutive seasons but also the first to have ten consecutive 200-hit seasons.

269. **Who was the first modern day player to have over 20 doubles, triples, and home runs in a single season?**

Just look to Frank "Wildfire" Schulte, who played right field for the Chicago Cubs in 1911, and amassed a total of 30 doubles, 21 triples, and a league leading 21 home runs, while driving in 107 runs, most in the league that year.

270. **Who was the first player to come to the plate in every inning, but one, in a nine-inning game?**

For this to happen the game had to be a wild and crazy game, as it was on Friday, August 28, 1992, when the 3rd place Milwaukee Brewers took on the Blue Jays at the SkyDome in Toronto.

It all started in the top of the 1st inning when RF Darryl Hamilton, batting in the second position in the batting order, struck out swinging against Toronto southpaw Jimmy Key. In the 2nd inning, with the Brewers ahead, 2-0, Hamilton drew a walk off Key which brought in the right-handed reliever Mike Timlin, who got Paul Molitor to ground out and end the inning.

In the 3rd inning, with the Brewers up, 3-0, Hamilton singled to center-field off Timlin. In the 4th inning, with the Brewers now ahead 7-1, right-hander Doug Linton relieved Timlin and up came Hamilton who lined a ground ball single to right field.

In the top of the 5th, with Milwaukee up 13-1, the Brewers get two hits, but no runs, and Hamilton doesn't get an at-bat.

That doesn't last long for in the 6th inning Hamilton leads off against southpaw Bob Macdonald, and flies out to right field. In the 7th Hamilton has better luck, and drives in a run with a line drive to short right field off Macdonald.

Now in the 8th inning, with the Brewers up 16-2, up comes Hamilton again, this time facing right-hander Mark Eichhorn, and he promptly lines a two-run single to right-center field.

Moving into the top of the 9th, and Milwaukee sitting on a 19-2 lead, in comes southpaw David "Boomer" Wells to relieve Eichhorn, and after giving up three runs and five hits, faces Hamilton for his 8th plate appearance and Wells gets Hamilton to hit into a force out at second base to end the Brewers hitting onslaught.

Milwaukee comes away with a 22-2 thrashing of the Blue Jays, setting an American League record of 31 hits, off six Toronto pitchers. Darryl Hamilton comes away with a 4-7 day at the plate, along with a walk, and 5 runs batted in.

But historically he became the first batter to come to the plate once in every inning but one, the 5th, in a nine inning game. It was a "Groundbreaker" kind of a day.

271. **Who is the first, and only, player in major league history to hit a home run in a regular season game, an All-Star game, a Division Series game, a Championship Series game, and a World Series, all in the same season?**

Sandy Alomar Jr. came from a family of major leaguers with Roberto, his brother, and Sandy Sr., his father, all having played in the big leagues. Sandy Jr. got off to a fast start in Cleveland, in 1990, by being named the American League Rookie of the Year, a member of the American League

All-Star team, and winning a Gold Glove.

But now we are talking about the 1997 season, when Sandy hit 21 regular season home runs, then followed that by hitting and a two-out, two-run home run off San Francisco Giants southpaw Shawn Estes in the 7th inning of the All-Star game, on July 8th at Jacobs Field to give the American League a 3-1 victory.

When the American League Division Series rolled around the Cleveland catcher came up in the 1st. inning of Game 1, on Tuesday, September 30th, at Yankee Stadium, and blasted a two-out, three-run home run to deep left field off Yankees right-hander David Cone. Alomar came back in Game 4, on Sunday, October 5th, out in Jacobs Field, and hit an 8th inning solo shot to deep right field off right-hander Mariano Rivera as Cleveland came away with a 3-2 victory.

Then Cleveland took on the Baltimore Orioles in the A.L. Championship Series, and Sandy continued his long-ball efforts in Game 4, on Sunday, October 12th, out in Jacobs Field, when he greeted Orioles right-hander Scott Erickson in the 2nd inning with a one-out, two-run home run into centerfield, as Cleveland pulled out an 8-7 win to take the ALCS in six games, sending them to the 1997 World Series against the Florida Marlins.

The story doesn't end there as Alomar again showed off his long-ball abilities on Sunday, October 19th down in Pro Player Stadium, where in Game 2 of the World Series he showed right-hander Kevin Brown the way downtown by blasting a two-out, two-run home run to deep left field in the 6th inning. Although the Marlins took home the championship flag in seven games, Alomar blasted two home runs in that losing cause.

That made him a "Ground Breaker" by hitting a home run not only in the regular season, but in the All-Star, ALDS, ALCS, games, and the World Series as well.

272. Who was the first batter, from opening day, to never have his batting average drop below .400 for the entire season?

We are obviously talking about a regular everyday player, and that would be St. Louis Cardinals second baseman Rogers "Rajah" Hornsby.

He opened up the 1924 season on April 24th by going 2-5 against right-hander Vic Aldridge of the Chicago Cubs, as the Redbirds came away with a 6-5 win.

He improved on that .400 batting average over the course of the season, and ended up the 1924 season with a .424 average, the highest major league batting average in the 20th century.

273. Who was the first catcher to have 200 hits, and hit 40 home runs in the same season?

In 1997 Mike Piazza, the Los Angeles Dodgers catcher, had 201 base hits, including 40 home runs, which drove in 124 runs, giving him a season batting average of .362 to become the first backstop to reach those numbers.

274. Who was the first player to drive in a run in thirteen consecutive games?

His batting streak began on Sunday, May 4, 1941 at Comiskey Park when Chicago White Sox's southpaw swinging right fielder, Taft "Taffy" Wright, drove in a run in a losing cause as his Sox lost to the Philadelphia Athletics, 17-11.

During the next twelve games he continued to drive in a run in every game, 22 in all, until his streak finally came to an end on Wednesday, May 21, 1941, down in Shibe Park when Philadelphia's Phil Marchildon, and Lum Harris shut down Taffy who went 0-4 with a walk, but not a run driven in as the Sox lost to The Athletics, 7-6.

Taffy was the first to drive a run for 13 consecutive games.

275. Who was the first player to pinch-hit a solo home run in his last major league at bat for the only home run, and run scored in his major league career?

On May 20, 1941, George Jumonville, a reserve infielder with the Philadelphia Phillies, was sent in to pinch-hit, by manager Doc Prothro, for Silas "Si" Johnson in the 6th inning with the Phillies down 4 to the Cardinals. Jumonville, in his 43rd and last major league plate appearance, hit southpaw Clyde "Hardrock" Shoun's pitch for a solo home run to give George his only home run, and only run scored, in his brief two-year stint with the Phillies. The Phillies did go on to win 6-4 in 11 innings.

276. Who was the first player to drive in 100 runs in a season, but not hit a home run?

Third baseman Lafayette "Lave" Cross of the Philadelphia Athletics had quite a season in 1902. His 191 base hits included 39 doubles and 8 triples that helped him to drive in 108 runs, and to also give him a .342

batting average.

With all of those base hits and 108 runs batted in Lave never did drive himself in, for none of those hits was a home run, and Lave became the first player to be so productive without the benefit of a round-tripper.

277. Who was the first player to hit into a triple play, but not be charged with a time at bat?

It was the first game of a doubleheader at Fenway Park, on Monday, September 26, 1927, when the visiting Washington Senators first baseman, Joe Judge, came up in the 5th inning with none out and Babe Ganzel on second, and Goose Goslin on first.

Judge hit a long fly ball to Ira Flagstead in deep centerfield for the first out with Ganzel moving to third after the catch. In those days, with the runner advancing after the catch, it was considered a sacrifice fly and not an official time at bat. Goslin also tried to advance, but was thrown out at second by Flagstead's toss to 2B Bill Regan. Ganzel, seeing the play at second, tried to come on and score, but Regan's throw to catcher Grover "Slick" Hartley nailed Ganzel for the third out, and there was Judge watching his fly ball be turned into a triple play, but the scorecard didn't charge him with a time at bat. It wasn't enough for the Red Sox as they dropped the first game 4-2, and the second game as well, 11-1. But that didn't stop Judge from being a "Groundbreaker" by being the first player to hit into a triple play without an official time at bat.

278. Who was the first player to hit a home run in his first major league at bat?

It was on opening day, April 16, 1887, that the southpaw swinging Baltimore Orioles centerfielder, Mike Griffin, in his first major league at bat, hit a home run, and added three extra base hits to lead the Orioles past the Philadelphia Phillies, 8-3.

279. Who was the first pitcher to have two base hits off two different pitchers in the same inning?

The explosions 24,363 fans heard at Fenway Park on July 4, 1948, were not firecrackers, but from the Red Sox bats as they pummeled the Philadelphia Athletics pitching staff for 20 hits and 19 earned runs as they, and their starter Ellis "Old Folks" Kinder, came away with an easy 19-5 win.

Kinder helped his cause by driving in two runs as he had three hits, two in the 6th inning. The first came off Charlie "Bubba" Harris and he came back up in that inning to bang out a second single, this off reliever Bill McCahan, to become the first pitcher to have two base hits in the same inning off two different pitchers.

280. Who was the first player to hit 30 or more home runs in his first four seasons?

Many a home run came off the bat of Mark "Big Mac" McGwire, and it all started in 1987, his first full year with the Oakland Athletics, when he led the American League with 49 home runs.

He followed that with 32 homers in 1988, 33 in 1989, and in his fourth season, in 1990, had 39 round-trippers.

Over the course of his 16-year career McGwire had two years over 40 with Oakland, 2 with 50 or more, one with Oakland, and the other when he split his season between the Athletics and the Cardinals in 1997, one over 60, when he led the National League with the St. Louis Cardinals, and again in 1998 with 70.

281. Who was the first pitcher to come to bat ten times in a single game?

His coming to bat ten times in a single game is a record I doubt will ever be broken. I am not sure any pitcher nowadays would go 26 innings. But that was not the case of Leon Cadore, the Brooklyn Robins right-hander who found himself locked in a 1-1 tie after 26 innings on Saturday, May 1, 1920, with Boston Braves right-hander Joe Oeschger.

After 3:50 had gone by and with the sun sinking in the sky, the umpires, who had been standing on their feet for almost four hours, were ready for a rest and a hot shower, and called the game.

A look at the box score showed that Cadore had come to the plate ten times, going 0-10, but had only struck out once. His mound opponent came to the plate, going 0-9 with 3 strikeouts. Cadore faced 96 batters, Oeschger 90. This wasn't about hitting, but more about the endurance of two pitchers locked in a duel that neither the 4,500 in attendance, nor the baseball world may ever see again.

282. Who was the first American League player to have seven consecutive pinch-hits?

The Texas Rangers were down 3-2 to the Minnesota Twins in the bottom of the 9th inning at Arlington Stadium on Monday, May 25, 1981 when, after scoring the tying run, and having the bases loaded with one out, utility infielder Bill Stein was sent up to pinch hit for LF Leon Roberts.

He faced Twins right-hander Doug Corbett and lined a single to center-field scoring 3B Buddy Bell from third to give the Rangers a 4-3 win, and with that base hit Stein became the first American League player to have seven consecutive pinch-hits

283. Who was the first major league player to strike out six times in a game?

It took 15 innings in a game that ended in an 8-8 tie against the Washington Senators, on July 25, 1913, for southpaw pitcher Carl "Zeke" Weilman, of the St, Louis Browns, to come to the plate and strikeout six times to be the first player to record a half dozen strikeouts in a single game, and in so doing he became first major league player to be awarded the titanium sombrero, symbolic of his six futile efforts to make contact with the horsehide.

284. Who was the first National League player to strike out six times in a game?

I wouldn't say that Don Hoak wanted this frustrating game stat to go any further than it has, but in talking about "Groundbreakers" the talented third baseman of the Chicago Cubs made it necessary by his game on May 2, 1956, when he faced eight pitchers, and went down on strikes on the deliveries of six of them. It was a 17-inning game so Hoak came up seven times, banged out a base hit once, but was fanned by six different New York Giants pitchers before his home crowd of 2,389 on that Wednesday afternoon at Wrigley Field, where the Giants edged out a 6-5 win.

285. Who was the first American League catcher to win a batting championship?

Joe Mauer, the fine hitting catcher of the Minnesota Twins, finished off the 2006 season by going 2-for-4 to hold off the charge by Robinson Cano and Derek Jeter of the Yankees to capture the batting championship with a .347 average, and became the first catcher in the American League to capture that award.

286. Who was the first player to get a base hit in a major league stadium that had the same name as the player?

On Sunday, April 7, 2002 Arizona Diamondbacks catcher Damian Miller came up in the top of the 2nd inning at Miller Park facing Milwaukee Brewers right-hander Ben Sheets and hit a ground ball single to become the first player to get a base hit in a stadium which bore his name. He came back in the 7th and got his second hit, a lined single to right field as Curt Shilling shutout the Brewers 2-0.

287. Who was the first teammates in major league history to both hit two home runs in the same inning of the same game?

On Thursday, May 2, 2002 the Seattle Mariners came into Comiskey Park, Chicago, with explosives in their bats, and started out in the 1st inning unleashing that power.

RF Ichiro Suzuki started off the game by getting hit by a pitch by the massive (6'10", 290 lb.) right-handed rookie, Jon Rauch, which brought up 2B Bret Boone who followed by hitting a two-run home run, scoring Suzuki. That brought up CF Mike Cameron who hit a blast that just cleared the centerfield wall beyond the outstretched glove of Kenny Lofton.

With six runs in, southpaw Jim Parque came on in relief of Rauch, and that brought up Boone for the second time, and he found Parque's first pitch to his liking and smashed his 2nd home run of the inning, scoring Suzuki, and making the score 9-0.

Cameron came up again and worked Parque to a full count before blasting his 2nd home run of the inning to deep centerfield, and increasing the lead to 10-0 before the White Sox had a chance to swing a bat.

RHP James Baldwin coasted to a 15-4 win and Cameron continued his hot hitting by hitting two more home runs to put him in the select company of those to have hit four home runs in one game. With his two home runs, following Boone's two in the 1st inning, made this duo the first teammates to each hit two round-trippers in the same inning.

288. Who was the first player to hit for the cycle in an interleague game?

On Friday evening, June 8, 2001, 27,770 fans came into Comerica Park to see the National League Milwaukee Brewers play the Detroit Tigers in their favorite lair. They didn't expect to see history being made by one of their own, when 2B Damion Easley put on a hitting show by being the first player to hit for the cycle in an interleague game.

It started in the bottom of the 3rd inning when Easley doubled to left field, off the Brewers right-hander Paul Rigdon, scoring 3B Jose Macias.

In the 5th Easley emptied the bases by hitting a 3-run home run off Rigdon, scoring Macias and CF Roger Cedeno.

In the 6th Easley singled to right field off right-hander Mike De Jean.

Then in the 8th inning he was facing another right-hander, Will Cunnane, and completed the cycle by hammering a triple through shortstop and into right field that gave Easley entrance into the "Groundbreakers" club, by being the first to accomplish the cycle in an interleague game, as the Tigers went on to a 9-4 victory.

289. Who was the first pair of teammates to switch-hit a home run in the same game?

We have to go north of the border to a game played at the SkyDome on Sunday, April 23, 2000, to find that the New York Yankees CF Bernie Williams hit a two-out, two-run 1st inning home run into the left-centerfield stands off Toronto's right-hander Frank Castillo. In the 2nd inning, with no outs, catcher Jorge Posada also hit a home run off Castillo, into the right field stands, to tie the game at 3-3.

That answers the first part of the question, but let's move on to the 4th inning when Williams hit a two-out, three-run home run to centerfield off southpaw Clayton Andrews. Two batters later Posada followed with a two-run home run to centerfield off Andrews as well.

The 20,485 fans who turned out never expected to see two teammates switch-hit a home run in the same game, but the historic experience didn't end there as Williams and Posada reprised their previous performance by having them both do it again, this time in the same inning!

290. Who was the charter member of the 2,500-500-100-200 Club?

Many of you have heard of the 30-30 Club and the 40-40 Club, but if you are not familiar with this club don't be puzzled for few have ever heard of it, much less know who its first member was. The club is open to any player who has attained over 2,500 base hits, 500 doubles, 100 triples, and 200 home runs in his major league career.

The club has a very select group of just eleven players, the latest being added in the 2011 season. It began its existence at the conclusion of the 1935 season when Babe Ruth was the first to qualify by having 2,873 base hits, 506 doubles, 136 triples, and 714 home runs.

He was followed by Rogers Hornsby in 1937, Goose Goslin in 1938, Lou Gehrig in 1939, Al Simmons in 1944, Stan Musial in 1963, Willie

Mays in 1973, George Brett and Robin Yount both joined the club in 1993, and its newest and eleventh member, Johnny Damon joined in 2011.

291. Who was the first catcher, of only three in major league history, to hit two home runs in one inning?

It was a Thursday evening game, on June 2, 1949, down in Shibe Park, when Philadelphia Phillies catcher Andy Seminick hit a solo home run in the 2nd inning off Cincinnati southpaw Ken Raffensberger. He followed that up in the 8th inning, when the Phillies broke the game open by scoring ten runs, as Seminick hit another solo home run of Raffensberger, and coming back up in that inning to hit a three-run blast off the Reds' reliever, southpaw Kent Peterson, giving Seminick three home runs for the game, and becoming the first catcher to hit two of them in the same inning. The Phillies took the game 12-3.

292. Who was the first player to have over 200 career pinch-hits?

When you needed a base hit you looked down your bench to see if the left-handed hitting Lenny Harris was there. The utility third baseman, outfielder, and pinch-hitter extraordinaire was the best chance you had as he had proven over his 18-year career which began with his major league debut on September 7, 1988 with the Cincinnati Reds. During that time he plied his trade, after leaving the Reds, with the Dodgers, Mets, Marlins, Diamondbacks, Rockies, Cubs, and Brewers.

He came to bat as a pinch-hitter 804 times and banged out 212 hits, to become the first player to reach the 200-hit mark coming off the bench.

Those 212 hits were part of his 1,055 career base hits which gave him a lifetime batting average of .269.

293. Who was the first player to hit an opening day home run in four consecutive seasons?

Lawrence Peter "Yogi" Berra of the New York Yankees began his "first to hit a home run on opening day" trick on Wednesday, April 13, 1955, at the Yankee Stadium, in the 6th inning, with a two-run homer against right-hander Bill Currie of the Washington Senators as the Yankees started their season off with a "laughter" winning 19-1.

On the next opening day, Tuesday, April 17, 1956, at Griffith Stadium, "Yogi" hit a two- out, two-run home run to centerfield in the 3rd inning off the Senators right-hander Camilo "Little Potato" Pascual as the Yankees came away with a 10-4 win.

The streak continued on opening day, Tuesday, April 16, 1957, at Yankee Stadium, with Berra hitting a solo home run to centerfield off Washington's southpaw Chuck Stobbs as the Yankees squeaked out a 2-1 win. The fourth and final one came against the Boston Red Sox, up in Fenway Park on Tuesday, April 15, 1958, when with no outs, Berra took right-hander Willard Nixon deep into right field to be the first of three players in history to hit a home run in four consecutive opening day games; and all three were catchers; Gary Carter did it with the Montreal Expos from 1977-80, and Todd Hundley with the New York Mets also did it from 1994-1997.

294. Who was the first, and only, veteran player to make only one plate appearance for his new team, and hit a walk-off home run?

On September 24, 1984, ten-year veteran catcher Jamie Quirk was purchased by the Cleveland Indians from the Chicago White Sox after having only three plate appearances with the Pale Hose.

Until Thursday, September 27th he hadn't come into a game with Cleveland, when he was inserted in the 9th inning in the 8th batting slot replacing Tony Bernazard, who had pinch-run for catcher Jerry Willard in the 8th inning, after Willard had singled off the Twins right-hander, Mike Smithson. With the scored tied at 3-3, and after Twins right-hander Ron Davis had struck out RF George Vukovich and 3B Pat Tabler to start the 9th up came Quirk who was quick to deposit Davis's pitch into the stands for a walk-off home run, in the only at bat for Quirk in his Cleveland career. Quirk remained on the roster till October 1st, and was released by the Indians on October 24, 1984.

295. Who was the first batter to hit back-to-back home runs in a game?

Let's go out to Comiskey Park on Thursday, July 13, 1961, where 43,960 fans turned out to see their White Sox come into the bottom of the 5th inning, down 4-0 to the Yankees, having seen White Sox right-hander Early "Gus" Wynn depart on the heels of a 4-run outburst by the Yankees in the 1st inning, and southpaw Frank "Beau" Baumann take over.

Yankee right-hander Bill Stafford started the inning off with the bottom of the order and saw catcher Sherm Lollar crush his pitch deep into the leftfield stands for a solo home run. The 9th batter, Frank Baumann followed suit and deposited a Stafford pitch deep into the centerfield stands to become the first battery to hit back-to-back home runs in major league history. It wasn't enough as New York defeated Chicago, 6-2.

296. Who was the first player to hit five grand slam home runs for five different teams?

Walker Cooper made his major league debut as a catcher with the St. Louis Cardinals on September 25, 1940, and during his 18-year big league career played for six different teams. With those teams he hit 173 career home runs, with all but one, the Pittsburgh Pirates, having been the beneficiaries of his grand slams while wearing their uniform. He made full bases empty while with the Cardinals, Giants, Reds, Braves, and Cubs to become a "Groundbreaker" when it came to clearing the bases for five different teams.

297. Who was the first, and only, player in major league history to hit a full-count, two-out, walk-off grand slam home run?

On Friday, May 17, 1996, down in Camden Yards, before 47,259 witnesses, the Baltimore Orioles came to bat in the bottom of the 9th inning down 13-10 to the Seattle Mariners.

The inning started off with Mariners' southpaw Norm "The Sheriff" Charlton walking 2B Roberto Alomar. He then struck out 1B Rafael Palmeiro, before giving up a double to left field to RF Bobby Bonilla, sending Alomar to third. Billy Ripken came in to bat for 3B Jeff Huson, and fouled out to 1B Paul Sorrento for the second out. Charlton then walked SS Cal Ripken to load the bases.

Now here comes the historic drama as catcher Chris Hoiles, with two outs, the bases loaded, down by three runs in the bottom of the 9th, works the count to 3-and-2, and crushes the next pitch for a walk-off grand slam home run, and the Orioles come away with a 14-13 win.

The first of its kind in major league history and Chris Hoiles was the first player to do it; a true "Groundbreaker."

298. Who was the first player to reach the 3,000-hits plateau by going 5-for-5 in the game that got him to 3,000?

We will have to go back to Minute Maid Park on Thursday, June 28, 2007, before a crowd of 42,537, when the Houston Astros played host to the Colorado Rockies.

Astros second baseman Craig Biggio came into the game with 2,997 base hits over his twenty seasons with Houston. Leading off in the bottom of the 1st inning right-hander Aaron Cook got him to ground out to 3B Garrett Atkins.

With the crowd on the edge of their seats awaiting a base hit to close in on 3,000 Biggio came up in the 3rd and singled to centerfield for hit 2,998.

In the 5th inning Biggio hit a drive down the third base line that Atkins went to his right, turned and fired to 1B Todd Helton, with the ball eluding his outstretched glove and bouncing beyond the Astros dugout. The official scorer ruled that Biggio had beaten the throw, and his advancement to second was on the throwing error.

In the 7th inning Biggio drilled a clean single to centerfield off Aaron Cook, and as the fans went into a frenzied pandemonium on his reaching the exalted figure of 3,000 Biggio was thrown out at second trying to stretch the hit into his 659th double.

Leading off the 9th inning, in a 4-4 tie, and facing right-hander Manuel Corpas Biggio singled to right field for his 4th base hit of the game, and his 3,001 career base hit. The game went into extra innings, which brought Biggio up in the 11th to face southpaw Brian Fuentes, and Biggio came through again, this time with a single to deep short for his 5th hit of the game and his 3,002nd of his career, clearly cementing him in the 3,000-hit club, and making him the 9th player to have that many for the same team, and the first player to have a five-hit game in reaching that figure.

The Astros came up with four runs in the bottom of the 11th for an 8-5 win.

299. Who was the first player to hit over 50 home runs in a season, and strike out less than 50 times?

Talk about a long-ball hitter with an eye, let's look at Johnny "The Big Cat" Mize, who in 1947 while playing first base for the New York Giants, smashed out 51 home runs while going down on strikes just 42 times, becoming the first "over and under" 50 player when swinging the bat.

300. Who was the first, and only, player to win a dozen batting titles?

This player, whom we have highlighted multiple times in this book, made his major league debut as an outfielder for the Tigers against the New York Highlanders at Bennett Field, Detroit, on Wednesday, August 30, 1905.

As you probably guessed we are speaking of Ty Cobb, who as a rookie batted .240, but for the next 23 seasons never saw is batting average fall below .300, leading the American League in batting from 1907-15, missed out in 1916 when he batted .371, losing the title to Tris Speaker's .386. He picked right up again by winning the title from 1917-19. He stands all alone when it comes to batting championships.

301. Who was the first player to hit a major league home run wearing short pants?

No, I am serious, it happened, on Saturday, August 21, 1976. The 32,607 fans who saw it happen out in Comiskey Park, in a game against the Baltimore Orioles, can attest to the play. Orioles southpaw Rudy May, opened the bottom of the 2nd inning, ahead, 3-0, over the White Sox, by walking 1B Lamar Johnson. He then got SS Bucky Dent to fly out to left field, and RF Jerry Hairston to fly out to center, bringing up 2B Jack Brohamer who deposited Mays' pitch into the right field stands for a two-run home run, scoring Johnson, to become the first player to hit a major league home run wearing short pants, which was the uniform of the day for the White Sox. Collared jerseys, Bermuda blue shorts and high knee socks were de rigueur for the Pale Hose for part of the '76 season. As Casey Stengel would say "You can look it up!"

302. Who was the first player, in the 19th century, to lead the league in batting average, hits, doubles, triples, home runs, runs scored, runs batted in, and in total bases in the same season?

Impossible? Not if you were Canadian-born James "Tip" O'Neill, who made his major league debut on May 5, 1883 with the New York Gothams (Giants) both as a pitcher and leftfielder.

He jumped to the St. Louis Brown Stockings (Browns) of the newly established American Association, who were in direct competition with the National League, during the 1884 season.

But it was the 1887 season which was so historic and unbelievable, for this 29-year old. He led the Browns to the pennant that year coming in 14 games ahead of the Cincinnati Reds.

His following personal statistics will show you why, with his league leading .345 batting average, 225 hits, 52 doubles, 19 triples, 14 home runs, 167 runs scored, 122 runs batted in and 357 total bases, all in 124 games played made him one of a kind, a "Groundbreaker."

303. Who was first, of four players, to have driven in more runs than

games played in a single season?

"Rajah rises again," when in 1925, Rogers Hornsby the St. Louis Cardinals Hall of Fame second baseman, again displayed his uncanny batting ability when he played in 138 games that season, but drove in 143 runs to be the first player to drive in more runs than games he played in. He also led the National League in home runs that year with 39.

The other three are also Hall of Fame residents, Hack Wilson, the Reds centerfielder did it in 1929 with 159 in 150 games, Mel Ott, the New York Giants right fielder also did it in '29 with 151 in 150 games, and the Philadelphia Phillies right fielder, Chuck Klein, had 158 in 156 games in 1930.

304. Who was the first, and only, player to collect over 200 pinch-hits and have over a .300 career batting average?

Leftfielder Bob "Fats" Fothergill made his major league debut with the Detroit Tigers on April 18, 1922. He was a consistent hitter, but he had a hard time cracking the solid Detroit outfield of Bobby Veach, Harry Heilmann, and Ty Cobb.

Fothergill, during the latter part of his career, became an excellent pinch-hitter and moved over to the White Sox, and finished up his 12 seasons by playing his last game on July 5, 1933 with the Red Sox, showing a career batting average of .325, 40th best in major league history, and having hit over .300 in 9 of his 12 seasons, including 5 where he exceeded .340. Of his 1,064 hits over 200 came as a pinch-hitter, so "Fats" was first in that department.

305. Who was the first player to come to bat three times in one inning?

When this game ended, after 3 hours and 1 minute, out in Cubs Park on August 25, 1922, the score looked more like the Chicago Bears having played the Philadelphia Eagles. In reality it was the Chicago Cubs coming away with a three-run margin to defeat the Philadelphia Phillies, 26-23.

Would one call this a woeful lack of good pitching or plethora of solid hitting? Either way it provided an opportunity for Cubs right fielder Marty Callaghan to become a "Groundbreaker" by coming to the plate three times, getting a pair of singles, and striking out the third time, in that 14-run, 4th inning, to become the first player to ever come to bat three times in one inning.

The line score is worth noting as Chicago went 26-25-0 and Philadelphia 23-26-0, as if errors weren't needed to help in the scoring.

306. **Who was the first player to hit over 200 home runs in both the American and National Leagues?**

Frank "The Judge" Robinson made his big league debut on April 17, 1956 with the Cincinnati Reds as a left fielder, but later played all three outfield positions, and later in his career 305 at first base. While with the Reds, Robinson had 324 home runs before being traded for three players to Baltimore in 1966. While with the Orioles he picked up an additional 179 before moving back to the National League for one season with the Los Angeles Dodgers where he added to his senior circuit total by blasting 19 more home runs.

Then it was back to the American League with the California Angels for the '73-74 seasons where added on another 50 homers. Then it was on to Cleveland from 1974-76, picking up an additional 14 home runs, before calling his 21-season career over on September 18, 1976, and going into the record books with 343 National League home runs, and 243 hit in the American League for a total of 586, averaging 34 homers per season being deposited in the hands of his fans.

The first player to exceed over 200 home runs in both leagues.

307. **Who was the first player to come to bat 13 times, and have just four hits for his entire season, a single, double, triple, and a home run?**

One has to say that 2B, SS, 3B Fred Manrique of the Montreal Expos made the most of his one season career with the Expos in 1985 when his batting stats showed 13 at bats with one single, one double, one triple, one home run, and one run batted in to go along with his one walk in his one year with the Expos to be the first to put up that oddity for his season record.

308. **Who was the first player in major league history to hit 30 home runs in 13 consecutive seasons?**

It came about on Tuesday, August 10, 2004, when Barry Bonds, the San Francisco Giants leftfielder, hit his 30th home run of the season, a solo shot to right center field of PNC Park in the 7th inning off Pittsburgh Pirates southpaw John Grabow, to become the first player to hit 30 home runs in 13 consecutive seasons. He started his run in 1992 with 34 home runs and continued it through the 2004 season.

309. Who was the first player to hit over 20 home runs in a season after having not hitting a single home run the previous season?

A solid .334 career hitter over his 27 seasons, Adrian "Cap" Anson went through the 1883 season with 36 doubles and 5 triples, but without a home run.

The 1884 season saw a turnaround for the Chicago White Stockings first baseman as "Cap" drove in 102 runs, helped by his 21 home runs, to have him be the first player to hit over 20 home runs the season after he was shut out of round-trippers.

310. Who was the first player to drive in 50 runs in a single month?

When the hallmark for driving in runs is 100 for a season, Chicago Cubs centerfielder, Lewis "Hack" Wilson exceeded the halfway point in just the month of August 1930, when he drove in 53 runs to be the first major leaguer to surpass the 50-mark in a single month. He not only ended the season with a league-leading 191 runs batted in, but also led the league with an awesome 56 home runs as well.

311. Who was the first designated hitter to have a 200-hit season?

Look no further than Paul "The Ignitor" Molitor, who in 1996 ignited the Minnesota Twins offense with 200 hits over 143 games as a designated hitter, and when adding in his 17 games at first base, gave him a league-leading 225 hits, 113 runs driven in, and 99 runs scored, with a .341 batting average for the season.

That combined with his 21-year career stats showed him with 3,319 base hits which works out to an even 200 hits over a 162 game season. Reason enough to see him inducted into the Hall of Fame in 2004.

312. Who was the first American League player to drive in 50 runs in one month?

Rudy York, a catcher and an infielder for the 1937 Detroit Tigers, in his first full season in the big leagues, drove in an even 50 runs in August, 1937, and went on to bat .307 for the season and drive in 103 runs to be the first in the American League to drive in 50 runs in a single month.

313. Who was the first, and only, National League player to hit four consecutive triples in a doubleheader?

It was on September 22, 1903 in Cincinnati, when the Reds hosted a doubleheader against the Philadelphia Phillies. In his last at bat in the opener Reds outfielder, "Turkey Mike" Donlin, laced a triple, but it had no bearing on the game as the Phillies came away with a 12-7 win. In the nightcap southpaw-swinging Donlin had three consecutive triples to give him four three-baggers in a row as Cincinnati came away with an 8-1 win.

314. Who was the first, and only, player to hit at least one triple in five consecutive games?

One of the most exciting plays in baseball is the sight of a runner racing around the bases for a triple. Well, John "Chief" Wilson, the right fielder of the Pittsburgh Pirates did it a league-leading 36 times during the 1912 season. And none more consistently than in a period of five consecutive games, beginning on Monday, June 17, 1912, at the Polo Grounds, against the New York Giants, when he hit his first triple in the streak. Tuesday, June 18th hit his second triple against the Giants. On Wednesday June 19th he was back home in Pittsburgh, and had his third straight triple game, this against the St. Louis Cardinals.

Thursday, June 20th saw Wilson in Cincinnati for a doubleheader against the Reds. In Game 1 he had another triple in a 6-4 win, and followed that with two triples in the nightcap that the Reds took 5-3.

There you have a "Groundbreaker" with five consecutive games with at least one triple, a record very hard to be beaten or tied.

315. Who was the first player to hit over 40 home runs, and yet drive in less than 100?

He wore number 3 on his broad back, and in his 22 seasons with Washington, Minnesota, and Kansas City, Harmon "Killer" Killebrew, hit 573 home runs, and drove in 1,584, but in the 1963 season the Twins left fielder hit 45 home runs, but only drove in 96, to be the first player to surpass 40 homers, while falling below 100 runs driven in for the season.

316. Who was the first player to have his strikeouts exceed his runs batted in by more than 100 over one season?

One could disparagingly call Detroit right fielder, Rob Deer, the "Sultan of Swing" in 1991, for he became the first player to have his strikeouts, which were a league-leading 175, exceed his runs batted in, which reached 64 in that season, by over 100.

Deer led the American League in strikeouts with over 150, four times, and fanned over 100 times per season in his eleven year career.

317. **Who was the first player to reach the 250,000th major league, regular season, home run mark?**

September 8, 2008, was a rainy Monday evening out in Comerica Park, Detroit, when the Oakland Athletics came in to play the first game of a three game series with the Detroit Tigers. Southpaw Giovanny "Gio" Gonzalez started on the mound for the visitors before a damp crowd of 37,981.

In the bottom of the 1st. inning Detroit's DH Gary Sheffield, came up and hit a two-out solo home run to deep left field which was the 249,999th regular season home run in major league history.

In the 2nd inning, with Detroit ahead 3-2, Sheffield was up again with catcher Brandon Inge, who had tripled, on third , RF Magglio Ordonez, who had walked on second, and 1B Miguel Cabrera, who had been hit by a pitch leading off first.

Then, after 133 years, and thousands of players before him, history was made as Sheffield blasted a grand slam home run deep into left-center field for the major leagues 250,000th regular season home run.

It would be Sheffield's 496th career home run, and his last home run with Detroit, as he went on to hit his 500th the following year with the New York Mets. Detroit came away with a 14-8 win, and Gonzalez's fourth loss, after one victory that season.

318. **Who hit the first home run in major league history?**

It happened on May 8, 1871 when third baseman Ezra Sutton of the Cleveland Forest Citys of the National Association, came up in the 4th inning and hit a pitch by Chicago White Stockings right-hander, George "The Charmer" Zettlein, over leftfielder Mart King's head, driving in his own hurler, Al Pratt, to become the first major league player to hit a round-tripper. It so happens that he came back to hit another in that game to make him the first to hit two in one game as well.

The National Association, in existence from 1871-75, was a group of teams of professional baseball players that had a number of its teams evolve into the creation of the National League in 1876. There are some in baseball who do not consider the teams in the National Association as major league players, although many players went on to have careers in the newly formed National League.

319. **Who was the first modern day player to get 200 hits in 7 consecutive seasons?**

This southpaw swinging third baseman, Wade Boggs by name, made his debut with the Boston Red Sox on April 10, 1982, and this hitting machine had 210 hits in 1983, and continued on through the 1989 season ringing up 200 or more hits in each of those seasons, highlighted by a league-leading 240 hits in 1985. When his 18-year Hall of Fame career ended on August 27, 1999, with Tampa Bay, his record showed 3,010 hits and a .328 batting average.

320. **Who was the first player to hit a home run for eleven different teams?**

Todd Zeile made his major league debut with the St. Louis Cardinals on August 18, 1989 as a catcher. During his 16 seasons in the big leagues you could find him at third base, first base, or behind the plate for 2,094 of his 2,099 games.

No matter the position he played he could hit the long ball, having hit 212 home runs while wearing the uniform of eleven different teams.

Starting with the Cardinals he went on to hit round-trippers for the Cubs, Phillies, Orioles, Dodgers, Marlins, Rangers, Mets, Rockies, Yankees, and the Expos, making him the first to round the bases unimpeded for eleven different ball clubs.

321. **Who was the first player in major league history to start off his season by hitting a home run in his first four games?**

The first four games of the 1971 season were a blast for San Francisco Giants centerfielder Willie Mays as he opened up the season at San Diego Stadium on Tuesday, April 6th against the Padres right-hander Tom Phoebus. In the top of the 1st inning the "Say Hey Kid" hit a solo home run to left field to get the season off on a positive note as Juan Marichal went on to shutout the Padres, 4-0.

The following day, Wednesday, April 7th, Willie waited until the 7th inning before unloading a one-out solo home run off Padres right-hander Al Santorini as the Giants went on to win, 7-3.

On Thursday, April 8th, the Giants were behind 4-1 going into the top of the 7th inning when Padre right-hander Steve Arlin gave up a single to Jimmy Rosario, pinch-hitting for righty Jerry Johnson, then walked RF Bobby Bonds and SS Chris Speier to load the bases, which brought in southpaw Dick Kelly in relief, and set the stage for Willie to do his thing. He didn't disappoint his teammates as he unloaded the bases with a grand slam home run to left field to give the Giants a 5-4 lead. They couldn't hold the lead as San Diego went on to a 7-6 win.

Now we come to Saturday, April 10th and the Giants find themselves in Busch Stadium, before a Redbird crowd of 26, 841. Willie's hot bat hadn't lost its power moving east to St. Louis as he crushed southpaw Jerry Reuss's 3rd inning pitch, after Chris Speier walked, for a two-out two-run home run to send the Giants on to a 6-4 win over the Cardinals.

In those four games Mays became the first player to hit a home run in the first four games of his season.

322. Who was the first player to hit a home run in eight consecutive games?

No player, until the 1956 season, went on a home run tear like Pittsburgh Pirates first baseman Dale Long did in that month of May.

Among his 27 home runs that season Long, went long, in eight consecutive games, hitting home runs on May 19th, one in each game on the 20th, then one on the 22nd, 23rd, 25th, 26th, and on the 28th he hit his 8th off Brooklyn Dodgers right-hander Carl Erskine in the 4th inning to become the first player to have eight consecutive home run games.

323. Who was the first American League player to hit a home run in eight consecutive games?

It took about 30 years for a player in the American League to duplicate Dale Long's home run streak until New York Yankees first baseman, Don Mattingly, made his 1987 season a memorable one while on his way to a 30-home run season. He homered in consecutive games from July 8th to the 12th and from the 16th through the 18th to be the first in his league to have such a streak.

Ken Griffey Jr., the Seattle Mariners outfielder, later became the third player to do it when he went on a home run barrage in July 1993.

324. Who was the first, and only, player to hit four home runs, and drive in twelve runs in the same game?

There have been twelve players in history who have hit four home runs in one game, but only one player, "Sunny Jim" Bottomley, with the 1924 St. Louis Cardinals, to be the first to have driven in 12 runs in one game. He did it at Ebbets Field on September 16, 1924 when he had three singles, a double, and two home runs as the Redbirds defeated the Brooklyn Dodgers 17-3

That was until Mark Whitten came along to do both. On Tuesday, September 7, 1993, in the second game of a doubleheader out in Riverfront Stadium, the St. Louis Cardinals centerfielder, Mark Whitten, before a crowd of 22,606 did both when he came up in the top of the 1st inning and hit a grand slam home run to deep left-centerfield, off Reds right-hander Larry Luebbers, scoring LF Lonnie Maclin, 3B Todd Zeile, and 1B Gerald Perry ahead of him.

In the 6th, with the Cardinals up, 5-2 over Cincinnati, he hit a 3-run homer off right-hander Mike Anderson, scoring Zeile and Perry again.

Whitten came up again in the 7th off Anderson, and again drove in Zeile and Perry with his third homer of the day to make the score 8-2.

The 9th saw Rob Dibble on the mound for the Reds, and after Perry had singled to center after one out, Whitten came up and treated the right-hander like he did his two predecessors by blasting a home run, his fourth of the game, and his twelfth run driven in as the Cardinals breezed to a 15-2 win. Whitten became a true "Groundbreaker" by being the first and only player to hit four home runs and drive in twelve runs in the same game.

325. Who was the first player to drive in 100 runs in a season?

Adrain "Cap" Anson, the first baseman for the Chicago White Stockings, in his 9th season in the National League, in 1884, drove in 102 runs in 112 games to be the first player to exceed the century mark. He went on to drive in over 100 runs for four consecutive seasons, 1884-87, and lead the league in that category eight times.

326. Who was the first player to hit two triples in the same inning?

We have to go back to Saturday, May 6, 1882 to the South End Grounds, where the Boston Red Stockings, before their hometown fans, crushed the Troy Trojans, 18-3.

In the 8th inning, Boston Red Stockings' left fielder, Joe "Ubbo Ubbo" Hornung hammered a pair of triples to be the first player to hit two triples in the same inning.

327. Who was the first player to hit a major league home run in Hawaii?

If you had been in the Aloha state at the Aloha Stadium, along with

40,050 fans you would have seen St. Louis Cardinals leftfielder Ron Gant come up in the 4th inning with none on and two outs, and blast a solo inside the park home run off San Diego Padres right-hander Alan Ashby. It didn't help as the Padres took the game, 8-2. So Gant stands out as a "Groundbreaker" by being the first to hit a home run in the 50th state.

328. Who was the first player to win four consecutive home run titles?

We have to go back to the early years before the American League, when, on September 21, 1895, Harry "Jasper" Davis made his major league debut at first base with the New York Giants. He moved over to the American League in 1901 with the Philadelphia Athletics where he spent sixteen of the next seventeen seasons.

When he completed his 22-year career on May 30, 1917 his career home run total was just 75. In those early years home runs were infrequent, but nevertheless Harry had four consecutive years with the Philadelphia Athletics where his power was apparent for he led the American League in home runs with 10 in 1904, 8 in 1905, 12 in 1906, and 8 in 1907, thereby setting the pace for those to follow.

329. Who was the first player to hit 40 home runs after the age of 40?

On Friday evening, September 17, 2004, out in SBC Park, Barry Bonds, the San Francisco Giants leftfielder came up in the top of the 3rd inning against San Diego Padres right-hander Jake Peavy and unleashed his 42nd and 700th career home run, a 392-foot solo shot to deep left-centerfield, at the age of 40 years, 55 days, to make Bonds the first player to exceed the 40 mark after the age of 40.

He had 45 home runs that season and finished his 22-year career on September 26, 2007 with 762 round-trippers.

330. Who was the first switch-hitter to hit 40 home runs in a season?

In 1956 Mickey Mantle, the Yankees centerfielder, and one of the most feared sluggers in baseball, proved that as he led the American League in runs batted in with 130, batting average with .353, and in home runs with 52, making him the first switch-hitter to hit over 40 home runs in a season.

331. Who was the first, of the four players, to have led the league in batting average, and home runs, but not in runs batted in one season?

This third baseman of the Chicago Cubs, Henry "Heine" Zimmerman had a career year in 1912, but failed to capture the Triple Crown by not having four more runs batted in.

He led the National League in base hits with 207, home runs with 14, and batting average with .372, but finished third in runs batted in with 99, behind the NL leader Honus Wagner's 102.

He ended up in good company with the Yankees Babe Ruth in 1924, Johnny Mize with the Cardinals in 1939, and Ted Williams with the Red Sox in 1941.

332. Who was the first, and only, batting champion to complete his season without hitting a triple, or stealing a base?

Manuel "Manny Being Manny" Ramirez lived up to his sobriquet at the conclusion of his 2002 season. The Boston Red Sox leftfielder and DH, banged out 152 hits, walked 73 times, hit 33 home runs, and won the American League batting crown with a .349 batting average.

That put him on base 225 times excluding reaching through an error or a force out, yet he couldn't manage a stolen base or a triple in his 532 plate appearances.

333. Who is the first, and only, player in major league history to hit 25 or more home runs in a season in four different decades?

"The Splendid Splinter", Ted Williams made his major league debut with the Boston Red Sox on April 20, 1939, and in his rookie year slammed 31 home runs.

From 1941-49, with three years taken out as a Marine fighter pilot in World War II, he hit over 25 home runs six times.

In the 1950's, again serving in the military during the Korean War, he had six seasons with 25 or more home runs. When he concluded his career on September 28, 1960 he hit his 29th home run of the season, in his last at bat, off Baltimore Orioles right-hander, "Fat Jack" Fisher, making him the only player to hit 25 or more home runs in four different decades.

334. Who was the first of the eight players who have won the batting title by more than 40 points?

It started back in 1901 when second baseman Nap Lajoie of the Philadelphia Athletics took the American League batting crown with a .426 average, besting second place finisher "Turkey Mike" Donlin, the leftfielder of the Baltimore Orioles, at .340.

Through the years eight different players have accomplished that margin a total of twelve times.

335. Who was the first, and currently only, player to win the National League batting title while playing in the American League?

This oddity did occur at the conclusion of the 1990 season when Willie McGee, the St. Louis Cardinals centerfielder, after playing 125 games, coming to bat 501 times, with a .335 batting average, and on his way to his second batting title, he had won one in 1985 with a .353 average, was traded on August 29, 1990 to the defending champion Oakland Athletics who desperately needed another strong bat to defend their title.

The Cardinals weren't going anywhere that season and received Daryl Green, Felix Jose, and Stan Royer in return, none of whom were any threat eclipse McGee's statistics.

McGee played only 29 games in Oakland, and came to bat 113 times, ending his season with the Athletics with a .274 average. He did, however, qualify for the NL batting title because he had enough plate appearances, 3.1 for every game played by the Redbirds that season to be named the 1990 National League batting champion. Willie's post game experience saw him bat just .222 in the ALCS against the Red Sox and .200 in the World Series, as Oakland was swept by the Cincinnati Reds.

336. Who was the first player to win back-to-back batting titles?

This "Groundbreaker" made his debut on May 5, 1871 with the Boston Red Stockings as a second baseman, and Charles Roscoe "Ross" Barnes batted .401 and led the league in runs scored with 66 in his rookie season in the National Association.

He followed that up in 1872 by leading the league with a .430 batting average as well as in hits with 99 and doubles with 28 in 230 at bats.

The following season he became the first to have consecutive batting titles when he again led the league in batting with a .431 average, in plate appearances with 340, hits, 138, doubles with 31, triples with 11 and in walks with 30.

337. Who was the first player to have 3,000 base hits by hitting more than 1,000 in both the American and National Leagues?

One of the more gifted multi-sport athletes in major league baseball,

THE GROUNDBREAKERS!

having been drafted by the San Diego Padres, the Atlanta Hawks in the NBA, and the Minnesota Vikings in the NFL, Dave Winfield selected baseball when drafted in the first round by the San Diego Padres, and made his debut in the outfield on June 19, 1973.

After 22 years with the Padres, Yankees, Angels, Blue Jays, Twins and Indians, this 12-time All Star ended his career with Cleveland on October 1, 1995 after 2,973 games with a .283 batting average, 465 home runs, and 3,110 hits, collecting 1,976 in the American League and 1,134 in the senior circuit to be the first to have 3,000 by having over 1,000 in each league.

338. Who was the first National League player to hit 100 career home runs after hitting one in his first major league at bat?

Carroll "Whitey" Lockman, playing centerfield for the New York Giants never imagined he would become a future "Groundbreaker" when he came to bat for the first time in the major leagues on that Thursday, July 5, 1945, afternoon at the Polo Grounds.

Batting third in the order he found a runner on with one out when he faced St. Louis Cardinals southpaw, George Dockins, and drove in his first two runs with a towering home run into the right field seats for his first major league home run. He finished his first debut by going 2-for-4, driving in four runs, making five put outs, and an assist. Not a bad introduction to the big leagues.

The 5,941 Coogan's Bluff fans, however, went sadly home as the Cardinals came away with a 7-5 win.

We now go to another Thursday, this on August 18, 1955. The scene is again at the Polo Grounds as 12,007 fans watched the Brooklyn Dodgers southpaw, Karl Spooner, face off against the Giants with Lockman now patrolling left field.

In the 3rd inning Whitey came up with one on, and two outs and hit his 12th home run of the season, and his 100th career home run to right field to make him the first National Leaguer to post 100 home runs after hitting his first in his initial time at bat in the bigs. Once again his heroics didn't help as the Dodgers came away with an 8-5 win.

339. Who was the first major league teen-ager to have two multi-homer games in a single season?

This 19-year old right-fielder would have many home runs in his 22-year career, 511 in fact, as Mel Ott's 1928 season saw him being the first teen-ager to have two multi-homer games along with his 18 home runs that season.

340. Who was the first player to have eight bases loaded triples in his career?

John Francis Collins, better known as "Shano", made his debut with the Chicago White Sox on April 21, 1910 playing both in the outfield and at first base. Not known as a long ball hitter having just 22 homers in his 16-year career, his forte became his ability to come up with the bases loaded, and clear them with a triple, which he did eight times while playing for the White Sox, and then when he changed his Sox, to play in Fenway with Boston, when he and Nemo Leibold were traded for Harry Hooper on March 4, 1921.

C. COVERING THE FIELD WITH LEATHER

1. Who was the first outfielder to complete a triple play?

Although there has been some dispute as to whether this was an unassisted triple play or not, he got three outs on the play. The "he" we are talking about was centerfielder Paul Hines of the Providence Grays in a game against the Boston Red Caps on May 8, 1878.

With runners on second and third with no one out in the 8th inning, Hines caught a liner over shortstop off his shoe tops, hit by Jack Burdock. He continued running in to tag third as both runners had passed third base, and to be doubly sure Hines fired to Charlie Sweasy at second to insure and complete the triple play.

The debate continues on these many years as to whether or not it was an unassisted triple play, but we here are calling it, and will let you all continue to debate it.

2. Of the nine catchers who have earned the Baseball Writers' Most Valuable Player Award who was the first?

Gordon "Mickey" Cochrane, known as "Black Mike," was in his first season with the Detroit Tigers after being traded on December 12, 1933 by the Philadelphia Athletics for Johnny Pasek and $100,000, had 32 doubles, scored 104 runs, drove in 76 and batted .320. With that, and his handling of the pitching staff, and having just seven errors in 593 chances for a .981 fielding average, made him the pick for MVP in 1934. He was elected to the Hall of Fame in 1947.

3. Who was the first, and only, outfielder to have over 7,000 putouts in his major league career?

Willie Mays, who patrolled centerfield for the New York/San Francisco Giants from 1951-1972 and finished off with the New York Mets in 1973, had 7,095 putouts and 195 assists in his 22-year National League career from 1951-1973

4. Who was the first, and only, outfielder to have over 400 assists?

Tris Speaker, who spent 20 of his 22-years, 1907-28, as an outfielder with the Boston Red Sox and Cleveland Indians had 449 career assists in his Hall of Fame career.

5. Who was the first catcher to openly wear shin guards?

Roger Bresnahan of the New York Giants, came out for the game against the Philadelphia Phillies at the Polo Grounds on April 11, 1907 wearing shin guards for the first time in major league history. This game was also the game in which the famous umpire, Bill Klem, made his major league debut.

6. Who was the first player to wear sunglasses in the field?

Paul Hines, who played twenty seasons in the big leagues, put on sunglasses in the 82 games he played centerfield, and presumably for the two at first base, when he played with the Providence Grays in the National League in 1882.

7. Who is the first, and only, catcher to catch four no-hit games?

Jason Varitek holds that distinct record starting with a no-hitter by Hideo Nomo against the Baltimore Orioles on April 4, 2001. Then came Derrick Lowe's no-hitter against Tampa Bay on April 27, 2002; followed by Clay Buchholz's no-hitter on September 1, 2007; and finally Jon Lester's no-hitter against the Kansas City Royals at Fenway Park on May 19, 2008.

Some will say Ray Schalk caught four, however his "first" went nine innings, without a hit, but Jim Scott lost it in the 10th with two hits by Washington, 1-0, so it doesn't count as an official no-hit game.

8. Who was the first National League first baseman to be involved in seven double plays in one game?

The Houston Astros pulled off seven double plays in a game against the San Francisco Giants on May 4, 1969, won by Houston, 3-1, with first baseman Curt Blefary setting a record by participating in all of them.

9. Who was the first major league catcher to earn the Gold Glove Award?

In 1957 Rawlings, the manufacturer of gloves for the major leagues, had a panel of sportswriters select a player at each position for the Gold Glove Award. Sherman Lollar, of the Chicago White Sox, was the first catcher to receive a Gold Glove Award. His stats tell you why. He had 500 chances, 494 put outs, and committed only one error in 820 innings for a .998 fielding average.

10. Who was the first player in the modern era to complete an unassisted triple play?

The credit for the first unassisted triple play in the modern era goes to

Cleveland shortstop Cornelius "Neal" Ball. It happened in the top of the 2nd inning of a doubleheader against the Boston Red Sox on July 19, 1909.

With shortstop Heinie Wagner on second base and first baseman Chick Stahl leading off first, Boston's second baseman Amby McConnell hit a sharp line drive to Ball who stepped on second to retire Wagner and then tagged Stahl as he thundered down from first to complete the first major league triple play in the 20th century.

Ball followed that up by coming to the plate in the bottom of the second to hit his first American League home run, an inside-the-park job as Cleveland went on to win the first game, behind Cy Young, 6-1. Boston won the nightcap 3-2.

11. Who was credited with the first double play in a National League game?

In the first National League game played, on April 22, 1876, in Athletic Park, Philadelphia, Athletics centerfielder Dave Eggler caught a fly ball and threw a Boston Red Stockings (Braves) runner out at home for the first double play in a National League game. Boston went on to win in the 9th 6-5, before 3,000 fans.

12. Who was the first player to win a Gold Glove Award in both the American and National Leagues?

Outfielder Tommie Agee won the American League Gold Glove Award in 1966 with the Chicago White Sox, and then again in 1970 with the New York Mets.

13. Who was the first major league catcher to catch 140 games in nine different seasons?

A tip of the cap goes to Jason Kendall, a workhorse of a catcher, who came up with the Pittsburgh Pirates in 1996 as a 22-year old rookie. He was rarely not behind the plate as the following will show; In 1997 he caught 142 games, 144 in '98, 147 in 2000, 143 in 2002 146 in 2003, 146 in 2004, 147 in 2005 when he went to the Oakland Athletics, 141 with Oakland in 2006 and then 149 in 2008 when he was with Milwaukee. He averaged catching 130 games per season over 15 years.

14. Who was the first modern day first baseman to play a complete nine-inning game without recording a single put out?

As unusual as it sounds John "Bud" Clancy, the Chicago White Sox first baseman, played the entire nine inning game on April 27, 1930 in a 2-1 White Sox win over the St. Louis Browns without recording a single put out.

15. Who was the first National League outfielder to have over 335 career assists?

This Pittsburgh Pirate outfielder, who spent the last four years of his 20-year career with Brooklyn, was known for his tremendous speed, base stealing ability (he led the National League ten times in this category), and outfield arm. That combination made Max "Scoops" Carey a fan favorite and resident of the Hall of Fame. He is not only the first outfielder to have over 335 career assists from 1910-1929, but holds the modern day National League career record of 339.

16. Who was the first player to commit over 100 errors in a single season?

I am not sure that the Cincinnati Red Stockings (Reds) shortstop, Frank Fennelly, would enhance his playing resume if he included his fielding in the 1886 season when he was charged with 117 errors over the course of 132 games.

To Frank's credit he did turn 54 double plays and have 169 putouts to go along with his 485 assists. We must remember, in defense of Frank, that the equipment and playing conditions were far more difficult than those we see today. Keep that in mind, Johnny Gochnauer and Al Brancato.

17. Who was the first player to play at least 1,000 games in the outfield, and 1,000 games in the infield in his career?

There have been four players who have accomplished this multi-task. Stan "the Man" Musial of the St. Louis Cardinals was the first with 1,896 games in the outfield and 1,016 at first base in his 22-year career from 1941-1963. And yes, he did have one mound appearance in his storybook career.

18. Who was the first outfielder to have double-digit putouts in a nine-inning game?

Back on September 17, 1945 the Brooklyn Dodgers came into Wrigley Field to play the Chicago Cubs. Art Herring, the Dodgers' right-hander, set down the Cubbies on three hits winning 4-0. The most notable part of the game, however, was the record that was set by Cub right-fielder Bill "Swish" Nicholson, who became the first outfielder to record double-digit putouts in a game when he made ten. That set a new record and his eleven chances accepted tied a major league record.

19. Who was the first player to record an unassisted triple play to end a game?

One has to go back to the 9th inning of a game on May 31, 1927 when Detroit Tigers first baseman Johnny Neun snared a line drive off the bat of Homer Summa, tagged Charlie Jamieson in the baseline, and then ran over to second base, tagging it, to retire Glenn Myatt who had left on his way to third.

That was a fitting way to give right-hander Harry "Rip" Collins his 1-0 win over the Indians, for it would be his only shutout of the season.

20. Who was the first player to record a triple play when two of the three outs were a pair of brothers?

What are the chances of one of the rarest plays in baseball happening on back-to-back days? Well it did, this time over in the National League. It occurred in the first game of a Memorial Day double-header, on Monday, May 30, 1927, out in Forbes Field. The victim this time was the Pittsburgh Pirates who were playing the Chicago Cubs.

In the 4th inning Cubs shortstop Jimmy Cooney caught a line drive off the bat of Paul "Big Poison" Waner. He quickly stepped on second base to retire younger brother Lloyd "Little Poison" Waner, before tagging Clyde Barnhart trying to get back to first.

It was a long day for both clubs as the Cubs won the opener 7-6 in ten innings, and the Bucs came back, with the help of three base hits by Lloyd Waner, to take the nightcap 6-5 in ten innings. Waner had seven base hits in that twin bill.

21. Of the 15 unassisted triple plays in major league history only two were recorded by a first baseman. Who was the first of the two to record an unassisted triple play?

The Groundbreaker" here was in the person of first baseman George Burns of the Boston Red Sox. In the 2nd inning of a game against the Cleveland Indians, on September 14, 1923 Burns speared a liner by Frank Brower, tagged Rube Lutzke who was moving off first, and then rushed to second base for the third out before Riggs Stephenson could get back, for the first triple play by a first baseman in major league history. The Sox went on to win it in 12 innings 4-3.

Interesting to note that of the fifteen unassisted triple plays in major league history, eight were by shortstops, five by a second baseman, and two by a first baseman.

22. Who was the first modern day National League player to record an unassisted triple play?

On October 6, 1923 shortstop Ernie Padgett, a rookie playing in only his second game of four that season for the Boston Braves, took a line drive off the bat of Philadelphia Phillies first baseman Walter "Union Man" Holke in the 4th inning, stepped on second base to double up Cotton Tierney, and tagged out Cliff Lee coming down from first.

The Braves went on to win this second game of a doubleheader 5-1.

23. Who was the first player to wear a baseball glove?

This has been a reason for debate for many years. Although it has been said that Art "Doc" Irwin has been credited with being the first player to wear a glove there is another school of thought that claims that Doug Allison, a catcher with the Cincinnati Red Stockings, had a local saddle maker make a glove for him in 1869. Heretofore players played bare handed, but as the distance between the pitchers' Square (mound) became closer to home plate, and the style of delivery changed it became practical to have some sort of protection.

On May 25, 1875, there was the newly founded St. Louis Brown Stockings, the first team to represent St. Louis, whose games were played in the Grand Avenue Grounds, the forerunner to Sportsman's Park. On that day Charlie Waitt, an outfielder and first baseman, became the first fielder to wear a fingerless glove. He initially was teased and taunted by the fans, and players alike as being a sissy. That eventually changed through the years, and evolved into what we see today.

24. Who was the first player to be credited with an assist?

This was bound to happen when the first, and only, due to rainouts in other cities, National League game was played, on April 22, 1876. The first assist was credited to Philadelphia Athletics 27-year old shortstop Davy "Wee Davy" Force, so named for his 5'4" 130 pound size. In that game the Boston Red Stockings came up with two runs in the bottom of the 9th to snatch victory from the home team, 6-5.

25. Who was the first left-handed catcher?

"Yaller Bill" Harbridge made his start on May 15, 1875, with Hartford, as an outfielder, catcher, and a three-position infielder. He stayed with the Dark Blues through 1877 when he moved on playing for four more teams during his nine-season career.

He played in a total of 401 games, 159 as a catcher, which qualified the lefty to be recognized as the first left-handed catcher in major league baseball.

26. Who was the first major league player to be killed trying to catch a popup fly ball?

This tragedy occurred on April 12, 1909 when 38-year old Philadelphia Athletics catcher, Mike "Doc" Powers, an eleven-year veteran, injured himself crashing into a wall while chasing a foul pop-up.

After the game, his first of the season, he complained of intestinal pains. He was operated on the next day, but would only survive until April 26th when the Holy Cross alumnus became the first major league death in the 20th century, caused by an on-field injury.

27. Who was the first modern day catcher to have three assists in one inning?

It happened in the 7th inning of a game against the Detroit Tigers, on August 3, 1914, when New York Yankees catcher, Les Nunamaker, threw out right fielder "Wahoo Sam" Crawford, and leftfielder Bobby Veach trying to steal, and then came back to pick off the other outfielder Hug "Bunny" High at second base, to become the first catcher in the 20th century to have three assists in one inning. New York lost to Detroit that afternoon, 4-1.

28. Who was the first catcher to have the opposition steal eight bases in one inning?

It had to be a long and embarrassing first inning for Cleveland Indians catcher, Steve O'Neill, when the Washington Nationals started the game off, on July 19, 1915, by running wild. The sore-armed catcher was certainly taken advantage of by speedy right fielder Danny Moeller who stole second, third, and then stole home, three of his 32 stolen bases that year.

Centerfielder Clyde "Deerfoot" Milan, who didn't come by that nickname without reason, chipped in with two of his 40 stolen bases that year. Even Russian-born catcher, Ed Ainsmith, followed Milan's example by swiping two bases, and finally shortstop George McBride added an eighth as the "Big Train". Walter Johnson, rolled to his 15th victory in an 11-4 win.

29. Who was the first catcher to allow 13 stolen bases in one game?

Here is a case of a team running wild on the base paths, and a catcher with a sore shoulder pressed into duty because the first string receiver, Red Kleinow, was out with an injury.

We're speaking here of a game between the last place Washington Nationals, and the New York Highlanders (Yankees), on June 28, 1907. The catcher in question is Branch Rickey who was taking over for Kleinow. The mayhem begins with Rickey's first attempt to throw to second base which ended up in right field.

Now baseball fans know that runners can steal bases on the pitcher as well as the catcher, and the Highlanders' right-hander, Lew "King" Brockett, proved a perfect example. In his eight innings of work Brockett didn't make it easy on Rickey with his deliberate windup, issuing nine walks and allowing 15 hits, which gave the Nationals plenty of chances to steal with 24 base runners.

Of the thirteen stolen bases that day only the pitcher, Tom Hughes, and second baseman John Perrine, were theft-less in the 16-5 Washington victory.

As baseball fans all know Branch Rickey will go on to make a name for himself in the halls of the executive offices of major league baseball.

30. What was the first team to use three catchers in one inning?

This happening was not by choice, but by necessity. On May 2, 1970 the Philadelphia Phillies were playing out in Candlestick Park, San Francisco, against the Giants. Going into the top of the 6th inning Phillies catcher, Tim McCarver, broke his hand while at bat, when a 2-1 foul tip caught him on his hands. Mike Ryan came in to replace him in the bottom of the 6th, and has his hand broken when he is spiked on a put out at home on Willie McCovey. A quick call is sent to the Phillies bench for a replacement for Ryan. Rookie Jim Hutto, heretofore an outfielder and third baseman, is called upon to assume the catching duties.

It was a tough day for the Phillies, losing two catchers in one inning, and also the game in nine, 7-1.

31. Who was the first catcher to win the Gold Glove Award, and the Silver Slugger Award in the same year?

In 1994 the Texas Rangers 22-year old catcher, Ivan "Pudge" Rodriguez, won the Gold Glove Award with 44 assists, 5 errors in 649 chances for a .992 Fielding Average. His Silver slugger Award came with a record of 16 home runs, 57 runs batted in, a batting average of .298 and a slugging percentage of .488 to be the first catcher to win both awards in the same year. He was also selected to the American League All-Star Game that year.

32. Who was the first catcher to catch three no-hitters and a perfect game?

Ray "Cracker" Schalk, a very fine defensive catcher and excellent fielder, caught for the Chicago White Sox from 1912 to 1928. He caught 1,727 games, three of which were no hitters. He was behind the plate for Joe Benz on May 31, 1914 when he no-hit Cleveland, 6-1, Eddie Cicotte when he did the same to the St. Louis Browns on April 14, 1917 winning 11-0, and then followed that by catching Charlie Robertson's 2-0 perfect game on April 30, 1922 at Detroit.

33. Who was the first catcher to record a put out at every base during his career?

The answer to that couldn't' be too surprising if you remember how catcher Ray Schalk, of the Chicago White Sox, was known for his aggressive backing up of plays behind each base. During his seventeen seasons he managed to make a put out at every base on the field.

34. Who is the first player, an outfielder, to be on the front end of two triple plays in the same season?

It all started with Cleveland tied at 3-3 with the Chicago White Sox on May 23, 1928. With White Sox third baseman Johnny Mann leading off third, first baseman Bud Clancy hit a short fly ball to leftfielder Charlie "Chuckoo" Jamieson who caught the fly, and then threw to catcher Luke Sewell to retire Mann trying to score from third after the catch. Sewell then threw to his brother Joe at second base, who caught Ray Schalk off the bag, and in desperation Schalk raced for third where he was tagged out by Johnny Hodapp.

The White Sox went on to win with a run in the 9th, 4-3.

On Saturday, June 9, 1928, at League Park, Charlie Jamieson started his second triple play in three weeks, this time the New York Yankees were the victims. In the 2nd inning with outfielder Ben Paschal on third base, and Tony Lazzeri on first, Jamieson grabbed a line drive hit by third baseman "Jumping Joe" Dugan. Jamieson then quickly threw to first baseman Lew Fonseca who tagged Lazzeri, and then fired home to Luke Sewell to catch Paschal trying to score. Even with the triple play Cleveland went down 7-3.

Charlie still was the first outfielder to start two triple plays in the same season, just three weeks apart.

35. Who committed the first error in National League history?

The first error committed in National League history was made on April 22, 1876, by Philadelphia Athletics third baseman Ezra Sutton on a wild throw to first base in a game against the Boston Red Stockings (Braves).

36. Who was the first catcher to catch two perfect games in his career?

It was a cold, damp night in Cleveland on May 15, 1981 when catcher Ron Hassey put on his "tools of ignorance" in preparation to being on the receiving end of right-hander Len Barker's pitches for the Indians against the Toronto Blue Jays. It wasn't a full workload that night as Barker didn't go to three balls on any Toronto batter, throwing 103 pitches, fanning 11, as he set down 27 in a row for a 3-0 perfect game.

Ten years later, on July 28, 1991, Hassey found himself in the other league playing for the Expos in a game at Dodger Stadium. When he positioned himself behind the plate that day to receive pitches from Dennis "El Presidente" Martinez he never realized he would become the first catcher in major league history to catch two perfect games. That's what happened as Martinez threw just 95 pitches, striking out 5, to set down the Dodgers 27 consecutive times, and Martinez had his first perfect game pitched, and Hassey his second behind the plate.

37. Who was the first catcher to wear eyeglasses while catching behind home plate?

Clint "Scrap Iron" Courtney, was the first catcher to wear glasses. He made his debut with the New York Yankees on September 29, 1951, his only game with them, before being traded to the St. Louis Browns on November 23, 1951, at the request of their manager, Rogers Hornsby.

He stayed with them through 1952-53 and moved to Baltimore when the Browns franchise was shifted there in 1954. Known as a tough and fearless battler, he had his physical moments on the field during his eleven seasons with Washington, Baltimore, Kansas City, and the Chicago White

Sox, ending up with a career .268 batting average.

38. Who is the first modern day outfielder, a centerfielder, to successfully start three double plays in one game?

You have to go back to Wednesday, April 26, 1905, in Exposition Park, Pittsburgh, when Jack McCarthy of the Chicago Cubs, started three successful double plays, the third of which ended the game, giving the Cubbies a 2-1 win over the Pittsburgh Pirates.

Jack O'Neill, the Cubs catcher, set a record for catchers by being the first, and at that time, the only, backstop to be on the receiving end of three double plays.

Just to keep the archives in order shortstop Jackson "Candy" Nelson did it back in 1887 in a Union Association game, but only two were completed at home plate.

39. Who was the first, and only, first baseman in major league history to go through an entire season without making an error?

This is a hard one to accept, but it did happen in the 159 games played at first base by Steve Garvey, of the San Diego Padres, when he played in 1,329.2 innings, over 159 games, accepting 1,319 chances, making 87 assists, but nary an error to be the first player at the initial sack to be able to make that claim.

40. Who was the first shortstop to play in 100 consecutive games without making an error?

Reynaldo "Rey" Ordonez, the Cuban-born shortstop of the New York Mets, committed an error on March 30, 2000 for the first time in 101 consecutive games. It occurred in the bottom of the 1st inning, in the second game of the season, in a game against the Chicago Cubs, played before 55,000 fans at the Tokyo Dome, Japan. Chicago centerfielder Damon Buford reached first on a misplayed ground ball by Ordonez. The Mets came away with a 5-1 victory.

During his nine-season career Ordonez made only 102 errors in 4,199 chances.

41. Who was the first catcher to be involved in a triple play where he made the first and third outs?

This totally unusual triple play happened to the Seattle Mariners on Saturday, September 2, 2006 in Tropicana Field, in the top of the 1st inning of a game against the Tampa Bay Rays.

The Mariners' CF Ichiro Suzuki led off the game with an infield single off southpaw J.P. Howell. 2B Jose Lopez walked. 3B Adrian Beltrie lined a single to right, scoring Suzuki, and sending Lopez to third. LF Raul Ibanez then struck out looking, but Adrian Beltre, who took off for second with the pitch, had catcher Dioner Navarro fire down to SS Ben Zobrist who applied the tag to Beltrie for the second out. On the throw to second Jose Lopez decided he could score, and raced for home, but Zobrist's throw back to Navarro nipped Lopez at the plate to complete the triple play.

For those of you scoring from home that series of plays is recorded as 2-6-2, the first of its kind in major league history.

The Mariners went on to win 4-3.

42. Who was the first outfielder to start 12 or more double plays from both left field and right field?

Samuel James "Jimmy" Sheckard, an excellent outfielder with a powerful right arm, started 14 double plays, for a record, from his right field position in 1899 with the Baltimore Orioles. Then while playing left field for the Chicago Cubs in 1911 he started an even dozen double plays, a another record at that position, to be the first to earn such honors at each position, and become a "Groundbreaker."

43. What was the first team to have its outfield play an entire game without a putout?

It took place before an Opening Day crowd of 30,000 at the Polo Grounds on April 15, 1909. Leon "Red" Ames, the New York Giants' right-hander was matched up in a pitching duel with the Brooklyn Superbas' right-hander, Irvin " Kaiser" Wilhelm. Ames had a no-hitter for nine innings, with Wilhelm matching him until the 8th, but then Ames lost his no-hitter in the 10th, then lost the game in the 13th, 3-0.

Meanwhile through all this brilliant pitching the Giants outfielders stood out there collectively awaiting a fly ball put out that never arrived.

44. Who was the first player to execute an unassisted triple play to end a game?

We'll go out to Citi Field on Sunday, August 23, 2009 when the New York Mets came up in the bottom of the 9th inning trailing the Philadelphia

Phillies 9-6, and facing RHP Brad "Lights out" Lidge.

The first batter, CF Angel Pagan, went all the way around to third on an error by 1B Ryan Howard. Then 2B Luis Castillo got on by an error on 2B Eric Bruntlett with Pagan scoring. 1B Dan Murphy singled to the right side sending Castillo to second and bringing up RF Jeff Francoeur, with still no out. Francoeur lined a ball to 2B Eric Bruntlett who snared the line drive, touched second to double up Castillo, and tagged Murphy who was running on the pitch at second for an unassisted triple play, the first to end a game in major league history.

45. Who was the first catcher to catch a no-hit game on consecutive days?

No one, least of all the Chicago White Sox, and I might add the St. Louis Browns catcher, Hank Severeid, ever dreamed they would become "Groundbreakers" when southpaw Ernie Koob took the hill for the Browns in the Mound City on May 5, 1917. Koob shutout the Pale Hose that day with a 1-0 no-hitter, with Severeid behind the plate calling the pitches.

On the next day, May 6th, the White Sox came out to face right-hander Bob Groom, and were equally inadequate at the plate as Groom shut them out, again with no hits, winning 3-0. And Hank was back behind the plate for the second consecutive day calling the pitches. His pitch calling had to be right on.

46. Who was the first player to throw out three runners at home in the same game?

That fielding honor goes to William "Dummy" Hoy, the centerfielder of the Louisville Colonels, when he erased three Philadelphia Phillies runners trying to score in a game on June 19, 1899, down in Philadelphia in an 11-3 Colonels victory.

47. Who was the first player to start two triple plays in one game?

It happened on Tuesday, July 17, 1990, at Fenway Park, when the Minnesota Twins, in spite of losing 1-0, turned a triple play in the 4th when RF Tom Brunansky, with the bases loaded, grounded to 3B Gary Gaetti who went around the horn to 2B Al Newman, and on to Kent Hrbek at first for the triple killing. In the 8th inning, after SS Tim Naehring doubled, and 3B Wade Boggs walked, 2B Jody Reed ended a chance for some runs when he grounded to Gaetti who again went around the horn to Newman and Hrbek for the second triple play of the game against the Boston Red Sox and a "Groundbreaker" day for Gary Gaetti.

48. Who was the first 50-year old catcher to play a big league game?

This battery still had life in it as "Orator Jim" O'Rourke, who had played some leftfield and at first base, along with being a catcher, was behind the plate, at age 54, in a game for the New York Giants on Thursday, September 22, 1904.

It was his 1,999th regular season game, and his 231st behind the plate. He went 1-4, for his 2,639th base hit, and became the oldest player in major league history to get a base hit, and scored his 1,229th run in his 23 seasons, and concluded his career that day with a .310 batting average, as the Giants clinched the 1904 pennant by defeating Cincinnati, 7-5.

He became a resident of Cooperstown when inducted by The Old Timers Committee in 1945.

49. Who was the first player to make all three continuous put outs, but receive no credit for an unassisted triple play?

This bizarre play occurred down in Griffith Stadium on September 19, 1929. In the bottom of the 8th inning the Washington Senators had 3B Jackie Hayes on second and RHP Fred "Firpo" Marberry on first when 1B Joe Judge came up and hit a sharp liner back at the St. Louis Browns RHP George Blaeholder, who instinctively threw his glove up, and partially deflected the ball toward 2B Oscar "Ski" Melillo who caught it for the first out. Melillo then tagged Marberry who was charging down from first for the second out, and then raced over and touched second before Hayes could scramble back to complete the triple play.

Melillo made all of the outs for the triple play, but was not given credit for an unassisted triple play because of the deflection, and it remains in the scorer's book as a 1-4-4-4 triple play! He was the first player to get no credit for his deed, but certainly respect from here. Washington went on to win 2-1.

50. Who was the first second baseman to commit nine errors in a 9-inning game?

Let's begin by saying that Andrew Jackson Leonard, born in County Cavan, Ireland, on June 1, 1846, certainly wasn't born into a baseball family, but that didn't stop him from playing the outfield, and second base for the Boston Red Caps on June 14, 1876 when in a game against the St. Louis Brown Stockings he became the first second-sacker to commit nine errors in a game where he, and his fellow infielders, made a total of 14 errors, and both infields combined made 22 errors, as the Brown Stockings romped to a 20-6 win.

51. Who was the first player to win a dozen consecutive Gold Glove Awards?

Willie Mays, the Hall of Fame centerfielder, won his first Gold Glove Award while with the New York Giants in 1957. He continued winning the award, after the team moved west, for the next eleven years, through 1968, while patrolling the outfield with the San Francisco Giants.

52. Who was the first catcher to use an oversize mitt to handle knuckle balls thrown by his battery mate?

Baltimore Orioles catcher Clint "Scrap Iron" Courtney came to the conclusion that he needed a bigger and better mitt to control the pitches of right-hander Hoyt Wilhelm, so, on May 27, 1960 he donned an oversize catcher's mitt to better control the whereabouts of "Old Sarge's" deliveries.

53. Who was the first modern day catcher to be charged with six passed balls in one game?

Sunday, August 30, 1987, before a crowd of 38,641 at Tiger Stadium, was not a day Texas Rangers' catcher, Geno Petralli, would fondly look back upon. Texas sent out their famed knuckleball specialist, right-hander Charlie Hough, to face Detroit's right-hander Doyle Alexander. Petralli knew catching the fluttering throws of Hough was always a problem and today's game would be no exception.

When the game was over and the final stats were in they were a bit bizarre. Neither Alexander nor Hough had allowed an earned run, both had given up just three hits, although Hough left after 7 innings, and right-hander Dwayne Henry pitched a scoreless 8th, allowing one hit, they each had struck out six, but the Tigers won the game 7-0!

The secret behind the Motown win was six walks, and a hit batsman by Hough, six passed balls by Petralli, and two Tigers' stolen bases, which was all Detroit needed with Alexander's pitching to come away with the win.

54. Who was the first catcher to be charged with over 300 errors in his career?

I guess when you have caught 1,195 games over 15 years, like Charles "Red" Dooin did from 1902 to 1914 with the Phillies, and from 1915-16 with the Reds and Giants, you might be expected to not be errorless, but "Red" became, like it or not, the first catcher to exceed 300 when his career ended with 320 miscues behind the plate.

55. Who was the first pitcher to record all three putouts in one inning?

It happened up in Fenway Park on September 26, 1940 when in the 4th inning Boston Red Sox right-hander Jim Bagby Jr. made all three putouts in the inning, but it wasn't enough as the Washington Senators rallied in the 9th to come away with a 6-5 win.

56. Who was the first National League pitcher to record all three putouts at first base in one inning?

Rick "Big Daddy" Reuschel, the Chicago Cubs right-hander, personally took care of the St. Louis Cardinals in the 3rd inning at Wrigley Field on Friday, April 25, 1975.

The first batter, catcher Ted Simmons, was retired on an unassisted groundout to Reuschel. 1B Keith Hernandez then grounded to 1B Pete LaCock and "Big Daddy" hustled over to first to take the throw and retire Hernandez. 3B Ken Reitz followed with another ground ball down toward first, and again Reuschel rumbled over to take the throw from LaCock and personally retired the side.

The Cards eked out a 4-3 win and Reuschel became a National League "Groundbreaker" by being the first in his league to personally retire all three batters at first base.

57. Who was the first player to pitch and catch in the same game, twice in a season?

Rick Cerrone, of the New York Yankees, covered the field with leather from both sides of the plate twice in the 1987 season. He did it the first time on Sunday, July 19th when he started the game down in Arlington Stadium against the Texas Rangers behind the plate. With things definitely not going the Yankees' way in the 8th inning, being behind 18-3, and three runs having scored in the inning, Rick switched positions, and took the mound in needed relief of southpaw Pat Clements, after he walked CF Bob Brower to load the bases. Mark Salas, came in taking DH Dave Winfield's spot in the batting order, and replaced Cerrone as the new catcher.

The first batter Cerrone faced was Texas shortstop Curt Wilkerson who flied out to left field. He then got RF Ruben Sierra on a force out, 1B Don Mattingly to SS Wayne Tolleson, with 3B Steve Buechele scoring on the play, and Browne moving to third. Up came Bobby Witt as a pinch-hitter for LF Pete Incaviglia, and Cerrone was called for a balk, scoring 2B Jerry Browne. Cerrone then struck out Witt and the Rangers went into the top of the 9th ahead 20-3, and the game ended that way. But not before Cerrone had a chance to cover the field with leather, from both sides of the plate.

The second opportunity, and the one that made him eligible to be a "Groundbreaker," happened out in Tiger Stadium, before a Sunday crowd of 44,673, on August 9, 1987, when in the bottom of the 8th inning, with the Yankees behind 15-4, manager Lou Piniella sent Cerrone to the mound to start the inning off replacing southpaw Dave Righetti. As in the last time Cerrone took over the pitching duties, Mark Salas took over behind the plate and took DH Dave Winfield's 4th slot in the batting order.

LF Tim Tolman was the first batter, and he walked. SS Alan Trammell flied out to Dan Pasqua in right field. CF Pat Sheridan grounded out to 1B Don Mattingly unassisted, with Tolman taking second. Then 3B Jim Morrison ended the inning by grounding out SS Bobby Meacham to 1B Don Mattingly.

The Yankees went down, 15-4, but Rick Cerrone became the first player to catch and pitch in the same game twice in one season. He truly covered the field with leather.

58. Who was the first player to start a triple play?

As legend goes, the very diminutive (5'3 ½") shortstop Richard J, "Dickey" Pearce of the St. Louis Brown Stockings started the first triple play in a game against the New York Mutuals, out in Sportsman's Park, on June 29, 1876, when he snared a low line drive by Joe Start, fired over to 1B Herman "Dutch" Dehlman for the second out, who, in turn, threw over to 3B Joe Battin to complete the triple play.

59. Who was the first player to establish the shortstop position in baseball?

In the early stages of baseball a player was stationed close to each base in the infield, and had a player called a short fielder who roamed behind the infielders and in front of the outfielders, much like the position used in playing softball.

Richard "Dickey" Pearce was that person, and while with the Brooklyn Atlantics in 1856 began to see the benefit of moving closer to the infield and occupying a spot between the second and third baseman, commonly known as the hole. Thus the position of shortstop was established, and Dickey Pearce had a long career in baseball, but just two in the major leagues, with the St. Louis Brown Stockings of the National League in 1876-77, but he certainly had a big impact on the game in this and other ways described in this book.

60. Who was the first player to wear a glove in the field?

Back in the early days of baseball many fielding errors were committed, and not till the introduction of a glove, and players stopped using just their bare hands, did the situation improve.

The first known player to introduce a glove to the game was Doug Allison, a catcher with the Cincinnati Red Stockings in 1870. With his hands continually subjected to pitches they were not a thing of beauty. He appeared on the field in 1870 wearing buckskin mittens, which gradually evolved into what we have today; shortly thereafter Al Spalding, the right-handed pitcher with the Chicago White Stockings, and a few others, donned make-shift gloves in 1876.

61. Who was the first catcher to catch a no-hitter in the American League, and a perfect game in the National League?

This witness to history, and surely a "Groundbreaker", was Baltimore Orioles catcher Gus Triandos when, on Saturday, September 20, 1958, he was behind the plate for Hoyt Wilhelm's 1-0 no-hitter against the Yankees before a crowd of 10,941 at Memorial Stadium.

Gus moved over to the National League, and with the Phillies at Shea Stadium, on Father's Day, Sunday, June 21, 1964, before a crowd of 32,026, in the first game of a doubleheader, he was the catcher for right-hander Jim Bunning when he threw his perfect game defeating the New York Mets 6-0.

Triandos not only caught one in each league, but as the catcher for two Hall of Fame pitchers.

62. Who was the first player to be on the front end of a triple play without having his bat ever touch the ball?

Impossible you say? Not when you read about the game played down in Tropicana Field on Saturday, September 2, 2006. Southpaw J.P. Howell started on the mound for the Tampa Bay Devil Rays, and faced Seattle's leadoff batter, centerfielder Ichiro Suzuki, in the top of the 1st inning, and gave up a ground ball single just out of reach of 2B Jorge Cantu. Seattle's 2B Jose Lopez then walked, and 3B Adrian Beltre singled to right center scoring Suzuki, and sending Lopez to third. LF Raul Ibanez then struck out looking, as Beltrie tried to steal second only to be nailed by catcher Dioner Navarro's throw to SS Ben Zobrist, covering, for the second out. Seeing the throw to second, Lopez took off for home and was cut down by SS Ben Zobrist's throw to the plate, completing the triple play, one in which a bat never touched the ball. Now can one say that Ibanez hit into a triple play or was the instigator?

63. Who was the first, and only, shortstop to ever play every inning of a doubleheader without having a ball hit to him?

We'll begin with the first game of a doubleheader down in Arlington Stadium, on Friday, June 25, 1976, when the Texas Rangers faced off against the Chicago White Sox, and throughout the first game Texas shortstop Toby Harrah played the entire nine innings without a chance for an assist or a putout. The line score showed 27 putouts and 8 assists, all by teammates.

He made up for his defensive inactivity by being productive at the plate by going 3-for-5 with a home run and a stolen base as the Rangers took the opener, 8-4.

In the nightcap the same denial for a defensive opportunity took place as Harrah didn't see a ball come to him as his teammates racked up 27 put-outs, and 12 assists, but none for Toby.

As in the first game his offensive ability surfaced, as he had two walks, went 3-for-3 at the plate, including a home run and drove in three runs as the White Sox rolled to a 14-9 win, and the 29,049 saw history being made as Toby Harrah became a "Groundbreaker".

64. Who was the first American League outfielder to start three double plays in a single game?

It wasn't a time for the Philadelphia Athletics to challenge the arm of Boston Red Sox centerfielder Ira "Pete" Flagstead in the second game of a Monday, doubleheader on April 19, 1926 at Fenway Park.

When the Athletics had a man on third, in this closely played game, a fly ball out to centerfielder "Pete", meant he caught the fly ball, and then let fly with a perfect strike to his catcher, John Bischoff, for the completion of the double play. He did that twice in the game, and completed his "trifecta" by catching another fly ball for the out and then throwing in to 3B Fred Haney, and on to 2B Mike Herrera , who relayed into Bischoff to complete the third double play that was started in the centerfield of Fenway by Flagstead.

65. Who was the first player to have over 40 putouts in a single game?

This hard to believe statistic happened on Saturday, May 1, 1920 at Braves Field when the famous game between the Brooklyn Robins and the Boston Braves before a meager crowd of 4,500, saw the longest game in history develop after the Robins picked up a run in top of the 5th and the Braves came back to tie it in their half of the 6th. It stayed that way as the two right-handers, Leon Cadore of Brooklyn and Joe Oeschger of Boston, toiled for 3 hours and 50 minutes and 26 innings before the umpires finally said enough.

When the scorecards were reviewed there was the Braves first baseman, Walter Holke, with 42 putouts and one assist for his day's work. His counterpart with the Robins, Ed Konetchy, had 30 putouts and no assists, but the "Groundbreaker" was Holke was the first player to record 40 or more putouts in one game.

66. Who was the first pitcher to win over 15 Gold Glove Awards?

When it came to defensive superiority no one could hold a glove to Jim "Kitty" Kaat the big southpaw who made his major league debut with the Washington Senators on August 2, 1959, and hurled for five other teams in both leagues, notably the Minnesota Twins, where he spent 13 of his 25 seasons, and came away with 16 Gold Glove Awards to go along with his 283-237, 3.45 Era.

67. Who was the first major league player to play an entire season without making an error?

Danny Litwhiler, made his debut in the outfield with the Philadelphia Phillies on April 25, 1940, and in 1941 led the National League in errors with 15. In 1942, after finding the error of his ways, he became the first major leaguer to go an entire season, playing in both left and right field, handling 317 chances in 151 games, without committing an error.

He extended his errorless ways for 187 consecutive games in the outfield over two seasons. He completed his eleven season career playing right field with the Cincinnati Reds on September 25, 1951 showing 37 errors in 1,057 games for a .982 fielding average.

Besides playing on the 1944 World Champion St. Louis Cardinals, Litwhiler was the inventor of the Jugs radar gun which measures the velocity of pitches.

D. ON THE BASEPATHS

1. Who scored the first run in major league history?

Tim McGinley, a 22-year old rookie outfielder and catcher, who played but one year with the Boston Red Stockings (Braves), crossed home plate on April 22, 1876 against the Philadelphia Nationals (Athletics) at Athletic Park, to be credited with scoring the first run in major league history. Boston went on to defeat Philadelphia 6-5 before 3,000 fans.

McGinley's career was short-lived for his last game was on July 25, 1876 when his three games as a catcher and six playing center field came to an end showing career stats of six hits driving in two runs in 40 at bats for a .150 average.

There are those who credit Weston "Wes" Fisler, infielder/outfielder of the Philadelphia Nationals with that score. Fisler's first National League game was on May 20, 1876 with the Philadelphia Nationals negating his ability to cross home plate on April 22, 1876.

2. Who was the first player to score the 1,000,000th run in major league history?

Bob Watson, first baseman of the Houston Astros, scored the one millionth run in major league history, at 12:32 P.M., in the second inning against the San Francisco Giants at Candlestick Park on Sunday, May 4, 1975.

Milt May, with an 0-2 count, and Watson on second base, hit John Montefusco's next pitch for a home run to drive in Watson with the historical run. The Giants went on to win the first game of the doubleheader 8-6.

3. There have been only six players in modern baseball history to score six runs in one game, who was the first?

On August 4, 1934 Mel Ott, New York Giant Hall of Fame right fielder, became the first modern day player to score six runs in a game when he had a walk, was hit by a pitch, hit two home runs, along with a double and a single, to score six time as the Giants rolled to a 21-4 thrashing of the Philadelphia Phillies in the second game of a doubleheader down in Philadelphia. The Phillies had taken the first game 5-4.

Ott would score six times again in the first game of a double header at the Polo Grounds on Sunday, April 30, 1944, against the Brooklyn Dodgers, when he collected two hits and walked five times as the Giants coasted to a 26-8 victory before 58,000 fans.

4. Who was the first player to steal a base in each of four decades?

Noted more for his bat than his base stealing prowess, Ted Williams stole his first two bases in 1939 as a rookie with the Boston Red Sox. He added 14 more in the decade of the forties, seven more in the fifties, and had his final stolen base in 1960 making him the first to swipe a bag in four decades.

5. Who was the first, and only player ever signed to a contract to be just a designated runner, and to never have an official at-bat in his two-year major league career, yet stole over 30 bases and scored over 30 runs?

Herb Washington, a world-class sprinter, was signed as an amateur free agent in 1974 by Oakland A's owner Charlie Finley. He appeared in 105 games over two seasons stealing 31 bases, being caught 17 times, and scoring 33 runs, yet he never stepped into the batter's box.

Interestingly in the 1974 World Series he appeared in three games as a pinch-runner without stealing a base or scoring a run. He was picked off first base by Los Angeles Dodgers right-hander Mike Marshall in Game 2, on October 13th, after entering the game as a pinch-runner for Joe Rudi in a crucial 9th inning situation.

6. Who was the first, and only, player to steal over 1,000 bases in his major league career?

Rickey Henderson, who played for nine different teams in both leagues, over his 25-year career, led his league in stolen bases twelve times, stole over 100 bases in three seasons, and ended his career with 1,270 American League stolen bases, and 136 in the senior circuit for his total of 1,406 career stolen bases.

7. Who is the first, and only, player to steal over 100 bases in three consecutive seasons, his first three in the major leagues?

Vince Coleman, the St. Louis Cardinals left fielder, came up to the majors in 1985 and stole 110 bases in his rookie season. He followed that up in 1986 with 107 stolen bases and ran his streak to 109 steals in 1987. He led the National League in steals in his first six consecutive seasons and ended his thirteen-year career with 762.

8. Who was the first pitcher to steal home in a modern day major league game?

George Barclay "Win" Mercer, a right-handed pitcher with the Washington Senators, who also played some third base, and in the outfield, stole home against the Philadelphia Athletics on August 10, 1901. It was one of his ten steals that season.

9. Who was the first player to steal six bases in one game?

Edward Trowbridge Collins, the Philadelphia Athletics second baseman, stole six bases in one game, on September 11, 1912, against the Detroit Tigers. Eleven days later, on September 22, 1912, he repeated the thefts by stealing another six bases in a game, this time against the St. Louis Browns, to become the first player to steal six bases in a game once and twice. He ended that season with 63 stolen bases. Although the record has been tied it has never been broken.

10. Who was the first player in modern baseball history to be issued a base on balls six times in a nine-inning game?

Jimmie Foxx, first baseman of the visiting Boston Red Sox, was issued six walks, one intentional, one semi-intentional, in his game at Sportsman's Park against three St. Louis Browns' pitchers on Thursday, June 16, 1938.

The Red Sox, and right-hander Johnny "Footsie" Marcum, came away with a 12-8 victory over fellow right-hander Ed "Babe" Linke before a crowd of just 1,028 fans.

11. Who was the first modern day player to steal over 100 bases in a season?

Shortstop Maury Wills of the Los Angeles Dodgers stole 104 bases in 117 attempts in the 1962 season to become the first modern day player to pass the century mark in thefts.

12. Who was the first player to never have an official at-bat in a game yet stole five bases and came around to score four runs?

If you said Rickey Henderson you would be correct, for in a game on Saturday, July 29, 1989, out in Oakland-Alameda County Stadium, LF Henderson walked four times and scored each time while stealing five bases off Mariners' southpaw Randy Johnson, and battery mate Scott Bradley. To no avail as the Mariners' prevailed, 14-6.

13. Who was the first major league player to be credited with sliding

into a base?

To find the answer to this obscure fact we have to go all the way back to the opening of the first National League season when the Chicago White Stockings left-handed outfielder Bob "The Magnet" Addy had developed the technique while playing for the Rockford ball club in 1866, and has been credited with being the first major league player to slide into a base.

14. Who was the first major league player to wear sliding pads, and among the first to slide feet first into a base?

Harry Stowe, who played under the name of Stovey, with Worcester, Boston, Philadelphia, Baltimore, and Brooklyn in his 14-year career, was credited with being the first player to wear sliding pads, and among the first players to slide feet first into a base.

15. Who was the first player to score three runs in the same inning?

That very unusual accomplishment went to Boston Red Sox catcher Sammy White, who in the 7th inning on June 18, 1953, in a game against the Detroit Tigers, won by the Red Sox 23-3, came around to score three times in that inning.

16. Who was the first, and hopefully the only, batter to hit a home run and then round the bases running backwards?

This bizarre incident occurred on Sunday, June 23, 1963, in the first game of a doubleheader, after Jimmy Piersall, then a centerfielder with the New York Mets, celebrated hitting his 100th career home run, and his only National League home run, a soft fly ball down the short right field line that carried into the stands at the Polo Grounds.

He then proceeded to run out his solo home run by circling the bases running backwards, and even slowing down to shake hands with the third base coach before continuing home, incurring the wrath of right-hander Dallas Green of the Philadelphia Phillies, the victim of the homer, who wasn't amused by Piersall's antics, nor was the National League Commissioner Ford Frick, who was one of the 19,901 in attendance, or manager Casey Stengel who was so mad that he released Piersall two days later.

17. Who was the first African-American umpire in the major leagues?

The first African-American umpire in the major leagues was Emmett Ashford who worked in the American League from 1965 to 1970. He officiated in the 1967 All-Star Game and the 1970 World Series. He retired after the 1970 season and died on March 1, 1980 in Marina Del Ray, California of a heart attack.

18. Who was the first pitcher to score seven runs in a nine-inning game?

"Blond Guy" Hecker, a right-handed pitcher with Louisville, scored seven runs in a game against Baltimore on August 15, 1886 as he went 6 for 7, including three home runs off right-hander Dick Conway, as Louisville rolled over Baltimore on Hecker's four-hitter.22-5.

19. Who was the first player to win the stolen base title in both leagues?

Ron LeFlore captured the American League theft title with 68 in 1978 with the Detroit Tigers. After moving over to the National League he led that league, swiping 97 bases while with the Montreal Expos in 1980.

20. Who was the first player to play in 1,097 games, come to bat 3,794 times before he stole his first base?

Certainly known for his prodigious power and home run ability, but not his speed on the bases, Cecil "Big Daddy" Fielder finally was credited with his first career stolen base while with the Detroit Tigers in 1996 when he thundered into second base safely as the throw from the catcher was juggled by the second baseman.

21. Who was the first major league umpire to collapse and die on the field during a game?

This tragic event took place on April 1, 1996, on the opening day of the season, at Riverfront Stadium, Cincinnati. After Cincinnati's starting pitcher, Pete Schourek retired the first two Montreal Expos batters in the first inning, Rondell White stepped into the batter's box and after the seventh pitch John McSherry said to the Reds catcher, Ed Taubensee, "time out for a second." He then turned and walked toward the screen behind home plate where the 6'2 ½, 328 pound, 51-year old McSherry collapsed and died as 53,000 fans watched in stunned silence.

22. Who was the first player to steal 7 bases in one game?

Grand theft took place on June 25, 1881 when Chicago White Stockings centerfielder George Gore came to the plate five times, scored every time, and stole second base five times and third base twice for a total of seven thefts in one game to be the first player to have that many stolen bases in one game, as Chicago went on to a 12-8 win over the Providence Grays.

"Sliding Billy" Hamilton, three years later, on August 31, 1894, ties this mark which hasn't been duplicated since.

23. Who was the first major leaguer to have twelve consecutive seasons of stealing 50 or more bases?

Leftfielder Lou Brock made his major league debut with the Chicago Cubs on September 10, 1961, and on June 15, 1964, in one of baseball's most talked about inept trading decisions, went to the St. Louis Cardinals with two journeyman players for outfielder Doug Clemens and pitchers Ernie Broglio and Bobby Shantz.

From then on his batting and base stealing abilities blossomed and from 1965 through 1976 his bases stealing abilities showed up in the record book as follows: 63, 74, 52, 62, 53, 71, 64, 63, 70, 118, 56, and finished off his streak in 1976 with 56 stolen bases; twelve consecutive years of over 50 stolen bases each year. When his career ended in 1979 he had swiped 938 bases to go along with his .293 career batting average. The Hall of Fame was quick to call and did in 1985.

24. Who is the first player to hold the team season stolen base record for two different teams?

Rickey Henderson set the Oakland Athletics team record in 1982 with 130 stolen bases. Moving east to the New York Yankees he stole 93 bases in 1988 to set another team record.

25. Who was the first, and only, modern day player to steal over 100 bases, and yet score less than 100 runs in one season?

That unusual accomplishment can be credited to the St. Louis Cardinals leftfielder, Vince Coleman, who led the National League in stolen bases in 1986 with 107, yet came around to score just 94 times, to be the first with those unusual statistics.

26. Who made the first successful steal of a base in National League history?

The first stolen base was credited to first baseman Tim Murnane of the Boston Red Stockings.

27. Who was the first player to get on base over 80 consecutive times in one season?

Ted Williams, the left fielder of the Boston Red Sox, and one of the greatest hitters in baseball history, got on base in 84 consecutive games in 1949. He did it by having 194 base hits, and leading the American League in walks with 162. He also led the league in doubles with 39, home runs with 43, runs scored with 150, and runs driven in with 159, with a batting average of .343 and a slugging average of .650, the latter also leading the league. No one has taken his place on the base paths in consecutive games more than The Splendid Splinter in a single season.

28. Who were the first modern day major league trainers to be called on to be umpires in a major league game?

The game between the Detroit Tigers and the St. Louis Browns was about to start at Navin Field in Detroit on Sunday, July 23, 1922, but the umpires were nowhere to be found. It seems Brick Owens and Tom Connolly scheduled to umpire the game had missed the train to Detroit.

So by mutual agreement Detroit's trainer Bits Bierhalter took over behind the plate and Dan Howley, the Browns' trainer, stationed himself at first base, and the game began.

The Tigers came away with an 11-6 win as RHP George "Hooks" Dauss bested RHP Wayne "Rasty" Wright.

29. Who was the first player to walk seven consecutive times?

It all started on August 17, 1938 when Detroit Tigers shortstop Bill Rogell drew a walk against the Chicago White Sox, and continued on until August 19th when he led off the game by drawing his 7th consecutive walk, against Oral Hildebrand of the St. Louis Browns.

30. Who was the first player to get on base more than 15 consecutive times?

During a stretch of six games in September 1957 Boston Red Sox slugger Ted Williams accomplished this amazing record of getting on base 16 consecutive times with two singles, nine walks, four home runs, and once by being hit by a pitch.

31. Who was the first player to draw five walks in a game twice in his career?

On May 21, 1930 Max "Camera Eye" Bishop, the Philadelphia Athletics second baseman, walked five times in the first game of a doubleheader with the New York Yankees at Shibe Park ,to become the first player to walk five times in one game, twice in his career. He will walk three times in the second game for a total of eight on the day, and to also be the first to draw more than six in one afternoon. The Athletics swept the twin bill, 15-7 and 4-1.

32. Who was the first umpire to work for a salary?

Mike Walsh, who had been an experienced umpire, joined the American Association in 1882 as that league instituted salaried umpires, whereby each was paid $140.00 per month with a $3.00 per diem.

Prior, umpires had worked either for a per-game fee or just did it for fun.

33. Who was the first Canadian-born major league umpire?

Robert D. Emslie was born in Guelph, Ontario on January 27, 1859, and made his debut with the Baltimore Orioles in the American Association. He spent three seasons in the major leagues as an outfielder and a pitcher. The right-hander had his best year on the mound in 1884 with a 32-17, 2.75 Era. record completing all 50 of his starts. He ended his career with a 44-44, 3.19 Era. before moving on to umpire in the International League in 1888-89 and in the American Association in 1890. He was a National League umpire in 1891 and spent 33 years as an active umpire before retiring at the end of the 1924 season.

He was best remembered for the historical call on September 23, 1908 when he was at second base at the Polo Grounds in the memorable New York Giants-Chicago Cubs "Merkle's Boner" game where Fred Merkle failed to touch second base. Home plate umpire, Hank O'Day, made the call for Emslie, who had worked 2,500 games prior, but claimed he ducked avoiding Al Bridwell's line drive to center and didn't see the play.

34. Who was the first player to be walked twice in the same inning in two different games in the same season?

Esoterically as this may be, George Selkirk of the New York Yankees, was walked twice in the same inning in two different games in 1936.

If you wondered who was the first in the National League you can look to second baseman Eddie Stanky when he was with the New York Giants in 1950.

35. Who was the first player to be walked over 2,000 times in his career?

It is not surprising to learn that Babe Ruth, having been walked 2,062 times in his career, was the first to exceed the 2,000 mark.

36. Who was the first, and only, player to have been walked over 2,500 times in his career?

The all-time leader in home runs, Barry Bonds, is also the first, and only, player to be walked over 2,500 times as he received 2,558 free passes in his 22-year career.

37. Who was the first modern day player to be picked off first base three times in one game?

You may be on, but not for long, must have been the thought going through the mind of Boston Braves southpaw, George "Lefty" Tyler, when the New York Giants outfielder, Benny Kauff, got on first base three times against him on May 26, 1916 up in Braves Field. Tyler proceeded to pick him off each of those three times as Kauff set a National League record of being the first player to be picked off first base three times in one game.

His mental errors didn't hurt as the Giants went on to win their 14th straight road game, 12-1, with Ralph "Sailor" Stroud recording his 20th and final major league victory.

38. When was the first time that six umpires, instead of the usual four, were assigned to be on the field for a World Series game?

This breakthrough on the base paths occurred on Tuesday, September 30th in Game 1 of the 1947 World Series between the Dodgers and Yankees. Commissioner Happy Chandler, instead of the usual four infield umpires, and two alternates in waiting, if needed, he assigned an additional one to each of the outfield foul lines as well.

Bill McGowan and Eddie Rommel from the American League; and Babe Pinelli and Larry Goetz of the National League handled the infield positions while Jim Boyer from the American League, and George Magerkurth from the National League had only outfield duty.

39. Who was the first, and only, player to successfully steal home seven straight times in one season?

In an act of thievery that will probably never be duplicated, the 1969 season for Minnesota Twins second baseman Rodney Carew shows him attempting 27 steals with 19 being successful.

What is incredible is of those successful stolen bases 7 were straight steals of home plate, none being on the front end of a double steal. The seventh and last steal of home that season happened on July 16th when in the 2nd inning of a game against the White Sox in Chicago, Carew stole home against southpaw Jerry Nyman. Stealing home is rare today and some of the recent great base stealers show a lack of success in that category.

Rickey Henderson had 1,406 career stolen bases, and Maury Wills had 586 stolen bases, but each only stole home once in their careers. Not even Lou Brock with 938, Tim Raines with 808, or Vince Coleman with 752 bases stolen, ever swiped home plate. That fact just highlights the enormity of Carew's 1969 performance.

40. Who was the first player to be ejected from a game, and to never ever have played in a major league game?

This bizarre event happened on Thursday, September 27, 1951 in the heat of the National League pennant race, which was finally decided by the famous "Shot Heard 'Round the World" home run by Bobby Thomson of the New York Giants.

The Brooklyn Dodgers were locked in a 3-3 tie going into the bottom of the 8th inning at Braves Field. Boston's LF Bob Addis led off with a single off Dodgers' southpaw, Preacher Roe, and after being advanced to third base by CF Sam Jethroe's single came charging home on 1B Earl Torgeson's ground ball to 2B Jackie Robinson, who fired home in an attempt to get Addis on a bang-bang play.

Home plate umpire Frank Dascoli called Addis safe, giving the Braves a 4-3 lead which they held for the win.

The Dodgers' catcher, Roy Campanella, went ballistic arguing Addis was out. The Dodgers bench gave Dascoli a hard time on the call as well, and Dascoli, after hearing enough from Campanella and the Dodgers bench, ejected him, and went over to the Dodgers' dugout and cleared the bench by throwing everyone out.

One of the players tossed was a young rookie outfielder who had been called up when rosters were allowed to be expanded after Labor Day. That player, although never playing in a major league game, made the National Basketball Hall of Fame as a star with the Boston Celtics, and later went on to be the head coach with the Los Angeles Lakers. We're talking about Bill Sharman.

41. Who was the first player to be a part of two triple-steals in the same game?

Look no further than League Park, Cleveland, on that Friday afternoon, July 25, 1930, when Connie Mack brought his Philadelphia Athletics into town to play the Indians. It started in the top of the 1st inning with Indians' right-hander Pete Jablonowski (he changed his name to Appleton in 1933) on the mound, and Joe "Mule" Sprinz behind the plate. When, with the bases loaded, and Jablonowski going into his windup, the heist was on. Athletics LF "Bucketfoot Al" Simmons came racing home safely from third, and RF Edmund "Bing" Miller swiped the then empty third sack while SS Edwin "Dib" Williams took second.

Then in the 4th inning with southpaw Milt Shoffner on the mound, and the Athletics leading by 4-0, Gordon "Mickey" Cochrane, the Athletics' catcher, thought he would duplicate Simmons' success from the 1st inning, and he swiped home while Simmons moved over to the vacated base at third, and 1B Jimmie Foxx went on down to second to accomplish, for the first time, two triple-steals in the same game, and "Bucketfoot Al", who had nine stolen bases on the year, and 88 in his 20-year career, not indicating gazelle-like speed became a "Groundbreaker" on that day for being the first player to be involved in two triple steals in one game.

The Athletics, behind Lefty Grove, who coasted to his 14th victory won a 14-1 laugher.

42. Who was the first catcher to allow 8 stolen bases in one inning?

On Monday, July 19, 1915, the Washington Nationals not only had their running shoes on when they came to Cleveland, but also must have had knowledge of the Indians' catcher, Steve O'Neill's, physical condition.

Washington came out running in the top of the 1st inning as Danny Moeller stole second, third, and home. The thievery didn't stop there as CF Clyde "Deerfoot" Milan, and catcher Eddie "Dorf" Ainsmith, each stole two bases, and SS George McBride picked up one on the ailing sore-armed O'Neill.

Those were the days when players rarely went on the disabled list, but toughed it out for each game. O'Neill was one of them and was considered one of the best and most durable catchers of his day, but with a very painful right arm, without much zing to his throws, the Washington base runners took advantage and made Steve O'Neill the first catcher to allow 8 stolen bases in a single inning.

Washington, behind Walter "The Big Train" Johnson, went on to an easy win, 11-4.

43. Who was the first player to steal home twice in the same game?

It happened back on June 28, 1910, when Chicago Cubs shortstop Joe

Tinker, who was immortalized along with second baseman Johnny Evers, and first baseman Frank Chance by Chicago native, and New York columnist, Franklin Pierce Adams, in his 1910 oft repeated reference to his eight-line poem which ended, "Tinker to Evers to Chance", caught national attention and quite possibly elevated Joe Tinker, a .262 hitter, into the Hall of Fame by the Veterans Committee in 1946.

That preface takes nothing away from Tinker on the aforementioned date as he became the first player to steal home twice in a game against the Cincinnati Reds, as the Cubbies rolled to an 11-1 win.

It is interesting to note that Tinker swiped 20 bases that season, with 10% coming in that particular game.

44. Who was the first player to be intentionally walked with the bases loaded?

We have to go back to August 21, 1881, in the 8th inning of a game against the Chicago White Stockings, when Jack Lynch, the Buffalo Bisons' right-hander, down 5-0, with no one out, gave up successive singles to RHP Fred Goldsmith, catcher Frank "Silver" Flint, and 2B Joe Quest to load the bases. That brought up LF Abner Dalrymple, who was a strong .323 hitter, and Lynch wanted no part of his swinging bat.

He felt it safer, to give up one run, by giving Dalrymple a free pass, and face CF George "Piano Legs" Gore, the next batter. Lynch threw seven balls outside (that was the required number for a walk back then) forcing in Goldsmith and bringing up Gore. Bad decision, for Gore rifled a double scoring Flint, Quest, and Dalrymple as Chicago went on to an 11-2 win. But Abner joins the "Groundbreakers" as being the first player to get an intentional pass with the bases loaded.

45. Who was the first modern day player to be intentionally walked with the bases loaded?

This unusual incident happened right after the turn of the century, on May 23, 1901.

It was the top of the 9th, and the Philadelphia Athletics scored two runs that inning to close the deficit to 11-7 to the Chicago White Stockings (Sox), but had the bases loaded and none out.

The next batter, 2B Nap Lajoie, who was on his way toward a Triple Crown, wasn't going to get a chance to add to those numbers as White Sox manager, and RHP, Clark "The Old Fox" Griffith inserted himself on the mound, and pitched four wide ones to Lajoie, forcing in the 8th Athletics run. He then retired RF Ralph "Socks" Seybold, 1B Harry "Jasper" Davis, on infield grounders, and disposed of the catcher, Morgan Murphy, to retire the side saving the 11-9 win. Lajoie, among his many accomplishments, became the first modern day player to get a free pass with the sacks full.

46. Who was the first player to be thrown out four times trying to steal in one game?

It was a Friday night at Riverfront Stadium on June 27, 1986, when 2B Robby Thompson of the San Francisco Giants, got too frisky when he thought he could swipe bases at will on the Cincinnati Reds catcher Bo Diaz. Bo had different ideas as he gunned down Thompson in the 4th, after he singled and was thrown out trying to steal.

In the 6th Thompson again singled, to drive in a run to give the Giants a 6-2 lead, but tried to advance himself only to be gunned down by Bo's rifle arm.

In the 9th, with the score tied 6-6, Thompson singled for the third time, and trying to get to second to be in scoring position, was again thrown out at second by Diaz.

Coming up in the 11th inning Thompson was struck out by John Franco, but reached first on the pitch that went beyond the grasp of Diaz. With Thompson looking to steal to set up the winning run, Franco fired to first just after Thompson broke for second, but Thompson wasn't quick enough, as Diaz nailed him at second to retire Thompson for the fourth time trying to steal in one game.

Robby may have been a "Groundbreaker" but at least his Giants came away with a victory in the 12th with 7-6 win.

47. Who was the first player to have 50 consecutive successful stolen bases?

Look to the fleet-footed St. Louis Cardinals leftfielder, Vince "Vincent Van Go" Coleman for that answer. He went from September 18, 1988 to Friday, July 28, 1989 stealing 50 consecutive bases before Montreal Expos catcher Nelson Santovenia took right-hander Pascual Perez's pitch in the top of the 4th and cut Coleman down trying to steal second base with his throw to SS Jeff Huson.

48. Who was the first American LeagueNational League player to steal second, third and home in the same inning?

John "Mugsy" McGraw, the fiery third baseman for the Baltimore Orioles, ran wild on the base paths in the 4th inning down in Baltimore on July 4, 1899 against the Boston Beaneaters. After getting on first he then stole second, third, and followed that by stealing home to be the first, of 50 players, 40 different ones, to steal all three bases in the same inning.

Honus "The Flying Dutchman" Wagner was a close second, for less than a month later, on August 1, 1899, while playing for the Louisville Colonels against the New York Giants, the Hall of Fame shortstop swiped all three bases, also in the 4th inning, and then went on to become the first National League player to accomplish that feat four times in his 21-season career.

49. Who was the first player to be caught stealing twice in the same inning?

Can't be, you say? Tell that to the 19,553 fans who saw it happen at Memorial Stadium on Saturday, June 15, 1974. This is how it went down. The Chicago White Sox came into the bottom of the 9th with a 3-1 lead over the hometown Orioles. Elrod Hendricks came up to pinch-hit for CF Paul Blair and singled. Don Baylor was sent in to run for him, and got caught trying to steal second by a throw from catcher Brian Downing. He got caught stealing, but there was an error by 2B Ron Santo, so there he stayed.

With 3B Brooks Robinson up, Baylor took off for third stealing the base. Presumably Baylor felt frisky with his base running, and as right-hander Cy Acosta delivered his pitch to Orioles catcher Andy Etchebarren, Baylor dashed for home, but was cut down for the second time in the inning, and he can sheepishly say he was the first major league player to be caught stealing twice in the same inning. The Baltimore effort wasn't in vain as they came away with a 4-3 win.

50. Who was the first player to steal home over 50 times in his career?

"The Georgia Peach", Ty Cobb, will not surprise too many being the first player to steal home over 50 times, when he pilfered an even 50 during his 22 years with Detroit, and added another 4 in his last two seasons with the Philadelphia Athletics.

Let the record show that in his 24 seasons Cobb stole a total of 897 bases, 869 with Detroit, and another 28 with the Athletics.

51. Who was the first National LeagueAmerican League player to steal second, third, and home in the same inning?

Letting Dave Fultz get on base was an invitation to a run on that Thursday afternoon of September 4, 1902, when the daring Philadelphia Athletics centerfielder got on first in the 2nd inning against the Detroit Tigers, and proceeded to steal second, then third, and dashed home to score, and became the first player to pilfer all three bases in the same inning. That was just one of the 13 runs Philadelphia scored as they rolled to a 13-4 win at Bennett Park.

52. Who was the first modern-day player to steal second, third, and home in the same inning?

On September 4, 1902, the Philadelphia Athletics centerfielder, Dave Fultz, pilfered those three bases successfully in the 2nd inning of a game against the Detroit Tigers, as Philadelphia rolled to a 13-3 win.

53. Who was the first player to safely get on base over 350 times, through base hits and walks, in one season?

Not many will be surprised to learn that Babe Ruth was that player, when in 1923 "The Sultan of Swat", who played all three outfield positions for the Yankees that season, also banged out 205 hits, and led the American League in walks with 170 to give him a total of 375 times safely getting on base.

54. Who was the first National League player to have over 200 base hits, and walk over 100 times in one season?

Look to "Stan the Man" Musial for this answer, when in 1949, and playing all three outfield positions that season for the St. Louis Cardinals, he collected a league-leading 207 base hits, and was given a free pass 107 times.

Then in 1953, where he played predominantly in left field, he had an even 200 base hits to go along with his league-leading 105 walks, to be the first in the senior circuit to do it in two different seasons.

55. Who was the first major league umpire to work in over 5,000 games?

That umpire would be who else but the "Old Arbitrator", Bill Klem, who began his umpiring career working a game between the Pittsburgh Pirates and the Cincinnati Reds in 1905. He served the National League for 35 years, umpiring in 5,374 games before stepping down from an active role after the 1940 season, and was then named Chief of the National League staff in 1941.

During his career he worked 18 World Series, and called balls and strikes in five no-hitters. Often referred to as "the Dean of Major League Umpires" Klem was the first to use an inside the shirt chest protector which is now standard equipment in baseball.

Elected to the Hall of Fame by the Committee of Baseball Veterans on July 27, 1953, he and American League umpire, Tom Connolly, were the first two umpires to be inducted to the Cooperstown shrine.

Klem died on September 16, 1951, at Doctors Hospital in Miami, at the age of 77, of a heart ailment.

56. Who was the first player to have more runs scored than base hits in a season?

This is an unusual statistic; it's rare, but it's happened more than once. It first occurred in 1930 when Philadelphia Athletics second baseman Max "Camera Eye" Bishop appeared in 130 games, banged out 111 hits, but came around to score 117 runs. The secret was Max's ability to draw the walk, which he did a league-leading 128 times, thereby making his modest .252 batting average escalate his on-base percentage to .426.

Over his 12-year career, 10 in Philadelphia, and 2 with the Red Sox, Bishop kept his hits-to-walks ratio very close, averaging 101 hits and 96 walks per season, so maybe they had a reason to call him, "Camera Eye."

57. Who was the first player to steal home five times in the first inning, and eight times during that season?

We have spoken earlier about his ability to steal without being arrested, and we return to speak again about the base stealing abilities of Ty Cobb. During the 1912 season he had 61 stolen bases, but what was so unusual was his theft of home. He stole home in the first inning of a game on April 20th, May 1st, May 13th, June 21st, and July 1st. He waited until later in the game to steal home on July 4th, August 1st, and September 6th.

58. Who was the first, and only, player to bite himself in the butt sliding into a base and then had to be removed from the game?

I am not putting the reader on. This actually happened to Clarence "Climax" Blethen, a 29-year old right-handed pitcher who made his major league debut with the Boston Red Sox on September 17, 1923. With the

Red Sox 37 games out of first place, "Climax" was called up to get some experience, and was used in five games, and 17.2 innings of relief.

His tenure there was brief, but long enough to relate this unusual story. During the 1923 season, Blethen would place his false teeth in his back pocket whenever he was in a game, which was seldom as he only had six plate appearances all year. In the only time he reached base in his career, in a game against Detroit, he was a runner on first and the next batter slapped a ground ball to short. "Climax" went sliding into second to break up the double play, but failed to remember that his teeth were in his back pocket, and his teeth took a bite out of his posterior so badly that he had to be taken out of the game due to excessive bleeding. "Climax" was "nipped" at second, but no word on the condition of his teeth.

59. Who was the first player to get on base by being hit by a pitch 50 times in one season?

The most important thing for a batter is to get on base, anyway they can, whether by a walk, a base hit, an error, or the most painful way, getting hit by a pitch. Admittedly, Ron Hunt, who played both second and third, made his debut on April 16, 1963 with the New York Mets, before moving on to the Los Angeles Dodgers, San Francisco Giants, Montreal Expos, and St. Louis Cardinals during his 12-year career, and was known for willingly accepting the hard way.

In fact he led the National League in getting hit by a pitch for seven consecutive seasons, (1968-74), hitting his high mark in 1971, when with the Expos, he "took one for the team", the hard way, by being plunked 50 times, double the amount of each of his previous three seasons.

What is interesting to note is that Hunt, during that season, got on base 145 times with base hits, and 58 times by being walked, showing that he got hit by a baseball one out of every three times he hit a baseball successfully. His teammates' pastime in the locker room must have been counting welts from the horsehide hits on his body, for when he played his final game on September 28, 1974 he had 1,429 base hits off opposing pitchers and they had 243 hits on him.

60. Who was the first, and only, player to have over a dozen seasons of swiping 50 or more bases?

If you said Lou Brock you would be very close, off by one season. It was "The Man of Steal", Rickey Henderson, who made his major league debut on June 24, 1979, and went on to exceed the 50 stolen base mark in 1980-86; 88-89, 90-91, 93, and 98.

61. Coming back to stolen bases, who was the first player to steal over 100 bases in consecutive seasons?

We're coming back to that same Rickey Henderson, who stole 130 bases in 1982 and 108 in 1983 while patrolling left field for the Oakland Athletics.

62. Who was the first player to steal the same base twice in the same inning?

We couldn't come this far and not introduce William Herman "Germany" Schaefer, and his antics of September 4, 1908. The multi-positioned Detroit infielder, in a game against the Cleveland Naps, found himself leading off first base with teammate Davey Jones leading off third. The Tigers wanted to pull a double steal that would allow Jones to score while "Germany" was drawing the throw to second. So off to second went Schaefer, only to not draw a throw from Cleveland catcher Nig Clarke, keeping Jones stuck on third.

Unhappy with the result Schaefer took off on the next pitch back to first and stole it safely with still no throw from Clarke. Then Schaefer took off a second time stealing second successfully once again, but this time allowing Jones to score. That gave Schaefer the distinction of being the first player to steal three bases, the same one twice, all in the same inning.

E. POWER AND SPEED

1. Who was the first, and only, player in major league history to win four home run titles and four stolen base titles?

I would have to say that the demonstration of power and speed doesn't become more evident than when you win four home run titles and four stolen base titles in your career like New York/San Francisco Giants centerfielder Willie Mays did in winning the home run title in 1955 with 51, then 49 in 1962, 47 in 1964 and 52 in 1965.

He then combined that with his speed and running agility when he led the National League in stolen bases with 40 in 1956, 38 in 1957, 31 in 1958, and 21 in 1959.

2. Who was the first player to have 200 home runs and 500 stolen bases?

"Little Joe" Morgan, the Cincinnati Reds second baseman on the "Big Red Machine," belted his 200th career home run on August 27, 1978 to become the first player to have 200 home runs and 500 stolen bases.

3. Who was the first major leaguer to hit over 50 doubles and steal over 50 bases in the same season?

Centerfielder, and Hall of Fame resident, Tris "The Grey Eagle" Speaker of the Boston Red Sox had 53 doubles and stole 52 bases in the 1912 season.

4. Staying with the thought expressed in the above item who, in 1998, became the first National League player to exceed 50 doubles and stolen bases in a single season?

It took until the 1998 season for the first, and only, National Leaguer to exceed 50 doubles and 50 stolen bases when Craig Biggio, the second baseman of the Houston Astros, led the senior circuit with 51 doubles and added on 50 stolen bases to his season's stats.

5. Who was the first player to lead his league in home runs and stolen bases in the same season?

You will have to take yourself back over 100 years, to 1903, to find 24-year old leftfielder Jimmy Sheckard of the Brooklyn Superbas leading the National League that year with 9 home runs and swiping 67 bases to become the first modern day power and speed champion.

6. Who was the first player to combine power and speed and create the 30/30 Club? (i.e. 30 home runs and 30 stolen bases in the same season)

The 30/30 Club was created, and its first member brought on in 1922, when Ken Williams, the leftfielder of the St. Louis Browns, finished his season with 39 home runs and drove in 155 runs, both of which led the American League, and had 37 stolen bases.

Interestingly once he became the charter member of the 30/30 Club he never repeated his entry credentials.

At this writing there are 10 American League and 24 National League members of the club.

7. Who was the first player after joining the 30/30 Club to renew his membership twice in both the National and American Leagues?

Bobby Bonds, the father of Barry Bonds, and also a right fielder for the San Francisco Giants, joined the 30/30 Club in 1969 with 32 home runs and 45 stolen bases. He renewed his membership in 1973 with 39 home runs and 43 stolen bases.

Moving over to the American League with the New York Yankees he became a member in the American League with 32 home runs and 30 stolen bases in 1975. He then moved out to California with the Angels in 1977, and there renewed his American League membership with a 37 home run, 41 stolen base season.

If there had been a third major league Bonds would have been a member there as well.

8. Who was the first, and only, player to collect 3,000 hits, 600 home runs, 100 triples, have 300 stolen bases, and bat over .300?

Willie Mays, the Hall of Fame centerfielder of the New York/San Francisco Giants, was the first, and only, player to reach the plateau of 3,000 base hits, 600 home runs, 100 triples, and 300 stolen bases. He closed out the last year and a half of his 22-year career with the New York Mets, with 3,283 hits, 660 home runs, 140 triples, and 338 stolen bases and a batting average of .302.

9. Who was the first player to hit 500 home runs and steal 500 bases?

That combination of power and speed belongs to Barry Bonds, the left-fielder of the San Francisco Giants, when on Monday, June 23, 2003, at

Pacific Bell Park, he stole his 500th base before 42,474 of his hometown fans after having gone well over 500 home runs in 2003.

10. Who was the first American League player to lead his league in home runs and stolen bases in the same season?

Ty Cobb, the Detroit Tigers centerfielder and hitter supreme, not only led the American League in home runs with 9, but stolen bases with 76 in that 1909 season to be the first in the American League to capture both titles in the same season.

While talking about leading your league in offensive categories let's not fail to mention that during that 1909 season he also led in runs scored with 116, runs batted in with 107, and in hits with 216, which gave him the batting title as well with a .377 average.

11. Who was the founder of the 40/40 Club?

Well I am not sure you can designate him as the founder, but he was the first player to have the credentials for entry into the club. We are speaking of the Oakland Athletics right fielder Jose Canseco, who hit 42 home runs and stole 40 bases in the 1966 season.

12. Who was the first player in the senior circuit to join the 40/40 Club?

The first National League player to reach the plateau of 40/40 was the San Francisco Giants leftfielder, Barry Bonds in 1996, when he hit 42 home runs and stole 40 bases.

13. To raise the exclusive 30/30 or 40/40 Club to even greater heights who were the first two players in each league to be members of an even more exclusive club, the 40/40/150 Club?

Raising the bar just a bit higher there are just two players in each league, at this writing, who are exclusive members of the 40/40/150 Club.

In the American League Jose Canseco had 158 ribbies in 1988 when he had 42 home runs and 40 stolen bases so he set the stage for this newly elevated level.

Joining him later was Alex Rodriguez in 1998 when he played shortstop with the Seattle Mariners, and put up home run numbers of 42, with 46 stolen bases, and 161 runs batted in.

Over in the National League Alfonso Soriano, the Washington Nationals leftfielder, joined Barry Bonds' 1996 numbers of 42/40/158 with his own of 46/41/159 in 2006.

14. Who was the first catcher to have twenty stolen bases, and hit twenty home runs in the same season?

In 1999, his ninth big league season, Texas Rangers catcher Ivan "Pudge" Rodriguez became the first catcher to ever hit twenty or more home runs (35), and steal over 20 bases (25) as he rolled to a 199-hit, 113 RBI , .332 season.

15. Who was the first player to have 20 stolen bases, 20 doubles, 20 triples, and 20 home runs in a single season?

Back in 1911 the Chicago Cubs had a right-fielder by the name of Frank "Wildfire" Schulte who was in his eighth year of patrolling the outfield of West Side Park when he combined power and speed that season to become the first player in history to record 20 doubles, triples, home runs and stolen bases in the same season.

Among his 173 base hits that year were 30 doubles, 21 triples, a league-leading 21 home runs, and 23 stolen bases, which earned him the National League's Most Valuable Player Award.

16. Who was the first player to have at least 200 base hits, 30 doubles, 20 triples, 25 home runs, and 25 stolen bases in the same season?

Just look down to the "City of Brotherly Love" and you will find Philadelphia Phillies shortstop, Jimmy "J-Roll" Rollins, there with those figures as his stat sheet for the 2007 season. It shows 212 base hits, 38 doubles, 20 triples, 30 home runs, and 41 stolen bases making him the first player to reach that plateau and a "Groundbreaker".

17. Who was the first player to hit 30 home runs, and steal 40 bases in one season?

Willie Mays became a multiple "Groundbreaker" after the 1956 season when he hit 36 home runs, and led the National League in stolen bases with 40.

18. Who was the first player to have a 40-home run and 50-stolen-base season during his career?

This may come as a surprise to some, but not to Chicago Cubs fans as one of their own, second baseman Ryne "Ryno" Sandberg, who made his debut with the Philadelphia Phillies on September 2, 1981, and was traded during the off season, on January 27, 1982, along with Larry Bowa to the Chicago Cubs for Ivan de Jesus, stole 54 bases in 1985, and came back to lead the National League in home runs with 40 in 1990, to become the first to display those power and speed numbers during his 16-year career where he racked up 9 Gold Gloves, 9 All-Star nominations, and a MVP Award in 1984, before he played his final game on September 28, 1997. He was elected to the Hall of Fame in 2005.

19. Who was the first second baseman in major league history to hit 30 home runs and steal 30 bases in a season?

Back in 2002 when the New York Yankees second baseman, Alfonso Soriano, was named to the All-Star team, and came in third in the MVP voting, there was good reason for he led the American League in five categories such as base hits with 209, and runs scored with 128, but more importantly in stolen bases with 41. When added to his 39 home runs he became the first second-sacker in major league history to exceed 30 in both power and speed categories.

20. Who was the first player to finish his career with 3,000 base hits and 500 stolen bases?

John Peter Wagner, not known by his given name, but more commonly referred to as "Honus," made his major league debut with the Louisville Colonels as a right-fielder on July 19, 1897. He spent the next three years with them until he was involved a large multi-player trade with the Pittsburgh Pirates on December 8, 1899.

Upon finishing his 21-year career with Pittsburgh, on September 17, 1917, he had amassed 3,420 base hits, and stolen 723 bases to become the first player to reach that 3,000-500 plateau. "The Flying Dutchman" became a "Groundbreaker, but more importantly became a member of the Hall of Fame in 1936.

21. Who was the first switch-hitter to have 300 home runs and 300 stolen bases?

With the power and speed of this switch-hitter it was not surprising when on Friday, June 15, 2012, Carlos Beltran, before a crowd of 42,001 Redbird fans, in the 2nd inning out in Busch Stadium, singled to right field off Kansas City right-hander Vin Mazzaro, and then took off for second base beating the throw from catcher Brayan Pena for his 7th stolen base of the season and 300th of his career. That went along with his already 300 home runs to make him the first switch-hitter to reach that plateau.

F. THE FRESHMAN CLASS

1. When the Rookie of the Year Award was started in 1947 who was the first player to be named?

When the first Rookie of the Year Award was established in 1947 the first recipient was first baseman Jackie Robinson of the Brooklyn Dodgers. In 151 games he had 701 at bats, collecting 175 hits including 12 home runs, and drove in 48 runs He led the National League in stolen bases with 29 and had a .297 batting average. He was elected to the Hall of Fame in 1962.

2. Throughout history there have been seven catchers named Rookie of the Year. Who was the first?

The first catcher to be named Rookie of the Year was Cincinnati Reds' Johnny Bench in 1968. In his 154 games he had 155 base hits, 15 home runs, drove in 82 runs with a .275 batting average. He was elected to the Hall of Fame in 1989.

3. Who was the first National League catcher to catch 100 games as a rookie?

Twenty-eight year old Toby Atwell caught 101 games as a rookie with the Chicago Cubs in 1952 handling 513 chances, 451 put outs and committing 12 errors for a .977 fielding average.

4. Who was the first unanimous winner of the Rookie of the Year Award in the American League?

On November 21, 1972 Carlton "Pudge" Fisk, the Boston Red Sox catcher, was the first unanimously named American League Rookie of the Year. With these statistics it would be hard to deny him the honor. He played in 131 games, had 134 hits, led the league in triples with 9, belted 22 home runs and had 61 runs batted in to go along with his .293 batting average.

5. Who was the first player to win the Rookie of the Year Award and the Most Valuable Player Award in the same year?

Centerfielder Fred Lynn, of the Boston Red Sox, was the first player to win both awards in the same season when he did it in 1975. The reason became obvious when his numbers showed him playing in 145 games, with 528 at bats, leading the league in runs scored with 103, and doubles with

47. He hit 21 home runs, drove in 105 runs, batted .331 and led the American League in slugging percentage with .566.

6. Who was the first rookie to record four base hits in one World Series game?

Freddie Lindstrom, rookie third baseman of the New York Giants, had four hits off Walter Johnson of the Washington Senators in Game 5 of the 1924 World Series. Lindstrom finished the seven game series with a .333 batting average and was elected to the Hall of Fame in 1976.

7. Who was the first player to hit 40 or more home runs in his rookie season?

The Oakland Athletics first baseman, Mark "Big Mac" McGwire, led the American League in home runs in his rookie year with 49. He also drove in 118 runs and finished the season with a slugging percentage of .618.

8. Who was the first, and only, rookie to hit four grand slam home runs in a single season?

Alexei "The Cuban Missile" Ramirez, the second baseman of the 2008 Chicago White Sox, had quite a freshman season as he was the first rookie to hit four grand slam home runs in a single season. His totals at the end of 2008 showed 21 home runs, 77 runs batted in 480 at bats for a .290 batting average.

9. Who was the first, and only, player to steal over 100 bases in his rookie season?

Leftfielder Vince "Van Go" Coleman, of the St. Louis Cardinals, led the National League in stolen bases with 110 in his rookie season of 1985. Just to show it was no fluke he went on to steal 107 and 109 in 1986-1987 and continued to lead the National League in stolen bases for the first six years he was in the league.

10. Who was the first American League rookie to strike out seven batters in a row in his initial major league start?

On September 1, 1978 right-hander Sammy Stewart, making his major league debut with the Baltimore Orioles, struck out all three Chicago White Sox batters in the 2nd and 3rd innings and one more in the top of the 4th to set a major league record for rookies. He went on to notch his first victory in a 9-3 win over the Pale Hose.

11. Who was the first American League rookie to strike out four batters in one inning?

It happened in the 9th inning, against the Detroit Tigers, on May 14, 1994, when rookie Paul Shuey, in his second major league appearance for the Cleveland Indians, struck out Chad Kreuter, Chris Gomez, then Travis Fryman swinging (but reached first base on the wild pitch), and finally Cecil Fielder for the fourth strikeout of the inning.

12. Who was the first rookie to win a batting title?

It happened in Minnesota in 1964 when Twins rookie right fielder Tony Oliva took the American League batting title with a .323 batting average. He also led the league in runs scored with 109, base hits with 217, and doubles with 43.

Although Oliva played in nine games in 1962, and seven in 1963 he appeared in too few not to be considered a rookie in 1964.

13. Who was the first, of the ten, third basemen to have won the Rookie of the Year Award?

Gil McDougald, of the New York Yankees, who primarily played third base in his rookie year in 1951, won the Rookie of the Year Award that year with his .306 batting average, 123 base hits, 14 home runs and 63 runs batted in.

14. Who was the first American League player to hit a home run in his first major league at bat?

Earl Averill, the Cleveland Indian's centerfielder, in his first major league at bat, hit an 0-2 pitch off Detroit Tigers' southpaw Earl Whitehill, on Opening Day, April 16, 1929 as the Indians won an 11-inning game 5-4.

15. Who was the first National League player to hit a home run in his first major league at bat?

This had to be the highlight of Joe Harrington's brief career. It happened on September 10, 1895 when the Boston Beaneaters second baseman hit a home run in his first time at bat in the major leagues. He went on to hit another that year and drive in 13 runs. Switching to third base in 1896 he managed one more home run in his final 54 games and ended his major league career with a total of three. That first one, though, made history.

16. Who was the first player to win the Rookie of the Year Award, and then follow that up the next year by winning the Most Valuable

Player Award?

That example of increased proficiency went to Cal Ripken Jr., the Baltimore Orioles shortstop, when in 1982 he won the Rookie of the Year Award by batting .264, hitting 32 doubles, 5 triples, 28 home runs, scoring 90 runs and batting in 93.

The following year he won the American League MVP Award with a .318 batting average, leading the league with 663 at-bats, in hits with 211, in doubles with 47, and in runs scored with 121. He also had 27 home runs that helped to drive in his 102 runs.

17. Who was the first rookie to win the Cy Young Award?

Fernando Valenzuela, the Mexican southpaw with the Los Angeles Dodgers, in his first full season on the mound in 1981, made the most of it. He led the National League in games started with 25, games completed with 11, in shutouts with 8, innings pitched with 192.1, and strikeouts with 180, compiling a 13-7 record to go along with his .248 Era.

Those statistics for his rookie season not only made him a shoo-in for the Rookie of the Year Award, but the coveted Cy Young Award as well, making Fernando the first rookie to win the Cy Young Award.

18. Who was the first rookie to hit a grand slam home run in a World Series?

We'll go back to Game 5 on October 9th of the 1951 World Series. In the top of the 3rd inning New York Yankees rookie third baseman, Gil McDougald, came to bat with the bases loaded facing New York Giants right-handed ace Larry Jansen with the game tied at 1-1.

He hammered Jansen's pitch into the left field stands of the Polo Grounds to break the tie and send the Yankees, and their southpaw Eddie Lopat, on their way to a lopsided 13-1 victory before 47,530 fans.

It was only the third grand slam home run, and the first by a rookie, in World Series history. Elmer Smith hit one for Cleveland in 1920 and Tony Lazzeri hit one in 1936 for the Yankees.

19. Who was the first player, in his rookie season, to have over a 30-game hitting streak?

In 1987 Benito Santiago, the San Diego Padres catcher, had an outstanding rookie year batting .300 with 164 hits, driving in 79 runs, and setting a record for a rookie by being the first to have a base hit in over 30 consecutive games, when he hit safely in 34 straight games, which to this day is the longest hitting streak by a catcher in major league history. That led him to be unanimously elected as the Rookie of the Year in '87.

20. Who was the first player to have over 200 hits in his rookie season?

The first player to have over 200 base hits in his rookie season was Jimmy "Buttons" Williams who played third base for the Pittsburgh Pirates in 1899, banging out 219 base hits including 28 doubles, a league leading 27 triples, and 9 home runs. He played the last nine of his eleven years as a second baseman and never duplicated his 200-hit season again.

21. Who was the first player to have over 700 at bats in his rookie season?

In the 1984 season Juan Samuel, the Philadelphia Phillies second baseman, led the National League, and became the first rookie to have 700 at bats when he had 701 and collected 191 base hits, led the league with 19 triples, but also led with 168 strikeouts.

22. Who was the first player to hit 35 or more home runs in his rookie season?

Back in 1930, rookie leftfielder Wally Berger of the Boston Braves amazed the batting world by hitting 38 home runs in his rookie year, the most ever hit by a player in his first year. He added to his batting prowess by driving in 119 runs with a .310 batting average.

It wasn't until 57 years later, in 1987, when rookie first baseman Mark McGwire of the Oakland Athletics came along and shattered that record by hitting 49 home runs, batting in 118 runs, and compiling a league leading .618 slugging average.

23. Who was the first player to hit a home run in his first two major league at bats?

There have been over 100 players who have hit a home run in their first major league at bat, but only one, rookie leftfielder Bob Nieman of the St. Louis Browns, hit one in each of his first two major league at bats. It happened on September 14, 1951, and Boston Red Sox southpaw Maurice "Mickey" McDermott was the victim. It didn't affect the outcome as Boston went on to win 9-6.

Nieman had only those two home runs that 1951 season, but ended up with 125 over his 12-year career.

24. Who was the first American League player to pinch-hit a home run

in his first major league at bat?

The first American League rookie to be called upon to pinch-hit, and come through with a home run in his first major league at bat, was Ace Parker of the Philadelphia Athletics in the 9th inning, on April 30, 1937, off Wes Ferrell of the Boston Red Sox. It had no impact on the game for Ferrell coasted to a 15-5 victory. Parker hit one more home run that season, but was better known for his football abilities where he ended up enshrined in the Football Hall of Fame.

25. Who was the first National League player, and pitcher, to hit a grand slam home run in his first major league at bat?

Not only did this player hit a grand slam home run in his first major league at bat, but this right-hander, making his first mound appearance, went on to pitch and win his game for the Philadelphia Phillies 13-4 over the New York Giants.

We are talking about "Frosty Bill" Duggleby, who hammered a pitch by New York Giants' southpaw Cy Seymour with the bases full, on April 21, 1898, to become the first player, and first pitcher, to hit a grand slam home run in his initial major league appearance at the plate.

26. Who was the first rookie to strike out eleven batters, and have two base hits in his major league debut?

It was a much heralded debut for right-hander Matt Harvey of the New York Mets when they brought him up from Buffalo to hopefully fit into their decimated rotation on July 26. 2012.

The right-hander didn't disappoint as he pitched his first major league game before a crowd of 22,010 at Chase Field, threw 106 pitches, 65 for strikes and fanned eleven Diamondbacks, and gave up three walks and three hits before he was relieved in the bottom of the 6th with a 3-0 lead.

He also displayed some prowess with the lumber as he hit a line drive double in his first big league at bat in the 2nd inning off southpaw Wade Wiley and followed that with a single in the 4th to be the first rookie to strike out eleven batters and pick up a pair of hits in his introduction to the big leagues. Four relief pitchers finished off the remaining 11 Arizona batters as the Mets went on to defeat the Diamondbacks, 3-1.

27. Who was the first player to lead the American League in home runs as a rookie?

Although Al "Flip" Rosen had played in just a few games in 1947-49 he wasn't a qualified rookie until the 1950 season when the third baseman played in 155 games with the Cleveland Indians, and his power and batting ability became apparent. That year he hit .287, scored 100 runs, drove in 116, and led the American League with 37 home runs, to become the first rookie to lead in that department.

28. Who was the first rookie pitcher to strike out as many batters in a game as years he was alive?

The pitcher we are talking about is "Rapid Robert" Feller, a 17-year old Cleveland Indians fire-baller who, on September 13, 1936, his rookie year, struck out 17 Philadelphia Athletics on his way to a 2-hit, 2 walk, 5-2 victory over 18-year old Randy Gumpert. Feller had 76 strikeouts in 62 innings of work that freshman season.

Interesting to note that the combined age of those two young pitchers in that first game of the doubleheader was just 35.

29. Who was the first player to drive in 100 runs in his rookie season?

We're declaring a tie in this category when in the 1924 season "Bucket-foot Al" Simmons, the Philadelphia Athletics centerfielder, and future Hall of Fame resident, drove in 102 runs as a rookie, and in the National League Glenn "Buckshot" Wright, the Pittsburgh Pirate shortstop, drove in 111 runs as a rookie in that season to become the first players to drive in over 100 runs in their rookie seasons.

30. Who was the first pitcher to win the Rookie of the Year Award?

The hard throwing right-hander, Don Newcombe, of the Brooklyn Dodgers compiled a 17-8, 3.17 ERA with 149 strikeouts in his rookie year in 1949.

31. Who was the first, and only, modern day pitcher to pitch a no-hitter in his first major league start?

Alva "BoBo" Holloman, the St. Louis Browns right-hander, threw a no-hitter in his first major league start on a rainy night in Sportsman's Park, St. Louis, on May 6, 1953, before a home town crowd of only 2,473, defeating the Philadelphia Athletics 6-0 in the only complete game of his abbreviated ten game 3-7, major league career. He did, however, get two hits and bat in three runs on that eventful eve.

32. Who was the first American League Player to win the Rookie of the Year Award?

In 1949, leftfielder Roy Sievers of the St. Louis Browns, played in 140 games, had a .306 batting average on 144 hits, 16 home runs and drove in 91 runs. That was enough for him to be named the first American League Rookie of the Year.

33. Who was the first modern day major league player to hit .400 in his rookie season?

It shouldn't be a surprise to learn that one of the greatest hitters in baseball history, "Shoeless Joe" Jackson, hit .408 in his rookie season with the Chicago White Sox in 1911. He played in 147 games, had 233 hits including 45 doubles, 19 triples, 41 stolen bases, 7 home runs and drove in 83 runs.

34. Who was the first rookie to pitch a no-hitter?

Nick Maddox, a 20-year old right-hander, in only his third game for the Pittsburgh Pirates, no-hit the Brooklyn Superbas (Dodgers) on September 20, 1907, winning 2-1, with all three runs in the game unearned. Brooklyn's Elmer Stricklett gave up only two hits in his losing cause.

Maddox went on to close out his season with a 5-1 record and a 0.83 Era.

35. Who was the first pitcher in major league history to serve up a game-losing walk-off home run to the first batter he faced in his major league career?

Welcome to the Big Time, "J.J.", was the sound heard when John "J.J." Trujillo, the 26-year old rookie right-hander of the San Diego Padres, came on in relief of right-hander Steve Reed in the top of the 10th inning, on June 11, 2002 at Camden Yards, Baltimore, and served up the first pitch of his major league career, to Tony Batista, the Baltimore Orioles' third baseman. Tony, blasted "J.J.'s" 2-2 pitch for his 16th home run of the season deep into the left field stands for a walk off solo home run giving the Orioles a 6-5 win in this inter-league game, and Trujillo the dubious distinction of being the first pitcher in history to give up a game-losing walk off home run to the first batter he faced in his big league career.

36. Who was the first rookie to lead the American League in runs batted in?

This player was signed as an amateur free agent by the Boston Red Sox in 1936, and made his major league debut on April 20, 1939. He had quite a rookie season batting .327 with 185 hits, 107 walks, scored 131 runs and became the first rookie to lead the American League in runs batted in when he drove 145 players home. He had many colorful nicknames given him, but if it had been up to me I would have given Ted Williams the sobriquet of "the chauffeur" because he drove so many fellow players home, 1,839, during his 19-year career.

37. Who was the first rookie to strike out six consecutive batters in his first major start?

The Brooklyn Dodgers called up southpaw Karl Spooner from their Fort Worth affiliate, and sent him out to pitch against the hated New York Giants, on September 22, 1954. All the rookie did in his introduction to the big leagues was to pitch a 3-0 shutout, striking out 15 Giants, a new major league rookie record. Six of those fanned Giants were in consecutive innings, the 6th and 7th, to put him in the Groundbreakers record book.

38. Keeping with the previous item, we now ask, who was the first pitcher to consecutively strike out the first six batters he faced in his major league pitching debut?

This effort didn't happen to start the game on April 12, 1962 against the Cincinnati Reds, but it did happen when the Los Angeles Dodgers starting pitcher Stan Williams, was lifted in the 2nd inning after allowing four runs, which brought on southpaw Pete Richert out of the bullpen for his major league debut. With two outs he got Vada Pinson to strike out swinging to end the inning.

Richert went on to strike out the next five Cincinnati Reds he faced; including four straight on swinging strikes in the 3rd inning to Frank Robinson, Gordy Coleman, which, because of a passed ball, allowed the Reds' first baseman to reach first base, then Wally Post and Johnny Edwards went down swinging to end the 3rd inning. In the top of the 4th 3B Tommy Harper took a third strike for the first out allowing Pete Richert to be the first pitcher to strike out the first six batters he faced in his major league debut and the first rookie to strike out four batters in one inning in his first start.

39. Who was the first pitcher to go 12-0 in his first dozen decisions on the mound?

George "Hooks" Wiltse, the New York Giants southpaw, made his major league debut on April 21, 1904, but didn't get his first starting assignment until May 29th, against the Brooklyn Superbas.

He went the rest of the summer pitching and winning games, until he was finally defeated by the Cincinnati Reds, on September 2nd, 7-3. That loss was his first, and made him the first pitcher to go 12-0 in his first dozen decisions, having him make one of the strongest first impressions in major league history. Wiltse finished off his rookie season with a 13-3 record and a 2.84 Era.

40. Who was the first rookie pitcher to voluntarily end his major league career after winning twenty games in his first season?

Henry Martin Schmidt, born on June 26, 1873, in Brownsville, Texas, was a 30-year old right-handed pitcher who made his major league debut on April 17, 1903, with the Brooklyn Superbas. He had a fine freshman season, starting 36 games and finishing 29, with five shut outs over 301 innings while striking out 96 for a 22-13 won-lost, 3.83 Era.

He rejected his 1904 contract saying he didn't like playing in the East, and would not return to the majors with the Superbas. He finished his pitching career on the Pacific Coast after playing only one year in the major leagues.

41. Who was the first player, in his major league debut, to create six outs and an error in three plate appearances?

The major league debut for Atlanta Braves shortstop Leo Foster, on Friday, July 9, 1971, at Three Rivers Stadium, was not pretty.

In the bottom of the 1st inning the leadoff batter, Pirates 2B Dave Cash hit a ground ball to Foster which, in his first chance, he turned into an error.

Then in his first major league at-bat, against right-hander Nelson Briles, in the 3rd inning, he flied out to centerfield. He came up to bat in the 5th inning and hit into a double play. Returning for his third and last at bat, in the 7th inning, he found singles by Hal King and Sonny Jackson putting runners on first and second. Poor Leo then emptied the bases, and ended the inning, by hitting into a triple play.

In the box score it showed Foster going 0 for 3, with an error and creating six outs, as the Pirates rolled to an 11-2 win.

So much for getting off to a fast start in your major league career. Foster did go on to spend three years in Atlanta before his last two with the Mets.

42. Who was the first player, in the first and only, major league game of his career, to strikeout, hit into a double play, and a triple play?

Up for "a cup of coffee" is a euphemism for an extremely short major league career, and Ron Wright exemplified that when he made his major league debut on Sunday, April 14, 2002. The Atlanta Braves drafted him in the 7th round of the 1994 amateur draft. He bounced around until the Mariners signed him on November 27, 2001.

The following season, in his first experience in the major leagues, Wright, penciled in as the designated hitter for Seattle, against the Texas Rangers in The Ballpark in Arlington, struck out looking on a pitch from Kenny Rogers in the 2nd inning.

Coming up in the 4th, after Ruben Sierra had doubled to left, and John Olerud singled Sierra to third base, Wright hit back to Rogers who threw to SS Alex Rodriguez for a force out on Olerud at second, and he threw home to catcher Bill Haselman to for the second out, who then threw down to 3B which went to Rogers covering, and he in turn threw to 2B Mike Young nailing Wright going into second for the third out, and a triple play was recorded. For those of you keeping score at home it went 1-6-2-5-1-4.

We now move to the 6th inning, and after Sierra and Olerud singled, that brought up Wright, who was responsible for four outs in two at-bats, and he hit a ground ball to SS Rodriguez who flipped to Young at second and his relay to 1B Rafael Palmeiro completed the double play.

In the top of the 7th with the Mariners down 5-1, manager Lou Piniella had seen enough of Wright doing wrong and had Mark McLemore pinch hit for him. McLemore went down swinging, and came back in the 8th and struck out for the second time. Even though Seattle ended up winning, 9-7, the combined DH slot that day showed three strikeouts, a double play, and a triple play, for a total of eight outs in five at bats.

That day, and the actions that were taken, was the final extent of Wright's DH major league career.

43. Who was the first rookie pitcher to make his debut, and start his

first game, not retire a batter, and never play in the majors again?

This is a sad tale about a rookie right-hander by the name of Henry Heitmann who, was stationed at the Brooklyn Navy Yard, but got the nod from the Brooklyn Robins skipper, Wilbert Robinson, to start the second game of a double-header at Ebbets Field against the last place St. Louis Cardinals on Saturday, July 27, 1918.

He was greeted by his first batter, CF Cliff Heathcliffe, with a single, then 2B Bob Fisher tripled, followed by another single by 1B Gene Paulette, and then another triple, this by SS Rogers Hornsby. That was all for Heitmann as right-hander "Ol' Stubblebeard" Burleigh Grimes came on, gave up a fifth run in that 1st inning, and then went on to pitch six innings giving up 10-hits and 8 runs as the Cardinals waltzed away with a 26-hit, 22-7 win.

Poor Harry's career came to a sudden stop after just four batters as his line score showed four hits, four earned runs, an 0-1 record, and a 108.00 Era.

44. Who was the first $100,000 minor league player to make his major league debut?

William "Willie" Kamm, after being purchased from the San Francisco Seals for $100,000, made his debut at third base with the Chicago White Sox on April 18, 1923 at Dunn Field in a 6-5 loss to the Cleveland Indians. Willie got himself a double and handled two chances flawlessly at third base and joined the Groundbreakers as the first $100,000 purchase of a minor leaguer in the major leagues. Willie ended his 13-year career with the Indians on May 21, 1935 with a career .281 batting average.

45. Who was the first player to hit an inside-the-park home run in his first official major league at bat?

There could be no greater thrill for a player in his first official major league at bat than to face a future Hall of Fame pitcher, and take him downtown. It happened to shortstop Johnnie LeMaster of the San Francisco Giants, when he came to bat in the bottom of the 4th inning, with one out, at Candlestick Park on September 2, 1975, and saw 1B Willie Montanez on second, via a double, and faced right-hander Don Sutton of the Los Angeles Dodgers.

LeMaster nailed Sutton's pitch out to the farthest section of Candlestick, and before it could be chased down and returned to the infield

LeMaster had scored an inside-the-park home run to help the Giants to a 7-3 victory. LeMaster had become a "Groundbreaker" before his first major league game was over by being the first player to hit an inside-the-park home run in his first major league at bat.

46. Who was the first pitcher to pitch a no-hitter in his first major league game?

Let's go back to pre-modern day baseball, to October 15, 1892, when Charles "Bumpus" Jones, a right-handed pitcher with the Cincinnati Reds took the mound, in the last game of the season, against the Pittsburgh Pirates, in his very first major league game.

"Bumpus was very impressive allowing for the fact that he gave up four walks, and his teammates gave up an error, which cost him a shutout, but "Bumpus, who fanned three, went on to a 7-1 win, pitching a no-hitter in the process, to join the "Groundbreakers" as the first pitcher to pitch a no-hitter in his first major league game.

Moving on to the New York Giants, "Bumpus" finished his brief, eight career appearances, on July 14, 1883 with a 2-4, .799 Era. record. But let's face it, he did what no one before or since has ever done. He pitched a no-hitter in his first major league game. Welcome to the "Groundbreakers."

47. Who was the first rookie to strikeout four batters in one inning in his major league debut?

This took place on April 12, 1962 when rookie southpaw Pete Richert came on in relief of right-hander Stan "Big Daddy" Williams, who had gone just 1.2 innings against the Cincinnati Reds out in Dodgers Stadium.

In the 3rd inning Richert struck out RF Frank Robinson, 1B Gordy Coleman (who reached base on a John Roseboro passed ball), LF Wally Post and finally catcher Johnny Edwards to become the first rookie to strike out four batters in one inning in his big league debut.

Richert went on to pitch 3.1 innings in relief, striking out seven while allowing no hits or runs on his way to an 11-7 Dodgers win.

48. Who was the first player to make five outs in two at bats in his major league debut?

July 9, 1971, at Three Rivers Stadium, should have been a memorable day for Atlanta Braves shortstop Leo Foster, in the positive sense, for it was the date of his major league debut. That wasn't the case, however, as he made an error, on his first chance, in the 1st inning, on Pittsburgh Pirates 2B Dave Cash's ground ball.

After flying out to centerfield in his first at bat, Foster came up in the 5th inning following CF Sonny Jackson's single, and hit into a double play, SS Gene Alley to 2B Dave Cash to 1B Bob Robertson.

In the 7th inning after catcher Hal King, and Sonny Jackson singled, Foster hit a shot to 3B Richie Hebner who went around the horn to Dave Cash and Bob Robertson for a triple play, and poor Leo just became the first player to make five outs in two at bats in his major league debut. His play didn't affect the game as Pittsburgh rolled to an 11-2 win.

49. Who was the first rookie to lose 19 straight games?

Right-hander Bob Groom, who would later go on to pitch a no-hitter for the St. Louis Browns, made his major league debut on Tuesday, April 13, 1909, for the Washington Senators, a game in which Washington was shutout 5-0, and things seemed to go downhill from there.

Groom went on to absorb 19 straight losses that season to lead the league in that category with a 7-26 record, and became the first freshman to lose that many straight games in his initial season in the big leagues.

50. Who was the first, and only, player to have five singles in his major league debut?

Take yourself back to Griffith Stadium, for a Tuesday afternoon game played before just 1,000 fans on May 16, 1933 when the Washington Senators rookie third baseman Cecil Travis made his major league debut against the Cleveland Indians not realizing that he would be quickly propelled into being a "Groundbreaker."

The 19 year-old southpaw swinging Travis faced five Indians' pitchers in that 12-inning, 11-10 Washington win, and ended his day with a .714 batting average to start his big league career by having five singles in his seven at bats, and scoring three runs in his major league debut to be the first rookie to have such a day at the plate.

51. Who was the first Rookie-of-the-Year Award winner to win the Most Valuable Player Award?

Jackie Robinson, the Brooklyn Dodgers first baseman won the Rookie-of-the-Year Award in 1947 and came back, as a second baseman, to win the Most Valuable Player Award two years later in 1949.

52. Who was the first Rookie-of-the-Year Award winner to win the Cy Young Award?

Don Newcombe, the big hard-throwing right-hander with the Brooklyn Dodgers won the Rookie-of-the-Year Award in 1949 with a 17-8, 3.17 Era, and went on to win the Cy Young Award in 1956 with a 27-7, 3.06 Era.

53. Who was the first modern day pitcher to pitch a shutout and also hit a home run in his major league debut?

On the evening of Thursday, August 23, 2001, Jason Jennings, the 22-year old rookie right-hander of the Colorado Rockies, made his major league debut at Shea Stadium against the New York Mets.

His debut was nearly perfect as he set down the Mets on five hits, 10-0, struck out eight, and went 3-for-5 at the plate including a 9th inning solo home run off Mets right-hander Donne Wall.

54. Who was the first and only player to win the batting title in his first two seasons?

Tony Oliva, the Minnesota Twins right fielder, made his major league debut on September 9, 1962, but played in only nine games that year and in just seven in 1963. So for the 1964 season he was still considered a rookie, but his bat proved otherwise as he led the American League, not only in batting with a .323 average, but also led in runs with 109, hits with 217, doubles with 43, and in total bases with 374, obviously making him the Rookie of the Year. He continued his hitting by capturing the batting title in 1965 with a .321 average making him the first player to capture two batting titles in his first two full seasons.

55. Who was the first player, making his first major league plate appearance, to be beaned, and to never get a chance to swing a bat in the major leagues?

This tragic occurrence happened in Dolphins Stadium on Saturday, July 9, 2005, before a hushed crowd of 22,863, when rookie outfielder, Adam Greenberg was sent up to pinch-hit for the pitcher, Chicago Cubs southpaw, Will Ohman, with no outs in the 9th inning, and the Cubbies up, 4-2.

On the first pitch he sees from Marlins southpaw, Valerio de los Santos, the pitch hits Greenberg in the head. Down he goes, and is carried off the field, to be replaced by Carlos Zambrano as a pinch-runner, but Greenberg is placed on the disabled list, then sent to the minor leagues, and finally released in November of that year. He will go in the record books, as appearing in a major league game, but there will be AB 1, and then 00000 alongside his career stats. He was the first player to step into the batter's box, never swing, and be carried off the field in his major league debut.

56. Who was the first player to hit a home run in his first major league at bat?

It was on Saturday, April 16, 1887, when Mike Griffin, the centerfielder of the Baltimore Orioles steeped up to the plate in the 1st inning to face right-hander Ed Seward of the Philadelphia Quakers. The left-handed hitting rookie blasted a home run to become the presumed first player to hit a home run in his first major league at bat.

I say presumed because on the same day outfielder George "White Wings" Tebeau of the Cincinnati Red Stockings, also hit a home run in his first major league at bat in a game against Cleveland.

57. Who was the first pitcher and player to hit a grand slam home run in his first major league at bat?

This bases clearing home run was hit by a Philadelphia Phillies right-handed pitcher, making his first mound appearance, and first plate appearance, by the name of "Frosty Bill" Duggleby, on April 21, 1898, when he connected for a grand slam home run off New York Giants southpaw James "Cy" Seymour as "Frosty Bill" went on to an easy 13-4 win.

58. Who was the first 20th century National League rookie to pitch a shutout in his first major league game?

The parents of Canadian-born Alex "Dooney" Hardy must have been proud when their son took the mound for the Chicago Cubs in his major league debut on September 4, 1902 against the Brooklyn Superbas. The 25-year old southpaw shut down Brooklyn, 1-0, to become the first 20th century National League pitcher to throw a shutout in his first big league game.

59. Who was the first, and only, rookie to drive in over 50 runs in a single month?

When the Detroit Tigers introduced a young 20-year old catcher to major league baseball on August 22, 1934 they knew they had a powerful bat coming into their lineup. He proved it in his first full season, in 1937, when Rudy York drove in 50 runs in the month of August, 1937, to become the first rookie, and the first American League player, to help himself to 50 ribbies in one month, as he went on to drive in 103 runs that season.

60. Who was the first rookie pitcher to start, and win, 20 games, be named the Rookie-of-the-Year, pitch 8 complete games, all in less than 200 innings?

This unusual combination of events happened to New York Yankees right-hander, Bob Grim, in 1954, when he started 20 games, went all the way in 8, had a 20-6, 3,26 Era., won The Rookie-of-the-Year Award, and all done in 199 innings on the mound.

61. Who was the first player to lead the league in triples and home runs in the same season?

This rookie made his major league debut on April 14, 1904 with the Brooklyn Superbas, and by the looks of his freshman year didn't take too many pitches. He was too busy swinging the lumber either at the horsehide or at the air. You see, right fielder Harry "Judge" Lumley, banged out 161 hits swinging from the port side, and led the National League in triples with 18, and in home runs with 9. When he wasn't hitting the horsehide a long way he was swinging at air, for Harry also led the senior circuit in strikeouts with 105.

62. Who was the first rookie to start a Game 7 of the World Series?

Although Charles "Babe" Adams, a 24-year old right-hander, made his pitching debut with the Pittsburgh Pirates on April 18, 1906, his only game that year, and pitched in only four more games until 1909, he was still considered a rookie that year, having gone 12-3 with a 1.11 Era. before being tabbed to start Game 1 of the 1909 World Series against the Detroit Tigers, where he came away with a 4-1 win.

He came back to win Game 5, 8-4, and was manager Fred Clarke's choice to start Game 7. Adams didn't disappoint as he pitched his third complete game, a 6-hit, 8-0 shutout of the Tigers, defeating right-hander "Wild Bill" Donovan for the World Championship, and becoming the first rookie to start a Game 7 in the Fall Classic.

63. Who were the first rookie batter mates to start a World Series game?

This was a very rare event, so much so that it took until Game 1 of the 1947 World Series, when on Tuesday, September 30th, before a crowd of 73,365 New York fans filled the Yankee Stadium to see right-hander Frank "Spec" Shea of the Yankees, with fellow rookie, Lawrence "Yogi" Berra, as his catcher, take on the Dodgers. These two became the first rookie batters to start a World Series game in major league history.

"Yogi" went 0-4 in the game, and "Spec" went five innings, and with the help of southpaw Joe Page getting the save, preserved Shea's 5-3 win.

64. Who was the first player to be named Rookie-of-The-Year, and also have his team win the World Series in the same season?

This rare occurrence happened to Gil McDougald, the 23-year old rookie third baseman of the New York Yankees, when after making his debut on April 20, 1951, went on to hit 14 home runs, and drive in 63 to go along with a .306 batting average, making him the 1951 American League Rookie-of-the-Year.

The Yankees went on to meet the New York Giants in the Series and in Game 5, at the Polo Grounds, on October 9th, before a crowd of 47,530, and the Yankees down, 1-0, in the 3rd inning, McDougald came up with the bases loaded, and unloaded them with a grand slam home run, deep into the left field stands to start the Yankees on a 13-1 rout, as the Yankees went on to win the World Series in six games, and brought down the curtain on the career of Joe DiMaggio.

65. Who was the first rookie to hit 30 home runs before the All-Star Game?

When the Oakland Athletics hosted the Boston Red Sox on Saturday, July 5, 1987 at the Oakland-Alameda County Stadium the 32,655 never realized they were about to see something never done before. When 1B Mark McGwire came up in the bottom of the 4th inning he took Red Sox right-hander Dennis "Oil Can" Boyd downtown to deep right-centerfield for "Big Mac's" 30th home run of the season. That solo shot made McGwire the first rookie to have 30 home runs before the All-Star Game.

66. Who was the first player in major league history to hit a home run from each side of the plate for his first three major league hits?

You can't burst out with your first two major league hits any better than rookie catcher Yasmani Grandel of the San Diego Padres.

This Cuban-born switch-hitter came up in the top of the 4th inning in a scoreless game against Colorado Rockies southpaw Christian Friedrich, on Saturday, June 30, 2012, out in Coors Field. His first hit was a solo home run to left-center field to give the Padres a 1-0 lead.

Coming back up in the top of the 6th, with Colorado leading 2-1, he faced right-hander Jeremy Guthrie, with one on, and deposited his pitch into deep left field for his second base hit and home run of his major league career. The Padres went on to an 8-4 win.

Not stopping there, after going 0-for-3 in a game out in Chase Field on Monday, July 2nd, against the Arizona Diamondbacks, he picked up his third career base hit by blasting a solo home run to deep left field in the 7th inning off southpaw Mike Zagurski as the Padres went on to win 6-2.

His first three base hits, all home runs from both sides of the plate, certainly make Grandel a "Groundbreaker."

1. Who was the first, and only, pitcher to give up a home run to his brother in a game, and then come back in the same game to hit a home run himself?

Rick Ferrell, the Boston Red Sox catcher homered off his brother, right-hander Wes of the Cleveland Indians, in the 4th inning on July 19, 1933.

Wes, showing he could go deep too, turned around in his half of the 4th and homered off Boston's right-hander Hank Johnson. They became the first brothers to do that in major league history.

In the career battle for home run leadership in the Ferrell family it was no contest as Wes was by far the better home run hitter with 38 home runs in 548 games compared to Rick's 28 in 1,884 games.

2. Who were the first brothers to hit a home run in the same game?

On September 4, 1927 Paul Waner led off in the 5th inning, for the first place Pittsburgh Pirates, by hitting a line drive that bounced into the short left field stands at Redland Field, Cincinnati for a home run. Fair balls that bounced into the stands were considered home runs in the National League until 1930. After Clyde Barhart was retired, his brother Lloyd duplicated his older brother by slicing an identical ball down the left line that also bounced in the stands for a home run.

The Pirates went on to defeat the Reds, and Dolf Luque, 8-4.

This brotherly feat will be duplicated on June 9, 1929 when the Pirates are playing the Brooklyn Dodgers and each brother hits a home run off starting right-hander Doug "Buzz" McWeeny. It is the second time in major league history that the two brothers homered in the same game. It wasn't enough, however, as the Dodgers prevail, 9-6.

3. Who were the first father and son to hit a home run in the same game?

It is unusual to have a father and son both being able to make it to the big leagues. It is even more rare to have them playing on the same team in the same game, which they did for the first time on August 31, 1990 when father and son teamed up in the same Seattle Mariners outfield in Safeco Field.

Now the Griffeys took it to an even higher level on September 14, 1990 while with the Seattle Mariners. On that day they faced right-hander Kirk

McCaskill of the California Angels. They started it off early by both Ken Sr. and Ken Jr. blasting back-to-back home runs in the first inning. They are the first father and son to do it in the same game, much less the same inning, and back-to-back!

4. Who was the first rookie to take his brother downtown? (Hit a home run off him).

George "Firebrand" Stovall, playing first base for the Cleveland Blues in 1904, hit a home run off his brother Jesse, a right-hander with the Detroit Tigers. It was the rookie's only home run of that season.

5. Who was the first, and only family to have five brothers all play in the major leagues?

This family of five was named Delahanty, and "Big Ed" was the first to be a major leaguer when he joined the Philadelphia Phillies on May 22, 1888, and had the longest career, 16years. He was followed in Philadelphia by Tom in 1894, then Jim went to Chicago in 1901, Frank to the New York Highlanders in 1905, and lastly Joe to the St. Louis Cardinals in 1907.

6. Who were the first father and son to be elected to the Hall of Fame?

Neither of these gentlemen played in the big leagues, but they both had an impact on how major league baseball was run and developed innovations that continue on today.

Leland Stanford McPhail, known as Larry, was born in Cass City, Michigan in 1890. He was known as being both an athlete and a scholar.

He was involved in World War I in a highly secretive, but unsuccessful, military mission in which he and a group were assigned to kidnap Kaiser Wilhelm. After the war he was in the retail business before moving over to major league baseball. In 1934 he became General Manager of the financially troubled Cincinnati Reds organization.

A very creative person, he introduced night baseball and air travel to major league baseball. He also was instrumental in building the foundations for the Reds rise to being pennant winners in 1939 and 1940.

He joined the Brooklyn Dodger organization in 1938 and installed lights in Ebbets Field, and brought in the popular Red Barber to broadcast the Dodger games. He, along with manager Leo Durocher, won the National League pennant for Brooklyn in 1941.

When Major League Commissioner Kenesaw Mountain Landis died in

1944 McPhail was instrumental in having Happy Chandler named the new Commissioner of Major League Baseball. After World War II he became President and General Manager of the New York Yankees, and installed lights in Yankee Stadium. He passed away in 1975 and was elected to the Hall of Fame in 1978.

Leland McPhail Jr., was the son of Larry, and was a front office executive for 45 years. In 1959 Lee joined the Baltimore Orioles as General Manager and was President of the club from 1960-65.

He then went to work in the Commissioner's office to help the new and inexperienced Commissioner William Eckert in 1966. He returned to New York and was named General Manager of the Yankees from 1967-73.

He then went on to replace American League president Joe Cronin in 1974 through 1983 and ruled on the famous "Pine Tar" incident with George Brett and the Yankees. Lee was elected to the Hall of Fame in 1998.

Lee's son, Andy, was the General Manager of the Minnesota Twins and later President of the Chicago Cubs.

7. Who was the first home plate umpire/catcher brother combination to appear in the same game together?

Tom Haller was a catcher for the Detroit Tigers and when he put his pads on and went out to home plate, to face the Kansas City Royals, on July 14, 1972. Who should be there but his brother Bill, the home plate umpire for that day's game. From all reports the game went along smoothly except the Royals won 1-0.

8. Who were the first, and only, brothers to hit back-to-back home runs off the same pitcher in the same game?

Hitting home runs in the same game wasn't unique to the Waner brothers, outfielders for the Pittsburgh Pirates, they had done it twice before. This, however, was different for it was the first time that Paul, and younger brother Lloyd, or anyone else, had hit back-to-back home runs off the same pitcher when southpaw Cliff Melton of the New York Giants served them up in the 5th inning on September 15, 1938.

That happened to be the last, of "Little Poison's" 27 career home runs in his 18 seasons.

9. Who was the first pair of brothers, in major league history, to collectively hit over 5,000 base hits in their careers?

As has been mentioned before in this chapter, "Big Poison" and "Little Poison", come to the forefront. These two Hall of Famers, Paul and Lloyd Waner, hold many accomplishments, but no one can exceed the base hit total of these two.

Paul had 3,152 base hits in his 20-year career and his brother, Lloyd collected 2,459 in his 18-year career for a total of 5,611.

10. Who formed the first brother battery in major league history?

James "Deacon" White came into baseball as a catcher with the Chicago White Stockings (Cubs) in 1876. He played with them a year before moving over to the Boston Red Stockings (Braves) in 1877, where he joined his brother Will, known as "Whoop-La", who had just come up as a rookie right-handed pitcher with Boston that year.

Deacon was rated the best barehanded catcher of his time, and carried a big stick as well, as he led the league in hitting, (.387), hits (103), triples (11), and RBIs (49) in that first year being a battery mate to his brother.

Will went on to have three 40-win seasons in his ten-year career in both the National League and American Association, and wound up with a 229-166 record in both leagues.

They also formed a battery when they both played for the Cincinnati Reds in the 1878 and 1879 seasons, with "Whoop-La" winning 30 and 43 games in those two years.

11. Who were the first father and son to each manage in the major leagues?

The first father and son to manage in the major leagues was George Sisler who managed the St. Louis Browns from 1924-26. His son, Dick, managed the Cincinnati Reds in 1964-65.

12. Who were the first brothers to hit home runs in the same World Series game, each for the opposing team?

This unusual event took place in the 1964 World Series. It started off in the 7th inning of Game7, on October 15th, when Ken Boyer, the St. Louis Cardinals third baseman hit a solo home run off New York Yankee southpaw Steve Hamilton.

Two innings later, in the top of the 9th, Yankee third baseman, Clete

Boyer, hit a solo home run off Cardinal right-hander Bob Gibson, for the first home runs hit by brothers, on opposing teams, in the same World Series game in major league history.

The Cardinals went on to take the World Championship in seven games.

13. Who were the first three brothers to bat in succession, in the same inning, for the same team in the major leagues?

On September 10, 1963, at the Polo Grounds in New York, the Alou brothers, all from the Dominican Republic, and all on the San Francisco Giants, were sent up to bat by manager Alvin Dark in the 8th inning against right-hander Carlton Willey of the New York Mets.

Jesus Alou, pinch-hitting for Jose Pagan, grounded out to shortstop. He was followed by Matty Alou, who came in to pinch-hit for the pitcher Bob Garibaldi, and struck out. The last of the Alou brothers, right fielder Felipe, hit back to the pitcher who threw to first for the final out of the inning, but not before a "first" in modern baseball history had been accomplished, with 14,945, including the author in attendance, to attest to the fact that for the first time on major league history all three brothers had batted in a row in this historic major league game.

14. Who was the first brother battery to appear in a World Series game?

On September 30th, in Game One of the 1942 World Series, right-hander Mort Cooper was on the mound while his brother, Walker, handled the catching duties to form the first brother battery to appear in a Fall Classic. They would do an encore performance in the 1943 and 1944 World Series as well.

15. Who were the first brothers to throw a no-hitter in the major leagues?

On Sunday, April 16, 1978, at Busch Stadium, Bob Forsch, the big right-hander of the St. Louis Cardinals, started it off when he no-hit the Philadelphia Phillies to win 5-0 for the first no-hitter in St. Louis by a Cardinal since Jesse Haines in 1924.

Not to be out-done by his younger brother, the equally strapping right-hander Ken, put the Forsch brothers in the record books on Saturday, April 7, 1979, when, at the Astrodome, with the Houston Astros, he threw a no-hitter to beat the Braves, 6-0, for the earliest no-hitter in major league history.

16. Who was the first modern day brother battery in the major leagues?

That distinction, as brief as it was, goes to the Thompson brothers of the New York Highlanders.

Rookie right-hander Tommy, having come on as the last of four New York pitchers on October 5, 1912, was on the mound making his final major league appearance, when his younger brother Homer, was behind the plate in his first and only major league appearance, making the Thompson boys the first brother battery in modern major league history.

That day also marked the last game played at Hilltop Park as the Highlanders would move to the Polo Grounds for the following season. New York came away with an 8-6 win over the Senators.

17. Who were the first brothers to pitch a combined shutout?

You will have to look out to the Windy City to find rookie Paul Reuschel, and his four-year veteran brother Rick, who on August 21, 1975 became the first brothers to pitch a combined shutout.

It happened against the Los Angeles Dodgers when younger brother Rick developed a blister on his pitching hand and had to be relieved by older brother Paul in the 7th inning, and he closed the door to home plate and the two brothers combined to shutout the Dodgers as the Chicago Cubs breezed to a 7-0 victory.

18. Who was the first father-son duo to play in the same major league game?

The father and son who teamed up to play together in the same game happened on August 31, 1990 when Ken Griffey Sr. took over in left field while son Ken Jr. was in centerfield for the Seattle Mariners in Safeco Field as they defeated the Kansas City Royals, 5-2, with each Griffey going 1-4 at the plate.

19. Who were the first modern day brothers to become battery mates?

These two Ireland-born players, catcher Jack O'Neill, who played for three teams in the major leagues from 1902-06, and his right-handed brother, Mike O'Neill, who played his entire career, 1901-1904 with the St. Louis Cardinals, formed a battery in 1902-03, when they both played for the Redbirds.

20. Who were the first African-American brothers to play in the major

leagues?

This may not quickly come to mind for one has to go back to 1884 when Moses Fleetwood "Fleet" Walker, a catcher for the Toledo Blue Stockings, born on October 7, 1856, had his major league debut on May 1, 1884. His brother Welday Walker, born on July 27, 1860, and a leftfielder with the Blue Stockings, made his first major league start on July 15, 1884. The brothers then played together for their only year in the major leagues, in 1884.

21. Who were the first brothers, who together, won 40 or more games for the same team in the same season?

If you thought one was Dizzy, and one was Daffy, you were right on both answers, for St. Louis Cardinal manager Frankie Frisch had to be excited when his brother tandem of Jay Hanna "Dizzy" Dean and his younger brother, by two years, Paul "Daffy," combined to win 49 games in the 1934 season. Dizzy had a 30-7 record and his younger brother Daffy went 19-11 for the National League champion St. Louis Cardinals.

22. Who were the first brothers to each win twenty games in a season?

The first brothers to reach the twenty win mark in a season were first southpaw Harry Coveleski, who was 22-12 in 1914 with the Detroit Tigers, and then followed by younger brother, right-hander Stan, who was 22-13 in 1918 with the Cleveland Indians.

23. Who was the first pair of pitching brothers to combine to win over 500 major league games?

It was interesting to see if the Perry brothers, Joe and Gaylord, would emerge as the first pair of brothers to reach the 500 wins level. The Niekro brothers, Joe and Phil, were certainly strong contestants for that honor.

When the results were in Jim Perry, having started his career in 1959 with Cleveland and finished it in 1975 with Oakland ended up with 215 career wins.

Meanwhile Phil Niekro began his career with the Milwaukee Braves in 1964, while Joe came up with the Chicago Cubs in 1967.

Gaylord, in the meantime, was in his first season, with the San Francisco Giants in 1962, and began adding to the victory list that his older brother had left. Then in 1972, after having been traded for southpaw "Sudden Sam" McDowell, he found himself over in the American League with Cleveland, and then later with Texas.

Gaylord kept racking up the victories until late in the 1984 season when Gaylord picked up four wins with the New York Yankees, the first of which allowed him to reach that magic 285 win total necessary to put the Perry brothers over the top with 500 wins to become the first brothers to reach that level.

Interestingly, when both careers ended Gaylord had 314 wins, Phil had 318, and both went to the Hall of Fame.

Their brother's records were impressive as well with Jim having 215 wins, and Joe 221. The Niekro's barely edged out the Perry's in career wins 539 to 529. But the Perry brothers arrived at 500 first.

24. Who was the first, and only, major league player to have as his brother the heavyweight champion of the world?

Joseph Aloysius Corbett was born on December 4, 1875, and made his major league debut as a right-handed pitcher on August 23, 1895 with the Washington Senators of the National League.

He moved over to the Baltimore Orioles in 1896-97, having a 27-8 record in '97, and finishing up his four-year career with the St. Louis Cardinals in 1904 with a lifetime record of 32-18.

His brother received much more notoriety as he was "Gentleman Jim" Corbett who became the Heavyweight Champion of the World when he knocked out John L. Sullivan in the 21st round, before a crowd of more than 10,000, in New Orleans, on September 7, 1892.

25. Who were the first brothers to shut out a team in both games of a doubleheader?

It was the afternoon of September 21, 1934 when those Dean brothers, "Dizzy" and "Daffy" (Paul), went up against the Brooklyn Dodgers. In the first game Dizzy took a no-hitter into the 8th inning, but then allowed three hits in an easy 13-0 win.

In the nightcap Paul cruised right along and threw a no-hitter, winning 3-0.

When Dizzy saw Paul's effort he came out with one of his typical fractured English, and often quoted remark, "If'n Paul had told me he was gonna pitch a no-hitter, I'd of throwed one, too."

26. Who were the first two pitching brothers to start a game against

each other as rookies?

In this highly unusual experience the Chicago Cubs, on September 29, 1986, started 20-year old rookie right-hander Greg Maddux against the Philadelphia Phillies 25-year old rookie right-hander Mike Maddux.

When the battle of the rookie brothers was over Greg came away with the win, 8-3. With that win Greg would come away with many more having a 23-year regular season career record of 355-227, 3.16 Era., 3,371 strikeouts in 5008.1 regular season innings, 8 All-Star Games, 20 Gold Gloves, 4 consecutive Cy Young Awards, (1992-95), and was considered the most dominant pitcher in the 1990's. It will be no one's surprise when he is elected to the Hall of Fame.

His brother, Mike, pitched for nine teams in his 15-year career, mostly as a middle inning reliever, and having a regular season career record of 39-37 with a 4.05 Era. over 861.2 innings.

27. Who was the first father to manage his two sons on the same team on the major league level?

The Ripken boys grew up together and listened to their Dad, Cal Sr., in their formative years. Then in 1987 Cal Sr., having been named the manager of the Baltimore Orioles, found that he had a second baseman, Billy, and a shortstop, Cal Jr., on his playing roster, and although he could no longer tell his two boys what to do off the field he sure could tell them what to do on the field, because Sr. was the first manager to manage his two sons on the same team in major league history.

28. Who were the first African-American brothers to play in the modern day major leagues?

Although these two brothers came close they never were in the major leagues at the same time. Solomon "Solly" Drake, came up as a centerfielder and made his major league debut on April 17, 1956 with the Chicago Cubs. After 65 games with Chicago he then went on to spend the 1959 season with both the Los Angeles Dodgers and the Philadelphia Phillies playing 76 games before his final game on September 27, 1959.

His younger brother Sammy, a second and third baseman, broke in with the Chicago Cubs on April 17, 1960. After spending the 1960-61 seasons playing in 28 games for Chicago he went over to the New York Mets as one of the players joining that new franchise in 1962, and played 25 games with them before his final major league game on September 30, 1962.

The Drakes can then be counted as being the first two modern day African- American brothers to play in the major leagues.

29. Who were the first brothers to play in all three outfield positions at the same time in the same game?

September 15, 1963 was a historic day in major league baseball when on that date the San Francisco Giants played the Pittsburgh Pirates in Forbes Field, Pittsburgh.

In the 9th inning of that game, for the first time in major league history, there were three siblings, all named Alou, patrolling the outfield for the Giants.

Felipe, the eldest was in right field, Matty, the speedster, was in center-field, and the youngest, Jesus, handled left field. The Giants came away with a 13-5 victory that day with the Alou brothers taking care of the outfield duties to become the first to play all outfield positions in the same game.

That worked out so well that two days later, on September 17th they were together again patrolling the outfield against the Atlanta Braves, win-ning again, this time 11-3.

On September 22nd, for the first time back at home in Candlestick Park, the brothers again shared the outfield with Felipe coming in to replace Wil-lie Mays in centerfield in the 7th inning while Matty was in left field and Jesus was covering right field. The Alous came to the plate in the 8th, but they go down 1, 2, 3, but it has no impact on the game for Willie McCovey hit three home runs, and the Giants defeated the Mets 13-4.

30. Who were the first pitching brothers to start against each other in a regular season inter-league game?

It was bound to happen sometime; brother versus brother in an inter-league game. It happened on Saturday night, June 20, 2009 out in Angel Stadium, Anaheim, when the Los Angeles Angels played host to the Los Angeles Dodgers and the Weaver brothers faced each other.

Older brother, Jeff (3-1) of the Dodgers, started against younger brother Jared (7-2) of the Angels in a battle of two right-handers who stood well over 6'4". Jeff prevailed although neither pitcher was sparkling with Jeff going 5-plus innings, giving up two runs and six hits while Jared went 5.1 giving up 6 runs, 10 hits as the Dodgers took the contest 6-4, before 44,148 including the proud parents.

31. Who was the first third generation major league player to play in the major leagues?

When you think of major league baseball tradition one must think of the Boone family. On September 3, 1948 Ray "Ike" Boone started off the family resume when he made his debut with the Cleveland Indians where he played for six seasons. He then went on to play for the Detroit Tigers, Chicago White Sox, Kansas City Athletics, and the Boston Red Sox before his final game on August 11, 1960.

In his 13 seasons he played a total of 1,373 games, at first base, third base and shortstop. He had 1,260 base hits, 151 home runs, 737 RBIs and a career batting average of .275.

His son, Bob, made his major league debut on September 10, 1972 as a catcher with the Philadelphia Phillies. One of the great catchers of his era Bob played 19 seasons in 2,264 games, 2,225 behind the plate, a few at third, first and as a DH, and banged out 1,838 hits, 105 home runs, 826 runs batted in for a .254 career batting average. His strength, however, was behind the plate where he was an All-Star four times and earned seven Gold Gloves.

Then along came the third generation major leaguers, Bret and Aaron. Bret started his big league career on August 19, 1992, at age 22 as a second baseman with the Seattle Mariners. He played 14 seasons with the Mariners, Reds, Braves, Padres, and Twins until he played his last game on July 30, 2005. During his career he had 1,775 base hits, 252 home runs, 1,021 runs batted in and a .266 batting average.

Now it's time for the fourth Boone, the youngest, Aaron, who played third and first for 13 seasons, making his big league start with Cincinnati on June 20,1997 and playing there for seven years before moving on to Cleveland, Florida, Washington, and Houston. His stats through 2009 show 1,017 hits, 126 home runs, 555 runs batted in and a .263 batting average.

Now there is the first three generation major league family and one that has made many vital contributions to the national pastime.

32. Who were the first brothers to play against each other in a World Series game?

You have to go back to the infamous World Series of 1920, when so many "firsts" were established. We'll get to those in other parts of this book, but for now, in this section let's talk about the Johnston brothers.

Doc, born Wheeler Roger Johnston, on September 9, 1887, he made his entrance into major league baseball on October 3, 1909 as a first baseman with the Cincinnati Reds.

Playing in the 1920 World Series against the Brooklyn Robins as the first baseman for the Cleveland Indians, and batted .273 in the seven game series, he faced his younger brother, Jimmy, who held down the hot corner for the Robins, but for only four games, having a .214 batting average in the Fall Classic. The Tribe went on to win the World Series that year 5 games to 2, but it didn't stop the Johnston brothers from saying they were the first brothers to face each other in the Fall Classic.

33. Who was the first grandfather-grandson combination to hit for the cycle?

When Philadelphia third baseman David Bell came up to the plate in the bottom of the 2nd inning against the Montreal Expos on June 28, 2004 little did he realize he would go down in major league history books as being the first grandson to join his grandfather in hitting for the cycle.

David doubled in that at bat, came back to hit a home run in the 4th, then singled in the 6th, and completed the cycle with a triple in the 7th.

Granddad David "Gus" Bell came up as an outfielder with the Pittsburgh Pirates on May 30, 1950 and played in the big leagues for 15 seasons When the Pirates visited Philadelphia on June 4, 1951, Gus hit for the cycle as Pittsburgh rolled over the Phillies 12-4 and started the cycle in motion for his grandson.

Gus's son, and David's father, "Buddy" Bell, had a very productive 18 season career with the Indians, Rangers, Reds, and Astros collecting 2,514 base hits, driving in 1,106 runs but never accomplished the cycle.

34. Who were the first brothers in American League history to face each other as starting pitchers in a game?

It happened on July 3, 1973 when the Cleveland Indians sent their ace right-hander Gaylord Perry to the mound to face off against his older brother Jim, of the Detroit Tigers.

In the battle of the two right-handed brothers age came out ahead, as Jim defeated his brother as the Tigers went on to a 5-4 win with the help of two Norm Cash home runs.

Gaylord lost this game, but in career statistics he came out ahead of his older brother with a 314-265, 3.11 Era. while Jim shows a 215-174, 3.45 Era.

35. Who were the first brothers to face each other on the mound in major league history?

If you go back to Thursday, June 26, 1924 at the Polo Grounds, you will see the Boston Braves sending former New York Giants right-hander, Jesse Barnes, out against brother right-hander, Virgil "Zeke" Barnes, of the New York Giants. "Zeke" didn't have a good game giving up four hits and an earned run after facing four batters in a third of an inning before being relieved by right-hander Claude Jonnard who went the remaining 8.2 innings to record an 8-1 win. Jesse took the loss and Virgil escaped any decision due to the arm of Jonnard and the bats of his teammates. It still went down as the first time in major league history where brother went up against brother in a mound duel.

Interestingly three days later on Sunday, June 29th, and still at the Polo Grounds, the brothers hooked up again, and this time Virgil went seven innings, giving up 10 hits and 4 runs to take the loss as Jesse pitched a complete game, also giving up 10 hits, but just a single run for a 4-1 win.

36. Who was the first American League player to hit a home run off a father and his son?

Ted Williams, the rookie leftfielder with the Boston Red Sox, blasted a home run off Chicago White Sox southpaw Thornton Lee, at Fenway Park, on September 19, 1939, one of 31 Williams would hit that year.

Twenty-one years later, on September 2, 1960, Williams faced the son of Thornton, right-hander Don Lee, of the Washington Senators, in the first game of a doubleheader, and did to the son what he had done to his father, and blasted a home run off of him as well, becoming the first player in major league history to hit a home run off a father and his son.

37. Who was the first National League player to hit a home run off a father, then off his son?

Andre "Hawk" Dawson, the Montreal Expos outfielder, matched his American League counterpart, Ted Williams, by taking a father "downtown" as he hit a home run off Pedro Borbon, the Dominican Republic-born right-hander of the Cincinnati Reds on June 10, 1977.

Showing no family partiality, on August 16, 1995, while with the Florida Marlins, Dawson gave young Pedro the same treatment as he did his father, by hitting a home run off the Atlanta Braves southpaw.

Who was the first African-American to be a third generation major league player?

If you look under "H" you will find the Hairston family.

Grandfather Sam started off the family lineage when he had a very brief career as a catcher for the Chicago Cubs in 1951. He was followed by his son, Jerry, who played six years in the outfield for the Chicago White Sox, and Pittsburgh Pirates from 1973-81. And then came grandson Jerry Jr. who played 13 seasons in the infield and outfield with the Baltimore Orioles, Texas Rangers, and the Cincinnati Reds. While we are talking about the Hairstons let's not forget brother Scott and nephew John who also all wore major league uniforms.

38. Who were the first brothers to be teammates on an All-Star team?

This brotherly get-together happened in 1941 when a pair of centerfielders made the All-Star team, their names being Dom "The Little Professor" DiMaggio of the Boston Red Sox, and older brother Joe, "The Yankee Clipper," of the New York Yankees teamed up on July 8th for the game out in Detroit.

39. Who were the first brothers to oppose each other in an All-Star Game?

I am sure the brotherly love aspect remained, but after that it was Carlos May, the outfielder of the Chicago White Sox, doing what he could to defeat older brother, Lee, the Cincinnati Reds first baseman in the July 23, 1969 game down in Washington as they became the first brothers to play in opposition to one another in an All-Star Game.

40. Who was the first major leaguer to have his father as a manager?

Earle Mack, the son of Connie Mack, played in his first game for the Philadelphia Athletics, under his father's management, on October 5, 1910 as a catcher, and had a good 2 for 4 day at bat. Playing in just two games at third base in 1911 and two more at first base in 1914 he concluded his five-game, three season career on October 1, 1914, showing two hits, one triple, one run batted in and a stolen base and a .125 batting average.

41. **Who were the first father and son to play in both the American and National Leagues, for the same teams in those leagues in two different eras?**

What goes around comes around or something like that. Jim Bagby Sr. pitched for the Cleveland Indians from 1916 to 1922, and then moved over to the senior circuit to pitch for the Pittsburgh Pirates, ending his career there in 1923.

His son, Jim Jr., pitched for the Indians from 1941 through 1945, and also ended his major league career pitching for the Pirates, in 1947.

42. **Who was the first family to have a father and son both pitch in a World Series?**

Look to the Bagby family for that answer. Father Jim "Sarge" Bagby pitched in two games for the Cleveland Indians in the 1920 World Series, pitching 15 innings against the Brooklyn Robins, winning one and losing one, with a 1.80 Era. as Cleveland took the series 5 games to 2.

Son Jim Jr. pitched three innings in the 1946 World Series for the Boston Red Sox, with no decisions, allowing 6 hits and an earned run, as the St. Louis Cardinals took the series 4 games to 3.

43. **Who was the first manager to pencil in his two sons in the starting lineup card for a major league game?**

Cal Ripken Sr. had the unusual and memorable experience of being the first manager to write in his son, Cal Jr., in the shortstop position, and his other son, Billy, at second base to start for the Baltimore Orioles in that Saturday, July 11, 1987 game at Memorial Stadium against the Minnesota Twins.

44. **Who were the first father and son to have a combined pitching career of winning 300 major league games?**

Mel Stottlemyre made his major league pitching debut with the New York Yankees on August 12, 1964, and pitched his entire eleven-year career in pinstripes, showing a 164-139 record.

On April 6, 1988 his son Todd, also a right-hander, made his debut with the Toronto Blue Jays. After seven years Todd went on to the Oakland Athletics, then the St. Louis Cardinals, Texas Rangers, and finished his fourteen-year career with the Arizona Diamondbacks, where his career record was 138-121, to make he and his father the first father and son combination to reach the 300-win plateau with 302.

45. Who were the first father and son, in modern day baseball, to hit for the cycle?

That honor began when Minnesota Twins leftfielder Gary Ward, on September 18, 1980, hit for the cycle against the Milwaukee Brewers.

Twenty four years later, on Wednesday, May 26, 2004, at Busch Stadium, Gary's son, Daryle, made the Ward family the first father-son to have hit for the cycle as the Pirates first baseman went four-for five with six runs batted in to lead his Pirates to an 11-8 victory over the St. Louis Cardinals.

46. Who were the first father and son to be behind the plate and call a no-hit game?

This is about as rare as rare can be when on August 13, 1969 Lou DiMuro called balls and strikes in the no-hit game that Jim Palmer pitched for the Baltimore Orioles as he beat the Oakland Athletics, 8-0.

On May 29, 2010 his son, Mike, was behind the plate calling the accuracy of the pitches thrown by Roy "Doc" Halladay, the big, strong All-Star right-hander of the Philadelphia Phillies, when he pitched a, 1-0, no-hitter against the Florida Marlins before 25,086 fans at Sun Life Stadium.

47. Who were the first cousins to hit over 1,300 home runs in their combined careers?

If you took a pair of southpaw swinging cousins, one in the American League, the other in the senior circuit, and combined Barry Bonds' major league record total of 762 home runs, with the 563 home runs hit by his cousin, Reggie Jackson, you would come up with a total of 1,325 home runs sent out of the park by these two sluggers.

48. Who were the first brothers to be battery-mates in both a World Series and an All-Star game?

St. Louis Cardinals right-hander Mort Cooper appeared in the 1942-43 World Series against the Yankees and in the 1944 World Series against the St. Louis Browns, and catching his pitches was his brother, Walker.

They both also appeared in 1942 and 1943 All-Star games, in New York and Philadelphia.

49. Who were the first brothers to each hit a home run in the same

regular season game while playing on opposing teams?

It was in a Friday afternoon game at the Polo Grounds on July 5, 1935, when Brooklyn Dodgers 2B Tony "Cooch" Cuccinello hit a solo home run in the 8th inning off New York Giants right-hander Leon "Shag" Chagon.

His brother, Al, who was playing third base for the New York Giants, watched his brother put one in the left field stands, and when he came up in the 9th inning he, too, joined his brother by hitting a two-run home run in the same spot, off Dodgers right-hander Johnny Babich, to make the Cuccinello brothers the first to each hit a home run in the same game, but for opposing teams.

50. Who was the first pitcher in major league history to give up a home run to three brothers?

I am pretty sure that Jesus Alou remembers the home run he hit off Chicago Cubs Hall of Fame right-hander Ferguson Jenkins when Jesus was patrolling the outfield for the San Francisco Giants in July 1967.

Ditto for brother Felipe, then with the Atlanta Braves, when he took Jenkins downtown in April of '68.

Then Matty got into the act, to make this item possible, when he homered for the St, Louis Cardinals in September of 1971 to make Jenkins the first pitcher to keep it in the family by giving up home runs to the three Alou brothers.

51. Who are the first, and only, brothers to win the Cy Young Award?

Older brother Jim was the first Perry to put the Cy Young Award on his wall when the right-hander led the American League in wins with a 24-12, 3.04 Era. record for the Minnesota Twins in 1970.

Younger brother Gaylord got his chance to match Jim in 1972, when the big right-hander led the league in wins with a 24-16, 1.92 Era., and in complete games with 29 while hurling for the Cleveland Indians.

Gaylord found himself with the San Diego Padres over in the National League in 1978, and duplicated what he did in the junior circuit by leading the NL in wins with a 21-6, 2.73 Era. which made he and Jim the first brothers to have the Cy Young Award gracing their trophy rooms.

52. Who was the first American League pitcher to make his major league debut pitching against his brother?

Among the crowd of 12,423 that were in Exhibition Stadium, Toronto, on that Thursday, May 31, 1979, I wonder if Mr. and Mrs. Underwood were there, and if so, were they on the edge of their seats to see the younger brother, Pat, go up against his older brother, Tom as the two southpaws faced off against one another.

The Detroit Tigers and Toronto Blue Jays became locked in a scoreless tie after seven innings. In the top of the 8th inning Detroit RF Jerry Morales blasted a solo home run off Tom to put the Tigers up by a run, and with southpaw, and Toronto native John Hiller, coming on in the 9th inning to register the final out, made Pat come away with a 1-0 win, as younger brother Pat, out dueled big brother Tom, in his first time on a major league mound.

53. Who was the first pair of brothers to hit their 100th home run on the same day?

Friday, August 3, 2012 was a big day in the Upton household for two of their sons reached a milestone in their careers as CF Melvin Emanuel, known as B.J., who made his major league debut with Tampa Bay on August 2, 2004, hit his 100th career home run on August 3, 2012 off Orioles right-hander Tommy Hunter, at Tropicana Field, a solo shot in the 4th inning as Tampa went on to a 2-0 win.

Then he had his brother, RF Justin, who made his first major league start, also on August 2nd, but in 2007, with the Arizona Diamondbacks, also hit his 100th round-tripper on the same day, August 3, 2012, down in Citizens Bank Park off Phillies right-hander Kyle Kendrick, a 2nd inning solo shot that helped Arizona triumph, 4-2.

Two brothers who broke into the majors on the same day of the month, three years apart, then hit their 100th career home run on the same day, two leagues apart, both being solo home runs, became the first brother act to step into the major leagues on the same day of the month, and hit their 100th career home run on the same day, August 3, 2012 to become "Groundbreakers."

54. Who were the first, and only, father and son combo to have each hit 50 home runs in a single season?

When Prince Fielder, the Milwaukee Brewers first baseman, hit a 1st inning two-run home run to deep right field off St. Louis Cardinals right-hander Branden Looper, and followed that with a second home run, another two-run shot to deep left field, this off right-hander Kip Wells, he helped the Brewers roll to a 9-1 win.

With Prince reaching the 50 home run level he became the youngest player, at 23 years, 139 days, to hit 50 home runs in a season, and joined his father, Cecil, who had hit 51 home runs in 1990 with the Detroit Tigers, as the first father and son to reach 50 home runs in a single season.

H. ALIGNING WITH THE STARS

1. What city hosted the first major league All-Star Game?

The first All-Star Game was played on July 6, 1933 in Comiskey Park, Chicago before 47,595 fans.

2. Who was the starting pitcher for the host American League in the first All-Star Game?

Vernon "Lefty" Gomez, of the New York Yankees, was the first starting pitcher in the first All-Star Game against the National League. He pitched three innings.

3. Who was the starting pitcher in the first All-Star Game for the National League?

Southpaw "Wild Bill" Hallahan, of the St. Louis Cardinals, was the starting National League pitcher in the first All-Star Game. He pitched two innings.

4. Who was the first winning pitcher in an All-Star Game?

Lefty Gomez, who pitched the first three innings, was credited with the first All-Star Game win.

5. What pitcher took the first loss in an All-Star Game?

"Wild Bill" Hallahan, who gave up one run in the 2nd inning, was charged with the first All-Star Game loss as the American League won the opener 4-2.

6. Who was the first player to come up to bat in the first All-Star Game?

John "Pepper" Martin, the third baseman of the St. Louis Cardinals, known as "The Wild Horse of the Osage", was the first player to bat in an All Star Game. He grounded out to future Hall of Fame shortstop Joe Cronin of the Washington Senators.

7. Who collected the first base hit in an All-Star Game?

Charles "Chick" Hafey, the Cincinnati Reds leftfielder, singled in the 2nd inning off Lefty Gomez for the first base hit in an All-Star Game.

8. Who hit the first home run in an All-Star Game?

It would not be hard to guess who this could be. With none out in the 3rd inning of the first All-Star Game Babe Ruth hit a two-run home run, with Charlie Gehringer on first base, to deep right field off "Wild Bill" Hallahan which gave the American League a three-run lead they would not relinquish.

9. Who drove in the first run in the first All-Star Game?

This one is not so easy to guess, in fact it would be very difficult. Of all the very talented batters on the field that day it was a pitcher, not certainly known for his bat, Lefty Gomez, who came through with a two-out single in the 2nd inning to drive in Jimmie Dykes with the first run of the All-Star Game.

10. Who was the first National League player to hit a home run in an All-Star Game?

Second baseman Frankie "The Fordham Flash" Frisch, with none on and two outs in the 6th inning, hit an Alvin "General" Crowder pitch for a home run into the deep right field stands for the first home run, in All-Star Game history.

11. Who hit the first double in an All-Star Game?

Harold "Pie" Traynor, Pittsburgh Pirate third baseman, hit the first double, off Lefty Grove, in All Star Game history.

12. Who made the first, and only, error in the first All-Star Game?

Lou Gehrig, first baseman of the New York Yankees, on July 6, 1933, made the first error in an All Star Game on a foul pop-in the top of the 5th by Dick Bartell.

13. Who was the pitcher credited with the first save in an All Star Game?

Robert Moses "Lefty" Grove came in to pitch the last three innings of the first All Star Game, allowing three hits, and striking out three, to record the first save in All-Star Game history.

14. Who recorded the first stolen base in All-Star Game history?

The first theft of a base in an All-Star Game was credited to Detroit Tigers second baseman Charlie Gehringer when he stole second base off "Wild Bill" Hallahan in the bottom of the 1st inning.

15. Who was the first American League manager in an All-Star Game?

Seventy-one year old Connie Mack, manager of the Philadelphia Athletics, managed the American League All- Stars in the first All-Star Game on July 6, 1933.

16. Who was the first National League manager in an All-Star Game?

John McGraw, at age 60, came out of retirement to manage the National League All-Stars in the first All-Star Game on July 6, 1933.

17. Who was the first pitcher to strike out the first four batters in an All-Star Game?

In a moving pre-game ceremony at Fenway Park, Boston on July 13, 1999 many of the game's all-time All Stars gathered on the infield as an ill Ted Williams was driven on the field in a golf cart to a thunderous ovation by the 34,187 fans as the players paid homage to "The Splendid Splinter", who then threw out the ceremonial "first pitch" to Carlton Fisk.

Boston Red Sox right-hander Pedro Martinez then dimmed the bats of some National League hitters when he took the mound to start that 1999 All-Star Game.

The first batter Barry Larkin went down on strikes as did Larry Walker, followed by Sammy Sosa. In the top of the 2nd Mark McGwire became the fourth National Leaguer to go down on strikes. Matt Williams then got on by an error by 2B Roberto Alomar which brought up Jeff Bagwell who with two strikes on him, saw Matt Williams break for second only to have Martinez blow a third strike past him, and "Pudge" Rodriguez nailed Williams with his throw to Alomar for a double play. Five of the six batters Martinez faced in his two innings of work went down on strikes.

The American League prevailed in this 70th All-Star Game, 4-1, and Pedro was named the MVP of the game, and also became the first American League starting pitcher to win an All-Star game in his home park.

18. When, if ever, was the first All-Star Game postponed?

The first All-Star Game to be postponed occurred on July 22, 1969, due to rain.

19. Who hit the first triple and scored the first National League run in All-Star history?

In the top of the 6th inning of the first All-Star Game, played in Chicago's Comiskey Park on July 6, 1933, pitcher Lon Warneke tripled to right field off Washington right-hander Alvin "General" Crowder. He then came home and scored the first National League run on a ground out by Johnny "Pepper" Martin, who then became the first National League player to drive in a run.

20. Who was the first player to win the Most Valuable Player Award, and not be selected for the All-Star team that year?

In 1935 Hank Greenberg, the first baseman for the Detroit Tigers, won the MVP Award with his final statistics for the year showing 203 hits, 121 runs scored, 36 home runs, 170 runs batted in, 389 total bases, and a .328 batting average, but was not selected for the mid-season classic. Interestingly, a player who couldn't make the All-Star team in mid-summer was a unanimous selection for MVP in the fall.

In 1956 this two-time MVP, four-time All Star was elected to the Hall of Fame.

21. Who was the first pitcher to win the coveted Cy Young Award in the same season he was not chosen for the All-Star Game?

Don Newcombe, the big 6'4", 220 pound right-hander of the Brooklyn Dodgers, was not selected for the 1956 National League All-Star team, yet when the season had ended "Newk" had not only won the National League's Cy Young Award with a record of 27-7, 3.06 Era., 5 shutouts, 139 strikeouts in 268 innings with 18 complete games, but the Most Valuable Player Award as well.

22. Who hit the first grand slam home run in an All-Star game?

On the 50th anniversary of the All-Star game, Fred Lynn, centerfielder of the Boston Red Sox, hit the first grand slam home run in All-Star game history, on a 2-2 pitch, with two outs in the 3rd inning in Comiskey Park, Chicago, off San Francisco Giants southpaw Atlee Hammaker on July 6, 1983, to cap a 7-run inning leading the American League to a 13-3 win, their first since 1971.

23. Who was the first player to appear in 24 All-Star games?

When Stan Musial, the St. Louis Cardinal outfielder, appeared in the All-Star game on July 9, 1963 in Cleveland, it marked his 24 appearance, setting a record for appearances in the mid-season classic.

24. Who was the first, and only, player to hit a home run in three consecutive All-Star games?

When Ralph Kiner, left fielder for the Pittsburgh Pirates, and no stranger to home runs, hit a home run in the All-Star Game on July 10, 1951, in Briggs Stadium in Detroit, it marked the third consecutive All-Star Game in which he homered, having done so on July 12, 1949 at Ebbets

Field, Brooklyn, and on July 11, 1950 at Comiskey Park, Chicago.

25. Who was the first umpire to call the opening half of the first All-Star Game, played in Chicago on July 6, 1933?

With the inaugural All-Star Game it was decided, to be fair to each league, to have the home plate umpire from one league call the first half of the game, and then be relieved for the second half by an arbiter from the other.

Bill Dinneen, of the American League, called the balls and strikes in the first half, and Bill Klem from the National League finished up the last half of the game.

26. Who was the first pinch-hitter in All-Star Game history?

In the top of the 6th inning of the inaugural game in 1933 outfielder "Lefty" O'Doul grounded out for catcher Jimmie Wilson to become the first pinch-hitter in All-Star Game history.

27. Who hit the first sacrifice in All-Star Game history?

The first sacrifice in All-Star Game history occurred in the bottom of the 6th when, after Joe Cronin singled to centerfield off Lon Warneke, Rick Ferrell laid down a sacrifice bunt advancing Cronin to second base. Cleveland centerfielder, Earl Averill, then singled to center scoring Cronin.

28. Who was the first player to represent five different teams in an All-Star Game?

Outfielder Moises Alou, son of Felipe, and nephew of Jesus and Matty, all former major leaguers, started his career in 1990 with the Montreal Expos, and his career in the All-Star Game began in 1994 when he represented the Expos, did the same with the Florida Marlins in 1997, the Houston Astros in 1998, 2001, the Chicago Cubs in 2004 and finally in his last All-Star appearance in 2005 with the San Francisco Giants. Alou then became the first player to represent five teams in the mid-season classic.

29. Who was the first player, of the three, to have hit safely in seven back-to-back All-Star Games?

It is not too surprising to learn that Mickey Mantle, New York Yankee centerfielder, who made his major league debut on April 17, 1951, and the following year went to the All-Star Game, and repeated for sixteen years from 1952-68. During that string he hit safely in seven back-to-back games from 1954 through 1960.

30. Who was the first player to hit three triples in his All-Star career?

Willie Mays, New York/San Francisco Giants centerfielder, was the first, and only, player to hit three triples in his career (24) All-Star appearances.

31. Who was the first player to hit a home run in his first at bat in an All-Star Game?

Max West, the Boston Braves outfielder, came up to bat in his first All-Star Game, on July 9, 1940, with two men on in the first inning, and crushed a Red Ruffing pitch for a three-run home run to become the first player ever to hit a home run in his first plate appearance in an All-Star Game.

32. Who was the first player to pinch-hit a home run in an All-Star Game?

In the 10th anniversary of the All-Star game, played at the Polo Grounds in New York, on July 6, 1942, Brooklyn Dodger catcher Mickey Owen came up in the 8th inning, with the National League down 3-0, to pinch hit for Chicago Cub right-hander Claude Passeau, and hit a home run into the left field stands for the only senior circuit run of the game as they lose to the American League 3-1.

What's interesting to note, is that Owen did not hit a home run during the regular season that year.

33. Who was the first, of three players, to have four hits in an All-Star Game?

Joe "Ducky" Medwick, the leftfielder of the St. Louis Cardinals, and ten-time All-Star, had a double in the top of the 4th inning, a single on the 6th, both off Tommy Bridges, then a double off Mel Harder in the 7th and finished up with a single off Harder in the 9th, scoring a run and driving in another on July 7, 1937, down in Griffith Stadium, to make him the first player in All-Star history to have four base hits in one All-Star Game.

Just for the record the other two were Ted Williams in 1946, and Carl Yastrzemski in 1970, both with the Red Sox.

34. Who was the first President of the United States to attend, and throw out the first pitch at an All-Star Game?

We were in our first year of World War II, when on July 6, 1942, President Roosevelt attended the All-Star Game at the Polo Grounds, in New

York, and became the first President to throw out the celebratory first pitch in the mid-summer classic.

35. Who was the first player to strike out three times in an All-Star Game?

In the famous July 10, 1934 All-Star Game where New York Giant Hall of Fame southpaw Carl Hubbell struck out five future Hall of Fame residents in a row; Babe Ruth, Lou Gehrig, and Jimmie Foxx to end the first inning, and then came back to strike out Al Simmons, and Joe Cronin in the second inning. It was the first of three strikeouts that Lou Gehrig would have that day to become the first player to strikeout out three times in an All-Star Game.

36. Who was the first player to steal home in an All-Star Game?

Harold "Pie" Traynor, third baseman of the Pittsburgh Pirates, before 48,363 fans as witnesses, was guilty of grand theft when in the 5th inning, of the 1934 All-Star Game, on July 10th he was on the front end of a double steal where he scored, and Mel Ott was able to take second on the back end of the steal. Mel Harder, of the Cleveland Indians, was on the mound to be the up-close witness, and victim of the first, and only, steal of home in All-Star history.

37. While speaking of stolen bases, who was the first player to steal two bases in one All-Star Game?

Not a stranger to this chapter, Willie Mays stole two bases in the 1963 All- Star Game in Cleveland, on July 9th, and was the first to do so in the mid-summer classic. He didn't stop there for he had two runs batted in, two runs scored, and a catch off Joe Pepitone against the center field fence that they are still talking about.

38. Who was the first player to be on the losing side in 15 All-Star Games?

Brooks Robinson, Hall of Fame third baseman with the Baltimore Orioles, had the unfortunate experience of being the first player to be on the losing side in 15 All-Star games.

39. When was the first All-Star Game played in which neither team made an error?

There must have been something about the quiet night life in New York City in 1934 for that was the first time, granted it was only the second All-

Star game played, where both teams must have been fully rested for neither team made an error.

40. What was the first year the All-Star Game winner determined the home field advantage for the World Series?

The World Series down through the years, from 1903 to 2002, with a possible exception, has alternated between the American League and the National League. The powers that be in Major League Baseball decreed that starting with the 2003 All-Star Game that the league that wins the All-Star Game becomes the host team for the World Series.

41. Who was the first batter to hit six home runs in his All-Star career?

Stanley Frank "Stan the Man" Musial, of the St. Louis Cardinals, holds that honor with six round-trippers in 24 games in the mid-summer classic.

42. Who was the first player to be selected for five All-Star games, and then came back to be an umpire in one after his playing days?

Lon "The Arkansas Hummingbird" Warneke, was a right-hander who pitched for the Chicago Cubs, and the St. Louis Cardinals for 15 seasons, from 1930-45. During his playing career he was selected for six All-Star games and upon his retirement from active playing became an umpire from 1949-55, and during that time became the first umpire to have played in an All-Star Game, and also was an umpire in one in 1952.

43. Who were the first father and son to umpire in an All-Star Game?

Though this could be placed in the "A Family Affair" chapter it certainly pertains to the mid-summer classic as well.

Ed Runge was an umpire in the 1955, '59, '61, and '67 All Star games. His son, Paul, followed in his father's footsteps, not only as an umpire, but one who worked the 1978, 1986, and 1994 All-Star games as well.

44. Who was the first, and only, pitcher to strike out five future Hall of Fame players in a row in an All-Star Game?

This was, no doubt, the most famous event in All-Star history. At least it continues to be talked about over these many years.

On July 10, 1934, before a crowd of 48,368, the second All-Star Game was played at the Polo Grounds in New York. On this day Lefty Gomez took the mound for the American League and his opponent was the southpaw ace of the New York Giants, Carl "King Carl" Hubbell. What followed was one of the most memorable pitching displays ever seen on a major league baseball field.

To set the scenario, Charlie Gehringer, the Detroit second baseman led off the game with a single, and moved to second on centerfielder Wally Berger's error. That brought up the Washington Senator's outfielder Heinie Manush, who drew a walk, putting men on first and second with no one out. That left Hubbell with the thought of getting out the heart of the American League order.

Next up was Babe Ruth who was totally fooled by the pinpoint positioning of Hubbell's screwball servings and went down swinging. Next up was another "tough out", Lou Gehrig, and he, too, went down swinging. On his return to the dugout he warned Jimmie Foxx as to what to expect. It didn't help as old "Double X" went down on strikes as well.

In the second inning Hubbell continued his mastery by striking out Al Simmons, and followed that by striking out Joe Cronin as well.

Five superb hitters, all future Hall of Fame residents set down in order by a future Hall of Famer. The next batter Bill Dickey got a single, but Lefty Gomez joined the air swatters by striking out and a memorable pitching performance went into the All-Star record books.

45. Who was the first player to hit a home run while representing each league in an All-Star Game?

The two-league All-Star homer king was Cincinnati Reds outfielder Frank Robinson who hit a home run in the 1959 All-Star Game for the National League in Los Angeles, and then again as a Baltimore Oriole in Detroit in 1971 for the American League.

46. Who was the first, and only, pitcher to be blown off the mound by the wind in an All-Star Game?

That embarrassment actually happened to San Francisco Giants' diminutive, 5'11", 165lb right-hander Stu Miller, who was not actually blown off the mound, but had his body sway under the pressure of a very high gust of wind, and was called for a balk in the July 11, 1961 All-Star Game played at Candlestick Park, San Francisco.

To set the record straight, and destroy the myth that he "was blown off the mound" as many believe, Miller entered the game in the 9th inning, relieving Sandy Koufax, with one out and runners on first and second. Rocky Colavito came up to the plate and as Miller was ready to throw his pitch a very strong gust of wind hit Miller and tended to make his body sway back and forth two or three inches. The American League bench seeing this yelled out "balk" as Colavito swung and missed the pitch. Home plate umpire, Frank Umont of the American League, took off his mask, and waived the base runners to second and third.

The National League, before a crowd of 44,415,went on to win the game, the first of two played that year, 5-4, in ten innings with Stu Miller the winning pitcher, wind and all.

47. When was the first time an All-Star Game was stopped due to rain?

It happened in the second All Star Game of 1961, played on July 31st at Fenway Park. With the game tied 1-1, and a crowd of 31,851, sitting in an increasing rainstorm the umpires stopped the game after the 9th inning and called the contest a tie.

The decision wiped out brilliant pitching performances by both sides as Rocky Colavito's home run in the 1st inning, and Bill White's single driving in Eddie Mathews in the 6th were the only the runs scored in the game.

48. Who hit the first inside-the-park home run in All-Star Game history?

This game had two "first" happenings on July 10, 2007 out in AT&T Park, San Francisco. The first, "first" was the case of Seattle Mariners centerfielder, Ichiro Suzuki, who singled in his first two at bats before crushing a pitch, by right-hander Chris Young of the San Diego Padres, in the 5th inning, that went out to the arcade in right center field, scoring 2B Brian Roberts.

Right fielder Ken Griffey Jr. looked up and waited for the carom to come off the 18-foot high red-brick wall. Instead it hit a green padded crease near the inside of the base of the third archway, and then caromed away from Griffey toward the corner. The speedy Suzuki was churning all the way, and before the ball could be retrieved and fired to the plate, Suzuki had hit the first inside-the-park home run in All-Star game history, putting the American League up, 2-1. The AL went on to a 5-4 win before a packed house of 43,965.

The second "first" happened upon the conclusion of the game when Ichiro Susuki became the first Japanese player to be named the MVP of the All-Star Game.

49. Who was the first player to receive the Most Valuable Player Award of an All-Star Game?

The first recipient of the All-Star Game MVP Award went to shortstop Maury Wills of the Los Angeles Dodgers, on July 10, 1962, down in Washington in the first of two All-Star games played that year.

Wills entered the game in the top of the 6th inning, scored the initial run for the National League, and came back in the 8th to score the third, and insurance run as the senior circuit went on to win 3-1, with Juan Marichal being the winning pitcher.

50. Who was the first player to win the All-Star Game MVP Award twice?

Willie Mays, "The Say Hey Kid," won his first All-Star Game MVP Award on July 9, 1963 out in Cleveland by driving in two runs, scoring two, stealing two bases and making a spectacular catch against the centerfield fence to take an extra base hit away from Joe Pepitone.

His second came on July 9, 1968 down in Houston when Willie scored on a double play in the first inning for the only run of the game, and the first 1-0 game in All-Star history giving the starting pitcher, Don Drysdale, the win.

51. When and where was the first shutout in All-Star Game history played?

The first shutout in All-Star Game history was recorded on July 9, 1940 at Sportsman's Park, St. Louis, when the National League won 4-0 behind the combined pitching of starter, Paul Derringer, followed by two innings of Bucky Walters, Whitlow Wyatt, Larry French, and ending with Carl Hubbell pitching the 9th.

The National League jumped off to a 3-0 lead in the first inning on Max West's homer off Red Ruffing to hold on for the first shutout in All-Star game history.

52. Who threw the first pitch in the first All-Star Game?

Since, if you have read this far, you know that the first All-Star Game was played out in Chicago's Comiskey Park on July 6, 1933, the National League being the visiting ball club. Toeing the rubber that day for the American League, was starting pitcher Vernon "Lefty" Gomez, the southpaw of the New York Yankees.

Because of his exploits that day he would enter the All-Star team of "firsts." (See above)

53. Who was the first American League batter in an All-Star Game?

The St. Louis Cardinals right-hander "Wild Bill" Hallahan threw the first pitch, in the bottom of the 1st inning, in that inaugural All-Star Game to leadoff batter Ben Chapman, the leftfielder of the New York Yankees, who grounded out third baseman Pepper Martin to first baseman Bill Terry.

Now you know who made the first assist and put out for the National League.

54. Who was the first player to ever be selected to start an All-Star Game as a write-in candidate?

In 1970 the fans were allowed, for the first time, to select a member of the National League All-Star team, and they chose Atlanta Braves leftfielder Rico Carty. Their selection wasn't perceptive in that July 14, 1970 game at Riverfront Stadium, for he was 0-1, but it sure was at the end of the season when Carty captured the batting title with a .366 average.

55. Who was the first pitcher to not retire a batter, or consummate a batter's at bat, and yet be credited with a win, in an All-Star Game?

Can't be, you say? Check out the All-Star Game of July 13, 1954 out in Cleveland where Bob "Smiley" Keegan, the Chicago White Sox right-hander got two out in the top of the 8th inning before being relieved by Washington southpaw Dean Stone. Stone found St. Louis Cardinals second baseman Red Schoendienst on third and New York Giants shortstop Alvin Dark on first, as he faced Brooklyn Dodgers centerfielder Edwin "Duke" Snider at the plate.

After running the count to 1-1 on Snider, Schoendienst dashed for home and was called out ending the inning. The American League came up in the bottom of the 8th to score three runs, and White Sox right-hander Virgil "Fire" Trucks came on to throw a scoreless 9th to make Stone, who was now probably in the showers, the pitcher of record, and winner of the 1954 All-Star Game, without retiring a single batter or having one even consummate an at bat.

Just for the record 6'8" Milwaukee Braves right-hander, Gene Conley, took the 11-9 loss in the highest scoring All-Star game in history.

56. Who was the first player to have over 100 runs batted in by the All-Star Game, and not be selected to the All-Star team?

In 1935 "Hammerin' Hank" Greenberg, the Detroit Tigers first baseman, had a torrid first half of a season by driving in 103 runs in his first 76 games, finishing up the 152 game season leading the American League with a total of 170.

That was good enough to win the American League MVP Award that season, but not be an All-Star selection.

57. Who was the first player to represent both Canadian major league teams as an All-Star?

The first player to represent both Canadian teams as an All-Star was the first to play for the Montreal Expos and the Toronto Blue Jays, Ron Fairly. The outfielder, first baseman was an All-Star in 1973 with the Montreal Expos and again in 1977 with the Toronto Blue Jays.

58. Who was the first pitcher to record "saves" in three All-Star Games?

Dennis "Eck" Eckersley, the right-handed relief artist of the Oakland Athletics, came on to record "a save" in the 1988 All-Star game in Cincinnati won by the American League, 2-1; in Chicago in 1990, saving a 1-0 shutout, and in Toronto, in 1991 in a 4-2 American League win.

59. Who is the first pitcher in All-Star Game history to start an All-Star Game while representing three different teams?

Roger Clemens started the 1986 All-Star Game while with the Boston Red Sox. He then started the 2001 game while wearing Yankee pin stripes, and when he moved over to the National League he was the starting pitcher in the 2004 game while with the Houston Astros.

60. Who was the first American League player to hit two home runs in an All-Star Game?

The answer is one you might expect, one who always answered the call, Theodore Samuel "The Splendid Splinter" Williams was the first player to hit two home runs in an All-Star Game.

The date and place was July 9, 1946 at Fenway Park Boston, a most appropriate place for "Teddy Ball Game" to show his stuff.

This was first All-Star Game to be hosted by the Fenway faithful and

Williams didn't disappoint.

His first home run was a long fly ball that carried into the centerfield seats off Kirby Higbe in the 4th inning.

His second was a bit more dramatic as Williams and Truett "Rip" Sewell, the Pittsburgh Pirate right-hander, known for his "eephus" pitch, was the talk of the National League, and carried over to this game.

Prior to the opening pitch Williams said to Sewell, "you can't throw me that pitch." In the 8th inning Sewell dismissed Williams' earlier remark. In one of the more dramatic moments in All-Star Game history Sewell, with one ball, two strikes on Williams, served up one of his special "eephus" pitches. It arched about twenty-five feet in the air before coming down in Williams' "sweet zone," and Williams attacked it and drove it into the right field bullpen.

That power display just added insult to injury as the American League rolled to a 12-0 victory, only the second shutout in All-Star history.

61. Since the All-Star Game began in 1933 who has been the first pitcher to start a game for both the American League and the National League?

In the history of the mid-summer classic only southpaw Vida Blue can make that claim. While with the Oakland Athletics in 1971 he started and was the winning pitcher for the American League, 6-4, in the '71 All-Star Game played in Detroit.

While still with Oakland Blue started for the American League in the 1975 game, but was not involved in the decision, won by the National League, 6-3.

Then in 1978, while pitching for the San Francisco Giants he started the All-Star Game for the National League, in San Diego, again not being involved in the decision in a game won by the National League, 7-3, making him the first pitcher to be the starting pitcher in an All-Star Game and representing both leagues.

62. Who was the first player to have 3,000 hits, yet be shutout in all his All-Star Games?

It wasn't difficult for Paul "Big Poison" Waner to get his share of base hits in the regular season, he had 3,152, but the Pittsburgh Pirates outfielder, in the 1933-34-35,37 All-Star games got the collar as he went 0 for 9.

63. Who was the first player to hit two triples in one All-Star Game?

Hitting two triples in one game is rare enough, but to do it against top-flight pitchers in an All-Star Game is something else. Not for Minnesota Twins first baseman Rod Carew, having led the American League in triples the year before with 16.

In this July 11, 1978 All-Star Game at Qualcomm Stadium, San Diego, he led off the 1st inning with his first triple to deep left-center field off starter Vida Blue, and then came back in the 3rd to hit one, off Blue again, to deep center field. They didn't help as Bruce Sutter and the National League went on to win, 7-3.

64. Who was the first pitcher to pitch in an All-Star Game, first in the American League, then over in the National League, and then back in the American League?

One might call this the flight of the Goose. Putting it in baseball terms it just represented the peregrinations of Richard "Goose" Gossage, the flame-throwing right-hander who made his major league debut with the Chicago White Sox on August 16, 1972, and represented them in the 1975-76 All-Star Game. Then in 1976 he was traded to the Pittsburgh Pirates and was selected to represent the National League in the mid-summer classic of 1977. Signing as a free agent with the New York Yankees in November, 1977 he represented the American League in the 1978, 80-82 All-Star games. Then, in 1984, it was back to the National League with the San Diego Padres where he was selected for the All-Star team in 1984-85.

His flighty nine-team, twenty-season, 124-107, 310 saves, 3.01 Era. pitching career finally ended with his induction into Cooperstown in 2008.

65. Where and when was the first All-Star Game played at night?

The first All-Star Game to be played under the lights took place on July 13, 1943 down in Shibe Park, Philadelphia right in the middle of World War II. The game began at 9:00 PM Eastern War Time so as to allow those working for the war effort to attend.

Red Sox second baseman Bobby Doerr's three-run home run in the 2nd inning got the American League off to a fast start as they went on to win 5-3, with Washington Senators right-hander, Emil "Dutch" Leonard getting the win and St. Louis Cardinals' right-hander Mort Cooper taking his second straight All-Star game loss.

"Double No-Hit" Johnny Vander Meer tied a record by recording six strikeouts in his 2.2 innings of relief. Vince DiMaggio, the Pittsburgh Pirates outfielder, and the oldest of the three DiMaggio brothers, just missed hitting for the cycle when he had a single, triple, and a home run in his three at bats, all in a losing cause.

The game was beamed via short radio to our troops throughout the world.

66. When was the first time that no New York Yankees player appeared in an All-Star Game?

This game relates back to question #65, for in the 1943 All-Star Game, down in Shibe Park, New York Yankee manager "Marse Joe" McCarthy, who had been roundly criticized in his six previous managerial efforts in this game, of having selected his own players to be the starters in the game, refrained from using any of the five Yankee players who had been selected for the All-Star roster.

67. Who was the first player to reach base five times in one All-Star Game?

The player the American League couldn't get out in the 1944 All-Star Game, played out in Forbes Field on July 11th, was southpaw swinging Chicago Cubs first baseman, Phil Cavarretta. He was the first player in All-Star game history to get on base five times when he singled, tripled, and walked three times as the National League rolled to a 7-1 victory.

68. Who was the first player to hit two home runs, each with a man on, in an All-Star Game?

Floyd "Arky" Vaughan, the Pittsburgh Pirate shortstop, had a big day before an All-Star game crowd of 56,674 on Tuesday, October 8, 1941, in Briggs Stadium, Detroit. Although Ted Williams hit his historic clutch 3-run walk off home run, with one out, in the bottom of the 9th, to snatch victory from defeat as the American League squeaked out a 7-5 win, Arky set a first-time record by belting two two-run home runs, one in the 7th, off Sid Hudson, scoring Enos Slaughter, who had singled before him, and again in the 8th, off Ed Smith, driving in Johnny Mize, who had doubled, to be the first in All-Star history to show off multiple home run power in the mid-summer classic.

69. Who was the first player to have a stolen base in an All-Star Game?

The first stolen base in an All-Star game happened quite quickly when American League All-Star second baseman Charlie "The Mechanical Man" Gehringer walked, and stole second base, in the 1st inning off St. Louis Cardinals' southpaw "Wild Bill" Hallahan in the inaugural game on Thursday, July 6, 1933 in Comiskey Park, before crowd of 47,595, none of whom pressed charges.

70. Who was the first National League right-hander to start and win an All-Star Game?

The first National League right-hander to start and win an All-Star Game happened on Tuesday, July 7, 1936, before a crowd of 25,556 at Braves Field.

Dizzy Dean of the St. Louis Cardinals started and pitched three scoreless innings as the National League scored twice in the 2nd inning. Carl Hubbell followed Dean and pitched three shutout innings as the Nationals scored twice in the 5th inning to hold a 4-0 lead before the American League scored three in the 7th as the senior circuit went on to win for the first time, defeating the Red Sox's Lefty Grove, 4-3.

71. Who was charged with the first passed ball in All-Star Game history?

The first passed ball in All-Star Game history came in the top of the 4th inning, on Tuesday, July 7, 1936, before a crowd of 25,556 at Braves Field, when with Lou Gehrig at the plate, a pitch, no doubt a screwball, from New York Giants southpaw, Carl Hubbell, got away from Chicago Cubs backstop, Charles "Gabby" Hartnett, allowing Detroit 2B Charlie Gehringer, who had singled, to advance to second, in a game won by the National League, 4-3.

72. Who was the first, of the six pitchers, to win both an All-Star Game, and then a World Series game in the same season?

Vernon "Lefty" Gomez was the winning pitcher in the 1937 All Star Game and came back in the 1937 World Series to win Games 1 and 5 for the New York Yankees in their five-game series against the New York Giants.

73. Who was the first National League pitcher to win both an All-Star Game and a World Series in the same season?

Paul Derringer, the Cincinnati Reds right-hander, was the winning pitcher in the 1940 All-Star Game when the National League was victorious, 4-0. He came back in the World Series to win Games 4 and 7 against the Detroit Tigers.

74. Who was the first player to score twenty runs in All-Star games during his career?

Willie Mays, the Hall of Fame centerfielder with the New York/San Francisco Giants, and New York Mets scored 20 runs in his 24 All-Star game appearances.

75. Who was the first, and only, player to play in an All-Star game representing four different teams?

Richard "Goose" Gossage, the big, hard-throwing right-hander, was the first, and only, player to represent and play for four different teams in an All-Star game. It started in 1975 when Gossage played that year in the All-Star game while representing the Chicago White Sox. In 1977 "Goose" found himself over in the National League with the Pittsburgh Pirates and playing in the All-Star game that year. Then Gossage is back in the American League and pitched in the 1978 and 1980 games while with the New York Yankees.

Moving ahead to 1984 "Goose" is now back in the senior circuit playing for the San Diego Padres and pitching in the All-Star game that year, as well as in the one the next year, 1985. Four teams, two leagues, and an All-Star regular to boot.

76. Which was the first All-Star game in which neither team made an error?

It happened quite late in the annual series when in the 15th mid-summer classic, held at Sportsman's Park, in St, Louis, before a crowd of 34,009, on July 13, 1948, neither team committed an error. The American League went on to win 5-2, but an error didn't come into play to determine the outcome, a first in All-Star game history.

77. Who were the first players to pull off a double steal in All-Star game history?

The two thieves who pulled off a double steal were 2B Charlie Gehringer, and LF Heinie Manush in the 1st inning of the 1934 All-Star game played at the Polo Grounds on July 10th.

Gehringer led the game off with a single, and Heinie Manush walked.

They both took off with Carl Hubbell on the mound and Gabby Hartnett behind the plate. With men on second and third and no out, one of the greatest pitching displays in baseball history took place.

Hubbell struck out Babe Ruth, Lou Gehrig, and Jimmie Foxx in order to end the inning. The AL went on to win that game 9-7.

78. Who was the first player to play for both leagues in an All-Star game?

Lynwood "Schoolboy" Rowe, the Detroit Tigers right-hander pitched the middle three innings for the American League in the 1936 All-Star game in Boston.

In 1947, then pitching for the Philadelphia Phillies, Rowe came in to pinch-hit for Warren Spahn in the game in Chicago.

79. Who was the first player to hit a home run in his first major league at bat, and in his first at bat in an All-Star game?

On September 12, 1986 Terry Steinbach made his major league debut with the Oakland Athletics, and in his first major league at bat, in Cleveland Stadium, hit a solo home run to left field in the 7th inning off Cleveland southpaw Greg Swindell. Cleveland went on to a 9-3 win in his initial game.

On July 12, 1988 Steinbach, for the first time, was voted to be on the American League All –Star team. In his first at bat, leading off the 3rd inning, in Riverfront Stadium, he hit a home run off the New York Mets right-hander, Dwight "Doc" Gooden. He became the first player to hit a home run in his initial major league at bat, and his initial All-Star game at bat. The latter making him the MVP of that 2-1 American League victory.

80. Who was the first rookie to draw the most votes for an All-Star game?

The Seattle Mariners rookie right fielder Ichiro Suzuki finished the All-Star voting with 3,373,035 votes when the voting closed on July 2, 2001.

81. Who was the first catcher to start an All-Star game in both the American and National Leagues?

He came up as a switch-hitting catcher making his debut with the St. Louis Cardinals on September 21, 1968. During his 13 seasons with the Redbirds Ted Simmons was voted on to the All-Star team in 1972-74, 77-79, but it was on Tuesday, July 11, 1978 at San Diego Stadium, before a crowd of 51,549 that he made his first start for the National League. The

NL took that game 7-3.

Simmons was involved in a seven- player trade with the Milwaukee Brewers on December 12, 1980 and found himself in the American League. He spent five seasons with the Brewers, playing multiple positions and being named to the American League All-Star team in 1981 and in 1983, when he was named as the starting catcher for the American League for the All-Star game played at Comiskey Park, before a crowd of 43,801 on Wednesday, July 6, 1983. The American League came away with a lop-sided 13-3 win.

Since Simmons became the first to catch for both leagues in a Mid-Summer Classic Terry Kennedy, the son of Bob Kennedy, has joined the club, while with the Padres in '85, and then with the Orioles in '87.

82. Who was the first, and only, player to be named to the All-Star team in every year he played in the major leagues?

Look no further than Giuseppe Paolo DiMaggio who was born on November 25, 1914 in Martinez, California, and made his major league debut as Joseph Paul DiMaggio on May 3, 1936 as an outfielder, and quickly became the regular centerfielder, with the New York Yankees.

During his 13 seasons with New York "The Yankee Clipper" was named to the American League All-Star team in each of those years until his final game on September 30, 1951 in the World Series against the New York Giants.

83. Who hit the first walk-off home run in All-Star game history?

Leave it up to Stan Musial, of the St. Louis Cardinals, to come through once again in the clutch, as he sent the fans home from Milwaukee County Stadium happy with a bottom of the 12th inning home run into the right field stands off Boston Red Sox right-hander, Frank Sullivan, to give the National League a 6-5 comeback victory in the All-Star game on July 12, 1955.

That just gave "Stan the Man" another star in a star-filled career as he became the first player to hit a walk-off home run in All-Star game history.

84. Who was the first rookie to be the winning pitcher in an All-Star game?

The scene was Wrigley Field, Chicago, on July 8, 1947, and the American League started Detroit southpaw Hal Newhouser against the host

National League. After three innings he turned it over to New York Yankees rookie right-hander Frank "Spec" Shea in the 4th who pitched the 5th, 6th, and 7th innings, and while in there benefited from a run in the 6th when Luke Appling scored as Joe DiMaggio banged into a double play, and in the 7th when Stan Spence singled home Bobby Doerr with the deciding run, as Washington right-hander Walt Masterson, and Yankee southpaw Joe Page held on for an American League 2-1 victory, and Shea, "The Naugatuck Nugget", became the first rookie to win an All-Star game.

85. Who was the first, and only, player to have two pinch-hits in an All-Star Game in the same season?

From 1959 through 1962 the major leagues played two All-Star games each season. In 1960 the first game was played on Monday, July 11th in Municipal Stadium, Kansas City. In the top of the 8th inning the St. Louis Cardinals' Stan Musial came in to pinch-hit for Pirates 2B Bill Mazeroski and lined a single off Detroit's right-hander Frank "The Yankee Killer" Lary. The NL went on to win 5-3.

In Game 2, played at Yankee Stadium on Wednesday, July 13th, the 38,362 on hand were privy to history as Stan Musial again came up to pinch-hit, this time in the top of the 7th, for the Los Angeles Dodgers right-hander, Stan Williams, and hit a two-out solo home run to deep right field off White Sox right-hander Gerry Staley to raise the National League lead to 4-0 as the senior circuit pitchers threw a 6-0 shutout. "Stan the Man" added another footnote to his resume by being the first player in All-Star Game history to have two pinch-hits in the same season.

86. Who was the first player to hit an All-Star game home run for three different teams?

Alfonso Soriano made his major league debut on September 14, 1999 with the New York Yankees.

Named as an All-Star while with the Yankees, he appeared in the mid-summer classic on Tuesday, July 9, 2002 in Miller Park, and hit a one out, solo home run, off Dodgers' right-hander Eric Gagne in the 5th inning of a game that was called after 11 innings at 7-7.

On Tuesday, July 13, 2004, down in Minute Maid Park, and now an All-Star with the Texas Rangers, he hit a two- out, three-run home run off Houston's right-hander Roger Clemens propelling the American League to a 9-4 win.

His third team, the Chicago Cubs, was the beneficiary of Soriano's bat when he hit a two-out, two-run home run off Mariners' right-hander, J.J. Putz, in the 9th inning out in A.T.&T. Park, but it wasn't enough as the American League squeaked out a 3-2 win.

I. THE BIG FALL SHOW

1. Who was the first batter to come to the plate in the first World Series game?

The first batter to step to the plate in the first World Series game, at that time called The Championship of the United States, was Clarence "Ginger" Beaumont, centerfielder of the Pittsburgh Pirates on October 1, 1903 at the home field of the Boston Americans (Red Sox), Huntington Avenue Baseball Grounds, Boston, before an overflow crowd of 16,242.

He led off, facing Denton "Cy" Young, and flied out to centerfielder Charles "Chick" Stahl. The Pirates went on to win the first game, 7-3.

2. Who hit the first World Series home run?

The first World Series home run couldn't have come any earlier for it happened in Game 1, on October 1, 1903, in the first World Series game ever played.

It was Pittsburgh Pirates right-fielder Jimmy Sebring who connected for the first World Series home run, a solo shot with one out, off Boston Americans' (Red Sox) right-hander Denton "Cy" Young in the 7th inning at the Huntington Avenue Grounds in Boston before a crowd of 16,242.

Right-hander Charles "Deacon" Phillippe, with ten strikeouts, and with the help of Sebring's four runs batted in, and third baseman Tommy Leach's four hits, carried him to a 7-3 win, and to make Phillippe the first pitcher to ever win a World Series game.

3. Who was the first manager to win a World Series?

When left fielder Fred Clarke, the playing manager of the Boston Americans, took his team to five wins out of the best of eight games, to defeat the Pittsburgh Pirates at the Huntington Grounds, before a small crowd of 7,455 on October 13, 1903, it was clinched by a four-hit, 3-0, shutout by "Big Bill" Dinneen. That made Clarke the first manager to win a World Series and put the winner's share of $1,182 in each of his player's pockets.

4. Who was the first manager to lose a World Series?

Like the Boston Americans the Pittsburgh Pirates were led by a playing manager, third baseman Jimmy Collins. The series started off well for Pittsburgh with their starter Deacon Phillippe pitching a six-hitter and Pittsburgh's power coming into play with right fielder Jimmy Sebring driving in four runs in a 7-3 opening game victory.

Boston came right back with "Wild Bill" Dinneen pitching a 3-hit shut-out, 3-0, tying the series.

With illness and injuries racking the Pirates staff Phillippe was called on time and time again and started five games, completed five, winning three but losing two.

Boston kept the pressure up and came away winning five of the eight and their first World's Championship, while Pirate skipper Jimmy Collins took the first World Series loss.

Interestingly, the Pirate players came away richer, for their losing share was $1,316,25 each, $134.25 more per player than Boston, because Pittsburgh President Barney Dreyfuss gave his share of the gate receipts to his players.

5. Who was the first National League player to be a designated hitter in a World Series?

The first National League designated hitter in World Series history occurred on October 16, 1976 when Dan Driessen, a first baseman/third baseman/outfielder for the Cincinnati Reds was penciled in on the lineup card as the designated hitter for Game 1, at Riverfront Stadium, as the Reds opened up the 1976 World Series against the New York Yankees.

Driessen came to bat 14 times in the series, had 5 hits, including two doubles, a home run, drove in one run, scored four times and stole a base for a .357 batting average in the four game sweep by the Big Red Machine over the Yankees.

6. Who was the first, and only, pitcher with a losing regular season record to start three games of a World Series?

This unusual assignment of having a pitcher with a losing regular season record start three games in a World Series happened in the 1973 World Series.

Jon Matlack, the New York Mets southpaw, was 14-16, with a 3.20 Era. in the regular season, and was selected by manager Yogi Berra to start Games One, Four and Seven against the Oakland A's. Matlack won Game 4, 6-1, but lost the other two.

Watching from the dugout was Tom Seaver who had a 19-10 record and led the National League in Era. with a 2.08, appeared in Games 3 and

6, with one losing decision.

7. Who was the first pitcher to lose two consecutive World Series games?

The pitcher who went into the record books by being the first pitcher to lose two consecutive World Series games started it off when, in Game 6 of the 1986 World Series between the New York Mets and the Boston Red Sox at Shea Stadium, right-hander Calvin Schiraldi came into the game in the 7th inning in relief of Roger Clemens. He pitched 2.2 shutout innings, and going into the 10th inning tied 3-3 had the benefit in the top of that inning of a Dave Henderson solo home run, and a single by Marty Barrett to drive in Wade Boggs and giving Boston a 5-3 lead going into the bottom of the 10th. When Wally Backman and Keith Hernandez were retired, the Mets were one out from Series elimination. Then Gary Carter singled to left, Kevin Mitchell, pinch-hitting for Mets' right-hander Rick Aguilera, singled to center field. With a 0-2 count on Ray Knight he lined a single to center to score Carter and make it 5-4, with Mitchell advancing to third.

In came Bob "Big Foot" Stanley, to replace Schiraldi and close out the World Series. He faced leftfielder Mookie Wilson, and with a 2-2 count fired a pitch way inside, driving Wilson to the ground, and getting away from catcher Rich Gedman for a wild pitch, with Mitchell scoring and Knight moving down to second.

Wilson got back up in the batter's box and awaited the tenth pitch of the at bat from Stanley. Wilson hit a slow ground ball up the first base line. As it approached first baseman Bill Buckner it just sneaked between his legs and rolled out to right field. Knight scored the final run and the Mets had defeated the Red Sox in Game 6, 6-5, in one of the most historic World Series games played, and with Schiraldi taking the loss.

Now for the rest of the story. In Game 7, on October 27th, at Shea Stadium, the Red Sox came back with southpaw Bruce Hurst, and he was given a three run lead in the top of the 2nd and carried it into the bottom of the 6th before the Mets picked up three to tie.

Schiraldi came on in relief in the 7th and was greeted by third baseman Ray Knight's home run to give the Mets the lead which they never relinquished, and the Mets overcame two runs in the top of the 8th with two of their own in the bottom of that inning to go on to an 8-5 win and the World Championship. Roger McDowell was the winner and Jesse Orosco received the save.

And yes, Calvin Schiraldi was the loser for the second consecutive day, the first time that has happened in a World Series.

8. Who was the first, and only, pitcher to throw a wild pitch in the bottom of the 9th inning to lose a World Series?

One has to go back to the 1927 World Series when the Pittsburgh Pirates faced the "Murderous Row" New York Yankees.

The Yankees had taken the first three games and heading into the fourth and final game, at Yankee Stadium, before a crowd of 57,909, were tied 3-3 with Pittsburgh, going into the bottom of the 9th inning.

Johnny "Big Serb" Miljus had come on in relief of 22-game winner Carmen "Specs" Hill in the 7th inning and provided strong relief until the 9th.

Then centerfielder Earle "The Kentucky Colonel" Combs walked, shortstop Mark Koenig beat out a bunt to advance Combs to second. Babe Ruth, after a wild pitch that advanced the runners, leaving first base open, was walked intentionally. With the bases loaded and no one out, and Lou Gehrig coming up next, Miljus struck out the next two batters. The next batter was Tony Lazzeri, and Miljus uncorked his second wild pitch to Lazzeri and Combs scored; game over, World Series over. The Yankees had swept the Pirates with a series ending wild pitch, the first in World Series history.

It also marked the first time that an American League team had swept the National League in a World Series.

9. Who was the first player to hit into three double plays in a World Series game?

1951 was a historic World Series, for it once again brought together two New York teams in a subway series, the Giants and the Yankees.

It also was the last sailing of "The Yankee Clipper" for the career of Joe DiMaggio would come to an end after the sixth game.

What it also did was to introduce two new young exciting players to major league baseball in the Fall Classic; Mickey Mantle of the Yankees, and Willie Mays of the Giants. These two would stand baseball on its head through the coming years with their great play and record setting performances.

Speaking to the latter, Willie, who was the 1951 National League Rookie-of-the-Year, would not have a great Game 4, on October 8th, at the Polo

Grounds. Beside going 0-4, he came up in the bottom of the 2nd inning, with Bobby Thomson on first via a walk, and hit a sharp grounder to Phil Rizzuto at short, who flipped to Gil McDougald at second, and then on to Joe Collins at first for the double play.

In the bottom of the 5th Willie was again up and again with Bobby Thomson on first via a walk. Willie bounced back to the mound where right-hander Allie Reynolds spun and threw to Rizzuto covering second, and the relay on to Collins gave Willie his second double play.

In the bottom of the 7th Willie kept the ball in the air and flied out to Joe DiMaggio in deep centerfield.

In the bottom of the 9th up came Willie, and who should be on first after a run-scoring single, but Bobby Thomson, and Monte Irvin was leading off third. It wasn't Willie's day for he hit another hard line shot to Rizzuto who fielded it, flipped it to McDougald, and then on to Collins, and Willie became the first player to hit into three double plays in one World Series game.

10. Who was the first player to end a World Series with a walk-off home run?

This game is still talked about with passion in baseball circles. On October 13, 1960 Bill Mazeroski, second baseman for the Pittsburgh Pirates, after seeing the New York Yankees tie the game in the top of the 9th inning, 9-9, came up in the bottom of the 9th inning of Game 7 at Forbes Field, and faced New York Yankees right-handed reliever Ralph Terry. He hit his 1-0 pitch deep over the left field wall for a walk-off home run to give Harvey Haddix, and the Pirates a 10-9 victory and the World Championship.

11. Who was the first, and only, player to get five base hits in one World Series game?

This rare occurrence happened in Game One, on October 12, 1982, at Busch Stadium, St. Louis before a crowd of 53,723. Milwaukee third baseman Paul Molitor had quite a day batting against Cardinal pitching as he went 5-6 with two runs driven in as the Brewers rolled to a 10-0 win behind the three-hit pitching of southpaw Mike Caldwell.

Molitor had an infield single in the 2nd, a single to centerfield in the 4th, a single to left field in the 6th, all off starter Bob Forsch. In the 8th he had a single off southpaw Dave LaPoint, and came back in the 9th with another single off right-hander Jeff Lahti to wind up his five base hit game, the first in World Series history.

12. Who was the first, and only, player to be named the Most Valuable Player from a losing team in a World Series?

Somehow this selection has bothered me. Let it take nothing away from the winner of the award, Yankee second baseman, Bobby Richardson, a solid ballplayer who had a great World Series. Going 11-30, driving in twelve runs with five extra base hits in the seven game series and batting .367, he should be applauded and recognized.

On the other hand, you have a player who had four extra base hits, drove in five, batted .320, and in the bottom of the 9th inning hit the winning, walk-off home run that brought his team, with one swing of the bat, the World Championship. I believe it is hard to top that for being the most valuable.

13. Who was the first Most Valuable Player of a World Series?

The Most Valuable Player Award for the World Series didn't begin until Brooklyn Dodger southpaw, Johnny Podres, defeated the New York Yankees for the second time in the 1955 World Series. His 2-0 shutout in Game 7 brought the first World Championship to Flatbush and was enough to make him the MVP for the series and the hero of Brooklyn fans throughout the borough.

14. Who hit the first walk-off home run in World Series history?

The first walk-off home run in World Series history occurred on October 5, 1949, in Game One at Yankee Stadium, when Yankee first baseman Tommy Henrich, who had gone 0 for 3 until the bottom of the 9th inning, hit a solo home run off Brooklyn Dodger right hander Don Newcombe to give the Yankees a 1-0 victory in the first game.

15. Who is the first manager in major league history to have managed in more than one World Series and to have never lost a game?

Terry Francona, the manager of the Boston Red Sox, defeated the St. Louis Cardinals in four games in the 2004 World Series and then came back in 2007 to sweep the Colorado Rockies in four games.

16. Who hit the first grand slam home run in World Series history?

On October 10, 1920 outfielder Elmer Smith of the Cleveland Indians, in the 1st inning of Game 5, of the historic 1920 World Series, hit the first grand slam home run in World Series history, off Brooklyn Dodger right-hander Burleigh "Ol' Stubblebeard" Grimes.

17. Who was the first, and only, player to turn an unassisted triple play in the World Series?

This story is repeated over and over again among baseball fans for it happened in, no doubt, the most historic game in a World Series ever played. Here is just one of the historic firsts from that game. If you doubt me, read on.

It took place in the 5ᵗʰ inning of Game 5 in the 1920 World Series, at Dunn Field, Cleveland, between the Cleveland Indians and the Brooklyn Robins (Dodgers).

With the Robins catcher, Otto "Moonie" Miller on first and second baseman Pete Kilduff leading off second, the Robins pitcher, southpaw Clarence Mitchell, came up against Jim "Sarge" Bagby Sr. He lined his pitch at shortstop Bill Wambsganss who snared it, stepped on second to retire Kilduff, and then tagged Miller as he came roaring down from first, to complete the first and only, triple play in World Series history. The local crowd of 26,884 went home happy as Cleveland came away with an 8-1 victory.

18. Who was the first pitcher to hit a home run in a World Series?

As we had mentioned previously the 1920 World Series was a historic one that created three "first time happenings." Here is the third.

Jim "Sarge" Bagby Sr., the Cleveland Indians right-hander, came up to bat on October 10ᵗʰ, in the 4ᵗʰ inning of Game 5 and faced Brooklyn Robins right-hander Burleigh "Ol' Stubblebeard" Grimes with one out, and two runners on, and cleared the bases with a 3-run home run into deep centerfield at Dunn Field to become the first pitcher to hit a home run in a World Series game.

Bagby had a good day at the plate going 2-4 with three runs batted in as Cleveland rolled to an 8-1 win.

19. Who was the first, and only, player to hit two doubles, two triples, and two home runs in one World Series?

First baseman, third baseman, designated hitter, whatever his assignment in the 1993 World Series, Paul Molitor of the Toronto Blue Jays always had a bat in his hand and he used it with great ability. In the six game series, won by Toronto 4-2 over the Philadelphia Phillies, Molitor went 12 for 24, with two doubles, two triples, and two home runs, drove in 8 runs, scored 10, walked three times and stole a base.

To absolutely no one's surprise he was presented with the World Series MVP Award.

20. Who was the first pitcher to pitch a perfect game in the World Series?

This question can be answered by most baseball fans, and many who just have a casual interest in the game. On Monday October 8, 1956, before Game 5, Yankee manager Casey Stengel had instructed pitching coach, Jim Turner, to place a baseball in the shoe of Don Larsen as his way of saying you are today's starting pitcher. Larsen had no idea he was pitching that day, especially after being hammered by Brooklyn in Game 2, and having spent the previous evening out partying. His arrival in the locker room told him differently.

His opponent that day for the Brooklyn Dodgers was a tough right-hander named Sal "The Barber" Maglie.

In the top of the 9th inning, at Yankee Stadium, before a crowd of 64,519, many more probably have claimed to have been there, though many had via television. Larsen, holding a slim 2-0 lead, was facing just three more batters for immortality. First up was right fielder Carl Furillo who flied out to fellow right fielder Hank Bauer. Next came catcher Roy Campanella, who grounded out, second to first, Billy Martin to Joe Collins. That brought up left-handed pinch-hitter Dale Mitchell, batting for Dodgers pitcher Sal Maglie. An 11-year veteran, and always a good hitter, with a career .312 batting average, and one of the toughest batters to strike out in major league history (119 in 3,984 at-bats) in what would be Mitchell's last major league at-bat.

Larsen had been unleashing mostly fastballs in setting down the first 25 batters in order, with 92 pitches. Now with his 93rd pitch he came in high and outside to Mitchell. The 94th pitch was a slow curve that broke over the plate for strike one. Pitch 95 was a slider that Mitchell swung at and missed for strike two. Larsen came back with a fastball on his 96th pitch that Mitchell sliced into the left field stands. The 97th and final pitch was a fastball, and Mitchell checked his swing, deeming it "a foot outside." Home plate umpire, Babe Pinelli, umpiring his final game before retirement, saw it differently, and raised his right arm for strike three, and the Dodgers went down 2-0, and fell behind in the series 3 games to 2.

With the call, catcher Yogi Berra leaped up and raced out to the mound to meet Larsen, jumping into the 6'4" right-hander's arms as the two did a dance on the Yankee Stadium mound. The crowd of 64,519, having been on the edge of their seats for 2 hours and 6minutes, erupted in a deafening roar as they had been witness to the first perfect game in World Series history.

So this 14-year journeyman pitcher for seven different franchises from 1953-67, with a career 81-91, 3.78 Era., and 849 strikeouts, and now wearing pin stripes from 1955-59, had made the biggest strikeout of his career, and had reached a pinnacle no other pitcher in World Series had attained -- the first perfect game in World Series history.

21. Who pitched the first, of the three, one-hitters in World Series history?

On Wednesday, October 10th, in Game 2 of the 1906 "Windy City" World Series, between White Sox centerfielder/manager Fielder Jones's "Hitless Wonders," and first baseman/manager Frank Chance's hard hitting Cubs, winners of 116 games that season, "Big Ed" Reulbach, the Chicago Cubs right-hander, took the mound at South Side Park III against his cross-town rival, White Sox southpaw Guy "Doc" White.

The Cubs got on Doc White for three runs in the 3rd, and another in the 4th and that was more than enough as the "Hitless Wonders" lived up to their name and "Big Ed" went on to deny the White Sox a base hit until the bottom of the 7th inning when, after third baseman George Rohe opened the inning with a walk, first baseman John "Jiggs" Donahue singled to center for the only hit for the Southsiders as Reulbach went on to win, 7-1, before a crowd of 12,595, and become the first pitcher to pitch a one-hitter in a World Series.

Interestingly, the second one-hitter in World Series history was pitched by another Chicago Cubs right-hander, Claude Passeau, when in Game 3, on October 5, 1945, out in Detroit, he allowed only a single to Tigers' first baseman Rudy York in the 3rd inning, and later a walk to catcher Bob Swift in the 6th in his 3-0 victory. Passeau then became the first to pitch a one-hit *shutout* in the Fall Classic.

22. Who was the first player to lead off a World Series game with a

home run?

It was in Game 2, of the 1903 World Series, on October 2nd, up in Boston, when Red Sox leftfielder Patsy Dougherty led off the game with a home run off Pittsburgh Pirate right-hander Sam Leever.

Patsy came back in the bottom of the 6th and hit another solo home run as he led the Red Sox, and their right-hander, "Big Bill" Dinneen to a 3-0 victory to tie the series at a game apiece.

23. Who was the first player to hit a home run in his first two World Series at bats?

Game 1, October 4, 1972, began a record setting day for Oakland Athletics catcher Gene Tenace. He came up to the plate in the top of the 2nd inning for his first at bat in a World Series, and found outfielder George Hendrick on first via a walk, and took Cincinnati Reds' right-hander, Gary Nolan deep into the left field stands of Riverfront Stadium, before a record Cincinnati crowd of 52,918.

He came back for his second at bat, in the 5th inning, with one out, and finding the bases clear, hit a solo shot deep into those left field stands for his second consecutive home run which was all that was needed for Ken Holtzman to record a 3-2 win.

Tenace's hitting didn't stop in Game 1 for he went on to be the big contributor in the Athletics seven game win over Cincinnati for the World Championship going 8 for 23 with four home runs and eight runs batted in for a .348 average, good enough for the MVP World Series Award.

24. Who hit the first World Series pinch-hit home run?

In a slugfest, before 33,098 at Ebbets Field, Brooklyn, in Game 3, on October 2, 1947, the New York Yankees were down 9-7 going into the top of the 7th inning and called on Yogi Berra to come and pinch-hit for fellow catcher Sherman Lollar. Facing him was right-hander Ralph Branca, and Yogi blasted a solo home run to be the first player to pinch-hit a home run in World Series history. That made the score 9-8 where it stayed, as the Dodgers took the game, one of three they would win as the Yankees took the series in seven games.

25. Who was the first, and only, player to hit five home runs in one World Series?

This came to pass in the 1977 World Series when, Reggie "Mr. October"

Jackson, of the New York Yankees, hit five home runs in that World Series.

The first came in Game 4, at Dodger Stadium, in the 6th inning with two outs. Jackson hit a solo home run off Dodger right-hander Rick Rhoden.

Moving on to Game 5, still at Dodger Stadium, Jackson came up facing Don Sutton, who had just given up a home run to Yankee catcher Thurman Munson. With the bases having been cleared by Munson, and with two out, Jackson followed with his home run which gave him his second home run of the series, but had no impact on the game as Sutton breezed to a 10-4 victory.

Now came the dramatic moments at Yankee Stadium in Game 6. Fans knew that Jackson could hit them out, he had shown that through games four and five, but today would be more impressive. With the Yankees ahead 3 games to 2 in the series someone had to step up, either on the Dodgers side to keep the series going, or on the Yankees side to close down the Fall Classic.

Here Jackson took over. In the bottom of the 4th inning Jackson came up with one on and no out and crushed a Burt Hooton pitch into the right field stands giving New York a 4-3 lead. Coming up in the 5th inning, this time facing right-hander Elias Sosa with one on and two out, he did what he had done in the 4th inning, by driving Sosa's pitch into the right field seats driving the 56,407 fans into ecstasy as the Yankees took the lead 7-3.

Reggie wasn't through, for in the 8th inning with the bases empty and no outs, Jackson took a slow knuckler from right-hander Charlie Hough and deposited it into the black bleacher section in deep center field for the eighth and final run in an 8-4 victory and the World Series Championship in 1977.

26. Who was the first, and only, St. Louis Browns player to ever hit a home run in World Series history?

Since the St. Louis Browns were spectators rather than players when the Fall Classic came around, it is safe to say that the first, and only, Browns player in franchise history who has, or ever will, hit a home run in the World Series was first baseman George McQuinn.

It happened in the 1944 World Series when there was an all-St. Louis Fall Classic, the Browns versus the Cardinals, dubbed the "St. Louis Show-down". In the six-game contest, all games won by the Cardinals were held in Sportsman's Park, the home field for both teams.

In the 4th inning of Game 1 McQuinn came up with two outs, after right-fielder Gene Moore had singled, and hit a two-run home run off Cardinal right-hander Mort Cooper. It proved to be the deciding factor for right-hander Denny Galehouse as his Browns won 2-1.

The 33,242 in attendance that day can claim who they witnessed the first, and only, World Series home run hit in St. Louis Browns history, thanks to George McQuinn.

27. Who was the first pitcher to win a Game 7, and a World Championship, in Brooklyn Dodger history?

If you said it was a 23-year old southpaw named Johnny Podres you would be correct. He took the mound for Game 7 on October 4, 1955, at the Yankee Stadium, before a crowd of 62,465, and went into the bottom of the 9th inning with a slim two-run lead.

Moose Skowron was first up and bounced back to Podres. Bob Cerv then flied out to Sandy Amoros in left field. Last hope was Elston Howard who bounced a grounder to Pee Wee Reese at short who flipped to Gil Hodges at first to end the game and the World Series, making the Brooklyn Dodgers 1955 World Champions.

For his eight-hit, two-walk, four-strikeout shutout effort he won the World Series Most Valuable Player Award.

28. Of the 32 players, to date, who have hit a home run in their first World Series at bat, who was the very first to do it?

If one goes back to October 7, 1925, to Game 1 at Forbes Field, Pittsburgh, we'll see Washington Senators' right fielder Joe "Moon" Harris come to bat against Pittsburgh Pirates right-hander Lee "Specs" Meadows in the 2nd inning, with one out, and take him downtown to be the first player to hit a home run in his first World Series at bat. It gave Walter Johnson an early one run lead as he went on to set down the Pirates 4-1 before a crowd of 41, 723.

29. Who was the first major league player to have played in the College World Series, and then in a Major League World Series?

Jackie Jensen played in the College World Series in 1947 with the University of California and went on to play in the outfield with the New York Yankees in the 1950 World Series.

30. Who were the first brothers to pitch and win all four World Series games?

If you want to win a World Series just look to the Dean brothers, Dizzy and Daffy, of the St. Louis Cardinals. They took matters into their own hands in the 1934 World Series against the Detroit Tigers.

Dizzy started Game 1, on October 3rd and won it 8-3 over General Crowder. Daffy (Paul) came back in Game 3 to beat Tommy Bridges 4-1. Dizzy came back to pitch in Game 5, on October 7th, but lost to Tommy Bridges 3-1. Daffy took on Schoolboy Rowe in Game 6 and beat him 4-3. With the series tied at three games Dizzy started Game 7, on October 9th, against Eldon "Big Six" Auker, winner of Game 4, and shutout the Tigers, cruising to an 11-0 victory, giving the Cardinals the World Championship and the Dean brothers two wins each to cover all the Cardinal victories in the World Series.

31. Who was the first pitcher to hit a grand slam home run in a World Series?

Southpaw Dave McNally, of the Baltimore Orioles, came up to bat in the 6th inning with two out in Game 3 of the 1970 World Series, on October 13, 1970, at Memorial Stadium.

Frank Robinson had flied out to left centerfield, and Paul Blair had singled to center when the call went out to bring in Cincinnati right-hander Wayne Granger to take over for Tony Cloninger. Brooks Robinson greeted Granger with a double to left field sending Blair to third. With first base open the Reds decided to intentionally walk Davey Johnson. Andy Etchebarren, next up, then struck out, which brought up Dave McNally. With a 4-1 lead, he saw a pitch he liked from Granger and deposited it deep into the left field stands for a grand slam home run, scoring Blair, Robinson, and Johnson to give the Baltimore Orioles an 8-1 lead which McNally took to a 9-3 win.

The crowd of 51,773 was witness to the first grand slam home run hit by a pitcher in World Series history.

32. Who was the first, and only, pitcher to win a World Series game in three different decades?

Leave it to Jim "Pancakes" Palmer of the Baltimore Orioles to pull this off. In the 1966 World Series he won the 2nd game beating Sandy Koufax with a 6-0 shutout of the Los Angeles Dodgers.

In the first game of the 1970 World Series against the Cincinnati Reds he bested Gary Nolan 4-3. Palmer then came back in Game 2, of the 1971 World Series, and with plenty of offensive support he beat the Pittsburgh Pirates 11-3.

In Game 3 of the 1983 World Series, against the Philadelphia Phillies, he again was dominant, taking a 3-2 win over Steve Carlton.

In six World Series appearances over three decades Palmer came away with a 4-1 record.

33. Who was the first player to play in a World Series, and then come back to umpire in a World Series game?

Right-hander "Big Bill" Dinneen, of the Boston Americans, one of the truly great pitchers of his day, with what now would be called the MVP, was a hero of the 1903 World Series when he won three games as Boston defeated Pittsburgh, 5 games to 3.

Eight years later, on Saturday, October 14, 1911, before a crowd of 38,281 at the Polo Grounds, in Game 1 of the World Series between the Philadelphia Athletics and the New York Giants, Dinneen became the first man to play in a World Series, and then come back to be the umpire in one, as he positioned himself as the first base umpire to start the first game of the 1911 World Series, won by the Giants, 2-1.

34. What teams were the first to face each other in the World Series?

Let's go back to 1903 when the owner of the American League leading Boston Americans (Red Sox), Henry Killea, was contacted by Barney Dreyfuss, the owner of the National League champion Pittsburgh Pirates to set up a best of nine series to determine the World Championship of major league baseball.

It was on October 1, 1903 that the Americans and the Pirates took the field at Huntington Avenue Grounds in Boston, before 16,242 excited fans to see who would be crowned the best in major league baseball.

Pirates right-hander Charles "Deacon" Phillippe, a twenty game winner the past three seasons, bested Denton "Cy" Young, who had posted 93 wins during the past three seasons, 7-3, in the first World Series game ever played.

Back in Boston, on October 13th, the eighth game of the series took place, with Boston having won the last three games and, four of the first seven.

Phillippe, who had pitched a complete game seven, but losing to Cy Young, but had won three games in the series, and had pitched four complete games, faced off against "Big Bill" Dinneen, who had pitched three complete games, winning two.

After one hour and thirty-five minutes, in a brilliantly pitched four-hit shutout, Dinneen set down the Pirates, 3-0, and the Boston Americans, by winning five games, became the first team to become World Champions.

35. Who was the first African-American to pitch in a World Series?

That distinction goes to Leroy "Satchel" Paige, the 42-year old ageless right-hander of the Cleveland Indians, who came on in relief of Russ Christopher to face the Boston Braves, with one out, and one on in the top of the 7th inning of Game 5, at Cleveland Stadium on October 10, 1948, before a crowd of 86,288.

He retired Warren Spahn on a fly ball to Larry Doby in centerfield. With Tommy Holmes up next Paige was called for a balk which moved Eddie Stanky to second. There he stayed as Tommy Holmes grounded out to short, Lou Boudreau to first baseman Eddie Robinson. Boston went on to win the game 11-5.

That was "Satchel's" only appearance in the series as the Indians captured the Championship, 4 games to 2.

36. Who was the first manager to win a World Series in both leagues?

George "Sparky" Anderson won the World Series as dugout skipper of the Cincinnati Reds with his team's 4 games to 3 win over the Boston Red Sox in 1975.

He came back with his "Big Red Machine" in 1976 to sweep the New York Yankees, 4-0.

Moving over to the American League he led the Detroit Tigers to the 1984 World Championship with his 4 games to 1 win over the San Diego Padres, to be able to say, "Been there, done that, in both leagues."

37. Who was the first African-American pitcher to win a World Series game?

Joe Black came into the big leagues with the Brooklyn Dodgers in 1952 at the age of 28, and had the best year of his six-year career as a rookie with a 14-3 record in relief, and 15-4 overall, to go along with his 15 saves and 2.15 Era.

He carried that fine rookie effort over to the World Series, in Game 1, on Wednesday, October 1, 1952, at Ebbets Field, before 34,861, pitching a complete game, six-hit, 4-2, win, allowing two walks, and striking out six to defeat the Yankees and right-hander Allie Reynolds to become the first African-American to win a World Series game.

38. Who was the first player to hit a home run with three different teams in the World Series?

The 1989 World Series, famous for the earthquake that interrupted play during the World Series, was the first time that San Francisco Giants shortstop Matt Williams had a chance to show off his home run hitting prowess in the fall.

On Friday, October 27th, Williams came up in the 2nd inning of Game 3, before a crowd of 62,138 at Candlestick Park, against Oakland Athletics right-hander Dave Stewart, and hit a two out solo home run to deep left field. It wasn't near enough as Oakland came away with a 13-7 win.

In 1997 Williams found himself in another World Series, this time as the third baseman for the Cleveland Indians. In the 8th inning of Game 4, in Jacobs Field, Williams came up facing Florida Marlins right-hander Jay Powell, and hit a two-run home run that just padded the Indians score as they went on to easily win the game 10-3.

On October 22, 2001 Williams was back in the National League, this time with the Arizona Diamondbacks, and facing Andy Pettitte, the stylish southpaw of the New York Yankees, in Game 2 at Bank One Ballpark in Phoenix. It was the 7th inning with Arizona clinging to a 1-0 lead, with two men on and one out when Williams cleared the bases with a three-run home run. That gave Randy Johnson a more comfortable margin as he went on to pitch a three-hit shutout winning 4-0.

It also gave Matt Williams the distinction of being the first player to hit a World Series home run for three different teams.

39. What two teams were the first to play in the World Series representing the same city?

The 1906 World Series brought together the Chicago White Sox, champions of the American League, and dubbed "The Hitless Wonders", against their cross-town rivals the Chicago Cubs, champions of the senior circuit, and winners of an unprecedented 116 wins that season.

The Cubs were the host for Game 1, played at West Side Park, before a crowd of 12,693. It was a great pitchers' battle with White Sox southpaw Nick Altrock allowing just one run on four hits, while his opposing pitcher, right-hander Mordecai "Three Finger" Brown gave up just four hits, but two runs, and the Pale Hose came away with a 2-1 victory.

Game 2 switched to the White Sox side of town, Southside Park, where the 12,595 fans saw pitching dominate as White Sox first baseman, John "Jiggs" Donahue singled in the 7th inning to spoil "Big Ed" Reulbach's no-hitter, with the Sox only run coming on a wild pitch and an error in the 6th inning. Cubs' third baseman Harry Steinfeldt went 3-3 and shortstop Joe Tinker had two hits and scored three runs as Reulbach breezed to a 7-1 victory.

Though the Cubs, with their 116-win regular season coming up against the "hitless wonders" were overwhelming favorites, they didn't measure up as expected and lost to their cross-town rivals 4 games to 2, as the White Sox became not only champions of the "Windy City" but World Champions as well.

Interesting to note that in this series, as in the previous one, covering 99 innings, not a home run was hit.

40. What opposing teams were the first to play all of their World Series games against each other in the same stadium?

The New York Giants met the New York Yankees in the 1921 World Series, the last of the five-out-of nine game series ever played. In 1913 the Yankees had made an agreement with the Giants to sub-lease the Polo Grounds, home of the Giants, for the games that they would play during the regular season until 1923, alternating home dates.

With both teams in the World Series that year each team played the role of home and visitor during, what was then, a nine-game series. The first game took place on October 5th and lasted for eight games with the Giants coming away as World Champions, 5 games to 3.

41. Who was the first pitcher to save a World Series game by coming on in relief?

Although the "save" statistic didn't exist back in 1906 southpaw Guy "Doc" White came on with one out in the 7th inning, in relief of "Big Ed" Walsh, for the Chicago White Sox on October 13th in Game 5, at West

Side Park, against the cross-town Cubs, and preserved the 8-6 lead Walsh had left him with, for the first "unofficial" save in World Series history. The White Sox went on to defeat the Cubs in six games.

42. What was the first team to lose the first two games of a World Series and come back to win the Series?

That comeback belonged to the New York Giants when they lost the first game of the 1921 World Series to Carl Mays, and the Yankees, 3-0, and also the second game by an identical score to Waite Hoyt.

They came back with a roar beating the Yankees in Game 3, on October 7th 13-5. They continued on with their winning ways by defeating their Bronx neighbors in Games 4, 6, 7, and 8 to take the World Championship, 5 games to 3.

43. Who was the first pitcher to pitch three shutouts in a best of seven World Series?

Without a doubt, the greatest pitching performances ever seen in a World Series happened back in the 1905 series between the New York Giants and the Philadelphia Athletics.

In Game 1, on Monday, October 9th, before a crowd of 17,955 down in Philadelphia, Christy Mathewson, in the initial class in Cooperstown, went for the Giants against southpaw "Gettysburg Eddie" Plank, another future Hall of Famer, who had won 24 games for Philadelphia during the regular season. Matty pitched a masterpiece, shutting out the Athletics 3-0, on four hits and allowing no walks.

Game 2, on October 10th, at the Polo Grounds, two future members of the Hall of Fame, Charles "Chief" Bender of the Athletics, went against Joe "Iron Man" McGinnity, the right-hander of the Giants. The 24,922 in attendance were treated to another gem, as the Athletics turned the tables, when the tall Chippewa Indian shutout the Giants 3-0 on four hits.

On October 12th, in Game 3, after a day of rain, giving both staffs a bit of rest, the series continued, down in Philadelphia, with the classic pitching of Mathewson, who again took the mound, this time against 18-game winner Andy Coakley. The results were much the same as Game 1 as Matty again shutout the Athletics with just four hits, helped by first baseman Dan McGann's three hits which drove in four runs in Matty's 9-0 victory.

Then on Friday, the 13th, in Game 4, back at the Polo Grounds, the Athletics called upon their future Hall of Fame pitcher, southpaw Eddie Plank, to stem the tide. Unfortunately the tide seemed to be going out for Plank for he met his match by opposing another future resident of Cooperstown, Joe McGinnity. The "Iron Man" throttled the Athletics offense, allowing just five hits, the same as Plank's great effort, but having the benefit of an error by SS Monte Cross in the 4th inning, gave the Giants their only run, McGinnity came away with his first shutout, 1-0.

With the Giants up three games to one, and the Athletics not scoring a run in their three previous defeats Chief Bender was called upon to save the series.

His opponent, in Game 5, on this October 14th afternoon, was none other than "Big Six", Christy Mathewson. The Bucknell graduate had had his way with Connie Mack's nine, and looked forward to closing out the series. Before a crowd of 24,187 at the Polo Grounds Matty set down the Athletics, 2-0, with a five-hit shutout to win the World Championship for the Giants, four games to one, to conclude the most brilliant individual, and two-pitcher pitching performance in World Series history.

There were three parts of this series that were unusual, and in turn, historic. Each game was decided by a shutout, the only time it has happened. The Giants mound staff didn't allow a run in their four victories, and Christy Mathewson's record over 27 innings showed 3 wins, 3 complete games, 13 hits, one walk, and 18 strikeouts, as he became the first pitcher to pitch three complete game shutouts in World Series history.

There is one more. This 1905 World Series was the first officially sanctioned championship series between the winners of the pennant in each league, and was reduced to a four-out-of seven series.

44. Who was the first player to have a career World Series batting average of over .400 (50 at-bat minimum)?

One of the most colorful ballplayers to play the game was John Leonard "Pepper" Martin, otherwise known as "The Wild Horse of the Osage," the fastest man on the field, who played third base and patrolled the outfield for the St. Louis Cardinals, from 1928-44.

Playing in the 1931 World Series, won by the Cardinals in seven games over the Philadelphia Athletics, "Pepper" went 12 for 24, scoring five runs, and driving in five. When the 1934 Cardinals, known as the "The Gas House Gang", one of the most colorful teams in baseball history, came back to the World Series that year they again captured the World Championship, in seven games, this time from the Detroit Tigers, with the Dean brothers, Dizzy and Daffy, each winning two games.

Martin had another big series that year as he went 11-31 with eight runs scored, and three batted in, for a combined World Series record of 55 at bats, 23 hits, 7 doubles, a triple, a home run, 7 stolen bases, scored 14 runs and drove in 8, for a World Series batting average of .418, to be the first player, with at least 50 at bats to have a career World Series batting average over .400.

That 1934 Cardinal team, "The "Gas House Gang", was a name given to a band of scrappy, tobacco chewing, rough, tough, vocal, covered with dirt, ballplayers (because their dirty uniforms resembled gas station attendants), went up against a formidable Tiger team that had won 101 games that year and were the favorites to capture the series. They were led by four future Hall of Fame residents, Hank Greenberg at first base, Charlie Gehringer at second, Leon "Goose" Goslin in left field, and Mickey Cochrane as the catcher, with 24-game winner Elwood "Schoolboy" Rowe as their leading pitcher.

But they proved no match for the band of rowdies nicknamed Dizzy (Dean), Daffy (Dean), Pepper (Martin), Lip (Durocher), Flash (Frisch), Ripper (Collins), Ducky (Medwick), Dazzy (Vance), Tex (Carleton) and Wild Bill (Hallahan).

45. Who was the first, and only, player to hit six doubles in any World Series, of any length?

Ervin "Pete" Fox, a veteran outfielder of 13 seasons with the Tigers and Red Sox, had 31 doubles as a sophomore right-fielder for the Detroit Tigers in 1934 and carried that over to the '34 World Series. There, up against the pitches of Dizzy and Daffy Dean, Bob Walker and Tex Carleton, Fox banged out 8 hits, two singles and six doubles for a .286 batting average, and became the first, and only, player to have a half dozen two baggers in any length World Series.

46. Who were the first brothers to have appeared and played in the same World Series?

Mr. and Mrs. Johnston must have been proud that kid brother Jimmy, who was born in Cleveland (Tennessee) and played third base for the Brooklyn Robins (Dodgers) would meet up with older brother Wheeler "Doc" Johnston, who was also born in Cleveland, and now would be holding down first base for Cleveland, the Indians that is, not Tennessee, in the 1920 World Series. Neither brother had much to write home about as far as statistics were concerned. "Doc" went 3-11, scored one run, and had a .273 batting average. His younger brother, Jimmy, went 3-14, scored two runs and batted .214. At least "Doc" went home flying the World Championship flag, and had bragging rights around the Thanksgiving table.

47. Who was the first pitcher to win 10 or more World Series games?

When it came to the World Series "The Chairman of the Board", as Edward "Whitey" Ford, the New York Yankee southpaw, was affectionately known, was almost a perennial. By appearing in the "Big Show" eleven times from 1950-64, he started 22* games, completed 7, won 10*, lost 8*, had 3 shutouts, pitched 146* innings, allowed 132* hits, 34* walks, struck out 94* and showed a very impressive 2.71 Era.

*Each asterisk represents he is the leader in that category.

An interesting note, Whitey has pitched in seven different National League venues in the World Series; Candlestick Park, Crosley Field, Dodger Stadium, Ebbets Field, Forbes Field, Milwaukee County Stadium, and Sportsman's Park.

48. Who were the first, and only, three players to share the World Series Most Valuable Player Award for the same World Series?

This one-time happening occurred in the 1981 World Series when the Los Angeles Dodgers defeated the New York Yankees 4 games to 2, and those who decide such things couldn't distinguish between third baseman Ron Cey who batted .350 with a homer and three runs batted in, outfielder Pedro Guerrero who had two homers, 7 RBIs and a .333 batting average, and catcher Steve Yeager who did yeoman-like work behind the plate in all six games, and contributed two home runs, 4 runs batted in, and hit .286.

So that trio became the first, and only, three players to share the World Series MVP Award.

49. Who was the first, and only, pitcher to start and win a World Series game for a National League team, and then for an American League team?

On October 10, 1970 southpaw Tommy John started Game 1 of the World Series for the Los Angeles Dodgers and defeated Ed Figueroa of the

New York Yankees, 11-5.

Moving ahead to the 1981 World Series we find the same Tommy John, on October 21st, and now wearing pin stripes, starting Game 2, at Yankee Stadium. Pitching shutout ball for seven innings he is relieved by Goose Gossage, and the two combine to defeat Burt Hooton of the Los Angeles Dodgers, 3-0, allowing just four hits; John getting the win, Gossage the save.

50. Who was the first player to play in a World Series in his first four years in the major leagues?

"The Yankee Clipper," Joe DiMaggio, came up to the New York Yankees as an outfielder in 1936. He stayed around for ten appearances in the World Series beginning in his rookie year of 1936, and continued on playing on in the World Series of '37, '38, and '39, which were his first four seasons in the major leagues. What a nice introduction to major league baseball and the "Big Show."

The Clipper, who was first, had two in pin-stripers who followed that four-year treat of playing in the fall when Elston Howard, (1955-58), and right-hander Johnny Kucks (1955-58) had the same experience of playing in four World Series in their first four major league seasons.

51. Who was the first player to have a dozen hits in a World Series?

With have to go back to the 1912 World Series between the New York Giants and the Boston Red Sox for this one. Charles "Buck" Herzog, the Giants third baseman, had quite a World Series as he went 12 for 30, including four doubles, a triple, scored 6, and drove in 4, to end up with a .400 average for the series, and the first to garner a dozen hits in the Fall Classic.

52. Who was the first player to be awarded first base on catcher's interference in a World Series game?

That very unusual happening occurred for the first time on October 15, 1925, in the 1st inning of Game 7, at Forbes Field, Pittsburgh, when Washington Senators' shortstop Roger Peckinpaugh was awarded first base by NL home plate umpire Barry McCormick, on Pittsburgh Pirates' catcher Earl "Oil" Smith's interference.

Interestingly this rarity has happened only four times in World Series history, in 1943 to Bud Metheny of the Yankees, in 1964 to Ken Boyer of the Cardinals, and in 1970 to Pete Rose of the Cincinnati Reds.

53. Who was the first player to strike out five times in one World Series game?

When New York Yankees right-hander George Pipgras stepped on the mound at Wrigley Field, Chicago, to start the bottom of the 1st inning of Game 3 of the 1932 World Series on October 1st, he never realized he would, at the end of the day, be in the record book with a "Platinum Sombrero" due to his bat, or lack thereof.

Pipgras, batting right-handed, and facing the Cubs' Charlie Root, Pat Malone, Jakie May, and Bud Tinning, came to the plate five times and became the first player to strike out five consecutive times in a World Series game to be the first player to earn the "Platinum Sombrero Award".

This award applies to a player who has struck out five times in one game, while a "golden sombrero" applies to a player striking out four times in a game.

Pipgras had the last laugh, however, as he had Babe Ruth and Lou Gehrig behind him who each whacked back-to-back home runs in the 5th inning, and each contributed one more home run in the game, which allowed George to come home with a 7-5 win and the third victory for the Yankees in their sweep of the Cubs.

54. Who was the first pitcher to pitch a shutout in World Series history?

Right-hander "Big Bill" Dinneen of the Boston Americans (Red Sox) shut out the Pittsburgh Pirates, 3-0, on three hits, striking out 11 batters, in Game 2 on October 2, 1903 to even the first World Series at a game apiece, at the Huntington Avenue Grounds, Boston.

He went on to again shut out Pittsburgh in Game 8, on October 13th, at home, in the final game of the Series, 3-0, on just four hits, as Boston took the first World Series 5 games to 3.

55. Who was the first player to hit two home runs in the same World Series game?

It happened in the same World Series where the first home run was hit, the 1903 World Series between the Boston Americans (Red Sox), and the Pittsburgh Pirates. On Friday, October 2, 1903, in Game 2, at Boston, the Americans elected to lead off the game, as was their choice back then, and their leftfielder, Patrick " Patsy" Dougherty, who had four regular season home runs, opened up the top if the 1st inning by hitting a solo home run off Pirates right-hander Sam "The Goshen Schoolmaster" Leever. "Patsy" followed that with his second solo home run, in the 6th, off right-hander

Fred "Bucky" Veil to become the first player to hit a pair of homers in a World Series game.

Bill Dinneen went on to shut out the Pirates 3-0, to even the series at 1-1.

56. Who was the first pinch-hitter to come to bat twice in the same inning of a World Series game?

This naturally had to happen in a big inning and that was certainly the case in the bottom of the 7th inning in Game 4, on October 12, 1929, when the Philadelphia Athletics manager, Connie Mack, with his team behind 8-0, called upon part-time first baseman "Tioga George" Burns, at the tail-end of his 16-year major league career, to pinch-hit for the pitcher Eddie Rommel.

Burns, not seeing much action in the twilight of his career, came to bat just twice in this World Series, and his plate appearances just happened to be in this same inning.

In his first at bat he popped out to short and when the Athletics batted around, in this 10-run inning, he came up again and this time struck out. Philadelphia went on to overcome one of the most famous and unbelievable eight run deficits in World Series history to win 10-8 over the Chicago Cubs. Those two efforts were, unfortunately, Burns' last two major league at bats in a successful 16-year career.

57. Who was the first player to score twice in the same World Series inning?

One of the most exciting and talented players of his time, and quite a character when he was active on the field, both as a player and a manager, and continued to amuse his listeners as a baseball announcer and analyst, was Frankie "The Fordham Flash" Frisch.

Frisch, the New York Giants' third baseman, on October 7th, in Game 3, of the 1921 World Series, at the Polo Grounds, opened up the bottom of the 7th inning, with the score tied, 4-4, with the New York Yankees, by lining a single to centerfield. He was driven home by leftfielder Emil "Irish" Meusel's double to right field.

With the rally on-going, pitcher Jesse Barnes singled to left field, center-fielder George Burns singled to center, and Frisch is walked. That brought up right fielder, Ross Youngs, who then tripled to the deep caverns of the Polo Grounds driving home Barnes, Burns, and Frisch, for the second time in the inning, as the Giants exploded for eight runs on their way to a 13-5 win over The Yankees.

The Giants continued their winning ways taking the World Series, 5 games to 3.

58. Here is a "series" of events worth noting. Who was the first player to play in a Little League World Series, a College World Series, the summer Olympic Games, the World Baseball Classic, and, the ultimate, the Major League World Series?

This is some list of accomplishments for a baseball player, and Boston Red Sox catcher and captain, Jason Varitek, can take a bow. As a 12-year old he played shortstop, third base, and catcher in the 1984 Little League World Series where his team from Altamonte Springs, Florida, lost to Seoul, Korea, 6-2.

In 1992 Varitek played for the United States in the summer Olympics. In 1994, in his senior year in college, he played for Georgia Tech in the College World Series, where his teammates were future major leaguers, shortstop Nomar Garciaparra, and centerfielder Jay Payton. Oklahoma defeated the Yellow Jackets in their first appearance in the College World Series in that championship game, 13-5. Varitek was named to the Baseball of America's All-Time College Team.

Then came 2004 and Varitek was behind the plate for the Boston Red Sox in their four-game sweep of the St. Louis Cardinals.

He followed that up by being selected to be a team member representing the United States in the World Baseball Classic. I think he was serious about being in a "series."

59. Who was the first player to collect four base hits in a World Series game?

It didn't take Pittsburgh Pirate third baseman, Tommy Leach, long to enter the record books by being the first player to have four hits in a World Series game.

Seeing that it happened in the very first World Series game in history he had no one to surpass. It happened on October 1, 1903, in Game 1, when Leach had two singles and two triples, going four for five, in the historical opener, all off Boston's great Denton True "Cy" Young, as the Pirates racked up 12 hits on their way to a 7-3 victory over the Boston Americans (Pilgrims, Red Sox).

60. Who were the first two players who had played in a Little League World Series game to now face each other in a Major League World Series game?

As strange as this could be Boston Red Sox catcher Jason Varitek, who had played in the 1984 Little League World Series, now batted against right-hander Jason Marquis of the St. Louis Cardinals, who had played in the 1991 Little League World Series where he no-hit Canada.

In Game 4 of the 2004 World Series Marquis, who had pitched one inning of scoreless relief in Game 1, came back to start Game 4, pitched six innings, giving up three runs in the Cardinal loss to Derek Lowe of the Red Sox.

61. Who was the first, and only, player to have six consecutive base hits in a World Series?

In the 1924 World Series Leon "Goose" Goslin, the leftfielder of the Washington Senators, coming off a 199-hit regular season continued his hitting when he collected eleven hits, six consecutively, in the exciting seven game series against the New York Giants. Goose started the streak in Game 3, on October 6th with a single in his last at bat. In Game 4, on October 7th, he went 4 for 4 with three singles and a home run. Then in Game 5, on October 8th, he picked up the last of his six hits to be the first player in World Series history to have six consecutive base hits.

62. Who was the first rookie to hit two home runs in a World Series game?

Charlie "King Kong" Keller, the rookie right fielder of the New York Yankees, took his home run abilities to the 1939 World Series against the Cincinnati Reds, and right-hander Gene "Junior" Thompson.

In Game 3 on October 7th, out in Crosley Field, before a crowd of 32,723, he took Thompson downtown in the 1st inning with a two-run shot, and followed that up with another two-run home run in the 5th inning to propel the Yankees to a 7-3 win, and become the first rookie to hit two home runs in a World Series game.

63. Who were the first two players to hit back-to-back home runs in World Series history?

Leon "Goose" Goslin and Joe "Moon" Harris, of the Washington Senators, teamed up in the bottom of the 3rd inning of Game 4 of the 1925 World Series to hit back-to-back home runs off Pittsburgh Pirates southpaw Emil Yde to become the first pair to accomplish this feat in a World Series.

64. Who was the first pitcher to play in over 15 World Series games without committing an error?

That fielding prowess belonged to Edward "Whitey" Ford, the stylish southpaw of the New York Yankees. His errorless streak began on October 7, 1950 in Game 4 against the Philadelphia Phillies, and continued until the bottom of the 4th inning in Game 6, out in Candlestick Park, against the San Francisco Giants, on October 15, 1962. In that inning Felipe Alou had singled and Willie Mays walked. With Orlando Cepeda at bat, and Alou leading off second, Ford tried to pick him off and the throw was bad, and Ford had committed the error that broke his streak at 18 consecutive errorless games.

65. Who was the first, and only, pitcher to pitch 10 or more complete World Series games?

There have been many great pitchers, and many great games pitched, in the history of the World Series, but Christy "Big Six" Mathewson of the New York Giants was the first to give his bullpen a day off ten times in his World Series pitching career.

Matty started a total of eleven games in the fall, and completed three in 1905, all shutouts against the Philadelphia Athletics, two in 1911, going eleven innings in a tie Game 3, but requiring one inning of relief in Game 4, three in 1912, going eleven innings in Game 2, and 9.2 in Game 8, and finished off with two more complete games in 1913.

66. Who was the first pitcher to give up six consecutive hits in a World Series game?

October 10, 1908 was rainy for the start of Game 1 of the World Series between the Detroit Tigers and the Chicago Cubs at Bennett Park, Detroit. Nothing, it seemed, could keep baseball fans from talking about how the Chicago Cubs came about winning their third straight pennant, by necessitating a playoff game between themselves and the New York Giants who were tied for the National League pennant, brought about by the historic "Fred Merkle boner" play.

The 19-year old New York Giants reserve first baseman, playing his first game of the year on September 23rd, replacing the injured veteran Fred Tenny, had followed a Harry "Moose" McCormick single with a single of his own sending McCormick to third in the bottom of the 9th inning.

Then Al Bridwell hit southpaw "Jack the Giant Killer" Pfiester's pitch into the outfield driving in Moose McCormick with what was presumed to be the winning run. Merkle had started toward second on the base hit, but upon seeing McCormick score turned and jogged toward the Polo Grounds centerfield clubhouse thinking there was no need to continue on to second for the winning run had scored.

Cub second baseman, Johnny Evers, didn't see it that way and screamed for the ball from centerfielder Arthur "Circus Solly" Hofman to get Merkle on a force at the bag. After a lengthy delay the umpires ruled Merkle had not touched second base and the Giants had not won. The game was declared a tie and ordered replayed on October 8th. Chicago won that game, 4-2, and the pennant by that one game.

Now all of the preceding sets the stage for the answer to the original question. In Game 1 of the World Series, southpaw "Twilight Ed" Killian started for Detroit and lasted just 2.1 innings, giving up four runs before Ed "Kickapoo Chief" Summers, who had won 24 games that season, came on in relief to finish the game. Going into the 9th inning and holding a narrow 6-5 lead he retired shortstop Johnny Evers, and then preceded to give up consecutive singles to Frank "Wildfire" Schulte, Frank Chance, Harry Steinfeldt, Solly Hofman's bases loaded single, followed by singles to Joe Tinker and Johnny Kling, then a sacrifice by Mordecai "Three Finger" Brown, before Jimmy Scheckard flied out to centerfield to end the five-run, six-hit inning that led to a 10-6 opening game Cubs victory and put Summers into the World Series record books by being the first pitcher to give up six straight base hits.

67. Who were the first two teammates to have served together, and were wounded together in Europe during World War I, who went on to play together in the World Series?

Ok, so this is a little esoterical, but very unusual nevertheless. First baseman Joe "Moon" Harris, and right-handed pitcher Johnny "Big Serb" Miljus had been bunkmates in the 80th Division, 320th Infantry, and served together in France in World War I. Both men were wounded in a major attack in the Argonne Woods, north of Verdun.

They were both gassed and Miljus was also bayoneted, but that didn't stop them from being teammates and playing in the 1927 World Series for the Pittsburgh Pirates in their four-game loss to the New York Yankees.

68. Who were the first two players, from the same team, to each steal home in a World Series.

We can go back to the 1921 World Series for this answer for it was New York Yankees third baseman Mike McNally who was the first of the two to swipe home.

In Game 1, leading off the top of the 5th inning McNally doubled into left field. Switch hitter, catcher Wally Schang, sacrificed him along to third. Carl Mays then struck out, bringing up centerfielder Elmer Miller. As right-hander "Shufflin' Phil" Douglas went into his windup McNally raced safely for home to give the Yankees a 2-1 lead. Then in the top of the 9th McNally singled to left field, and decided to try out his base stealing skills against right-hander Jesse Barnes, and was successful for his second stolen base of the game.

In Game 2, McNally's teammate right fielder "Long Bob" Meusel must have gotten the itch from McNally. With the Yankees ahead 1-0, Meusel singled to centerfield sending Babe Ruth, who was on first via a force out, to third as the throw to cut him down came too late, and Meusel moved into second.

First baseman Wally Pipp grounded out to Johnny Rawlings at second, scoring Ruth, as Meusel advanced to third. With second baseman Aaron Ward up, Meusel took off for home and scored to become the second teammate, and the first pair to successfully steal home in a World Series.

69. Who was the first pitcher to win three games in a World Series, but then have his team lose the World Series?

This unfortunate experience reared its ugly head very early in World Series history for it happened in the very first one played, between the Boston Americans (Red Sox) and the Pittsburgh Pirates in 1903.

In Game 1 the Pirates sent Charles "Deacon" Phillippe to the mound against Denton True "Cy" Young. With both pitchers going all the way the

"Deacon" and his flock came out winning, 7-3.

Phillippe then pitched and won Games 3 and 4, but lost games 7 and 8, one to Cy Young, and the final game to "Big Bill" Dinneen, who pitched a masterful four-hit shutout, 3-0, as the Americans took the first World Championship 5 games to 3, making Phillippe the first pitcher to win three games, yet lose the World Series.

70. Who were the first team, and manager, to lose three straight World Series?

Unfortunately for the fans of Motor Town their Detroit Tigers, under manager Hughie Jennings, were swept by the Chicago Cubs in the 1907 World Series, lost again to the Cubs in five games in the 1908 World Series, and made it three straight failures in 1909 when they bowed to the Pittsburgh Pirates in seven games.

71. Who was the first, and only, player to compete in a World Series in both Wrigley Field and Comiskey Park, in Chicago?

In 1918, with the United States still involved in World War I in Europe, the government ordered Major League Baseball to conclude its regular season by Labor Day, meaning the 1918 World Series would start, and be completed, in September, for the first and only time in history.

Game 1, on September 1st, which was played in Comiskey Park, home of the White Sox, and not the Cubs home park of Weegham Park, (later to be renamed Wrigley Field when the Wrigley family purchased the team), was because the Cubs wanted the greater seating capacity of 32,000 at Comiskey, as opposed to 18,000 at Weegham Park

Opening day provided a battle of the southpaws as Babe Ruth took the mound for the visiting Red Sox and James "Hippo" Vaughn for the Chicago Cubs.

The game's only run scored in the 4th inning when first baseman John "Stuffy" McInnis singled to left field scoring second baseman Dave Shean, as Ruth went on to pitch a six-hit shutout besting Vaughn's five-hitter to open up the six game series with a 1-0 win.

Ruth then pitched eight innings in Game 4, on September 9th, back in Fenway Park, defeating "Shufflin' Phil" Douglas, 3-2, when the go-ahead run scored in the 8th inning after Wally Schang's single, a passed ball by "Reindeer Bill" Killefer sending Schang to second with Harry Hooper at bat, Hooper's sacrifice bunt, and a throwing error on the play by Douglas which scored Schang.

With the Cubs scoring twice in the 8th Babe Ruth's record scoreless innings streak is stopped after 29.2 innings.

To fully answer the question; when Babe Ruth moved to the Yankees he played in five more National League parks in a World Series, finally coming back to Chicago for the 1932 World Series against the Cubs, where he completed the circle by playing in Wrigley Field for Games 3 and 4, on October 1st and 2nd, after playing in Comiskey Park back in 1918.

72. Who was the first manager to win back-to-back World Series titles?

I have to presume that the nickname "The Peerless Leader", given to Frank Chance, player/manager for the Chicago Cubs, certainly had merit for he displayed it by being the first manager to win back to-back-World Series titles when he took the Cubs to victories over the Detroit Tigers by sweeping them in 1907, and then defeating them in five games in 1908.

In those series he led by example by batting .333 over those nine games.

Cooperstown must have thought the same for he was inducted into the Hall in 1946.

73. Who was the first pitcher to win a World Series game played at night?

World Series at night became a reality when on Wednesday, October 13, 1971, in Game 4, in Three Rivers Stadium, Pittsburgh, Pirates rookie right-hander Bruce Kison came on in relief of southpaw Luke Walker, with two out in the first inning, when Baltimore scored three runs, and pitched 6.1 innings of one-hit ball.

With the score tied, 3-3, in the bottom of the 7th, first baseman, Bob Robertson, leading off the inning singled to centerfield, as did catcher Manny Sanguillen. After pinch-hitter Vic Davalillo reached base on an error of a fly ball to deep right-center, reserve catcher Milt May, batting for Bruce Kison, singled to right-center field off right-hander Eddie Watt, and Robertson scored with the lead run. Right-hander Dave Giusti came on and shut the door in the 8th and 9th for the save, and Bruce Kison, with a 4-3 win, became the first pitcher in history to win a World Series night game.

74. Who was the first pitcher to strike out ten batters and walk none in

a World Series game?

This particular game seems to have come up more than once. It was, of course, the very first World Series game in history, and as such, we must expect first time things to happen.

Well it did in this case, with Charles "Deacon" Phillippe, whom we have written about in prior notes. The Deacon took pitching to a high level when, on October 1, 1903, in Game 1 of the very first World Series, he struck out ten Boston Americans (Red Sox), and did not walk a batter in his 7-3 victory over Boston to be the first, but not maybe the last, pitcher in World Series history to strike out 10 batters, but allow no one to get a free pass.

75. Who was the first pitcher to win a World Series Game in the first Yankee Stadium?

From 1913 to 1923 the New York Highlanders (Yankees) had shared the Polo Grounds with the New York Giants. The 1923 World Series had brought the two teams together for the third year in a row, with the Giants having taken seven of the last eight games in a row, there was one tie.

This year the venue changed with the Yankees having moved across the Harlem River from the Polo Grounds into the Bronx.

Game 1 of this series was played in the new Yankee Stadium, on October 10, 1923, before a crowd of 55,307 and pitted Giants right-hander John "Mule" Watson, who had come over from the Braves in mid-season, against 17-game winner, Yankee right-hander Waite "Schoolboy" Hoyt.

Watson lasted two innings, giving up three runs, before being relieved by right-hander Wilfred "Rosy" Ryan. Hoyt lasted just 2.1 innings, giving up four runs, before he was relieved by right-hander Leslie "Bullet Joe" Bush.

Going into the top of the 9th inning with the score tied, 4-4, Giant centerfielder Casey Stengel came up, with none on and two out, and blasted a Bush pitch for an inside the park home run as the Giants, and Ryan, came away with a 5-4 win, making everything "Rosy" as he became the first pitcher to win a World Series game in what would later be called "The House That Ruth Built."

76. Who was the first player to hit three home runs in one World Series game?

When one thinks of the possible candidates, one stands out above all the rest as the best possibility. That is George Herman "Babe" Ruth. In his 10

World Series, playing in 41 games, coming to bat 129 times and hitting 15 home runs it is not surprising that in Game 4, on October 6, 1926, against the St. Louis Cardinals, in Sportsman's Park, before a crowd of 38,825, he would be the one to do it.

Babe came up in the top of 1st inning with none on and two out and blasted right-hander Flint Rhem's pitch into the right field stands. Coming back in the 3rd inning, with two out, he again took Rhem downtown with a solo shot into the deep centerfield stands. Not stopping there, for when Herman "Hi" Bell came on in relief, he took no pity on this right-hander by hitting his third home run of the game, this time with one on and one out, deep into the centerfield stands for his third home run of the game leading the Yankees to a 10-5 win and knotting up the series at 2-2.

Ruth hit his fourth home run of the series, in Game 7, with a solo shot into the right-centerfield stands, off Jesse Haines, in the 3rd inning. It wasn't enough, however as the Cardinals won the game 3-2, and took the series in seven games.

77. Who was the first National League player to hit a grand slam home run in the World Series?

A couple of American League players had done it as we mentioned earlier, but it was this unlikely batter, who was not known for the long ball, or such heroics, but nevertheless stepped up. "Iron Hands" Chuck Hiller, the San Francisco Giants second baseman, with the score tied, 2-2, in the 7th inning of Game 4, on October 8, 1962, came up to the plate.

After Jim Davenport walked, Matty Alou, pinch-hitting for shortstop Jose Pagan, doubled to left field sending Davenport to third. That was all for Yankees right-hander Jim "Mummy" Coates, who was relieved by southpaw Marshall "Sheriff" Bridges, who then intentionally walked Bob Nieman. Ernie Bowman was sent in to run for Nieman. Harvey Kuenn popped out to third base, which brought up Chuck Hiller, who promptly deposited Bridges' pitch into the stands in deep right field for a grand slam home run, scoring Davenport, Alou and Bowman to send the Giants to a 7-3 win, and making Chuck Hiller the first National League player to hit grand slam home run in World Series history.

78. Who was the first, and only, player to end Game 7 of a World Series, by being thrown out trying to steal?

The man who had been so instrumental in bringing his team to a World

Series became the goat of the 1926 World Series. With two down in the 9th inning, of Game 7, and the St. Louis Cardinals holding a narrow 3-2 lead, Grover Cleveland Alexander faced the Bambino, Babe Ruth, and after running the count to 3-2 walked him to put the tying run on first. That brought up the clean-up hitter Bob Meusel, who was trying to create some kind of rally and advance Ruth, but he was denied the opportunity when the Babe took off for second base. He got a slow start and Cardinal catcher Bob O'Farrell's throw to shortstop Tommy Thevenow was right on target, nailing Ruth for the final out, giving the Redbirds a 3-2 win and ending the Fall Classic, as the Cardinals took the seven game series and the World Championship.

79. Who was the first player to have two multi-homer games in one World Series?

If you look at the scorecard of the 1980 World Series between the Philadelphia Phillies and the Kansas City Royals you will see the name of Royals first baseman, Willie Mays Aikens, there under home runs. In Game 1, at Veterans Stadium, on October 14th, in the 3rd inning, after Hal McRae had singled to centerfield, Aikens hit a two-out, two-run blast off right-hander Bob Walk. Aikens came up in the top of the 8th inning and followed George Brett's double by blasting his second two-run home run of the game, again off Bob Walk.

Moving on to Game 4, on October 18th, at Kaufman Stadium, Kansas City, Aikens came up in the bottom of the 1st inning, with one out, facing right-hander Larry Christenson, who had just given up a triple to George Brett, and sent the ball deep into the right field stands giving the Royals a 2-1 lead. That was all for Christenson who was replaced by another right-hander, Dickie Noles. Moving into the bottom of the 2nd inning, with Kansas City now ahead, 4-1, after a big first inning, the crowd of 42,363 was again brought to its feet as Aikens took Noles downtown with a two-out solo shot into the deep right field stands, making it 5-1, as the Royals went on to a 5-3 win, and making Willie Mays Aikens the first player to hit multiple home runs in two different games in a World Series.

80. Who was the first player to be awarded a home run in a World Series game by instant replay?

Something spooky happened on this Halloween night down in Citizens Bank Park, Philadelphia. It took place on Saturday, October 31, 2009, in the 4th inning of Game 3, when 46,061 fans, for the first time in World

Series history, had to wait for television to document a call by the umpires.

To set the stage, the New York Yankees were behind 3-0, when Yankees first baseman, Mark Teixeira, drew a one-out walk off Phillies southpaw Cole Hamels. Then on a 0-1 count on Alex Rodriguez, the third baseman, drilled a Hamels' pitch just to the left of the right-field foul pole, where the ball bounced back on the field. The umpires ruled it a ground-rule double, with Tiexeira being held up at third, and A-Rod waved on to second base. There, A-Rod quizzically questioned whether it was a home run or a double. Yankee manager Joe Girardi rushed out on the field calling for a home run.

After a brief mound conference, the four umpires walked off the field to review the call on replay television. Upon their return they overturned the original call and declared A-Rod's base hit to be a two-run home run. The replay showed that the ball had hit a television camera, owned by Fox, and major league baseball, which extended over the chain link fence that formed the top of the wall, but jutted out onto the field. The Yankees had reduced the Philadelphia lead to 3-2, and would go on to win the game 8-5. It was the first time in World Series history that an umpire's call was subjected to, and reversed by, an instant replay camera in World Series history.

81. Who was the first player to strikeout a dozen times in a World Series?

That dubious distinction happened to a very fine ballplayer, the fleet-footed leftfielder, and switch-hitting lead-off hitter of the Kansas City Royals, Willie Wilson, at Veterans Stadium on October 21, 1980.

His 12th strikeout occurred in his 26th Series at bat, when Philadelphia Phillies popular southpaw reliever, Frank "Tug" McGraw fanned Wilson for the final out in the 4-1 win of the 6th and final game of the 1980 World Series. This series was of particular note for it was the first World Championship in the long history of the Philadelphia Phillies.

82. Who was the first player to have a "baker's dozen" strikeouts in a World Series?

In an earlier segment we talked about Willie Wilson being the first player to strike out a dozen times in a World Series. Well Ryan Howard, the big, slugging first baseman of the Philadelphia Phillies, added another notch by being the first player in World Series history to have a "baker's dozen" strikeouts. It happened in the 8th inning of Game 6 of the 2009

World Series when southpaw Damaso Marte struck out Howard, the 13th time he had gone down on strikes in six games, against New York Yankee pitching.

83. Who was the first full-time designated hitter to be named the MVP of the World Series?

There were a couple of "firsts" in this series. Hideki Matsui, the designated hitter for the New York Yankees in the 2009 World Series against the Philadelphia Phillies, was selected the Most Valuable Player in the Series. He was the first DH to ever be given the World Series MVP Award, and he was also the first Japanese-born player to receive the award as well.

84. Who was the first relief pitcher in World Series history to pitch exactly one inning, strike out three batters, and give up a home run?

This unusual series of events happened for the first time in Game 4, on October 14, 1970 at Memorial Stadium, Baltimore, when in the top of the 8th inning Orioles' ace Jim Palmer, ahead 5-3, against the Cincinnati Reds, gave up a single to left field to leadoff hitter, Tony Perez and another single in the same spot to Johnny Bench, sending Perez to third.

That brought in right-hander Eddie Watt, who promptly gave up a home run to deep left field to first baseman Lee May, scoring Perez and Bench, to put Cincinnati ahead 6-5.

Watt then struck out Bernie Carbo, gave up an infield single to Tommy Helms, and proceeded to strike out Clay Carroll, and Darrell Chaney to end the inning, but not before giving up one home run, and striking out three batters. He became the first pitcher to accomplish that unusual combination in a World Series game. Baltimore went on to win that game 9-3, and take the World Series in five games.

85. Who was the first relief pitcher to lose three World Series games?

It took southpaw Eddie Watt, of the Baltimore Orioles, three different World Series experiences to register the losses. In 1969 he took the loss in Game 5, on October 16th at Shea Stadium, in a 5-3 win for Jerry Koosman, as the New York Mets closed out the World Series, 4 games to 1.

In 1970, in Game 4, on October 14th, down in Baltimore, he came on in relief of Jim Palmer, giving up a home run to Cincinnati's Lee May in the 8th inning for the 6-5 loss in the Orioles only loss to the Reds in the five game series.

In the World Series of 1971 against the Pittsburgh Pirates, Watt pitched 1.1 innings of relief, in Game 4, on October 13th, in relief of Joe Dobson and Grant "Buck" Jackson, and took the loss as Pirate catcher Milt May delivered a tie-breaking, run-scoring pinch single to bring the Pirates back from a 3-0 deficit to a 4-3 win. Three years, three World Series, five games, 5.2 innings pitched, 10 hits, one walk and eight strikeouts later he showed a 0-3 World Series record. Eddie had been through the wars.

86. Who was the first player to be hit by a pitch twice in one World Series game?

A bit sore, but always ready to crouch behind the plate, Yogi Berra, the New York Yankee catcher, was involved in three hits in Game 3, on October 2, 1953, at Ebbets Field, Brooklyn.

The crowd of 35,270 saw Dodger right-hander, Carl Erskine, walk Yogi in the top of the 2nd inning, and have him move to second on a wild pitch to Mickey Mantle, but move no further as the Yankees went down.

In the top of the 4th inning Berra got his first "hit" as Erskine plunked him with a pitch, but moved no further as Erskine retired Mantle on strikes and got Gene Woodling to pop out to Pee Wee Reese at short.

In the 6th Berra got his second "hit," and some revenge, as he singled to right field off Erskine. Going into the top of the 8th inning, with Brooklyn up 2-1, Hank Bauer singled to centerfield bringing up Berra, who promptly got his third "hit" when plunked by Erskine for the second time in the game. Mickey Mantle then struck out, but Gene Woodling singled to center scoring Bauer and tying the score at 2-2. Billy Martin grounded out to second, Jim Gilliam to Gil Hodges to end the inning and leave the game tied.

Brooklyn took the game 3-2, with Yogi going only 1 for 1 on the day, but was on base four times with a walk, single, and being hit by pitches twice to be the first player to "take two for the team." in World Series history.

87. Who was the first player to be hit by a pitch three times in a World Series?

Pittsburgh Pirates centerfielder, Max "Scoops" Carey, shouldn't be criticized if he thought he was stepping onto a set of railroad tracks instead of into the batter's box on October 7, 1925, in the 1st inning of Game 1 against the Washington Senators in Forbes Field, Pittsburgh. Carey came to the plate only to be greeted, and hit by "The Big Train." Walter Johnson, a twelve-time twenty-game winner and high-speed right-hander of the visiting Senators wasn't a headhunter, but he did hit 205 batters in his 21-year career.

Down to first base went Carey, and being no slouch at stealing bases, he had led the National League nine times in thefts, and ended his 20-year career with 738, no doubt had thoughts of getting even by stealing second. Catcher Herold "Muddy" Ruel was alert to "Scoops" for he gunned him down trying to steal, on a rocket throw to shortstop Roger Peckinpaugh.

In the bottom of the 4th it was Johnson's time to get even by not allowing Carey to get on, so he struck him out. Now we go to the bottom of the 9th and Johnson is holding on to a 4-1 lead and facing Carey once again. "The Big Train" is a little off track and hits Carey with another pitch, but no harm is done other than another "strawberry" on "Scoops" body as Johnson goes on to defeat the Pirates 4-1.

Now we go back to the 1st inning again, this time in Game 3, and Carey is facing right-hander Alex Ferguson, who was no stranger to the major leagues, having played for the Red Sox and the Yankees in his over five years of pitching, and had been purchased from the Yankees back on August 17th. Nats' second baseman, Eddie Moore walked, bringing up Carey who, no doubt still smarting from Johnson's fastballs, now took one from Ferguson to make him the first player to have been hit a total of three times in one World Series, (by two different pitchers in two different games).

88. Who was the first player, in a World Series, to drive in as many runs as the entire opposing team combined?

This exceeds credulity, but as Casey Stengel once said, "you can look it up," in response to a reporter's challenge to one of Casey's statements. In the 1928 World Series, where the New York Yankees swept the St. Louis Cardinals, to be the first American League team to sweep a team from the senior circuit, they were led by more than one player, but their first baseman, Lou "Iron Horse" Gehrig was totally dominant.

He had 6 hits in 11 at bats, hit 4 home runs, scored 5, walked 6 times and had a batting average of .545. Now here is the kicker: he drove in two runs in Game 1, three in Game 2, 3 more in Game 3 and one in Game 4 for a total of 9 runs batted in, which was as many as the entire St. Louis Cardinal team, which also had 9 driven in during the entire four-game series.

89. Who was the first player to have as many errors in a seven-game

World Series as games played?

We are back again to the 1925 World Series where the Pittsburgh Pirates squeezed out a World Series victory over the Washington Senators in seven games.

The series is remembered, and has been talked about, down through the years for the unbelievable display, or lack thereof of defensive capabilities.

The Washington Senators committed nine errors in that World Series and one player, shortstop Roger Peckinpaugh, made an error in Game 1, two in Game 2, one in Game 3, one in Game 5, one in Game 6 and finished off the series by making his 7th miscue in Game 7.

He became the first player in World Series history to make seven errors in one World Series. Not something someone would recommend for a Gold Glove.

90. What were the first teams to play in a World Series where neither team hit a home run and every game pitched resulted in a shutout?

This happened early in World Series history when in the 1905 World Series the New York Giants faced off against the Philadelphia Athletics, and with the great pitchers who faced each team it was not too surprising that no home runs were hit. What was surprising was that every single game played was a shutout.

The Giants' staff of Christy Mathewson, Joe "Iron Man" McGinnity, and Leon "Red" Ames allowed Connie Mack's nine just 25 hits, with five doubles, and no triples, striking out 25, which resulted in a total of three runs, none earned, in the five game series won by the Giants.

Philadelphia had three fine pitchers themselves with Charles "Chief" Bender, Andy Coakley, and southpaw "Gettysburg Eddie" Plank Unfortunately their star, southpaw George "Rube" Waddell, didn't pitch due to a supposed sore shoulder.

The other three allowed the Giants 32 hits, 7 doubles, no triples, struck out 26, but allowed 15 runs, 8 earned for a fine 1.47 combined Era. Bender shut out the Giants, and Joe McGinnity in Game 2, 3-0.

That was not good enough, for the Giants' trio, with a combined 0.00 Era., pitched four shutouts; Mathewson beat Plank in Game 1, 3-0; beat Coakley in Game 3, 9-0, and beat Bender in Game 5, 2-0. McGinnity won Game 4, 1-0, beating Plank. This World Series, and rightly so, is still considered the most brilliant individual and two-team pitching performance in World Series history.

91. What was the first team to collect 20 base hits in a single World Series game?

This explosion of hitting prowess happened in Game 3, on October 7, 1921, by the New York Giants, as they defeated the New York Yankees 13-5, with two Giants, centerfielder "Tioga George" Burns, and catcher Frank "Pancho" Snyder each collecting four hits in the 20-hit attack.

92. Who was the first player to hit 4 home runs in a World Series, twice?

Not a stranger to the long ball, having hit 407 regular season home runs, and eleven in World Series competition, Edwin "Duke" Snider, the Brooklyn Dodgers centerfielder, hit a two-run home run in Games 1 and 5, and a pair of solo home runs in Game 6 of the 1952 World Series against New York Yankees pitching, only to see the Dodgers bow in seven games.

Snider was back in the 1955 World Series, again facing Yankees pitching, and hit a solo shot in Game 1 and a 3-run home run in Game 4, and then came back in Game 5 with a pair of solo home runs to make him the first player to hit four home runs in two different World Series. His efforts helped to bring the first World Championship to Flatbush.

93. Who was the first pitcher to lose consecutive deciding games in World Series history?

This unfortunate and embarrassing event happened to a good pitcher, one who had helped his team get to the Big Fall Show. It started in the 1908 World Series between the Chicago Cubs and the Detroit Tigers.

Chicago won Game 1, and in Game 2, on October 11th, Orval Overall's four-hitter defeated Detroit's 18-game winner "Wild Bill" Donovan, 6-1.

These two pitchers came back to face each other in Game 5, on October 14th in Detroit, with the Cubs holding a 3-1 lead in games. Overall again came away with a win, 2-0, pitching a three-hit shutout, and striking out 10, to take the deciding game and the World Championship, four games to one, with both pitchers going all nine innings, and "Wild Bill" taking the heartbreaking loss.

Let's move ahead to 1909, and we again find Detroit back in the Big Fall Show, this time against the Pittsburgh Pirates. The Pirates take Game 1 out in Pittsburgh, 4-1. In Game 2 "Wild Bill" is the starting pitcher and defeats Howie "Red" Camnitz, 7-2.

On October 16th, out in Detroit, the series is tied at three games apiece. The Pirates send Charles "Babe" Adams, a winner of Games 1 and 5, to the mound against Donovan in the deciding game. Adams came away with six-hit shutout, winning 8-0, and Pittsburgh became the World Champions, and "Wild Bill" Donovan became the first pitcher in World Series history to lose consecutive final games in the Big Fall Show.

94. Who were the first Cy Young Award winners to start against each other in a World Series game in the year they won the award?

It all came about in Game 1 of the 1968 World Series out in St. Louis, on October 2nd, when Cardinals right-hander Bob "Hoot" Gibson took the mound against fellow right-hander Denny McLain of the Detroit Tigers.

McLain had won the 1968 American League Cy Young Award with his brilliant 31-6, 1.96 Era. record wherein he led the junior circuit in wins, with a winning percentage of .838, games started with 41, complete games with 28, and in innings pitched with 336.

Gibson also had a stellar year, winning the National League Cy Young Award with a 22-9 won lost record, and a league leading miniscule 1.12 Era., 268 strikeouts and 13 shutouts.

Both pitchers won their respective league's Most Valuable Player Award as well.

Getting back to the game Gibson set down the Tigers on five hits, shutting them out, 4-0, and striking out 17 batters to set a World Series record. McLain, the first 30-game winner since Dizzy Dean did it for the Cardinals with his 30-7 record in 1934, was relieved in the 6th by Joe Dobson.

Gibson went 2-1, with a 1.67 Era., and McLain 1-2, with a 3.24 Era. in the series, but Detroit went home with a 4 games to 3 win.

95. Who was the first player to agree with gamblers to fix the 1919 World Series?

The World Series of 1919 is better known today as the "Black Sox Scandal." It all began when Chicago White Sox first baseman Charles "Chick" Gandil, described by his contemporaries as a "professional malcontent," and was once also described by a historian; "There was a mean streak in him that ran from his toes to his crown."

Gandil made his major league debut on April 14, 1910 with the Chicago White Sox which didn't go well, and he was sent to Montreal of the International League.

On May 26, 1912 Gandil was traded by Montreal to the Washington Senators, and it was at this time that he met bookie and gambler, Joseph "Sport" Sullivan who later, when Gandil moved to the White Sox, became a key figure, along with Gandil to fix the 1919 World Series.

It was on a September day in 1919 that Sullivan approached Gandil and fellow teammate, Eddie Cicotte, at their Boston hotel, and suggested that a syndicate be formed of seven or eight players to throw the series to the National League champion Cincinnati Reds. Also in the wings with Sullivan was Arnold Rothstein, a New York gambler and racketeer, as well as Thomas "Sleepy Bill" Burns, a former major league southpaw pitcher, with a connection to the players, and Billy Maharg, a gambler with underground connections.

Sullivan, using his persuasive manner, backed by a generous amount of cash, said he would pay $10,000 to each of the players who would be involved. Gandil's salary that season was $4,000. Gandil was to be the contact for the gamblers as well as being responsible for recruiting and paying the players involved in the fix. For that effort Gandil received $35,000 for his role in fixing the World Series, won by Cincinnati 5 games to 3. That was quite a sum over and above his salary that year.

When the story of the fix surfaced Gandil and seven White Sox teammates were indicted. The jury found the eight players not guilty, but the new Commissioner of Major League Baseball, Kennesaw Mountain Landis, who had just taken over for Ban Johnson, didn't see it that way and wanted to clean up baseball, and imposed a lifetime suspension from professional baseball on all the eight players involved; Leftfielder "Shoeless Joe" Jackson, utility man Fred McMullin, pitchers Eddie Cicotte, and Claude "Lefty" Williams, first baseman "Chick" Gandil, centerfielder Oscar "Happy" Felsch, shortstop Charles "Swede" Risberg, and third baseman George "Buck" Weaver.

96. Who was the first manager to be ejected from a World Series game?

The first manager, in this case, the first player-manager, to be ejected from a World Series game happened on Thursday, October 20, 1910 at the West Side Grounds in Chicago, before a crowd of 26, 210 fans.

It was Game 3 of the series between the Athletics and the Cubs, and it was brought about by a one-out, three-run home run, hit by Philadelphia Athletics right-fielder, Danny Murphy, when he drove a Harry "Rocks" McIntyre pitch against a sign in deep centerfield in the 3rd inning with third baseman Frank "Home Run" Baker, and first baseman Harry "Jasper" Davis on board.

Manager and first baseman, Frank "The Peerless Leader" Chance, vehemently protested the awarding of a home run, and claimed it should have been called a ground rule double. Umpire Tom Connolly thought otherwise, and had enough of Chance's protesting and ejected him from the game.

"The Peerless Leader" not only lost the argument, and the game, 12-5, but did gain the recognition as being the first player, and/ or manager; however you want to characterize it, to be ejected in the Fall Classic.

97. Who was the first National League pitcher to pitch a no-hitter in the post season?

On Wednesday, October 6, 2010, in Game One of the National League Division Series, Philadelphia Phillies right-hander Roy Halladay made his first post season appearance, and immediately broke into the post-season record books when he no-hit the Cincinnati Reds, winning 4-0, before a home crowd of 46,411 at Citizens Bank Park.

Halladay, in allowing one walk, faced just 28 batters, using his sharp fastball, and devastating curve, to strike out eight batters as he threw 104 pitches, 79 for strikes. He contributed with the bat as well when his single in the 2nd inning drove in a run. Reds right-hander Edinson Volquez took the loss.

No-hitters weren't unusual for Halladay that season as he pitched a perfect game down in Florida against the Marlins on May 29, 2010.

98. Who was the first pitcher to pitch 27 consecutive innings in a World Series and not allow an earned or an unearned run?

This outstanding pitching performance was performed in the 1905 World Series when New York Giants Hall of Fame right-hander, Christy Mathewson, shut out the Philadelphia Athletics, on October 9th, in Game 1, defeating Eddie Plank, 3-0.

On 12th, in Game 3, Matty came back and once again gave up only four hits when he shut out the Athletics, 9-0.

Back in Game 5, on October 14th, Mathewson gave up six hits in pitching his third consecutive shutout, defeating Chief Bender, 2-0.

It's tough to beat that effort.

99. Who was the first rookie to be inserted in the third batting slot in a World Series game?

Think no longer, for it was Lawrence Peter Berra, lovingly known as "Yogi", who after debuting with the New York Yankees on September 22, 1946, and playing in just seven games, not qualifying as a rookie, did bat .364 that season.

Coming back in 1947, which would now qualify as his rookie season, he played in 83 games, some as a catcher, and an outfielder, but when the 1947 World Series started against the Brooklyn Dodgers "Yogi" played both behind the plate, and in the outfield, and was inserted in the 3rd slot in the Yankees batting order, the first rookie to be given that honor in the Fall Classic.

100. Who was the first National League rookie to be inserted in the 3rd slot in the batting order in a World Series game?

Just as Yogi Berra was the first rookie to play in the Fall Classic and bat in the 3rd position in the batting order, it took until the 2010 World Series for it to happen in the senior circuit. The San Francisco Giants' catcher Gerald "Buster" Posey, who batted .305 with 67 runs batted in during his rookie season, took on that honor in Game 2, on October 28th, against the Texas Rangers, in AT&T Park in San Francisco.

101. Who was the first player, a pitcher, to hit a grand slam home run in an American League Championship Series game?

When Baltimore Orioles southpaw Mike Cuellar took the mound on Saturday, October 3, 1970, at Metropolitan Stadium, against the Minnesota Twins in the opening game of the 1970 ALCS little did he think he would be the offensive weapon that would create a seven-run 4th inning to help him rout the Twins 10-6.

That is exactly what he was as the lefty swinging pitcher came to bat in that inning with one out, and the bases loaded with Elrod Hendricks, Davey Johnson, and Mark Belanger, and emptied them with a grand slam home run down the right field line that was aided by a 29 mph wind that carried it fair, off right-hander Jim Perry. It was the first home run hit by a pitcher in the LCS and the only homer a pitcher would hit in the ALCS in the 20th century.

102. Who was the first pair of rookies to start a World Series game as battery mates?

This is a rarity, and because it was so unusual, it didn't happen until Game One of the 1947 World Series when, on Tuesday, September 30th, before a crowd of 73,365 at Yankee Stadium, the New York Yankees faced the Brooklyn Dodgers. It was a "first" in World Series history, for the battery that started the game for the Yankees that day were a pair of rookies, 26-year old right-hander Frank "Spec" Shea, "The Naugatuck Nugget" started on the mound, and his battery mate was 22-year old Lawrence "Yogi" Berra who, although he made his major league debut on September 22, 1946, and appeared in just seven games that season, was considered a rookie in 1947 as well. It was the first time that a battery of rookies started a World Series game in its history.

Shea was the winning pitcher, defeating Dodgers right-hander, Ralph Branca, 5-3, as "Spec" went five innings with the southpaw Joe "The Gay Reliever" Page pitching the final four innings for the save.

103. Who was the first pair of National League rookies to form the battery that started a World Series game?

It took 63 years, since it originally happened to a pair of American League rookies in1947, for a pair of rookies to be the starting battery for the National League in a World Series.

It happened down at The Ballpark in Arlington on Sunday, October 31, 2010 when 21-year old southpaw rookie Madison Bumgarner of the San Francisco Giants, took the mound against the Texas Rangers, with 23-year old rookie Gerald "Buster" Posey behind the plate. Bumgarner pitched a 3-hit shutout, defeating right-hander Tommy Hunter 4-0.

104. Who was the first rookie catcher to bat cleanup in a World Series game?

In Game 4 of the 2010 World Series, on October 31st, the San Francisco Giants inserted rookie catcher Gerald "Buster" Posey in the cleanup slot against the Texas Rangers to become the first rookie to bat in that prestigious position in the batting order in a World Series.

105. Who is the first, and only, player to hit three home runs in a World Series game twice?

Look no further than George Herman Ruth who duplicated his 1926 Game 4 feat on October 9th, in Game 4 of the 1928 World Series, here again, in Sportsman's Park III, this time before a crowd of 37,331.

With the Yankees behind 1-0, Ruth led off the top of the 4th inning with a home run into deep right field off Cardinal starter right-hander "Wee Willie" Sherdel.

In the 7th inning, with the Yankees behind, 2-1, Ruth hit another solo home run into deep right field, again off Sherdel. The Babe came up in the 8th inning, with the Yankees ahead 5-2, and blasted his third solo home run into the right field stands, this time off future Hall of Famer, Grover Cleveland "Pete" Alexander; just another of the Babe's long list of batting accomplishments.

106. Who was the first player to appear in three consecutive World Series with three different teams?

Don Baylor, an outfielder, first baseman, and designated hitter, appeared in three World Series during his 19-year career, and he bunched them all within a three-year period when he appeared in 1986 with the Boston Red Sox against the New York Mets. He followed that in the following season when he was a member of the Minnesota Twins in the 1987 World Series against the St. Louis Cardinals. In 1988 he found himself in the World Series with the Oakland Athletics playing the Los Angeles Dodgers, and became a "Ground Breaker" by being the first player to appear in three consecutive Fall Classics with three different teams.

107. Who was the first player to hit a grand slam home run in a game which his team lost?

He did the best he could but it wasn't enough as New York Yankees catcher "Yogi" Berra came up the top of the 2nd inning of Game 2 of the 1956 World Series, on Friday, October 5th, at Ebbets Field, and silenced the home crowd of 36,217 by driving a Don Newcombe pitch deep into the right field stands scoring the Yankees starter Don Larsen, LF Enos "Country" Slaughter, and CF Mickey Mantle ahead of him to give the Yankees an early 6-0 lead. That didn't last long as the Brooklyn Dodgers came back with six runs in their half of the inning as they went on to pound seven Yankees pitchers for twelve hits and came away with a 13-8 win. "Yogi" remains a "Groundbreaker" by being the first to hit a grand slam for a losing cause.

108. Who was the first National League player to hit a home run in his first two World Series at bats?

Game 1 of the 1996 World Series took place at Yankee Stadium on

Sunday evening, October 20, 1996 when the Yankees played host to the Atlanta Braves. And what cordial hosts they were, especially to Braves left-fielder Andruw Jones.

In the top of the 2nd inning Jones made his first World Series at bat and found catcher Javy Lopez on first after a single to centerfield. Jones lashed southpaw Andy Pettitte's pitch deep into left field for a two run home run putting the Braves up 2-0.

In the top of the 3rd, and with right-hander Brian Boehringer having replaced Pettitte earlier in the inning, Jones came up for his second at bat and found 1B Fred McGriff and Javy Lopez on base and took Boehringer downtown for a three-run home run, his second round-tripper in his first two World Series at bats, which put the Braves up 5-0.

Atlanta, and right-hander John Smoltz, went on to a "laughter" to open the series by winning 12-1. Jones went on to be the first in the senior circuit to hit a home run in his first two World Series at bats.

109. Of the three relief pitchers to have been named the MVP of a World Series, who was the first?

We'll go back to the 1974 World Series between the two west coast teams, the Oakland Athletics and the Los Angeles Dodgers, where Oakland right-hander Rollie Fingers was involved in three of the four wins the Athletics had in defeating the Dodgers in seven games.

Fingers pitched a total of 9.1 innings of relief, winning Game 1, and saving Game 3 and Game 5, compiling a 1.93 Era. in the process to then be named the first relief pitcher to be awarded the MVP in a World Series.

110. Who was the first pitcher to strike out the side in a World Series game?

On October 1st in the 2nd inning of Game One of the 1903 World Series, Pittsburgh Pirates right-hander Deacon Phillippe struck out Freddy Parent, Candy LaChance, and Hobe Ferris of the Red Sox in order to become the first pitcher, of the 35 who would follow, to set down the side on strikes in the Fall Classic.

111. Who was the first, and only, pitcher in a World Series to strike out the side in order, twice in the same game, and doing it against the same three batters?

It is not surprising to learn that southpaw Sandy Koufax of the Los

Angeles Dodgers on October 2nd, in the 1963 World Series against the New York Yankees struck out Tony Kubek, Bobby Richardson, and Tom Tresh in order in the 1st inning of Game One, and then came back to strike out the same trio of batters in the 4th inning as well to stand alone in that feat.

112. Who was the first pitcher to strike out the side on three different occasions in the World Series?

With seven pitchers striking out the side twice in their World Series career only Orlando "El Duque" Hernandez can lay claim to doing it three times. On October 23, 1999 the Yankees right-hander struck out three Atlanta Braves in the 1st inning of Game One, then came back in the 3rd inning to strike out three other Braves.

The following year, on October 24, 2000, in the 1st inning of Game 3 he struck out three New York Mets in order to be the first pitcher to strike out the side three times in a World Series.

113. Who was the first, and only, player to have played on a team that swept a World Series in both the National and American Leagues?

This rarity began at Riverfront Stadium on Tuesday, October 10, 1990 when the Cincinnati Reds, and right-hander Jose Rijo, shutout the Oakland Athletics, 7-0 in Game 1 of the World Series with Paul O'Neill patrolling right field.

The Reds took Game 2, 5-4, in 10 innings to move the series out to Oakland on Friday, October 19th where the Reds continued their dominance by winning Game 3, 8-3. The following day Jose Rijo was back to clinch the title by winning 2-1 to sweep the World Series.

The 1998 World Series finds O'Neill again in right field, but now with the New York Yankees, and in the Fall Classic against the San Diego Padres. The Yankees took Game 1 on Saturday, October17th, 9-6, came back the next day to take Game 2, 9-3. The series moved out to Qualcomm Stadium for Game 3 which New York won 5-4. In Game 4, before 65,427, southpaw Andy Pettitte shutout the Padres, 3-0, to give O'Neill his second World Series sweep.

We now move to Turner Field for Game 1 of the 1999 World Series against the Atlanta Braves, and O'Neill remains on a roll as the Yankees continue their winning ways in the Fall by sweeping the Braves, winning the first two down at Turner Field, 4-1 and 7-2, and coming back to Yankee Stadium to finalize the sweep, 6-5, and 4-1, to make Paul O'Neill a

"Groundbreaker" by being the first, and only player to have played on a team that has swept their opponent in both leagues.

114. Who is the first, and only, pitcher to have won a World Series game for three different teams?

Curt Shilling, the big, hard-throwing right-hander had his first World Series victory when with the Philadelphia Phillies he shutout the Toronto Blue Jays, 2-0, on five hits, in Game 5 of the 1993 World Series on October 21st.

He followed that up on October 27th in the 2001 World Series when he defeated the New York Yankees, 9-1, in Game 1, while pitching for the Arizona Diamondbacks.

Then in Game 2 of the 2004 World Series, on October 24th, Schilling beat the St. Louis Cardinals, 6-2, at Fenway Park while pitching for the Red Sox. As an add-on, and still in Beantown, Schilling dispatched the Colorado Rockies, 2-1, on October 25th in the 2007 World Series.

115. Who was the first player in World Series history to have three doubles in his first three times at bat?

On October 27, 2010, before a crowd of 43,601, San Francisco Giants second baseman Freddy Sanchez faced off in Game 1 of the World Series, at San Francisco, against southpaw Cliff Lee and banged out a double in his first three appearances against the Texas Rangers star to be the first to achieve such a batting record. Sanchez went on to go four for five and drive in three runs as RHP Tim Lincecum bested the Rangers 11-7.

116. Who was the first outfielder to complete an unassisted double play in a World Series?

We have to go back to a cold afternoon with 32,694 in attendance at Fenway Park, on Tuesday, October 15, 1912 when the 7th game of the World Series (Game 2 had been tied at 6-6, and was called in the 10th inning at Fenway due to darkness, making this the first World Series needed to go eight games), was played between the New York Giants and the Boston Red Sox with Boston leading the series three games to two.

Going into the top of the 9th inning with the Giants up 10-4, Giants 2B Buck Herzog, leading off, drew a walk from Red Sox right-hander Charley "Sea Lion" Hall. Catcher Art Wilson lined a single to centerfield, and Herzog raced around to score on an errant throw to third base to give the Giants an 11-4 lead with Wilson moving to second on the play. Shortstop

Art Fletcher then stroked a soft liner to centerfield where Tris Speaker raced in to snare the short fly, and seeing Wilson, who had been on second, racing around trying to score on what he thought was a single, continued running and touched second base to double up Wilson completing the first unassisted double play in World Series history.

The series went to Game 8 where the Red Sox won the final game, 3-2, and the series 4 games to 3, with two runs in the 10th inning, with Smoky Joe Wood besting Christy Mathewson.

117. Who was the first player to hit two triples in a World Series game?

Since October 1, 1903 was the date of the very first World Series game it is not surprising that a number of "firsts" were recorded. Pittsburgh Pirates third baseman Tommy Leach took advantage of that fact by establishing two "firsts" when he banged out four hits, two of them were triples, along with two singles, to become the first to have not only four hits, but two triples in a World Series game.

118. Who were the first pitchers to win three games in a World Series?

We go back to the 1903 World Series when Pittsburgh right-hander Charles "Deacon" Phillippe won Games 1, 3, and 4, and the right-hander of the Boston Americans, "Wild Bill' Dinneen, took Games 2, 6, and 8.

119. Who was the first player to hit a home run from both sides of the plate in an ALDS game?

The New York Yankees centerfielder Bernie Williams hit a home run from both sides of the plate in Game 3 of the American League Division Series, against Seattle, on October 6, 1995, to be the first player to switch hit home runs in the same playoff game.

He came back in 1996, against the Texas Rangers, to repeat that performance in Game 4 of the ALDS on October 5th, to not only be the first to do it in a playoff series, but to do it twice in his career.

120. Who was the first player to hit a home run from both sides of the plate in a NLDS game?

The Atlanta Braves switch-hitting third baseman, Larry Wayne "Chipper" Jones, did it in a 6-4 Braves win against the Chicago Cubs in Game 4, at Wrigley Field, on Saturday, October 4, 2003.

He hit his first, a two-run home run to left field off right-hander Matt

Clement in the 5th inning scoring 2B Marcus Giles before him. He followed that with a two out, two-run homer in the 8th off southpaw Mark Guthrie, again to left field, and again scoring Giles.

121. What team was the first to *not* win a World Series game?

The first team to not win a World Series game began on Tuesday, October 8, 1907, when in Game 1, the Detroit Tigers played a 3-3 tie with the Chicago Cubs with the game called because of darkness in the 12th inning at Chicago.

From then on the Cubs brought out the broom and swept the Tigers away with a four-game sweep as Cubs' pitchers Jack Pfiester, Ed Reulbach, Orval Overall, and Mordecai "Three Finger" Brown slammed the door on the Tigers, and Detroit became the first team to be swept in a World Series.

122. What team was the first to play in four consecutive World Series?

John McGraw's New York Giants was the first team to make it to the World Series in four consecutive years, from 1921-1924.

123. What teams were the first to play all of their World Series games in the same ballpark?

The 1921 World Series between the New York Giants and the New York Yankees was played at the Polo Grounds in New York. Both teams used the Polo Grounds for a time until the Yankee Stadium was completed in 1923.

In the 1944 World Series the St. Louis Cardinals and St. Louis Browns played their World Series games in Sportsman's Park, St. Louis.

124. Who was the first player to pinch-hit a grand slam home run in post-season history?

It happened in Game 3 of the National League Division Series with the Cincinnati Reds up two games to none against the Los Angeles Dodgers on Friday October 6, 1995 at Riverfront Stadium.

In the bottom of the 6th inning, with Cincinnati up 3-1, 1B Hal Morris singled through the right side of the infield off right-hander Kevin Tapani. Catcher Benito Santiago singled to left field, and that was all for Tapani. Southpaw Mark Guthrie came in and walked 2B Bret Boone to load the bases.

That brought up Mark Lewis to pinch-hit for 3B Jeff Branson, and he didn't disappoint as he hit the first pitch for a grand slam home run to left-centerfield to make it 7-1, Cincinnati, as they went on to win 10-1, and swept the Dodgers in the best 3-out of 5 series.

Mark Lewis became a "Groundbreaker" by being the first pinch-hitter to blast a grand slam home run in the post season.

125. Who was the first pitcher to lose three World Series games?

There seems to be, and is, more to this story for it involved the infamous 1919 World Series, better known as the "Black Sox Scandal."

Claude "Lefty" Williams of the Chicago White Sox lost Game 2, Game 5, and Game 8 of the 1919 World Series to the Cincinnati Reds, and with that 0-3 record showed a 6.63 Era. That makes Lefty eligible, by virtue of that embarrassing statistic, as being the first pitcher to lose three games in a World Series, but the subject deserves no further mention.

126. Who was the first pitcher to get two base hits in the same inning of a World Series game?

It happened in Game 7 at Navin Field, on Tuesday, October 9, 1934, before a crowd of 40,902, when in a scoreless top of the 3rd inning RHP Dizzy Dean doubled to left field off Detroit's RHP Elden "Submarine" Auker, and came around to score the Cardinals first run when 2B Frankie Frisch, with the bases loaded, hit a three-run double to right field.

Later in the inning Dean came up again, this time against the third pitcher of the inning, southpaw Elon "Chief" Hogsett, and singled down third to drive in catcher Bill DeLancey. With that base hit Dizzy became the first pitcher to have two base hits in the same inning of a World Series game.

St. Louis, with that seven-run 3rd, went on to win as Dizzy pitched a six-hit, 11-0, shutout as the Tigers fell in seven games.

127. Who was the first player in World Series history to start each of the first three games at a different position?

The 1992 World Series between the Toronto Blue Jays and the Atlanta Braves opened up on Saturday, October 17th in Atlanta-Fulton County Stadium.

The Blue Jays' Joe Carter played Game 1 at first base, and batted in the third slot in the order. Game 2 was back in Atlanta on October 18th but Joe Carter, still batting third, was now playing left field. Game 3 moved to the SkyDome in Toronto and there was Carter, batting third again, but now patrolling right field. He stayed in right field for Games 4 and 5, but was back at first base for Game 6 as Toronto took the series in six games, but Joe Carter became the first player to start the first three games of the fall classic at three different positions.

128. What teams were the first to play a World Series game before a televised audience?

September 30, 1947 the Brooklyn Dodgers came to Yankee Stadium to play the Yankees in Game 1 of the World Series before 73,365 fans at the ballpark, and untold thousands in the areas of New York City, Schenectady, Philadelphia, and Washington, D.C where the fans in those areas were the first to see this historic event on television.

129. Who was the first African-American to play in a World Series?

When Jackie Robinson was penciled in the lineup card and took the field at first base for the Brooklyn Dodgers for Game 1 of the 1947 World Series on September 30th, he became the first African-American to play in the Fall Classic.

130. Who was the first player to be in the starting lineup of a World Series game, but never appear on the field?

On October 13, 1917 in Game 5 of the World Series, out in Comiskey Park Chicago, New York Giants right-fielder, Jim Thorpe, football star and noted Olympic athlete, was listed as batting 6th in the starting lineup, for his only postseason "appearance" of his major league career.

When it came time for him to bat in the top of the first inning Thorpe, a right-handed hitter, was strategically replaced for a pinch-hitter, the left-handed hitting outfielder, Dave Robertson, after the White Sox lifted southpaw Ewell "Reb" Russell in favor of right-hander Eddie Cicotte. Thorpe's name was penciled in as the right-fielder, batting 6th, but it never happened.

131. Who was the first player-manager to hit a home run in a World Series?

Leftfielder Fred "Cap" Clarke not only led the Pittsburgh Pirates to their first World Championship in 1909, but also became the first player-manager to hit a home run in the Fall Classic.

He started in the 4th inning of Game 1, on October 8, 1909, at Forbes Field, the first World Series played in that historic park, when Clarke hit a game-tying home run off Detroit Tigers right-hander "Wabash George" Mullin. The Pirates took the opening game, 4-1, behind right-hander Charles "Babe" Adams.

He hit another in Game 5, this one coming off right-hander "Kickapoo Ed" Summers, also in the 4th inning. Clarke hit the only Pirate home runs in the series.

132. Who was the first American League player-manager to hit a home run in a World Series?

It was Game 2, on Sunday, October 5th, of the 1924 World Series, in Griffith Stadium, when the Washington Senators manager and second baseman, Stanley "Bucky" Harris, connected with a solo shot to deep left field in the 5th inning, off the New York Giants southpaw, Jack Bentley, for the first home run by an American League player-manager in World Series history.

Coming back in Game 7, on Friday, October 10th, he hit another solo home run, this in the 4th inning off Giants right-hander Virgil "Zeke" Barnes as Washington went on to win their first, and only, World Championship with a run in the bottom of the 12th inning, when CF Earl McNeely doubled off reliever Jack Bentley scoring catcher Muddy Ruel with the winning run, 4-3.

133. Who was the first, and only, pitcher to twice pitch a complete 7th game in a World Series?

When it came down to the 7th and deciding game of the 1964 World Series, on October 15th out in Sportsman's Park, the St. Louis Cardinals were locked at three games each with the New York Yankees.

The Redbirds sent their right-handed ace Bob "Hoot" Gibson up against the Yankees right-handed rookie Mel Stottlemyre Sr., winner of Game 2.

Gibson pitched his 2nd complete game in the series, winning 7-5, striking out 9 to give him 31 over the 27 innings he worked, and giving the Cardinals the World Championship.

In 1967 the Cardinals were back in the Fall Classic, this time facing the Boston Red Sox. With Boston winning Game 6 and forcing a 7th game, St. Louis designated Gibson as their man to capture the World Championship. He went up against Boston's ace right-hander Jim Lonborg, winner of Games 2 and 5. Red Sox bats were quickly quieted by Gibson as he pitched a complete game allowing just three hits and striking out ten as St, Louis came away with a 7-2 victory and the World Championship.

Gibson gave the Cardinals two clutch performances, in '64 and '67, to make him the first to win two complete 7th games in the World Series.

134. Who was the first player to have 10 or more base hits in a World Series with 2 different teams?

This Hall of Famer not only did it with two teams, but playing in two different positions. We are talking about Paul "The Ignitor" Molitor, who played in the 1982 World Series at third base for the Milwaukee Brewers against the St. Louis Cardinals, and peppered the mound staff of the "Mound City" for 11 singles in his 31 at bats for a nifty .355 average, but the Cardinals took the series in seven games.

The 1993 World Series saw Molitor on the Toronto Blue Jays lineup card as the designated hitter, and he surely lived up to that title as he had 6 singles, 2 doubles, 2 triples, and two home runs in his 24 at bats, for an unbelievable .500 batting average while driving in 8 runs and scoring 10 against Philadelphia Phillies pitching as Toronto took the World Championship north of the border after six games.

135. Who was the first pitcher to collect his first two major league career victories in the post season?

If you are going to win your first major league game there is no better stage than in the post season. Right-hander Francisco (K-Rod) Rodriquez of the Anaheim Angels made his big league debut on September 18, 2002, but he was winless until Game 2 of the American League Division Series, on Wednesday, October 2, 2002, in Yankee Stadium, when K-Rod was called in to relieve right-hander Kevin Appier, with the Yankees ahead 6-5, and pitched a scoreless 6th and 7th inning.

In the top of the 8th the Angels pushed across three runs and went on to win 8-6. That gave K-Rod his first major league win.

His taste of victory followed him out to Edison Field in Anaheim on Friday, October 4th when, in Game 3, he came on in relief of southpaw Scott Schoeneweis, with the Angels down 6-5. K-Rod pitched a scoreless 7th and 8th innings, striking out four Yankees. In the bottom of the 7th the Angels tied the game at 6-6.

In the 8th the Angels exploded for three runs and went on to win 9-6.

RHP Troy Percival came on in the 9th to close out the win for Rodriguez. K-Rod's career pitching record now stood at 2-0, and he had yet to win a regular season game, but he can always say he was the first pitcher to have his first career wins happen in the post season.

136. Who was the first player to hit home runs in the first two games of a post season series twice in his career?

It began on Tuesday, September 30, 1997 at Game 1 of the American League Division Series at Yankee Stadium when Yankees shortstop Derek Jeter hit a two-out solo home run to deep right field in the 6th inning off Cleveland Indians right-hander Eric Plunk.

Jeter came back in Game 2, on Thursday, October 2nd, again at Yankees Stadium, and hit a solo home run to centerfield in the 9th inning of Jose "Joe Table" Mesa.

Moving on to the 2002 ALDS at Yankee Stadium, on Tuesday, October 1st for Game 1 against the Anaheim Angels, Jeter came up in the 1st inning with one out and hit a solo home run to left-centerfield off Angels south-paw Jarrod Washburn.

In Game 2, on Wednesday, October 2nd, Jeter came up in the 3rd inning with one out, and hit another solo home run, this into the left field seats off right-hander Kevin "Ape" Appier, to make the Yankees' captain the first player to hit a home run in the first two games of a post season series, twice in his career.

137. Who was the first player to have as many as eight total bases in one World Series game?

On October 1, 1903 the World Series was introduced to baseball fans and the Pittsburgh Pirates 3B Tommy Leach saw that it got off to a fast start. He came into Game 1 and banged out four hits, two triples and two singles as he went 4-for-5 against the great Cy Young of the Red Sox as Pittsburgh took the opener in Boston, 7-3.

In winning the first Fall Classic, 5 games to 3, Leach ended up with 17 total bases in 33 at bats, driving in 7 runs.

138. Who was the first pitcher to have 3 base hits in one World Series game?

It happened in Game 3, on October 20, 1910, when Philadelphia Ath-letics right-hander "Colby Jack" Coombs took a liking to Chicago Cubs pitching and went 3-for-5, driving in 3 runs in the process as Philadelphia rolled to a 12-5 win as they defeated the Cubs and went on to win the World Championship in five games.

139. Who was the first player to have 5 hits in the ALCS?

When Baltimore Orioles centerfielder Paul "Motormouth" Blair took the field for Game 3 of the ALCS on October 6, 1969 against the hometown Minnesota Twins he didn't think he would be would be the first player to have five hits in a post-season game.

When the Orioles came away with an 11-2 win there was Blair having gone 5-for-6 with two doubles and three singles that was the catalyst for victory.

140. Who was the first pitcher to win five World Series games?

When it comes to great pitching performances in the regular season or the post-season, New York Giants Hall of Fame right-hander Christy Mathewson has set the standard.

Putting aside his 373 regular season victories for the moment, he is the first pitcher to win five World Series games, the first three with his brilliant performance in the 1905 World Series where Matty shutout a very talented Philadelphia Athletics team in Games 1, 3, and 5, giving up just 14 hits, striking out 18, and walking just one over 27 innings.

He continued on to the 1911 World Series where he added to his wins on October 14, 1911 in Game 1 against the Philadelphia Athletics Hall of Fame right-hander Charles "Chief" Bender defeating him, 2-1.

Then in the 1913 World Series, in Game 2, Matty was again facing the Athletics, and this time the Hall of Fame southpaw, "Gettysburg Eddie" Plank on October 8th in Game 2, and again came through as his run scoring single in the top of the 10th inning added a run in the three-run inning to give Matty his 5th World Series win, and another shutout, as the Giants won, 3-0.

141. Who was the first player to win a World Series with a team in both leagues?

Look no further than John "Stuffy" McInnis, a first baseman who made his major league debut on April 12, 1909 with the Philadelphia Athletics, and went on to be on the 1911 and 1913 World Champion Philadelphia Athletics when they beat the New York Giants. The Athletics lost to the Boston Braves in the 1914 World Series, but McInnis moved over to the

Boston Red Sox in 1918 and again found himself on a World Series winner when they beat the Chicago Cubs in the 1918 World Series.

The 1925 season found "Stuffy" over in the National League with the Pittsburgh Pirates, and sure enough there was "Stuffy" in the Fall Classic once again, and again he came away as a member of a World Champions team as the Pirates defeated the Washington Senators in seven games. That made McInnis the first player to play on a World Championship team in both leagues.

142. Who was the first player to be named the Most Valuable Player in a World Series, but then played for a different team the following season?

Since the World Series MVP Award wasn't formally established until 1955, there have just been five players who have won the award, and then switched teams the following season.

It happened for the first time after the 1986 famous 6-game series between the New York Mets and Boston Red Sox, when the Mets third baseman, Ray Knight, won the award with a .391 batting average, five runs driven in, and a .440 on base percentage. On November 12, 1986 he was granted free agency and signed on with the Baltimore Orioles for the 1987 season.

143. What World Series teams were the first to be picketed by the American Indian Movement?

When you recall the teams in that 1995 Fall Classic, where the Atlanta Braves defeated the Cleveland Indians in six games, it isn't too surprising to learn that these two teams were the target for picketing and verbal abuse.

The American Indian Movement was a civil rights organization founded in 1968 to supposedly help urban American Indians who had been displaced by government programs. The national leadership of these so-called "do-gooders" was disbanded in 1978.

144. Who was the first player, in a World Series, to steal two bases on the same pitch?

It seems the unusual was part of the 2009 World Series, for on Sunday, November 1st, in Game 4, Phillies closer, right-hander Brad "Lights Out" Lidge, came in at Citizens Bank Park in the 9th inning with the score tied at 4-4, and got Hideki Matsui to pop-up, Derrick Jeter to strike out, and was one out away from ending the inning. Only Johnny "Caveman" Damon stood in his way.

A nine-pitch duel took place whereby Damon, with a 1-2 count on him, then fouled off four of Lidge's pitches, including a foul tip that just squirted below catcher Carlos Ruiz's mitt. With Lidge's next pitch, a 3-2 fastball on the outside corner, the southpaw swinging Damon lofted a soft single to left field.

As the switch-hitting Mark Teixeira came walking to the plate, to face the right-hander Lidge, the Phillies, as they had in the past, moved into their shift against the southpaw swinging first baseman. Shortstop Jimmy Rollins moved over to the right side of second base. Third baseman Pedro Feliz moved to his left closer to second, into the area vacated by Rollins.

Now as Damon led off first base there was a very good possibility that he would try to steal second, especially since Lidge wasn't known for his proficiency at holding runners on. Damon knew this as well and it didn't take him long to make up his mind, for on the first pitch Damon got a huge jump and took off for second as Feliz went over to cover second. Lidge's slider, his best pitch, went into the dirt, and catcher Carlos Ruiz had a hard time gripping it, and his throw to the bag was late, and not strong. Feliz had to scramble just to hang on to the baseball which came in on the wrong side of second, and Damon slid in safely.

Regaining his feet the 35-year old Damon saw no one covering third base, and dashed for the hot corner with Feliz in hot pursuit, but to no avail as Damon went in safely to become a "Groundbreaker" by being the first player to steal two bases on the same pitch in World Series history, as 46,145 fans sat in stunned disbelief.

That had to be unsettling, and no doubt, changed the complexion of the game, for two pitches later Lidge then hit Teixeira on the arm with a pitch, Alex Rodriguez doubled to left, and Jorge Posada singled to left-center, and closed out the inning by being thrown out Raul Ibanez to 2B Chase Utley trying to stretch his single. The Yankees went on to score three runs in the 9th to come away with a 7-4 win, on their way to their 27th World Championship.

145. Who was the first player to commit three errors in the same inning of a World Series game?

It was a classic matchup of two future Hall of Fame residents, Baltimore Orioles right-hander, Jim Palmer, against the Los Angeles Dodgers southpaw Sandy Koufax on Thursday, October 6, 1966 in Game 2 out in Dodger Stadium, before a crowd of 55,947.

Going into the top of the 5th inning the two teams were locked in a scoreless tie. 1B Boog Powell led off with a single to left field. 2B Davey Johnson fouled out to catcher John Roseboro. Then CF Paul Blair hit a routine fly ball out to centerfielder Willie Davis who lost the ball in the sun, and both runners were safe on the error.

The Orioles catcher, Andy Etchebarren then hit a fly ball into short centerfield which Davis bobbled and then dropped it. Powell scored, and when Davis rushed his throw to third base it sailed high, and Blair scored on the throwing error, the third of the inning by Davis.

SS Luis Aparicio then laced a double to left field scoring Etchebarren from third and Baltimore won Game 2, 6-0, on their way to a four-game sweep.

146. Who was the first player to strike out in the 9th inning, in consecutive years, to end the final game of an American League playoff series, and end his team's chances of going to the World Series?

On Friday, October 22, 2010, down in The Ballpark in Arlington, before a crowd of 51,404, the Texas Rangers were hoping to close out Game 6 over the New York Yankees in the ALCS, and go to their first World Series.

Leading 6-1 in the top of the 9th inning Rangers right-hander, Neftali Feliz, was called in to close out the game for right-hander Colby Lewis, who started and was in complete command for the first eight innings.

Feliz, throwing big-time heat, sent leadoff hitter CF Curtis Granderson down swinging. He followed that by getting 2B Robinson Cano to ground out to first base. That brought up 3B Alex Rodriguez, who when he joined the Rangers in 2001, stated he was there to lead Texas to the World Series. Ten years later he didn't lead them to a World Series, but he made it possible by watching an 83 mph curveball freeze him for a called strike three sending the Texas Rangers to the World Series to meet the San Francisco Giants.

Let's move on to the Yankee Stadium on Thursday evening, October 6, 2011, where the Yankees were hosting the Detroit Tigers in Game 5 of the ALDS before a crowd of 50,960.

The teams were tied two games apiece. Going into the bottom of the 9th inning with Detroit holding on to a slim 3-2 lead, Detroit sent in right-hander Jose "Papa Grande" Valverde to relieve right-hander Joaquin Benoit who went the previous 1.2 innings. "Papa Grande" was certainly that as he got Granderson to fly out to left field, Cano to line out to center, which brought up A-Rod, who had gone down swinging in the 7th, and the huge right-hander ended the Yankees hopes of going further in the post season by getting Rodriguez to go down swinging again. In two consecutive seasons A-Rod crushed the hopes of his teammates by eliminating them by striking out to end the playoff.

It was Valverde's 51st perfect save of the season sending Detroit down to Texas for the ALCS.

147. Who was the first player to hit a walk-off grand slam home run in post-season history?

The 51,227 fans who jammed The Ballpark at Arlington on Monday afternoon, October 10, 2011, for the third game of the ALCS were treated to an exciting game, and were witnesses to baseball history.

The Detroit Tigers, who led 3-2 going into the bottom of the 7th, saw that disappear when RF Nelson Cruz hit a solo home run to deep left field off RHP Max Scherzer to tie the game at 3-3.

It stayed deadlocked until the bottom of the 11th inning when right-hander Ryan Perry, the 5th Detroit pitcher, came in replacing RHP Jose Valverde, who had pitched the 9th and 10th. DH Michael Young, led off the inning with a ground ball single to left field. 3B Adrian Beltre followed with long single to center. Then catcher Mike Napoli singled to center with the runners moving up to load the bases.

That set the stage for Nelson Cruz who did what any good right-handed hitter would do in the clutch; he blasted Perry's pitch into the left field stands for a game-winning, walk-off grand slam home run, the first in the history of the post-season.

With that 7-3 win Texas took a two-game lead as the teams headed to Detroit for Game 3.

148. What team was the first to win four consecutive games to sweep a World Series?

There will be some question about the answer to this query as the Chicago Cubs played Game 1 of the 1907 World Series on October 8th at their West Side Park against the Detroit Tigers only to see the game end in a tie in the 12th inning, 3-3.

The following day, still in Chicago, the Cubs took Game 2, 3-1, and went on to win Games 3, 4, and 5, for a 4-game sweep of the Tigers to win the World Championship.

Now for all those Boston Braves fans; on October 13th they won Game 4 of the 1914 World Series against the Philadelphia Athletics, 3-1, at Fenway Park, where the series was played that year, to become the first team to sweep a World Series in four *consecutive* games.

149. Who was the first pitcher to give up a natural cycle to four successive batters in the same inning in playoff history?

The 2011 American League playoffs created a few first time happenings, and this "Groundbreaker" event is a classic.

Let's go into the bottom of the 6th inning of Game 5 of the ALCS, on Thursday afternoon, October 13, 2011, before a crowd of 41,908 at Comerica Park.

With the Texas Rangers and Detroit Tigers tied at 2-2, Tigers RF Ryan Raburn opened up the inning, facing southpaw C.J. Wilson, with a single to left-centerfield. Then 1B Miguel Cabrera lined a ball down the line that hit the third base bag, and bounced over 3B Adrian Beltre's head and down the line for a double, scoring Raburn. DH Victor Martinez followed with a sinking line drive deep to right field that the Rangers' Nelson Cruz dove for, but missed, and the ball rolled down the line for a triple. Then LF Delmon Young crushed his second home run of the game, a two-run shot to deep left-center, and fifth of the post season, scoring Martinez, and completing the first natural batting cycle in post season history.

The Tigers came away with a 7-5 win to be down 3-2 in games and heading to Texas for Game 6.

150. Who was the first player to win the MVP Award in the League Championship Series and the World Series in the same year?

In 1979 the National League LCS saw a three game sweep by the Pittsburgh Pirates over the Cincinnati Reds, led by Willie "Pops" Stargell, the big Pirates first baseman, as he went 5-for-11, for a .455 batting average, hitting two home runs, scoring twice, and driving in six runs to win the Most Valuable Player Award.

Moving on to the World Series, against the Baltimore Orioles, Willie kept his hot bat smoking against the American League champions by going 12-for-30, for a .400 average, including two doubles and three home runs, driving in seven runs and scoring seven, on his way to becoming the first player to capture both awards in the same year, as the Bucs beat the Birds in seven games.

151. Who was the first player to win the World Series MVP Award and then make the last out in a later World Series?

One of the most memorable and dramatic World Series concluded out in Forbes Field, in Game 7, on October 13, 1960, when Pirates second baseman Bill Mazeroski, came up in the bottom of the 9th inning with the score tied 9-9, and faced Yankees right-hander Ralph Terry, and hammered his pitch for a solo tie-breaking home run to give the Pirates a 10-9 victory and the World Championship.

Yankees second baseman Bobby Richardson had a great series, going 11-for-30 for a .367 average, hitting a pair of doubles and triples along with a home run, driving in 12 runs, and was named the most valuable player of the series. The first player in history to win the Most Valuable Player Award while playing for a losing team.

I find it quite interesting that a player who had two doubles, two home runs, scored four runs, and drove in 5, and batted .320, and came up in the clutch, in the bottom of the 9th inning, to drive in the winning run with a walk-off solo home run to make his team the World Champions was overlooked, and a player on the losing team, who, granted, had an outstanding series, however, did not strike the winning blow is considered the most valuable player in the series.

Moving on to Game 7 of the 1964 World Series at Busch Stadium before a crowd of 30,346, on Thursday, October 15th, the New York Yankees came into the top of the 9th inning down, 7-3, to the St. Louis Cardinals right-hander Bob Gibson, who struck out LF Tom Tresh, gave up a solo home run to 3B Clete Boyer, then struck out PH Johnny Blanchard, batting for RHP Pete Mikkelsen, then allowed another solo home run to SS Phil Linz, which brought up Bobby Richardson who ended the World Series by popping up to 2B Dal Maxvill to make the St. Louis Cardinals World Champions.

152. Who was the first player to pinch-hit, and drive in the winning run of Game 1 of the World Series, and come back in Game 2, again as a pinch-hitter, and drive in the first, and leading run, and his

team's only run of the game off the same pitcher?

It started on Wednesday evening, October 19, 2011, before a crowd of 46,406, out in Busch Stadium, in Game 1 of the World Series, between the Texas Rangers and the St. Louis Cardinals. Coming up in the bottom of the 6th inning, with the score tied, 2-2, to pinch-hit for RHP Chris Carpenter, Allen Craig found 3B David Freese on second after his line drive double to right field, and 2B Nick Punto on first via a walk, and facing Rangers righty reliever Alexi Ogando, who had just come in, replacing southpaw C.J. Wilson. Craig ripped a line drive single down the right field line scoring Freese with the go-ahead run as the Cardinals held on for a 3-2 win.

The following evening, October 20th, Allen Craig is again called upon to pinch-hit, this time in the 7th inning, for southpaw Jaime Garcia who had been locked in a scoreless pitching duel with Rangers right-hander Colby Lewis. After Lewis had given up singles to Freese and Punto, Alexi Ogando was called upon to preserve the shutout.

Craig greeted Ogando the way he did the night before by lacing a single to right-center field, scoring Freese and sending Punto to second, putting the Cardinals up 1-0.

The Rangers pitching held up as they punched across two runs in the top of the 9th to win, 2-1, and even the Series at a game apiece.

Craig had done his part as a pinch-hitter, and became the first player in a World Series to come up in consecutive games as a pinch-hitter and drive in the winning run in the first game and come back the next game to put his team ahead by driving in their only run, all off the same pitcher.

153. Who was the first National League player to hit three home runs in a World Series game, and off three different pitchers?

In a World Series that wasn't void of records Albert Pujols, the St. Louis Cardinals first baseman, made sure to continue the trend. In Game 3, on Saturday evening October 22, 2011, down in The Ballpark at Arlington, he raised the level up a few notches starting in the top of the 6th inning by hitting a 1-1 count for a three-run home run to left field off Rangers right-hander Alexi Ogando.

Coming up in the 7th and facing southpaw Mike Gonzalez he crushed the first pitch into centerfield for a two-run home run.

Then in the 9th, with southpaw Darren Oliver on the mound, Pujols made history by hitting a 2-2 pitch into the left field stands for his third consecutive home run, and all off three different Texas pitchers. That not only sent Pujols into the record books, but propelled the Redbirds into a 2-1 lead in games, as they came away with a 16-7 victory, and the most runs scored in a World Series game in their history.

154. Who was the first player in World Series history to have a base hit in four straight innings?

We are still on Albert Pujols, and in the same Game 3, on October 22, 2011, before a crowd of 51,462, down in Texas. He came up in the 4th inning and singled to left field off southpaw Matt Harrison. In the 5th he singled to centerfield off right-hander Scott Feldman.

As mentioned in item #153, he then homered to left field off Alexi Ogando in the 6th, came back to homer off Mike Gonzalez in the 7th and finished off his four straight hit streak with his home run in the 9th off Darren Oliver. It's just another entry for Pujols in the "Groundbreakers Club."

155. Who was the first player to have 14 total bases in a World Series?

If you have been reading the two former items it will be easy to discern that we are speaking again about Albert Pujols. His two singles and three home runs in Game 3 of the 2011 World Series added up to 14 total bases.

156. Who was the first National League player to have five base hits in one World Series?

This is getting to be a bit repetitive because Albert Pujols surfaces again, and this time he took a page out of Paul "The Ignitor" Molitor's book from the 1982 World Series, at Busch Stadium in Game 1, when Molitor banged out five singles in six at bats playing third base for the Milwaukee Brewers as they went on to shutout St. Louis, 10-0.

Pujols equaled that 5-hit performance by having two singles and three home runs in Game 3, on October 22, 20011.

157. Who was the first National League player to drive in 6 runs in a World Series game?

The script never changes in this drama for we are back to the same game, Game 3, of the 2011 World Series, and as the crowd of 51,462 sat in awe of Pujols' performance in other at bats when they looked at their scorecard they saw his performance that game had duplicated that of the Yankees 2B Bobby Richardson, who had the same number of runs batted in, in Game 3 of the 1960 World Series.

I think after five items on Albert Pujols, where his final line score of 5-for-6, with 3 home runs, 4 runs scored, 6 driven in, and 14 total bases we can safely move on.

158. Who was the first player to be caught stealing twice in the same World Series game?

Of the nine players who followed right-fielder Frank "Wildfire" Schulte of the Chicago Cubs in this category, none can take away his "Groundbreaker" title that he earned on Monday, October 17, 1910 in Game 1, at Shibe Park when in the top of the first inning, with one out, Schulte singled to left field off Philadelphia Athletics right-hander "Chief" Bender.

With CF Solly Hofman up Schulte broke for second, but was thrown out by catcher Ira Thomas's throw to 2B Eddie Collins.

In the 4th Schulte drew a walk, and again tried to swipe second base, with Solly Hofman up, only to be foiled again by Thomas's strong throw to Eddie Collins.

That made "Wildfire" the first player to be thrown out twice attempting to steal a base, in the same World Series game, one that Bender and the Athletics went on to win, 4-1.

To take this one step further raises the question, who was thrown out twice in the same game, twice in the same World Series? And the answer still remains, "Wildfire" Schulte.

We just have to go to Game 5, this on Sunday, October 23rd, at the West Side Grounds in Chicago. It's the bottom of the 3rd and with the score knotted at 1-1 Schulte singled to centerfield off right-hander "Colby Jack" Coombs. Next up was Hofman, and Schulte, with wildfire in his shoes, decided second base was going to be his, and raced down the base path only to find that catcher Jack Lapp had a strong arm as well as he nailed "Wildfire" with his throw to Eddie Collins.

In the bottom of the 5th, with the Cubs down 2-1, with one out, LF Jimmy Sheckard singled to center. Schulte followed with a ground ball to SS Jack Barry who forced Sheckard at second, setting up Schulte to try his thievery once again. With Coombs' pitch "Wildfire" was off and running only to be gunned down once again by Lack Lapp's accurate throw for the third out. Philadelphia went on to take Game 5, 7-2, and the World Series in five games.

Schulte went on to become a "Groundbreaker" on two occasions, once to get caught stealing twice in the same game, and the first to be caught twice on two occasions in the same World Series.

159. Who was the first player in World Series history to have a pair of tying or go-ahead base hits in the 9th inning or later in the same game?

On Thursday evening, October 27, 2011, out in Busch Stadium, in Game 6 against the Texas Rangers, St Louis Cardinals third baseman David Freeze thrilled the overflow crowd of 47,325 with one of the most dramatic two at-bats in World Series game memory.

When he came up in the 9th inning, with the Cardinals down 7-5, and found 1B Albert Pujols on second after a double, and LF Lance Berkman on first via a walk, and down to the last strike in the game, he hit a two-run triple off Rangers right-hander Neftali Feliz, to deep right field, just over a leaping Nelson Cruz, scoring Pujols and Berkman and tying the score at 7-7, the fourth tie of the game.

In the 10th inning LF Josh Hamilton put Texas up, 9-7, with a two-run home run off right-hander Jason Motte. In the bottom of the 10th 2B Ryan Theriot grounded out to third driving in SS Dan Descalso with the Redbirds' 8th run. Lance Berkman, also down to his last strike, then tied the game at 9-9 with a single to center scoring Jon Jay.

That set the stage for more of Freeze heroics as the game went into the bottom of the 11th tied at 9. Right-hander Scott Feldman came in to face Freese as the leadoff batter, and served up a home run ball that Freese deposited 428-feet away into the grassy incline behind the centerfield wall for a 10-9 win, and tying the series at 3-3.

Freeze with two swipes of the bat became the first player in World Series history to have a game-tying hit, and follow that with a game-winning hit from the 9th inning on. His batting made him a game-breaker as well as a "Groundbreaker" over the course of three innings.

160. When was the first time in World Series history that a team had its pitching staff have three blown saves in one game?

Look no further than Game 6, on Thursday evening, October 27, 2011, out in Busch Stadium, when the Texas Rangers not only let that game slip away from them, but possibly the World Championship as well, as right-handers Alexi Ogando, (2 walks in one-third inning), Neiftali Feliz, (a walk, two hits, two runs in one inning),and Scott Feldman, (a walk and a walk-off winning home run in two-thirds of an inning), all co-operated with the St. Louis Cardinals' batters to keep them alive by allowing three blown saves, to play Game 7 on Friday, October 28th with an 11th inning win 10-9.

That proved to be the impetus to have St. Louis capture the World Championship with a 6-2 victory the next day.

161. Who was the first pitcher to win five games in the same post season?

With the creation of the playoff system for the ALDS and NLDS along with the LCS, the opportunity to win more post season games increased beyond the World Series.

In 2001 southpaw Randy "Big Unit" Johnson, of the Arizona Diamond-backs, went up against the Atlanta Braves' best when he defeated right-hander Greg Maddux, 2-0, in Game 1 of the NLCS, on October 16th, at Bank One Ballpark. He came back on October 21st to defeat southpaw Tom Glavine, in Game 5, at Turner Field, 3-2, to send Arizona to the World Series against the New York Yankees.

Johnson kept his winning efforts alive in Game 2 of the World Series, on October 28th by shutting out the Yankees, and defeating southpaw Andy Pettitte at Bank One, 4-0. In Game 6, on November 3rd, he had an easy go as he cruised to a 15-2 victory over Andy Pettitte, again out in Bank One.

He came back on November 4th, in Game 7, still in Bank One, and defeated Yankee ace closer, right-hander Mariano Rivera, 3-2, to give the Diamondbacks the World Championship, and make the "Big Unit" the first pitcher in major league history to win five games in the same post season.

162. Who was the first pitcher to give up a walk-off home run in the World Series to the only batter he faced in that game?

In Game 3, on Saturday, October 10, 1964, before a crowd of 67,101, at the Yankee Stadium, John Keane, St. Louis Cardinals manager, sent up Bob Skinner, in the top of the 9th inning, with the score tied, 1-1, to bat for southpaw Curt Simmons, who had pitched a four-hitter for eight innings. Skinner flied out to deep center field to end any chance for the go-ahead run.

Going into the bottom of the 9th right-hander George "Barney" Schultz took over for Simmons, and the first batter he faced was CF Mickey Mantle, who promptly greeted Schultz with a long solo home run deep into the right field seats to give the Yankees, and Jim "Bulldog" Bouton, a 2-1 victory. The Cardinals went on to take the World Series in seven games, but Barney Schultz became a "Groundbreaker" the hard way, by being the first pitcher in World Series history to give up a walk-off home run, to the only batter he faced in the game.

163. Who was the first player to come to the plate in the World Series with his team one-out from elimination, and drive in the winning walk-off run to preserve the series for another game?

This moment in history takes us back to Wednesday afternoon, October 25, 1911, before a crowd of 33,228, at the Polo Grounds, when the Philadelphia Athletics went into the bottom of the 10th inning tied with the New York Giants, 3-3, in Game 5.

Hall of Fame southpaw "Gettysburg Eddie" Plank came on to start the inning for Philadelphia, and gave up a double down the left field line to 2B "Laughing Larry" Doyle.

CF Fred Snodgrass hit back to Plank, who missed getting Doyle at third on a fielder's choice, allowing Snodgrass to be safe at first.

With runners at the corners RF John "Red" Murray hit a short fly to right field for the first out with Doyle holding third. That brought up 1B Fred Merkle who then hit a fly ball to deep right field which allowed Doyle to tag up, and score the winning run, and make Merkle the first player to bring his team back from elimination, in the World Series, by one swing of his bat, to play Game 6 another day.

The final game took place on Thursday, October 26th down in Shibe Park, before a crowd of 20, 485.

It became "a laugher" for Hall of Famer Charles "Chief" Bender and the Connie Mack-led Athletics, as they banged out 13 hits off right-hander Leon "Red" Ames, southpaw George "Hooks" Wiltse, and Hall of Fame southpaw Richard "Rube" Marquard, to coast to a 13-2 win and the World Championship. For those keeping score at home, the second time it happened was in the 10th inning of the 1986 New York Mets-Boston Red Sox World Series.

164. Who was the first player to have a walk-off base hit to win a World Series game?

We'll take you back to Game 4, on Saturday, October 22, 1910, to the West Side Grounds in Chicago, before a crowd of 19,150, where the Philadelphia Athletics were tied, 3-3, with the Chicago Cubs going into the bottom of the 10th inning. Right-hander "Chief" Bender was on the mound for the Athletics, facing the bottom of the Chicago order. He got the lead-off batter, SS Joe Tinker, to pop-up to SS Jack Barry. Cubs' catcher Jimmy Archer then doubled to left field. RHP Mordecai "Three-Finger" Brown grounded out to Jack Barry at short with Archer moving over to third. LF Jimmy Sheckard then drove home Archer with a sharp single to centerfield for the winning run as Chicago nipped Philadelphia, 4-3, sending the series to Game 5 where Philadelphia became World Champions in five games by winning, 7-2.

165. Who was the first player to hit a grand slam home run in a World Series game after hitting over 40 home runs in the regular season?

This rarity began in the 1988 season when right-fielder Jose "The Chemist" Canseco hit a league leading 42 home runs and drove in 124 runs to win the MVP Award that year and to help lead the Oakland Athletics into the World Series against the Los Angeles Dodgers.

In Game 1, at Dodger Stadium, on Saturday, October 15, 1988, the Athletics led off the top of the 2nd inning down 2-0. With one out Dodgers right-hander Tim Belcher gave up a single to left field to 2B Glenn Hubbard, then walked RHP Dave Stewart, and 3B Carney Lansford. After striking out CF Dave Henderson, Canseco came up and blasted a grand slam home run to deep centerfield to give Oakland a 4-2 lead, and all the runs they would score that day as Kirk Gibson hit that dramatic two-run home run, pinch-hitting for RHP Alejandro Pena, in the bottom of the 9th, off Hall of Fame right-hander Dennis "Eck" Eckersley, to give the Dodgers a 5-4 win as they went on to take the Series in five games.

166. Who was the first, and only, player to hit a home run off Babe Ruth in a World Series?

Over the course of Babe Ruth's truncated ten-year pitching career he surrendered home runs to eight different American League players. The ninth player to take Ruth downtown was Henry "Hi" Myers, the 27-year old centerfielder of the Brooklyn Dodgers, in Game 2, of the 1916 World Series, played at Braves Field, on Monday, October 9th when in the top of the 1st inning, with two out Myers hit a solo home run into the deep right-centerfield stands for their only run of the game as the 47,373 on hand saw one of the great pitching duels in World Series history as a pair of southpaws, the Dodgers' Sherry Smith dueled the Red Sox's Babe Ruth over 13 innings, locked in a 1-1 tie, until the bottom of the 14th inning when Boston's Del Gainer pinch-hit a single to left field to drive in pinch-runner Mike McNally, to give Ruth, and the Red Sox a 2-1 win.

167. Who was the first pitcher to strike out four batters in one inning of a World Series game?

Let's go back to the fifth and final game of the 1908 World Series on Wednesday, October 14th out in Bennett Park, Detroit, where, with the smallest crowd in World Series history, just 6,210, watched the Chicago Cubs right-hander Orval Overall take the mound in the bottom half of the 1st inning, with a 1-0 lead, and walk the Tigers' leadoff batter LF Matty McIntyre. SS Charley O'Leary then struck out. CF "Wahoo Sam" Crawford singled to center sending McIntyre to second. RF Ty Cobb struck out, as did 1B Claude Rossman, who reached first by a wild pitch on strike three. Now with the bases loaded 2B William "Germany" Schaefer went down on strikes as Overall became the first pitcher to strike out four batters in one World Series inning.

168. Who was the first player to hit a World Series home run in the 21st century?

When the Chicago White Sox met the Houston Astros in Game 2 on Sunday, October 23, 2005, at Cellular Field, Chicago, little did the 41, 432 in attendance imagine they would see a first in the 21st century. It occurred in the bottom of the 7th inning with the Pale Hose on the lower end of a 4-2 Houston lead. Astros right-hander Dan Wheeler came in to start the inning, replacing southpaw Andy Pettitte and after getting the first out, gave up a double to centerfield to SS Juan Uribe, and followed with a strikeout of LF Scott Podsednik, before walking 2B Tadahito Uguchi.

Next up was RF Jermaine Dye who was hit by a pitch to load the bases. That brought in right-hander Chad Qualls to replace Wheeler and face 1B Paul Konerko who crushed a two-out grand slam home run into left field for the first World Series grand slam in the 21st century and gave the White Sox a 7-6 victory on their road to a four-game sweep and the World Championship.

169. Who was the first player to twice have four hits in a World Series game in the same World Series?

The first two batting positions got the Milwaukee Brewers off to a fast start in Game 1 of the 1982 World Series against the St. Louis Cardinals, on Tuesday, October 12ᵗʰ at Busch Stadium. 3B Paul Molitor went 5-for-6, and SS Robin Yount went 4-for-6 as the Brewers came away with 17 hits and a 10-0 win.

Yount kept his bat ablaze by coming back in Game 5, on Sunday, October 17ᵗʰ, back in County Stadium, going 4-for-4 to be the first player to have two four-hit games in one World Series. It was enough for the "The Brew Crew" to take that game, 6-4, but the Redbirds went on to take the Series in 7.

170. Who was the first African-American National League umpire to be the home plate umpire in a World Series game?

When Game 4 of the 1993 World Series was over on Wednesday, October 20ᵗʰ down in Veterans Stadium, Philadelphia, there could have been no one more tired and glad to see it end, than home plate umpire Charlie Williams.

With both the Toronto Blue Jays and the Phillies racking up runs like the national debt, the Blue Jays topped the Phillies, 15-14. Poor Charlie, having his baptism behind the plate in the Fall Classic, called balls and strikes on 101 batters, saw 29 players cross the plate all over a span of 4 hours, 14 minutes. It was time for Charlie to be sent to the showers.

171. Who was the first Cy Young Award winner to be relieved by another Cy Young Award winner in a World Series?

This "first time happening" took place down in Veterans Stadium, Philadelphia in Game 3, on Friday, October 14, 1983. It began in the top of the 5ᵗʰ inning, with two-out, when Baltimore Orioles right- fielder Ken Singleton came in against the Phillies ace, Steve Carlton, to pinch-hit for Baltimore's starter, and 1979 Cy Young winner, southpaw Mike Flanagan, with the O's down, 2-0.

Singleton went down looking to end the inning and in came right-hander Jim "Cakes" Palmer, a Cy Young winner in 1973, 75-76, to relieve Flanagan to start the bottom of the 5ᵗʰ and pitched a scoreless 5ᵗʰ and 6ᵗʰ innings, receiving the win as the Orioles picked up a run in the 6ᵗʰ, and two in the 7ᵗʰ to win that day, 3-2, and took the series in five games. That game represents the first time a Cy Young winner relieved another Cy Young winner in a World Series game.

172. Who was the first rookie pitcher to throw two complete game wins in a League Championship Series?

On Friday, October 9, 1992, Pittsburgh Pirates right-hander Tim Wakefield, who had just made his major league début on July 31, 1992, was named the starter in Game 3 of the NLCS against the Atlanta Braves at Three Rivers Stadium on Friday, October 9, 1992. He went all the way pitching a five-hitter to win, 3-2.

Relying on that win manager Jim Leyland named him to start Game 6 on Tuesday, October 13th at Atlanta-Fulton County Stadium and with Pirate batters giving him heavy run support he went all the way for his second complete game as the Pirates easily won 13-4, making Wakefield the first rookie to pitch two complete game wins in the National League Championship Series.

173. Who was the first pitcher to strike out the side on nine pitches in a World Series Game?

It happened in Game 5 of the 1985 World Series when Kansas City Royals manager Dick Howser gave the starting assignment to southpaw Danny Jackson out in Busch Stadium before 53,634 excited Redbird fans. Going into the 7th inning, with a 4-1 lead, Jackson faced 3B Terry Pendleton and struck him out swinging.

Next up was St. Louis Cardinals catcher Tom Nieto, and he looked at three pitches for the second out. That brought pinch-hitter Brian Harper, batting for right-hander Todd Worrell, and he, too, went down swinging as Kansas City took Game 5, 6-1, and the World Series in seven games.

174. Who was the first player in major league history to have six multi-hit games in a League Championship Series?

This second baseman was acquired on July 27, 2012 by the San Francisco Giants from the Colorado Rockies, and his new team took him into his second post season, the first having been with the Oakland Athletics in 2006.

Marco Scutaro had a "Groundbreaker" experience when he had his first multi-hit game in Game 1, of the 2012 LCS, on Sunday. October 14th, at AT&T Park when he went 2-for-5 against the St. Louis Cardinals, who took the game, 6-4.

In Game 2 he went 2-for-3, and followed that on Wednesday, October 17th, where he went 2-for-5, at Busch Stadium. In Game

3, again at Busch Stadium, Scutaro went 2-for-5, and carried that hitting groove into Game 4, on Thursday, October 18th, by going 2-for-4. Game 5 saw him only have a single as the Giants blanked the Redbirds, 5-0.

Coming into Game 6 Scutaro had his 5th multi-hit game by going 2-for-3 back in AT&T Park, and finished off his record six multi-hit game by going 3-for-4, as the Giants took the deciding Game 7, on Monday, October 22nd, before 43,056 of their faithful, 9-0.

J. RESIDENTS OF COOPERSTOWN

1. In what year were the first players inducted into the Hall of Fame in Cooperstown?

The National Baseball Hall of Fame and Museum, located at 25 Main Street, Cooperstown, New York, was created to honor the most worthy individuals, whether they be players, managers, umpires, executives or others, who have made notable contributions to major league baseball.

Many of the great artifacts and memorabilia from days passed are housed here for the many visitors to see.

Elections to the Hall began in 1936, the first inductions didn't begin, however until the Hall was finally completed in 1939.

2. Who were the first players, in the original five, to be inducted into the Hall of Fame?

There were five players originally inducted into the Hall of Fame in 1939 with Ty Cobb, Detroit Tigers, receiving the most votes, 98.23%. Babe Ruth, New York Yankees, had 95.13% of the votes, Honus Wagner, Pittsburgh Pirates, 95.13%, Christy Mathewson, New York Giants, 90.71%, and Walter Johnson, Washington Senators, 83.63%.

3. Who was the first major league manager to be elected to the Hall of Fame?

John McGraw, who managed the Baltimore Orioles in 1899 and 1901, and the New York Giants from 1902 to 1932, won 2,763 games while losing 1,948, taking the Giants to 55 World Series games in nine World Series. In 1937 he became the first manager to be elected to the Hall.

4. Of the fourteen catchers residing in the Cooperstown Hall of Fame who was the first to be enshrined?

William "Buck" Ewing, who played for 18 seasons from 1880-97 in the National League with the Troy Trojans (Giants), New York Giants, Cleveland Spiders, and Cincinnati Reds with a career batting average of .303.

5. Who were the first father and son to be inducted into the Hall of Fame?

These two inductees didn't wear uniforms, but were top baseball executives. Father, Larry McPhail was a lawyer, president of the Brooklyn Dodgers, and the New York Yankees, innovated night baseball, and the televising of regular season games, and flying teams between games. He was inducted into the Hall in 1978.

He was followed by his son, Lee, who was a front office executive for 45 years. He was director of player personnel with the Yankees, president and general manager of the Baltimore Orioles, worked in the Commissioner's office, and was the Executive Vice President and General Manager of the Yankees, and finally president of the American League. He was inducted into the Hall in 1998.

6. Who was the first pitcher to have played over 25 seasons, won more than 250 games, and was never elected to the Hall of Fame?

Southpaw Tommy John pitched for six teams in both the American and National Leagues for 26 years from 1963 to 1989, compiling a career record of 288-231, 162 complete games, 2,245 strike outs, but has yet to be elected to the Hall.

7. Who is the first position player to play over 25 years and not be elected to the Hall of Fame?

James "Deacon" McGuire played for 26 years, from 1884 to 1912, for ten teams in the American Association, National League and the American League, catching 1,611games, and playing 137 games at five other infield and outfield positions with a career batting average of .278, but not enough credentials to join others in Cooperstown.

8. Who was the first, and only, player to have his Hall of Fame plaque mention that he won the Triple Crown?

There are eleven players who have won the Triple Crown in their careers who are in the Hall of Fame, but the first, and only, player to have that feat mentioned on his Hall of Fame plaque is Carl Yastrzemski of the Boston Red Sox.

9. Who was the first Negro League player to be elected to the Hall of Fame in Cooperstown?

LeRoy "Satchel" Paige, played in the Negro Leagues before he joined the major leagues with the Cleveland Indians on July 9, 1948. He stayed with Cleveland in 1948-49, and then was with the St. Louis Browns from 1951-53, before finishing with the Kansas City Athletics in 1965. He had a major league career record of 28-31 with a 3.29 Era. The Negro League Committee voted him into Cooperstown, as a player, in 1971.

10. Who was the first, and only, player who became a member of the Hall of Fame, to hit his 500ᵗʰ home run off a pitcher who was to be a fellow member of the Hall of Fame?

On July 14, 1967 Eddie Mathews, then with the Houston Astros, hit his 500ᵗʰ career home run off San Francisco Giants right-hander Juan "The Dominican Dandy" Marichal. They will be able to talk about it in future Hall of Fame reunions.

11. Who was the first reliever elected to the Hall of Fame?

James Hoyt "Old Sarge" Wilhelm, who pitched for 21 seasons, made his debut with the New York Giants on April 18, 1952. Playing for nine teams in both leagues he had only 52 starts, but switching to the relief role appeared in a total of 1,070 career games, pitching 2,254.1 innings, recording 227 saves, winning 143 and losing 122, with an Era. of 2.52. In 1985 he became the first reliever to be elected to the Hall of Fame.

12. Who was the first Hispanic player to be enshrined in Cooperstown's Hall of Fame?

Roberto Clemente, the Pittsburgh Pirates right fielder from 1955-72, born August 18, 1934 in Carolina, Puerto Rico, was the first Hispanic player to be enshrined in the Hall of Fame, posthumously, on August 6, 1973.

13. Who was the first African-American player inducted into the Hall of Fame?

That honor was easily arrived at when Jackie Robinson, the first modern day African-American major leaguer, who played three infield positions with the Brooklyn Dodgers from 1947-56, played his last game on September 30, 1956, after ten seasons.

His career totals showed him playing in 1,382 games, with 1,518 base hits, 947 runs scored, 734 driven in, 137 home runs, and 197 stolen bases, and a career batting average of .311. He was inducted into the Hall of Fame on July 23, 1962.

14. Who was the first umpire to be elected into the Hall of Fame?

Actually there were two inducted on July 27, 1953. Thomas Henry Connolly, born December 31, 1870 in Manchester, England, moved at age 13, with his family to America, settling in Natick, Massachusetts.

Generating an immediate interest in baseball, he began his career as a major league umpire in the National League in 1898. Back in those early days he was the only umpire on the field.

Connie Mack recommended him to the American League and he moved over there in 1901, and worked the first games played at Fenway Park, Comiskey Park, Shibe Park, and Yankee Stadium. On October 1, 1903 he umpired in the first World Series between the Boston Red Sox and the Pittsburgh Pirates. In June 1941 he was made Umpire in Chief in the American League.

The other umpire inducted on that July day was William "Bill" Klem, born on February 22, 1874 in Rochester, New York, nicknamed "The Old Arbitrator", a term he enjoyed, but certainly not the other, "Catfish," which would have you thrown out post-haste.

Many will say that Klem was the most famous of all the umpires. He certainly was colorful and flamboyant during his career that spanned from 1905, after he was introduced to National League president Harry Pulliam in 1904, by umpire Hank O'Day, to 1941. He was appointed Umpire in Chief of the National League that year.

As a display of Klem's "rabbit ears" we go back to October 1, 1914, when in response to name calling from the New York Giant bench, he threw out the entire bench, all 24 players.

He was one of the first umpires to use arm signals to indicate his calls, and the first to wear an inside chest protector.

There were no more deserving umpires to enter the Halls of Cooperstown that July 27th than Connolly and Klem.

15. Who was the first American Association player to be elected to the Hall of Fame in Cooperstown?

John "Bid" McPhee was one of the finest second baseman in the American Association. He made his major league debut on May 2, 1882 with the Cincinnati Red Stockings, and continued with Cincinnati when they joined the National League in 1890 as the Reds. During his eighteen-year major league career he compiled a record of 2,258 hits, 1,072 runs batted in, 568 stolen bases and a .272 batting average. He was elected to the Hall of Fame by the Veterans committee in 2000.

16. Who was the first, and only, pitcher to be inducted into the Hall of

Fame with under 100 career wins?

It took from 1939 until 2006 for a pitcher with under 100 victories to become a resident in the Cooperstown Hall of Fame. That distinction went to Bruce Sutter who ended his twelve-year career after 661 games, in which he finished 512, resulting in a 68-71 won-lost record. But let's wait a moment, he also had 300 saves and a 2.83 career Era.

17. Who was the first Native-American selected to the Hall of Fame?

The first, and only, Native-American to be inducted into the Cooperstown Hall of Fame was a tall, 6'2" Chippewa Indian pitcher for the Philadelphia Athletics, Charles Albert "Chief" Bender. His father was German and his mother was a Chippewa, and he grew up on the reservation in Minnesota. He attended the well-known, and famous Carlisle Indian School in Carlisle, Pennsylvania.

He began his major league career with the Philadelphia Athletics on April 20, 1903, at the age of 19 winning his first game, in relief that day, over Boston's Cy Young and went on to register a 17-14 record as a rookie. He pitched a no-hitter against Cleveland, winning 4-0, on May 12, 1910.

He spent his first twelve years with Philadelphia before moving to Baltimore in the Federal League for a year, and then moving on to the Phillies and the Chicago White Sox, where he finished his 14-year career with a record of 212-127 in the regular season and 6-4 in the World Series.

The Veterans Committee selected him for the Hall in 1953, and he passed away just a few weeks before his induction, on May 22, 1954, at age 70.

18. Who was the first pitcher in the Hall of Fame to hit a home run in his first major league at bat?

This exclusive accomplishment by James Hoyt Wilhelm, is just one of many by the right-handed Hall of Fame knuckleballer. On April 23, 1952 Wilhelm came on to pitch in his first major league game going 5.1 innings in relief in a 9-5 New York Giants win in relief against the Boston Braves at the Polo Grounds.

In his first major league at bat, in the 4th inning, Wilhelm sliced a Dick Hoover pitch into the right field stands for his first hit, first home run, and his first run batted in covering 432 at bats in 1,070 games over his 21-year career that, by the way ended just days before his 50th birthday.

Wilhelm had started his major league at the late age of 29 after serving and seeing considerable combat in World War II.

Wilhelm pitched a no-hitter against the Yankees on September 2, 1958 winning 1-0. His 124 wins in relief is a record for relief pitchers, as is his being the first pitcher to appear in 1,000 games (1,070), and the first pitcher to have saved over 200 games (227) in a career.

19. Who was the first, and only, man to be elected into both the Major League Baseball Hall of Fame and the National Football League Hall of Fame?

Here is a man who has walked down the halls of the superior athlete not once, but three different times. Robert "Cal" Hubbard not only is the only man to be elected to both the Major League Baseball Hall of Fame, and the National Football League Hall of Fame, but in addition to the College Hall of Fame, in his distinguished athletic career.

That career started at little Centenary College and Geneva College where this bulk of a man, 6'3", 250 pounds, crushed the opposition as a tackle.

Moving into the professional ranks he starred as an end, linebacker, and tackle with the 1927 Champion New York Giants, including the 1928 and '36 seasons, as well as the Green Bay Packers in 1929-33, 35, and the 1936 Pittsburgh Pirates of the NFL. He was named to the official All-NFL team in 1931-33.

His baseball career started as a minor league umpire during the summers when he wasn't playing football. When he retired from football he joined the American League as an umpire and rose to supervisor of American League umpires, a post he held for 15 years. Hubbard died on October 17, 1977, just a year after his election to Cooperstown by the Veterans Committee on February 2, 1976.

20. Who was the first player of the Jewish faith to be elected to the Hall of Fame?

His talents on the field made Detroit Tigers first baseman-outfielder "Hammerin' Hank" Greenberg an easy selection for Cooperstown in 1956. With his career batting average of .313, with 1,628 base hits, and 331 home runs, 1,051 runs scored, and 1,276 batted in, leading the league in doubles twice, and home runs and runs batted in four times, being the American

League MVP twice, and a four-time All-Star in his thirteen-year playing career, interrupted by three years in the Navy during World War II, there's no telling what his final numbers would have been.

21. Who was the first pitcher to be inducted into the Hall of Fame with a losing record?

William Arthur "Candy" Cummings, a diminutive, and somewhat frail right-hander, had a won-lost record of 16-8 in 1876 with the Hartford Dark Blues in the National League before moving over to the Cincinnati Reds in 1877 where he concluded his major league career with a 5-14 record to be one shy of .500 with a two-year 21-22 career record.

How can that be, one might ask? Well he was elected to the Hall of Fame by the Old Timer Committee in 1939 based on the self-professed claim that he was the inventor of the curve ball which he said he discovered while throwing clam shells out over the water in Massachusetts as a teenager.

22. Who was the first player to be inducted into the Hall of Fame with a waiver of the mandatory five-year waiting period after retirement?

It was not too difficult to come up with the answer of Lou Gehrig, New York Yankees first baseman. He was signed as a free agent, and brought up to the Yankees on September 23, 1923, and batted .423 in his first 29 at bats that year. The next season he played two games for the Yankees before being sent to Hartford. He came back up for good to the Yankees in 1925. He soon replaced Wally Pipp at first base, and then went on to play in 2,130 consecutive games over his 13-year career.

On June 3, 1932, against the Philadelphia Athletics, he became the first player in the 20th century to hit four home runs in one game. He went on to win the Triple Crown in 1934 with a .363 batting average, 49 home runs, and 165 runs batted in.

On April 30, 1939, after playing in just eight games, and having been diagnosed with amyotrophic lateral sclerosis (now commonly called "Lou Gehrig's Disease") he played his last game. On June 19, 1939, on his 36th birthday, with his body wracked with pain and weakness, he retired from baseball.

On July 4th, in a very touching moment at Yankee Stadium, Gehrig's uniform #4 was retired, the first time in baseball history that a player had his number retired. His well-quoted, and moving, speech followed the proceedings.

Then in December 1939 he was unanimously elected, in a special election by the Baseball Writers Association, to the Hall of Fame.

At 10:10 P.M. on June 2, 1941, in the Bronx, "The Iron Horse" passed away at age 37.

23. Who was the first player, who was not a pitcher, to be elected to the Hall of Fame, who never batted .300 in any season?

When one thinks of a Hall of Fame player they generally think of a starting pitcher with 200 or more wins or a player with a .300 batting average or prodigious home run totals.

Neither was the case here for the first player to be elected to the Hall of Fame with a career of never batting .300 in any full season happened in 1954 when a diminutive 5'5", 155 pound shortstop by the name of Walter "Rabbit" Maranville was elected to Cooperstown.

Being a bit of a flake, and endearing himself to the fans and photographers, with his comic antics, "Rabbit" received his nickname for his speed and rabbit-like leaps into the arms of his biggest teammate. He did have a fine fielding ability, and was noted for his basket catches of high infield flies.

That being said, his offensive statistics might be considered a bit ordinary for he came to bat in his 23-year career, 15 with the Boston Braves, 10,078 times and picked up 2,605 hits, with 380 doubles, 177 triples, and just 28 home runs, with 22 of them inside-the-park, drove in 884 runs and had a .258 career batting average, and never leading in any offensive category throughout his career. He set a major league record of coming to the plate 672 times, the league high, without hitting a home run, either in or out of the park.

Credit must be given to him when it came to the glove however, for here he was among the league's top fielding shortstops where he is first among all shortstops in putouts with 5,139, second in total chances with 13,124, and third in assists with 7,534.

When you add in his overall fielding statistics at short, second, and third, those numbers increase to 16,091 chances, 6,413 put outs, and 8,967 assists.

Put it all together and it did get him elected to the Hall in 1954.

24. Who was the first switch-hitter to be elected to the Hall of Fame?

There have been a number of switch-hitters elected to the Hall of Fame including the very first, second baseman Frankie "The Fordham Flash" Frisch, who after being a four-letter athlete at Fordham University, came up with the New York Giants, and made his debut on June 17, 1919, having never played in the minor leagues.

A superb fielder with great base path speed he led the National League three times in stolen bases, batted over .300 in thirteen seasons, won the MVP in 1931, and was the starting second baseman in the first All-Star Game.

After playing in exactly 1,000 games, and appearing in four World Series as a Giant, John McGraw traded him to the St. Louis Cardinals, along with Jimmy Ring, for another future Hall of Famer, Rogers Hornsby.

In St. Louis he was in his element being part of the famous Gas House Gang, and managed them from 1933-38, appearing in four more World Series.

He retired in 1937 after 19 years with 2,880 hits for a .316 career average. He later went on to manage both the Pittsburgh Pirates and Chicago Cubs. He was elected to Cooperstown in 1947, the first switch-hitter to be so honored.

25. Who was the first, and only, Hall of Fame member to lead his team to a World Series after he was elected to the Hall of Fame?

This resident of Cooperstown started out as an infielder and outfielder, and when he came up to the major leagues in 1946, with the Cleveland Indians, their manager, Lou Boudreau, converted him to a pitcher, not immediately endorsed by the rookie. By 1948, Bob Lemon was comfortable enough to throw a no-hitter, on June 30, 1948, defeating the Detroit Tigers, 2-0, be named to the All-Star team, and winning Games 2 and 6 of the 1948 World Series, defeating the Boston Braves, to help bring the World Championship to Cleveland.

His 13-year pitching career saw him with a 207-128, 3.23 Era. record, and also rank one home run behind the great hitting pitcher Wes Ferrell with 37 home runs.

After retiring as a player Bob Lemon moved over to managing the Kansas City Royals from 1970-72 and, in the interim was elected to the Hall of

Fame in 1976 as a player.

He went on to manage the Chicago White Sox in 1977, where he was awarded his second manager of the year award, and through 74 games in 1978, before being axed by Chicago. He moved to New York to manage the Yankees for the last 68 games in 1978, after Billy Martin was fired by George Steinbrenner.

There, he took New York to a seven-game ALCS victory and into the World Series where they defeated the Los Angeles Dodgers in six games to win the World Championship. With that win Lemon became the first resident of Cooperstown to lead his team, after he was elected to the Hall of Fame, to a World Series.

26. Who was the first player elected to the Hall of Fame who had hit a home run in his first major league at bat?

Earl Averill Sr., not to be confused with his son, Earl Jr., who played seven years as a catcher in the big leagues, made his major league debut on Tuesday, April 16, 1929, at League Park, as a centerfielder with the Cleveland Indians. He came to bat in the 1st inning, before the home crowd, against six-year veteran southpaw Earl Whitehill of the Detroit Tigers, and on an 0-2 count went into the record books as he blasted a solo home run to be the first resident of Cooperstown to hit a home run in his first major league at bat. Averill went on to hit 238 in his 13-year career.

27. Who was the first Hall of Fame resident to hit his first major league home run off a future fellow Hall of Famer?

This rookie had been called up from the New York Giants Minneapolis farm team in 1951, and went hitless in his first twelve major league at bats.

On Monday May 28, 1951, in a game at the Polo Grounds against the great southpaw with the high leg kick, of the Boston Braves, Warren Spahn, Willie Mays came up in the 1st inning, before a crowd of 23,101 and hit a mammoth two-out solo home run over the left field roof for his first, of 660, career home runs.

When Spahn was asked about the pitch to Mays he said, "It looked pretty good for the first 60 feet."

28. Who was the first pitcher to throw a no-hitter at the age of 40?

Denton True "Cy" Young, the Boston Red Sox right-hander, born on March 29, 1867, threw a no-hitter on June 30, 1908 at Hilltop Park, New

York defeating the New York Highlanders (Yankees) 8-0, to become the first 40-year old pitcher to pitch a no-hitter.

29. Who was the first Hall of Fame resident to be born on Christmas Day?

The first resident of the Hall of Fame to get his birthday and Christmas presents on the same day was James "Pud" Galvin, who was born on December 25, 1855 in St. Louis. His career spanned 14 seasons, from 1879-92, with Buffalo, Pittsburgh, and St. Louis, winning 361 games, losing 309, and pitching 5,941.1 innings, with 639 complete games, and 57 shut outs. He became a resident in the Hall in 1965.

30. Who was the first, and only, player to have hit a home run in each of the innings, one through sixteen in his career?

Hall of Fame resident, Willie Howard Mays, is the first player to have hit a home run in each of the innings, one through sixteen in his career. Of his 660 home runs he has taken 267 different pitchers downtown in 22 different ballparks.

31. Who was the first pitcher to pitch 27 major league seasons?

"The Ryan Express", the sobriquet given to Lynn Nolan Ryan, was known throughout his major league career which started on September 11, 1966 with the New York Mets, as being one of the hardest throwing and durable pitchers in the history of the game.

The right-hander easily holds the record for career strikeouts with 5,714, but when he hung up his spikes on September 22, 1993, after 5,386 innings pitched over 27 seasons, and with 324 wins, he knew he stood alone as being the first pitcher to have pitched that many years in the history of major league baseball.

32. Who is the first player to be a resident of Cooperstown who had the unusual distinction of being an outfielder who threw from the left, but batted from the right?

Rickey "Man of Steal" Henderson, who made his debut on June 24, 1979, at the age of 20, with the Oakland Athletics, who was known for his power and speed, went on to play 25 seasons for nine teams in both leagues, two of them in New York.

In all those 3,081 games he always threw from the left and hit from the right.

33. Who was the first of the Hall of Fame residents to play in four leagues during his career?

"Sir Hugh" Duffy was an outfielder who made his major league debut on June 23, 1888 with the Chicago White Stockings (Cubs) in the National League. He jumped to the Chicago Pirates of the Players League for the 1890 season, leading that league in games, plate appearances, at bats, runs, and hits.

Then he moved on to the Boston Beaneaters (Braves) in the American Association for 1891, leading that league in runs batted in with 110. He then jumped to the Milwaukee Brewers in their first year in the American League in 1901, and finally finished his peregrinations with the Philadelphia Phillies, playing in his final game on April 13, 1906.

That's quite a career -- six teams, and four leagues, all in 14 seasons. He can't quite be called "a man for all seasons" but "a man for four leagues" seems more appropriate.

His final stop after the four leagues was Cooperstown, where he was inducted by the Old Timers Committee as a player in 1945.

34. Who was the first Hall of Fame pitcher to give up a home run to the first batter he faced in the major leagues?

On April 15, 1959 right-hander Bob Gibson made his major league debut for the St. Louis Cardinals in the 7th inning at the Los Angeles Coliseum against the Dodgers. The first batter he faced was third baseman Jim Baxes who promptly homered.

35. Who was the first member of the Hall of Fame to hit two grand slams in one game?

Tony Lazzeri, the New York Yankees second baseman, hit a grand slam home run off southpaw George Turbeville in the 2nd inning of a game played before 8,000 fans on May 24, 1936 in Shibe Park against the Philadelphia Athletics. He came back in the 5th inning and hit another grand slam, this off right-hander Herman Fink. He added a third solo home run in the 7th off southpaw Woody Upchurch to give him 15 total bases in the game the Yankees rolled over Philadelphia 25-2.

36. Who was the first Hall of Fame resident to have two sons follow him into the major leagues?

George Sisler, inducted into Cooperstown in 1939 after playing first base with the St, Louis Browns, Boston Braves, and Washington Senators from 1915-1930, was the 1922 Most Valuable Player, and ended his career with a .340 batting average.

He sired two sons, Dick, who played first base and left field with the St. Louis Cardinals, Philadelphia Phillies, and Cincinnati Reds from 1946-1953, and right-handed pitcher Dave who played from 1956-62 with the Boston Red Sox, Detroit Tigers, Washington Senators and Cincinnati Reds.

37. Who was the first pitcher to win the Cy Young Award, the League Most Valuable Player Award, the Gold Glove Award, and was named to the All-Star team in the same year?

A pitcher can't have a better season than the one right-hander Bob "Hoot" Gibson of the St. Louis Cardinals had in 1968.

Gibson pitched 304.2 innings, had a 22-9 won-lost record, and led the National League in strikeouts (268), in hits per 9 innings (5.8), shutouts (13) and in earned run average with 1.12. He also was awarded the Gold Glove Award, and named to the All-Star team that year as well, and who could possibly have left him off. He concluded his brilliant 17 season pitching career with 251 wins against 154 losses and a 2.91 Era. which made him a resident of Cooperstown in 1981.

38. Who was the first Hall of Fame first baseman to defeat Hall of Fame pitcher Walter Johnson in a pitching match-up?

When "Gorgeous George" Sisler made his major league debut on June 28, 1915, it was as a southpaw pitcher. During his rookie year, with the St. Louis Browns, he went up against Walter Johnson on the mound, and defeated "The Big Train". After a 5-6, 2.35 mound record, Sisler, as most people know, went on to become a Hall of Fame resident as a first baseman in 1939.

39. Who was the first 40-year old pitcher to win 20 games?

It shouldn't be surprising to learn that Denton "Cy" Young, in 1907, had a 21-15, 1.99 Era. at age 40 for the Boston Americans.

Just to prove it was no fluke, and that he still had plenty left in his right arm, he came back in 1908, at 41, to have an impressive 21-11, 1.26 Era. for Boston.

40. Who was the first 40-year old pitcher to pitch a no-hitter?

"Cy" Young comes back in the picture when on June 30, 1908, while pitching for the Boston Red Sox he no-hit the New York Highlanders (Yankees), 8-0, to be the first pitcher to have a no-hitter after his 40th birthday.

41. Who was the first, and only, modern day pitcher to no-hit the same team twice in his career?

Adrian "Addie" Joss, the Cleveland Naps right-hander, pitched a perfect game against the Chicago White Stockings on October 2, 1908, winning 1-0.

He came back against the White Stockings on April 20, 1910 to inflict the same embarrassment on Chicago by pitching his second no-hitter against them, also winning, 1-0. Addie, wasn't "Joss" another pitcher, he was the first to no-hit the same team twice.

42. Who was the first Hall of Fame resident to appear in over 600 games as a designated hitter?

Reggie Jackson, who played in 2,820 games in his 21-year career; 10 seasons with Oakland, 5 with the Yankees, 5 with the Angels, and 1 with Baltimore, was penciled in on the scorecard 638 times as a designated hitter.

43. Who was the first Rookie-of-the-Year to be inducted into the Hall of Fame?

The first player to win the Rookie-of-the-Year Award and then be inducted into Cooperstown was the Brooklyn Dodgers second baseman Jackie Robinson, who won the R.O.Y. Award in 1947 and was inducted into the Hall of Fame in 1962.

44. Who was the Hall of Fame pitcher who gave up the first, and only, inside-the park home run, of the 755 that were hit by fellow Hall of Famer, Hank Aaron?

What are the chances of this entry ever happening? Well it did on Wednesday, March 10, 1967, when Hank Aaron stepped to the plate in the top of the 8th inning down in Connie Mack Stadium after Mike de la Hoz pinch-hit for Clay Carroll, and singled to left field. With two outs Hank Aaron stepped into the batter's box to face Phillies' right-hander, and future Hall of Fame resident, Jim Bunning.

Aaron wasted no time in not being cordial to his soon-to-be fellow resident by walloping an inside-the-park home run to deep centerfield that drove in de la Hoz and give "Hammerin Hank" his first and only inside-the park home run of the 755 he hit in his great career.

The Braves went on to take the game, 7-2.

45. Who was the first future Hall of Famer to get his 3,000[th] career base hit off another future Hall of Famer?

This unusual occurrence happened at the Metrodome in Minnesota, on September 16, 1993, when Twins right-fielder, and 2001 Hall of Fame inductee, Dave Winfield, in his 20th season, drove a run-scoring single to left field in the 9th inning off Oakland Athletics right-hander, and 2004 Hall of Fame inductee, Dennis "Eck" Eckersley.

Winfield got his first base hit on June 19, 1973 with the San Diego Padres, at age 21, having just come out of the University of Minnesota. He finished with 3,110 hits, 199 as a designated hitter.

46. Who was the first player with 3,000 hits to be elected to the Hall of Fame?

Actually the question should have been framed "players" for there were two elected after the Hall of Fame was founded in 1936, by a Special Committee appointed by Commissioner Kenesaw Mountain Landis.

Among the first five immortals enshrined in 1936; Babe Ruth, Christy Mathewson and Walter Johnson, and two others, each of whom had collected over 3,000 hits, Honus "The Flying Dutchman" Wagner, the Pittsburgh Pirates shortstop, who had 3,420 hits before his final game with the Pirates on September 17, 1917, and Detroit Tigers centerfielder, Ty "The Georgia Peach" Cobb, who finished up the last two years of his 24-year career, with the Philadelphia Athletics on September 11, 1928 with 4,189 base hits, each received 215 votes to become the first 3,000-hit club members to be inducted into the Hall of Fame.

A few years later the voting was turned over to the Baseball Writers Association of America where it rests today.

A Special Veterans Committee of twelve was later created to go back in the 19th Century, and consider players eligible for enshrinement. It was by their decision that Adrian "Cap" Anson, who finished out his 27-year career with the Chicago Colts on October 3, 1897 with 3,435 hits, was inducted by The Old Timers Committee in 1939.

47. Who is the first, and only, player to have more than 3,000 hits, and

to have them be equally divided, half hit at home, and half hit on the road?

"Stan the Man" Musial who made his major league debut with the St. Louis Cardinals as a 20-year old outfielder on September 17, 1941, played his entire 22-year career in St. Louis, and joined the 3,000-hit club on May 13, 1958 with a pinch-hit double, and ended his career on September 29, 1963 with exactly 3,630 base hits, equally divided by hitting 1,815 on the road and the same number at home. No one else can make that claim.

48. Who is the first resident of Cooperstown, and only player in major league history, to have his 3,000[th] hit come as a pinch-hitter?

It was on the afternoon of Tuesday, May 13, 1958, out in Wrigley Field, when with the Chicago Cubs came into the top of the 6th inning leading the St. Louis Cardinals, 3-1.

RF Gene Green led off by lining a double to right field off the Cubs right-hander, Moe Drabowsky. Catcher Hal Smith then grounded out which brought up the Redbirds right-hander "Toothpick Sam" Jones.

Manager Fred Hutchinson wanted that runner on second brought home, and who better to call on than Stan "the Man" Musial, who was sitting on 2,999 career base hits.

The crowd of 5,692 wasn't expecting to see history made on this day, but Musial came through with a screamer to left-center field for a double scoring Green to narrow the Cub lead to 3-2, and Musial went into the record books by being the 8th player to join the elite 3,000-hit club, and the first and only player, to do it as a pinch-hitter.

As the crowd acknowledged the accomplishment, Frank Barnes, right-handed reliever and pinch runner, was sent in to pinch-run for Musial. The Cards went on to score 4 runs in that inning on the way to a 5-3 win.

49. Who was the first player to be elected to the Hall of Fame having played a regular season major league game in shorts?

I know you are probably thinking I have lost my mind, and are stretching for a joke. Not the case. In 1976 right-hander Richard "Goose" Gossage, of the Chicago White Sox, pitched two scoreless innings, in the 8th and 9th, to preserve the victory for Terry Forster, and was credited with a save in the White Sox 5-2 win over the Kansas City Royals at Comiskey Park on

Sunday, August 8, 1976.

With Bill Veeck's White Sox being the first to wear shorts and high knee stockings to go with their collared shirts as the new uniform, the "Goose" can say he stands alone as a "Groundbreaker" in being the first resident of Cooperstown to have worn shorts in a major league game.

50. Of the 295 residents of the Cooperstown Hall of Fame who was the first to be the son of a major league player?

On Sunday, July 24, 2011, second baseman Roberto Alomar, the brother of Sandy Jr. who played 20 years in the big leagues, and the son of Sandy Alomar who played 15 years in the major leagues, was inducted into the Hall of Fame.

Roberto was instrumental in helping the Toronto Blue Jays win two World Championships in 1992 and 1993.

He was also the third Puerto Rican player to enter the hallowed halls of Cooperstown joining Orlando Cepeda and Roberto Clemente.

51. Who was the first, and only, pitcher to strike out over 100 batters in 20 seasons, but never lead either major league in strikeouts over the course of a season?

This Cooperstown resident made his pitching debut on April 14, 1966 for the Los Angeles Dodgers, and right-hander Don "Black and Decker" Sutton stayed with them for 15 seasons before taking the mound for Houston in 1981-82, and then moving over to the American League with California, Milwaukee, and Oakland before finishing out his 23-season career with the Dodgers on August 9, 1988.

Sutton, who was inducted into the Hall of Fame in 1998, recorded 324 wins, 256 losses, and 3,574 career strikeouts, but never led the league in the latter category.

52. Who was the first pitcher to toss a no-hitter for three different teams, in three different decades, and in two different leagues?

Who else, but the "Ryan Express", Nolan Ryan. Anyone who has thrown seven no-hitters in his career certainly has to come to mind when trying to answer this question.

Ryan had his first no-hitter while with the California Angels on May 15, 1973 in his 3-0 win over the Kansas City Royals. He came back two months later, on July 15th to no- hit Detroit, 6-0.

On September 28, 1974, still with California, he threw his third no-hitter, this against the Twins, 4-0. On June 1, 1975 he didn't allow a hit when he beat the Orioles, 1-0. His fifth no-hitter came when the flame-throwing right-hander was over in the National League with the Houston Astros, on September 26, 1981, when the Los Angeles Dodgers fell victim to his no-hit pitching, 5-0. That took care of the second decade, and the second league.

Moving into his third decade, and back in the American League, with the Texas Rangers he pitched his 6th no-hitter, a 5-0 win, over the Oakland Athletics, on June 11, 1990. His 7th and final no-hitter was against the Toronto Blue Jays, on May 1, 1991 when he and his Texas Rangers came away with a 3-0 win.

There you have it, the first pitcher to have seven no-hitters, each against a different team, in three different decades, pitching for three different teams, in both the American and National Leagues.

When the "Ryan Express" hung up his spikes his pitching resume showed 27 years on the mound, 324 wins, 5,714 strikeouts, seven no-hitters, an eight-time All-Star, and one World Championship.

More than enough credentials to become a resident of the Hall of Fame, which happened in 1999.

53. Who was the first Hall of Fame pitcher to win 25 games in a season three times, yet never win a Cy Young Award?

This "Dominican Dandy", Juan Marichal by name, made his pitching debut for the San Francisco Giants on July 19, 1960, and in 1963 posted a 25-8, 2.41 Era. In 1966 he had a 25-6, 2.23 Era., and the right-hander, with the high kick followed that in 1968 with a 26-9, 2.43 Era. But nary a Cy Young Award in sight.

He was not only the first not to win the award with 25 wins, he was also the first not to win it after three seasons of 25 or more wins.

54. Who was the first Hall of Fame resident to hit 40 home runs in a season, yet fail to drive in 100 runs?

At the present time only four residents of the Hall of Fame can lay claim to the unusual statistic of having hit 40 or more home runs in a season in which they drove in less than 100 runs. So if you check you will see that

Edwin "Duke" Snider, the Brooklyn Dodger centerfielder, who became a resident in 1980, hit 40 home runs in 1957 while driving in just 92 runs to be the first while Mickey Mantle, Hank Aaron, and Harmon Killebrew fill out the quartet.

55. Who is the first Cooperstown resident to pitch, and win a game in his teens and in his 40's?

The newly inducted, class of 2011, resident of the Hall of Fame in Cooperstown, Rik Aalbert "Bert" Blyleven, was born on April 6, 1951 in Zeist, Netherlands, and made his pitching debut with the Minnesota Twins on June 5, 1970, at age 19, and went on to have a 10-9 record that year.

Moving forward to 1992, we see the right-hander finishing off his 22-season career with the California Angels, and there, at the age of 41, he racked up his 287th career win to make Blyleven the first pitcher to record major league wins as a teenager and as a 40-year old.

56. Who was the first pitcher to lead his league in losses, and in earned run average in the same season?

This 1946 Hall of Fame inductee not only led the American League with 40 wins for the Chicago White Sox in 1908, but also in losses with an 18-20 record in 1910. What stands out is the fact that "Big Ed" Walsh also led the American League that year with a miniscule 1.27 Era. to be the first pitcher in the junior circuit to lead is such strangely divergent categories.

57. Who was first pitcher to win the Triple Crown for a last place team?

When you were the competitor that this southpaw was you gave your very best each time you took the mound, even if your ball club was headed for a last place finish in the National League with a 59-97 record.

That's was Steve "Lefty" Carlton's mindset in that 1992 season with the Phillies when he easily won the pitching Triple Crown by winning almost half of his team's games, as "Lefty" did when he not only led the league in wins with a 27-10 record, but in Era. with a 1.97, games started with 41, completed games with 30, innings pitched with 346.1, and strikeouts with 310. The only thing he didn't lead in was selling scorecards, but you can rest assured he brought the fans in to buy them when he took the mound in the "City of Brotherly Love" or in any other city in the National League.

For his efforts that season he was voted to the All-Star team, and won the coveted Cy Young Award. For some unbeknownst reason he came in 5th in the MVP voting.

But Cooperstown gave him his due by enshrining him to the Hall of Fame in 1994.

58. Who was the first player to have ten consecutive seasons of 30 home runs and 100 runs batted in?

On May 1, 1925 a young catcher made his major league debut with the Philadelphia Athletics named Jimmie "Double X" Foxx.

He caught and played in the outfield until moved to first base in 1927 where he soon became a fixture, and his bat began to thunder in 1929 when he hit 33 home runs and drove in 118 runs.

He kept that hitting production up with the Athletics until they traded him to the Boston Red Sox on December 10, 1935. Foxx continued his tremendous hitting through the 1940 season and wound up going twelve consecutive seasons with 30 or more home runs, hitting 58 in 1932, and leading the American League four times, driving in over 100 runs in 13 consecutive seasons. A true "Groundbreaker" and also a fence buster.

59. Who was the first pitcher to give up a lead-off home run, and then retire every batter, in order, after that?

Much to the surprise of the 6,856 in attendance on Thursday, May 13, 1954 at Connie Mack Stadium, when Cincinnati Reds third baseman Bobby Adams, opened up the ball game with a solo home run to deep left field, did the Reds manager, Birdie Tebbetts, or the fans, believe that was to be the only batter who would safely touch a base for Cincinnati the rest of the afternoon.

The Phillies right-hander, Robin Roberts, saw to that as he set down the next 27 batters in a row to come away with a one-hit, 8-1 victory over right-hander Harold "Corky" Valentine.

60. Who was the first, and only pitcher to defeat the Boston Braves, the Milwaukee Braves, and the Atlanta Braves?

While we were on the subject of Robin Roberts in the previous item, it seemed only fitting that we bring him in again for this one and only experience.

During his 19 years on the mound, from 1948 to 1966, he beat the Braves 12 times in Boston before seeing them vacate Boston for Milwaukee, where he won 21 times, and then move on to Atlanta, when on August 29,

1966, while with the Chicago Cubs, he notched his final career victory, 4-2, giving him the opportunity to be the first to defeat the Braves in all three cities.

61. Who was the first pitcher to win back-to-back Cy Young Awards?

The Cy Young Award was first given out in 1956 upon the passing of its namesake on November 4, 1955 at the age of 88.

It was designed to be awarded to the best pitcher in the major leagues that season. In 1965 Sandy Koufax, the brilliant southpaw of the Los Angeles Dodgers, won it with a 26-8, 2.04 Era., and 382 strikeouts.

The following year Koufax had a 27-9, 1.73 Era., 317 strikeout season, and again won the award to become the first pitcher to win it in consecutive years.

In 1967 it was decided to change the award by giving out two separate awards, one to the best pitcher in the American and National Leagues.

62. Who was the first modern day pitcher to win over 100 games in both the American and National Leagues?

The first pitcher to be that successful in both leagues after the turn of the 20th century, made his major league pitching debut on July 20, 1955 for the Detroit Tigers. Right-hander Jim Bunning stayed in the Motor City for nine seasons compiling a 118-87 record, and throwing a no-hitter against the Red Sox, before moving over to the National League in a trade with the Philadelphia Phillies for the 1964 season.

In his six seasons with the Phillies he won 89 games including a perfect game against the New York Mets. Then on to Pittsburgh for two years winning 14 games before playing briefly with the Los Angeles Dodgers in 1969 winning 3 games before coming back to the Phillies where on August 11, 1970 he defeated the Houston Astros, 6-5, to become the first modern day pitcher to win 100 games in each league before ending his career on September 3, 1971, and showing a National League record of 106-97, and a combined career record 224-184.

63. Who was the first player to drive in over 100 runs in 13 consecutive seasons?

When Lou Gehrig drove in 107 runs in 1926 he went on a streak that continued on through the 1938 season, when he drove in 115 runs to be the first player to do it over 13 consecutive seasons.

His fellow Cooperstown resident, Jimmie Foxx, duplicated that effort from 1929 through the 1941 season. There is a third player, not in the Hall of Fame just yet, named Alex "A-Rod" Rodriguez who has accomplished the same feat from 1998-2010.

64. Who was the first relief pitcher to win the Cy Young Award, and the Most Valuable Player Award in the same season?

The first relief pitcher to capture both awards in the same season was the tall, mustached, Hall of Fame right-hander of the Milwaukee Brewers, Rollie Fingers, who in 1981 posted a 6-3, won-lost record, with a 1.04 Era., and came on in 47 games, saving a league-leading 28 games, to propel the Brewers into the ALDS, where he won one of the two games, as the Brewers bowed to the Yankees in five.

His efforts over the season were impressive enough for him to be named the American Leagues' Most Valuable Player, and the first relief pitcher to capture both titles.

65. Who was the first Cooperstown resident to hit a home run, but then have it taken away from him by an umpire?

If you think that Hank Aaron officially had 32 home runs in 1965 you would be correct, but unofficially you could say he had 33, giving him 756, not 755 for his career.

You see on Wednesday night, August 18, 1965, out in Busch Stadium, "Hammerin' Hank" came up in the 8th inning with his Milwaukee Braves tied with the Cardinals, 3-3, and hit southpaw Curt Simmons' pitch on top of the roof for an apparent solo home run.

Home plate umpire Chris Pelekoudas had other thoughts for he didn't watch the flight of the ball, but rather the placement of Aaron's feet, and called Aaron out for being out of the batter's box when he hit the ball. The Cardinals catcher, Tim McCarver, got credit for the put out, and Aaron, a deduction in his home run totals. Luckily, the Braves didn't need the run as they went on to a 5-3 win.

66. Who was the first Hall of Fame resident to be the first known, or publicly admitted, grandfather to hit a major league home run?

To the baseball world he was known as "Stan the Man", but in the Musial household he was known as "Gramps" or some similar endearing name for a grandfather.

For on Tuesday, September 10, 1963, out in Busch Stadium, 13,883 of the faithful, saw Musial come up in the bottom of the 1st inning, after Cardinals' shortstop, Dick Groat, had singled, and deposit Chicago Cubs right-hander, Glen Hobbie's pitch into the stands for a two-run home run to make "Stan the Man" the first publicly admitted grandfather to take a hurler downtown.

It was the first run of eight for the Redbirds as Bob Gibson went on to shutout the Cubbies, 8-0.

67. Who was the first player to hit three grand slam home runs in 96 hours?

This "Iron Horse" went on a home run tear in "grand fashion" in the summer of 1931, and with help of his teammates, who loaded the bases as he came to bat made New York Yankees first baseman, Lou Gehrig, the first player to clear the bases with home runs four times in 96 hours.

It started on Saturday, August 29, 1931 down in Shibe Park when Gehrig blasted his 36th home run off Philadelphia's Lefty Grove in the 6th inning, but the Athletics came away with a 7-4 win.

On Sunday, August 30, up in Braves Field he hit his 37th home run, but not with all the bases occupied, as the Yankees came away with a 14-4 win.

On Monday, October 31st, Gehrig was at home in Yankee Stadium, and hit his 38th home run, and second grand slam, in the 5th inning, off Washington Senators southpaw Lloyd "Gimpy" Brown, but it wasn't enough as the Nats went on to a 6-5 victory.

On Tuesday, September 1st, again at Yankee Stadium, he found himself coming up with the bases load in the 3rd inning, and emptied the bases with his 40th home run of the season, and his third grand slam in four days as he hammered a pitch off Boston right-hander, "Big Ed" Morris, to give the Yankees a 4-1 win over the Red Sox, and become a "Groundbreaker" by being the first to hit four grand slams in just 96 hours.

68. Who was the first pitcher to lose all four of his only major league decisions, and be elected to the Hall of Fame?

Impossible you say? No, not when you look over their resident roster and see the name of southpaw Tom LaSorda, who made his pitching debut on August 5, 1954 with the Brooklyn Dodgers, going 0-0 with a 7.62 Era.

in eight games over his two-year stay in Flatbush.

On March 2, 1956 he was purchased by the Kansas City Athletics, appearing in eighteen games, with a 0-4, 6.15 Era., and made his last mound appearance on July 8, 1956, after a less than stellar mound career, and moved to the dugout.

LaSorda, who always claimed he bled "Dodger Blue", took over the managerial reins in Los Angeles in 1976, and took the team to four pennants, and World Series victories in 1981 over the Yankees in five, and came back in 1988 to defeat the Oakland Athletics in five games.

It is interesting to note that Lasorda won as many games against the Athletics in that World Series as he had pitching for them as a player.

Speaking of wins Lasorda retired from the dugout after 3,040 games with a 1,599-1439, .526 record, and received the Manager-of-the-Year Award in 1983 and '88. The Veterans Committee elected him to the Hall of Fame as a Manager in 1997.

69. Who is the first player to win the MVP Award in consecutive years, and not be in the Hall of Fame?

In the early sixties this players name was on the tongues of many in the baseball world, and was highlighted by his home run performance in 1961.

Let's step back to 1957 when Roger Maris, born Roger Maras, made his major league debut in the outfield on April 16th, as a 22-year old outfielder with the Cleveland Indians.

On June 15, 1958 he was traded to the Kansas City Athletics in a five-player deal. On December 11, 1959 he again was traded, this time to the Yankees in a seven-player deal, and it would be the following year, 1960, that he came into his own by leading the league in runs batted in with 112, while hitting 39 home runs, and batting .283, giving him the MVP Award.

Then came that historic year, 1961, when Maris broke the home run record of Babe Ruth by hitting 61 home runs, driving in league leading 141 runs while batting .269. The MVP Award that year went to him for the second consecutive year. I would say that the Yankees got more back in what Roger did than the $32,000 he was paid that year. Interesting to note that Roger's salary jumped to $70,000 in 1962 after that record-breaking season of '61.

With all that the Hall of Fame Committee, while recognizing those two fine years, did not deem him worthy of taking up residence in Cooperstown.

70. Who was the first pitcher to be the starting pitcher for his team in over 15 opening day games?

Tom Seaver, who was enshrined in the Hall of Fame in 1992, was the first pitcher to start over 15 opening day games when he started 11 games for the New York Mets, 3 while with the Cincinnati Reds, and his final 2 when he went over to the American League with the Chicago White Sox in 1984-85.

71. Who was the first Cy Young Award winner to be elected to the Hall of Fame?

Warren Spahn, the Milwaukee Braves southpaw with the high leg kick, led the National League in wins with a 21-11 won-lost record to go along with his league leading 18 complete games, which earned him the 1957 Cy Young Award, and be the first resident of Cooperstown to hold that honor.

72. Who was the first, and only, pitcher to toss a shutout for his 300th major league win?

Among his 318th career wins right-handed knuckleballer Phil Niekro tossed a four-hit shutout against the Toronto Blue Jays up in Exhibition Stadium on Sunday, October 6, 1985 for his 300th career victory, and his 16th of the season as the New York Yankees defeated Toronto 8-0.

73. Who was the first rookie to hit three home runs in a single game, and later be inducted into the Hall of Fame?

We have to go back three cities, when the Braves played their home games in Boston, and to EbbetsField, Brooklyn, on Saturday, September 27, 1952 when 3B Eddie Mathews came up in the top of the 3rd inning and found Braves right-hander Virgil Jester on base after stroking a single to right, and drove him in with a two-run homer to right field off Dodgers right-hander Joe Black.

Mathews came back to lead off the 6th with a solo home run off right-hander Ben Wade, and followed that up leading off the 8th with another solo home run off Wade to give the rookie three home runs as the Braves rolled to an 11-3 win.

After a 17-year career, and 512 home runs later, Mathews was inducted into Cooperstown in 1978.

74. Who was the first player to open both games of a double header

with a home run?

It happened on Friday, May 30, 1913 down in Griffith Stadium when right fielder Harry Hooper of the Boston Red Sox opened the first game against the Washington Senators with a home run, but it wasn't enough as the Senators took the opener, 4-3.

In the nightcap Hooper started that game off with a solo home run as the Red Sox eked out a 1-0 win. Hooper, after his 17-year career with the Red Sox and White Sox, was inducted into the Hall of Fame, by the Veterans Committee in 1971.

75. **Who was the first Hall of Famer to retire as a World Series Champion?**

When New York Yankees centerfielder Joe DiMaggio hung up his spikes after the Yankees World Series victory over the New York Giants on October 10, 1951 he became the first resident of Cooperstown, when he was inducted in 1955, to retire as a World Series Champion.

76. Who was the first player to hit a home run for his 3,000th base hit?

It took until Saturday, August 7, 1999, down in Tropicana Field, when the Tampa Bay Devil Rays third baseman Wade Boggs came to the plate, before 39,512, with one out in the bottom of the 6th inning with CF Chris Haney on base via a line single to left field, and hit a one out, two-run home run to deep right field for his 3,000th base hit to be the first player to reach that exclusive plateau with a home run.

77. **Who was the first Hall of Fame member to hit his first, and last, major league home run on the same date?**

This unusual happening started on Thursday, September 27, 1923 at Fenway Park when Lou Gehrig, the Yankees first baseman, who made his debut on June 15, 1923, hammered his first home run, a 1st inning, two-run shot, off Boston Red Sox right-hander "Wild Bill" Piercy, as the Yankees went on to an 8-3 win.

Then 15 years to the day, on Tuesday September 27, 1938, now at the Yankee Stadium, before 2,773 fans, Gehrig hit his 29th home run of the season, and his 493rd and last of his career, a solo shot in the 5th inning off Washington Senators right-hander Emil "Dutch" Leonard.

K. A LOOK INTO THE DUGOUT

1. Who was the first manager to watch his son play as a major league player while his father watched him from the dugout?

Although it was brief, Earle Mack played in just five games as a first baseman, third baseman, and as a catcher, with the Philadelphia Athletics in 1910, 1911, and 1914 while his manager/father viewed his efforts from the dugout.

2. Who was the first major league manager to win 10 pennants?

John McGraw of the New York Giants won the National League pennant ten times: 1904-05, 1911-13, 1917, 1921-24.

3. Who was the first, and only, manager to manage his teams to over 2,000 victories, but never to have played the game at the major league level?

"Marse Joe" McCarthy managed the Chicago Cubs, New York Yankees, and the Boston Red Sox to 2,126 wins in his 24-year career. His playing career as a second baseman took place from 1907-21 in the minor leagues with Toledo, Buffalo, and Louisville.

4. Who was the first, and only, player with the Seattle Pilots to go and become a major league manager?

Mike Ferraro played in just five games, with only four at bats, for the Pilots in 1969 before being traded to the Baltimore Orioles. He later went on to replace Dave Garcia as manager with the Cleveland Indians in 1983. After a 40-60 record he was released and later coached with the Kansas City Royals before replacing Dick Howser, who had to resign as manager due to a brain tumor, and finished out the season as skipper there with a 36-38 record.

5. Who is the first major league manager to win two or more World Series without losing a game?

Terry Francona, manager of the Boston Red Sox, swept the St. Louis Cardinals in the 2004 World Series, and then swept the Colorado Rockies in the 2007 Fall Classic, to be the first undefeated manager in winning two World Championships.

6. The New York Yankees have had 41 managers, 32 different names, in

their storied existence, who was the first?

The first manager of the New York Yankees, known as the Highlanders after they moved from Baltimore, and were first organized, was playing-manager and right-handed pitcher Clark Calvin Griffith, known as "The Old Fox." He left Chicago and came to New York to take over as manager in 1903 and remained at the helm until shortstop Norman "The Tabasco Kid" Elberfeld took over for the last half of the 1908 season when Griffith had a falling out with ownership.

7. Who was the first manager of the New York Mets?

Charles Dillon Stengel, better known as "Casey," had managed the Brooklyn Dodgers from 1934-36, the Boston Bees (Braves) 1938-43, the New York Yankees from 1949-60 before taking over the newly established National League franchise in New York, the Metropolitans (Mets) in 1962. He stayed until the end of the 1965 season and had a 175-404, won-loss record.

8. Who was the first manager of the Philadelphia Athletics?

Cornelius Alexander McGilicuddy, known to baseball fans as Connie Mack, took over ownership of the fledging American League franchise and led the Athletics from their first year in 1901 through 1950.

Known as "The Tall Tactician" he was a quiet, even-tempered, tight-fisted and gentlemanly person who was always addressed and referred to as "Mr. Mack."

An interesting note to Mack's tenure was that he was never ejected from a game in his 50 years as the Athletics manager. His lifetime managerial record showed him winning nine pennants and five of the eight World Series his team appeared in. Over his career the Athletics won 3,776 games while losing 4, 025, both major league records. He was inducted into the Hall of Fame in 1937.

9. Who was the first African-American to be hired as a major league manager?

Frank Robinson, who played first base, and the outfield in the American and National Leagues for 21 seasons with Cincinnati and Baltimore, as well as the Dodgers, Angels, and Indians was the first African-American to be named a major league manager when he was named skipper of the Cleveland Indians on October 3, 1974.

The 39-year old outfielder-first baseman doubled as a player in 1975-76. The Indians went 79-80, finishing 4th in 1975 and his three year record from 1975-1977 was 186-189.

In 1981-84 he moved over to the senior circuit to manage the San Francisco Giants, and became the first African-American manager in the National League. He stayed managing the Giants for four years before moving back to the American League and the Baltimore Orioles from 1988-91.

In 2002-2004 he was back in the National League at the helm of the Montreal Expos, and remained two more years with them as they moved south to become the Washington Nationals.

10. Who was the first player-manager to hit a home run in his first at bat as a manager?

Frank Robinson, player-manager of the Cleveland Indians, inserted himself as the designated hitter on April 8, 1975 and hit a solo home run off New York Yankee right-hander "Doc" Medich in the bottom of the first inning.

11. Who was the first father-son to manage in the major leagues?

The first father and son to manage in the major leagues started when first baseman George Sisler played for the St. Louis Browns from 1915-27 and managed them as well from 1924-26, and continued on when his son, Dick, who was a first baseman and outfielder with the Cardinals, Phillies, and Reds from 1946-53, took over the managerial reins in Cincinnati in 1964-65.

12. Who was the first African-American to manage a team to the pennant?

Clarence "Cito" Gaston not only led his team, the Toronto Blue Jays, to a pennant he also led them to two World Championships, the first ones outside of the United States.

He defeated the Atlanta Braves in six games, in 1992, and repeated again in 1993 against the Philadelphia Phillies, also defeating them in six games before 52,195 of the Canadian faithful in the Skydome.

13. Who was the first manager to be thrown out of both games of a doubleheader?

If you didn't already know this it may come as a surprise for there are a number of managers who would quickly fit this category. Mel Ott, manager of the New York Giants, and a very well liked, polite, and respected person throughout his playing career, wouldn't be one of them. He got the thumb on June 9, 1946, out in Forbes Field, in a doubleheader loss to the Pittsburgh Pirates; 2-1 to southpaw Fritz Ostermueller, in the first game, and a 5-1 loss to "Tobacco Chewin' Johnny" Lanning in the nightcap, for protesting calls. Umpires Tom Dunn and George Magerkurth had had enough of "Master Melvin", and tossed him out of both games, making him the first Skipper to be banished for a twin-bill.

14. Who was the first player-manager to pinch-hit a home run?

Joe Cronin of the Boston Red Sox, pinch-hit a 3-run home run on June 15, 1943 against the Philadelphia Athletics.

15. Who was the first pair of seventy-year old major league managers to start a season?

When the 2005 season started, two teams had managers whose age was seventy years young. Frank Robinson of the Washington Nationals was 70 and Jack McKeon of the Florida Marlins 75. Just a few weeks later, on May 12th, Felipe Alou of the San Francisco Giants turned 70 to make the pair a trio.

16. Who was the first manager in major league history to manage three 600 career home run hitters?

Dusty Baker had managed Barry Bonds with the Giants in San Francisco, Sammy Sosa in Chicago with the Cubs, and on June 9, 2008 Ken Griffey Jr. hit his 600th home run while Dusty watched from the Cincinnati Reds dugout.

17. Who was the first Asian-American manager in major league history?

On November 19, 2008 Don Wakamatsu, a fourth-generation Japanese-American, who had been a former Oakland Athletics bench coach, was named the new manager of the Seattle Mariners.

18. Who was the first in-season replacement manager to take over a team that was ten or more games below .500, and lead his team to a record of at least 30 games above .500 during that season?

When the Colorado Rockies brought in Jim Tracy to replace Clint Hurdle on May 29, 2009, with the team wallowing ten games below .500 at 18-28, Tracy led his team to a 74-42, .638 record for the rest of the season which was at least 30 games above .500.

19. Who was the first manager to resign, and yet win the Manager of the Year Award on the same day?

On November 5, 1997 Davey Johnson, manager of the Baltimore Orioles, resigned as manager after Orioles owner Peter Angelos refused to give him a vote of confidence after saying that Johnson would be back to manage in 1998. Hours later Davey Johnson was named the American League Manager of the Year.

20. Who was the first manager to shift his players to the right side of the field in order to stop Ted Williams?

It may have been thought about before the first game of a doubleheader between the Boston Red Sox and the Cleveland Indians on July 14, 1946, but it was implemented at the start of the second game that day.

In the first game, Ted Williams, one of baseball's greatest hitters, came to bat with the bases loaded and Cleveland ahead 5-0, and promptly hit a grand slam home run. He followed that with a 3-run home run and finished off with his third home run, a solo shot in the 8,[th] giving him three home runs, and eight runs driven in for the game, as Boston defeated the Tribe 11-10.

In the second game Cleveland player-manager Lou Boudreau shifted all of his players, including himself at shortstop, except the third baseman and the leftfielder to the right side of the diamond in order to stop Williams. This became known as "The Boudreau Shift" and it worked in the second game as Williams grounded out and walked twice while completely ignoring the shift and the Red Sox went on to sweep the doubleheader by winning 6-4.

21. Who was the first manager to be fired during spring training?

When the Chicago Cubs went through a dismal 5-15 won-lost spring training record in 1954 player-manager Phil Cavarretta gave his owner, Phil Wrigley, his honest assessment of the team's chances for the new season. Upon hearing it Wrigley then fired Cavarretta for his "defeatist attitude." The three-year player-manager was replaced by the popular former third baseman Stan Hack.

It turns out Phil's assessment was on target as the Cubbies had a 64-90, .416, 7th place finish that season.

22. **Who was the first member of the 500 home run club to become a major league manager?**

Mel Ott, of the New York Giants, who became the player-manager of the team in 1942, hit his 500th career home run for the Giants on August 1, 1945. His 511 career home runs were a long-standing National League record.

23. **Who was the Hall of Fame player-manager to hit the first pinch-hit extra inning grand slam home run in major league history?**

Rogers Hornsby, player-manager of the Chicago Cubs, came out of the dugout to pinch-hit an 11th inning, two-out, grand slam home run in the first game of a doubleheader at Wrigley Field, on Sunday, September 13, 1931, off Braves right-hander Bruce Cunningham, to give the Cubs an 11-7 win over Boston.

24. **Who was the first manager to have three pitchers start both games of a doubleheader in the same season?**

It was a shock to the baseball world when the adored New York Giants 32-year old right-hander Christy Mathewson was traded to the Cincinnati Reds on July 20, 1916 along with Bill McKechnie and Edd Roush for Buck Herzog and Red Killefer. Matty, who took on the role as player and skipper wasn't well, and would play his final game on September 4, 1916, and later pass away after a lengthy stay in a nursing home in Saranac Lake, New York at age 45 on October 7, 1925.

But let's get back to the original story of his one year managerial stay. On Tuesday, June 19, 1917, Matty had right-hander Horace "Hod" Eller start both ends of a doubleheader against the Cubs. Hod lost the first game, 2-1 but came back to win the second game 6-2.

Then on Sunday, July 1st he asked Fred Toney to do the same against the Pirates in Cincinnati and with better luck, as Toney allowed 3 hits in each game, all singles, to come away with 4-1 and 5-1 wins.

Matty tried this again on Wednesday, September 26th when he sent Pete Schneider against the Boston Braves at Redland Field. He lost the opener, 1-0 after retiring after 8 innings for a pinch-hitter, but came back to go the distance in the second game, but lost, 3-0.

So Matty stands alone as the first manager to have three of his pitchers start both games of a double header in one season.

25. Who was the first African-American manager of a New York team?

The first African-American manager of a New York team appeared in the dugout of the New York Mets in 2005 in the person of Willie Randolph. Willie had started his playing career as a second baseman with the Pittsburgh Pirates in 1975 before moving to the Yankees in 1976 and stayed there for 13 years before finishing out his 18-year career with two years with the Dodgers, a short stay with Milwaukee and his final one with the Mets.

26. George Steinbrenner, the mercurial owner of the New York Yankees, hired and fired twelve managers during his tenure as an owner. The 13th hire, Joe Girardi, at this writing, is still in command of the Yankee dugout. Who was the first manager Steinbrenner hired and fired?

After the 1973 season Ralph Houk, who had been at the helm of the Yankees from 1961-63, and came back from 1966-73, up and quit when Steinbrenner took over. Steinbrenner's first hire was Bill Virdon in 1974, and he stayed till 1975 when Billy Martin was hired and started the merry-go-around that would continue for some time.

27. Who was the first manager to be ejected over 100 times from a ball game?

The first manager to be ejected over 100 times in his managerial career was John "Little Napoleon" McGraw who was the skipper for the Baltimore Orioles in the National League in 1899 and again with them in 1901-02 in the American League, which covered a span of 345 games.

Moving over to lead the New York Giants for the next 30 years, and 4,424 games, his total career managerial record of 4,769 games saw "Muggsy" ejected 117 times.

Now those were his ejections as a manager. If you add the number of times he was ejected in his 1,099 games in his playing career you can just add another 14.

If you were surprised by McGraw's 117 ejections let us take you a step further to a recent skipper who has eclipsed Muggsy's figure and currently holds the major league record for ejections. Bobby Cox, who was at the helm of the Toronto Blue Jays from 1982-85, and in his two stints with the Atlanta Braves, 1978-81, 1990-2010 covering over 5,800 games has been told by umpires to "go take a shower skipper, and cool off" 154 times.

28. Who was the first major league manager to win 3,000 games?

Beginning his baseball career as a catcher in 1886 with the Washington Statesmen in the National League, Cornelius Alexander McGillicuddy (Connie Mack), played every position but third base and as a pitcher in his eleven year career spanning 723 games with Washington, the Buffalo Bisons in the Players League, and the Pittsburgh Pirates back in the National League.

With that experience he began his managerial career while with Pittsburgh in 1894, staying in that position as a player-manager through 1896. In 1897 he worked partly in the front office while handling the managerial duties of the Milwaukee club in the Western League.

When the newly established American League was created in 1901 he was named the manager of the Philadelphia Athletics and managed that ball club, always in a business suit, never in uniform, for the next 50 years winning a record 3,731 games while losing 3,948 and guiding them to nine pennants and five World Championships.

29. Who was the first manager to lead his team through an entire 162-game schedule without ever being out of first place?

In 1990 the Cincinnati Reds, managed by Lou Piniella, played the entire 162-game season without ever being out of first place during that record-setting season as they clinched the National League West by five games on September 29th when the Los Angeles Dodgers lost to the San Francisco Giants 4-3.

They opened their season with an 8-4 win over the Houston Astros on April 9th and never looked back as they won the first nine games of the season. The Reds distributed their wins evenly by having a 46-35 home record and a 45-36 away record.

They defeated the Pittsburgh Pirates in the League Championship Series 4 games to 2, and went on to sweep the Oakland Athletics in the World Series.

30. Who was the first manager to manage two sons at the same time on the major league level?

Proud as he certainly was to have two sons playing on the same field for him every day Cal Ripken Sr. was the skipper of the Baltimore Orioles for one game in 1985, then for a full season in 1987 and for six games in 1988 before Frank Robinson took over for the remainder of the season.

During his tenure Billy Ripken played second base while older brother Cal Jr. was in the midst of his record playing consecutive game streak at shortstop.

31. Who was the first major league manager to lead three different National League teams, in three different cities, to the World Series?

This is a classic example of a routine utility player having a great insight into, and knowledge of, the game of baseball. "Deacon" Bill McKechnie played for eleven undistinguished years with five teams until his retirement in 1920, but it wasn't until he took over the reins of a major league club that his talent as a manager became exposed.

In mid-1922 he took over for George "Moon" Gibson as skipper of the Pittsburgh Pirates and brought them up from 5th place to a tie for third with the Cardinals. After finishing in third place in 1923 and 1924 he brought the Pirates to his first pennant in 1925, and a seven game victory over the Washington Senators in the World Series.

Moving on to St. Louis as a coach he took over as manager at the end of the 1927 season replacing Bob O'Farrell who failed to win the pennant that year by a game and a half.

In 1928 he won the National League pennant beating out John McGraw's New York Giants by two games, but went on to lose the World Series in four games to the New York Yankees.

McKechnie moved on to Cincinnati in 1938 after a less than successful eight years with the Boston Braves, and had to wait until 1939 with Cincinnati before he won his third pennant, but was swept again by the Yankees in the World Series.

He came back to please the Queen City fans in 1940 by winning 100 games and easily finishing ahead of the Brooklyn Dodgers for the National League pennant. His World Series fortunes were much improved as his Reds defeated the Detroit Tigers in seven games for the 1940 World Championship.

That completed the trio of cities and teams that made "Deacon Bill" McKechnie the first manager in major league baseball history to take three different teams in three different cities to a pennant.

32. Who was the first manager to win 100 games in his rookie season?

Gordon "Mickey" Cochrane had a Hall of Fame playing career as a catcher with the Philadelphia Athletics from 1925 to 1933 before being traded to the Detroit Tigers on December 12, 1933 for journeyman catcher Johnny Pasek and $100,000.

Arriving in the Motor City Cochrane took over the managerial reins as a rookie manager and continued his catching duties for the 1934 season. He did well in both departments for he batted .320, drove in 76 runs and stole 26 bases, as he led his team to a 101-53 record and into the World Series where they bowed to the infamous St. Louis Cardinals, "Gas House Gang" in seven games.

33. Who was the first, and only, manager of the Seattle Pilots?

This answer will be brief because the tenure of the Seattle Pilots in the American League was equally brief. On opening day April 11, 1969 the Seattle Pilots had their first and only opening day in history. It was against the Chicago White Sox before a crowd of 14,993 excited fans.

Walking out to present the opening day lineup, wearing number three on the back of his jersey, was manager Joe Schultz. A baseball purple heart was in order for poor Joe, for after the season ended his team had a record of 64-98 for a .395 average and a 6th and last place finish, 33 games behind the division winning Minnesota Twins.

34. Who was the first manager to win a World Series in both leagues?

George "Sparky" Anderson was the dugout skipper when his Cincinnati Reds won the World Series in seven games against the Boston Red Sox in 1975. He came back in the 1976 World Series, with the "Big Red Machine" to sweep the New York Yankees, 4-0.

Moving over to the American League with Detroit he led the Tigers to the 1984 World Championship with his 4 games to 1 win over the San Diego Padres.

35. Who was the first manager to lose the opening game of the season and promptly resign as manager before the next game?

Eddie Sawyer, who had been the skipper of the Philadelphia Phillies from 1948 to 1952, and taking the "Whiz Kids" to the 1950 World Series, came back to manage the team for 70 games in 1958, a full season in 1959, and was in the dugout on opening day in Cincinnati to start the 1960 season on April 12th. The Reds downed the Phillies that day 9-4. The team had an off day on April 13th and that must have given Sawyer time to reflect back on the season so far. For on April 14th the Phillies made the surprising announcement that Sawyer, at age 49, had resigned after just one game. Gene Mauch was appointed the new manager, but Sawyer remains the first manager to quit after the first game of the season.

36. Who was the first modern day manager of an African-American player?

This one is a bit tricky. On April 9, 1947 Leo Durocher, the manager of the Brooklyn Dodgers, was suspended by Major League Baseball Commissioner Happy Chandler for the 1947 season for "conduct detrimental to baseball." A last minute interim manager had to be quickly selected to begin the season and Brooklyn coach Clyde "Sukey" Sukeforth was chosen. He was in the Dodgers' dugout on opening day on April 15,th the same day that Jackie Robinson made his major league debut against the Boston Braves. Sukeforth came away with a 5-3 win that day and came back on April 17th with a 12-6 victory to give him a perfect two-day managerial career record for after that Burt Shotton was named the full-time manager.

But no one can take away from "Sukey" the experience of being the first manager of an African-American major league ballplayer.

37. Who was the only manager to manage three brothers in a World Series?

He did it in two leagues, with two teams, and in two World Series, but Alvin "Blackie" Dark or "The Swamp Fox" as he was also known, had the privilege of managing Matty and Felipe Alou when they played the outfield for the San Francisco Giants in the 1962 Fall Classic. He also was at the helm when the other brother Jesus, played under Blackie when the Oakland Athletics won the 1974 World Championship by defeating the Los Angeles Dodgers in five games in an all-West Coast World Series.

38. Who was the first Japanese-American to become a manager in the major leagues?

On November 19, 2008 Don Wakamatsu, a fourth generation Japanese American, who had been a former Oakland Athletics bench coach, was named the manager of the Seattle Mariners, and became the first Japanese-American to be the skipper of a major league team. He guided the Mariners to a third place finish in the Western Division of the American

League, compiling an 85-77 won-lost record in the 2009 season. In 2010 his Mariners had the second poorest record in the American League on August 9th and were last in the Western Division with a 42-70, .375 record. The Mariners replaced him on that date with interim manager with Daren Brown, the manager of the Triple A Tacoma ball club.

Wakamatsu 274 game record as a major league manager was 127-147, .464.

39. Who was the first manager to win the Manager of the Year Award in both the American League and the National League?

The first manager to capture the title of Manager of the Year in both leagues began when Bobby Cox won the award with the Toronto Blue Jays in 1985 when he took the Jays to a 99-62 record to finish first in the American League East.

Bobby's second came in 1991 when he led the Atlanta Braves to a first place finish in the National League West in 1991 with a 94-68 record.

40. Who was the first manager to lead two different teams to the World Series?

Pat Moran was a catcher and a third baseman who made his major league debut behind the plate for the Boston Beaneaters on May 15, 1901 and played his final game on June 5, 1914 with the Philadelphia Phillies on June 5, 1914.

Moran took over the managerial reins of the Phillies in 1915, and in that rookie season as a manager took the Phillies to their first pennant and World Series, where they were defeated by the Boston Red Sox in five games. He remained at the helm in Philadelphia through 1918, when in the following year, 1919, he managed the Cincinnati Reds to their first World Series and a World Championship when they defeated the Chicago White Sox, in that infamous series, 5 games to 3.

Moran was what we call today, "old school," where he was a sound believer in the fundamentals with an emphasis on a strong defense. He believed in playing your best players every day, throughout the game, and going to his bench only when necessary. His pitchers were known for racking up more innings where control was emphasized rather than throwing heat.

41. Who were the first two managers to fill out their scorecards with the names of 45 players to play in one game?

The game on Tuesday, September 5, 1978, at Wrigley Field, had to be one where the opposing managers came down with writer's cramps as Herman Franks penciled in 24 of his Chicago Cubs, six of them pitchers, and Dick Williams followed closely behind with 21 Montreal Expos, sending eight of his staff to the mound, to finally see a game, after 3 hours, 20 minutes, to its conclusion, won by the Expos, 10-8.

That day, and that game, was the first that sent 45 players onto the field to bring a game to its conclusion in nine innings.

42. Who was the first manager to manage 1,000 winning games?

Harry Wright, the English-born centerfielder and pitcher, made his debut as a player-manager on May 5, 1871 with the Boston Red Stockings. He continued on in both capacities with the Boston Red Caps in 1876 and through the 1877 season before settling into just the dugout where he managed the Boston Red Caps through the '81 season.

He moved to the Providence Grays for the 1882-83 seasons before taking over the managerial reins in Philadelphia with the Quakers from 1884 to 1889, and finished his 23-year career with the Phillies from 1890 to 1893, but not before becoming the first manager to win 1,000 games when he recorded than historic win with the Phillies early on in the 1891 season.

43. Who was the first pitcher to win the National League pennant as a player-manager?

This 25-year old right-handed pitcher, who also played centerfield and first base, by the name of Al Spalding, took over the managerial reins of the Chicago White Stockings in 1876 after winning 204 games on the mound for the Boston Red Stockings, and took them to a 52-14 record and first place, to make him the first pitcher-manager to win the NL championship. It is very important to note that Spalding's mound record that year was 47-12.

His second year at the helm, in 1877, and where his mound record was just 1-0, didn't turn out as well as the White Stockings ended up in 5th place with a 26-33 record.

44. Who was the first manager to win back-to-back World

Championships and not be inducted into the Hall of Fame?

Bill "Rough" Carrigan, after completing his studies at the College of the Holy Cross, made his major league debut on July 7, 1906 as a catcher with the Boston Americans (Red Sox).

In 1913 he took over as player-manager of the Boston Red Sox and two years later, in 1915, won 101 games to take the American League flag, and then brought them to a World Championship by defeating the Philadelphia Phillies in five games.

He followed that in 1916 by again winning the American League pennant, and then went on to his second consecutive World Championship, defeating the Brooklyn Robins in five games. Those credentials weren't enough, however, to make him a resident in Cooperstown.

45. Who was the first manager to have pennant winners in both leagues?

It is interesting to note that "Marse Joe" McCarthy was one of the few successful managers to have never played in the major leagues. That didn't stop him from being a successful manager, however.

In 1926, at age 39, he took over the managerial duties of the Chicago Cubs and brought them to no better than third place, until 1929, when the Cubs captured the National League flag with 98 wins, but lost in the fall to the Philadelphia Athletics in five games.

He moved over to the Yankees as their skipper in 1931 bringing them to a 2nd place finish. In 1932 he won it all, not only the American League pennant, but the World Championship flag as well.

Starting in 1936 he ran off not only four consecutive AL pennants, but four World Championships as well. He didn't stop there having a 7th pennant and 6th World Championship in 1941. His Yankees won the 8th pennant for "Marse Joe" in 1942, but not the World Series as he bowed to the St. Louis Cardinals in five games. His last pennant, and World Championship happened in 1943, before he moved on to finish up his managerial career with the Boston Red Sox from 1948-50.

In his 24 years in the dugout, he no doubt, qualifies, with 9 pennants and 7 World Series titles, in both leagues, to being a "Groundbreaker" when it comes to winning pennants in both leagues.

46. Who was the first modern day manager to pilot two teams to pennants in the same league?

You will have to go back to 1915 when Pat Moran brought the Philadelphia Phillies to a pennant in 1915, and then led the Cincinnati Reds to the National League flag in 1919.

47. Who was the first American League manager, since 1901, to lead two teams to a pennant in the same league?

Shortstop Joe Cronin led the Washington Senators to the American League pennant with a 99-53 record in 1933 as a player manager, and then went up to Boston as a player-manager in 1935, and led the Red Sox, from the dugout, to the pennant in 1946, with a 104-50 record, having given up his playing career a year earlier.

48. Who was the first, and only, manager to win the pennant in his first and only year as a manager?

George Wright, was a shortstop and second baseman, who made his playing debut on May 5, 1871 with the Boston Red Stockings, and spent five years with them and three years with the Red Caps, before moving to Providence to become the player-manager with the Grays in 1879. He took them to the National League title that year with a 59-25, .702 record in the first and only year he ever managed a major league ball club.

He went back to the Red Caps for the 1880-81 seasons before finishing out his 12-year playing career with Providence in 1882 with a .301 career batting average.

49. Who was the first manager to manage a team in the World Series that he had not managed for the entire season?

Rogers Hornsby came over as a playing-manager to the Chicago Cubs in 1930, and continued managing them through 99 games in 1932 compiling a 53-46, .535 record that season. With the team not responding to Hornsby's stern discipline he was replaced by Cubs first baseman "Jolly Cholly" Grimm, who guided the Cubs, as the player-manager, for the remaining 55 games with a 37-18, .673 record, and won the National League pennant by four games over the Pittsburgh Pirates.

Charlie's good fortune ended there as the Cubs dropped the World Series to the New York Yankees by being swept in four games. "Jolly Cholly" remains, however, the first manager to manage a team in the World Series, but for only part of that regular season.

50. Who was the first man to win a World Championship in his first full season as manager?

Hall of Fame centerfielder, Tris "The Grey Eagle" Speaker, took over the managerial position in addition to his playing centerfield for the Cleveland Indians at age 31 in 1919. He replaced Lee Fohl who after 79 games, had a 45-34 record. Speaker, over the final 61 games, had a 40-21 record taking them to a 2nd place finish behind the Chicago White Sox.

In his first full season, in 1920, Speaker, with his .388 batting average and five other regulars batting over .300, took the Indians to the American League pennant with a 98-56 record two games ahead of the White Sox.

They faced off against the Brooklyn Robins (Dodgers) in the World Series, and with Speaker batting .320, and Stan Coveleski hurling three complete game wins, took the World Championship in seven games in Speaker's first full season at the helm.

51. Who was the first National League manager to win a World Championship in his first full year as a manager?

Infielder Rogers Hornsby made his major league playing debut with the St. Louis Cardinals on September 10, 1915, and began leading the league in batting in 1920, and kept that streak going for the next six years until the 29-year old second baseman took over the managerial duties from Branch Rickey, 38 games into the 1925 season inheriting a 13-25 record.

Powered by his league leading .403 batting average, "Rajah" took the Redbirds over the next 115 games to a 77-76, 4th place finish.

In 1926, his first full season as a player-manager, he brought the Cardinals to a National League flag with an 89-65 record, two games ahead of the Cincinnati Reds.

Facing the New York Yankees in the Fall Classic Hornsby, with the right arms of Hall of Famers Grover "Pete" Alexander and Jesse "Pop" Haines, each winning two games, defeated the Yankees in seven games to give Rogers "Rajah" Hornsby a World Championship in his first full season as a manager.

52. Who was the first manager to lead his team to more than 3,000 wins?

There have been a number of fine managers who have led their team to over 2,000 wins, some to over 2,500, but when it comes to that 3,000 plateau there is only one man standing, Cornelius Alexander McGillicuddy, known as Connie Mack, "The Tall Tactician," but referred to, and addressed as, Mr. Mack by his players, and those others around him. He took over the helm of the Pittsburgh Pirates in the National League in 1894, and won 149 games during his three-year stay there.

With the formation of the American League in 1901 he moved over to manage the Philadelphia Athletics in the new league and spent the next 50 years leading the Athletics to 9 pennants and 5 World Series Championships while winning 3,582 games, losing 3,814. His 53-year managerial record comes out to 3,731-3,948, .486.

53. Who was the first manager to have six 100-victory seasons?

"Marse Joe" McCarthy, never played in the major leagues, but started out managing the Chicago Cubs in 1926, and remained in the Windy City for five years before moving to New York, in 1931, to manage the Yankees. It was here, during his 16 years in the Bronx that he led the Yankees to 100-win seasons six times; 1932 (107), 1936 (102), 1937 (102), 1939 (106), 1941 (101), and 1942 (103). He took them to 1,460 wins before moving to Boston, in 1948, to take over the reins of the Red Sox till 1950, coming close to 100 wins twice with them by winning 96 games in 1948-49.

54. Who was the first manager to manage two different American League teams in the same city?

Now just how could that possibly happen? Very simple, just follow the path of Joe "Flash" Gordon, former Yankee second baseman, who took over in Cleveland managing the Indians from 1958-60.

After 95 games in Cleveland he moved on to Detroit and finished out the last 57 games of the 1960 season in the Motor City guiding the Tigers.

In 1961 he took over in the dugout for the Kansas City Athletics and guided the former Philadelphia team for 60 games until another former Yankee, Hank Bauer, took over the team.

Gordon was not in a major league dugout again until 1969 when the Kansas City Royals were formed, and he took on the duties as the skipper. He led them to a 4th place finish with a 69-93 record, but remains today as the first manager to manage two different American League teams in the same city.

55. Who was the first Puerto-Rican born manager in the major leagues?

On June 23, 2010 Edwin Rodriguez, who had been managing the Marlins Triple A team in New Orleans, was named interim manager of the Florida Marlins after the franchise fired then manager Fredi Gonzalez after a 34-36 record to open his fourth season with Florida.

Five days later, on June 28th, the Marlins made Ponce-born Rodriguez their full-time manager, and he guided the team to a 46-46 record over the rest of the 2010 season, becoming the first Puerto-born manager in big league history.

56. Who was the first manager to win a World Championship in his first full season as a manager?

Tris "The Grey Eagle" Speaker, who took over the managerial reins of the Cleveland Indians from Lee Fohl after 79 games into the 1919 season, brought the Indians to a 2nd place finish, 3 ½ games behind the pennant winning White Sox.

Starting off the 1920 season as the full-time manager Speaker led the Tribe to a 98-56 record two games better than the White Sox, and then went into the World Series and took the World Championship, defeating Brooklyn Dodgers, 5 games to 2. The Grey Eagle soared over the baseball world as the first skipper to win the World Series in his first full year as manager.

57. Who was the first National League manager to win a World Championship in his first full year as manager?

In 1925, after a 13-25 start Branch Rickey turned over the managerial duties to his star second baseman Rogers Hornsby who had a better year with the bat, leading the National League in batting with .403 average, home runs with 39, and 143 runs batted in than he did managing the team as his Redbirds ended up in 4th place behind the pennant-winning Pittsburgh Pirates.

The following year, 1926, when he was in complete command over the ball club for the entire season "Rajah" not only brought his Cardinals to the National League flag, two games better than Cincinnati, but took them into the Fall Classic, and defeated the New York Yankees in seven games to become the first National League manager in his first full year to win a World Championship.

58. Who was the first manager of the Texas Rangers?

In 1969 one of the finest pure hitters in the history of baseball decided to put his knowledge and experience to work in the dugout, and Ted Williams accepted the position of skipper of the Washington Senators.

Taking a very mediocre team to a 86-76 record, and 4th place finish that year he went on to lead the Senators for two more years until, after a punishing $2.6 million in financial losses after three years of operating an expansion team in the nation's capital, and little chance of attracting an increase in the fan base, owner Bob Short left Washington for the Dallas-Fort Worth area after the 1971 season to create the Texas Rangers.

His manager came along, and "The Splendid Splinter" took the reins of the Rangers through the 1972 season to become the first manager in their franchise history.

A cellar dwelling season of 54-100, along with continued financial losses, due to an attendance of 662,974, well below the break-even point, their leading hitter, high-priced Frank Howard, went to Detroit, and Williams, also with a handsome salary, resigned on the advice of GM Joe Burke, at the conclusion of that season. Dorrel "Whitey" Herzog came on to guide the Rangers for the following season.

59. Who was the first major league manager to retire immediately after winning the World Series?

This 67-year old, with 33 years of success as a manager, and after bringing his team, the St. Louis Cardinals, to the 2011 World Championship, after many thought it couldn't be done, decided that after 2,728 victories, six pennants, three World Series titles, two with St. Louis, and one with Oakland, he would step down. Tony LaRussa leaves in good company for the only other managers ahead of him on the victory list are John McGraw with 2,763 wins, ten pennants, and three World Series titles after 33 years at the helm, and Connie Mack with 3,731 victories, nine pennants, and five World Series titles in his 53-year managerial career.

60. Who was the first manager to be ejected from a game, for the first time in his baseball career, for arguing a call, after 28 seasons, and over 3,600 games as a player or a manager?

A strange thing happened in the bottom of the 4th inning on that Wednesday evening, July 18, 2001, out in Shea Stadium. The Mets 1B Todd Zeile hit a single to left field off Florida Marlins RHP Chuck Smith, and after CF Jay Payton flied out to center, SS Rey Ordonez doubled to left sending Zeile to third, RHP Kevin "Ape" Appier then hit into a fielder's choice to short, and Ordonez and Zeile both ended up on third base. A confused third base umpire, Kerwin Danley, called Zeile out, then called Ordonez out as well, which would have ended the inning, bringing Mets manager, Bobby Valentine, out on the field to protest the call. After ten minutes of conversation Valentine convinced the umpires that they made a mistake and they returned Zeile to third.

That quickly brought out Marlins manager, Tony Perez, to argue the reversal in the call. The umpires wanted no more conflicts, and promptly ejected Perez from the game. Now Tony had played 526 minor league games, 2,777 regular season games, and 47 postseason games, and had managed 257 games without being tossed from a game, until that moment. Just imagine the rage that must have ensued in the dugout when 3B Joe McEwing then doubled to left field driving in Zeile. The game went into the bottom of the 11th when the Mets pushed across a run to win 4-3.

61. Who was the first manager of the Montreal Expos?

Gene Mauch came up as an infielder with the Brooklyn Dodgers in 1944, and played nine seasons with them, as well as the Pirates, Cubs, Braves, Cardinals and Red Sox.

He started his managerial career with the Phillies in 1960 and stayed with them until the 1969 season when he was named the first manager of the newly formed Montreal Expos, where he stayed seven years, and over 1,127 games had a 499-627 record. He later went on to manage the Twins for five seasons and the California Angels for six.

62. Who was the first manager to wear the uniform of eight teams in his managerial career?

Runway fashion models don't change their working clothes more often than Stanley "Bucky" Harris, the former Washington Senators/Detroit Tigers second baseman.

In 1924 Harris took over the reins of the Washington Senators as a player-manager, and stayed with them as skipper till the 1929 season when he took on a similar role with the Detroit Tigers. He left Detroit to manage the Red Sox in 1934, but found himself back in Washington as manager from 1935-1942.

In 1943 he was in Philadelphia managing the Phillies for a year. After a three-year absence he returned to the dugout to manage the Yankees in 1947-48, before returning to Washington for five years at the helm of the Senators once again, from 1950-1954. He ended his second home, in the dugout, back in Detroit managing the Tigers for the 1955-56 seasons before calling it a career after 29 years, 4,410 games managed, 2,158 games won, two pennants and a World Series title with Washington, and a pennant and World Series victory with New York.

63. Who was the first American League manager to step down after managing just one game during the middle of the season?

In 1977 Frank Lucchesi took the Texas Rangers to a 31-31 record when Eddie Stanky was called in to replace him on June 22nd and took the Rangers to a 10-8 win over the Minnesota Twins. He then promptly quit the next day as skipper after just that one game, to be replaced by interim manager, Connie Ryan the next day, June 23rd.

64. Who was the first player or manager to never register a hit or a win?

This is a bizarre story that could be applied to a number of categories, but since it started on the playing field, and ended in the dugout we have included it in this category.

This 6'3, 220 pound outfielder/first baseman, by the name of Lawrence "Moose" Stubing, was a minor league player from 1956-69 in the Pittsburgh Pirates, New York/S.F. Giants, St. Louis Cardinals and California Angels organizations. He made his major league debut with the Angels on August 14, 1967 at age 29. He appeared in five games with them as a pinch-hitter, had five at bats, and struck out four times.

He played his final game for California on August 29, 1967, but that didn't end his association with the team for went on to manage for them in the minor leagues, and came back up to the big leagues as their coach. He was there when Cookie Rojas was fired in 1988, and at the age of 50, took over the managerial reins for the remaining eight games of the season, and lost every game to become the first player to never register a base hit and the first manager to manage at least eight games without a win.

L. FROM FOREIGN SHORES

1. Who was the first pitcher to win a regular season major league game on foreign soil?

Montreal's southpaw Dan McGinn was the winning pitcher in the first home game played in Expos history, before 29,184, on April 14, 1969. McGinn had come in to relieve starting pitcher Larry Jaster who went 3.2 innings giving up seven runs. McGinn went the remaining 5.1 innings with the help of Mack Jones three-run home run in the 1st. inning off Nelson Briles, and his single in the 7th driving in Coco Laboy breaking a 6-6 tie, and taking the Expos to an 8-7 victory over the St. Louis Cardinals to record the first win of a major league game played outside the United States.

2. Who was the first Canadian-born major league player?

First baseman Bill Phillips, born in St. John, New Brunswick, Canada in April 1857, became the first Canadian-born major leaguer when his career started on May 1, 1879 with the Cleveland Blues where he stayed until 1885. He then played for the Brooklyn Trolley Dodgers through 1887 before finishing up in 1888 with the Kansas City Blues.

His ten-year career showed him playing in 1,038 games with 17 home runs among his 1,175 base hits for a career .273 batting average.

3. Who was the first Australian pitcher to win a major league game?

Graeme Lloyd, the Milwaukee Brewers 6'8" lefthander, was the first Australian player to win a major league game when he defeated the Texas Rangers, 5-4, on April 30, 1993.

Interestingly, he pitched the next day, May 1st, to again defeat the Rangers, this time 4-3, in 12 innings.

4. Who was the first Puerto Rican-born player to play in the major leagues?

Hiram Gabriel "Hi" Bithorn, was born in Santurce, Puerto Rico on March 18, 1916. He pitched in his first major league game for the Chicago Cubs on April 15, 1942.

In his four seasons, interrupted by service in World War II, he played in 105 games, started 53, completed 30, with 8 shutouts, and five saves. Over the course of 509 innings he racked up 185 strikeouts and had a career

34-31 record with a 3.16 Era.

"The Pride of Puerto Rico" was honored in 1962 when the biggest ballpark on the island was built and named for him. Hiram Bithorn Stadium has hosted many baseball games, the 1979 Pan American games, World Boxing matches, and many musical events, and is located next to Roberto Clemente Stadium.

It wasn't until 1954 that a Puerto Rican player made his American League debut.

5. Who was the first American League player to come to the plate in a major league game played in Canada?

Outfielder Ralph Garr, of the Chicago White Sox, was the first American League player to step to the plate in Canada, when he came up to bat in a game against the Toronto Blue Jays on April 7, 1977.

6. Who was the first major leaguer to be born on the island of Jamaica?

Charles Theodore "Chili" Davis was born on January 17, 1960 in Kingston, Jamaica and came up to the major leagues as a centerfielder with the San Francisco Giants in 1982. He played 19 years in the big leagues for five different teams either in the outfield or as a designated hitter. He played in 2,436 games, driving in 1,372 runs with 2,380 base hits and 350 home runs for a .274 career batting average.

7. Who was the first major league player to hit a home run in a game played outside the United States?

Montreal Expos' Mack Jones, on opening day, hit the first home run in Jarry Park, Montreal, Canada, a three-run blast in the 1st inning, on April 14, 1969 off Nelson Briles of the St. Louis Cardinals.

8. Who was the first player to hit a major league grand slam home run in Canada?

Charles Dal Maxvill, the light-hitting shortstop of the St. Louis Cardinals, took Expos starting pitcher Larry Jaster downtown early with a grand slam home run in a game, on April 14, 1969, that was eventually won by Montreal 8-7.

It was the first of his two home runs hit that season and added to his total of 6 for his 14-year, 3,443 at bats career. But he still can claim that feat of being the first to hit a grand slam in a game outside the United States.

9. Who was the first Australian major league player to be named to the

All-Star team?

Dave Nilsson played eight seasons with the Milwaukee Brewers as a catcher, outfielder and first baseman. He batted .309 in 1999, his last season in the majors, and was named to the National League All-Star team that year.

10. Who were the first Australians to make up the first All-Australian battery?

With twenty four Australians having been in the major leagues it took until April 13, 1994 for them to have their own major league battery, when Milwaukee Brewer southpaw Graeme Lloyd, born in Victoria, took the mound in the bottom of the 9th inning with one out against the Texas Rangers, in relief of Jeff Bronkey. Dave Nilsson, from Brisbane, was his catcher and the first All-Australian battery was formed.

11. Of the many players from the Dominican Republic who have played in major league baseball who was the first?

Third baseman Ozzie Virgil, born in Monte Cristi, D.R., was the first Dominican to play in the major leagues when he made his major league debut with the New York Giants on September 23, 1956.

During his nine-year career with five teams as a catcher, infielder and outfielder he had a .231 career batting average.

12. Who was the first player born in South Korea to play in the major leagues?

Right-hander Chan Ho Park who was born on June 3, 1973 in Kongju, South Korea, made his major league pitching debut with the Los Angeles Dodgers on April 8, 1994 coming in pitch in the 9th inning of a game against the Braves, and respectfully bowing to the umpire upon reaching the mound. The Dodgers would lose 6-0 as the Braves' Kent Mercker pitched a no-hitter in his first complete game in the majors.

Playing for five teams in his 17-year career Park posted a 121-96 won-lost record with a 4.36 Era.

13. Who was the first Japanese-born player to appear in a major league game?

Southpaw pitcher Masanori Murakami, born on May 6, 1944 in Otsuki, Japan, made his pitching debut with the San Francisco Giants in a 4-1 loss in New York to the Mets. His major league debut would be impressive for in his first eleven innings he would not allow a run.

He pitched in 54 games over two seasons, but he felt uncomfortable pitching in a foreign country, and retuned to Japan after his final game on October 1, 1965, with a 5-1, 100 strikeouts in 89.1 innings, 3.43 Era. record.

14. Who was the first Latin American pitcher in the major leagues?

The first major league pitcher born in Latin America was right-hander Adolfo "Dolf" "The Pride of Havana" Luque, who was born in Havana, Cuba on August 4, 1890. He made his major league debut on May 20, 1914 for the Boston Braves in a 4-1 loss to the first place Pittsburgh Pirates.

Over his twenty-year career with the Braves, Reds, Robins, and Giants he would pitch 3,220.1 innings, with 26 shutouts, and 1,130 strikeouts for a 194-179, 3.24 Era. record.

15. Who was the first foreign-born player to win the Rookie of the Year Award?

The first foreign-born player to win the Rookie of the Year Award was shortstop Luis Aparicio of the Chicago White Sox in 1956. Born in Maracaibo, Venezuela on April 29, 1934, he played for 18 seasons with the Pale Hose, Baltimore Orioles, and the Boston Red Sox having a career batting average of .262.

What makes Aparicio stand out was his very slick fielding along with a cannon arm. Although batting .266 in his freshman year, he led the American League in stolen bases with 21, and continued on for the next nine years as the stolen base leader.

He provided the perfect infield combination along with second baseman Nellie Fox.

With Aparicio leading off and Nellie Fox batting second the two combined for an excellent hit-run combination. Cooperstown thought so with the induction of both of them into the Hall of Fame.

16. Who was the first foreign-born player to win the American League batting championship?

The first foreign-born player to win the American League batting championship was second baseman Roberto "Bobby" Avila, born on April 2, 1924 in Veracruz, Mexico. His 189 base hits, 112 runs scored and his .341 batting average helped the Cleveland Indians win the pennant in 1954.

The Tribe was disappointed in the World Series, however, by being swept by the New York Giants.

Well-educated, he turned to politics in his native country and later became President of the Mexican League.

17. Who was the first foreign-born player to win the Cy Young Award?

After being with the Cincinnati Reds, St. Louis Cardinals, and the Houston Astros in the National League, Mike Cuellar moved over to the Baltimore Orioles in 1969 where the southpaw had a 23-11 record in 290.2 innings, striking out 182 and posting an Era. of 2.38. That effort tied the Las Villas, Cuba native with Detroit right-hander Denny McClain, and they shared the American League Cy Young Award.

18. Who was the first foreign-born player to win the Most Valuable Player Award?

The ballots were in and the honor of being the first foreign-born player to win the MVP Award went to Zoilo " Zorro" Versalles, born on December 18, 1939, in Veldado, Cuba. The flashy shortstop was the sparkplug, and key member of the Minnesota Twins offense in their pennant-winning year of 1965. His .273 batting average along with his league leading 666 at bats, 45 doubles, 12 triples, and 126 runs scored as well as his 27 stolen bases and 19 home runs, and Gold Glove Award combined to make him the choice for the 1965 MVP Award.

During his twelve-year career he played for five teams concluding with the Atlanta Braves on September 28, 1971.

19. Who was the first foreign-born player elected to the Hall of Fame?

Pittsburgh Pirates right fielder Roberto Walker Clemente, born on August 18, 1934, in Carolina, Puerto Rico was an easy selection for the Hall of Fame committee when he was inducted by a special election in 1973.

He was a brilliant fielder and no one had a better arm as many an opposing runner trying to take an extra base will attest to. He won four batting titles, batting .351 in 1961; .339 in 1964; .329 in 1965; and .357 in 1967.

On September 30, 1972 Clemente lined a double off New York Mets southpaw Jon Matlack, at Three Rivers Stadium, for his 3,000[th] and final career base hit. His career batting average was .317 with 240 home runs and 1,305 runs batted in. Named to the All-Star team twelve times, he was the National League MVP in 1966.

His career ended when he was killed in a tragic airplane accident on New Year's Eve 1972 while bringing relief supplies to earthquake victims in Managua, Nicaragua.

20. Who was the first foreign-born pitcher to win twenty major league games in a season?

As mentioned previously in this section Dolf Luque was not only the first Latin American pitcher in the major leagues he was also the first foreign-born twenty-game winner.

One has to go back to 1923 when "The Pride of Havana" led the National League in wins with 27 while losing 8, and carried a league best Era. of 1.93 for the Cincinnati Reds.

Interestingly, just the year before Dolf led the National League in losses with 23 while winning 13. Over his 20-year career with the Reds, Dodgers, and Giants he had 193 wins and 173 losses.

21. Who was the first foreign-born player to reach 3,000 career base hits?

Once again a familiar name comes up, this time in the person of Roberto Clemente. On September 30, 1972, at Three Rivers Stadium, the rifle-armed right fielder for the Pittsburgh Pirates lined a double off New York Met southpaw Jon Matlack in the 4th inning for his 3,000th career base hit in a 5-0 whitewash win for Dock Ellis and the Pirates.

22. Who was the first Australian to play in the major leagues?

Way back in 1884 "Uncle Joe" Quinn, born in Sydney, Australia, came into the major leagues as a first baseman with St. Louis in the Union Association. He stayed with St. Louis when they moved into the National League with the then named Browns.

He played seventeen years, mainly as a second baseman for Boston, St. Louis, Baltimore, Cleveland, Cincinnati, and Washington. His career batting average was .261 with 1,797 base hits. He also was a player/manager with St. Louis in 1895, and with Cleveland in 1899.

23. Who was the first player to play on foreign soil for both Canadian major league teams?

Ron Fairly broke into the majors as a 19-year old outfielder with the Los Angeles Dodgers on September 9, 1958. He was traded after just over eleven years to the Montreal Expos on June 11, 1969. The Expos traded him after just over five years to the St. Louis Cardinals on December 6, 1974 for the 1975 season. The Oakland Athletics purchased him from the Redbirds on September 14, 1976 where he remained briefly until February 24, 1977 when he was traded by Oakland to the Toronto Blue Jays. In December 1977 he was traded by Toronto, after playing just 132 games for them, to the California Angels, where he finished out his 21-year, six-team career as a first baseman and designated hitter, in 1978, and being able to say that he was the first player to play for both Canadian teams.

24. Who was the first major league player to be born in Vietnam?

Right-handed pitcher Daniel Peter Graves, known as the "Baby-Faced Assassin", was born on August 7, 1973 in Saigon, South Vietnam, to a Vietnamese mother and a U.S. serviceman.

He made his major league pitching debut on July 13, 1996 with the Cleveland Indians in a lop-sided Indians 19-11 victory over Minnesota.

After pitching for eleven seasons with the Indians, Cincinnati Reds and the New York Mets he wrapped up his 11-year career on May 9, 2006 with Cleveland showing a career record of 43-44 won-lost record with an Era. of 4.05.

25. Who was the first Canadian-born player to play for the Montreal Expos?

It seemed appropriate that a Canadian be a member of the first Canadian major league team so right-hander Claude "Frenchy" Raymond, born in St. Jean, Quebec, Canada, and having pitched just over nine years in the big leagues for the White Sox, Milwaukee/Atlanta Braves, Houston Colt 45's/Astros was released by the Atlanta Braves to the newly established Montreal Expos on August 19, 1969 in exchange for cash.

One of the few major leaguers to wear glasses Raymond went on to have an 8-16 record in his three years with the Expos, and a 46-53, 3.66 Era. career record. Raymond went on to broadcast Expos games after his playing days were over.

26. Who was the first Japanese-born player to win his league's Rookie of the Year Award?

Right-hander Hideo Nomo, born on August 31, 1968 in Osaka, Japan, made his major league debut with the Los Angeles Dodgers on May 2, 1995. He was voted National League Rookie of the Year, at age 26, by starting 28 games, leading the National League in shutouts with three, and strikeouts with 236, along with 19 wild pitches, while pitching 191.1 innings, for a 13-6, 2.54 Era. to become the first Japanese-born player to win the Rookie of the Year Award.

His twelve-season career, ending with the Kansas City Royals on April 18, 2008 in 2008, showed him playing for seven teams with a career record of 121-109, and an Era. of 4.24.

27. Who was the first major league player to hit a home run in three different countries?

Will Steve Finley of the San Diego Padres please stand up and take a bow. When the Padre outfielder hit a home run on August 16, 1996 against the New York Mets in Monterrey, Mexico to defeat New York in a 15-10 slugfest, he became the first player to hit a home run in three different countries having hit them in both the United States and Canada.

28. Who was the first Taiwan-born major league player to hit a home run in a major league game?

It happened on June 13, 2007, in the 2nd inning, when with one out and the bases empty Hong-Chich Kuo, the southpaw pitcher for the Los Angeles Dodgers, born on July 23, 1981 in Tainan City, Taiwan, hit a solo home run in his third major league season to become the first player born in Taiwan to hit a major league home run.

Kuo is still pitching, but has not hit a round-tripper since. His appearance in 140 games and 222.1 innings, since his debut on September 2, 2005, has kept him more on the mound than at the plate. He does sport an 11-14, 3.56 Era. since coming to the big leagues.

29. When was the first time that three pitchers, each born in a different Asian country, pitched in the same game for the same major league team?

This rare occurrence happened on May 17, 2008 out in Los Angeles with the Dodgers playing at the Angels. The Dodgers started right-hander Chan Ho Park, born June 30, 1973 in Gongju, South Korea. Before the game was over he was followed by two Asian teammates, southpaw Hong-Chih Kuo, born on July 23, 1981 in Tainan, Taiwan, and right-hander Takashi Saito who was born on February 14, 1970 in Sendai, Miyagi, Japan to form the first Asian trifecta playing in a major league baseball game.

30. Who was the first major leaguer to play in Japan?

The answer to this question kind of comes out of left field, maybe better stated from the mound. Right-hander Phil Paine made his major league debut as a pitcher for the Boston Braves on July 14, 1951. He then served in the military during the Korean War and having been stationed in Japan had the opportunity to pitch for the Nishitetsu Lions in the Nippon Professional League on August 23, 1953. He pitched nine games for the Lions before returning to the Braves, now in Milwaukee, for the 1954 season. Moving over to the St. Louis Cardinals for the 1958 season, he finished out his career pitching for the last time on September 19, 1958. He was traded on December 4, 1958 to the Dodgers, along with Wally Moon, for Gino Cimoli, but decided to call it a career. During his six seasons in the big leagues Paine had a 10-1 won-lost record, pitching in 150.1 innings with 101 strikeouts and a 3.24 Era., but remains today as the first big leaguer to play in Japan.

31. Who were the first Japanese-born major league players, pitcher and batter, to face each other in a major league game?

This face-to-face meeting took place on April 13, 2001, in Anaheim, when Angels five-year veteran right-handed reliever Shigetoshi "Shiggy" Hasagawa, born on August 1, 1968 in Kobe, Japan, faced Seattle Mariners rookie left-handed hitting right fielder, Ichiro Suzuki, born on October 22, 1973, in Kasugal, Japan, with two outs in the 9th inning and gave up an infield single to bring about the first time two Japanese players faced each other in the major leagues. Shiggy picked up the win in that All-Asian confutation as the Angels took a home victory 4-3.

32. Who was the first pitcher to win a major league game South of the Border?

On August 16, 1996, in Monterrey, Mexico, in the first major league game played outside the United States or Canada, southpaw Fernando "El Toro" Valenzuela was the winning pitcher, benefiting from four San Diego Padres home runs in a wild 15-10 victory over the New York Mets.

33. Who was the first Colombian-born player in the major leagues?

We have to go way back to April 23, 1902 to a game where Luis Manuel "Jud" Castro, born in Medellin, Colombia, but educated at Manhattan College in New York City, was called in by Connie Mack's Philadelphia Athletics at Baltimore Orioles Park in the 9th inning, to replace Nap Lajoie at second base. It seems that the Pennsylvania court system exercised an injunction order with anyone except the Phillies for Lajoie's services. Castro played in 42 games that season for Mr. Mack.

34. Who was the first Canadian-born pitcher to pitch a no-hitter?

Dick Fowler was born on March 30, 1921 in Toronto, Canada, and the right-hander made his major league debut with the Philadelphia Athletics on September 13, 1941. Called into the Canadian army in 1943, he didn't return to the major leagues until 1945. In his first start, after rejoining the Athletics, at Shibe Park, Philadelphia, on September 9, 1945, he faced the St. Louis Browns, and pitched a no-hitter winning 1-0, for his only victory of that season, to become the first Canadian major leaguer to pitch a hitless game.

35. Who was the first Quebec-born player to play with the Montreal Expos?

Jean Claude "Frenchy" Raymond, a right-handed pitcher, was born in St. Jean, Province of Quebec, Canada on March 7, 1937 and made a very brief major league debut with the Chicago White Sox on April 15, 1959. On May 11th of that year he was sent to the Milwaukee Braves and played for them for three years before moving on to Houston. From there to the Atlanta Braves and finally ending up being purchased by the Montreal Expos from the Braves on August 19, 1969, where he finished out his career on September 15, 1971 with a 46-53 record.

36. Who was the first Canadian-born pitcher to win 20 games in a season?

Many of you no doubt said Ferguson Jenkins. Although "Fly" had seven 20-game winning seasons, and did come from Canada, the honor goes to Russ Ford, born April 25, 1883 in Brandon, Manitoba, Canada.

The right-hander made his major league debut on April 28, 1909 pitching three innings and giving up three earned runs for the New York Highlanders. He quickly erased any thoughts of him not being a winning pitcher in 1910, when he had a 26-6 record to become the first Canadian-born pitcher to win twenty games in the big leagues.

Ford played five seasons with New York before spending the last two with Buffalo and ended up with a career 99-71. 2.59 Era. record.

37. Of the many Mexican-born players to have played in the major

leagues, who was the first?

Centerfielder Mel Almada, born in Huatabampo, Mexico, was the first from his country to play in the big leagues when he debuted with the Boston Red Sox on September 8, 1933.

He played seven seasons in the American League with Boston, Washington, and the St. Louis Browns before playing his final game on October 1, 1939 with the Brooklyn Dodgers. His career totals showed 706 base hits, 15 home runs, 197 runs batted in, for a .284 batting average.

Although his figures don't match some of the other more successful Mexican players he still was the "groundbreaker" for Mexican baseball players in the major leagues.

38. Who was the first major league player to be born in Afghanistan?

Right-hander Jeff Bronkey, was born in Kabul, Afghanistan on September 18, 1965, and was drafted in the second round of the 1986 amateur draft by the Minnesota Twins.

He was released by the Twins on January 3, 1990 and signed as a free agent on May 25, 1990 with the Texas Rangers. He made his major league pitching debut on May 2, 1993 with Texas, and appeared in 21 games with them before being traded to the Milwaukee Brewers on January 13, 1994. Playing in 24 games with the Brewers in 1994-95 he played his final major league game on August 12, 1995, and was released by the Brewers on October 9, 1995.

His career record shows a 2-2 won-lost, 4.04 Era. record, walking 29 and striking out 36 batters.

39. Who was the first Canadian to win the Cy Young Award?

Hall of Fame resident Ferguson Jenkins, the right-hander of the Chicago Cubs, who was born in Chatham, Ontario, became the first Canadian born player to win the Cy Young Award when he led the National League in wins with a 24-13 record, and also led in complete games with 30, and innings pitched with 325 in1971.

40. Who was the first Latin-American-born player to play in the major leagues?

The first Latin-American-born player to play major league baseball was Esteban "Steve" Bellan, who was born in Havana, Cuba, and made his debut as a third baseman with the Troy Haymakers on May 9, 1871, and later played at short, second, and in centerfield, before moving to the New York Mutuals in 1873.

41. Who was the first Latino to strike out 3,000 batters?

Right-hander Pedro Martinez, who made his pitching debut on September 24, 1992 with the Los Angeles Dodgers, and pitched in both leagues with the Dodgers, Expos, Red Sox, Mets, and Phillies for 18 seasons ended up his career in 2009 with 3,154 strikeouts.

42. Who was the first Latin-American-born pitcher to pitch a perfect game?

Right-hander Dennis "El Presidente" Martinez, besides being the first Nicaraguan-born player in major league baseball, was the first Latino to pitch a perfect game. He made his major league debut on September 14, 1976 with the Baltimore Orioles, and on July 28,1991 he pitched the 13th perfect game in major league history when, with the Montreal Expos, he shut down the Los Angeles Dodgers, 2-0.

During his 23 seasons "El Presidente" pitched 3,999.2 innings for the Orioles, Expos, Indians, Mariners, and Braves winning 245 games, losing 193, with a 3.70 Era.

43. Who was the first major league player to be born in a Latin-American country?

Esteban "Steve" Bellan was born in Havana, Cuba on October 1, 1849, and made his major league debut as a third baseman with the Troy Haymakers of the National Association, which was the predecessor to the National League, on May 9, 1871.

He played his final game on June 9, 1873 with the New York Mutuals, and during his 3-year career played third base, second base and centerfield and compiled a .251 batting average with 43 runs batted in.

44. Who was the first modern day player to be born in Latin America?

The first modern day player born in Latin America was Luis "Jud" Castro who was born in Medellin, Columbia on November 25, 1876. He attended Manhattan College, in New York prior to making his major league debut as a second baseman for the Philadelphia Athletics on April 23, 1902. His career lasted for 42 games, ending on September 27, 1902, with a .245 batting average, with one home run and 15 runs batted in.

45. Who was the first Hispanic to play in an All-Star game?

Born in Caracas, Venezuela, Alfonso "Chico" Carrasquel of the Chicago White Sox was the starting shortstop for the 1951 American League All-Star team. In his ten-year career "Chico" was named an All-Star four times.

46. Who was the first Hispanic to own a major league team?

Arturo "Arte" Moreno, a native of Tucson, Arizona, made history on May 15, 2003 when he purchased the 2002 World Champion Anaheim Angels for $180 million from the Walt Disney Company, and became the first Hispanic to own a major league sports team in the United States.

In an initially unpopular move to the fans and the city of Anaheim, he changed the name of the team to the Los Angeles Angels of Anaheim. That change gave him a bigger geographical identity and once Moreno was established his practices were widely accepted and he remains a very popular owner.

47. Who was the first Hispanic to pitch a no-hitter?

On June 15, 1963, before a Saturday afternoon crowd of 18, 869, at Candlestick Park, "The Dominican Dandy" right-hander Juan Marichal of the San Francisco Giants, won his 10th game of the season when he pitched a no-hitter defeating Dick Drott and the Houston Colt '45s, 1-0, allowing two walks and striking out 5. The winning run came in the 8th inning on a pair of doubles by Jim Davenport and Chuck Hiller, two of the only three hits given up by Drott, as Marichal became the first Latin American to pitch a no-hitter in the major leagues.

48. Who pitched the first major league season no-hitter in Canada?

On Monday, October 2, 1972, Bill Stoneman the Montreal Expos right-hander, shutout the New York Mets without a hit, 7-0, at Jarry Park to become the first pitcher to pitch a no-hitter on foreign soil.

49. Who was the first major league manager born in the Dominican Republic?

Felipe Alou, who was born in Haina, Dominican Republic, came up with the San Francisco Giants in 1958 and played 17 seasons with five clubs in both leagues before he switched over to the managerial side after his playing days.

He became the manager of the Montreal Expos in 1992 and stayed at the helm until 2001. He then moved to his first team, the San Francisco

Giants, from 2003-2006.

During his 14-year career as a manger his record was 691-717, .491 average. Considering his first ten years were spent with an expansion team his duties guiding a team were pretty good.

50. Who were the first Japanese-born pitchers, one to be credited with a win, and the other to be credited for the save in the same game?

We have to go down to The Ballpark at Arlington on Sunday, April 14, 2002, when Seattle right-hander Shigetoshi "Shiggy" Hasegawa, born in Kobe, Japan, came on in relief of right-hander Ryan Franklin who had come on to start the bottom of the 7th in relief of southpaw John Halama with the Mariners ahead 7-5, and found two runners on through a pair of walks given up by Franklin to the first two batters he faced. Hasegawa got out of the inning allowing two runs, one on a ground out, and the second on a single by LF Rusty Greer, but Texas had tied the game at 7-7.

In the top of the 8th the Mariners picked up two runs and went ahead 9-7. In the bottom of the 8th Hasegawa struck out DH Ivan Rodriguez, but CF Gabe Kapler hit a screeching line drive down the left field line, and after RF Kevin Mench grounded out, manager Lou Piniella decided to bring in Tokyo-born right-hander Kazuhiro Sasaki to pitch to pinch-hitter Carl Everett. Everett grounded out to second, and Sasaki had gotten out of the inning. He followed that with a scoreless 9th to gain his 3rd save, and have Hasegawa's record go to 2-0, as Seattle went on to win, 9-7.

That marked the first time in major league history that two Japanese-born players each picked up a win and a save in the same game.

51. Who was the first Japanese-born player to come to bat against a fellow countryman on the mound in major league history?

Kasugai-born met Kobe-born on Friday, April 13, 2001, before a crowd of 31,087, at Edison Field, Anaheim. Angels right-hander Shigetoshi "Shiggy" Hasegawa, who had come on in the top of the 8th inning in relief of southpaw Scott Schoeneweis had two outs in the 9th when up to the plate stepped southpaw swinging RF Ichiro Suzuki from Kasugai, Japan for the first meeting of two Japanese-born players in major league history. Ichiro performed, as usual, by banging out a ground ball single before CF Mike Cameron flied out to left field to end the inning. The Angels rallied for two runs in the bottom of the 9th to win, 4-3, and give Hasegawa, 1-0, his first win of the season, and another countryman, Kazuhiro Sasaki, 0-1, his first loss of the season.

52. Who was the first Curacao-born player to be named to the All-Star team?

Willemstad, Curacao-born Andruw Jones made his major league debut with the Atlanta Braves on August 15, 1996, as an outfielder, and quickly was positioned as their regular centerfielder. He was named to his first All-Star team in 2000 and became the first to represent his homeland in the mid-summer classic.

53. Who was the first Latin-American pitcher to pitch in a World Series game?

His name is no stranger to this section of the book for right-hander Dolf Luque, of the Cincinnati Reds, came on to pitch the 8th inning, in relief of fellow right-hander Ray Fisher, on October 3rd, in Game 3 of the infamous 1919 World Series against the Chicago "Black Sox."

He re-appeared on the mound in Game 7, on October 8th, coming on in relief of Fisher, once again, to pitch the last four innings of that game to become the first Hispanic pitcher to pitch in a World Series.

54. Who was the first Mexican pitcher to win 20 games in a season?

If you were one of the 27,641 at the Houston Astrodome on Monday, September 22, 1986, you witnessed Los Angeles Dodgers southpaw Fernando Valenzuela, born in Sonora, Mexico, strikeout five Astros batters, and give up just two hits, winning 9-2, as he became the first Mexican pitcher to win 20 games in a season.

55. Who was the first player to play in the major leagues, then play in Japan, and return to play back in the major leagues?

On April 13, 1965 Davey Johnson made his major league debut as an infielder with the Baltimore Orioles. From 1973 to 1975 he was a second baseman with the Atlanta Braves until his release. Johnson then went to Japan and played for the Yomiuri Giants in the Japanese League in 1975-76 before signing as a free agent with the Phillies in 1977, and staying there till August 6, 1978 when he was traded to the Chicago Cubs for Larry Anderson.

56. Who was the first foreign-born pitcher to win over 280 major league games?

North America won out over Europe as right-hander Ferguson Jenkins, born in Chatham, Ontario, Canada on December 13, 1942, and broke in with the Philadelphia Phillies on September 10, 1965, went on to pitch 19 years with the Phillies, Cubs, Rangers, and Red Sox. He racked up 284 wins, and 226 losses on his way to the Hall of Fame in 1991.

A few years later Rik Aalbert "Bert" Blyleven, born in the Netherlands, and pitched for Minnesota, Texas, Pittsburgh, Cleveland, and California, finished his 22-year career on October 4, 1992 with a 287-250 record and an address in Cooperstown in 2011.

M. FRANCHISE FIRSTS

1. What was the first all-professional baseball team?

The Cincinnati Red Stockings, who were incorporated on June 23, 1866 in a downtown Cincinnati law office, had ten salaried players, and were the first all-professional baseball team. They played their games at Lincoln Park Grounds, with the first one happening on May 4, 1869 when they defeated the Great Westerns, a team from Cincinnati, 45-9. It was the first of 57 games for the team that season which concluded with a 57-0, record, the first and only perfect season in baseball history.

In 1870 the team continued its winning ways winning about 24 more before their first franchise loss, to the Brooklyn Atlantics, 8-7, in 11 innings on June 14, 1870.

2. What were the teams that played in the first National League game?

The first National League game was played on April 22, 1876 between the Boston Red Stockings (Braves) and the Philadelphia Athletics at the Jefferson Street Grounds, Philadelphia.

Before a crowd of about 3,000 fans, in a very poorly played game, 20 errors were made, but with Boston scoring twice in the 9th inning they came away with the first victory in the new league, 6-5.

Diminutive, 5'9", 140-pound right-hander Joe Borden was the winning pitcher in the new league's first game.

3. What franchise was the first to use turnstiles to enter a ball park?

In 1878 the Providence Grays, who found it unusual to have more than 1,000 fans attend their games, instituted the practice of having turnstiles installed for the first time, as 6,000 fans rotated through the gates of the Messer Street Grounds to watch the Boston Braves win 1-0.

4. What major league fanchise was the first to be expelled from the National League?

The first year in the National League for the Philadelphia Athletics started off with an Opening Day loss to the Boston Americans, 6-5, in a game that featured twenty errors. As the losses mounted and the team stumbled to a 14-45, .237, record and a 7th place finish under manager Al Wright, 34 ½ games out of first place, things continued to go downhill.

Crowds dwindled because of the lack of quality of play, and various other public events such as the Centennial Exposition, the Fireman's Parade and the Regatta. Usually when a team was out of contention oftentimes they would just postpone games or just cancel them.

The team, not having train fare to make a final western swing, prompted team President G. W. Thompson to prevail upon the Chicago and St. Louis franchises to come to Philadelphia to play the final two series with his club. In return he offered 80% of his gate receipts to them. When both clubs declined Thompson had little choice but to cancel the eight game road trip as well as the last three games of the season against the New York Mutuals.

This wasn't looked upon favorably by the league, and they voted to expel the team from the league in their December meeting. It would be six years before Philadelphia would again have a National League franchise.

5. What was the first franchise to lose the pennant because of a rain-out?

In 1908 the Detroit Tigers won the American League pennant with a record of 90-63 over the Cleveland Indians record of 90-64, a margin of ½ a game, all due to a Detroit rainout.

Cleveland naturally was upset and protested to the owners. A new rule was introduced after the 1908 season which specified that any game, having a mathematical bearing on the pennant race, had to be made up.

6. What was the first franchise to have its players wear a number on their uniforms?

The 1916 Cleveland Indians were the first American League team to have numbers applied to their uniform sleeves. Some years later other teams followed the practice.

7. Who was the first, and only, member of the Kansas City Royals to have his uniform number retired?

This shortstop and second baseman made his major league debut on April 11, 1961 with the Kansas City Athletics. On May 25, 1963 Dick Howser was traded with Joe Azcue to the Cleveland Indians for Doc Edwards and $100,000. After spending four seasons with Cleveland, Howser was traded by the Indians to the New York Yankees on December 20, 1966. He played his final game with the Yankees on September 27, 1968. In 1978 he became the manager of the New York Yankees for one game, and after a brief hiatus was back at the helm of New York for the entire 1980 season, winning 103 games and bringing them to the American League Championship Series where they were swept in three games by Kansas City, who went on to become World Champions.

George Steinbrenner fired Howser after that season, presumably for losing to Kansas City. Howser then went into the real estate business in Florida.

From 1981 through 1986 he guided the Royals to a 404-365 record and took them to the American League pennant and a World Championship over St. Louis Cardinals in 1985. He never finished lower than second place during his seven-year managerial career.

Howser, as manager of the defending champions, the Kansas City Royals, managed his last major league game, the 1986 All-Star Game at the Astrodome in Houston. Complaining of feeling sick he was diagnosed with a brain tumor and underwent surgery. Howser passed away on June 17, 1987 in Kansas City. The much beloved manager had his uniform number #10 retired, the only one retired by the franchise in its history.

8. Who was the first pitcher in Milwaukee Brewers' history to pitch a no-hitter?

Milwaukee Brewers first no-hitter was pitched by Juan Nieves against the Baltimore Orioles on April 15, 1987. Nieves struck out seven and walked five with no runners going beyond first base.

9. What was the first franchise to have the attendance for a World Series game exceed 90,000?

On October 4, 1959 the Los Angeles Dodgers hosted the Chicago White Sox in Game 3 of the World Series. With a seating capacity of 94,000 the game drew a near capacity crowd of 92, 394.

10. What franchise was the first to play host to the first modern day perfect game?

The first franchise to play host to the first modern day perfect game came about on May 5, 1904 when Cy Young threw a perfect game for the Boston Americans against the Philadelphia Athletics on May 5, 1904, winning 3-0, at The Huntington Avenue Grounds in Boston Massachusetts.

11. Where and when was the first New York Highlanders (Yankees) game played?

The New York Highlanders played their first game in Washington at the American League Park in Washington, D.C. on April 22, 1903, as manager Tom Loftus's Washington Nationals came away with a 3-1 victory over manager-pitcher Clark Griffith's Highlanders.

12. What pitcher pitched the first perfect game in Oakland Athletics history?

You have to go back to May 8, 1968 to find 22-year old right-hander Jim "Catfish" Hunter, before his home crowd, striking out eleven batters, including Harmon Killebrew three times, on his way to a 4-0 perfect game against the Minnesota Twins. It was the first American League perfect game in 46 years.

"Catfish" aided the offense as well as he drove in three of the four runs that day.

13. What was the first franchise to have their pitchers pitch no-hitters on consecutive days?

The Chicago White Sox ran up against some great pitching on May 5, 1917 when St. Louis Browns southpaw Ernie Koob, with the aid of George Sisler driving in the only run, pitched a no-hitter defeating Eddie Cicotte and the White Sox, 1-0.

Three interesting sidelights to this game; it would be the last shutout the 24-year old Koob will pitch; just in the previous month, on April 14th, Cicotte had pitched a no-hitter against these same Browns, winning 11-0; and a first inning questionable base hit by White Sox third baseman Buck Weaver is changed to an error after a lengthy discussion among the umpires and players. The writers' association will later make a ruling that a scorer's decision on a play cannot be reversed.

Let's move on to the following day, May 6, 1917. In the first game of a doubleheader between these two teams the Browns pull out an 8-4 win in 10 innings with Browns' right-hander Bob Groom pitching the last two hitless innings.

This point is important, for in the second game of that double-header who should be the starting pitcher but the same Bob Groom, who then went on to pitch the second no-hitter by a Browns' pitcher, in consecutive days, white-washing the Sox, 3-0. In so doing the White Sox set a record by having only 23 official at-bats in 9 innings.

That three game sweep, in which the Pale Hose were held hitless in two of the three, may have added to their 54 losses on the season, but their 100 wins were ten better than runner-up Boston for the American League flag, and a 4-games-to-2 victory over the New York Giants in the World Series.

14. Who pitched the first no-hitter in Philadelphia Phillies history?

Just go back before the turn of the previous century to July 8, 1898 when right-hander Frank "Red" Donahue pitched a no-hitter down in Baker Bowl, Philadelphia defeating the Boston Beaneaters (Braves), 5-0, allowing just four base runners and only one to reach second base.

15. What team was the first to win a major league baseball game played outside of the United States or Canada?

They were the very first, but certainly not the last, when on August 16, 1996, the San Diego Padres, with four home runs, defeated the New York Mets, 15-10, down in Monterrey, Mexico, in the first regular season game played outside of the United States or Canada.

The following day the Mets come back for a South-of-the-Border 7-3 win over San Diego.

16. What was the first team, playing in an indoor stadium, to have their game rained out?

Hard to believe? Oh, it happened, on June 15, 1976, when the first indoor facility for playing baseball in the major leagues, the Houston Astrodome, had to call off a game between the Houston Astros and the Pittsburgh Pirates due to ten inches of heavy rain accompanied by very strong winds that flooded the area and prevented players, fans, umpires and stadium workers from getting to the arena.

17. When did the New York Yankees win their first World Championship?

In 1923, after losing to the New York Giants in the 1921 and 1922 World Series, the New York Yankees defeated the Giants in six games to become World Champions for the first time.

18. What teams were involved in the first game called because of the sun?

We have had games called because of the rain, or an early season snowstorm, but now the sun? Yes fans it happened on May 6, 1892, when right-hander John Clarkson of the Boston Beaneaters was locked in a scoreless 14-inning duel with Cincinnati Reds right-hander Elton "Icebox" Chamberlain in Crosley Field.

Clarkson had given up four hits to the Reds while Chamberlain had allowed five, when the angle of the blinding sun began bothering both pitchers and the batters, and in the interest of safety, umpire Jack Sheridan called the game. The Cincinnati Enquirer validated the arbiter's decision by stating it a just and sensible one.

19. What was the first team in major league history to hold a defending league champion scoreless over a three game series?

When the Philadelphia Phillies came into the "Big Apple" for a three game series with the New York Mets on Tuesday, May 25, 2010 they didn't realize that the Mets had their whitewash brushes out, ready to use them.

The brushes came out that day with right-hander R.A. Dickey blanking the 2009 N.L. champions, 8-0. The following day, with the brushes still wet, southpaw Hisanori Takahashi came away with a 5-0 win. Then on Thursday right-hander Mike Pelfrey joined his fellow starters with a 3-0 whitewash to make the Mets the first team to hold the National League Champions scoreless in a three-game series.

20. What was the first National League team to win a World Series after being down three games to one?

It was the first team that was up 3 games to 1, and then lost the first World Series played in 1903, when Boston came back to defeat them 5 games to 3.

We are speaking about the Pittsburgh Pirates in the 1925 World Series against the Washington Senators. Washington won games 1, 3, and 4 before the Pirates came roaring back to sweep the last three to win the World Series, 4 games to 3.

21. Who was the first San Diego Padre to hit 50 home runs in a season?

The first San Diego Padre to hit 50 home runs in a season was left-fielder Greg Vaughn who hit an even 50 and drove in 119 runs in that 1998 season.

22. Who was the first San Diego Padre to hit a home run in an All-Star game?

On July 9, 1996 third baseman Ken Caminiti came up in the 6th inning with none out, and hit a solo home run into deep right-centerfield of Veterans Stadium, off Texas right-hander Roger Pavlik, as the National League went on to a 6-0 victory.

23. What American League team was the first to score 1,000 runs in a

154-game season?

The first American League team to score 1,000 runs in a season happened in 1930 when the New York Yankees scored 1,062 runs in their 154 games.

24. What was the first *modern* day National League team to score 1,000 runs in a 154-game season?

It seems that 1930 was a run scoring season, for the St. Louis Cardinals topped the 1,000 run mark as well as the Yankees, when they crossed the plate 1,004 times in their 154 games that year.

25. Who was the first New York Yankee to lead the American League in runs batted in and home runs in the same season?

It comes as no surprise to learn that Babe Ruth was the first Yankee, and first player, to do many things. One of which was to be the first Yankee to lead the league in runs batted in with 137, and in home runs with 54 in 1920. Not having to validate that achievement he went on to repeat those two batting titles in 1921, 23, 26, and '28. Interesting to note the year that he didn't lead in those two categories was in 1927 when he hit 60 home runs. He came up eleven shy in RBIs to teammate Lou Gehrig with 164.

26. What team was the first to turn two triple plays in one game?

It happened up in Fenway Park, Boston on July 17, 1990, when in the bottom of the 4th inning third baseman Wade Boggs walked, second baseman Jody Reed doubled to right, and Minnesota Twins right-hander Scott Erickson walked first baseman Carlos Quintana. Right fielder Tom Brunansky then hit a ground ball to Twins third baseman Gary Gaetti who touched third, and went around the horn to Al Newman at second, who relayed on to Kent Hrbek at first for the triple play.

In the 8th inning Red Sox shortstop Tim Naehring opened the inning by doubling to left off southpaw John "Candy Man" Candelaria, who then walked Wade Boggs. Jody Reed came up and duplicated the play of the 4th inning by grounding down to Gaetti who, again, went around the horn to complete the second triple play of the game, and put the Minnesota franchise in the record books by being the first team to turn two triple plays in the same game.

The Red Sox fans went home happy as Boston, and southpaw Tom Bolton, won, 1-0, and the 34,113 in attendance can say they were witnesses to major league history, something that will be difficult to duplicate.

27. What pitcher won the first game in Texas Rangers history?

It happened on Sunday, April 16, 1972, in the second game in the franchise's history when right-hander Pete Broberg, before a crowd of 6,556 in Anaheim Stadium, beat the California Angels 5-1, giving up just five hits, to become the first pitcher to record a win in Texas Rangers history.

28. Who was the first pitcher in San Diego Padres history to steal a base?

On Sunday, May 13, 1979, right-hander Randy Jones, after reaching first on an error, stole second base in the bottom of the 3rd inning, against the New York Mets battery of Mike Scott and John Stearns, to be the first Padre pitcher to swipe a base in their history, as San Diego went on to a 5-4 victory.

29. Who was the first African-American player on the Boston Braves?

Centerfielder Sam "Jet" Jethroe, who went on to be the National League Rookie-of-the-Year, made his debut on April 18, 1950 and went 2-4 with a home run to lead the Braves, and Warren Spahn, to a 4-1 win over the New York Giants at the Polo Grounds.

30. What player hit the first home run in New York Mets history?

First baseman Gil Hodges, hit the first home run in New York Mets history, a solo shot into the left field stands of Busch Stadium, in the 4th inning off right-hander Larry Jackson, on Wednesday, April 11, 1962. The Mets, and Roger Craig, went on to lose that first game in their franchise history to the St. Louis Cardinals, 11-4.

31. What was the first American League team to hit four home runs after two were out?

Going into the top of the 4th inning out in Tiger Stadium on Saturday, July 18, 1998, Detroit held a 3-2 lead over the Boston Red Sox, but not for long. Right-hander Frank Castillo got the first out, then CF Damon Buford doubled to left field. Catcher Scott Hatteberg walked, 3B Mike Benjamin grounded out with the runners moving up. Then 2B Donnie Sadler hit his first major league home run, deep down the left field line, scoring Buford and Hatteberg. RF Darren Lewis followed with a solo home run to deep left field to make it 6-3. The DH, Midre Cummings, drew a walk bringing on right-hander Dean Crow to relieve Castillo. He gave little relief to the Tigers cause as SS Nomar Garciaparra greeted him with a two-run home run to deep left field, scoring Cummings to make it 8-3. Then big 1B Mo

Vaughn cracked Crow for a solo home run to deep right field to make it 9-3. LF Troy O'Leary, no doubt looking to continue the homer streak finally ended the inning by striking out swinging, but Boston went on to a 9-4 win. The Red Sox franchise became "Groundbreakers" by entering the record books as being the first team to go on a four-homer spree after two were gone in the inning.

32. What pitcher threw the first no-hit game in Minnesota Twins history?

On April 27, 1994 Minnesota Twins right-hander Scott Erickson struck out 5 and walked 4 while pitching the first no-hitter in the history of the Metrodome, and the first by a Twins pitcher in their 27-year history, defeating the Milwaukee Brewers, 6-0.

33. Who hit the first home run in Three Rivers Stadium in Pittsburgh?

Unfortunately for the Pirates the honor of hitting the first home run in their new stadium went to Cincinnati Reds third baseman Tony Perez, when on Thursday, July 16, 1970, he hit his 30th home run into the left field stands off Doc Ellis in the 5th inning, with one on and two outs, as the Reds, behind Clay Carroll, took the game 3-2.

Hometown hero Willie Stargell followed up in the 6th inning, with a two-out solo home run, his 17th, into the right field stands, off Gary Nolan for the Stadiums second, and the Pirates first one.

34. Who got the first base hit in Three Rivers Stadium in Pittsburgh?

Richie Hebner, the Pirates third baseman, got his team off to a good start by becoming the first player to get a base hit in the new stadium when he got an infield single off Cincinnati's Gary Nolan in the bottom of the first inning on July 16, 1970.

35. Who got the first base hit in Boston's Fenway Park?

Harry Meiggs Wolter, a reserve right fielder and first baseman of the New York Highlanders (Yankees) banged out the first base hit in the newly opened Fenway Park on April 20, 1912. It would be Wolter's one of eleven hits that season as the Red Sox went on to an 11-inning 7-6 win before a crowd of 27,000, handing the Yankees their 6th straight loss as right-handed spit-baller Thomas "Bucky" O'Brien combined with Charlie "Sea Lion" Hall to top southpaw Jim "Hippo" Vaughn.

36. Who hit the first home run in Fenway Park history?

Red Sox first baseman Hugh "Corns" Bradley was the first player to hit a home run in Fenway Park history when he hit a 3-run shot over the left field wall helping the Red Sox to a 7-6 win over the Philadelphia Athletics on April 26, 1912.

37. Who hit the first major league home run in Milwaukee County Stadium?

On April 14, 1953 centerfielder Bill Bruton of the Milwaukee Braves waited until the 10th inning to hit the first home run in Milwaukee's County Stadium, when he connected off the St. Louis Cardinals' right-hander Gerry Staley, giving the Braves a 3-2 victory. The ball just made the stands as it tipped off Cardinals right-fielder Enos "Country" Slaughter's glove and was initially ruled a double. It would be Bruton's only home run of the season.

38. Who were the first American League player and team to hit a home run in Milwaukee County Stadium?

On May 15th in the first game, of the twenty that would be played there in 1968-69 by the Chicago White Sox, Chuck Hinton, the California Angels right-fielder, took Sox southpaw Wilbur Wood deep to left field in the 9th inning with a one out solo home run that gave the Angels a 4-1 lead. White Sox first baseman Tommy McGraw would hit a solo home run in the bottom of the 9th for the second home run of the game in an Angels 4-2 win.

39. Who was the first New York Giants pitcher to throw a no-hitter?

On September 27, 1888 right-hander Ed "Cannonball" Crane became the first pitcher in New York Giants history to throw a no-hitter when he shut down the Senators without a hit, striking out five, on his way to a seven inning 3-0 victory at the Polo Grounds. Crane retired the last six batters in the game on ground balls back to the mound before darkness required the game to be called.

40. Who threw the first no-hitter in Arizona Diamondbacks history?

It was "Big Unit" time on May 18, 2004, at Turner Field, when the 6'10" southpaw, Randy Johnson, not only threw the 17th perfect game in major league history, but the first no-hitter in Diamondbacks history as he set down the Atlanta Braves, 2-0.

To add to that day's accomplishments Johnson was just the 5th pitcher in history to toss a no-hitter in both the American and National Leagues, and the oldest pitcher, at age 41, to ever throw a perfect game.

41. Who was the first player, and the team he played for, to get the first hit, and home run in the new Jacobs Field, in Cleveland?

On Monday, April 4, 1994, Jacobs Field opened to an enthusiastic crowd of 41, 459, but the thunder and prestige of the home team getting the first base hit, and the first home run, fell to their guests, the Seattle Mariners, and their leftfielder Eric Anthony who hit a two out solo home run down the deep right field line in the 3rd inning off right-hander Dennis "El Presidente" Martinez.

The Indians prevailed and went on to win, 4-3, with another "Eric", right-hander Eric Plunk getting the win in relief.

42. What pitcher threw the first no-hitter in Seattle Mariners franchise history?

This was his first, but not his last, when on June 2, 1990, southpaw Randy Johnson, the tallest pitcher in major league baseball at 6'10", walked 6, and struck out 8 on his way to a 2-0 no-hit win over the Detroit Tigers to become the first pitcher in Seattle Mariners history to pitch a no-hitter.

43. Who was the first Chicago Cubs player to hit a home run in an All-Star Game?

It came in the 5th inning of the 1936 All-Star Game, before 25,556 fans, at Braves Field, Boston when Chicago Cubs outfielder Augie Galan hit a solo home run off Detroit Tigers' right-hander Lynwood "Schoolboy" Rowe in the 5th inning of the game won by the National League 4-3.

44. Who was the first pitcher to win 20 games in a season in New York Mets history?

In the 1969 season right-hander Tom Seaver won 25 games, while losing 7, to become the first 20-game winner in Mets history.

45. Who was the first Minnesota Twin to reach 3,000 hits?

On September 16, 1993, twenty years from his rookie season, right-fielder Dave Winfield stroked his 3,000th base hit, a single off Oakland's Dennis Eckersley, to become the 19th player to reach that mark. Winfield will end up his career on October 1, 1995 with 3,110 hits.

46. In the first game played in Yankee Stadium history, who was credited with the first victory?

New York Yankee right-hander Bob Shawkey defeated Boston Red Sox right-hander Howard Ehmke, allowing just three hits in a 4-1 win on April 18, 1923, to be the first pitcher to win a game in Yankee Stadium history.

47. Who was the winning pitcher in the first game played in the New York Giants newly reconstructed Polo Grounds on June 28, 1911?

New York Giants right-hander, Christy Mathewson, ten weeks after a fire destroyed the old Polo Grounds, 6,000 fans show up for the inaugural game to see "Big Six" allow nine hits in defeating right-hander Al Mattern, and the Boston Rustlers, 3-0.

48. Who hit the first Yankee Stadium home run?

It happened on opening day, April 18, 1923, before a crowd of 74, 217 on a balmy spring day that saw the new Stadium's first home run hit off the bat of Babe Ruth in the 3rd inning off Boston Red Sox right-hander Howard Ehmke as the Yankees win, 4-1.

49. Who hit the first home run in Atlanta's Fulton County Stadium?

This player, who later made a name for himself as a manager after 18 years playing first and third base and catching is just what Atlanta Braves catcher Joe Torre did by hitting the first home run in the new Stadium, a solo shot in the bottom of the 5th inning off Pittsburgh Pirate southpaw Bob Veale, on April 12, 1966.

He came back in the bottom of the 13th inning to crush his second solo home run of the game, this off Pirate right-hander Don Schwall. It wasn't enough to overcome the two outs, two-run home run by Willie Stargell, off Braves right-hander Tony Cloninger, in the top of the 13th that saw the inaugural game go to the Pirates, 3-2.

50. Who was the first player to hit a home run in Cincinnati's Riverfront Stadium?

The Atlanta Braves were the Opening Day guests of the Cincinnati Reds on that Thursday, April 4, 1974 at Riverfront Stadium and their left-fielder Hank Aaron didn't wait long to invoke guest privileges as he came up in the top of the first inning, and after Reds right-hander Jack Billingham had walked RF Ralph Garr, and given up a single to 1B Mike Lum, and got 3B Darrell Evans to fly out, promptly blasted a Billingham pitch into the left-centerfield stands for a three-run home run, and claim the title of being the first player to hit a home run into the seats of Riverfront Stadium.

The Reds did have a successful opening day as they went on to defeat the Braves, 7-6, with a run in the bottom of the 11th inning on a wild pitch by Lee "Buzz" Capra, scoring Pete Rose.

51. Who was the first player to hit a home run in the new (2008) Washington Nationals Stadium?

On Sunday, March 30, 2008, 39,389 fans welcomed the Washington Nationals to their new ball park, appropriately called, Nationals Park. Their foe that day were the Atlanta Braves and although the Nationals got off to a fast start by putting up two runs in the bottom of the 1st inning it wasn't until the top of the 4th that Braves 3B Chipper Jones drove a solo home run, the first in Park history, deep into the centerfield stands, off southpaw Odalis Perez, to put the game at 2-1. It stayed there until each team picked up a 9th inning run, with Washington scoring the final winning run, with two outs, for a 3-2 victory.

52. What was the first, and only, franchise to go an entire season without hitting a home run?

As hard as this is to believe it did happen, not to the "hitless wonders" of 1919 (Chicago White Sox), but to the homer less Chicago White Stockings of 1877.

Their year wasn't that great with a 26-33 season record, finishing next to last, 15.5 games behind the 1st place Boston Red Stockings, but to play in 59 games, the season at that time, and not have somebody run around the bases unimpeded is certainly a record that won't be broken.

53. Who was the first Afro-American player to play for the New York Yankees?

The first Afro-American to play for the Yankees was Elston "Ellie" Howard who made his major league debut on April 14, 1955 as an out-fielder, playing in 75 games, and 9 as a catcher, and went on later to play some first base as well.

In 1963 he became the first Afro-American to win the American League MVP Award, as a catcher, with 28 home runs and 85 runs batted in to go along with his .287 average.

54. Who christened Busch Stadium in St. Louis with the first home run?

On Thursday, May 12, 1966, the St Louis Cardinals played their first game in their new ball park, Busch Stadium II, before a crowd of 46, 048, and had to go to the 12th inning before they came away with a 4-3 win over the Atlanta Braves.

In the top of the 6th inning Atlanta leftfielder Felipe Alou led off the inning by hitting a home run off Cardinals right-hander Ray Washburn, on a 1-2 pitch, to become the first player in the new stadium's history to homer.

Then in the top of the 8th inning, with the score tied at 2-2, Alou hit a 2-2 pitch for his second home run of the game, this coming off right-hander Tracy Stallard, giving him the Busch Stadium home run title, at 2, at least for the day.

55. Who became the first pitcher to start a game for the New York Mets on their Opening Day of Shea Stadium?

There were 50,312 fans who came to opening day of the Mets new home field, Shea Stadium, on Friday, April 17, 1964. Cuban right-hander Ed Bauta faced off for the Mets against Pittsburgh Pirates right-hander, and winning pitcher that day, Bob Friend, who also had the distinction of being the winning pitcher in the last game ever played by the New York Giants at the Polo Grounds on September 29, 1957. Pittsburgh took this opener, when they picked up a lone run in the top of the 9th on a single to center by Bill Mazeroski driving in Willie Stargell for the 4-3 win.

56. Who was the first player in the history of the Washington Senators franchise to hit 30 or more home runs in a single season?

In the long history of the Washington franchise it took until 1957 before leftfielder-first baseman Roy "Squirrel" Sievers led the American League in home runs with 42, and also in runs batted in with 114. Sievers would also come back to hit 39 home runs in 1958.

57. Who was the first player in Pittsburgh Pirates franchise history to hit 30 or more home runs in a season?

Hall of Fame leftfielder-first baseman Ralph Kiner, who made his major league debut with the Pittsburgh Pirates on April 16, 1946, and went on the lead the National League in home runs his rookie season with 23, continued his home run prowess in 1947, by again leading the league in home runs with 51 making him the first Pirate to hit the 30-home run mark.

In Kiner's ten-season, three-team, career he averaged 36.9 home runs per season.

58. Who was the first player in White Sox franchise history to hit 30 or more home runs in a single season?

"Beltin" Bill Melton, predominantly a third baseman, but with 82 games in his 10-year career in the outfield, had back-to-back years with the Chicago White Sox with over 30 home runs when he hit 33 in 1970, and came back in '71 to lead the league with 33.

59. What was the first American League franchise to sign and play an Afro-American player?

A 22-year old southpaw swinging centerfielder with the Newark Eagles by the name of Larry Doby was called up and signed as a free agent with the Cleveland Indians on July 2, 1947, and made his major league debut three days later on July 5th. He then became the first African-American player in the junior circuit. He was inducted into the Hall of Fame by the Veteran's Committee, as a player, in 1998.

60. Who was the first player in Florida Marlins history to have 200 or more hits in a single season?

Speedster Juan D'Vaughn Pierre made his big league debut on August 7, 2000 as a centerfielder with the Colorado Rockies. On November 16, 2002 he was sent to the Florida Marlins in a multi-player trade, and in his first season in Florida became their first player to exceed the 200-hit level for a season when he banged out 204 base hits. He led the National League in hits the following season with 221.

61. Who was the first player to hit 30 or more home runs in the long history of the Cincinnati Reds?

Right-fielder Ival "Goodie" Goodman made his major league debut with the Cincinnati Reds on April 16, 1935, leading the league in triples his first two years with 18 and 14. It wasn't until 1938 when his long ball began to reach the stands that he hit an even 30 home runs, to be the first Reds' player to hit 30 home runs in a season. He never came close to that figure again in his ten-year career.

62. Who was the first Boston Red Sox player to hit 30 or more home runs in a season?

Just put a "double x" alongside the year 1936 for that was the season that Hall of Famer Jimmie "Double X" Foxx put up numbers in the home run column that showed he hit 41 to become the first Red Sox player to reach the 30 plateau.

He had already proven he could hit a ton while with the Philadelphia Athletics when he had totals of 33, 37, 30, 58, 48, 44 and 36, leading the league in that category three times before coming to Boston from Philadelphia in a four player trade and cash on December 10, 1935. Foxx ended his 20-year career in the National League, with the Phillies on September 23, 1945 with his record showing him hitting over 30 home runs in 12 seasons and having 534 home runs in his career.

63. Who was the first player in Houston Astros history to hit 30 or more home runs in a season?

James Sherman Wynn, otherwise known as Jimmy Wynn, "The Toy Cannon," playing the outfield in his major league debut with the Houston Astros on July 10, 1963 had to wait until his fifth season in Houston to break out and become the first in Astros history to put 30 or more hits into fair territory for home runs when he had 37 round-trippers in the 1967 season.

64. Who was the first player in Detroit Tigers franchise history to hit 30 or more home runs in a season?

Hank Greenberg signed as a free agent in 1929 and came up to the Detroit Tigers making his major league debut, in one game, as a 19-year old pinch-hitter on September 14, 1930.

From there this first baseman's career took off as he came back to Detroit in 1933 and batted .301 with 12 home runs. In 1935, after hitting 26 home runs the year before he exploded for 36 round-trippers to lead the American League and become the first Tiger to reach the 30-home run seasonal mark in their history. "Hammerin' Hank" wasn't finished with home runs for he went on to hit 40, 58, 33, 41, and 44 before his 13-year career ended on September 18, 1947 with Pittsburgh, showing 331 career home runs.

65. Who was the first player in Philadelphia Phillies franchise history to hit 30 or more home runs?

It should come as no complete surprise to learn that right fielder Charles

Herbert "Chuck" Klein who made his major league debut with the Philadelphia Phillies on July 30, 1928, and followed up his freshman season by leading the National League in home runs, with 43 in his second season should not be the first in Phillies franchise history to pass the 30-home run mark.

In fact after hitting those 43 he continued on hitting 40 the next year and then led the National League with 31, 38.and 28, before completing the next three seasons with over 20 home runs.

The left-handed hitting power hitter continued on his streak of 20 or more home runs from 1929 through 1936.

Klein ended his 17-year career with the Phillies, on June 11, 1944, with exactly 300 home runs to have the Veteran's Committee put him into the Hall of Fame in 1980.

66. Who was the first player in Braves franchise history (Boston, Milwaukee, and Atlanta) to hit 30 or more home runs in a single season?

When right-fielder Wally Berger made his major league debut with the Boston Braves on April 15, 1930 he never realized he would not only be the first player in Boston Braves history to hit 30 or more home runs, nor did he think he would be the first rookie to hit as many as 38 home runs in a season, but he did both.

67. Who was the first player to come to bat in Yankee Stadium when it originally opened on April 19, 1923?

Paradoxically, it was Wilson "Chick" Fewster, who had been a Yankee infielder up until July 23, 1922 when he and three others were traded along with cash for 3B "Jumping Joe" Dugan and OF Elmer Smith to the Boston Red Sox, who was the leadoff batter and played shortstop for the visiting Boston Red Sox on that opening day.

68. Who was the first player to hit for the cycle in Chase Field, home of the Arizona Diamondbacks in Phoenix?

On Monday, September 1, 2008, Arizona shortstop Stephen Drew, in a game against the St. Louis Cardinals, went 5 for 5, with 12 total bases, to become the first player to hit for the cycle in Chase Field.

69. What team was the first to commit six errors in a single World Series game?

The Chicago White Sox, on that Saturday afternoon of October 16th, out in the West Side Grounds, before 23,257 Windy City fans, were certainly trying to win that 6th game of the 1906 World Series against their cross town rivals the Chicago Cubs, but their fielding abilities certainly didn't show it.

"Big Ed" Walsh saw he and his 2B Frank Isbell make errors in the 1st inning, SS George Davis commit one in the 3rd, 3B George Rohe have miscues in the 4th and 6th innings, and Isbell come back with his second error of the game and the 6th as a team.

Nonetheless Walsh prevailed as the Pale Hose took the game 8-6 and went on to take the series 4-2, and become World Champions.

70. What Tampa Bay Rays player drove in the franchise's very first winning run in an American League Championship Series?

On Saturday, October 11, 2008, going into the bottom of the 11th inning at Tropicana Field, with the Boston Red Sox tied with the Tampa Bay Rays at 8-8, Mike Timlin came on to relieve Jonathon Papelbon for Boston. He walked Dioner Navarro, and rookie speedster Fernando Perez came in to run for him.

Then Ben Zobrist walked, and on an infield out both runners moved up. Akinori Iwamura was intentionally walked loading the bases for B.J. Upton who lifted a sacrifice fly to J.D. Drew in right field, scoring Perez with the winning run and giving Tampa Bay their first ALCS victory, 9-8.

22-year old rookie southpaw David Price, who made his major league debut less than a month earlier, on September 14th, received the win.

71. Who was the first, and only, player to play in the very first game for two different teams in the same league in the same city?

Cuban right-hander Diego Segui made his debut on April 12, 1962 with the Kansas City Athletics, spent the 1966 season with Washington before going back to Kansas City in 1967, and moving with the Athletics to Oakland for the 1970 season. On October 15, 1968 he was drafted by the newly formed Seattle Pilots, from Oakland, as the 14th pick in the 1968 expansion draft.

The expansion Pilots were created in December 1967 as part of an agreement between the American League and Missouri politicians that allowed Charlie Finley's Athletics to move to Oakland and allow the establishment of the Kansas City Royals in their place.

Diego Segui appeared in the Pilots first game, against the California Angels, down in Anaheim Stadium, before a crowd of 11,390, on April 8, 1969. He came on in relief of Marty Pattin in the 6th inning and faced 13 batters, allowing two hits, one earned run, walked two, and struck out 4 until walking Roger Repoz to start the 9th. Right-hander Jack "Chief" Aker came on to replace him. The Pilots won their first game, 4-3, and Marty Pattin was the winning pitcher.

The Pilots franchise lasted for only one year, 1969, playing in what one must consider an appropriate name for their ball park, especially in the Pilots' case, Sicks Stadium.

The franchise was underfunded in the executive area, and untalented on the field, showing a record of 64-98 (.395).

The franchise dissolved in March of 1970 and was moved to Milwaukee where it played under the name "Brewers" Segui bounced around from the Brewers to Oakland to the Cardinals to the Red Sox to the Padres, and was finally purchased from San Diego by the Seattle Mariners on October 22, 1976, and the 40-year old local favorite, who made the first appearance for the Seattle Pilots in 1969, came full circle on April 6, 1977, when before his home crowd of 57,762, at the Seattle Kingdome, Segui started against the California Angels southpaw, Frank Tanana, and lasted just 3.2 innings giving up five hits, six runs, four earned, three walks, struck out 3 in facing 22 batters, before right-hander John Montague came on to finish up the game with Tanana throwing a nine-hit, 7-0 shutout.

Segui made his final major league appearance, after a 0-7 record with the Seattle Mariners, on September 24, 1977. The first, and only, player to play in the very first game for two franchises (teams) in the same league in the same city.

72. What was the first American League franchise to produce both back-to-back Most Valuable Player Award winners, and Cy Young Award winners in the same years?

Take yourself back to 1981 when Roland "Rollie" Fingers, the right-handed reliever, of the Milwaukee Brewers won the Cy Young Award by leading the American League in saves with 28, along with his 1.04 Era., completing 41 games, and having a 6-3 record over 78 innings. The MVP voters thought that strong enough reason to make him the 1981 MVP as well.

The following year, 1982, Milwaukee right-hander Pete Vuckovich won the Cy Young Award with an 18-6, 3.34 Era. record, and leading the American League with a .750 winning percentage.

His teammate, shortstop Robin Yount, not only won the Most Valuable Player Award with a .331 batting average, a league leading 46 doubles, and 210 base hits, and also had 29 home runs and 114 runs batted in as well, winning a place on the All-Star team and a Gold Glove Award as well.

There you have it, two MVP Awards, two Cy Young Awards, in consecutive years by one franchise. That's a franchise first.

73. What expansion team was the first to have a 13-game winner in its initial year?

Gene Brabender, the big right-hander, who after three years with the Baltimore Orioles, was traded to the newly formed expansion Seattle Pilots on March 31, 1969, and paid early dividends as he became the first pitcher to win 13 games with an expansion club when he went 13-14, with a 4.36 Era. for the last place 1969 Seattle Pilots.

74. Who threw the first shutout in Seattle Pilots' franchise history?

As the Pilots opened up their first, and only, major league season, on Friday, April 11, 1969, 14,993 fans at Seattle's Sick's Stadium see right-hander Gary Bell pitch a 9-hit shutout, striking out 6, and allowing 4 walks to the visiting Chicago White Sox.

75. Who hit the first World Series home run in Tampa Bay Rays franchise history?

Game One of the 104th World Series, was played on October 22, 2008, at Tropicana Field, St. Petersburg, Florida, between the Tampa Bay Rays and the Philadelphia Phillies.

In the bottom of the 4th inning leftfielder Carl "The Perfect Storm" Crawford hit a solo home run off Phillies southpaw Colebert "Cole" Hamels which was not only the Rays first World Series home run, but their first run batted in the history of the franchise.

Philadelphia took the first game 3-2 and the World Series in five games, for their second World Championship in their 125-year history.

76. Who had the first base hit in Tampa Bay World Series history?

Second baseman Akinori Iwamura led off the first inning of Game One of the 2008 World Series, on October 22nd, by beating out a base hit to first baseman Ryan Howard of Philadelphia.

77. Who was the first San Francisco Giants pitcher to lead the National League in strikeouts?

Choosing your answer carefully you will find that right-hander Tim Lincecum led the National League in strikeouts with 265 in 2008.

Hopefully you were not fooled by the fact that Christy Mathewson, in 1903-05; Rube Marquard in 1911; Carl Hubbell in 1937; and Bill Voiselle in 1944, all led the National League in strikeouts when the Giants called New York home.

78. What team was the first to hit five home runs in one inning?

It happened on Tuesday, June 6, 1939, at the Polo Grounds, before an afternoon crowd of 7,405. After the New York Giants had knocked south-paw Johnny Vander Meer out after retiring just two batters in the 1st inning, he was followed by right-hander Ray "Peaches" Davis. LF Jo-Jo "The Gause Ghost" Moore hit a solo home run off Davis in the 2nd inning, and RF Mel Ott hit a 3-run blast off Davis in the 3rd. Going into the 4th inning the Giants were ahead 6-0 and then they really unloaded upon Cincinnati pitching in the 4th inning, after two were out.

Catcher Harry Danning started off the home run parade with a home run off right-hander Davis, RF Mel Ott singled, 1B Zeke Bonura walked, and CF Frank Demaree then cleared the bases when he blasted a three- run home run.

In came right-hander Wes Livengood in relief of Davis. He walked 3B Tony Lazzeri, and 2B Burgess "Whitey" Whitehead followed with a two-run home run, one of his two all season. Up came RHP Manny "Gyp" Salvo who proceeded to hit an inside-the-park home run into the deep confines of the spacious Polo Grounds outfield for his only career home run.

Next up, for the second time in the inning, was leadoff hitter LF Jo-Jo Moore, who deposited one of Wes Livengood's pitches deep into the upper deck of the right field stands for his second four-bagger of the game, and the Giants 5th home run of the inning, all after two outs, as the Giants become the first team to blast five homers in one inning.

Needless to say Wes wasn't "Livengood" after this inning, and the Giants rolled to a 17-3 win over the Reds.

79. Who did the New York Giants play host to on the opening of their new stadium, the Polo Grounds, on April 22, 1891?

It was not only opening day for the New York Giants' new stadium, the Polo Grounds, located at 157th Street and 8th Avenue, but Opening Day of the 1891 National League season.

The Giants played host to the Boston Beaneaters, before a crowd of 17,355, and lost a heartbreaker in the 9th inning, 4-3 on an error by center-fielder George Gore. This site would be the home of the Giants from this day on till 1957 when the team moved to San Francisco and would then be the home of the New York Mets in 1962-63.

80. What were the first teams involved in the first-ever televised Major League game?

We have to go back to August 26, 1939 when the first televised Major League game was broadcast on station, W2XBS that was later to become WNBC-TV.

It was a doubleheader played in Ebbets Field, Brooklyn, between the Brooklyn Dodgers and the Cincinnati Reds with the "voice of the Dodgers" Red Barber as the announcer.

The coverage was a far cry from today's standards with one stationary camera placed down the third base line to pick up the infield plays, and a second stationary camera placed high up over home plate allowing for a broad view of the entire field.

Obviously the experiment of televising games became a huge success, and the concern about hurting attendance has long since been dismissed.

In the first game of the doubleheader, Cincinnati won 5-2, with the Dodgers coming back to capture the nightcap, 6-1.

81. What were the teams involved in the first three-game pennant playoff in Major League history?

Take yourself back to the 1946 season when after 154 regular season games the St. Louis Cardinals and the Brooklyn Dodgers were locked evenly in first place with a 96-58 record.

The National League had set up a best-of-three format to determine the pennant winner. The first game was played on October 1, 1946 at Sportsman's Park, St. Louis, before 26, 012 fans, with the Redbirds winning 4-2, with Howie Pollet besting Ralph Branca, and Cardinal rookie catcher Joe Garagiola having three hits and driving in two runs.

The second game, played on October 3rd in Ebbets Field, Brooklyn, before a crowd of 31,437 Flatbush fans, went to St. Louis as well, as right-hander Murry Dickson gave up five hits in 8.1 innings, and Harry Brecheen finished it off for the save, defeating southpaw Joe Hatten, 8-4, with Enos "Country" Slaughter's two-run triple a big blow.

The Cardinals went on to defeat the Red Sox in that famous Game 7, with Harry Brecheen recording his third series victory.

82. Who was the first player to hit a home run out of Dodger Stadium?

The Pittsburgh Pirates, and their leftfielder Willie "Pops" Stargell, can take credit for this one when, on August 5, 1969, he hit his 18th home run of the season, a solo shot in the 7th inning, out of the right field section of Dodger Stadium, off Dodgers' right-hander Alan Foster, helping the Pirates to an 11-3 win.

83. What was the first American League team, and the players involved, to hit four consecutive home runs in an inning?

This batting barrage happened on July 31, 1963, when the Cleveland Indians, at home against the Los Angeles Angels, in Cleveland Stadium, in the second game of a doubleheader, did what the Milwaukee Braves had done just two years earlier.

It began with two outs in the bottom of the 6th inning against the newly acquired right-hander from Detroit, Paul Foytack. 2B Woodie Held started it off with his home run into the left field stands, and he was followed by RHP Pedro Ramos who also deposited one into the left field stands, his second of the game, having hit one off right-hander Eli Grba in the 3rd inning into the right field seats.

Next up was LF Tito Francona who hit the third straight home run, this into the right field stands, and SS Larry Brown finished it off with the fourth consecutive four-bagger, this to left field off the battered Foytack.

The Cleveland Indians made history that day, but only 7,288 paying customers bore witness to it.

84. What team hit the first home run in National League history?

The Chicago White Stockings, who became the Cubs, had a second baseman, Ross Barnes, who on May 2, 1876, hit the first home run in National League history. It was an inside-the-park shot off Cincinnati Red Legs right-hander William "Cherokee" Fisher. It was the slightly built, right-handed hitter's only home run that year, and the first of two in his four-year major league career.

85. What major league team was the first to shutout out the opposition?

The first major league shutout happened in the first game played by the Chicago White Stockings (Cubs), on April 25, 1876, when right-hander Al Spalding, who was also their manager, shut out the Louisville Grays 4-0, in the Louisville Baseball Park.

86. What was the first franchise to win a National League pennant?

It started on February 2, 1876 with the creation of the National League, and later the major leagues as it is known today. The Chicago White Stockings, the oldest continuous franchise in major league baseball, which through the years has also been known as the Colts, Orphans, and now the Cubs, was then owned by William Hulbert, and managed by Albert Spalding. The team won the first National League pennant by defeating the Hartford Dark Blues and the St. Louis Brown Stockings (Browns) by six games, with a 52-14, .788 record to become the first franchise to capture the National League flag.

87. Who was the first player to hit a home run over the centerfield wall in the new Memorial Stadium in Baltimore?

It comes as no surprise to learn that the big, 6'4 ½", 230 pound southpaw swinging left fielder John "Boog" Powell, blasted a solo home run off equally large, 6'6", 200 pound, Red Sox right-hander Don Schwall deep over the centerfield wall of Memorial Stadium, in the 7th inning of the second game of a doubleheader on June 22, 1962, as the Orioles defeated the Red Sox, with two runs in the bottom of the 9th, 4-3.

88. What was the first franchise to host a World Series game on artificial grass?

When Game One of the 1970 World Series opened on October 10th at Riverfront Stadium, the Cincinnati Reds were the host to the American

League champion Baltimore Orioles in the first World Series game played on artificial grass, and the first at Riverfront Stadium.

First baseman "Boog" Powell's two-run home run, and solo shots by catcher Elrod "Ellie" Hendricks and 3B Brooks Robinson brought the Orioles back from three runs down to a 4-3 victory over right-hander Gary Nolan, spoiling Cincinnati's initial fall classic game. Baltimore continued the punishment by going on and taking the series in five games.

89. Who hit the first home run for the California Angels in their first regular season game played in Anaheim Stadium?

Leftfielder Frederic "Rick" Reichardt wasted no time in christening the Angels home field on Tuesday, April 19, 1966, when in the 2nd inning, with one out, he hit a solo home run into deep centerfield off Chicago White Sox southpaw Tommy John in their opening day, 3-1 loss.

90. Who was the first player to play over 23 seasons with the same franchise?

Brooks Robinson, the Hall of Fame third baseman with the Baltimore Orioles, played his entire 23-plus year career with the Orioles.

91. What two teams played in the first night game in American League history?

On May 16, 1939 the Philadelphia Athletics hosted the Cleveland Indians down in Shibe Park, Philadelphia in the first night game played by American League teams.

92. What was the first team to have players from ten different countries on their roster?

That international group of players that represented ten different nations was on the 2006 Los Angeles Dodgers. They came from the United States, Canada, Panama, Cuba, Dominican Republic, Mexico, Japan, Venezuela, South Korea, and Taiwan. One can also throw in a player from the U.S. Commonwealth of Puerto Rico on that squad.

93. Who was credited with the first home run hit in a night game in Wrigley Field?

After a New York Mets, Chicago Cubs game was called, after four innings, because of rain at Wrigley Field, on August 8, 1988, and all the results and statistics were cancelled, the game was rescheduled and played the following night, on Tuesday, August 9th.

It was then that New York Mets centerfielder Lenny Dykstra, before a crowd of 36,399, came up in the top of the 5th inning, with 2B Wally Backman on first and with one out, crushed a two-run home run into the right field seats off right-hander Mike Bielecki.

It was the first home run with the lights on in Wrigley Field history.

94. Who was the first Chicago Cubs player to hit a home run in a night game at Wrigley Field?

The Cubs fans had to wait two weeks, till August 22, 1988, before one of their own, catcher Damon Berryhill, came up in the bottom of the 2nd inning and found LF Rafael Palmeiro on first base via a single.

Berryhill hit a 0-1 pitch by Houston right-hander Mike Scott into the left field seats, driving in Palmeiro with the game's first run and giving the 30, 417 Cubs fans watching something to tell their children about as they witnessed the first night game home run hit by a Cubbie in Wrigley Field history.

The rest of the evening didn't turn out that well for Cubs fans as the Astros won with three runs in the top of the 10th, 9-7.

95. Who was the first player to hit a grand slam home run in New York Mets history?

That honor went to Roderick "Hot Rod" Kanehl, a big fan favorite because of his hustle, who patrolled all three outfield positions, and all four infield positions for the Mets from 1962-64. Batting right-handed Kanehl hit that first grand slam in team history on July 6, 1962 into the left field stands of the Polo Grounds off St. Louis Cardinals southpaw Bobby Shantz in the 8th inning, driving in SS Elio Chacon, RF Joe Christopher, and CF Jim Hickman as the Mets went on to beat the Cardinals, 10-3, behind right-hander Roger Craig, and before 14,515 new fans.

96. Who hit the first home run in the debut of Yankee Stadium in 1923?

The first home run hit in Yankee Stadium history happened in the 3rd inning, on April 18, 1923, when Babe Ruth hit a 3-run home run off Boston Red Sox right-hander Howard Ehmke, as the Yankees went on to a 4-1 win before an opening day crowd of 74,217.

97. Who made the first error in Yankee Stadium history?

The same opening day crowd of 74,217 that saw Babe Ruth hit the first home run in Yankee Stadium history, on April 18, 1923, saw him make the first error as well as he dropped a fly ball out in right field in the 5th inning.

98. Who got the first base hit in Yankee Stadium history?

The first base hit in Yankee Stadium history happened early on opening day, August 18, 1923, when Boston Red Sox first baseman "Tioga George" Burns singled off right-hander Bob Shawkey in the 2nd inning.

99. Who was the first Yankee player to get a base hit in Yankee Stadium history?

The first Yankee to get a base hit in Yankee Stadium history was second baseman Aaron Ward when he singled in the 3rd inning off Red Sox right-hander Howard Ehmke.

100. Who was the first Cincinnati Reds player to receive the Most Valuable Player Award in an All-Star Game?

The California Angels played host to the 1967 All-Star Game. The National League, on Dick Allen's 2nd inning solo home run, had the lead until Brooks Robinson tied the game with his solo home run in the 6th inning.

The game stayed tied, while 30 batters were going down on strikes, until Cincinnati's 3B Tony Perez won the longest All-Star Game in history with his dramatic 15th inning solo home run off Kansas City Athletics right-hander, Jim "Catfish" Hunter.

101. Who was the first New York Yankee pitcher to win a World Series game in Yankee Stadium?

It was in the 5th game of the 1923 World Series, on October 14th, that right-hander Leslie "Bullet Joe" Bush set down the New York Giants, on three hits, all by Emil "Irish" Meusel, to win 8-1, and record the first World Series win by a Yankee pitcher in Yankee Stadium.

102. What the team gave the New York Yankees their first loss in Yankee Stadium?

The Yankees' first loss at Yankee Stadium was on Sunday, April 22, 1923 when Washington Senators righthander Walter "The Big Train" Johnson went 7.1 innings, and southpaw George Mogridge finished up, to defeat Bob Shawkey 4-3.

103. What was the first, and only, major league team to have a 26-game winning streak?

It started on Thursday, September 7, 1916 at the Polo Grounds when New York Giants southpaw Ferdinand "Ferdie" Schupp started the Giants on their historic winning streak as he stopped the Brooklyn Robins, 4-1.

After that the Polo Grounders continued to roll along winning game after game for the next twelve games, before they met up with the Pittsburgh Pirates in a doubleheader on Monday afternoon, September 18th. Ferdie Schupp came up big again in the first game shutting out the Pirates 2-0.

In the 5th inning of the second game Benny Kauff, the diminutive centerfielder, belted an inside-the-park home run into the vast expanse of the Polo Grounds for a 1-0 Giant lead. Holding that lead going into the top of the 9th inning Pirate Hall of Famer, shortstop Honus Wagner, lifted a sacrifice fly driving in the tying run. The skies then open up and the game is called after nine innings, 1-1. Giant manager John McGraw is beside himself, but the tie stands and the streak remains unbroken.

On September 25th the Giants swept a doubleheader 1-0, and 6-2, over the St. Louis Cardinals. That was their 21st straight win which broke the previous winning streak of 20 established by the Providence Grays in 1884.

The streak continued from there with the Giants on the winning side until Game 27, on September 30th, the second game of a doubleheader, the 9th during their winning streak, when a series of miscues and some long balls by the Boston Braves ended the unprecedented winning streak at 26, all at home, as the Boston Braves George "Lefty" Tyler handed the Giants an 8-3 loss.

Now prior to the 26-game winning streak the Giants had started a long winning streak earlier, on May 9th, after defeating the Pittsburgh Pirates 13-5, and it went for 17 consecutive wins until the Philadelphia Phillies put an end to it by beating the "men of McGraw" 5-1 on May 30th.

Now with those two long winning streaks the Giants ended up in 4th place, with an 86-66 record, seven games behind the Brooklyn Robins.

Some interesting sidelights to this streak is that during it the Giants pitchers threw 23 complete games, 10 of them shutouts, winning seven games by one-run, and played 15 errorless games, and turned 15 double plays.

In the early part of their winning streak they played an exhibition game against the New York Yankees, and were successful there as well, winning 4-2, although that game was not part of their consecutive winning record.

In deference to Windy City fans they will, no doubt, be looking to their Cubbies who had 21 straight winning games from September 4th to the 29th, 1935; a tip of the runner-up cap to them.

104. What was the first major league franchise to host and play a night game?

Minor League night games had been played for some time before they came to the Major Leagues. Due to the prompting of Larry MacPhail, the general manager of the Cincinnati Reds, the National League agreed to offer their eight teams the opportunity to each play seven night games in 1935. The Cincinnati Reds jumped at the chance and installed lights in Crosley Field.

After a day of rain the first night game was played on Friday, May 24, 1935, before a crowd of 20,422, and the opposition was the Philadelphia Phillies.

The lights of Crosley Field came on when President Franklin Roosevelt ceremoniously pushed a button in the White House, and the game was about to begin.

The Reds sent right-hander Paul Derringer against Philadelphia's right-hander Joe Bowman. The first batter to come up to the plate that night was Phillies second baseman Lou Chiozza.

The Reds scored a run in the bottom of the 1st inning on SS Billy Myers double and RF Ival Goodman's single. They picked up another run in the 4th on 1B Billy Sullivan's single and catcher Gilly Campbell driving him in. The top of the 5th inning the Phillies picked up their sole run when catcher Al Todd was driven in by his battery mate, Joe Bowman.

The final line score showed Cincinnati with two runs and four hits, and the Phillies with one run on six hits as Derringer picked up the first night game win, and Joe Bowman the loss.

Today the majority of games are played at night, but it all started back on that May 24th evening.

105. What team was the first to apply a player's name, as well as his number, to the back of their uniforms?

The Chicago White Sox, in 1960, broke new ground with the addition of the player's name as well as his number placed on the back of the uniform. Many teams eventually followed this trend, with a few still declining to affix names. As of this writing the San Francisco Giants, New York Yankees, and the Boston Red Sox refrain from showing players' names.

106. What was the first team to have three players hit consecutive home runs in the same inning?

One would have to go back to a game played on May 10, 1894 when the St Louis Cardinals' (known as the Browns that year) centerfielder Frank Shugart, third baseman George "Doggie" Miller, and catcher Henry "Heinie" Peitz hit consecutive home runs in the 7th inning against the Cincinnati Reds, but to no avail, as St. Louis lost 16-9.

107. What was first visiting team to play a night game in Yankee Stadium?

The first night game played in the Yankee Stadium occurred on Tuesday, May 28, 1946, before a crowd of 49,917, when right-hander Emil "Dutch" Leonard of the Washington Senators, defeated right-hander Clarence "Cuddles" Marshall and the Yankees 2-1.

108. Who hit the first World Series home run in Yankee Stadium history?

New York Giants outfielder, Charles Dillon "Casey" Stengel, decided the first game of the 1923 World Series, on October 10th, when the lefty swinging Stengel unloaded an inside-the-park home run in the 9th inning off "Bullet Joe" Bush for a 5-4 Giant win.

109. What was the first franchise to have two pitchers strike out over 300 batters in the same season?

It is not that surprising, when two strikeout pitchers take the mound for the same team in the same season, that opponents' bats will begin to wave and create a big breeze.

That is what happened in the 2002 season for the Arizona Diamondbacks when right-hander Curt Shilling struck out 316 batters, and his teammate, southpaw Randy "Big Unit" Johnson topped that with 334 strikeouts. Arizona is the first franchise in major league history to have two pitchers with 300 strikeouts in the same season.

110. What was the first franchise, in regular season history, to fire its manager after August 1ˢᵗ with his team in playoff position?

As unusual as it seems it happened on September 15, 2008 when Milwaukee Brewers manager Ned Yost, with the Brewers having an 83 and 67 record, had lost seven of their last eight games to fall back into a tie with the Phillies for the National League wild card lead, decided they had enough, and fired Yost.

111. Who was the first player to hit a home run completely out of Baltimore's Memorial Stadium?

We had previously mentioned Boog Powell being the first to hit a home run over the centerfield wall in Memorial Stadium, but this is a bit different.

On May 8, 1966, when Frank Robinson, the Orioles right-fielder, hit a pitch off Cleveland right-hander Luis Tiant that traveled 451 feet, cleared the stands and completely left Memorial Stadium, it was a first.

The Cuban right-hander will remember it well, for it broke his 27-inning scoreless streak, and cost him the game, 8-3.

112. Who hit the first inside-the-park home run in the new Yankee Stadium?

In the newly rebuilt Yankee Stadium there were a lot of home runs hit in the first few weeks, but no one had hit one with the ball staying within the confines of the field.

Not until Friday, May 15, 2009, when the Yankees played host to the Minnesota Twins.

The story has a very tender side to it. Earlier on that day Yankee centerfielder Brett Gardner visited Children's Hospital in New York and visited a young girl, whom he didn't personally know, who was stricken with a deadly disease. In thankfulness for the visit the young girl gave Gardner a bracelet and told him if he kept it he would hit a home run.

Gardner accepted the gift and returned to the Stadium for that evening's game. Not knowing if he was going to play in the game that evening he was a spectator in the dugout until the 4ᵗʰ inning when Johnny Damon was ejected after an umpire dispute.

Gardner took his place and when he came to the plate with two out in the bottom of the 7ᵗʰ inning he was facing reliever Jesse Crain. He hit a 0-2 pitch down the left field line that took a funny bounce and skipped past leftfielder Denard Span and bounced around in the corner. Gardner, a speedster, seeing the ball bounce and ricochet around Span, put himself in high gear and raced around the bases and slid home safely prior to the throw to the plate.

This young girl's prophecy came true for Gardner for he had hit a home run, and not only that, but hit the first inside-the park home run in the new Yankee Stadium.

113. What was the first team to have 20 members inducted into the Cooperstown Hall of Fame?

The first team to have twenty members inducted into the Cooperstown Hall of Fame was the New York/San Francisco Giants. They have 23 or 24, depending on who wants to argue the validity of a particular player. The list follows:

Dave Bancroft	Christy Mathewson
Roger Bresnahan	Willie Mays
Orlando Cepeda	Willie McCovey
George Davis	Joe "Iron Man" McGinnity
Frankie Frisch	John McGraw
Carl Hubbell	Johnny Mize
Monte Irvin	Mel Ott
Travis Jackson	Gaylord Perry
George Kelly	Amos Rusie
Freddie Lindstrom	Bill Terry
Juan Marichal	Hoyt Wilhelm
Rube Marquard	Ross Youngs

114. What was the first team in major league history to hit ten home runs in a single nine-inning game?

The thunder of booming bats was never more apparent than on Monday, September 14, 1987 at Exhibition Stadium, when before a crowd of 27,446; the Toronto Blue Jays crushed six Baltimore Orioles pitchers for a major league record ten home runs in an 18-3 rout.

Leading the parade of four baggers was Blue Jay catcher Ernie Whitt who had three, followed by 3B Rance Mulliniks and LF George Bell with two each, and CF Lloyd Moseby, and his replacement in centerfield, Rob Ducey, and DH Fred "Crime Dog" McGriff all having one.

This game also saw the consecutive innings streak of Cal Ripken end at 8,243 when he was removed for pinch-runner, Ron Washington, in the 8th inning.

115. What was the first team to take their radio announcer out of his booth and activate him to their pitching staff?

It could only happen to the hapless St. Louis Browns whose winning percentage (.383) in 1947 was almost as low as their attendance. To bolster that attendance on the season's last day, Sunday, September 28, 1947, and in a desperate attempt to entice fans to come to Sportsman's Park, the Browns activated their popular radio announcer, 36-year old Dizzy Dean to be their starting pitcher.

With 15,910 fans on hand Dizzy took the mound against the Chicago White Sox southpaw Eddie Lopat, and allowed only 3 hits, and walked one, in his scoreless four innings of work, and added a clean single in his only time at bat.

A pulled muscle in his leg forced Dizzy to leave the game, replaced by right-hander Glen Moulder, and his Hall of Fame career came to a close that day.

The game remained scoreless until the 9th inning when the White Sox scored 5 runs in the top of the 9th, and the Brownies came back with two of their own, but it was too little, too late and St. Louis went down to their 95th loss, 5-2, ending their season in 8th place, 38 games behind the 1st place Yankees.

The Browns drew just 320,000 fans that season, about half of what they drew in 1946, with a low point coming on September 25th when a very sparse crowd of 315 showed up to see them lose to Cleveland, 4-3.

116. What was the first American League team to lose three straight World Series?

Unfortunately for Motor City fans their beloved Detroit Tigers, under manager Hughie Jennings, were swept by the Chicago Cubs in the 1907 World Series, lost again to the Cubs in five games in the 1908 World Series, and made it three straight failures in 1909, when they bowed to the Pittsburgh Pirates in seven games.

117. What was the first major league team to use a public address announcer?

This innovation occurred on Sunday, August 25, 1929 at the Polo Grounds in New York when the New York Giants became the first major league team in history to use a public address announcer in its game with the Pittsburgh Pirates.

It was obviously set up quite differently than one might imagine by today's standards. The home plate umpire, Cy Rigler, was wired for sound wearing a microphone and metal-plated shoes as he stood on a metal sheet. His calls were broadcast over speakers for the 20,000 fans' edification and enjoyment. These things have to start sometime, somewhere, and this was the place, and time.

Giant fans left happily as their heroes came away with a 10-5 win as right-hander Larry Benton defeated southpaw Jesse "The Silver Fox" Petty.

118. Who was the first woman public address announcer for a major league team?

It seems the Giants had the breakthrough on public address announcers, no matter the gender.

It all came to pass in 1993 when the San Francisco Giants held an open audition and hired Sherry Davis to be their first female public address announcer at Candlestick Park. She remained in that position until 2000 when a local morning radio talk show host, Renal Brooks-Moon, replaced Sherry.

119. What was the first team to host a World Series game played in a domed stadium?

The first indoor World Series game took place in the Minnesota Metrodome on October 17, 1987, when the Minnesota Twins hosted the St. Louis Cardinals in Game 1, winning 10-1, in a seven game series that was won by the Twins.

120. Who hit the first inside-the-park home run in Shea Stadium history?

Many Pittsburgh fans will happily remember that Pirate slugger Willie Stargell is credited with hitting the first home run, and also getting the first base hit, in Shea Stadium history, but few will recall that it was Met second baseman, Ron Hunt, who had just 39 home runs in his entire twelve-year career that hit the first inside-the-park home run.

It came in the 8th inning, with two outs, and the bases empty, on June 5, 1966, with the Mets behind 15-2, that future Hall of Famer southpaw Sandy Koufax, of the Los Angeles Dodgers, served up the fat pitch to Hunt in an eventual 16-3 rout.

121. What team was the first to win a pennant on a wild pitch?

Nothing could be more heartbreaking than to throw a wild pitch which, not only cost you the game, but the American League pennant as well.

It happened on October 10, 1904, on the final day of the season, when the Boston Red Sox came down to Hilltop Park, with the American League pennant on the line, to play the New York Highlanders (Yankees) in a doubleheader before 30,000 excited fans.

With the score tied 2-2 in the top of the 9th inning, and Red Sox catcher Lou Criger on third base, right-hander "Happy Jack" Chesbro, who had won a league-leading 41 games that season, uncorked one of his famous spitballs that sailed for a wild pitch allowing Criger to score the go-ahead run, 3-2.

That was all the edge "Big Bill" Dinneen needed as he shut down the Highlanders in the bottom of the 9th for his 23rd win, and his 37th consecutive complete game, setting an American League record, but more importantly clinching the pennant for Boston.

New York won the second game as Red Sox right-hander George "Sassafras" Winter took a 1-0 loss, but too late, as Boston had captured the flag by 1 ½ games.

122. What team was the first to draw one million fans for the season?

The New York Yankees were the first team to draw one million fans when they had 1,289,422 fans come through the turnstiles during their 1920 season at the Polo Grounds.

123. What was the first team to have over 100 batters come to the plate in a single game?

The parade of batters to home plate occurred in a night game at Shea Stadium on Wednesday, September 11, 1974, when the New York Mets played host to the St. Louis Cardinals before a crowd of 13,460.

The game went a major league record of 25 innings, for a game under the lights, and didn't end until 3:13 am after seven hours and four minutes of playing time when CF Bake McBride scored with the winning run in the top of the 25th inning for a 4-3 St. Louis victory.

103 Mets stepped to the plate during the game while 99 Cardinals came to bat. Right-hander Sonny Siebert, the seventh Cardinal pitcher, picked up the win, while right-hander Hank Webb took the loss.

124. What team was the first to have three of its players play together at the same time, each of them playing only for this team throughout their 20 year career?

This might take a bit of hard thinking, and being a resident of the Windy City, might be a help. There were three players with the Chicago White Sox that during their twenty-year careers with the Pale Hose played together on the same team at the same time, from 1930-33.

Luke Appling, their Hall of Fame shortstop, played twenty seasons from 1930 to 1950 retiring with 2,749 base hits and a .310 batting average.

Urban "Red" Faber, their Hall of Fame right-hander, who won 254 games in his twenty years, from 1914-33; and fellow Hall of Fame right-hander Ted Lyons, who won 260 games in his 21 years, from 1923-42, 46 all slipped on the Pale Hose together as teammates.

125. Who was the first player in Tampa Bay Rays' history to hit for the cycle?

B.J. Upton made history at Tropicana Field in St. Petersburg, Florida, on Friday night, October 2, 2009, when he became the first Tampa Bay player in history of that young franchise to hit for the cycle.

He wasted no time by blasting a bases loaded triple to right-centerfield off New York Yankees southpaw ace, C.C. Sabathia, in the first inning. In the 3rd inning Upton hit a Sabathia pitch for a double off the left field wall.

When right-hander Jonathan Albaladejo came on in relief of Sabathia, Upton continued his hitting by adding a two-run home run in the 4th, which put the Rays up 11-1, leaving him with just a single to complete the cycle.

When Upton came to the plate in the 5th inning, for his fourth at bat, he was now facing right-hander David Robertson, and after falling behind in the count, 1-2, he lined the next pitch into right field to the elation of the 22,704 faithful fans who witnessed Tampa Bay history, as B.J. Upton became the first to hit for the cycle in their history. He did it in his first four at bats, all in the first five innings, as he ended up with five hits, and drove in six runs, as the Rays walloped the Yankees 13-4.

126. What was the first team to have its pitching staff pitch 148 complete games in a 154 game season?

This is a statistic, which in today's climate is unfathomable, but nevertheless happened when the 1904 Boston Pilgrims (Red Sox) staff took the mound. This mound corps, with a combined Era of 2.12, was headed up by "Cy" Young who had a record of 26-16, with 40 out of 41 games completed, then "Big Bill" Dinneen, 23-14, with all of his 37 starts completed, followed by southpaw Jesse Tannehill at 21-11, with 30 complete games out of 31 started, then Norwood Gibson, 17-14, with 29 complete games out of 32, and finally George Winter with an 8-4 record completing 12 of his 16 starts.

That's 148 complete games pitched out of their 154 games played, by a mound staff that greatly contributed to their 95-59 first place finish in a season where their abilities couldn't be displayed in the World Series that was never played that year, because the National League Champion New York Giants, winners of 106 games, and having their two pitching aces, Christy Mathewson and "Iron Man" Joe McGinnity win a combined 68 games, refused to play the upstart American League, being vindictive toward Ban Johnson, and unwilling to lend credibility to the American League by agreeing to the postseason games.

With the kind of mound numbers the Boston starters put up that season I am surprised that the Pilgrim bullpen didn't file for unemployment insurance.

127. What were the first franchise and the first Stadium to host every game of the World Series?

The 1921 World Series was a series of many "firsts." Among them was the first time in major league history that all the World Series games were played in the same ballpark.

The reason being was that it was the first time the New York Yankees appeared in a World Series, and they played it in their home park which just happened to be the Polo Grounds, the home of their rival in the Fall Classic, the New York Giants.

The Giants won the series, 5 games to 3, as southpaw Art Nehf, defeated right-hander Waite "Schoolboy" Hoyt in the deciding game 1-0.

The Yankees didn't get their own park until the 1923 season.

128. What team was the first to lose the first two games of the World Series, and come back to win the World Championship?

As mentioned previously the 1921 World Series had many "firsts." One notable one was the fact that the New York Giants lost Game 1, on October 5th to the New York Yankees, 3-0. They then went down in Game 2, on October 6th, by the same score as Waite Hoyt pitched a three-hitter and losing pitcher Art Nehf gave up only two hits.

The Giants took Game 3, 13-5, and Game 4, 4-2, with the Yankees winning Game 5, 3-1.

Then the Giants came back to sweep the last three games, in the eight-game series, with Art Nehf pitching a four-hit shutout, 1-0, to win the World Championship.

129. What was the first major league team to forfeit an Opening Day game?

The 1907 Opening Day game, between the New York Giants and the Philadelphia Phillies, on April 11th, was preceded by a heavy snowstorm in New York on the eve of the game. To prepare for play the groundskeepers at the Polo Grounds shoveled the snow from the field to the outer edges in foul territory.

During the course of the game the Giants fell behind, 3-0, and disappointed Giants fans began throwing snowballs at each other in the 7th inning, and continued throughout the game, moving around the field as the game progressed, and eventually causing a delay in the game.

In the 9th inning, with the snowball fight continuing, the fans realized there were no police to stop them and then accelerated their snowball fight onto the field making it impossible to continue the game.

Unfortunately one of the snowballs landed on the dean of all arbiters, Bill Klem. That was enough for him as he called the game and forfeited it to the Phillies.

130. What team was the first to be shutout in major league history?

One has to go all the way back to the origins of the National League to come up with this one. It was on April 25, 1876 that the Louisville Grays played their very first game and came face-to-face with Chicago White Stockings right-hander Al Spalding, who not only blanked the Grays, 4-0, for the first shutout in major league history, but Spalding went on to lead the league with 47 wins that season.

131. Who was the first African-American to pitch for the New York Yankees?

Southpaw Alphonso "Al" Downing was signed to an amateur free agent contract with the New York Yankees prior to the 1961 season, and made his major league pitching debut on Wednesday, July 19, 1961 in Griffith Stadium, Washington, when he started against Senators' right-hander, Dick Donovan.

His introduction to the big leagues was brief as he struck out two in the 1st inning and retired the side. In the 2nd inning he faced five batters, giving up a single, three walks, and hit a batter, before right-hander Hal "Porky" Reniff came on in relief. Downing was charged with one hit, three walks and five earned runs as Washington went on to score seven runs, on four hits, and two Yankee errors in the inning, and rolled to a 12-2 win.

132. Who was the first Yankee to play an entire season without making an error?

This flawless fielding leftfielder, Roy White by name, went the entire 1971 season, playing in 145 games, in 1,284.1 innings, having 320 chances, making 313 put outs, having seven assists and starting one double play.

His errorless streak went for 204 games before making an error.

133. Who was the first African-American to play for the Pittsburgh Pirates?

Second baseman Curtis Roberts was signed by Branch Rickey in October 1953, after three years with the Denver Bears in the Class A Western League.

He made his major league debut with the Pittsburgh Pirates on April 13, 1954. He spent just one full season with the Pirates, playing in 134 games and batting .232, with one home run, and 36 runs driven in. He came back in 1955 to play in just six games and had a .118 batting average. His final game took place on June 8, 1956 after playing in 31 games, getting 11 hits, and having a .177 batting average.

134. Who was the first pitcher to win a night game at Ebbets Field?

The first night game played at Ebbets Field, Brooklyn, was on June 15, 1938 between the Dodgers and the visiting Cincinnati Reds.

This game and day became historic for on that night, before 38,748 fans, Cincinnati southpaw Johnny "The Dutch Master" Vander Meer, pitched his unprecedented second consecutive no-hit game defeating the Dodgers, 6-0. Just four days earlier, on June 11th, he had no-hit the Boston Braves, 3-0, at Cincinnati.

135. Who was the first player to hit a "splash-down" home run into China Basin, popularly known as "McCovey's Cove", at Pacific Bell Park, San Francisco?

In the bottom of the 6th inning, on Monday, May 1, 2000, before a crowd of 40,930, with the Giants ahead 6-0, over the New York Mets, CF Calvin Murray greeted Mets' southpaw reliever Rich Rodriguez with a single, and 3B Bill Mueller followed with his single.

That brought up LF Barry Bonds who crushed Rodriguez's first pitch deep into right field, over the wall, and into a splashdown finish in the water of McCovey's Cove for his 11th home run of the season.

The Giants continued on to a 10-3 win for southpaw Shawn Estes over fellow southpaw Bill Pulsipher.

136. Who was the first New York Yankee to lead the American League in home runs?

Quite possibly your first answer should be re-thought for the player in question was far better known as the player who came down with a migraine headache and, on June 2, 1925, reportedly asked Yankee manager Miller Huggins for a day off, than for being a home run slugger. The story goes that Lou Gehrig, the player whom first baseman Wally Pipp suggested to Huggins to sign out of Columbia University, would end up being the one to replace him.

Pipp made his major league debut with the Detroit Tigers on June 29, 1913. On February 4, 1915, the tall broad-shouldered first baseman, was purchased by the Yankees from Detroit and had a modest success with the bat driving in 60 runs and batting .246.

The following season, 1916, though he was known as an excellent bunter, holding the Yankee team record with 226 sacrifices, he saw his long ball hitting ability perk up as he led the American League with 12 home runs, two ahead of teammate, Frank "Home Run" Baker.

Pipp repeated as AL home run champion in 1917, with 9, one ahead of Detroit's Bobby Veach. That gave Pipp the title of being the first Yankee to be crowned the "King of Swat."

137. **What team was the first to have players banned from professional baseball for throwing games?**

The victims of the first gambling scandal in Major League baseball happened to a charter member of the National League, the Louisville Grays, in their second season, who were the favorites to win the 1877 pennant that year.

They saw the Boston Red Caps (Braves) go on a long winning streak, winning 20 of its last 21 games, while the Grays, who had been in first place by 5 ½ games, lost 8 games in a row, then split their next eight, and saw Boston go on to win the pennant by seven games.

At the end of the season investigations took place and their right-handed pitcher Jim Devlin, who had a 35-25, 2.25 Era. record that season, and their shortstop, Bill Craver, leftfielder George Hall, and utility man Al Nichols, were all accused of throwing games.

The announcement of their banishment for life came in an article in the Louisville Courier-Journal on October 30th, and the scandal was then referred to as the "crime of 77."

The team was devastated and unable to continue, and closed down after the announcement.

138. **What was the first National League team to go 18 consecutive games without having their pitching staff give up four or more runs?**

The streak began on September 4, 2010 when the Los Angeles Dodgers had scored a 5-4 victory over the San Francisco Giants in the previous game.

From that day forward, to September 25, 2010, the Giants mound staff, whether the team won or not, didn't allow the opposition to score more than four runs in any game.

All streaks come to an end, and it happened in an unusual slugfest, albeit in the Colorado Rockies home park, where balls fly all over the place in the mile high atmosphere, and the Rockies had their way with Giants pitching in a 10-9 slugfest.

139. It wouldn't be fair not to pose the same question, about the major league record, by asking what team holds the record for the most consecutive games of not allowing over four runs per game.

Look back in the record books and you will see that the Chicago White Sox mound staff held their opponents to less than four runs per game for 20 straight contests in 1917.

140. What franchise was the first to have five pitchers all record their 200th victory while pitching for them?

It all started with right-hander "Smiling Mickey" Welch when he recorded his 200th victory with the New York Giants during the 1886 season. He was followed by another right-hander, Amos "The Hoosier Thunderbolt" Rusie during the 1897 season. Then came the third right-hander, Christy "Big Six" Mathewson, when he won his 200th victory during the 1908 season.

The fourth pitcher was a southpaw, "King Carl" Hubbell, "The Meal Ticket", when he arrived at the double century level during the 1938 season. The fifth and final one of the group was Juan "The Dominican Dandy" Marichal who won his 200th with the San Francisco Giants in 1970.

141. When the New York Mets opened their new Citi Field Stadium on Monday, April 13, 2009, who was their first starting pitcher?

The 6'7" right-hander, Mike Pelfrey, took the mound as the starting pitcher on that opening night, before 41,007 fans. His first pitch was a called strike.

142. Who was the first batter to come to the plate in the New York Mets' new Citi Field Stadium?

The first batter to come to the plate in the new Citi Field was center-fielder Jody Gerut of the San Diego Padres.

143. Who had the first base hit in Citi Field history?

This, and other questions, can be answered by using the name of just one player, centerfielder Jody Gerut, for it came very quickly when as the leadoff batter for San Diego he hammered Mike Pelfrey's pitch for a home run in the top of the first inning.

With that swing the answer to who had the first base hit, the first home run, the first run batted in, and the first run scored in Citi Field history was answered.

144. Who was the Mets' player to have the first base hit in Citi Field history?

Third baseman David Wright was the first Mets player to garner a base hit when he doubled in the bottom of the first inning off San Diego Padres' right-hander Walter Silva on April 13, 2009.

145. What was the first visiting team to open the new Yankee Stadium on April 16, 2009?

The Cleveland Indians were the New York Yankees' opponent at the inaugural game in the new Yankee Stadium on April 16, 2009. They were joined by an excited crowd of 48,271.

146. Who were the starting pitchers for the first game in the new Yankee Stadium?

The New York Yankees started southpaw C.C. Sabathia, the American League Cy Young winner in 2007 while with Cleveland, and the Cleveland Indians countered with their 2008 American League Cy Young winner, southpaw Cliff Lee.

147. Who was the first player to come to bat in the opening day game at the new Yankee Stadium?

Cleveland centerfielder Grady Sizemore was the first batter to come to the plate. He took the first two pitches as balls, then a strike, before grounding out to first baseman Mark Tiexeira unassisted.

148. Who was the first strikeout victim in the opening day game at the new Yankee Stadium?

C.C. Sabathia struck out first baseman, Victorio Martinez swinging, in the top of the first inning.

149. Who was the first Yankee to come to bat in the opening day game at the new Yankee Stadium?

Shortstop Derrick Jeter was the first Yankee batter, and after taking the first pitch for ball one, hit the second pitch for a fly ball out to centerfielder Grady Sizemore.

150. Who was the first Yankee (and the first player) to have a base hit in the new Yankee Stadium?

New York Yankee leftfielder, Johnny Damon, hit a breaking ball off Cleveland southpaw Cliff Lee to centerfield, for a single in the first inning, for the first base hit in the new stadium.

151. Who was the first Mets pitcher to record a win in Citi Field?

The first Mets victory at the new Citi Field was recorded by lefthander Oliver Perez as the Mets defeated the San Diego Padres, 7-2, on April 15, 2009, before a crowd of 35,581.

152. Who was the first Mets player to hit a home run in Citi Field history?

Third baseman David Wright hit the first Mets home run in Citi Field history in the 5th inning on April 13, 2009, off San Diego right-hander Walter Silva.

153. Who recorded the first victory in Citi Field history?

The first pitcher to record a win at Citi Field was San Diego right-hander Edward Mujica, on April 13, 2009, who also won his first game of the 2009 season.

154. Who was the pitcher to be charged with the first loss in Citi Field history?

That dubious honor went to Mets' right-hander Brian Stokes, when he came on in relief in the 6th inning with the score tied 5-5, and had SS Luis Rodriguez's fly ball misplayed by RF Ryan Church for a three base error. With one out, Pedro Feliciano came on in relief of Stokes, got the second out, and then balked while pitching to 2B David Eckstein bringing in Rodriguez with the deciding, but unearned, run. San Diego went on to win 6-5, and Stokes took the first Citi Field loss.

155. Who drove in the New York Mets' first run in Citi Field?

Second baseman Luis Castillo drove in catcher Brian Schneider in the 2nd inning of the initial game there on April 13, 2009 for first Mets run in Citi Field history.

156. Who hit the first grand slam home run in Citi Field history?

The first grand slam home run hit in Citi Field history came from an unlikely source, backup catcher Omir Santos of the New York Mets, filling in for injured Brian Schneider. Santos came up in the bottom of the 1st inning against the Florida Marlins right-hander, Anibal Sanchez, on April 25, 2009, before a home crowd of 38,573, and found the bases loaded with Gary Sheffield who had singled to center, David Wright who had singled to right field, and Fernando Tatis, who had walked.

Santos two days shy of his 28th birthday, gave himself, and his teammates, an early birthday present by hitting a Sanchez fastball four rows into the left field stands for his first big league home run, and first career RBIs, and went down in Mets history for being the first player to hit a grand slam home run in the newly-built Citi Field.

That six-run 1st inning, along with John Maine's two-hitter, was enough to lead the Mets to a 7-1 victory.

157. Who hit the first grand slam home run in the new Yankee Stadium?

The first home run with the bases loaded in the new stadium's history happened on opening day, April 16, 2009, when Cleveland Indians centerfielder, Grady Sizemore, came to the plate, before 48,271 fans, in the 7th inning with the score tied 1-1, and found RF Ben Francisco on third, catcher Kelly Shoppach on second, and LF Trevor Crowe on first.

He hopped on southpaw Damaso Marte's pitch and drove it into deep right field for a grand slam home run, one of nine runs the Indians would get that inning, to blow the game open on their way to a 10-2 victory.

158. Who made the first Yankee error in the new Yankee Stadium?

Third baseman Cody Ransom committed the first Yankee error on a bad throw of a ground ball hit to him by Indians 2B Tony Graffanino in the top of the 6th on opening day, April 16, 2009.

159. Who hit the first Yankee home run in the new Yankee Stadium?

The first Yankee home run came in the bottom of the 5th inning when catcher Jose Posada hit a solo home run, with two outs, off Cliff Lee to tie the game at 1-1.

160. Who was the pitcher credited with the first Yankee win in the new Yankee Stadium?

The Yankees won their first game in their new stadium on April 17, 2009 defeating the Cleveland Indians, 6-5, with right-handed reliever Brian Bruney recording the victory.

161. Who was the first Seattle Pilots player to hit a home run in their abbreviated history?

With the new franchise struggling to gain an identity in the American League any accomplishment was warmly welcomed. So it fell upon the shoulders of outfielder Mike Hegan, (the son of Jim Hegan, the Cleveland Indians catcher from 1941-57), who made his debut with the Yankees on September 13, 1964 as a first baseman/outfielder, and now was a member of the Seattle Pilots by virtue of being purchased on June 14, 1968 from the Yankees to fill out the roster of the new Seattle franchise.

Playing right field on opening day, April 8, 1969, before a California Angels crowd of 11,930, in Anaheim Stadium, Hegan came up in the 1ˢᵗ inning and faced right-hander Jim "Red" McGlothlin, with Tommy Harper on second via a double, and no one out, and greeted Red with a long two-run home run to right field for the first home run in the history of the freshman franchise.

With a 4-run first inning Seattle went on to win over the Angels, 4-3.

162. What was the first National League franchise to strand 18 runners on base in a single game?

Shoulda, coulda, doesn't explain how the Pittsburgh Pirates, on September 8,1905, managed to have 23 base runners, and fail to have more than three come around to score, against the Cincinnati Reds.

The Pirates had 15 hits, and were given 8 walks by Cincinnati right-hander, Charlie Chech, and still could not bring more than three home as the Reds took an 8-3 win.

163. What was the first team to have a game called because of no, not rain, snow, darkness nor earthquakes, but gnats?

This may be a bit unusual, but nonetheless factual. On September 15, 1946, after the Brooklyn Dodgers lost the opening game of a doubleheader to the Chicago Cubs, 4-3, in 10 innings, the second game is halted at the end of the 5ᵗʰ inning when a swarm of gnats invade Ebbets Field, and the umpires decided they had seen enough and called the game, certainly not disputed by the Brooklyn ball club as they came away, behind Kirby Higbe's one-hitter, 2-0.

164. What was the first team to have its games rained out for ten consecutive days?

Enough of giving my players a rest, let's get on with the season, or let's start building an ark. That had to be the feelings of Billy Murray, the skipper of the Philadelphia Phillies, when his team continued on an unexpected sabbatical, of being rained out for ten consecutive days on August 19, 1909.

165. Who did the Texas Rangers defeat for their first franchise playoff victory, in their home field at Arlington Park?

The Texas Rangers defeated the New York Yankees, 7-2, in Game 2 of the American League Championship Series on Saturday, October 16, 2010, down in Arlington Park, before a crowd of 50,362 to witness the first playoff victory in Texas Rangers franchise history. Right-hander Colby Lewis defeated fellow right-hander Phil Hughes.

166. Who hit the first home run in Montreal Expos history?

Surprisingly, the first home run hit on behalf of the Montreal Expos franchise came from a pitcher, southpaw pitching and hitting, Dan McGinn. It happened on Tuesday April 8, 1969 at Shea Stadium, when McGinn hit a solo home run, with one out, off New York Met right-hander Tom Seaver in the 4th inning to narrow the Met lead to 6-4. In this wild game the Expos went on to win, despite 4 runs in the bottom of the 9th by the Mets, 11-10.

167. What was the first major league team to win 10,000 games in their franchise history?

The Giants franchise, which was established in 1883, as the New York Gothams, then the New York Giants, before moving to the west coast to become the San Francisco Giants, were the first franchise to go over the 10,000 wins mark in major league history.

To date they have won 10,522 games in their storied history, followed by the Chicago Cubs, who were started in 1876, and played as the Chicago Orphans, Colts, White Stockings, and Cubs, and currently have won 10,311 games since the formation of the National League in 1976.

168. What franchise was the first to host a major league interleague game?

The first interleague game was played on June 12, 1997, when the Texas Rangers hosted the San Francisco Giants, down in The Ballpark in Arlington, Texas. The visitors came away with a 4-3 victory.

169. Who was the first New York Mets player, in their franchise history, to have over 200 base hits in a season?

Centerfielder Lance "One Dog" Johnson was signed as a free agent by the New York Mets on December 15, 1995, and brought his productive bat with him from the Chicago White Sox, where he led the American League in hits in 1995 with 186.

In the 1996 season he led the National League in hits with 227, as well as in triples with 21 to become the first Met in franchise history to have over 200 base hits.

170. Who was the first Arizona Diamondback to have over 200 base hits in a season?

Leftfielder Luis "Gonzo" Gonzalez was traded by the Detroit Tigers to the Arizona Diamondbacks on December 28, 1998, and immediately showed Detroit it had made a bad trade when "Gonzo" led the National League in base hits with 206 in 1999, batting .336, to become the first Diamondback in their franchise history to have 200 or more hits in a season.

171. Who was the first batter to hit a fair ball out of Forbes Field, Pittsburgh?

On May 25, 1935, Babe Ruth, playing with the Boston Braves, hit the first fair ball out of Forbes Field in Pittsburgh, clearing the right field grandstand, measured at 600 feet, for his third of the game, and his 714th and final career home run. It came off right-hander Guy "The Mississippi Mudcat" Bush. His first two of the game came off Pirate right-hander Charles "Red" Lucas.

172. Who was the first batter to step to the plate on opening day at Shea Stadium, 1964?

On Tuesday, April 17, 1969 the New York Mets played host to the Pittsburgh Pirates and a crowd of 50,312 crammed the ball park for the first game played at Shea Stadium. Short stop Dick Schofield was the first batter to step to the plate, and he faced right-hander "Fat Jack" Fisher who got him to pop out to 2B Larry Burright.

The Pirates, with a run in the top of the 9th took the game 4-3, with RHP Bob Friend the first winning pitcher, and righty Ed Bauta taking the first loss in the new stadium.

173. Who was the winning pitcher for the Texas Rangers when they clinched their first American League pennant?

The Texas Rangers, established after coming from Washington in 1961, had played 7,959 games as a franchise, winning 3,747, but none so important as the one they won on Friday, October 22, 2010 when, before a home crowd of 51,404 excited fans at Rangers Ballpark at Arlington, they defeated the New York Yankees, 6-1, in Game 6 of the American League Championship Series to become 2010 American League Champions, and advance to the World Series for the first time in their franchise history.

Rangers' right-hander Colby Lewis allowed just three hits, striking out seven in his eight innings on the mound until he gave way to right-handed reliever Neftali Feliz, who closed out the 9th inning by striking out Alex Rodriguez, looking for the final out.

174. What was the first, and only, major league team to complete, not a triple play, but a quadruple play?

Impossible you say? Never happened! Oh, but it did. Let's go back to July 1, 1903, to the Polo Grounds in New York, when the St. Louis Cardinals came in for a game against the New York Giants.

In the top of the 6th inning St. Louis had the bases loaded with no one out. CF Homer Smoot hit a shallow fly ball to Roger Bresnahan in centerfield for the first out. Clarence Currie, the Cardinals right-hander, tried to score after the catch, but Bresnahan's rifle throw to catcher John Warner nipped him at the plate for the second out. Warner, seeing RF Patsy Donovan trying to take second on the throw to the plate, fired down to SS George Davis who applied the tag for out number three, a triple play!

But hold on, there is more to the story. Davis, in possibly a temporary mental lapse, seeing Cardinals 2B John Farrell steaming home from second base, must have believed the ball was still in play, for he threw back to Warner, who saw Farrell charging down the line on him, and applied the tag on him for the fourth out!

Obviously, only the first three outs go in the record book, but we've allowed the fourth one to go into this book.

175. What team was the first to turn triple plays on consecutive days?

We have to go way back to June 6, 1908 out in Bennett Park, Detroit, when the Boston Red Sox came up in the top of the 3rd inning, with 2B Amby McConnell on first and 3B Harry Lord on second. RF "Catus Gavvy" Cravath, with the hit and run on, lined out to Tigers' 3B Germany Schaefer who fired over to SS Red Killefer at second, doubling up Lord, who in turn threw to 1B Claude Rossman to get Amby McConnell to complete the triple play.

We now move ahead a day, to June 7th, same teams, and same venue. In the top of the 1st inning, the Red Sox load the bases. CF Denny Sullivan is on first base, 1B Bob Unglaub on second, and RF Gavvy Cravath on third.

Boston SS Charles "Heinie" Wagner came to the plate and chopped a ground ball to Germany Schaefer at second who tagged Sullivan coming down from first. He then threw on to 1B Sam Crawford retiring Wagner for the second out. On the play Cravath scored from third, but Unglaub, in trying to follow Cravath home, had Crawford send the ball home to catcher Ira Thomas who applied the tag for the triple play, the second in two consecutive days by the Detroit Tigers infield, and the first time in major league history.

Gavvy Cravath had the unique distinction of hitting into the first one and being on base and scoring in the one the next day.

176. Who was the winning pitcher in the first World Series win in Texas Rangers franchise history?

After losing the first two games of the 2010 World Series to the San Francisco Giants, in San Francisco, the Rangers returned home to The Ballpark in Arlington on October 30th, and behind the excellent pitching of right-hander Colby Lewis, and the outstanding closing out of the game by 22-year old Neftali Feliz, retiring the final three batters in the 9th, brought the Texas Rangers their first World Series win in their franchise history.

177. What was the first team to play an entire regular season home stand against the same team in consecutive games?

This bizarre scheduling occurred in 1904 when the Detroit Tigers hosted the St. Louis Browns, at Bennett Park, for eleven consecutive games, playing doubleheaders on September 8th, 9th, 10th, and 11th, then a single game on the 12th, followed by a doubleheader on the 14th, coming away with a 5-6 record before going on the road to play a scoreless tie with the Cleveland Blues on the 15th.

178. What was the first team to play 9 consecutive doubleheaders in a season?

They should have given the person who drew up the 1928 Boston Braves schedule a sobriety test, or a sanity test.

It all started on September 4th with a doubleheader in Boston against the Brooklyn Dodgers. The following day they played another twin-bill against the Dodgers. The Braves then went down to Philadelphia playing doubleheaders against the Phillies on September 7th and 8th. They returned home to play doubleheaders against the New York Giants on September

10th and 11th, 13th and 14th, before the Cubs moved in to play the 9th consecutive doubleheader on the 15th.

All told the Braves played 32 twin-bills in their 153-game schedule. I can't imagine the pitchers had anything left of their arms at season's end.

179. What was the first franchise to have their team record more strikeouts than base hits in a season?

This may be a hard one for Brewers fans to swallow, but in 2001 the Milwaukee Brewers became the first team to exceed their base hits with strikeouts.

The stats show 1,399 times that the bat missed the ball to 1,378 when the bat hit the ball fairly.

Shortstop Jose Hernandez did his part in making this franchise first by leading his team with 185 whiffs.

180. Who was the first pitcher to record a win at the new Target Field in Minneapolis?

It happened on Friday night on April 17, 2010, in the first night game at Target Field. Twins right-hander Scott Baker went up against the 2009 Cy Young winner, right-hander Zach Greinke of the Kansas City Royals. The Twins came away with a 10-3 rout to christen the new stadium in a proper fashion.

As an aside, the last home night game they played outdoors was at Metropolitan Stadium on September 25, 1981 before a cool crowd of 38,532.

181. What eight teams   represented the American League in their inaugural season?

The first teams to open up the inaugural season of the American League, in 1901, were the Baltimore Orioles, Boston Americans, Chicago White Stockings, Cleveland Blues, Detroit Tigers, Milwaukee Brewers, Philadelphia Athletics, and the Washington Senators.

Today those Americans are called the Red Sox, the White Stockings are the White Sox, the Blues are the Indians, the Athletics are in Oakland, the Washington Senators are now the Minnesota Twins, and that Milwaukee Brewers team is now the Baltimore Orioles.

182. **What was the first American League team to sweep the World Series from a National League team?**

The year was 1927, and the New York Yankees went by the sobriquet of "Murderers Row" and led by skipper Miller Huggins swept the Pittsburgh Pirates, led by Donie Bush, in four games.

183. **What was the first major league team to sweep two consecutive fall classics?**

The Yankees continued their dominance of 1927, when in 1928, Miller Huggins' team swept the St. Louis Cardinals, led by "Deacon Bill" McKechnie, in four games, to become the first team to sweep two consecutive World Series.

184. **Who was the first winning pitcher in the Oakland Athletics inaugural game in their new home at Oakland-Alameda County Coliseum?**

It wasn't a pleasant welcome to their new home on the west coast for the Athletics after 54 years in Philadelphia, and 13 years in Kansas City when they faced the Baltimore Orioles in their inaugural game on April 17, 1968, before 50,164 excited fans.

Southpaw Dave McNally was the primary reason as he threw a two-hitter to defeat Lew Krausse Jr. 4-1.

185. **What National League team was the first to offer "rain checks"?**

It is generally accepted that the Detroit Wolverines, in the 1880's, were the first team to offer "rain checks" to fans. They were only good for the game being played the next day at Recreation Park.

186. **What were the first teams to play in the first recorded baseball game?**

On June 19, 1846 Alexander Cartwright's New York Knickerbockers lost to the New York Baseball Club, 23-1, in a four- inning game played at the Elysian Fields, Hoboken, New Jersey.

187. **What team was the first to wear a uniform?**

These same New York Knickerbockers were the first to don a uniform when they dressed as a team in 1849.

188. **Who was the first rookie in Boston Red Sox history to be the**

starting pitcher on opening day?

That unusual honor went to Jim Bagby Jr. who started the 1938 season off, before 10,500 fans, on April 18, 1938 in Fenway Park against the New York Yankees, and their right-handed ace, Red Ruffing.

Bagby, a right-hander, went six innings giving up four runs, three earned, on 5 hits and left leading 8-4. Southpaw Archie "Happy" McKain came on to pitch three scoreless innings in relief, allowing one hit, for the save.

189. Who was the first Montreal Expos pitcher to pitch a no-hitter in Olympic Stadium?

Right-hander Charlie Lea, was born in Orleans, France, on Christmas day 1956, and made his pitching debut with the Expos on June 12, 1980.

A year later, on May 10, 1981, in the second game of a doubleheader, Lea pitched a no-hitter, against the San Francisco Giants, striking out 8, and winning 4-0 at Olympic Stadium.

190. Who was the first pitcher in modern day Baltimore Orioles franchise history to pitch a no-hitter?

The first Orioles no-hitter was pitched on Saturday, September 20, 1958, before a crowd of 10, 941 at Memorial Stadium, when right-hander Hoyt Wilhelm pitched a 1-0 no-hitter against the New York Yankees, beating southpaw Bobby Shantz.

191. Who was the first Baltimore Orioles pitcher to win 20 games in a season?

Southpaw Steve Barber went 20-13, with an Era. of .275 in 1963 to become the first in Baltimore Orioles franchise history to win twenty games in a season.

192. Who was the first Baltimore Orioles player to hit for the cycle?

Third baseman Brooks Robinson became the first Baltimore Orioles player to hit for the cycle when on July 15, 1960, at Comiskey Park, before 43,704 fans, he went 5-5, with three runs batted in, off southpaw Billy Pierce, and reliever Turk Lown, as the O's rolled to a 5-2 win over the Chicago White Sox.

193. Who was the first New York Yankees player to hit a home run in his first major league at bat?

On September 11, 1966 first baseman John Miller made his major league debut at the plate in Fenway Park, Boston, and hit a home run that led to a 4-2 Yankees win over the Red Sox.

He stayed with the Yankees for 23 plate appearances showing a .087 batting average before being released.

He surfaced again in 1969 with the Los Angeles Dodgers, playing left field and three infield positions, before his final game on September 27, 1969 when in his last major league at bat he hit his second career home run before being given his walking papers with a .211 average. This less than stellar career made him the first player to hit a home run in his first major league at bat, as well as in his last major league at bat, with no others in between.

194. Who was the first Texas Rangers player to hit a home run in World Series history?

It happened in the 2nd inning of Game 3, on October 30, 2010, at The Ballpark at Arlington when Texas first baseman Mitch Moreland hit a two-out, two on, home run to deep right field off San Francisco Giants south-paw, Jonathan Sanchez, before a hometown crowd of 52,419.

That blast propelled the Rangers to their first World Series game win in their history, 4-2.

195. What franchise was the first to score ten or more earned runs in a game?

On June 5, 1882 the Boston Red Caps defeated the Detroit Wolverines 10-2 to become the first team to score ten or more runs in a game with all of them being earned.

196. What was the first team to introduce a formal "Ladies Day"?

Way back in the summer of 1897 the Washington Senators, in an effort to entice ladies to come to the ballpark, introduced the first formal Ladies Day. The ladies were not charged an admission fee that day, and well over one thousand ladies stormed the gates to see, not baseball, but their charismatic star, the dashing ladies' man, right-hander George "Winnie" Mercer pitch.

The game was without incident, however, until the 5th inning, when Mercer objected vehemently to a pitch he thought should have been called a strike. This erupted into heated words and verbal abuse by Mercer heaped upon the esteemed umpire, Bill Carpenter, who after hearing enough, ejected the Senators right-hander from the game.

That was more than the ladies could stand as they verbally attacked Carpenter, and when the game ended with Washington going down in defeat the still upset ladies, denied of their heartthrob since the 5th, attacked Carpenter, tore his clothing, punched him, hit him with their parasols as Carpenter had to fight his way through the angry mob to the protection of the clubhouse.

197. What were the first teams to play in a game that scored as many as 19 runs in a single inning?

It happened on Sunday, April 10, 1977, in Fenway Park, when the Cleveland Indians went into the top of the 8th inning tied 3-3 with the Boston Red Sox. Before they had three outs they had scored 13 runs off RHP Bill Campbell, RHP Jim Willoughby, and southpaw Tom House to go ahead 16-3.

Then in the bottom of the 8th Boston fought back and scored six runs of their own, to bring the game to 16-9.

Cleveland went on to win 19-9 with three more runs in the 9th, off RHP Tom Murphy, but for the first time in modern baseball history one inning, and two pitching staffs, allowed 19 runs in one inning, and 14,931 fans were witnesses.

198. What were the first franchises to have their World Series delayed due to an earthquake?

On October 27, 1989 the World Series resumed after a ten-day delay because of the Loma Prieta earthquake during warm-ups, prior to Game 3, between the San Francisco Giants and the Oakland Athletics at Candlestick Park in San Francisco, on October 17, 1989. Oakland went on to win Game 3 that day, 13-7, over the Giants, and sweep the World Series in four games.

199. What was the first major league team to lose 10,000 games in their franchise history?

Sunday, July 15, 2007, was a noteworthy date in major league history, but it was certainly not celebrated down in Citizens Bank Park in Philadelphia. For on that date the Phillies lost to the St. Louis Cardinals, 10-2, and 44,872 fans bore witness to the Phillies 10,000th regular season loss since the franchise took shape back in 1883. They became the first professional sports team to reach that dubious plateau.

200. Who was the first player to hit a grand slam home run in the history of the Chicago White Stockings?

Larry Corcoran, a right-handed pitcher, and a part-time outfielder and shortstop, for the Chicago White Stockings went 4-for-4, including a bases loaded home run in a game against the Worcester Ruby Legs in Chicago, on June 20, 1882, to become the first player on the White Stockings to hit a grand slam home run in their history.

201. What team was the first to have the entire regular starting lineup bat over .300 for the year?

Look down to Philadelphia where the Phillies played their games at the Philadelphia Baseball Grounds and the University of Pennsylvania Athletic Field.

They finished the 1894 season with a .555winning percentage, but, as a team, batted .349 with 1,732 hits in 4,967 at bats, and had a slugging percentage of .476.

1B Jack Boyle batted .301, 2B Bill Hallman .309, 3B Lave Cross .386, SS Joe Sullivan .352, outfielders Ed Delahanty .407, Billy Hamilton, .404, Sam Thompson .407, catcher Mike Grady, .363, and pitcher Jack Taylor, .333, along with their often used reserve outfielder, Tuck Turner, .at .416.

202. Who pitched the first no-hitter in the history of Camden Yards?

It happened very early in the season, on April 4, 2001, when Hideo "The Tornado"Nomo, making his first start with the Boston Red Sox, shut down the Baltimore Orioles in front of their hometown fans at Camden Yards, 3-0.

203. What team was the first to pitch a no-hitter in an inter-league game?

The Houston Astros used six pitchers on June 11, 2003 to no-hit the New York Yankees, the most ever for a no-hitter.

Roy Oswalt started for Houston, but had to leave in the 2nd inning with a strained groin. He was followed in order by Peter Munro, Kirk Saarloos, Brad Lidge, and Octavio Dotel, who tied a record by striking out four Yankees in the 8th inning, and Billy Wagner finished up, as Houston rolled to an 8-0 win.

The Yankees tied an American League record by striking out eight consecutive times.

204. Who threw the first no-hitter in Comerica Park history?

The first no-hitter pitched in Comerica Park happened on June 12, 2007 when the big Detroit Tigers right-hander, Justin Verlander, set down the National League's Milwaukee Brewers, 4-0.

205. What was the first team to use four pitchers to pitch a no-hitter?

Sunday, September 28, 1975 was the final day of the regular season. The Oakland Athletics faced off against the California Angels, at the Oakland Coliseum, and started their ace southpaw Vida Blue who went five innings. They followed him with Glenn Abbott for an inning, then Paul Lindblad for an inning, and in the 8th and 9th closed out the game with Rollie Fingers, who like his predecessors kept the Angels hitless, and the Oakland staff, with Vida Blue credited with his 22nd win, had pitched a combined 5-0 no-hitter, much to the pleasure of skipper Alvin Dark.

206. Who pitched the first no-hitter in Busch Stadium?

Bob Forsch, the big St. Louis Cardinals right-hander, pleased the Sunday home crowd of 11,495 on April 16, 1978 when he held the Philadelphia Phillies hitless winning his third game of the season, 5-0, and being the first in Busch Stadium II history to throw a no-hitter.

207. What was the first franchise to win a World Series after being no-hit twice in the same season?

It started on May 5, 1917 when the St. Louis Browns' southpaw Ernie Koob no-hit the Chicago White Sox 1-0.

It continued on to May 6th when Brown's right-hander Bob Groom also no-hit the White Sox, for the second consecutive day, 3-0.

When the end of the regular season came around the White Sox had taken the American League pennant and went up against the New York Giants.

They captured the World Championship by downing the men of McGraw in six games and became the first team in history to be no-hit, not only twice in the same season, but on consecutive days, and go on to win the World Series.

208. Who pitched the first no-hitter in Coors Field history?

In a hitters' park, like Coors Field, a no-hitter, always difficult under normal circumstances, takes on a new dimension.

That didn't bother Hideo "The Tornado" Nomo on September 17, 1996 when the Dodgers' right-hander from Osaka, Japan shut down the Colorado Rockies without a hit, 9-0, to become the first pitcher to hold the Rockies' bats hitless in Coors Field history.

209. What were the two teams involved in a series in which each game in the series was a no-hitter?

Harry "The Hat" Walker and his Houston Astros came into Crosley Field to begin a two-game series against the Cincinnati Reds on Wednesday April 30, 1969.

Jim Maloney won his third game of the season that day when he slammed the door on the Astros' hitters as he pitched a 10-0 no-hitter.

On the following day, Thursday, May 1st, Don Wilson, paid the Reds back with a no-hitter of his own as he held Cincinnati hitless to come away with a 4-0 win.

The first time a series, albeit just two games, were decided by no-hitters by each team.

210. Who pitched the first no-hit game in Colorado Rockies history?

For all Rockies' fans right-hander Ubaldo Jimenez, who made his debut on September 26, 2006 with Colorado, became their hero on April 17, 2010, when down at Turner Field, before 32,602, he pitched the first no-hitter in Colorado Rockies franchise history when the Atlanta Braves fell victim to his pitches, 4-0, as Jimenez went 3-0 on the season.

211. Who threw the first no-hitter in Chicago's Comiskey Park?

Right-hander Vern Kennedy, in his sophomore season with the Chicago White Sox, became the first pitcher to throw a no-hitter in Comiskey Park when he blanked the Cleveland Indians, 5-0 on August 31, 1935.

212. Who was the first brother battery in Boston Red Sox history?

On Thursday, September 19, 1929, Boston Red Sox right-hander Milt Gaston took the mound at Fenway Park against Willis Hudlin of the Cleveland Indians.

His battery mate that day was his older brother Alex, who became part of the first brother battery in Red Sox history.

Milt won his 11th game of the season with his brother behind the plate, defeating the Indians, 3-2.

213. What franchise was the first to hire a woman to do play-by-play on television?

In 1976 Harry Caray, the Chicago White Sox broadcaster, saw Mary Shane in the press box on a number of occasions, and asked her if she would like to do some play-by-play which she did.

On January 4, 1977 WMAQ radio and WSNS-TV, the flagship stations for the White Sox, hired her to do the play-by-play broadcast with Caray, Lorn Brown, and Jimmy Piersall, of the games on television.

With that assignment, Mary became a "Groundbreaker" as she became the first woman to handle the play-by-play on television in major league baseball history.

Poor Mary, as the depth of her knowledge about baseball situations, and her lack of experience became apparent, Mary's contract was not renewed prior to the conclusion of the season.

She later went on to become a sportswriter for the Worcester Telegram.

214. What was the first modern day team to score a run in every inning of a 9-inning game?

It was on June 1, 1923 down in Baker Bowl, Philadelphia, when the New York Giants went on a consistent scoring spree as they scored a run in every inning of the game; 4 in the 1st, 2 in the 2nd, 1 in the 3rd, 1 in the 4th, 5 in the 5th, 5 in the 6th, 1 in the 7th, 2 in the 8th, and 1-run in the 9th to finalize their 22 run, 23 hit scoring spree against a very overmatched Phillies pitching staff.

Such a happening is expected once in every 451,834 games.

215. What was the first team to hit four consecutive home runs in an extra-inning game?

We'll take you out to Municipal Stadium on Saturday, May 2, 1964 where the Kansas City Athletics hosted the Minnesota Twins before a small crowd of 8,159. The game went into extra innings tied at 3-3 when RF Tony Oliva opened up the top of the 11th inning with a home run off Kansas City right-hander Dan Pfister. 1B Bob Allison followed with a home run to make it 5-3. CF Jimmie Hall also liked the pitches of Pfister as well, and blasted a home run to make the score 6-3. That brought in right-hander Vern Handrahan to face one of the great home run hitters of his time, LF Harmon Killebrew, who wasn't about to watch others homer so he greeted Handrahan with one of his own to finish out the inning giving the Twins a 7-3 lead going into the bottom of the 11th where Twins southpaw Gerry Arrigo set down the Athletics to gain the win.

216. What team was the first to score over 20 runs in an opening day game?

The Cleveland Indians batters were in mid-season form on opening day, Tuesday, April 14, 1925, at Sportsman's Park, when they hammered the St. Louis Browns 21-14, to become the first team in major league history to score more than 20 runs on opening day.

217. What was the first team in major league history to lose 100 games in the season after winning the World Series?

In 1997 the Florida Marlins had a 92-70 record in the regular season, and went through the playoffs, and into the World Series where they became World Champions by defeating the Cleveland Indians in seven games.

The following year wasn't as glorious as they became the first team to lose over 100 games after winning the World Series, when they finished the 1998 regular season with a 54-108 record.

218. What team was the first to score at least one run in every inning of a game?

Back on August 15, 1889 the Cleveland Spiders walloped the Boston Beaneaters 19-8, and in so doing scored at least one run in every inning of the game.

219. What team was the first to score over 35 runs in a single game?

Back before the turn of the previous century, in Chicago, on June 29, 1897 the Chicago Colts had their way with the Louisville Colonels, when they trounced them 36-7, becoming the first team to score that many runs in a single game.

220. What was the first modern day team to score 30 runs in a single game?

It was the first game of a double header down in Camden Yards in Baltimore on August 22, 2007, when the Texas Rangers, behind 3-0 in the 4th inning scored five runs, then added nine more in the 6th, ten more in the 8th and finished off the 9th inning with another six runs to light up the scoreboard with 30 runs on their way to a 30-3 "laughter" against the Orioles.

The Rangers continued with their hot bats by sweeping the double-header, winning the second game 9-7.

221. What was the first team to sweep a series from the other team, and never score a run in the first seven innings of any of the games?

Let's go back to Friday, August 31, 2001, in Fenway Park, when the New York Yankees came in for a three game series with the Boston Red Sox.

In that game the Yankees were behind, 1-0 going into the 8th inning when they came up with two runs, and followed that with a single run in the 9th to come away with a 3-1 victory.

On Saturday, September 1st the Red Sox picked up a run in the bottom of the 1st and held the lead until the Yankees tied it in the top of the 8th with a run, and then came back in the 9th to score the deciding run in a 2-1 victory.

The final game of the series continued on to Sunday, September 2nd when Mike Mussina, lost his perfect game, and his no-hitter with Carl Everett's base hit in the bottom of the 9th, but held on as Enrique Wilson, in the top of the 9th drove in Clay Bellinger, running for Tino Martinez, to give the Yankees a 1-0 win, and a sweep in Fenway, without scoring a run before the 7th inning in any of the games played in that series, and became the first team in major league baseball to lay claim to that record.

222. Who was the first Los Angeles Angels pitcher to pitch a no-hit game?

On Saturday evening, May 5, 1962, before a crowd of 15,886, south-paw Robert "Bo" Belinsky took the mound for the Angels out in Dodger Stadium, against Steve Barber of the Baltimore Orioles. With a single run in the 1st and 2nd innings it was all the runs needed as Belinsky went on to pitch the first no-hitter in Los Angeles Angels franchise history.

223. Who was the first Colorado Rockies player to hit a grand slam pinch-hit home run?

It happened on Tuesday, May 4, 1993 when in the top of the 8th inning out in Wrigley Field, Chicago, Jim Tatum came up to pinch-hit for Rockies centerfielder Alex Cole with Colorado behind 5-4, and found catcher Joe Girardi on third, SS Vinny Castilla on second, and 2B Eric Young on first.

Tatum hit a pitch by the Cubs southpaw Dan Plesac deep into the left field stands for the first pinch-hit grand slam home run in Rockies franchise history. The Rockies went on to take that slugfest 14-13 in eleven innings.

224. Who hit the first home run in Detroit's new ballpark, Navin Field, in 1912?

It took eleven days before someone finally hit a home run in the Detroit Tigers' new Navin Field, and it was a St. Louis Browns rookie second baseman, Del Pratt who did it. It was in the top of the 2nd inning with no one on, and it was a very weird and unusual home run. Pratt hit Tigers right-hander Ed Willett's pitch to left-center field where it took a fluke bounce off the concrete wall and skipped through the side door of the left field scoreboard where it was irretrievable.

For all you Tigers fans the first player wearing your uniform to hit a home run in Navin Field occurred on June 10, 1912 when shortstop Donie Bush hit an inside-the-park homer off Washington Senators southpaw Joe Engel.

225. Who hit the first inside-the-park grand slam home run in Milwaukee Brewers franchise history?

On Saturday May 30, 1970, up in County Stadium, Milwaukee Brewers second baseman Roberto Pena came up in the bottom of the 1st inning with Milwaukee behind 2-0 to the Detroit Tigers and found the bases loaded with two out.

He quickly changed that score as he hit a Les Cain pitch to deep centerfield scoring SS Ted Kubiak, RF Ted Savage, and CF Hank Allen, with Pena also coming around to score on the first inside-the park grand slam home run in Milwaukee Brewers franchise history. The Brewers went on to top the Tigers 9-7.

226. Who was the first player in Texas Rangers history to successfully steal home?

It happened out in Metropolitan Stadium on Saturday, May 27, 1972 when, in the top of the 2nd inning, with the Rangers down, 1-0, SS Toby Harrah doubled to centerfield off Minnesota Twins right-hander Dick Woodson. He moved to third on a sacrifice by the Rangers right-hander Dick Bosman. CF Elliott Maddox then drew a walk. With RF Joe Lovitto at the plate the double steal was on with Harrah racing home successfully, and Maddox going down to second. When catcher George Mitterwald's throw went wild Maddox raced on to third. Before the inning was over

Texas had racked up nine runs and waltzed to an easy 16-2 win.

227. What franchise was the first to hire a full-time African-American coach?

On May 29, 1962, the Chicago Cubs, who had previously employed John Jordan "Buck" O'Neil as a scout, announced he would become the first major league African-American coach.

228. Who was the first Atlanta Braves player, in their franchise history, to hit an inside-the-park home run?

The Atlanta Braves were behind 2-1 to the Cubs in the top of the 9th inning at Wrigley Field, on Sunday, May 29, 1966, when with one out Eddie Mathews tied the game with an inside-the-park solo home run deep to right field off right-hander Ferguson Jenkins.

The Cubbies won it in the bottom of the 10th, 3-2, on a solo home run deep into the right-centerfield stands by Ron Santo.

229. Who hit the first pinch-hit grand slam home run in Florida Marlins franchise history?

It took a rookie to make Marlins history, when on Friday, May 7, 1999, outfielder Bruce Aven was sent up by manager John Boles to pinch-hit for his pitcher, right-hander Dennis Springer, in the 7th inning with one out in Dodger Stadium. The bases were loaded and the Marlins were down, 3-1, as Aven stepped in against the Dodgers right-hander Alan Mills. He promptly emptied the bases with a grand slam home run to deep left field scoring 1B Derrek Lee, CF Todd Dunwoody, and catcher Jorge Fabregas propelling the Marlins to a 6-3 win, and a place in the record book for Aven as being the first player in Marlin history to pinch-hit a grand slam home run.

230. What was the first team, in the modern era, to establish their spring training site in their home city?

On May 7, 1996 the Tampa Bay Devil Rays announced that their 1998 spring training site would be located right in Tampa Bay.

231. Who was the first player to hit for the cycle in Los Angeles Dodgers history?

It didn't happen before the home crowd, but rather in Shea Stadium on Thursday, May 7, 1970, against the New York Mets. 1B Wes Parker doubled to center in the 2nd, and homered in the 7th off Ray Sadecki, then singled to right in the 8th off Cal Koonce, and finished off the cycle with a triple to centerfield off Jim McAndrew as the Dodgers broke a 4-4 tie with three runs in the 10th to win, 7-4.

232. Who hit the first pinch-hit home run in Kansas City Royals franchise history?

It was a big 3-run home run, part of a 5-run 9th inning rally, that sent the Royals to a 7-6 win over the Detroit Tigers at Tiger Stadium on Tuesday, May 6, 1969. Bob "Hawk" Taylor was sent up to pinch-hit for SS Juan Rios, and facing the hard-throwing reliever, Dick Radatz, the right-fielder drilled a fast ball to deep left-center field to drive in 2B Jerry Adair and 1B Chuck Harrison to become the first Royal in their franchise history to pinch-hit a home run.

233. What was the first National League team to travel by air to a major league city?

On Tuesday, May 7, 1940, the Brooklyn Dodgers travelled to Chicago, by air, from St. Louis, after playing the Cardinals, to play a single game with the Chicago Cubs on May 9th.

234. Who was the pitcher credited with the first home victory for the Milwaukee Brewers?

It was on a Wednesday, May 6, 1970, in County Stadium, when right-hander Bobby Bolin took the mound against the Boston Red Sox's southpaw, Gary Peters, and came away with a 4-3 win for the first Brewers home victory.

235. Who hit the first grand slam home run for the Cleveland Indians when they moved into their new home in Jacobs Field in downtown Cleveland?

This happened quickly as Kansa City Royals right-hander Doug Linton served up a grand slam home run to Cleveland 1B Paul Sorrento in the first inning at Jacobs Field, scoring DH Eddie Murray, 3B Jim Thome, and RF Manny Ramirez, to add to the 8-run outburst that propelled the Indians to an easy 10-0 win for right-hander Orel Hershiser.

236. Who hit the first inside-the-park home run in Houston Colt 45's franchise history?

On Thursday, May 10, 1962 RF Roman Mejias got Houston off to a fast start by hitting the first inside-the park home run in the young franchise's history when in the bottom of the 1ˢᵗ inning, with two outs, he blasted a pitch off Los Angeles Dodgers right-hander Don Drysdale to deep center-field in Colt Stadium, and came around to score the first run of the game. The lead was short-lived as the Dodgers went on to a 6-2 win.

237. What two teams played in the first major league game in history in which the players on both teams wore numbers on the back of their jerseys?

This historic game happened on Monday, May 13, 1929 when out in League Park in Cleveland, the Indians and the New York Yankees players took the field with each of the players, for the first time, wearing a number on the back of their uniform jersey. Cleveland, behind right hander Willis Hudlin's six-hitter took the game 4-3.

238. Who hit the first inside-the park home run in New York Mets franchise history?

New York Mets fans, as well as former Brooklyn Dodgers fans, will applaud this significant effort by "one of their own" as Gil Hodges hit the first inside-the-park home run in Mets franchise history when in the bottom of the 8ᵗʰ inning, with no outs, 1B Gil Hodges crushed Cubs' southpaw Dick Ellsworth's pitch to deep centerfield in the Polo Grounds, and raced home with a solo home run that tied the game at 5-5. The Mets went on to the 11ᵗʰ inning when they pushed across a run for a 6-5 win over the Chicago Cubs on that Wednesday, May 16, 1962.

239. Who was the first Kansas City Royals pitcher to pitch a no-hitter before their home crowd at Royals Stadium?

It was a Saturday evening on May 14, 1977 and the Texas Rangers were in town and 29,978 fans turned out to see right-hander Jim Colburn face off against the Rangers right-hander Tommy Boggs. It was a Royals' night as Colburn set down Texas, 6-0, without a hit, giving up only one walk, and striking out 6, to be the first Royals pitcher to send the home crowd home talking about this historic game.

240. What team was the first to record an American League shutout?

The first American League shutout was a three-hitter pitched by rookie southpaw Wyatt "Watty" Lee of the Washington Senators as he white-washed the Boston Somersets, 4-0, on May 15, 1901.

241. Who hit the first inside-the-park home run in Colorado Rockies franchise history?

Ellis Burks, the Colorado Rockies centerfielder, came up in the bottom of the 6th inning at Mile High Stadium on April 15, 1994, and found 3B Charlie Hayes standing on second after his double deep down the left field line. Facing Montreal Expos' southpaw, Jeff Fassero, Burks drove his pitch deep down the right field line driving Hayes home as Burks circled the bases to score the second run of a 4-run inning, and the Rockies first inside-the-park home run, as the Rockies went on to a 9-2 win over Montreal.

242. Who was the first player to ever hit a home run that cleared the roof at Briggs Stadium?

It came about on Thursday, May 4, 1939 when the Boston Red Sox came in to play the Detroit Tigers. In the 4th inning, with SS Joe Cronin on first base, Ted Williams in his first at bat in Detroit, crushed right-hander Alfred "Roxie" Lawson's pitch high and deep over the right field seats to clear the roof at Briggs Stadium.

In the 5th inning Williams came back to hit a three-run home run off another right-hander, Bob Harris, to have him drive in 5 of the 7 runs needed to tame the Tigers, 7-6.

243. What was the first team in major league history, to sweep a regular season series of three or more games with each of the three winning pitchers recording their first major league victory?

Cleveland Indians manager Eric Wedge brought his team into the Yankee Stadium for a three-game series starting on Tuesday, April 17, 2007. In the first game the Yankees sent their rookie southpaw, Chase Wright, to the mound and after pitching five innings, and having an 8-3 lead, turned it over to the bullpen, who held Cleveland scoreless, and Wright came away with his first major league victory as New York added two runs for an 10-3 win.

On Wednesday, April 18th the Yankees sent another rookie southpaw, Kei Igawa, to tame the Tribe and after six innings, and a 9-2 lead, he had the bullpen finish it off without any further scoring, giving Igawa his first major league victory.

Next it was Sean Henn, another southpaw, not a rookie, but in his third year, who came on in the top of the 9th and relieved right-hander Kyle Farnsworth with the Indians ahead 5-2. Going into the bottom of the 9th with

Cleveland now up, 6-2, the Yankees rallied for six runs and came away with an 8-6 win, and Sean Henn his first major league victory.

So there were three pitchers, each earning their first major league win in consecutive games.

244. What was the first franchise to have two pitchers win their 200th career game in consecutive games?

This unusual occurrence began on April 11, 2004 when New York Yankees right-hander Mike Mussina won his first game of the season, a 5-4 victory over the visiting Chicago White Sox, for his 200th career win.

The Yankees next game was on Wednesday, April 14th, and right-hander Kevin Brown took the mound at the Yankee Stadium and set down the Tampa Bay Devil Rays, 5-1, for his third straight win of the 2004 season and the 200th in his 18 seasons.

245. What team was the first to sweep both New York teams in the same season?

One could call this the Coors Field "Subway Sweep" as the Colorado Rockies swept the visiting New York Yankees on June 19, 20, and 21, 2007, and then turned around to sweep the visiting New York Mets on July 2nd, 3rd, and 4th to be the first team to sweep both New York teams in the same season.

246. Who was the first pitcher to win a major league game for the expansion Los Angeles Angels?

The expansion Los Angeles Angels made their major league debut on Tuesday, April 11, 1961 against the Baltimore Orioles down in Memorial Stadium before an opening day crowd of 37,352.

Right-hander Eli Grba started for the Angels, against right-hander Milt Pappas, and he was given an early lead in the top of the 1st inning when after two outs, RF Albie Pearson walked, and 1B Ted Kluszewski hit a two-run home run deep down the right field line. LF Bob Cerv followed that with a solo home run to deep right-center and Grba had himself an immediate 3-0 lead.

In the top of the 2nd inning, with Pearson and 2B Bob Aspromonte on, and the Orioles now down, 4-0, right-hander John Papa replaced Milt Pappas. Kluszewski greeted Papa with his second home run, a three-run blast to deep right field. Baltimore went into the bottom of the 2nd inning down

7-0, and never recovered as the Angels came away with their first win in franchise history, 7-2, and Eli Grba credited with being the first pitcher to win a game for the newly formed Angels.

247. Who was the first batter in Minnesota Twins franchise history to hit for the cycle?

It won't come as much of a surprise to learn that on Wednesday, May 20, 1970, Twins second baseman Rod Carew, down in Municipal Stadium, Kansas City, went 4-for-5 as he singled in the 1st inning off right-hander Bob Johnson, then hit a solo home run in the 3rd, and a double to left field in the 5th, all off Johnson, and followed that up with a triple in the 8th off right-hander Al Fitzmorris to complete the cycle as the Twins rolled to a 10-5 win over the Royals.

248. Who hit the first pinch-hit home run in Atlanta Braves franchise history?

It came in the bottom of the 7th inning on Saturday, May 21, 1970, down in Atlanta Stadium, with the Braves down 6-5 to the Chicago Cubs, when Braves manager Bobby Bragan sent Hank Aaron up to pinch-hit for RF Gary Geiger with two outs. Hammerin' Hank sent a pitch by southpaw Billy Hoeft into the left field stands for his 15th homer of the year to tie it up at 6. The Cubs went on to win the game with a run in the 10th, 7-6.

249. Who was the first Yankee to pitch a regular season perfect game?

It came before a partisan crowd of 49,820 on Sunday, May 17, 1998 at Yankee Stadium, when southpaw David "Boomer" Wells struck out eleven Minnesota Twins on his way to pitching the first regular season perfect game in New York Yankees history, winning 4-0.

250. Who pitched the first no-hitter in Houston Colt .45's history?

It came on Friday, May 17, 1963, before a crowd of 8,223 at Colt Stadium, when Colts right-hander Don Nottebart went up against the Philadelphia Phillies. He faced 31 batters, walking 3, and fanning 8, and shut them down without a base hit to come away with a 4-1 win for the first no-hitter in Colt .45's history.

The lone Phillies run scored in the 5th inning on a two-base error by SS J. C. Hartman on 1B Don Demeter's ground ball, a sacrifice by catcher Clay Dalrymple, moving Demeter to third, and a sacrifice fly by 3B Don Hoak.

251. What was the first team in modern day history to have five players

collect four hits each in one game?

It was a hitter's delight, but a pitchers nightmare, on Tuesday, May 13, 1958 out in the Los Angeles Coliseum as the San Francisco Giants hitters had their way with five Dodgers' pitchers starting with right-hander Don Newcombe, and including southpaw Sandy Koufax.

CF Willie Mays led the way, going 5-for-5, with two home runs off Newcombe, two triples, and a single, also walking once and stealing a base and driving in four runs. SS Daryl Spencer had two home runs, a triple and a double, and drove in six runs. 1B Orlando Cepeda had a home run and three singles driving in a pair of runs. Catcher Bob Schmidt had a double and three singles and a run batted in. 2B Danny O'Connell completed the five-some with four singles and a run driven in.

When the dust cleared the Giants had scored in 7 of the 9 innings, and came away with a 16-9 win, and banging out 26 hits on the day.

252. What was the first team in modern baseball history to have two players hit a grand slam home run in the 1st inning?

The 15,829 fans who turned out in Metropolitan Stadium on Wednesday, July 18, 1962 to see their Minnesota Twins play the Cleveland Indians were treated to an historic time in baseball history.

It started in the bottom of the 1st inning when Cleveland right-hander Barry Latman walked the first batter, CF Bill Tuttle. 1B Vic Power singled to left field and 3B Rich Rollins singled to right, scoring Tuttle. LF Harmon Killebrew walked, bringing up RF Bob Allison who cleared the bases with a grand slam home run, scoring Power, Rollins, Killebrew and himself giving the Twins a 5-0 lead. Then catcher Earl Battey followed with a solo home run making it 6-0.

That was all for Latman who was replaced by fellow right-hander Jim Perry. The Twins continued to show no pity as 2B Bernie Allen singled to left field, but SS Zoilo Versalles and southpaw Dick Stigman were retired. Up came Tuttle again and he again walked. Power singled to right scoring Allen and sending Tuttle to third. Rollins walked to load the bases for Killebrew who promptly unloads on Perry for the second grand slam home run of the inning, scoring Tuttle, Power, Rollins and Killebrew. Allison pooped out to Woodie Held at short to end the 7-hit, 11-run 1st inning and give southpaw Dick Stigman a comfortable way to pitch himself, and the Twins to a 14-3 win.

253. Who was the first Milwaukee Brewer to hit two home runs in the same inning?

It came before a Twins hometown crowd of 26,733 at the Hubert H. Humphrey Metrodome in the 6th inning on Friday, May 17, 1996, when RHP Jose Parra gave up a leadoff solo home run to Brewers DH Dave Nilsson, and when he came to bat later in the inning he found LF Greg Vaughn who had been hit by a pitch, and 1B John Jaha who had singled, on base. He drove them home with his second round-tripper of the inning, this to deep right-centerfield, off right-handed reliever Erik Bennett, to increase the Brewers lead to 12-1. With that 11-run inning, and Scott Karl holding the Twins scoreless the rest of the way, the Brewers southpaw coasted to his third win of the season.

254. What was the first franchise to have four pitchers make their major league debut in the same game?

Without having the benefit of an explanation by Tigers' skipper Alan Trammell I can only give you the facts of this very unusual decision of having four of his pitchers make their major league debuts within the same 9-inning game.

Let's go back to Wednesday, April 2, 2003 at Comerica Park, in just the second game of the season, when the Minnesota Twins came into Detroit and the Motor City Nine decided to start their rookie right-hander, Jeremy Bonderman, make his major league debut against the Twins' 4-year veteran right-hander Joe Mays.

Bonderman had a rough couple of innings giving up a run in the 1st, 2 in the 2nd, retired the side in the 3rd, but got whacked for 3 runs in the 4th.

Rookie southpaw Wilfredo Ledezma came on in the 5th and pitched two innings, giving up not a single hit or run. In the top of the 7th, with Minnesota up, 6-1, the third rookie, right-hander, Chris Spurling, made his debut and pitched a scoreless inning.

Then it was rookie right-hander, Matt Roney's turn to get a taste of major league bats, and he came in for the 8th inning and gave up a hit and a run, making it 7-1 Twins.

In the 9th Trammell called upon his 6-year veteran right-hander, Matt Anderson, and he helped the Twins to an 8-1 win by giving up two hits and a run.

Looking back on that game the 21,123 fans saw a "Groundbreaker" moment as it was the first time that four pitchers from the same team, Bonderman, Ledezma, Spurling, and Roney, all made their big league debut in the same game.

255. What teams were the first to have their players hit back-to-back-to-back home runs in the same game?

This baseball rarity began before a crowd of 20,480 at Kauffman Stadium on Sunday, April 9, 2000, when a trio of Minnesota Twins unloaded on Kansas City's right-hander Brad Rigby in the top of the 6th inning.

With the Twins ahead, 6-0, 3B Corie Koskie led off the inning with a ground ball single between first and second. 1B Ron Coomer drove him home with a two-run home run to left-centerfield. LF Jacque Jones followed with a solo home run to right field. That brought up the catcher Matt LeCroy, and he took Rigby's pitch downtown, into the leftfield stands for the third successive homerun of the inning off Rigby. When the inning was over the Twins had increased the lead to 10-0.

Going into the bottom of the 8th inning, and Minnesota up 13-0, "Everyday Eddie" Guardado came on with two on and two outs, to finish up, replacing Twins southpaw, Eric Milton, who had just given up singles to catcher Brian Johnson and SS Rey Sanchez.

Luis Ordaz came in to run for Sanchez. Guardado then walked LF Johnny Damon to load the bases, bringing up 2B Carlos Febles who singled to right field scoring Johnson and Ordaz with Damon taking third. Then came CF Carlos Beltran who cleared the bases with a three-run home run to centerfield, scoring Damon, and Febles.

That set the stage for RF Jermaine Dye who also liked Guardado's pitches and crushed the ball into the right field seats for a solo home run. That was all for Guardado, as right-hander Hector Carrasco came on to stop the run rampage. That wasn't going to happen if DH Mike Sweeney had a say, and he did, as he hit the third consecutive home run of the inning, into the right field stands, to close the score to 13-7, where it ended, but not before both teams had been the first to have three of their players hit back-to-back-to-back home runs in the same game.

256. What was the first American League franchise to have four players each hit over 30 home runs in the same season?

When the 2000 season ended the Anaheim Angels lineup showed third baseman Troy Glaus as the home run champion with 47, followed by 1B

Mo Vaughn with 36, LF Garret Anderson with 35, and RF Tim "Kingfish" Salmon with 34, which made the Angels the first American League team to have four players with thirty or more home runs on the season.

257. What was the first team to have its players hit four consecutive home runs in one game?

On Thursday, June 8, 1961, the Milwaukee Braves took their heavy hitters into Crosley Field to play Cincinnati and, after being behind 10-2, they decided to take it out on two of the Red's pitchers in the top of the 7th inning.

2B Frank Bolling led off the inning with a single to left field. 3B Eddie Mathews took right-hander Jim Maloney downtown for a two-run home run into deep right field, scoring Bolling. Then CF Henry Aaron followed Mathews, and copied him by drilling a solo home run to deep left field, and that was all for Maloney and manager Fred Hutchinson called upon southpaw Marshall "Sheriff" Bridges to come in and put a stop to this power display. The first batter the "Sheriff" faced was 1B Joe Adcock who took a page out of his teammates' book and crushed a home run deep into the centerfield stands for the third round-tripper of the inning. Next came LF Frank Thomas who liked what he saw off Adcock's bat and duplicated it by also blasting a solo home run deep into those centerfield stands for the fourth consecutive home run by the Braves in the inning to make them the first team to have their players hit home runs in four successive at bats.

The display of power wasn't enough as Cincinnati went on to a 10-8 win.

258. What teams were the first to play each other with each team having a player in the game with over 500 career home runs?

On Sunday, August 25, 1945, in the first game of a doubleheader, it was a first-time chance for the 26,355 in attendance at the Polo Grounds to not only see two future Hall Of Fame players, but with both of them having over 500 home runs in their career, playing in that game.

The New York Giants playing-manager, Mel Ott, was in his usual spot in right field having hit his 500th career home run with them on August 1st, and who connected for a grand slam home run off Phillies' right-hander, Charlie Sproull, in the 6th inning of this game.

The Philadelphia Phillies had 37-year old Jimmie Foxx, who had hit his 500th home run while with the Boston Red Sox on September 24, 1940, come up as a pinch-hitter, and be struck out by Giants' right-hander Bill Voiselle, who went on to pick up the win 14-5, as the Giants went on to also win the nightcap, 4-2.

259. What teams were the first to play each other with each side having a career 600 home run player in the starting lineup?

It was on Tuesday, April 27, 1971 at Atlanta County Stadium when the San Francisco Giants came east to play the Braves, and brought along their 600-home run centerfielder, Willie Mays, to play against the Atlanta Braves right fielder, Henry Aaron, who eventually moved to first base from right field in the top of the 7th.

The 13,494 in attendance were looking for the long ball from both of these Hall of Fame players, but that would only happen to their fan favorite, as "Hammerin Hank" hit his 8th home run of the season, a one-out two-run homer off right-hander Gaylord Perry in the 3rd inning.

When the game ended the scorecard showed Aaron going 2-for-5, with a double and a home run, and Willie with a double and three singles, the last one the game-winning hit giving the Giants a 6-5 win.

260. What team was the first in major league history to have a different catcher hit a walk-off home run in successive games?

The New York Mets went into the bottom of the 9th inning at Citi Field, on Friday, May 7, 2010, tied at 4-4 with the San Francisco Giants. Right-hander Sergio Romo came on to start the inning in relief of right-hander Denny Bautista and got the leadoff batter, RF Jeff Francoeur, on a ground-out to third. He then walked 1B Ike Davis which brought up Mets' catcher, Rod Barajas, who smashed a walk-off home run deep down the leftfield line, scoring Davis for a 6-4 win.

The following day, on Saturday, May 8th, backup catcher Henry Blanco, opened the bottom of the 11th inning in a 4-4 tie with San Francisco and blasted a walk-off solo home run deep into the left field stands off right-hander Guillermo Mota to give the Mets a 5-4 win, and made them the first team in history to have two of their catchers hit walk-off home runs in successive games.

261. What team was the first to complete seven double plays in a nine-inning game?

No one was charged with murder, but there were seven twin-killings on Friday afternoon August 14, 1942, in Shibe Park when the Philadelphia

Athletics' batters created them by either grounding into them, via Yankees SS Phil Rizzuto-to 2B Joe Gordon-to 1B Buddy Hassett twice, or 3B Red Rolfe-Gordon-Hassett, or Gordon-Rizzuto-Hassett or Hassett-Dickey-Rolfe, or providing them by having two striking out-throwing out situations for New York Yankees catcher Bill Dickey firing to SS Phil Rizzuto to catch an errant base runner. Even righty reliever Johnny "Grandma" Murphy started one on a comebacker as he went to Rizzuto and on to Hassett. Whichever way you looked at the scorecard, it was a first, for it said seven double plays, and a not so surprising Yankees win, 11-2.

262. What was the first National League team to hit into seven double plays in a nine-inning game?

You have hopefully read the previous entry on the first team to complete seven double plays in nine innings, so here is a first for the senior circuit.

On Sunday, May 4, 1969 down in the Astrodome, before a crowd of 27,801, the Houston Astros put on a fielding clinic against the San Francisco Giants, and the "Boys by the Bay" were complicit in making it happen.

In the top of the first inning LF Jim Ray Hart hit into a SS Denis Menke to 2B Joe Morgan to 1B Curt Blefary double play. In the 3rd RHP Horace "Dooley" Womack got catcher Dick Dietz to hit into an around the horn double play, 3B Doug Rader to 2B Joe Morgan on to 1B Curt Blefary. In the 4th Womack got 3B Bobby Etheridge to hit into a short-to-second-to first double play.

The twin-killings continued on into the 5th when Womack got RF Frank Johnson to be doubled up Morgan to Blefary. In the 7th inning it was RHP Fred Gladding's turn as he had his mound opponent, right-hander Juan Marichal, hit into a Menke to Blefary double play. The Giants continued to get men on base, and then to have them snuffed out when in the 8th Gladding had 2B Ron Hunt go the Blefary to Menke route for the Astros' 6th double play of the game.

It's never over till it's over as Yogi used to say, and Bobby Etheridge proved the point by breaking up a last chance for a rally when hit into his second, and the seventh, and final double play of the game when his ground ball went from Morgan to Menke to Blefary as the Astros took the game with twice as many double plays as runs, 3-1, as the Giants wasted 9 hits and 4 walks to give Juan Marichal his second loss.

263. What team was the first to be shut out in four consecutive games?

This item will not be warmly received in Beantown as their beloved Boston Americans' bats fell conspicuously silent beginning on Thursday, August 2, 1906, when they went into Chicago to play the White Sox. They were shut out that day 3-0. They came back on Friday, August 3rd to be shut out by the Pale Hose, 4-0. On Saturday, August 4th the whitewash was again applied by the White Sox when they shut out the Americans, 1-0.

They sheepishly sneaked off to Cleveland on Monday, August 6th to play the Indians and found silent bats there as well, as they were shut out for the fourth successive game to be the first team to see goose eggs on the scoreboard four days in a row, and in two cities.

This wasn't an anomaly, for the Americans were shut out 28 times in their 105 losses in 1906, and had a losing streak of twenty in a row from Tuesday, May 1st to Thursday May 24th.

264. What was the first, and only, team to play an entire season without hitting a home run?

We will have to give some leeway here to the 1877 Chicago White Stockings (Cubs) for the schedule was not as lengthy as today. They came in 5th place in the National League that season with a 26-33 record.

Their players had 2,330 plate appearances, 2,273 bat bats, 633 hits, including 79 doubles, and 30 triples, but not one home run.

They scored 366 runs, including 21 in a game on Tuesday, August 7th, but just couldn't get the long ball so they hold the dubious record of being the first, and only team to show a zero at the bottom of their season's stat sheet when it came to home runs.

265. What team was the first to score 10 runs in a game before an out was recorded?

This is historical, but doesn't take us too far back in baseball lore as it occurred on Friday, June 27, 2003 at Fenway Park when the Boston Red Sox were host to the interleague Florida Marlins.

The Marlins started the game off with a run in the top of the 1st inning. When the Red Sox came up in the bottom half of the inning it seems they were ready to embarrass their guests as they shook Marlins starting pitcher right-hander Carl Pavano for 6 hits, and 6 earned runs, including a three-run home run by LF Manny Ramirez. After Pavano, having faced just 6 batters, it was time for a change. In came the second of five pitchers in the game, southpaw Michael Tejera who did no better as he gave up 4 hits, a walk, and 5 earned runs, mimicking his starter in that he didn't get a man out either.

Then in came right-hander Allen Levrault, who got the first batter he faced, SS Nomar Garciaparra, to hit a foul pop-up behind the plate that Marlins' catcher Ivan Rodriguez snared for the first out, after 50 minutes and 91 pitches, and 10 runs had scored. When the inning finally ended the Red Sox were up 14-1.

Levrault went three innings giving up 6 hits, 5 walks and 6 runs before giving way to another right-hander, Kevin Olsen, in the bottom of the 4th, who also went three innings giving up 9 hits and 4 runs before the fourth right-hander, Blaine Neal, arrived in the bottom of the 7th with the score 20-5. Neal struggled the last two innings to get through the game, giving up 3 hits, 1 walk, and 4 runs, and the Red Sox, behind right-hander Byung-Hyun Kim, and four other pitchers, getting an inning of work each, cruised to a 25-8 victory, and made the Red Sox the first team in history to score ten runs before they made an out.

266. What was the first franchise to inaugurate spring training for their ball club?

After the 1885 season, even though the Chicago White Stockings nosed out the New York Giants by two games to capture the National League pennant, manager Cap Anson ordered his team to report to him at Hot Springs, Arkansas for spring training prior to the 1886 season, for the purpose of getting his players in shape and to lose the fat bellies they had acquired.

It must have worked for Chicago captured the NL flag that year by two and a half games over the Detroit Wolverines.

267. What was the first, and only, franchise to win consecutive pennants in two different leagues?

In 1889 the Brooklyn Trolley Dodgers were playing in the American Association and captured the pennant that year with a 93-44 record narrowly besting the St. Louis Browns 90-43 record.

In 1890 Brooklyn entered the National League as just the Brooklyn Dodgers, and again was successful by capturing the NL flag that year besting the Chicago White Stockings, and became the first franchise to capture the pennant in two different leagues.

268. What team was the first to have their pitching staff start over 90 consecutive games without a complete game being pitched?

"The Bullpen Never Sleeps" might be another way of saying in their bullpen the pitchers must have been weary, and their arms aching, as the New York Yankees started a streak in 1991 of not having their staff pitch a complete game until the following season, when on Saturday, April 18, 1992, at the Yankee Stadium, in their eleventh game of the season, and their 93rd without a complete game, southpaw Greg Cadaret, with the benefit of a 14-run assault on four Cleveland Indians pitchers went all the way for a 9-hit shutout, 14-0, that ended the Yankees embarrassing record of being the first team to go over ninety games without having to call on the bullpen to finish off all nine innings.

269. What team was the first to score ten runs in the 9th inning for a walk-off win?

As that sage in pinstripes, "Yogi" Berra, so aptly opined, "It ain't over, 'til it's over."

That must have been the thought process that the Detroit Tigers had in their American League debut on that Opening Day of the 1901 season, on April 25th.

The 10,023 who turned out that Thursday at Bennett Park were witness to the greatest opening day rally one could hope for as their home team spotted the Milwaukee Brewers a 7-0 lead after three innings, and a 13-4 lead going into the 9th inning thanks to their seven errors, including three by their shortstop Norman "The Tabasco Kid" Elberfeld.

Thanks to first baseman Frank "Pop" Dillon's four doubles, which tied a major league record, with two of those doubles coming in a 10-run, 9th inning, and the final one, off right-handed reliever Bert "Pete" Husting, driving in the winning run, giving the Tigers a walk off, 14-13 inaugural win.

270. Who was the first Toronto Blue Jays player to have his number retired?

On Sunday, July 31, 2011, at the Rogers Centre, the Toronto Blue Jays, in a pre-game ceremony retired the uniform number of their Hall of Fame second baseman Roberto Alomar. He was instrumental in helping Toronto achieve back-to-back World Championships in 1992-93, and during his five years with the Blue Jays, from 1991-95, he was selected to the All-Star team five times, won five Gold Glove Awards and batted .302.

271. What franchise was the first to outfit their players with short pants as part of their uniform to wear for the upcoming season?

Leave it up to the flamboyant, innovative, an unpredictable owner, Bill Veeck, to come up with the idea of having his Chicago White Sox ballplayers dress in collared uniform shirts, and instead of the customary below the belt uniform knickers and high stockings, or as some like to wear, extended pants to their ankles, switch to wearing short pants and knee socks for the 1976 season. The players looked like a masculine girls' softball team.

The new uniforms didn't make their first appearance until August 8, 1976, when the White Sox came out on the field before a Sunday crowd of 15,997, at Comiskey Park, for the first game of a doubleheader against the Kansas City Royals. Southpaw Terry Forster got the Pale Hose win, to become the first pitcher to win a major league game wearing shorts.

The second appearance of these Bermuda blues happened on Saturday, August 21st, before a home crowd of 32,607, again out in Comiskey Park, against the Baltimore Orioles. In a shoot-out, the White Sox, in the bottom of the 12th inning, had 2B Bill Stein single home catcher Jim Essian for the winning run, with southpaw Dave Hamilton picking up the 11-10 win.

The third and final appearance of this relatively successful stunt by Veeck came to a close on Sunday, August 22nd after the first game of a doubleheader with the Baltimore, won by right-hander Pete Vuckovich, 7-3, over the Orioles. The 16,991 in attendance were the last to see a major league team win or lose in short pants. Commissioner Bowie Kuhn, not amused by the practice saw that it wasn't continued.

272. What team was the first to score 11 runs in one inning, on only one hit?

This ranks among the near impossible, but it happened on Wednesday, April 22, 1959 out in Municipal Stadium, Kansas City, before a meager crowd of 7,446, when the Chicago White Sox had a field day against three Athletics' pitchers.

Right-hander Tom Gorman started off the top of the 7th inning behind 8-6. Then came two infield errors, and a single to right field by LF Johnny Callison, which scored two runs. The third error of the inning was charged to Roger Maris on the play in right field.

Then Gorman issued a walk to SS Luis Aparicio, who promptly stole second base, and then another walk. He then got behind pinch-hitter Earl Torgeson, and midway in pitching to him, Gorman was replaced by right-hander Mark Freeman who finished with Torgeson by walking him, with Callison scoring. Then a walk, and another walk, then a groundout, followed by another walk with a run scoring, which brought in the third pitcher of the inning, southpaw George "Lefty" Brunet, who walked his first two batters, each scoring another run, then he hit Callison, up for the second time in the inning, with a pitch, scoring a run, then issued another walk scoring a run, then got a strikeout, followed by two more walks, each scoring a run. With the bases loaded CF Jim Landis ended the mound misery by bouncing back to Brunet who threw to 1B Kent Hadley to mercifully end the inning. The scorecard for the inning must have carried over to the next page to show 11 runs, 10 walks, 1 hit batsman, 3 errors, a stolen base, and a lone single for a 19-6 lead. The final line score read an easy 20-6 victory for right-hander Bob Shaw, and a franchise first credited to the Pale Hose.

273. What franchise was the first to put the players' names on the back of their uniforms?

In 1960 the Chicago White Sox must have thought that the numbers on their players' uniforms weren't identity enough, and their actions must have negatively influenced the sale of scorecards, for they outfitted each player with not only his number, but his name on the back of his uniform.

274. Who was the first player to clear the hedge in centerfield for a home run at Baltimore's Memorial Stadium?

For the first time in franchise history, on Saturday, August 10, 1957, the hedge in deep centerfield at Baltimore's Memorial Stadium, was cleared by a 460-foot home run off the bat of New York Yankees centerfielder Mickey Mantle on a pitch delivered with one out, and one on, in the top of the 1st. inning off Orioles right-hander Ray "Farmer" Moore. That helped take New York to a 6-3 win before a crowd of 36,366.

275. What franchise was the first to have two players to each hit a home run from both sides of the plate in the same game?

It was before a crowd of 20,485 at the SkyDome in Toronto, on Sunday, April 23, 2000, when Bernie Williams, the New York Yankees centerfielder, took Blue Jays right-hander Frank Castillo downtown in the 1st. inning with a two-out, two-run home run to left-center field. In the 2nd inning Castillo again gave up a home run, this time a solo shot, with no outs, to catcher Jorge Posada to right field.

In the 4th inning rookie southpaw Clayton Andrews fell victim to a blast by Williams with a two-out, three-run homer to centerfield. Posada followed that with a two-run home run to centerfield to make the Yankees the first franchise to have a pair of players to each hit a home run from both sides of the plate in the same game.

276. **What was the first franchise to have two players collect over 200 base hits, and 100 walks in the same season?**

We turn to the Windy City for this one, for in 1930 Woody English, who played both shortstop and third base for the Chicago Cubs that season, had 214 hits to go along with his 100 walks to match his teammate Hack Wilson, who patrolled centerfield, and had 208 hits and a league-leading 105 free passes to have the Cubbies become the first, and only franchise to have a pair of players exceed both marks in the same season.

277. **Who was the first player to clear the roof for a home run at Comiskey Park, Chicago?**

In Chicago White Sox history no one had cleared the roof at Comiskey Park in Chicago until August 16, 1927, when Babe Ruth came to the plate in the 5th inning, with no outs, and before 20,000 fans, blasted his 37th home run of the season, a solo shot that cleared the roof for the first time, off White Sox right-hander Alphonse "Tommy" Thomas. New York went on to win 8-1, behind southpaw Herb "The Knight of Kennett Square" Pennock.

278. **What franchise was the first to have a payroll where the average player's salary was in excess of $2,000,000?**

The New York Yankees payroll in 1995 showed them to be the first franchise to have the average player's salary exceed two million dollars. Their team salary of $58,200,000 showed Jack McDowell as the highest paid at $5,400,000, followed by Danny Tartabull at $5,300,000; Jimmy Key at $4,873,700; Wade Boggs at $4,724,316; and Don Mattingly at $4,420,000.

The team finished 2nd in the American League East with a 79-65, .549 record, and losing in five games to the Seattle Mariners in the League Divisional Series.

279. What was the first team to win a game while not getting a base hit?

It's pretty hard to believe, and that's what the Cincinnati Reds players, and the 5,426 fans in attendance said when on Thursday, April 23, 1964, down in Colts Stadium, the Houston Colt .45's right-hander Ken Johnson faced 31 batters, gave up 2 walks, but not a single base hit, but lost, 1-0.

His mound opponent, southpaw Joe Nuxhall, pitched a 5-hit shutout, walking one, and also faced 31 batters. Nuxhall won his first game of the season while Johnson lost his first after two wins.

It all came to a conclusion after eight scoreless innings when, in the top of the 9th 2B Pete Rose hit back to Johnson who mishandled the ball and "Charlie Hustle" ended up on second base. Then 3B Chico Ruiz grounded out sending Rose to third, where he then scored when CF Vada Pinson grounded to 2B Nellie Fox, who committed an error allowing Rose to score with the winning run. Nuxhall shut down Houston in the 9th and Cincinnati came away with the first major league win, in history, without the benefit of a base hit.

280. What was the first American League team to win a game in which they went hitless?

Let's go back to April 30, 1967, to Baltimore's Memorial Stadium, where a Sunday crowd of 26,884 settled in for the first game of a double-header with the Detroit Tigers. On the mound that day for the hosting Orioles was southpaw Steve Barber. Opposing him for the Motown nine was right-hander Earl Wilson.

Going into the top of the 9th inning Baltimore was up 1-0, on a sacrifice fly by SS Luis Aparicio, scoring LF Curt Blefary, who had walked, with the only run of the game.

Up to this point Barber had not allowed a base hit and the crowd sat anxiously awaiting history to be made by one of their own.

1B Norm Cash led off with a walk, Dick Tracewski pinch-ran for Cash. Then Barber walked SS Ray Oyler, moving Tracewski to second. Jake Wood was then sent in to run for Oyler. That brought up RHP Earl Wilson, who had given up just two hits in his 8 innings on the mound, and he sacrificed the runners over, which brought up Willie Horton to pinch-hit for 2B Dick McAuliffe, and he hit a foul pop-up for the second out. With CF Mickey Stanley the next batter Barber unleashed a wild pitch scoring Tracewski with the tying run, and moving Wood to third. Barber then walked Stanley for his 10th walk of the game, and that quickly brought in the right-handed reliever Stu Miller. Miller got 3B Don Wert to hit into a fielder's choice with Aparicio tossing to 2B Woody Held for the third out, but Held couldn't hold on to the ball and Stanley was safe at second, and Wert at first, but more importantly, Wood scored on the play for the go-ahead run. Miller then got RF Al Kaline to ground into a force out at second and the unbelievable inning was over. The line score showed 2 runs, 0 hits, 1 error, and 2 left on base.

The bottom of the 9th went easily as Tigers right-hander Fred Gladding came on in relief of Wilson and set down 3B Brooks Robinson, RF Frank Robinson, and 1B Mike Epstein in order to preserve the win for Earl Wilson and give the local fans something they hoped to see going into the 9th inning, a no-hitter by Steve Barber, but not with the result that ensued. The first team in the American League to have their staff, Barber 8 2/3 and Miller 1/3 innings pitch and lose a no-hitter, as Detroit became the first team to win a ballgame, 2-1, without getting a base hit.

281. What two teams were the first to play a triple-header in one day?

We have to go back to September 1, 1890, when at 10:30 am, the Brooklyn Bridegrooms took on the Pittsburgh Innocents (Pirates) in the first game and raced off to a 10-0 lead until the 9th inning when the Innocents came alive, and scored 6 runs, and had the bases loaded with two outs.

Then up came 3B George "Doggie" Miller to provide a dramatic ending as he cleared the bases with a triple to left field and raced around second as CF Darby O'Brien recovered the ball and threw to SS Germany Smith who had run out from short to take the relay, and then spun and fired home, and the hustling Doggie was narrowly thrown out at the plate trying to make it a game-tying home run. Brooklyn, behind right-hander "Parisian Bob" Caruthers, came away with a close 10-9 win.

The second game was also a nail-biter, but the Bridegrooms pulled off a 3-2 victory. The 3rd and final game of the day saw southpaw Dave Anderson take the mound again for the Innocents after losing the second game, and although he pitched a complete game, Brooklyn, behind right-hander Adonis Terry swept the first triple-header ever played, 8-4. That last loss gave Pittsburgh its 22nd straight loss, which would reach 24 before its next victory.

282. What were the first, and only, teams to play a triple-header in the

20th Century?

Once again Pittsburgh was involved, this time against the Cincinnati Reds, on Saturday, October 2, 1920, after the order to play was handed down by National League President John A. Heydler after Pirates owner Barney Dreyfuss, who had been refused by Reds manager Pat Moran to comply with Dreyfuss's wishes, bowed to the league president's order. The Pirates were battling for the pennant and time and schedule was running out to get these games in, and the weather was not cooperating.

The first game started at noon and the Reds wasted no time blasting southpaw ace Wilbur Cooper for ten hits and eight runs in 2-2/3 innings, and cruised to a 13-4 win.

The second game was close until the 7th inning when Cincinnati exploded for seven runs to go on to a 7-3 win, pounding Pirates right-hander for 14 hits.

The third game of this triple-header started late in the afternoon and saw Pittsburgh score three runs in the 1st inning and add three more in the 6th while Pirates' rookie righty "Jughandle Johnny" Morrison tamed the Reds with four hits.

After one hour, one minute of play, darkness descended on the Steel City after the 6th inning, and the umpires called the game with Pittsburgh on top. 6-0. The 24-inning tripleheader took just five hours to complete and became the first, and the last of its kind.

283. What team won the first game played at Braves Field?

The Boston Braves opened Braves Field on August 18, 1915, as a crowd of 46,500 jammed into the ballpark to see Braves right-hander Dick "Baldy" Rudolph defeat the St. Louis Cardinals, 3-1, and become the first team to win at their new ballpark.

284. What was the winning team in the first night game ever played at the Polo Grounds?

Although the first major league night game occurred on May 24, 1935 in Cincinnati, the inaugural night game under Coogan's Bluff didn't happen until Friday, May 24, 1940, when 20,260 fans anxiously awaited their first look at their hometown heroes under the arcs. The Boston Braves were the visiting team, and right-hander "Sailor Bill" Posedel was the mound opponent of Giants right-hander Harry "Gunboat" Gumbert.

The Giants got off to a fast start on the bats of LF Jo-Jo-Moore's 1st. inning home run, followed by 2B Al Glossop's 2nd inning solo home run, and SS Billy Jurges' two run homer right after Glossop's blast, as the Giants went on to a comfortable 8-1 win.

285. What was the first, and only, team to hit three grand slam home runs in the same game?

On Thursday, August 25, 2011, at the Yankee Stadium, the afternoon crowd of 46,369 never expected to see this kind of hitting display put on by the Yankees against the pitching staff of the Oakland Athletics. The crowd was taken out of the game early as Oakland jumped off to a 7-1 lead after three innings against right-handed starter Phil Hughes and righty reliever Cory Wade.

The crowd then saw catcher Russell Martin blast a solo home run off right-hander Rich Harden in the bottom of the 4th to make it 7-2, and little did they know that history was soon coming down the line.

In the 5th DH Derrick Jeter singled, CF Curtis Granderson walked, 1B Mark Teixeira struck out, and 3B Alex Rodriguez singled softly to left field with Jeter stopping at third. That brought up 2B Robinson Cano who wiped the bases clean with a grand slam home run, off Harden, to deep right field, scoring Jeter, Granderson, and Rodriguez before him to make it 7-6 Oakland. That was all for Harden as southpaw Craig Breslow came on pitch.

In the 6th inning the first thing Breslow did was to hit the leadoff batter, Granderson, with a pitch. He then got Teixeira to line out to left field, which was all manager Bob Melvin needed to see, and rookie right-hander, Fautino De Los Santos, was called in to pitch to A-Rod. He walked him, which moved Granderson to second, and brought up Cano. De Los Santos unleashed a wild pitch with the runners moving up, before De Los Santos got Cano swinging for the third strike. Melvin then gave the signal to catcher Anthony Recker to intentionally walk RF Nick Swisher and load the bases. Martin, who had hit a solo home run in the 4th off Harden, didn't wait very long before he blasted his second homer of the game, a line drive deep down the right field line, for the Yankees second grand slam in two innings, making the score 10-7. When SS Eduardo Nunez singled to center that was all for De Los Santos as southpaw Jordan Norberto came on and got Jeter to hit a soft grounder to short that SS Cliff Pennington took, and fired home to Recker to end the inning.

The home run barrage wasn't over for the Oakland mound staff, for in the bottom of the 8th inning, with the Yankees ahead, 16-8, they continued to pour it on when Francisco Cevelli, batting for Cano, singled to left field off right-hander Bruce Billings, who had come on to replace Norberto in the 7th, and with one out, Martin doubled to center moving Cervelli to third, Nunez walked, and LF Brett Gardner singled to left, scoring Cevelli and moving Martin to third and Nunez to second. Jeter went down swinging. Granderson came up, and you guessed right, he blasted a grand slam home run to deep left-center field, the Yankees third of the game, scoring Martin, Nunez, and Gardner to make the score 21-8. Southpaw Brian "T-Rex" Fuentes came in to replace Billings, and Andruw Jones, who had come on in the 8th inning replacing Teixeira, hit a solo shot to left field to give the Yankees a 22-8 lead which they held until the 9th, when they gave up a single run, in this 22-9 lopsided win, and sending the Oakland pitching coach to the couch with a jar of aspirin.

286. What was the first team to have four of their players hit their 500th career home run while playing for them?

This is A Tale of Two Cities, no, not London and Paris, but New York and San Francisco.

The characters in this historical, but factual version, could all hit the dickens out of a baseball and proved it when it all started in New York when the Giants Hall of Fame rightfielder "Master Melvin" Ott became the first National League player to reach the 500 home run plateau on Wednesday, August 1, 1945, before a crowd of 19,318 at the Polo Grounds when he connected with a solo shot into the right field stands off Boston Braves right-hander Johnny Hutchings in the 3rd inning for his 11th round-tripper of the season and the 500th of his 511 career home runs. The Giants cruised on to a 9-2 victory.

The scene now shifts to the City by the Bay, after the Giants moved their franchise to San Francisco, and Willie Mays was playing down in the Houston Astrodome, before a crowd of 19,827, against the Astros right-hander Don Nottebart. Willie came up in the 3rd inning and hit his 47th season, and 500th career, home run into centerfield. The Giants went on to a 5-1 win, and Willie went on to hit 660 career home runs.

The third member of this story was none other than Willie "Stretch" McCovey, who was playing first base in the first game of a doubleheader on

Friday, June 30, 1978 down in Atlanta Fulton County Stadium. He came up in the top of the 2nd inning, before a crowd of 14,429, and blasted a solo shot for his 7th home run of the season, and the 500th of his career, off Braves southpaw Jamie Easterly. It wasn't enough as the Braves squeaked out a 10-9 win.

Now we come to the fourth Giants player to reach the coveted 500 level in home runs. It took place on Tuesday, April 17, 2001 at Pacific Bell Park, before 41,059 of the faithful, when in the bottom of the 8th inning, after SS Rich Aurilia tripled to right-centerfield, Barry Bonds crushed right-hander Terry Adams pitch for a no out, two-run home run for his 6th of the year, and the 500th of his to be 762 career home runs, giving the Giants a 3-2 win, and making the Giants the first franchise to have four players hit their 500th home run wearing their uniform.

287. Who was the first batter in Minnesota Twins franchise history to hit three consecutive home runs in the same game?

The popular Twins right fielder Bobby Allison became the first in Minnesota franchise history to hit three consecutive home runs in a single game when he hit a 3-run blast, in the 5th inning off Jim "Mudcat" Grant, the Cleveland Indians right-hander, on Friday, May 17, 1963, at Cleveland Stadium, and followed that with a solo shot in the 7th off right-hander Jerry Walker, and finished it off by hitting a two-run home run in the bottom of the 8th off southpaw Ron Nischwitz as the Twins rolled to an 11-4 victory.

288. What teams played in the first night game at Sportsman's Park?

The first night game to be played at Sportsman's Park came on Friday, May 24, 1940 when the St. Louis Browns played host to the visiting Cleveland Indians before a crowd of 24,827 fans.

Indians right-hander Bob "Rapid Robert" Feller was matched up against the Browns right-hander Eldon "Big Six" Auker, and both pitchers went all the way with Feller giving up 7 hits and Auker 9 as Cleveland came away with a 3-2 win, with Feller hitting his first major league home run, a solo shot in the 3rd inning.

289. What teams were the first to field 13 future Hall of Fame players in the same game?

Little did the 40,000 fans who turned out for the doubleheader played down in Shibe Park on Thursday, May 24, 1928 realize what an historic event they were about to witness in the first game. The New York Yankees had come to town and fielded six future Hall of Fame players with Earl Combs in centerfield, Babe Ruth in left, Lou Gehrig at first base, Tony Lazzeri at second, Leo Durocher at shortstop, and right-hander Waite Hoyt coming on in relief in the 9th inning to get the final two outs in the Yankees 9-7 win.

The Philadelphia Athletics field was an equally impressive group with seven of their players, Ty Cobb in right field, flanked by Tris Speaker in center, Mickey Cochrane behind the plate handling the pitches of Lefty Grove, and having Al Simmons, Eddie Collins, and Jimmie Foxx stepping to the plate as pinch-hitters. Philadelphia came back to take the nightcap 5-2.

290. What was the first major league team to have more than 16 consecutive losing seasons?

On Monday, September 7, 2009, out in PNC Park, 14,673 of the faithful turned out to see their Pittsburgh Pirates establish a new record for futility as Cubs southpaw Ted Lilly defeated the Bucs, 4-2, to hand them their 10th defeat in their last 11 games, their 82nd of the season, (54-82) to assure them of having the dubious distinction of becoming the first team in major league history, and the first in North American professional sports, to have 17 consecutive sub .500 seasons as they ended up with a 62-99 record. As of this writing the Pirates are about to extend that losing season record to 19.

Interestingly their last winning season came in 1992, when they went 96-66, which put them in the National League Championship Series, which they lost to Atlanta in five games.

291. What was the first National League team to use 10 pitchers in a 9-inning game?

That Friday evening game, on September 7, 2007, out in Coors Field, must have taxed the patience of the 27,247 in attendance as they waited 3 hours and 25 minutes for pitcher after pitcher to come in and toe the rubber for their beloved Colorado Rockies when their team never was behind in the game necessitating a more effective hurler.

Clint Hurdle, the Rockies manager, had to remove his starting right-hander Elmer Dessens with one out in the 3rd inning after he strained his left hamstring while walking San Diego Padres RHP Justin Germano. In came southpaw Mark Redman, and the parade of pitchers began. Four pitchers later, with the Rockies up 5-3, in came RHP Matt Herges, and he became the winning pitcher, pitching just 2.1 innings before pitcher #6 came in. Three innings, and four pitchers later, RHP Ramon Ortiz came on and pitched the 9th to give the Rockies an easy 10-4 win, using as many pitchers as runs they scored, by using 10 pitchers who gave up a total of 4 runs, 5 hits, and 8 walks. Across the field, in the Padres' dugout, skipper Bud Black used six pitchers so the game ended up with as many pitchers being used, collectively, 16, than all the other position players that started the game for both teams.

292. What team was the first to leave 20 base runners on base in a 9-inning game?

"I wanna' come home" must have been the cry of the 20 New York Yankees base runners that were stranded on base on Friday, September 21, 1956 up in Fenway Park, for after 15 hits, and 9 walks off right-handed starter Frank Sullivan, and fellow right-handers George Susce, and Ike Delock, along with 4 Red Sox errors, they could muster up just 7 runs, leaving the bases loaded three times, as Boston went on to defeat the pennant-bound Yankees, 13-7.

293. What was the first team to leave 16 runners on base, over 9 innings, and still be shutout?

I thought the object of this game was to have runners come around and score must have been the reaction of the 25,618 fans sitting in Busch Stadium on that Friday evening, May 24, 1994, when their hometown Cardinals were locked in a 0-0 tie, and had left 14 runners on base, through 8 innings, against the visiting Philadelphia Phillies.

The tie was soon broken as the Phillies came up with 4 runs in the top of the 9th to send the Redbirds up for one last try to bring somebody, anybody, home with a run. That wasn't to be for although they got singles from 1B Gregg Jefferies and 3B Todd Zeile, right-hander Doug Jones then slammed the door and the Phillies came away with a 4-0 shutout and the Cardinals, with two left on in the 9th, became the first team to leave 16 runners aboard while being shutout.

294. What team was the first to win a game in Braves Field, Boston?

After previously playing their home games at Fenway Park the Boston Braves, under manager George Stallings, opened up their new ballpark, Braves Field, on Wednesday, August 18, 1915, before an overflow crowd of 46,500. The first visiting team was the St. Louis Cardinals, under the managerial reins of Miller Huggins.

Braves right-hander Dick "Baldy" Rudolph took the mound and came away with the first victory for the Braves in their new home, defeating the Cardinals, 3-1.

Later on, in 1936, when the All-Star game was played there, and from that time until April 29, 1941 it was officially known as the "Bee Hive".

295. Who was the first pitcher to throw a no-hitter in Chicago White Sox history?

We have to go back to the first game of a doubleheader played on Saturday, September 20, 1902 in Chicago's South Side Park, where right-hander James "Nixey" Callahan became the first pitcher in White Sox history to pitch a no-hitter when stopped the Detroit Tigers, 3-0.

296. What was the first modern day team to commit seven errors in one inning?

The 8th inning for the Cleveland Naps, on September 20, 1905, against the Chicago White Sox, wasn't very productive as they committed seven errors that led to 8 runs as the Pale Hose came from behind for a 9-6 victory. The faux pas were evenly divided as LF Otto Hess, CF Harry "Deerfoot" Bay, RF Elmer Flick, SS Terry "Cotton Top" Turner, 3B Bill Bradley all had one each, and the catcher Nig Clarke contributed a pair.

297. What team was the first to turn two triple plays in one game?

The 34,113 who turned out at Fenway Park on Tuesday, July 17, 1990 were witness to a once in a lifetime experience when the Minnesota Twins, in spite of losing 1-0, to the Boston Red Sox, did something no other team in history had done.

They turned a triple play in the 4th inning when RF Tom Brunansky, with the bases loaded, grounded to 3B Gary Gaetti who went around the horn to 2B Al Newman, who relayed on to Kent Hrbek at first for the triple killing.

In the 8th inning, after SS Tim Naehring doubled, and 3B Wade Boggs walked, 2B Jody Reed ended a chance for some badly needed runs when he grounded to Gaetti who again went around the horn to Newman and Hrbek, for the second triple play of the game, and the first repeat of one in the same game in major league history, obviously a Groundbreaker for the

Twins.

298. Who was the first owner to have a boat built to house and transport his team?

As wacky as this sounds that's not the way Chicago White Sox President Charles "The Grand Old Roman" Comiskey saw it when, with his team conducting spring training in New Orleans prior to the 1905 season, and being a very big boat enthusiast, ordered the construction of a houseboat by The Racine Boat Manufacturing Company, of Muskegon, Michigan, for the express purpose of housing and transporting, his team during the 1905 spring training season.

299. What was the first franchise to have their players complete a triple steal twice in the same game?

We have to go back to Friday, July 25, 1930 when the Philadelphia Athletics ran wild on the bases at League Park, Cleveland. In the top of the first inning Hall of Fame LF Al "Bucketfoot" Simmons was on third base, RF Edmund "Bing" Miller was on second, and SS Dib Williams was leading off first. That's when the first heist was on as Indians' right-hander Pete Appleton went into his windup, Simmons, who was off with the pitch, raced successfully for the plate and scored, as Miller and Williams moved up a base.

Going into the 4th inning, and leading 4-0, the Athletics erupted for six runs helped when catcher, Gordon "Mickey" Cochrane, was perched on third, Simmons on second, and 1B Jimmie "Double X" Foxx on first.

Again the Athletics took advantage of Appleton, and his battery mate, Joe "Mule" Sprinz, as Cochrane successfully raced for home, Simmons went to third, and "Double X" wound up on second for the second triple steal of the game, as Philadelphia put up six runs to give Bob "Lefty" Grove his 14th win with an easy 14-1 decision.

300. What was the first team to raise a white flag immediately after some of its games ended?

If you have been out in Wrigley Field, Chicago, and witnessed a Cubs victory, you would have seen a pure white flag, with a large "W" on it, raised to designate and celebrate a Cub "win" immediately after the Cubs home game ended with a victory. The flag, which is raised on the left side of the scoreboard by a member of the scoreboard staff, waves in the breezes of the Windy City for a few hours before being taken down, with the flag being changed after each Cubs win. These are called "White Flag Days" by the north-side faithful.

If the Cubbies should lose, a flag with a large white-lettered "L" on a blue background, is flown on the right hand side of the scoreboard. Should the Cubbies split a doubleheader both flags are shown.

These flags are very symbolic for Cubs fans, and have been since the construction of the scoreboard, by then Cubs owner, Philip K. Wrigley, in 1937, and the introduction of the flag raising ceremony shortly thereafter.

301. What franchise was the first to have players with 300, 400, and 500 career home runs playing for them on the same day?

If you had been one of the 23,407 fans down in The Ballpark in Arlington on May 11, 2003, when the Texas Rangers fielded SS Alex Rodriguez, with 309 career home runs, RF Juan Gonzalez with 417, and 1B Rafael Palmeiro with 499. That is until the 7th inning when Palmeiro blasted a two-out, three-run home run into the right field seats off Cleveland Indians right-hander Dave Elder, for his 10th home run of the season, and the 500th of his career propelling the Rangers to a 17-10 win, and making the Rangers the first team in major league history to have players with 300, 400, and 500 career home runs on the field in the same game.

302. What team was the first to commit six errors in a World Series game?

This memorable game took place on Saturday, October 13, 1906 at the West Side Grounds in Game 5 between the Windy City rivals, the White Sox and the Cubs. The Pale Hose did the best they could to give the game to the Cubbies, but came away with an 8-6 win anyway.

The White Sox made two errors in the 1st inning, one by right-hander "Big Ed" Walsh and the other by 2B Frank Isbell. In the 3rd inning SS George Davis made an error, as did 3B George Rohe in the 4th and 6th innings. In the 8th Frank Isbell came back for his second error of the game, and the record-breaking 6th of the game to make the Pale Hose red-faced over their fielding habits by being the first franchise to err an even six times over nine innings.

303. What team was the first to play an entire season and commit fewer than 200 errors?

It was an historic season in more ways than one for the 1906 Chicago Cubs. They not only won the National League pennant by twenty games over the second place New York Giants, with a record of 116-36, but won more regular season games than any other team in history. They also led the National League with the fewest errors, 194, to become the first team in major league history to commit fewer than 200 errors in a season.

304. Who was the first St. Louis Cardinals player to hit a walk-off home run, in extra innings, in their postseason history?

Their centerfielder, Jim Edmunds, joined the "Groundbreakers" club on Wednesday, October 20, 2004 at Busch Stadium, before a hometown crowd of 52,144, when in Game 6 of the NLCS, he came to bat in the bottom of the 12th inning, against the Houston Astros right-hander Dan Miceli, with the score tied at 4-4. He walked the first batter, 1B Albert Pujols, got 3B Scott Rolen to pop out behind the plate to catcher Brad Ausmus, bringing up CF Jim Edmunds who blasted an 0-1 Miceli pitch to deep right-center for a two-run home run, scoring Pujols, and sending the Cardinals to a 6-4 win. They also won Game 7, winning 5-2, to send them into the World Series against the Boston Red Sox, with Edmunds being the first player in Redbirds' history to hit a walk-off home run in extra innings in the post season.

305. Who was the first franchise owner, after winning the pennant, to boycott the World Series?

For the first and only time in major league baseball history John T. Brush, the owner of the New York Giants, along with his manager, John McGraw, in a vindictive display against Ban Johnson, the President of the newly formed American League, with whom they had a long-standing personal dispute, refused to meet the Boston Americans in the 1904 World Series.

Neither of them was willing to lend credibility to Johnson, and the new league, by agreeing to meet them in the post season.

The Giants, winning 106 games, easily won the National League flag by thirteen games over the Chicago Cubs, and had a pair of future Hall of Fame pitchers, Christy Mathewson and Joe McGinnity, who had won 68 games between them that season. Boston's staff wasn't shoddy by any means with Cy Young, Bill Dinneen, and Jesse Tannehill showing 70 victories among them as well.

The following year, 1905, after another easy pennant win by nine games over Pittsburgh, McGraw agreed to meet the Philadelphia Athletics in what most describe as the greatest pitching display in World Series history.

Each of the five games were a shutout as Mathewson won three, McGinnity one, and the Athletics' Chief Bender one as the Giants became World Champions in five games.

306. What were the first two teams to play an entire nine-inning game in less than 60 minutes?

Now before we start thinking about this let's remember games were not interrupted by commercials so they moved along at a decent pace, especially with Bill Klem behind the plate.

One instance that made this a "Groundbreaker" moment took place in the first game of a Sunday doubleheader at the Polo Grounds, on September 28, 1919, when right-hander Jesse "Nubby" Barnes of the New York Giants went up against right-hander Lee "Specs" Meadows, of the Philadelphia Phillies.

The Phillies jumped off to a 1-0 lead in the 1st inning, but Barnes slammed the door, and the Giants came away with a 6-1 win in a record 51 minutes. The first teams in history to allow their 14,000 fans an uninterrupted trip to the rest rooms, and concession stands in under an hour.

Barnes faced just 33 batters, giving up five hits, while Meadows gave up thirteen hits to the 37 batters he faced, but there wasn't much time spent with the batters stepping out to adjust their equipment, or take practice swings between pitches.

307. What team was the first to have 50 total bases in a single game?

We'll take you down to Shibe Park on Friday, June 3, 1932, where a paltry crowd of 5,000 saw a baseball game whose final score resembled a football game, as the New York Yankees defeated the Philadelphia Athletics in a batting barrage, 20-13. Five Philadelphia pitchers gave up 23 base hits good for 50 total bases as 1B Lou Gehrig hit four home runs for 16 total bases, followed by 3B Tony Lazzeri with a home run and 11 total bases, CF Earle Combs and LF Babe Ruth each had a home run and 6 TB's, RF Ben Chapman had 4, catcher Bill Dickey with 2, and 2B Jack Saltzgaver, LHP "Lefty" Gomez, and RHP Gordon "Dusty" Rhodes each with one.

The Athletics held up their side with 13 hits good for 27 total bases with 1B Jimmie Foxx, and catcher Mickey Cochrane, each having homers and a combined 11 total bases. With 77 total bases over nine innings those 5,000 fans witnessed history, unlikely to be repeated.

308. What was the first National League team to score 1,000 runs in a single season?

We have to go back to the 1893 season when the fourth place Philadelphia Phillies scored 1,011 runs in that 129-game season, just surpassing the first place Boston Beaneaters who won the pennant by scoring 1,008 runs.

309. Who hit the first home run in the new Polo Grounds?

On April 14, 1911 the wooden Polo Grounds was destroyed by fire. The field was replaced with a double-deck grandstand with a horseshoe design to accommodate the configuration of Coogan's Hollow, giving it shorter left and right field lines, and a tremendously deep centerfield reaching 505 feet from home plate.

In the interim the Giants played twenty-nine games at Hilltop Park until Wednesday, June 28, 1911, when the new Polo Grounds re-opened., Before 10,000 fans Christy Mathewson and the New York Giants shut out the Boston Rustlers, 3-0, with their 2B "Laughing Larry" Doyle hitting the first home run in the new park, off southpaw Alonzo "Al" Mattern.

A total of 6,660 home runs were hit in Polo Grounds history, with the Giants' rightfielder, Mel Ott hitting 323 of his 511 career home runs there.

310. Who hit the first home run in Ebbets Field, Brooklyn?

The first game played at Ebbets Field was on Wednesday, April 9, 1913, when the Philadelphia Phillies shutout the Brooklyn Superbas (Dodgers), 1-0. The first home run wasn't hit there until Saturday, April 26, 1913 when LF Casey Stengel hit one of his seven that year, in a 5-3 win over the Giants.

311. Who were the first team, and its batter, to bat against the first use of a yellow baseball in the major leagues?

On Tuesday, August 2, 1938 the Brooklyn Dodgers hosted the St. Louis Cardinals at Ebbets Field in a doubleheader. In the first game the Dodgers introduced a yellow baseball for the first time, and right-hander "Fat Freddie" Fitzsimmons threw his first "yellow pitch" to Cardinals' centerfielder Terry Moore. Brooklyn took the first game 6-2, but not before Johnny Mize hit a 7th inning solo home run of the first yellow baseball in major league history into the anxious hands of a fan in the stands for a home run.

312. What was the first, and only, team to hold their spring training camp in Bermuda?

The New York Yankees traveled to, and held their spring training camp in Hamilton, Bermuda prior to the 1913 season.

313. What was the first team to hold their spring training in Cuba?

The New York Giants, and their manager Bill Terry, decided to take their team to Cuba for their spring training camp in 1937.

314. What was the first team to be taken to the Dominican Republic for spring training?

In 1948, when the Dodgers played in Brooklyn, they took their team down to the Dominican Republic for their spring training camp.

315. What was the first franchise, in the modern era, to win 80% of their home games?

If you went to the home games down to Shibe Park, Philadelphia to see Connie Mack's Athletics play in 1931 you were a witness to history, as the American League Champions won 60 of their 75 games played there that season to become the first team in the modern era to have an .800 record at home, while posting a 47-30 record on the road, which gave them a pennant-winning 107-45 record, 13.5 games ahead of the 2nd place New York Yankees.

Their winning ways didn't impress the St. Louis Cardinals who took the Fall Classic in seven games.

316. What was the first, and only, franchise in the modern era, to win 80% of their away games in a single season?

It mattered not where the 1906 Chicago Cubs played that season as skipper Frank Chance took his team to the National League pennant with a record 116-36 record, with a 56-21 record before his hometown fans at the West Side Grounds, and an unheard of 60-15, .800 record on the road. That was too much for the second place New York Giants who were 20 games back and beyond telescope range of the Boston Braves who ended up 66.5 games behind in last place. Those numbers didn't faze their cross-town rivals, the American League Champion White Sox, who took the World Series in six games.

317. What franchise was the first to play, and win, a baseball game played on ice skates?

One might have called the Philadelphia Athletics "the frozen field nine" on that Saturday afternoon of February 4, 1861, when they played, and defeated, the Charter Oak Club of Brooklyn, on the frozen Litchfield Pond out in South Brooklyn, New York, by the crazy score of 36 to 27 with all the players wearing ice skates. Each team was allowed to have 10 players with the extra being a back- up catcher.

318. What franchises were the first to be approved to change their home uniforms to "pinstripes"?

At the National League annual meeting, held on Tuesday, February 14, 1911, the New York Giants and the Philadelphia Phillies were granted permission to come up with a new style of home uniform of white flannels with thin vertical stripes.

These uniforms predated the now widely recognized pinstripe home uniforms worn by the New York Yankees.

319. What was the first major league team to wear numbers on their uniform?

Back on June 26, 1916 the Cleveland Indians, in a game against the Chicago White Sox, out in League Park, came out before their home crowd with large numbers pinned to their left sleeves which corresponded to those on the scorecard.

The honor of being the first major league batter to come to the plate wearing a number on his uniform was Canadian-born southpaw swinging leftfielder Jack Graney.

Although the Indians were the first major league franchise to experiment with numbers on their uniforms the experiment lasted just a few weeks. In the 1917 season it was tried again, this time on the right sleeve only to have the practice abandoned.

320. What was the first American League team to start off a game with three consecutive home runs?

It was quite a shocking welcome Texas Rangers right-hander Colby Lewis received when he opened up the bottom of the 1st inning in the first game of a double header against Baltimore down in Orioles Park at Camden Yards on Thursday, May 10, 2012.

The first batter he faced was left fielder Ryan Flaherty who greeted Lewis with a home run to deep right field. The next batter was shortstop J.J. Hardy who did the exact same thing, only to deep left field. The third batter was right fielder Nick Markakis who wanted in on the fun and blasted another home run, down the left field line for the third consecutive home run making the Orioles the first American League team in history to open up a game with three consecutive home runs. All three hit on only five pitches thrown by Lewis. The O's took the game 6-5.

A similar thing happened at the Great American Ballpark in Cincinnati when the Milwaukee Brewers teed-off on Reds southpaw Phil Dumatrait in the top of the 1st inning on Sunday, September 9, 2007, as 2B Rickie Weeks opened up the game with a home run to deep centerfield, and SS J.J. Hardy (yes, he was involved again) blasted a home run to right field, and 3B Ryan Braun made it a three-some as he blasted the third consecutive home run, this to centerfield, to open up a game. The Brewers coasted to a 10-5 win.

321. Who hit the first Texas Rangers home run in Arlington Stadium?

The first player to christen the new ballpark for the Texas Rangers was that huge Rangers first baseman Ron Frank Howard, who on Friday April 21, 1972, unloaded a solo home run with two outs to deep centerfield off California Angels southpaw Clyde Wright, before 20,105 excited new fans, as Texas came away with a 7-6 win.

322. Who had the first base hit in Texas Rangers history?

It almost didn't happen before that opening day crowd of 13,916 out in Anaheim Stadium on that Saturday afternoon of April 15, 1972. Angels' right-hander Andy Messersmith was on the mound for California and was on his way to a no-hitter until Texas catcher Hal King led off the top of the 7th inning by stroking a single to right field for the first base hit by a Texas Ranger in their franchise history. SS Toby Harrah got the hang of it, and in the top of the 8th inning, he too, lined a single to right field for the sum total of the base hits as California, and Messersmith came away with a 1-0, two-hitter.

323. Who was the first Texas Rangers player in their franchise history to be selected for an All-Star Game?

It came in their first year of existence when shortstop Toby Harrah was selected as a member of the American League squad for the All-Star game that was played down in Atlanta on July 25, 1972.

The game was the 7th in All-Star game history to go into extra innings and was won by the National League in the 10th inning, 4-3.

324. What teams were the first to play an extra-inning game in which not one strikeout was recorded by either team?

It was on Tuesday, July 7, 1931, out in Sportsman's Park, when the players of both teams, the St. Louis Browns, and the visiting Chicago White

Sox, had their eyes on the ball for it wasn't until the top of the 12th inning with the score tied 8-8 that Chicago broke through for two runs to take their lead into the bottom of the 12th where right-hander Hal McKain came on to set the Brownies down to give right-hander Urban "Red" Faber the win, 10-8.

What made this game so different, and a first time event, was that although both teams had 13 hits, St. Louis southpaw Walter "Lefty" Stewart, who went 9 innings, and right-hander Chad Kimsey who went the last three, couldn't strikeout a batter. That can also be said about right-handers Tommy Thomas, "Red" Faber, and Hal McKain of the Pale Hose who also couldn't register a strikeout making it 72 putouts in the game but not once did the home plate umpire have to shout out, "Strike three!".

325. What team was the first in major league history to have each of their four infielders hit at least 25 home runs in the same season?

It happened down in Dolphin Stadium on Friday, September 12, 2008 when third baseman Jorge Cantu led off the bottom of the 4th inning by hitting his 25th home run of the season to deep left-center field off Washington Nationals right-hander Shairon Martis in a 2-1 Marlins victory. When the season concluded he ended up with 29 while teammates 1B Mike Jacobs had 32, 2B Dan Uggla also hit 32, and SS Hanley Ramirez topped them all with 33, to make the Marlins the first team to have their four infielders all hit over 25 home runs that season. Those four accounted for 126 of the 208 home runs hit by Florida in 2008.

326. What team was the first to have eight players on the active roster who had hit 200 or more career home runs?

During in the 2012 season the New York Yankees had eight players on their active roster who could claim to have hit over 200 home runs during their careers. It came to pass later in that season when Nick Swisher and Curtis Granderson exceeded that mark, and as of this writing they each have 205 round-trippers to join Eric Chavez (245), Derek Jeter (255), Raul Ibanez (267), Mark Teixeira (337), Andruw Jones (433), and Alex Rodriguez (646).

327. What team was the first to have six players in its history who have hit over 300 home runs while playing for that team?

The New York Yankees didn't come by their sobriquet, "The Bronx Bombers", without reason, and the following players during their history have gone over the 300 mark in home runs while wearing Yankee pinstripes.

Leading the pack is obviously Babe Ruth with 659, followed in order by Mickey Mantle with 536, Lou Gehrig with 493, Joe DiMaggio 361, Yogi Berra 358, and Alex Rodriguez with 302.

328. What was the first National League team to have five players in its history to have hit over 300 home runs while playing for them?

The first franchise to have had five players hit over 300 home runs while playing for them would be the Braves of Boston, Milwaukee, and Atlanta as Hank Aaron (who else) leads the pack with 733 of his 755 career home runs coming while wearing a Braves uniform. Next in line would be Eddie Mathews with 493, then Chipper Jones with 468, Dale Murphy with 371, and followed by Andruw Jones with 368.

329. What franchise was the first to have four players in its history to have hit over 400 home runs while playing for them?

Moving on to the 400 home run level we find the New York/San Francisco Giants being the first franchise in major league history to have four of their players having hit over 400 home runs while wearing the Giants uniform.

We start with Willie Mays who hit 646 home runs in his 21 years with the Giants before moving back to New York, with the Mets, where he finished his career with 660. Then we come to Barry Bonds who smacked 586 with the San Francisco Giants in his 15 years by the Bay, after hitting 176 with the Pittsburgh Pirates, for his career total of 762. Mel Ott, who played his entire 22-year career with the Giants in New York hit 511, and Willie McCovey, in his 19 years with San Francisco, hit 469 of his career 521 home runs there.

330. What was the first modern day team to have over 1,700 hits in a single season?

All of their hitting prowess didn't help the 1921 Detroit Tigers very much for although they were the first team to pass the 1,700 mark with 1,723 base hits with Harry Heilmann getting 237, Bobby Veach, 207, and Ty Cobb 197, leading the way, and batting .316 as a team, they still ended up in 6th place with a 71-82 record.

331. What team was the first in American League history to have teammates finish first, second, and third in the batting race for the season?

Look no further than north of the border to the 1993 World Champion Toronto Blue Jays who, with a .279 team batting average, had 1B John

Olerud bat .363 to win the batting title, DH Paul Molitor finish second with a .332 average, and 2B Roberto Alomar come in third with a .326 average.

332. What team was the first in major league history to come back from an 0-2 deficit in a 5-game League Division Series by winning three consecutive road games?

It all started in San Francisco on Saturday, October 6, 2012 out in AT&T Park when the Cincinnati Reds, the Central Division winners, came away with a 5-2 win in Game 1 over the Western Division winners, the San Francisco Giants.

Cincinnati went on to take Game 2, the following day, 9-0, sending the series back to the Great American Ballpark in Cincinnati where the Giants took Game 3 on Tuesday, October 9th, 2-1.

Game 4 saw the Giants continue their winning ways behind right-hander Tim Lincecum, 8-3. In Game 5, on Thursday, October 11th right-hander Matt Cain, before 44,142 disappointed Reds' fans, saw him win the deciding game, 6-4, and propel the Giants into the NL Championship Series against the St. Louis Cardinals.

333. What was the first team in major league post season history to have the starting pitcher drive in a run in three straight elimination games?

The first four games of the 2012 National League Championship Series saw the St. Louis Cardinals, after dropping Game 2 to the San Francisco Giants, ahead 3 games to 1, and heading back to Busch Stadium for Game 5 hoping to wrap up the NLCS and go on to meet the Detroit Tigers in the World Series.

In Game 5, on Friday, October 19, 2012, the Giants came up in the top of the 4th inning in a scoreless game and began putting runs on the board off Cardinals' right-hander Lance Lynn. LF Gregor Blanco, who had walked earlier, and had moved around to third, set the stage for Giants southpaw Barry Zito, who hit a swinging bunt single down the third base line bringing home Blanco with the 4th run of the inning as the Giants went on to a 5-0 win.

Game 6, on Sunday, the 21st, was back at AT&T Park, and in the bottom of the 2nd, with the Giants up 1-0, right-hander Ryan Vogelsong came up with 1B Brandon Belt leading off third after tripling to center field, and brought him home with a sharp ground ball that SS Pete Kozma couldn't handle for the 2nd run in a 4-run inning that took the Giants to a 6-1 win.

Now we go to the 7th and deciding game on Monday night, October 22nd. In the bottom of the 2nd inning right-hander Matt Cain came up with LF Gregor Blanco on second, via a single to right, and having moved to second on a ground out, was able to score when Cain lashed a single to center off right-hander Kyle Lohse, scoring Blanco with the second run of game, and with five more added in the 3rd the Giants rolled, before 43,056 of their faithful, to a 9th inning, where with two out, and rain pounding down on the field 2B Marco Scutaro spread his arms and looked skyward awaiting the pop-up by Matt Holliday that would seal the easy 9-0 win and give the Giants their 22nd National League Championship. With that win coupled with the last three consecutive winning games over Cincinnati, San Francisco won its record-tying 6th elimination game in the post season.

Those three pitchers, Zito, Vogelsong, and Cain can help put to rest that the 9th slot in the batting order can't produce runs.

1. Who was the first player, of only two, to play for eight different teams and also win the Most Valuable Player Award?

This well-traveled star played three different infield and all three outfield positions for eight different teams during his 13 seasons in both the American and National Leagues.

Of course we are talking about Kevin Mitchell, who was signed by the New York Mets in 1980 as an amateur free agent, and made his major league debut with them on September 4, 1984. He was traded to the San Diego Padres for the 1987 season, but played there for 62 games before being traded up the coast to the San Francisco Giants. In 1989, with the Giants, he had his really big year by leading the National League in home runs (47), runs batted in (125), total bases (345), and slugging percentage (.635), which led to him being named the Most Valuable Player in the National League that year.

From San Francisco he was traded further up the coast to the Seattle Mariners for the 1992 season. He played 99 games there before being traded at the end of that season to the Cincinnati Reds where he played in 1993-94. He was granted Free Agency on October 25, 1994. Is the pace getting too dizzy for you? Hang on, there's more.

Then it was back to the American League, as the Boston Red Sox signed him as a free agent on March 8, 1996. After 27 games with the Red Sox he was traded by them on July 30, 1996 back to the Cincinnati Reds, where he played in 37 games before he was again granted Free Agency, on November 18, 1996. Mitchell's peregrinations don't end just yet. Stay with me.

On December 13, 1996 he signed as a free agent, going back again to the American League, this time with the Cleveland Indians for the '97 season. He played just 20 games with the Tribe batting .153 before they released him on June 3, 1997. The calendar pages turned and who should show up but Kevin Mitchell, as the veteran right-handed hitter signed on as a free agent with the Oakland Athletics. His 51 games with Oakland were his last in the majors as he banged out 29 hits, two home runs, and drove in 21 runs, for a .228 batting average and on August 3, 1998 he played his last game, for he was released on August 7th and his wanderings around the two leagues certainly adroitly identified Mitchell by his nickname of "World" for it seemed that he traveled much of it in his 13-year career with eight different teams, including two World Series, with the Mets in '86, and the

Giants in '89 to go with his two All-Star appearances in 1989-90.

2. Who was the first African-American player to win the American League Most Valuable Player Award?

The first African-American player to be named the American League's Most Valuable Player occurred in 1963 when Elston Howard, who was purchased by the New York Yankees from the Kansas City Monarchs on July 19, 1950, and made his New York Yankee debut on April 14, 1955, and played left field, first base, and caught for New York from 1955 to 1967, won the award with a .287 batting average, having 140 base hits that included 21 doubles, 6 triples, 28 home runs and 85 runs batted in.

He was traded to the Boston Red Sox on August 3, 1967 for Pete Magrini and Ron Klimkowski. After catching 109 games, and playing in 113, for the Red Sox in 1967-68, he finished out his playing career, after 14 seasons, on September 29, 1968, and was released on October 29, 1968 showing a career batting average of .274.

3. Who was the first player to win four consecutive Most Valuable Player Awards?

Barry Bonds not only won four consecutive MVP Awards, 2001-2004, but he is the first to have won six all together with his winning the award in 1990 and 1992.

4. Who was the first player to come to bat in a televised major league game?

Billy Werber, third baseman for the Cincinnati Reds, was the leadoff batter against the Brooklyn Dodgers at Ebbets Field, Brooklyn, in the first televised major league game, played on Saturday, August 26, 1939. The game had an estimated 3,000 viewers.

5. Who was the first major league umpire to wear eyeglasses on a major league field?

Eddie Rommel, an 18-year veteran umpire in the American League, donned eyeglasses for the first time, when he was the third base umpire in a game between the Washington Senators and the New York Yankees, down in Griffith Stadium, on April 18, 1956.

6. Who was the first, and only, major league player to win a battlefield commission in World War II?

Hall of Fame lefthander Warren Spahn, after fighting and being wounded, was awarded a Purple Heart, and the Bronze Star for bravery, in the Battle of the Bulge. At the Ludendorff Bridge, as a combat engineer, he was awarded a battlefield commission in June 1945 for his heroic exploits; the first and only major leaguer to earn such a distinction.

The southpaw with the high kick came up with the Boston Braves and didn't record his first major league win until 1946 at the age of 25. There would be 362 more victories as he became the mainstay of the Boston Braves staff for two decades winning 20 games 13 times, recording a 4-0 no-hitter against the Philadelphia Phillies on September 16, 1960, and a second, 1-0 against the San Francisco Giants on April 28, 1961. At the completion of his 21-year career no lefthander had won more games in major league history.

7. Who was the first African-American player in the major leagues?

No, it wasn't Jackie Robinson, who played first, second, and third base for the Brooklyn Dodgers and made his major league debut on April 15, 1947.

It was Moses Fleetwood Walker, a catcher who made his major league debut on May 1, 1884 with the Toledo Blue Stockings in the American Association, which was considered a major league team at the time. Fleet played only a year, playing in his final game on September 4, 1884, having a .263 batting average over 42 games, but his league leading 72 passed balls and 37 errors may have contributed to his brief career. He still is recognized as being the first African-American major league player, and the last, until 63 years later when Jackie made his historic debut.

Fleet had a younger brother, Welday Walker, who played 5 games in left field in 1884, having a .222 batting average, with the Blue Stockings.

8. Who was the first player to die as a result of on-field activity?

On opening day, April 12, 1909, Philadelphia Athletics' catcher, Mike "Doc" Powers injured himself by crashing into a wall while chasing a pop-up. Complaining of intestinal pains he was taken to the hospital and operated on the following day, but the 38-year old, 11-year veteran would pass away on April 26, 1909.

9. Who was the first player to wear a fraction as his uniform number?

On August 19, 1951 the St. Louis Browns played the first game of a doubleheader with the Detroit Tigers, losing 5-2. Browns owner Bill Veeck, known for his wacky promotions to encourage slipping attendance, had signed Eddie Gaedel, a 3'7", 65-pound vertically challenged person, to a major league contract.

In between games of the doubleheader Veeck had the ground crew roll out a very large birthday cake, in what was called a celebration of the American League and Falstaff Brewery. Out of the cake popped little Eddie Gaedel wearing a diminutive Browns uniform with the number 1/8 on the back of the jersey.

In the first inning of the nightcap who should come up to the plate, pinch-hitting for leadoff hitter Frank Saucier, and wearing his St. Louis Browns uniform with 1/8 on the back but Eddie Gaedel.

Home plate umpire Ed Hurley, questioning the appearance of Gaedel, was then assured by manager Zack Taylor that Gaedel had signed a valid major league contract.

On the mound for Detroit was southpaw Les Cain, trying unsuccessfully, to holdback his laughter without a lot of success. He proceeded to throw four consecutive balls, out of the minute strike zone, walking Gaedel. Off little Eddie went on to first base, but only momentarily as manager Zack Taylor quickly inserted outfielder Jim Delsing to run for him. Detroit swept the doubleheader winning the second game 6-2.

Although Gaedel was allowed to come to bat in Veeck's latest stunt American League President Will Harridge banned Gaedel, and all such "little people" from the league the following day, and ruled that Gaedel's name and his major league record should not appear in the final 1951 averages. He is, however, listed in the Baseball Encyclopedia, you can look it up.

10. Who was the first position player to win the Most Valuable Player Award while leading the league in strikeouts?

Jimmie Foxx, the Boston Red Sox first baseman, won the MVP award in 1933 while leading the American League with 93 strikeouts. He also led the league with 48 home runs, runs batted in with 163, and with a batting average of .356 and a slugging average of .703.

He also was the MVP in 1932 with equally impressive numbers, sans the strikeouts leadership.

11. Who was the first female public address announcer in major league baseball?

Sherry Davis, on March 10, 1993, became the first female public address announcer when the San Francisco Giants hired her for that work at Candlestick Park.

12. Who was the first African-American to play in the American League?

Larry Doby was signed as a free agent with the Cleveland Indians on July 2, 1947, and made his major league debut on July 5th, playing his first six games at first base, second base, and shortstop. He was moved to right field in 1948 and moved over to centerfield in 1949 where he became a fixture. He was traded to the Chicago White Sox on October 25, 1955, staying there until traded by Chicago to the Baltimore Orioles on December 3, 1957. He was traded back to Cleveland in 1958 and traded again, in 1959, to Detroit, where he was then purchased by the White Sox from Detroit, on May 13, 1959, for $30,000, and finished out his 13-season career playing six games at first and in the outfield, and hanging up his spikes for the final time on July 26, 1959. The Veterans Committee elected him into the Hall of Fame in 1998.

13. Who was the first major league player to appear on the cover of Sports Illustrated?

The first major leaguer to grace the cover of the first issue of Sports Illustrated, on August 16, 1954, was Milwaukee Braves third baseman Eddie Mathews shown swinging at a pitch at a night game in Milwaukee's County Stadium.

14. Who was the first player to play all nine positions in one major league game?

Cuban-born shortstop Bert Campaneris took part in a promotion at Municipal Stadium, Kansas City, on Wednesday, September 8, 1965, to stir up attendance for Kansas City Athletics' games, by playing all nine positions against the California Angels.

Campy started out at his usual shortstop position, and then moved in each succeeding inning from there to 2B, 3B, LF, CF, RF, 1B.

When on the mound in the 8th inning he pitched ambidextrously, throwing right-handed against right-handed batters, and switching to being a southpaw to left-handed batters. The first batter he faced that inning was his right-handed hitting cousin, centerfielder Jose Cardenal, who he got to pop out. He allowed one run in the inning.

In the 9th inning, with Campy catching, he had a collision with Angels' catcher Ed Kirkpatrick at home plate, and had to be replaced by Rene Lachemann. The Angels went on to win the game in the 13th inning, 5-3, but Campaneris can boast that he was the first player to play every position in a major league game. A couple of other players have done the same thing, but Campy was the "Groundbreaker" by being the first.

15. Who was the first, and only, player to have his name and birth date on the back of his uniform?

Carlos May, outfielder, first baseman, and designated hitter for the Chicago White Sox for 8 ½ years of his 10-year career, was born on May 17, 1948 in Birmingham, Alabama, and made fans aware of that fact by wearing his name and birth date, "May, 17," on the back of his uniform, the only one so far, to have been able to do such a thing.

16. Who was the first major league baseball player to appear on the front of a Wheaties box?

In 1934 Lou Gehrig, the New York Yankees first baseman, was the first non-fictional person to appear on the front of a Wheaties box.

17. Who was the first player to play 1,000 games in both the American and National Leagues?

Frank "The Judge" Robinson who played 1,502 games for the Cincinnati Reds, and 103 with the Los Angeles Dodgers for 1.605 in the National League, also played 827 with the Baltimore Orioles, and 276 with the California Angels for a total of 1,203 games in the American League giving him a grand total of 2,808 for his 21 seasons in the big leagues. The first to break the 1,000 game played mark in both leagues.

18. Who was the first player to wear sunglasses in the field?

Paul Hines, who made his major league debut with the Washington Nationals on April 20, 1872, and after moving on to play centerfield with the Providence Grays from 1878-1885, decided to don shades and became the first major leaguer to wear sunglasses when he took the field in 1882. He finished out his career on July 3, 1891 back with Washington.

19. Who was the only major league player to be killed in World War I?

Third baseman, Edward Leslie Grant, known as "Harvard Eddie" Grant, of the New York Giants, whose last game, of his 10-year career in the major leagues, was on October 6, 1915, before he was called off to war. He was killed on October 5, 1918 in the Argonne Forest, France. A five-foot tall monument with a brass plaque, honoring him, was erected on the centerfield wall at the deepest part of the Polo Grounds, in front of the team offices and clubhouse, which was situated between the left field and right field bleachers.

20. Who was the first, and only, player to save the life of a fan at a ball game?

George "Doc" Medich, a medical student at the University of Pittsburgh, and a right-handed pitcher with the Texas Rangers, saved the life of a 61-year old man who had suffered a heart attack prior to a game in Baltimore in1978. He jumped into the stands and applied heart massage until the medics could get to the stricken man who went on to live several more years.

21. Who was the first player in major league history to win the Rookie of the Year Award, the Cy Young Award, and the Most Valuable Player Award?

Right-hander Don Newcombe of the Brooklyn Dodgers, won the Rookie of the Year Award in 1949, and the Cy Young and Most Valuable Player Awards in 1956.

22. Who was the first person to have a plaque erected in his memory, and placed in what is now called "monument park" in Yankee Stadium?

On May 30, 1932, a plaque in memory of Miller Huggins, the Yankee manager from 1918 to 1929, was dedicated at Yankee Stadium. It was the first of many monuments erected to past Yankees in the Stadium.

23. For all you serious trivia buffs, who was the first major league player to commit suicide?

This esoteric and morbid bit of baseball history revolves around Frank C. Ringo, a journeyman catcher, centerfielder, and third baseman who made his major league debut on May 1, 1883 with the Philadelphia Quakers. He played four seasons in the big leagues with Philadelphia, Detroit, and Kansas City in the National League, and eighteen games with Pittsburgh in the American Association. He played his last major league game on September 18, 1886 with the Kansas City Cowboys with a career .192 batting average. He went down to the minor leagues and played there until, at age 28, he ingested a lethal dose of morphine on April 12, 1889 in Kansas City, Missouri to become the first major league player in history to take his own life.

24. Who was the first National League player to win back-to-back Most Valuable Player Awards?

Ernie Banks, known as "Mr. Cub," was signed as an amateur free agent in 1953 and made his major league debut on September 17th that year. The 22-year old shortstop was an immediate hit with Cub fans for his hard playing, and love for the game. Always in consideration for the MVP Award he was awarded it in 1958 when he led the league in at bats (617), home runs (47), runs batted in (129), slugging percentage (614), and total bases (379) to go along with his .313 batting average.

He came right back in 1959 to win the MVP Award for the second consecutive year with a .304 batting average and a league leading 143 runs batted in, the first player in the senior circuit to do it in back-to-back years.

25. Who was the first player to be suspended for a racial remark?

On July 29, 1938, in a pre-game interview at Comiskey Park, Chicago, WGN radio announcer Bob Elson asked New York Yankee outfielder Jake Powell what he did in the off-season.

Powell said he was a Dayton, Ohio policeman and stayed in shape by cracking (racial slur) blacks over the head with his nightstick. Black leaders demanded that Powell be barred from baseball for life.

Major League Commissioner Kenesaw Mountain Landis, after having heard of the racial slur, suspended Powell for ten days.

Factually, Powell never worked for the Dayton police department, but his comment was considered by Powell as a joke. Obviously a bad one.

26. Who was the first major league player to have his home run verified by "instant replay"?

In the 9th inning of a night game, down in Tropicana Field, against the Tampa Bay Rays, on Wednesday, September 3, 2008, New York Yankees third baseman Alex Rodriguez hit a pitch thrown by Troy Percival, very high down the left field line over the foul pole that hit the lower catwalk. Third base umpire Brian Runge called the ball fair for an apparent home run. Catcher Dioner Navarro immediately protested and Tampa Bay manager Joe Maddon came on the field to argue the ball was foul. The umpires huddled to discuss the play and at 10:19 three of the four umpires left the field to review the play on television in a room behind the Yankees dugout. They emerged 2:15 minutes later and crew chief umpire Charlie Reliford ruled that Rodriguez had hit his 549th career home run as the Yankees went on to win 8-4. It was the first instance of major league baseball using the replay camera to confirm a ruling on the field.

27. Who was the first major league player to have his uniform number retired?

On July 4, 1939 the New York Yankees retired the uniform number, 4, at Lou Gehrig Appreciation Day in Yankee Stadium. At this writing 15

Yankees, and over 120 major league players, have had their uniform numbers retired in appreciation of their exploits on the field.

28. Who was the first, and only, major league player not to be born in a country or on any land?

This is totally bizarre, but entirely true. Right-hander Edmund Joseph Porray, who began his career on April 17, 1914, and started three games on the mound for the Buffalo Buffeds (Blues) in the Federal League, and ended his career on May 1, 1914, with a 1-1 won-lost, 4.35 Era. record, was born, as his birth certificate states, on December 5, 1888 "At sea-on the Atlantic Ocean." He did pass away however on land, on July 13, 1954 in Lackawaxen, Pennsylvania. You can look it up!

29. Who was the first player to have his ethnicity used to name a major league baseball team?

Louis "Chief" Sockalexis, a Penobscot Indian, was one of the first Native Americans to play in the major leagues. He was born on October 24, 1871 on Indian Island, Old Town, Maine. He came to the Cleveland Spiders as a rightfielder on April 22, 1897, after attending the College of the Holy Cross, with a huge reputation after stories about his prowess with a bat for Poland Springs in the Maine summer league was made known.

The Spiders, after having a horrendous year in 1899, when they won 20 games and lost 134, and finished 84 games out of first place, and 35 games out of eleventh place in that twelve team league compiling the worst full-season record of any team in the history of major league baseball, and it began to show in the dissolution of their fan base.

In 1915, after playing in the newly formed American League as the Cleveland Blues, Bronchos (Broncos), and Naps from 1903 to 1914, the Cleveland paper sponsored a contest in 1915 asking fans to suggest a new name for the team. A fan came up with the suggestion that the team be named after the first Native American to play in the major leagues, the popular rightfielder, Lou "Chief" Sockalexis who had played for the Cleveland Spiders from 1897-1899, and finished his playing days on May 13, 1899, with a .313 career batting average.

The name "Indians" was embraced and it stands today in tribute to Chief Sockalexis.

30. Who was the first major league player to wear eye glasses?

Will "Whoop-La" White, the brother of James "Deacon" White, was a right-handed pitcher, and the first major leaguer to wear glasses. He made his major league debut on July 20, 1877 with the Boston Red Stockings, moving to Cincinnati in1878 to complete his ten season pitching career, with a one year stop over with the Detroit Wolverines in 1881, and pitching his final game on July 5, 1886. He had an impressive career, winning 229 games, losing 166 for a .580 winning percentage, striking out 1,041 batters, with 36 shutouts and a handsome 2.28 Era.

31. Who was the first major league baseball player to play in a Super Bowl?

Tom Brown, a first baseman, outfielder, and pinch-hitter, played his first major league baseball game for the Washington Senators on April 8, 1963 and 60 more that year.

I have to presume that he envisioned becoming a big baseball star, and not for what his destiny would be.

Having been blessed with being a dual professional athlete he found his other athletic love, playing professional football, which brought him to playing safety for Vince Lombardi's Green Bay Packers in Super Bowl I and Super Bowl II.

32. Who was the first unanimous selection for the National League Most Valuable Player Award?

It was the former San Francisco Giant, and then the stellar first baseman of the St. Louis Cardinals, Orlando "Baby Bull" Cepeda, who was selected to be the first unanimous Most Valuable Player in the National League when he won the award in 1967 with 183 hits, 25 home runs, a league-leading 111 runs driven in to go with his .325 batting average.

33. Who was the first player to win the Most Valuable Player Award in both the American and National Leagues?

Outfielder Frank "The Judge" Robinson won the National League MVP Award in 1961 with the Cincinnati Reds by batting .323, with 37 home runs, and 124 runs batted in.

On December 9, 1965 he was traded by Cincinnati to the Baltimore Orioles for three players, one of whom was Milt Pappas, for the Reds felt that the 30-year old Robinson was showing signs of aging.

It seems Robinson didn't feel the same way for he went on with Baltimore to win the American League MVP, and Triple Crown, in 1966 by leading the league in batting with .316, home runs with 49, and runs batted in with 122, and runs scored with another 122.

In his six years with Baltimore "the aging" Robinson only had an additional 179 home runs, and appeared in five All-Star games before he was inducted into the Hall of Fame in 1982. No one, to date, has duplicated that feat.

34. Who was the first African-American umpire to call a major league game?

Emmett Ashford started working as an umpire in the minor leagues in 1951 before being elevated to the AAA Pacific Coast League in 1954, where he worked until the 51-year old arbiter was called up by the American League to call a major league game on April 11, 1966.

With his flamboyant style for showmanship he delighted the fans, but was not always appreciated by the more serious of the baseball community, who considered him a bit of a showboat.

Nevertheless he continued with his different style of umpiring, and spent the next five years giving his opinion as to balls and strikes, whether batted balls where fair or foul, and who was safe on a base.

Ashford had his dream come when he was asked to work the 1967 All-Star game, and topped it off by working the 1970 World Series between the Cincinnati Reds and the Baltimore Orioles. He retired at the end of that season.

35. Who was the first player drafted in the first free agent amateur draft that was instituted on June 8, 1965?

Robert "Rick" Monday was the first overall selection in the inaugural major league player draft on June 8, 1965, and was drafted by the Kansas City Athletics, and signed on June 15, 1965.

He made his major league debut in centerfield on September 3, 1966, and played in the outfield for the Athletics from 1966-71, both in Kansas City, and when they moved to Oakland. He was traded by Oakland to the Chicago Cubs on November 29, 1971, and stayed with them from 1972-76 when, on January 11, 1977, the Cubs traded him to the Los Angeles Dodgers where he played the outfield and first base for them from 1977-84 including the 1977, '78 and '81 World Series. On June 20, 1984 he played his final big league game, and was released two days later by the Dodgers.

His 19-year career shows two All-Star Game selections, in 1968 and '78, and 1,619 base hits. 241 home runs and 775 runs batted in for a .264

batting average.

36. Who was the first player to earn $1,000,000 per season?

The first "Millon Dollar Man," according to records, was Nolan Ryan, the right handed Hall of Fame pitcher who received that salary in 1979 when with the California Angels.

37. Who was the first major league player to wear a batting glove?

Ken "The Hawk" Harrelson, nine-year American League first baseman-outfielder (1963-71), was credited with being the first player to wear a batting glove. Although it has been said that rightfielder-first baseman Rusty Staub (1963-85) was the first to wear golf gloves on a regular basis.

38. Who was the first player to play in every inning of every game for his team, which included the regular and postseason, for a total of 171 games, in one season?

The new "Iron Man," Cal Ripken Jr., the Baltimore Orioles shortstop, began this historic string of games and innings on April 4, 1983, and continued it through the regular season of 162 games and 1,452.1 innings, followed by the four games, and 37 innings of the ALCS against the Chicago White Sox, and then on into the five-game, 45-inning World Series against the Philadelphia Phillies, ending on October 16th at Veterans Stadium, for a total of 171 games, and 1,534.1 innings.

39. Who were the first teammates to win the National Leagues' Cy Young Award and the Most Valuable Player Award in the same season?

We tip our caps to southpaw Warren Spahn for winning the Cy Young Award, and also to his Milwaukee Braves teammate, Hank Aaron, when they both took home their prize in 1957.

40. Who was the first, and only, major league pitcher to pitch a no-hitter, and then as an umpire call one from behind the plate, and four more in his arbiters career?

This unusual circle of events started off in the first game of a doubleheader on September 27, 1905 when right-hander "Wild Bill" Dinneen, of the Boston Red Sox pitched a 2-0 no-hitter against the Chicago White Sox.

Moving ahead to May 12, 1910, when Dinneen, after finishing a twelve year career on August 26, 1909 with the St. Louis Browns, had become a major league umpire. He was on the field for Chief Bender's 4-0 no-hit victory, for the Philadelphia Athletics over the Cleveland Indians on May

12, 1910. On July 4, 1912 Detroit's right-hander, "Wabash George" Mullin, pitched a 7-0 no-hitter over the St. Louis Browns, and "Wild Bill" was there as one of the umpires. Dinneen's third no-hitter took place on June 3, 1918 when Boston Red Sox southpaw Hubert "Dutch" Leonard threw a 5-0 no-hitter against the Detroit Tigers.

That takes us to September 4, 1923 when New York Yankees right-hander "Sad Sam" Jones set down the Philadelphia Athletics, down in the Quaker City 2-0, without recording one strikeout, and Dinneen was behind the plate calling every pitch to be the first to have pitched a no-hitter, and the first to behind the plate to call one.

There's one more, and it came three days later, on September 7,[th] again down in Philadelphia, when Boston Red Sox right-hander Howard Ehmke deprived the Athletics of a hit, winning 4-0. That gave Dinneen the distinction of being the first umpire to work five no-hit games and the first to call one from behind the plate after pitching one from the mound in his interesting career.

41. Who was the first former major league player to become president of the league?

Joe Cronin who signed as a free agent with the Pittsburgh Pirates just before the 1925 season, made his first major league start on April 29, 1926 at second base before moving to both short and second in his two years with Pittsburgh. He was purchased by Kansas City, in the American Association, on April 1, 1928, before being purchased from them by the Washington Senators in July of that year for $7,500, where he became their regular shortstop, and had his finest year in 1930 with a .346 batting average, 127 runs scored, and 126 batted in. The Sporting News named him Player of the Year, the forerunner to the MVP Award now given out.

He became their playing manager in 1933-34, and piloted the Senators to the AL pennant in 1933, at the young age of 27, only to lose the World Series to the New York Giants in five games, in Washington's final World Series appearance.

On October 26, 1934, Washington owner Clark Griffith traded his nephew, (Cronin had married Griffith's niece in 1934), to the Boston Red Sox for infielder Lyn Lary and $225,000.

In 1935 Cronin became a playing manager for the Red Sox taking them to a World Series in 1946 where they lost to the St. Louis Cardinals in seven games, best known for the mad dash around the bases by Cardinals rightfielder Enos "Country" Slaughter scoring from first after Harry Walker's base hit, and Johnny Pesky's hesitation in throwing the ball back into the infield to cut off Country at the plate in the 7th game.

Always a good hitter, Cronin was named the American League all-star shortstop seven times. On April 19, 1945 he played his final game for the Red Sox after breaking his leg, and his 20-year career showed 2,124 games, 2,285 hits, 515 doubles, 118 triples, 170 home runs, with 1,424 runs batted in and a .301 batting average. With those offensive numbers, and his premier fielding abilities he was elected to the Hall of Fame in 1956.

He moved into the front office of the Red Sox in 1948, staying there until he was selected to be the president of the American League by the owners in 1959. He then became the first former player to become the president of one of the two major leagues.

42. Who was the first, and only, player from the National League's inaugural season in 1876 to play in a 20th century game?

On September 22, 1904 the New York Giants clinched the NL pennant behind Joe McGinnity, beating the Reds 6-5. Behind the plate was "Orator Jim" O'Rourke, a 19-year veteran and former Giant star who had been out of the game since 1893, and was invited by John McGraw to play in the clincher. The 54-year, 10-month old had a single in four at bats and scored a run.

43. Who was the first president of the newly established National League?

William Hulbert was the dominant personality in the formation of the National League on February 2, 1876, and became its president in 1877. He remained in that capacity until his death in 1882. He was a stern taskmaster and went so far as to expel both the Mutual of New York team, and the Philadelphia Athletics franchises from the league after the first season for not completing their assigned schedules.

44. Who was the first Commissioner of Major League Baseball?

The new position of Commissioner of Major League Baseball was established in November 1920 after the owners got together and unanimously elected an acting Federal Judge, by the name of Kenesaw Mountain Landis, to begin serving in that capacity on November 12, 1920.

He was responsible for restoring the integrity of the game in the eyes of the public after the scandal that had come to light following the 1919 World Series between the Cincinnati Reds, and what was to be forever known as the "Chicago Black Sox," in reality a White Sox team that had some of its players conspiring to throw the World Series.

Landis, having complete authority, ruled with a strong hand, and he remained as commissioner until his death in 1944.

45. Who was the first President of the United States to recommend to a major league team that they sign a young man to a baseball contract?

On April 12, 1958 President Dwight D. Eisenhower, who was a friend of Pittsburgh Pirate general manager, Branch Rickey, recommended the son of the doorkeeper at the White House, Preston Bruce, to him as a future prospect. Young Preston Bruce was signed and sent to Lincoln, Nebraska, in the Western League. Could you file that under an Executive Order? Just asking.

46. Who was the first major league player to be paid $100,000 per year?

The player who received what in 1947 was an incredible salary, was Hank Greenberg, who had come up to the Detroit Tigers for one at bat as a pinch-hitter on September 14, 1930, and didn't get into another game until 1933, when he played his first full season at first base, and remained with Detroit until January 18, 1947 when he was purchased by the Pittsburgh Pirates for $75,000. Upon joining the Pirates he signed a contract for the upcoming season for $100,000, and thus became the first major league player to break the 100 grand per year salary barrier.

47. Who was the first, and only, player to be named Rookie of the Year, and receive the Most Valuable Player Award in the same year?

Fred Lynn, the centerfielder of the Boston Red Sox, who was selected in the second round of the 1973 amateur draft made his debut with Boston on September 5, 1974, playing in just 15 games. In 1975 he was inserted in centerfield on a full-time basis and performed outstandingly. He led the American League in runs scored with 103, doubles with 47, slugging with .566, while hitting 21 home runs and driving in 105, and batting .331. Those numbers were enough to earn him not only the Rookie of the Year Award, but the Most Valuable Player Award as well, not to mention a Gold Glove and an All-Star selection. Fred Lynn was the first player to come away with those two prestigious awards in his rookie year.

48. Who was the first player to hit a home run, and get credit for it, but wasn't allowed to run it out, nor get credit for scoring the run?

Most fans would say this is impossible, and it certainly sounds that way, but it did happen on September 26, 2008. In the bottom of the 6th inning in a game against the Los Angeles Dodgers, Bengie Molina, the San Francisco Giants catcher, hammered a pitch which seemed to carom off the right field wall at AT&T Park. The umpire called it a fair ball and in play, but Molina, not known for being a speedster, stopped at first base with what he thought was an apparent long single.

Giants' skipper Bruce Bochy immediately sent infielder Emmanuel Burriss out to first to run for the slow-running Molina before anyone could intervene. Bochy continued his discussion with the umpires as to how the base hit should be ruled. Then when Bochy saw green paint on the ball that was thrown in he quickly called for the newly instituted replay rule which had just been created, and inserted in the rule book on August 27th. It now allowed umpires to review home run calls. They used instant replay and ruled the hit a home run, but refused to allow Molina to re-enter the game to run out his home run. The Giants protested the decision.

When the umpires inspected the ball it showed that the ball had hit in Levi's landing, an awning where the top is green and the rest looks like brick. If the ball hits the green top it is a home run, if it hits the brick it is still in play. The smudge of green paint showed that the ball had hit the green awning and bounced back onto the field. With that evidence the umpires re-enforced their decision to award Molina with a home run.

Now it gets sticky. Since Burriss was already in the game as a runner for Molina he asked the first base coach Roberto Kelly whether he should now circle the bases or should Bengie come back out and run out his home run. Kelly told Burriss to go ahead and circle the bases and score the run.

When Buriss came back to the dugout he was greeted by Molina with "a good swing" and they all laughed at this bizarre episode. The official scorer credited Molina with a home run and Burriss with a run scored.

For those of you keeping score at home you can credit Molina with a home run, and driving in two runs even though he wasn't officially in the game at the time of the decision, and Burriss with scoring a run now that he was.

The Giants had originally played the game under protest, but they went ahead to win 6-5 in the 10th inning nullifying the protest.

49. Who was the first player to hit a grand slam home run, but only be credited with a single in a championship game?

It happened in the longest postseason game ever played, Game 5 of the

1999 National League Championship Series in Shea Stadium, New York.

With the Atlanta Braves ahead 3-2 in the bottom of the 15th inning the Mets Shawon Dunston led off with a single and stole second base. Matt Franco then walked, and manager Bobby Valentine sent in Roger Cedeno to run for Franco. Edgardo Alfonso sacrificed the runners to second and third. The next batter, John Olerud, was intentionally walked to load the bases. Todd Pratt then walked, forcing in the tying run to make it 3-3, and bringing up the third baseman, Robin Ventura, to face the Braves rookie right-hander Kevin McGlinchy. Ventura worked the count to 1-1, and hit the next pitch high and far into the right field stands for a grand slam home run. Roger Cedeno crossed home plate with the winning run.

Pratt, seeing Cedeno score the winning run, reversed his path toward home and ran back to congratulate Ventura, holding him up, as the other Mets players, erupting with joy raced on the field and mobbed Ventura as he rounded first base preventing him from being able to circle the bases and complete his home run trot, for which was truly deserving, and was thus credited with just a single.

50. Who was the first modern day player to spend twenty or more years with the same ball club?

Walter "The Big Train" Johnson came up to the Washington Senators in 1907 and pitched in 801 games, starting 666, and completing his 21-year career in 1927 with 417 wins and 279 losses, with 110 shutouts, all with his original team, Washington.

51. Who was the first, and presumably the last, at least for quite some time, to be the first major league player to have his first, middle, and last name begin with the letter "U"?

In the history of major league baseball we have had some very unusual given names, nick-names, and an assortment of different initials, but this player holds a very distinctive place in the Major League Baseball Encyclopedia. For he stands alone, does this right-hander pitcher, because no one, after many thousand names within this great book, has his full and complete name entirely made up beginning with the letter, "U."

We're speaking, of course, about Ugueth Urtain Urbina who was born on February 15, 1974 in Caracas, Venezuela, and signed by the Montreal Expos as an amateur free agent in 1990. Five years later, on May 9, 1995, he made his pitching debut with Montreal. On July 31, 2001 he was traded to the Boston Red Sox, and from there went on to play for the Texas Rangers,

Florida Marlins, appearing in their 2003 World Series, the Detroit Tigers and finished his 12-year career on October 2, 2005 with the Philadelphia Phillies.

52. Who was the first, and only, player to miss the entire season the year following his winning the Most Valuable Player Award?

That unfortunate happening occurred to George Sisler, the St. Louis Browns first baseman, who won the Most Valuable Player Award for his outstanding 1922 season. He led the American League, in batting with a .420 average (batting over .400 for the second time, having batted .407 in 1920), in runs scored with 134, in base hits with 246, triples with 18, stolen bases with 51, and he also batted in 105 runs, had 42 doubles, hit 8 home runs, and only fanned 14 times in 654 at bats.

The following year, in 1923, he was stricken with sinusitis which affected his optic nerve and his eyesight, causing him to miss the entire season. Sisler went on to play for 15 seasons finishing out his last three years with 20 games with Washington in 1928, and then on to the Boston Braves in 1928-29, and playing his final game with them on September 22, 1930.

His great career made him an easy inductee to the Hall of Fame in 1939.

53. Who was the first player to win the Most Valuable Player Award when playing for a losing team?

In 1958 the Chicago Cubs shortstop, with the well-known sobriquet, "Mr. Cub", Ernie Banks, had quite a year. He led the National League in games played (154), at bats (617), home runs (47), runs batted in (129), slugging percentage (.614) and total bases (379), putting that together with his .313 batting average. That made him the first player to win the MVP Award while playing for a team with a losing record as his Cubbies ended the season with a 72-82 won-lost record which put manager Bob Scheffing's team in 5th place.

54. Who was the first player to win back-to-back Most Valuable Player Awards?

The first player to win the MVP Award in consecutive years was Philadelphia Athletics first baseman Jimmie (Double X) Foxx, when his first award came in 1932, at the age of 24, after a season of leading the American League in five major offensive categories: runs scored (151), runs batted in (169), home runs (58), slugging (.749) and total bases (438), which shouldn't come as a total surprise when you factor in his 213 base hits for a .364 batting average, just three percentage points behind the batting leader that season, Red Sox first baseman, Dale Alexander who hit .367.

"Double X's" value just continued to rise as the burly right-handed power hitter continued to rack up numbers in 1933. He led the American League in home runs (48) and runs batted in (163), but also in strikeouts with 93, however his leading the junior circuit in total bases (403), and a slugging figure of .703, to go along with his .356 batting average, which gave him his first batting title, two total bases titles, two home run titles, two runs batted in titles, and more importantly two back-to-back MVP titles, made him the first to ever accomplish consecutive MVP titles. No wonder the Hall of Fame extended an invitation to him to become a resident in 1951.

55. Who was the first player to win his league's home run title and then be released the following season?

This is not that unusual for there have been a few occasions where this has happened, The first time it occurred was back in 1901 when Napoleon "Nap" Lajoie, the second baseman of the Philadelphia Athletics, led the American League with 14 home runs. It goes deeper than that, for Nap not only won the home run title, but led the American League in their first year of existence by also being first in that season in runs (145), hits (232), doubles (48), runs batted in (125), and total bases (350) along with the aforementioned 14 home runs, and an unbelievable .426 batting average to go along with his .463 on base percentage.

Now in those years the Most Valuable Player Award was just beyond the thoughts of the baseball mavens, but if it hadn't been Nap would have won in a walk away. Now imagine a franchise today allowing a player with those credentials to jump from one team to another as Lajoie did from the Phillies to the Athletics. Philadelphia did just that on April 21, 1902. A few weeks later, on May 31, 1902, Lajoie signed on with the Cleveland Bronchos (Indians). Playing 13 seasons with Cleveland with a .339 batting average he certainly was a welcome addition to that franchise.

I guess it is safe to say that the Athletics had long overdue second thoughts for they purchased Lajoie from Cleveland in January 1915, and he remained with them, until closing out his 21-year Hall of Fame career with them in his final game on August 26, 1916.

His final statistics show 3,251 base hits, 648 doubles, 1,504 runs scored, and 1,599 runs batted in, and a .339 batting average.

56. Who was the first major league catcher to wear glasses?

The first catcher to wear glasses was Clint "Scrap Iron" Courtney, but that didn't stop him from being a battler behind the plate or on the base paths.

He is long remembered for an on-field brawl with New York Yankees middle infielders, Phil Rizzuto and Billy Martin, after a collision at second base while Courtney was with the St. Louis Browns.

Courtney made his major league debut with the New York Yankees playing in his initial, and only, major league game with them on September 29, 1951. On November 23rd of that year he was traded to the St. Louis Browns where The Sporting News, un- officially, considered him to be the Rookie of the Year in 1952, and remained with the Browns, who became the Baltimore Orioles in 1954, until being sent on to the Chicago White Sox in December of that year. From the White Sox to the Washington Senators, back to the Orioles he went before being traded to the Kansas City Athletics. Courtney returned to his original team in April 1961 and played his final game of his 11-season career with the Orioles on June 24, 1961 ending with a .268 career batting average. "Scrap Iron" remains to this day as being the first catcher to wear glasses.

57. Who was the first person to create and publish the first baseball box score?

Interestingly, the first baseball box score was originated by an English-man, Henry Chadwick, who was born on October 5, 1824 in Exeter, England. He and his parents then emigrated to Brooklyn, New York.

Back in England, as a boy, Chadwick played the English game of "round-ers", which some consider the precursor to baseball. In 1856 Chadwick watched a baseball game between New York's Eagle and Gotham clubs that piqued his interest, and he became a fan. He requested the New York Times, with whom he was working reporting cricket matches, and other New York newspapers to allow him to cover baseball games.

As time progressed so did his technique in reporting games and he cre-ated the box score, which he adapted from the cricket scorecard. The first box score was a grid with nine rows for players' names, and nine columns for innings. The box score contained the first abbreviation for a strike out, using the last letter, "K" for the term "struck" as in "struck out" and a better scoring system, with the introduction of statistics that measured a play-ers' batting average, and earned run average, which clarified the distinction between runs caused by a batter's skill or that of a fielder's inability, that made reporting a game more thorough and interesting.

His writings expanded with him writing numerous instructional manuals on the game, and extended to editing multiple baseball guides.

In 1860 he prepared baseball's first guide and edited it annually including the Spaulding Guide from 1881 to 1908. In an 1863 issue of the New York Clipper appeared what we know today as the "box score." His tireless efforts, including his work as an influential member of baseball's early rules committees, did more to enlarge the popularity of the game during its early growth, and he since has been known to many as "The Father of Baseball."

In 1868 Chadwick wrote the first hard-cover book on baseball entitled, "The Game of Base Ball". He was elected to the Hall of Fame by the Veterans Committee in 1938, the only writer not in the writers' wing.

58. Who was the first president of the American League?

Byron Bancroft "Ban" Johnson was born in Norwalk, Ohio on January 5, 1864. He studied law at Marietta College in Ohio and later became a sportswriter for the Cincinnati Gazette. In 1894 Johnson, and his good friend Charlie Comiskey, who had been fired as the Cincinnati Reds manager that year, took over the running of the Western League with Johnson as president. Their league was known as being very well run and in 1900, after some crafty maneuvers, Johnson changed the name to the American League, launching it as a major competitor to the National League and in 1901 they claimed the league had major status.

He searched and solicited very wealthy people to bankroll his teams, He appointed managers, conducted trades, levied fines and suspended players and even arranged schedules to minimize travel costs. He even went so far as to rule it permission able for the New York Highlanders (Yankees) to draft right-hander Jack Quinn away from the Richmond Virginias on September 1, 1908 much to the strenuous objections of White Sox owner Charles Comiskey.

When Judge Kenesaw Mountain Landis came in as Commissioner of Baseball, after the Black Sox scandal, Johnson's dictatorial reign was over, however he did remain as American League president until October 17, 1927 when he was strongly persuaded to resign.

His fiery, uncompromising attitude made him successful and he was credited with recruiting President William Howard Taft to be the first president to throw out the first ball on opening day.

59. Who were the players involved in the first tie for the Most Valuable Player Award in the National League?

It took from 1931, when the MVP Award was established, to 1979 when the first tie took place, when Willie "Pops" Stargell, the Pittsburgh Pirates first baseman, tied for the award with St. Louis Cardinals first baseman Keith Hernandez.

Now Hernandez led the National League in batting with .344, in doubles with 48, and runs scored with 116. He also had 11 home runs and 105 runs batted in.

Stargell didn't lead the league in any specific category, except he was a very strong force in leading the Pirates to the pennant, and then to a World's Championship victory over the Baltimore Orioles in seven games.

To my way of thinking I believe this sharing of the MVP Award should have taken place in earlier years, and in the other league.

60. Who was the first major league player to be killed by a pitch?

On August 16, 1920, in a game against the New York Yankees at the Polo Grounds, Cleveland Indians shortstop Ray Chapman was severely beaned in the temple by a fast ball thrown by Carl Mays, and collapsed. As the ball rolled toward third base, Mays, thinking the ball had hit Chapman's bat, fielded the ball and threw to Wally Pipp at first base.

The home plate umpire, Tom Connolly, quickly called for a physician, and Chapman was taken to St. Lawrence Hospital with a 3 ½ inches depressed skull fracture and operated on. He died the following morning at 4:40 AM before his new wife, Kathleen, who had rushed in from Cleveland, could be with him.

Chapman, immensely liked and respected by players throughout the league, announced this would be his final year before retiring, was batting .303 and was on his way toward a career year in hits, runs, doubles, home runs, and runs batted in.

Joe Sewell was brought up as his replacement and Sewell went on to play 14 years in the major leagues and went on to be elected to the Hall of Fame in 1977.

61. Who was the first player to spend his entire career, of over 20 years, with the same team?

That loyal player was Adrian "Cap" Anson who joined the Chicago White Stockings (Cubs) in 1876 and played for them for 22 years, retiring after the 1897 season. He had a .329 career batting average and led the National League in batting with a .399 average in 1881, and in 1888 with a .344 average as well as leading the league in runs batted in seven times.

He, no doubt, got one of the best choices in rooms in the Hall when he was one of the earliest inductees in 1939.

62. Who was the first Heisman Trophy winner to play in a major league game?

The Heisman Trophy is given to the outstanding college football player of the year. Vic Janowicz, one of the last great single-wing tailbacks, out of Ohio State, was the winner of that award in 1950. He was the first to receive that honor and then to go on to play in the major leagues. He was one of a number of "bonus babies" in the fifties and signed with the Pittsburgh Pirates as an amateur free agent on December 15, 1952, making his major league debut as a catcher on May 31, 1953. After a mediocre rookie year where he caught 35 games, he returned in 1954 playing in just 18 games as a third baseman, and two in the outfield, playing his final game on September 10, 1954 before returning to the NFL's Washington Redskins, where unfortunately his football career ended tragically in 1956 in an automobile accident.

63. Who was the first to play in both a Rose Bowl Game and a World Series?

This two sport athlete was well-known for his baseball ability, but prior to that he played for the University of California as an All-American running back in the 1949 Rose Bowl game against Northwestern.

On October 13, 1949 Jackie Jensen was traded by Oakland, in the Pacific Coast League, along with Billy Martin, to the New York Yankees. The 23-year old right fielder made his debut with the Yankees on April 18, 1950, and played in 45 games before appearing in one game, with no official at bats, in the 1950 World Series in the Yankees' sweep of the Philadelphia Phillies.

It soon became apparent that he would develop into a fine ballplayer, and some had hopes that he would eventually replace Joe DiMaggio in centerfield.

A fellow by the name of Mickey Mantle put that idea to rest and Jensen went down to the Washington Senators on May 3, 1952 in a five player exchange, and stayed there until December 9, 1953 when the Senators traded him to the Boston Red Sox for southpaw Mickey McDermott and outfielder Tom Umphlett.

In his 11 seasons Jensen led the American League in runs batted in three times, stolen bases and triples once, and had 199 home runs. He played his final game, with the Red Sox, on October 1, 1961 cutting his career short due to his fear of flying, and ended with a career batting average of .279. He was named to three All-Star teams and was the American League's Most Valuable Player in 1958.

64. Who was the first player to pitch in 100 games and have 1,000 base hits?

I'll bet you probably came up with Babe Ruth. A very good guess, but he was much too late to be the first. If you are looking for a number two in this category you would be right on.

Southpaw James Bentley Seymour, better known as "Cy", played his first game in the big leagues on April 22, 1896 with the New York Giants, when at age 23 he pitched in 11 games that season and had a 2-4 record. He continued on the mound through the 1902 season and finished his six season pitching career with a 61-56 won-lost record, and a 3.71 ERA, while pitching in 141 games.

Before the start of the 1901 season Seymour jumped to the Baltimore Orioles where he played centerfield and stayed until July 1902 when he was released, and signed on immediately with the Cincinnati Reds. On July 12, 1906 the Giants purchased him from the Reds for $12,000.

On August 24, 1910 he was purchased by Baltimore from the Giants and stayed with them until February 25, 1913 when Seymour signed on as a free agent with the Boston Braves, playing the last, on July 17, 1913, of his 39 big leagues games with them before being released on July 19th. In his 16-year career Seymour played in 1,529 games, had 1,724 base hits, drove in 799 runs, and had a .303 batting average to make him the first player to pitch in 100 games and have 1,000 base hits in his major league career.

Now to satisfy those of you who are curious, and who had an intelligent, but incorrect thought, the Babe had, from 1914 to 1935, 163 games on the mound, and 2,873 base hits

65. Who was the first player to win the National League Championship Series Most Valuable Player Award more than once?

In the 1978 National League Championship Series the Los Angeles Dodgers defeated the Philadelphia Phillies 3 games to 1, and a big reason was Dodgers first baseman Steve Garvey who had seven hits, a double, triple, and four home runs driving in 7 runs to win the MVP.

Proving he could do it for a second time, Garvey, now playing for the San Diego Padres, was a huge factor in the Padres 3 games to 2 victory over the Chicago Cubs in the 1984 NLCS. He batted .400 in that series with eight hits, including a double and a home run, and drove in seven runs in that series as well. He then became the first player to walk away with the MVP Award twice in the NLCS.

66. Who was the first owner to have his initials put on his major league team's uniform?

Charles Brofman, the founder of the Montreal Expos in 1968, the first major league baseball team outside of the United States, but who later sold in 1990, was honored by having his initials sewed on the uniform of the Expos.

67. Who was the first black coach in major league baseball?

John "Buck" O'Neil, a star first baseman with the Kansas City Monarchs in the Negro National League, was first hired as a scout for the Chicago Cubs in 1955, and later on in 1962 was hired by the Cubs to be the first black coach in the major leagues.

68. Who was the first American League player to be a unanimous selection for the Most Valuable Player Award?

There have been three different names given for the Most Valuable Player Award since its inception in 1911. From 1911 to 1914 it was referred to as the Chalmers Award. From 1922 to 1929 it was called the League Award, and starting in 1931 the Baseball Writers Association of America made the selections.

During those years the first player to be named a unanimous selection happened in 1935 when "Hammerin Hank" Greenberg, the Detroit Tigers first baseman, was selected unanimously by the Baseball Writers Association as the American League's Most Valuable Player.

He tied for the American League lead in home runs, with Jimmie Foxx, with 36, led in runs batted in with 170, and in total bases with 389 to go along with his .328 batting average as he led Detroit to the 1935 World Series, and the Tigers win over the Cubs in six games.

69. Who was the first National League player to be selected unanimously as the Most Valuable Player?

The year following the unanimous selection of an American League player as the MVP the senior circuit did the same thing. New York Giant southpaw "King Carl" Hubbell, dubbed "The Meal Ticket" took the 1936 Most Valuable Player honors unanimously with his league leading 26-6, 2.31 ERA, and .813 winning percentage. He completed 25 games and had three shutouts in his 304 innings pitched.

70. Who was the first player to use flip-down sunglasses in the outfield?

Although there are those who claim that Harry Hooper was the first player to use flip-down sunglasses in the outfield, it was a few years before his claim that Pittsburgh Pirate leftfielder Fred Clarke had used smoked glasses hinged to the bill of his cap around 1911, according to research done by SABR member Maria Vacarro. Max Carey, who came up in 1911 as a leftfielder with Pittsburgh, has also been credited with that practice.

71. Who was the first player Lou Gehrig replaced to start on his way to his 2,130 consecutive game playing streak?

It all began on Monday, June 1, 1925 at the Yankee Stadium with the New York Yankees behind to the Washington Nationals, with Walter "The Big Train" Johnson on the mound. In the 9th inning Yankee manager Miller Huggins sent Lou Gehrig up to pinch-hit for shortstop "Pee Wee" Wanninger.

Interestingly "Pee Wee" had replaced Everett "Deacon" Scott at short on May 5th. Scott, who had been the Yankees shortstop since coming over from the Red Sox in a multi-player trade on December 20, 1921, brought his own consecutive game played streak with him which had started on June 20, 1916, and ended with Wanninger taking over at short after 1,307 consecutive games.

The following day, June 2nd, Huggins inserted Gehrig at first base replacing Wally Pipp, who had held that position for eleven seasons, to give him a rest. The rest, as they say, is history for "The Iron Horse" went on to play 2,130 consecutive games, and held that record until September 6, 1995 when Cal Ripken Jr. of the Baltimore Orioles broke it with 2,131 consecutive games, playing against the California Angels.

Ripken's streak began on May 30, 1982 and continued on for 2,632 consecutive games until Ripken, himself, took his name off the official starting lineup on September 20, 1998, the final Orioles game of the 1998 season.

72. Who was the first pitcher to pitch in just one game, which he won, batted only once, for a base hit, and left the major leagues with a 1.000 winning percentage; a 1,000 batting average; and a 1.000

fielding percentage?

Now you are not really expected to solve this question unless you just happened to come across the name of John A. (born Kolonauski) Kull, a left-handed pitcher who appeared in, and won, one game in relief on Saturday, October 2, 1909 for the Philadelphia Athletics in a 6-5 win over Washington at Shibe Park.

He pitched the final three innings, allowed three hits, one earned run, five walks, struck out four, hit one batter, had one flawless assist, and had a single that drove in two runs in his only time at bat. His career statistics show a 1-0 pitching record for 1.000, a 1 for 1 batting average for 1.000. Talk about a piece of trivia.

73. Who was the first public address announcer at a baseball stadium?

In 1901 the first American League game was played at American League Park in Washington, D.C. On hand that day was E. Lawrence Phillips who strolled the left and right field lines using a megaphone to announce the batteries for that day's game, and later the entire home and visiting team lineups to the fans. Phillips would handle the megaphone duties for 28 seasons before his retirement in 1928.

There were three other "megaphone announcers" around this time: George Levy, who handled the New York Giants, and Highlanders (Yankees) games; Wolfie Jacobs up in Boston; and Pat Pieper out in Wrigley Field, Chicago. Phillips, to this day, is recognized as being the first public address announcer at a baseball stadium.

74. Who was the first player to introduce the bunt to baseball?

One of the most important players of the 19th century, Richard J. "Dickey" Pearce, was born on February 29, 1836, and began his career with the Brooklyn Atlantics in 1856, and played for twenty years in the National Association before finishing out his career playing in 1876-1877 with the St. Louis Brown Stockings (Browns) of the National League.

As a 5'3" 161 pound player he was nevertheless fleet afoot and an excellent fielder. He created what he termed "the tricky hit" which is now called "the bunt."

75. Who was the first player to create the position of shortstop?

During his early career, shortstop Dickey Pearce played all over the infield until he personally established the position of shortstop. He, and pitcher Jim Creighton, are considered by many to be the first two to be paid as baseball players. There are some who disagree and mention Al Reach. We will not get into all of that here.

Speaking of Jim Creighton, considered by historians to be the game's first superstar, deserves more space here. He was one of the earliest and brightest stars in baseball and considered to be the greatest of his day, the first great pitcher. He played for only two seasons, famous for his efforts on behalf of the Brooklyn Excelsiors from 1860 to 1862, he demonstrated all the attributes that defined his position.

Tragically, Creighton, who was also a good hitter, hit a home run on October 18, 1862 playing against the Union Club of Morrisania, New York. John Chapman, in the on deck circle, heard a snap as Creighton hit the ball and questioned him upon touching home plate.

Creighton said it was just his belt snapping. That wasn't the case. Four days later this rising young star was dead. He had ruptured either his spleen or bladder in hitting that home run, and had bled to death at the age of 21 ½.

76. Who was the first person to originate the term applied to enthusiastic and loyal followers of a team, i.e. "fans."?

Interestingly it was a German immigrant who applied the term "fanatics" to those people who came out to see America's future national pastime. Chris Von der Ahe knew nothing about baseball, but knew the advantages of having the people going to, and coming from, the game stopping in to his saloon near Sportsman's Park.

Alfred H. Spink, who later became the founder of The Sporting News, approached Von der Ahe to take an interest in the St. Louis Brown Stockings by buying $1,800 worth of stock and having the beer concession in the ballpark.

It wasn't long after that Von der Ahe bought out Spink and the remaining partners after seeing the enthusiasm of the people coming to the games. He referred to them as "fanatics." The Brown Stockings (Browns) manager Ted Sullivan liked the term, but shortened it to "fans," and the term has not only stayed down through the years, but has become an important part of the lexicon of those who love and follow the game.

77. Who was the first player to coin, and use, the term, "good field, no hit"?

This term is attributed to one of the first Cuban-born players to play in the major leagues, Mike Gonzalez, a catcher, who made his big league debut, in his only game with the Boston Braves, on September 28, 1912 before being released the following April. He went on to the Cincinnati Reds for the 1914 season and before his 17-year career was over played for the Chicago Cubs, New York Giants, and three stints with the St. Louis Cardinals before his final game with the Red Birds on September 7, 1932.

After his playing days were over he became a coach and was in the third base coaching box waving Enos Slaughter home on that famous mad dash around the bases after Harry "The Hat" Walker's double in the 8ᵗʰ inning of the 7ᵗʰ game brought "Country" home in that deciding game over the Boston Red Sox.

The Cardinals asked Mike to scout a player playing in the winter league. After watching him he judged the player to be outstanding defensively, but a liability as a batter. He sent a wire back of his appraisal to the Cardinals stating simply, "good field, no hit." That reference is still in common use today.

78. Who was the first President of the United States to throw out the "first ball" on Opening Day of the baseball season?

This tradition goes all the way back to April 14, 1910 when the Washington Nationals manager Jimmy McAleer suggested to President William Howard Taft that he throw out the ceremonial first pitch before the Opening Day game with the Philadelphia Athletics.

President Taft, with Mrs. Taft, and Vice President James S. Sherman with him at the game, became the first President to throw out the first ball on Opening Day.

Walter Johnson caught the first pitch and went on to pitch the first of his 14 Opening Day games for Washington, striking out nine on his way to shutting out the Philadelphia Athletics, and their southpaw Eddie Plank, 3-0.

79. Who was the first umpire to receive a salary?

It has been credited to Michael "John" Walsh, who was born in Ireland in 1850, and was the first umpire to be paid a salary to officiate a game. Heretofore an umpire was paid on a per game basis. He was the first umpire in the National League's first season in 1876 and was an umpire for eleven major league seasons. He umpired 304 games from 1875 to 1888 in three different leagues and called three no-hitters.

80. Who was the first, and only, major league player to play on two championship teams, in two different sports, in two different

seasons, in two different cities?

This 6'8" right-hander came in second in the National League Rookie-of-the-Year voting in 1954, and went on to play for the Milwaukee Braves through the 1958 season, winning the 1957 World Series when Milwaukee defeated the New York Yankees in seven games. On March 31, 1959 Gene Conley was traded to the Philadelphia Phillies in a five player deal.

His alternating lifestyle had him pitching eleven years in the major leagues ending with the Boston Red Sox in 1961, and six seasons of professional basketball where he won three Championship rings with the Boston Celtics as a backup center and forward.

In April 1961, just two weeks after he helped defeat the St. Louis Hawks in Game 5 he was on the mound pitching the 9th inning for the Red Sox in a 6-1 victory over the Washington Senators and contributed by driving in a run much to the delight of his Celtic teammates Bill Russell and K.C. Jones who were in the stands rooting them on.

81. Who was the first player to bring a hair dryer into a major league clubhouse?

The egocentric and sartorially conscious first baseman of the New York Yankees, Joe Pepitone, who spent the last four years of his 12-year career with the Astros, Cubs, and Braves, and upon joining the Cubs, brought a hair dryer into the Chicago clubhouse, and with him on the road in hopes of keeping his hair just right.

82. Who was the first player to bat in front of both Mickey Mantle and Sadaharu Oh?

The first player to bat in front of two of the biggest home run hitters in baseball, and presumably the beneficiary of being driven home quite a few times, was leftfielder Roy White when he was with the New York Yankees, batting in front of Mickey Mantle, and in the twilight of his baseball career when he went to play in Japan with the Yomiuri Giants, and batted in front of Sadahru Oh, the home run king, with 868, in Japan.

83. Who was the first player to play for four teams in a single season?

Frank Huelsman, a right-handed hitting leftfielder, never really got a chance to unpack and find a comfortable bed. You see he came up and played his first major league game on October 3, 1897 with the St. Louis Cardinals. He played in one other game for them for a total of seven at bats before being sent down.

He resurfaced with the Chicago White Sox in 1904 and played in four games before being purchased by the Detroit Tigers on May 30, 1904. He played four games with Detroit before he was on the road again this time when he was purchased by the St. Louis Browns on June 16, 1904. His stay there was equally brief playing in just 20 games before the Browns traded him along with Hunter Hill to the Washington Senators for Charles Moran on July 14, 1904.

I would presume that Huelsman, like so many others who go to Washington, not the team, find a home and stay longer than their talents should allow. He did play with Washington during the 1904 and 1905 seasons amassing 800 plate appearances in 205 games before bidding adieu to the major leagues as he played his last game on October 5, 1905.

Through all of Frank's peregrinations his career totals show three seasons, 235 games, 205 with Washington, 4 with the White Sox, two with the St. Louis Cardinals, 20 with the St. Louis Browns, and 4 with Detroit, and a .258 batting average, having him become the first player to play for four teams, in one season, and all before airline travel and frequent flier miles were ever a twinkle in a travelers' eyes.

84. Who was the first pitcher to be ejected from a game for wearing earrings on the mound?

Sound crazy? Of course it does, but then when you think of this era of flashy jewelry being displayed by ballplayers there may be something to it.

On August 25, 2001 Mariners' southpaw Arthur Rhodes came on in relief of Kazuhiro Sasaki, who had injured his arm in the 9th inning out in Seattle, and who should he face but Omar Vizquel, the Cleveland Indians shortstop. Vizquel called the umpires attention to the glistening jewelry of Rhodes, complaining that the sunlight was reflecting off the reliever's right earring. Rhodes yelled back at Vizquel, and was ready to do battle with him, but before punches were thrown Mariners' manager Lou Pinella restrained Rhodes, and third base umpire Tim McClelland told Rhodes to get off the diamond and take his diamonds with him.

There went the chance for a sparkling performance by Rhodes that day, who had to watch from the dugout as Seattle defeated Cleveland in eleven innings, 3-2.

85. Who was the first player to four times witness a fellow player hit

four home runs in one game?

You just gotta be in the right place at the right time, as the saying goes. And right-hander Billy Loes, one of the better flakes, in the blizzard of pitchers to have stepped on the mound, was witness to this unusual event. It started when Loes came up with the Brooklyn Dodgers and saw teammate, and first baseman, Gil Hodges crush four pitches off four different Boston Braves pitchers for home runs on August 31, 1950 at Ebbets Field.

Still with Brooklyn, on July 31, 1954, Loes watched Milwaukee first baseman Joe Adcock do it just a bit differently as he hit his four home runs, at Ebbets Field, off four different *Dodgers* pitchers.

Moving over to the Baltimore Orioles he again witnessed an opposing player smash four home runs when Cleveland right fielder Rocky Colavito became just the second American League player, Lou Gehrig was the first, to hit his four home runs consecutively, when he did it on June 10, 1959 at Memorial Stadium.

His fourth and final four-bagger game happened when Loes was on the mound, pitching a complete game for the San Francisco Giants, at the end of his 11-year career, when, on April 30, 1961, before a crowd of 12,263 at County Stadium, Milwaukee, he was aided by centerfielder Willie Mays' home runs in the first, third, sixth and eighth innings as Willie drove in eight of the fourteen runs the Giants scored in a 14-4 rout of Milwaukee.

86. Who was the first, and only, player in major league history to win the pitching title for wins in a season, and the batting title for the highest batting average?

This multi-faceted player was Guy Jackson Hecker, a right-handed pitcher, first baseman, and outfielder who made his major league debut on May 2, 1882 with the Louisville Eclipse in the American Association. In 1884, his third year, Hecker had an outstanding season on the mound leading the league in nine categories; wins with 52, a 1.80 Era., total games 75, games started 73, complete games 72, innings pitched 670.2, strikeouts 385, batters faced 2,649, and base hits allowed 526. One must remember that the pitching distance back then was just 50 feet, not the 60'6" as it is today.

When it came to hitting Hecker was a heck of a hitter, and in addition to his 336 games on the mound, played 75 games in the outfield and 322 at first base. In 1886, with the Louisville Colonels, and playing all three of his positions, he had 378 plate appearances, banged out 117 base hits, drove in

48 runs, stole 25 bases and posted a league leading .341 to win the battle title.

After his release by the Louisville Colonels on September 17, 1889, he played his final season, in the National League, with the Pittsburgh Alleghenys (Pirates) playing in 86 games, in his three positions before hanging up his spikes on September 30, 1890.

The Hecker family, to this day, can still lay claim that Guy was the first player to lead his league in wins one year, and come back to league it again in batting average.

87. Who was the first player who led his league in slugging, home runs, bases on balls, errors, and being hit by a pitch, and caught stealing, but in each category in a different season?

Jack Fournier, a first baseman and outfielder, who started his major league career on April 13, 1912 as a first baseman with the Chicago White Sox was a leader, in fact he was a leader in four different categories, not just in the same season. Although he played 15 seasons and had a career .313 batting average he managed to lead his league in a number of categories, not just at the same time.

Let's start in 1925 when Jack, with the White Sox, led the American League in slugging percentage with a .491 record and also the hit by pitcher statistic with 15.

Moving back to 1920 with the St. Louis Browns, Fournier got in the way of 12 pitches to reestablish his ability to get on base by taking a pitch for the team by being hit by a pitch 12 times. The following year, 1921, Jack must have been slow afoot for he led the American League in being caught 22 times while trying to pilfer a base.

Not to be deterred Fournier was destined to league the league, some league, in some category, and in 1924, when he was over playing for the Brooklyn Dodgers in the National League, he was again a league leader by playing in 154 games, and to win the home run championship that season with 27 round-trippers.

Then came the 1925 season and the best that Jack could do was to lead the National League in bases on balls when he strolled 86 times. In the 1926 season with Brooklyn, and the 1927 season, his final one, with the Boston Braves he was not a leader in any statistic. Jack can always say he was the first to lead the league in a given category, not just a multiple leader in a major one.

88. Who was the first former baseball player to become a baseball play-by-play announcer?

John Gladstone "Jack" Graney, who was born on June 10, 1886 in St. Thomas, Ontario, made his major league debut on April 30, 1908 as a southpaw pitcher for the Cleveland Naps (Indians), pitching just 3.1 innings in two games that season. Not appearing in the majors again, until he re-joined the Indians in 1910, when he took over in right field, and played there until 1911, when he moved over as the regular left fielder when "Shoeless Joe" Jackson joined the Indians.

Graney continued to roam the Indians' outfield for 13 seasons, and as their lead-off batter, and with his ability to draw walks, which gave him a high on-base percentage even with his modest batting average, saw him lead the American League in bases on balls in 1917 and 1919, and in doubles in 1915. He ended his 14-year career with 1,178 base hits, 420 runs batted in, and a rather soft .250 batting average, but an above average on base percentage of .354.

When Graney ended his playing career on June 28, 1922 he embarked on a new one, and moved over to the Indians broadcast booth to be a play-by-play broadcaster. With that move he became the first former major league player to be a play-by-play baseball announcer in the United States. He called the Indians' games from 1932 to 1944, had a year off, and resumed his broadcasting of games from 1946 to 1953.

89. Who was the first major league player to appear in a game with a number on his uniform?

The first player to appear in a game with a number on his uniform is profiled in item 88. The event goes back to June 26, 1916 when the Cleveland Indians introduced numbers on their uniforms on an experimental basis in a home game against the Chicago White Sox. The numbers were placed on the sleeves of the Cleveland uniforms, and they corresponded with the names in the scorecards. On that day lead-off batter, leftfielder Jack Graney was the first major league player to appear in a game with a number on his uniform.

In 1929 both the Indians and the Yankees started wearing numbers on their uniforms. The Yankees leftfielder, Earle "The Kentucky Colonel" Combs, who batted leadoff for New York, was assigned #1, and became the first player to come to the plate with a number, not on his sleeve, but on the back of his uniform.

Each Yankees player, depending upon where they were in the batting order, followed with the next number. That is why Babe Ruth, who batted third, wore #3, and Lou Gehrig, who batted fourth, wore #4.

90. Who was the first batter to face Babe Ruth in his pitching career?

When Cleveland's lead-off batter, leftfielder Jack Graney, stepped into the batter's box on July 11, 1914 to face a rookie southpaw of the Boston Red Sox by the name of George Herman "Babe" Ruth he became the first batter that Ruth would face in his long and distinguished career, on the mound, and of course, later at the plate. "Firsts" were not uncommon for Jack Graney as items #87, 88 and this current one will attest.

91. Who were the first players to be the subjects of a motion picture?

One has to go back to the very early days of the motion picture to come up with the names of second baseman Nap Lajoie and centerfielder Harry "Deerfoot" Bay of the Cleveland Indians who went through some baseball motions for a motion picture camera during a post season exhibition series against the Cincinnati Reds in 1903.

92. Who was the first major leaguer to play all three major professional sports?

Ernest Alonzo Nevers made his major league baseball debut on April 26, 1926, as a right-handed pitcher with the St. Louis Browns, having a less than awesome major league baseball career over his three years with them, pitching 178.1 innings in 44 games, and compiling a 6-12, 4.64 Era. record.

What makes Nevers' athletic career unique and compelling is that although considered big and clumsy in his youth, even to the point of being used as a tackling dummy for his high school football team, where he learned strength and toughness. He developed into a fine basketball, football, and baseball player as he matured. Playing college football at Stanford the 6-foot, 205 pound fullback could do it all, run, block, tackle, pass and punt. In his two years of playing at Stanford, including the 1925 Rose Bowl, where he played the entire 60 minutes, carrying the ball 34 times and rushing for 114 yards, gaining more yardage than Notre Dame's "Four Horseman" combined, earned him the MVP Award, and national fame. In 1951 he was inducted into the College Football Hall of Fame. In 1962 Sports Illustrated called him the greatest college football player of all time.

In December 1925 Evers began his professional football career playing a series of gate-producing exhibition games against Red Grange and the Chicago Bears. Shortly after he signed with the Duluth Eskimos in the NFL, and later played fullback with, and coached, with the Chicago Cardinals from 1929 to 1931.

In late 1925, early '26, Nevers switched over to play professional basketball in Chicago.

During his five seasons with the Chicago Cardinals he was named the All-Pro fullback five times, and in 1963 was inducted as a charter inductee into the Professional Football Hall of Fame.

Ernie Nevers, one of America's greatest athletes, played all three major professional sports and is the first player to do so, and be inducted into both the college and professional football Halls of Fame.

93. Who was the first player to be credited with receiving a salary for playing professional baseball?

The first player credited with being the first salaried professional baseball player was a speedy, left-handed batting and throwing centerfielder, second baseman and shortstop, and the first great Jewish ballplayer, by the name of Lipman Emanuel Pike, who was born in New York City on May 25, 1845.

In July 1866, when the Philadelphia Athletics paid him $20 a week to handle the hot corner, he accepted, and thus became the first player to be credited as salaried.

On May 9, 1871, at the age of 26, he made his major league debut with the Troy Haymakers in the National Association as a player-manager playing in centerfield, and at first and second base. In 1872, when he was with the Baltimore Canaries, he led the league in games with 56, in home runs with 7, and in runs batted in with 60, while batting .298.

In 1873, and still with the Canaries, Pike either asked for, demanded, or his team voluntarily agreed, to pay him the princely salary of $1,200 for the season, making him the first salaried player in professional baseball. He responded by leading the league in home runs with 4, and had a good year by driving in 51 runs. Having a regular paycheck must have sat well for Pike for in 1874 he led the league in doubles with 22, and in slugging with .504, while batting an impressive .355.

Pike played a total of ten seasons, one each with six teams, and two seasons with the Cincinnati Red Stockings, and Baltimore Canaries, and played his final game, at age 42, on July 28, 1887, with the New York Metropolitans in the American Association with a career batting average of

,322, driving in 332 runs while scoring 434.

94. Who was the first major league player to be killed in World War II?

Elmer John Gedeon, who was born on April 15, 1917, in Cleveland Ohio, upon graduation from the University of Michigan signed a major league contract with the Washington Senators in the spring of 1939. He was called up to the majors appearing in his first game on September 18, 1939 at the age of 22. This centerfielder played four games in center and one in right field, coming to bat 15 times, getting 3 hits, scoring a run, and batting in another for a career .200 batting average.

Called into the service during World War II he piloted a B-26 bomber that was hit by flak over St. Pol, France, on April 20, 1944, in air combat and he was killed instantly. Only his co-pilot was saved after bailing out. Gedeon became the first major league player to be killed in action during that war. He is buried in Arlington National Cemetery, Arlington, Virginia.

The second player to be killed in action, and the first in the Pacific Theatre, was Philadelphia Athletics catcher, Harry Mink O'Neill, who made his only major league appearance in a game on July 23, 1939.

Harry was 27 years old when he was killed on Iwo Jima, in the Marianas Islands, on March 6, 1945. Harry was buried in Arlington Cemetery, Drexel Hill, Pennsylvania.

95. Who was the first player to have his uniform number retired by three teams?

Here is a pitcher who had his uniform number retired by not only three teams, but to have an easy entrance into the residency of Cooperstown, as he did in 1999, receiving 491 out of 497 votes. We are speaking of #34, Nolan Ryan, who was drafted in the 12th round of the 1965 amateur draft by the New York Mets, and made his pitching debut on September 11, 1966. Granted the record of this 19-year old in his first year was less than one would hope for with a two game Era. of 15.00, but the Mets hung with him for five seasons.

A pitcher with so much heat, with so much potential talent, he was traded by the Mets on December 10, 1971 along with three others to the California Angels for third baseman Jim Fregosi. That deal is still talked about to this day.

Once in California Nolan Ryan began to blossom and his pitching career accelerated toward stardom. In his 27 seasons with the Mets, California, Houston, and Texas he had 324 wins, 292 losses, an Era. of 3.19, striking out an unheard off 5,714 batters, having 61 shutouts, issuing 2,795 walks over 5,386 innings made him the obvious favorite to have his uniform number retired by the California Angels, the Houston Astros, and the Texas Rangers with whom he played his last game, on September 22, 1993. He stands alone to be the first to have his number retired by three former teams, and as an aside, be enshrined in Cooperstown.

96. Who was the first player to win the American League Most Valuable Player Award, in the first year the official league award was given?

St. Louis Browns first baseman, George Sisler, was the first American League player to be the recipient of the Most Valuable Player Award in the first year the official league award was given.

In 1922, the year of his award, he led the league in runs scored (134), base hits (246), triples (18), stolen bases (51) and batting average (.420). In addition he drove in 105 runs while establishing a then American League record consecutive game hitting streak with 41 consecutive games.

97. Who was the first player to win the National League Most Valuable Player Award, after it became the official league award?

The first National League player to win the Most Valuable Player Award, after it became the official league award, was right-handed pitcher Charles Arthur "Dazzy" Vance who made his major league debut on April 16, 1915 with the Pittsburgh Pirates starting on the mound and pitching 2.2 innings, giving up 3 hits, 5 walks, and 3 earned runs before the New York Yankees purchased him from the Pirates later in the month.

In 1915 and 1918, while with New York, he appeared in 10 games pitching in 30.1 innings before being sent down. Just before the 1922 season Dazzy was purchased by the Brooklyn Robins from New Orleans in the Southern Association.

Vance came into his own with Brooklyn, staying with them for 12 seasons with a 190-131 won-lost, and a 3.24 Era. record.

His biggest year was 1924 when he led the league with a 28-6, 2.16 Era., pitching 30 complete games, and striking out a league high of 262 batters.

For that effort Dazzy was named the MVP for the 1924 season.

98. Who was the first, and only, player to play for the same franchise in three different cities?

It all started just before the 1949 season when Eddie Mathews was signed by the Boston Braves as an amateur free agent. It wasn't until April

15, 1952, however, until that dream of a major league career became a reality when the 20-year old Mathews made his debut at third base playing in 145 games and leading the league in strikeouts with 115 and batting .242 in that freshman year.

In 1953 the Boston Braves moved their franchise to the mid-west and became the Milwaukee Braves. The change of scenery and a year of maturity bode well for this future Hall of Famer for he had a very good year leading the National League in home runs with 47, and had 135 runs batted in to go along with his .302 average.

In 1966 the Milwaukee Braves decided to move south and the Atlanta Braves were established, and Mathews was still wearing a Braves uniform, this time with his third city across his chest when on the road.

On December 31, 1966 Atlanta traded Mathews to the Houston Astros where he stayed until Houston traded him, on August 17, 1967, over to the American League to join the Detroit Tigers. He played in 67 games with Detroit over the next two seasons, finishing out his 17-year career on September 27, 1968, and was released by them on October 28, 1968.

He was a member of the 500-home run club with a career total of 512, and was elected to The Hall of Fame in 1978.

Mathews remains the first player to play for the same franchise in three different cities.

99. Who was the first pitcher to pitch in the major leagues, and have over a 20-year gap until he again pitched in the big leagues?

It's difficult to imagine, but as Casey Stengel use to say, "You can look it up." Paul Schreiber, a right-handed pitcher, made his major league debut, as a 19-year old, on September 2, 1922 with the Brooklyn Robins finishing out the second game of a doubleheader against the New York Giants, at the Polo Grounds, in relief of Leon Cadore, and Al Mamaux. Before a crowd of 40,000 Schreiber, without getting a decision, pitched a scoreless inning, and allowed two hits as the Robins lost 5-2.

Schreiber came back in 1923 to pitch in nine games, finishing five in relief over 15 innings, allowing seven earned runs and nine hits.

Schreiber finally returned to the major leagues, this time as a batting practice pitcher for the New York Yankees. In 1945, at the age of 42, while a coach with the Yankees, he came out of retirement as a player when he came on in relief in two games, pitching 4.1 innings, giving up two earned runs, four hits, and two walks. He pitched his final game on September 8, 1945,

22 years after his last major league appearance, making him the first player to have over a 20-year gap in his active major league career.

100. What were the first major league teams to play a game in the shadow of the Pyramids, outside Cairo, Egypt?

Under the heat of a North African desert sun the New York Giants and the Chicago White Sox played an exhibition game, on February 1, 1914, in the shadow of the Pyramids, outside of Cairo, Egypt. In a game the following day a triple play will be executed, that's a baseball term, not a political event.

101. Who was the first, and only, player to hit a fair ball out of Roosevelt Stadium, Jersey City?

Roosevelt Stadium was the home of the New York Giants farm club, the Jersey City Giants. When attendance began to slide, due to the advent of televised baseball, and three major league teams in the New York Metropolitan area the "Little Giants" moved to Ottawa, Canada in 1951. From then till 1956 no professional games were played there. That changed when, on December 1, 1955, the Brooklyn Dodgers announced they had made an agreement with the governing body of Jersey City to play seven regular season games, and one exhibition game in Roosevelt Stadium in 1956. They extended that by also agreeing to play seven regular season games in 1957 and 1958 as well, for an agreed upon annual rental of $10,000.

The first game played in Roosevelt Stadium by the Dodgers took place on April 19, 1956 as the Dodgers, before a modest crowd of 12,214, beat the Philadelphia Phillies, 5-4.

The seventh game of that home stand came on Wednesday, August 15, 1956 when the "Big Giants," from across the river in Manhattan, drew the largest home crowd of the season when 26,385 turned out to see New York Giants southpaw Johnny Antonelli shut out the Dodgers, on two hits, and winning, 1-0, on the bat of Willie Mays who hit a one out, solo home run, in the 4th inning off right-hander Don Newcombe, to become the first player to hit a fair ball clear out of Roosevelt Stadium.

102. Who was the first owner to be banned from baseball for life?

Horace Fogel, who was the owner of the Philadelphia Phillies, was tried by the National League directors on October 17, 1912, and found guilty, and banned forever from major league baseball, in November, for "undermining the integrity of the game," when he charged that Cardinals' manager Roger Bresnahan used substitutes, and the National League umpires, specifically William Brennan, who made questionable calls to insure that the New York Giants won the 1912 pennant.

On January 11, 1913, following the expulsion of Horace Fogel from baseball William H. Locke and William F. Baker bought the Phillies.

103. Who was the first umpire to be banned for life from major league baseball?

Richard Higham, in 1882, was banned for life for conspiring with gamblers to fix games.

104. Who was the first player, upon retirement to produce silent films for over twenty years?

Outfielder and first baseman, "Turkey Mike" Donlin, who played his last game on October 1, 1914, after 12 years, with a .career .333 batting average, went on to Hollywood to produce silent films, passing away on September 24, 1933.

105. Who was the first player to pinch-run, and then pinch hit, later in the same game?

Catcher Pat Collins of the St. Louis Browns, as a courtesy extended by Philadelphia Athletics' manager Connie Mack, was allowed to run for third baseman Homer Ezzell in a game on June 8, 1923, a game won by Philadelphia 6-5.

It seems that Ezzell had an urgent call of nature, and had to run to the locker room. Later in the game Collins came back to pinch-hit and walked. True, I am not making this up.

106. Which players formed the first "Z" battery to play in the major leagues?

Anyone with a flashlight knows about A, AA, and D batteries, and some knowledgeable baseball buffs know of the "Q" battery, right-hander Dan Quisenberry, and his sometimes battery mate, Jamie Quirk with the Kansas City Athletics.

But, if you want to catch up on your "Z's" read along. It was down in Memorial Stadium on that Monday, July 1, 1957, before a crowd of 45,276 that saw the Baltimore Orioles go into the top of the 10th inning locked in a 2-2 game with the New York Yankees. Right-hander George Zuverink had come on to pitch after Bob Hale had pinch-hit for southpaw Ken Lehman in the 9th.

His battery mate became 18-year old Frank "Noodles" Zupo, who had come in to replace Joe Ginsberg who had been pinch-hit for in the 9th by Joe Durham, who struck out swinging.

Zuverink got SS Gil McDougald to ground out to second for the first out, but that brought up CF Mickey Mantle who quickly deposited a pitch into the right field stands or his 22nd homer of the season giving New York a 3-2 lead which they kept as Whitey Ford went all the way by closing down the O's in the 10th.

But the fans saw the first "Z" battery in major league history.

107. Who was the first number one pick in the amateur draft not to make it to the major leagues?

Unfortunately Steve Chilcott was the first pick in the draft on June 7, 1966 and never made it to the big leagues.

108. Who was the first pitcher to ever play for four different divisions in the same season?

Right-hander Dan Miceli, who made his major league debut on September 9, 1993 with the Pittsburgh Pirates had a well-traveled 14-year career in both the American and National Leagues ending his career with a 43-52 record on September 29, 2006 with the Tampa Bay Devil Rays.

What sets Miceli apart, and makes him a "Groundbreaker" occurred during the 2003 season. He started the season with the Colorado Rockies in the NL West, but was released on May 13th. Two days later, on May 15th, he signed as a free agent with the Cleveland Indians in the AL Central.

On June 25th he was sent to the New York Yankees, AL East, as part of a conditional deal. On June 29th, the Yankees shipped him back to the National League, to the Houston Astros, NL Central, as part of a conditional deal. He stayed with Houston until May 21' 2005 when he signed with the Rockies, and then on to the Tampa Bay Devil Rays in 2006.

With his peregrinations during the 2003 season Miceli is the first pitcher to spend his season in four different divisions. For those purists Dave Kingman had a similar traveling experience in 1977.

109. Who was the first player to have his hometown name as his uniform number?

"Big Bill" Voiselle made his major league debut with the New York Giants on September 1, 1942. He picked up the moniker of "Big Bill" because of his 6'4" 200 pound body, but asked for, and received, a uniform number of "96", for the strapping right-hander was born in the town of 96,

South Carolina, to become the first player to identify his name by his number on the scorecard while advertising his birthplace on his back as well.

110. Who was the first major leaguer to jump to the "outlaw" Mexican League?

On February 19, 1946, New York Giants outfielder-first baseman Danny Gardella, with players returning from World War II, and seeing himself being demoted to the minor leagues, Gardella joined the newly formed Mexican League, who were offering generous salaries to lure newly returning military veterans to their new league.

In April 1946 MLB Commissioner Happy Chandler imposed a ban of at least five years on anyone jumping to Mexico. After a potential lengthy legal battle, and Chandler offering amnesty to the players who had gone to Mexico, Gardella, supposedly settled for $60,000, and after disenchantment settled in with the Mexican League he signed with the St. Louis Cardinals, and after one-at bat with them in 1950, was sent to the minors. He still remains as the first major leaguer to jump south of the border to the short-lived Mexican League.

111. Who was the first player to play in four different leagues?

On May 11, 1883 Edward Enoch Bakley, who was known as Jersey Bakley, by having been born in Blackwood, New Jersey, made his debut with the Philadelphia Athletics in the American Association as a pitcher and right fielder. In 1884 he played in the Union Association with the Philadelphia Keystones as well as the Wilmington Quicksteps, and the Kansas City Unions. In 1888 we found Jersey with the Cleveland Blues back in the American Association. In 1889 he stayed with Cleveland, this time in the National League, with the Spiders. In 1890 Jersey jumped to the Cleveland Infants in the Players League to make him the first player to play his career in four different leagues.

112. Who was the first United States President to throw out the Opening Day first pitch with both his left hand and his right hand?

It was Opening Day, on April 18, 1950, in Griffith Stadium, Washington, when President Harry Truman threw out the ceremonial first pitches, one left-handed and the other right-handed, then settled in his seat to watch the Senators defeat the A's 8-7. A faithful and rugged fan, Truman, when a slight rain began to come down in the 6th inning, just put on his raincoat and stayed till the end of the game.

113. Who was the first and only player to win the Triple Crown and

then be traded in the off season?

Philadelphia Phillies right-fielder Chuck Klein not only won the Triple Crown in 1933, he led the National League in 8 different offensive categories, when he racked up the following numbers: 223 hits, 44 doubles, 28 home runs, 120 runs batted in, .368 batting average, .422 OBP, and a .602 SLG, 1.025 OPS, and 365 total bases.

With the Phillies needing cash, and Klein making $17,500, he was traded on November 21, 1933 to the Chicago Cubs for 1B-OF Harvey Hendrick, LHP Ted Kleinhans, SS Mark Koenig and $65,000. The Cubs obviously thought he was worth more for they paid him $30,000 for the 1934 season.

114. Who formed the first major league battery whose last names began with the letter "Q"?

On Sunday, April 13, 1980 the Kansas City Royals played host to the Detroit Tigers at Royals Stadium. Southpaw Paul Splittorff, with Jamie Quick as his battery mate, started for Kansas City and went 6.1 scoreless innings before being relieved by right-hander Dan Quisenberry which then created the first major league "Q" battery in major league history, as the Royals eked out a 3-2 win.

115. Who were the first Afro-American pitcher, and batter, to face each other in a major league game?

It happened on Friday, July 8, 1949, at Ebbets Field, when Brooklyn Dodgers right-hander Don Newcombe faced New York Giants second baseman Hank Thompson leading off in the top of the 1st inning.

116. Who was the first, and only player, by his actions at Ebbets Field, to become the inspiration for a scene in a Hollywood movie?

Interestingly, one might say it was the forerunner to the scene from the movie "The Natural", but it didn't come from a power hitter, but from Boston Braves leftfielder Carvel "Bama" Rowell. This bizarre happening occurred in the second game of a double header between the Boston Braves and the Brooklyn Dodgers at Ebbets Field on Memorial Day, Thursday, May 30, 1946.

In a 7-run, 2nd inning, of the second game of a doubleheader, Braves leftfielder, Bama Rowell came up and smashed a double off Dodgers right-hander Hank Behrman that shattered the large Bulova clock that sat high atop the right field scoreboard, at exactly 4:25 PM, sending a shower of glass down upon Dodgers' right-fielder Dixie Walker.

One hour later the clock stopped, but Bama may have put a stop to the clock, but his hit may have become an inspiration for a scene in the movie, "The Natural." The Braves, after being shutout in the opener, 5-0, by right-hander Kirby Higbe, took the nightcap, 10-8, thanks to that 7-run 2nd inning.

The Bulova Watch Company had promised a free watch to any batter who hit the clock. It wasn't until 41 years later that Rowell received his prize when he was honored at "'Bama' Rowell Day" in his birthplace at Citronelle, Alabama.

117. **When was the first day in major league history that eight teams were all involved, for better or worse, in games that ended in a 1-0 score on the same day?**

It seems that September 2, 2001 was shutout day in major league baseball as the Yankees beat the Red Sox, 1-0, at Fenway Park, the Baltimore Orioles beat the Seattle Mariners 1-0, down in Baltimore, and over in the National League the Houston Astros defeated the Brewers 1-0, in Milwaukee, while the Arizona Diamondbacks were shutout by the Padres, 1-0, in San Diego, which completed a most unusual day in the major leagues, a first of its kind.

118. **Who was the first player in major league history to be part of a quartet of consecutive home runs twice, once in each league?**

This unusual experience happened for the second time to Boston Red Sox outfielder J.D. Drew on Sunday, April 22, 2007, in the bottom of the 3rd inning at Fenway Park against the New York Yankees.

LF Manny Ramirez started off the power display by hitting a home run to deep left-center field off rookie southpaw Chase Wright. RF J.D. Drew followed with his home run to deep right-center. 3B Mike Lowell was next and he hammered the third home run off Wright to deep left field, and catcher Jason Varitek completed the quartet by hitting a home run to the same spot as Lowell. It was a welcome to the big leagues for the shocked and shelled rookie as he became the victim of four consecutive round-trippers. These quickly wiped away the Yankees' three run lead at the time as the Red Sox went on to win 7-6.

The first time Drew was part of a quartet of consecutive home runs occurred on Monday, September 18, 2006 at Dodger Stadium, when Drew patrolled right field for Los Angeles in a game against the San Diego Padres.

In the bottom of the 9th inning, and behind 9-5, the Dodgers sent up 2B Jeff Kent against right-hander Jon Adkins, who had come on in relief of right-hander Scott Linebrink to start off the 9th, and preserve the Padre lead. He took Adkins downtown to start off the come-from-behind effort. He was followed by RF J.D. Drew who did the same. Next up was catcher Russell Martin, but manager Bruce Bochy decided to bring in his ace, Trevor Hoffman, to save the day. But Martin had other ideas, and he became the third consecutive Dodger to hit a home run. That brought up LF Marion Anderson, and he rounded out the home run quartet by blasting the fourth consecutive home run, which tied the game at 9-9 and sent the game into extra innings where the Padres came up with a run in the 10th, but Los Angeles came back with two in their bottom of the 10th to win 11-10.

119. Who was the first player to endorse non-sporting goods merchandise?

We have to go back well over a century to find that John "Buck" Freeman, who made his major league debut as a southpaw pitcher for the Washington Senators on June 27, 1891, but was reassigned to right field, had a banner year in 1899 when he hit 25 triples, drove in 122 runs as he established a new major league home run record by hitting 25. His reward for those fancy statistics was to have his picture appear in various newspaper ads endorsing Squinksquillet's suspenders. My, have players come a long way since then.

120. Who was the first player to play over 8,000 consecutive innings of major league baseball?

Cal Ripken Jr., the Baltimore Orioles shortstop, had played in every inning of the game on June 5, 1982, and continued playing every inning of every game until the 8th inning of a blowout game at Exhibition Stadium, on September 14, 1987, where the Orioles were being routed, 18-3, by the Toronto Blue Jays. His manager, and father, Cal Ripken Sr. pulled his son off the bases and inserted pinch runner, Ron Washington, to be the player who replaced Cal after 8,243 consecutive innings. A record that I am quite sure will not be broken. But then they said that about the consecutive game record as well.

121. Who were the first major league players, both deaf mutes, to face each other at the plate in a game?

This is a very unusual, but gratifying story. On May 16, 1902 Cincinnati

Reds centerfielder William "Dummy" Hoy led off at the plate, and opposing him on the mound was Luther "Dummy" Taylor, a right-handed pitcher for the New York Giants.

Hoy greeted Taylor with a "I'm glad to see you" in sign language, and both players realized this historical moment in baseball history when two players were representing their team on the playing field, but neither could hear nor speak.

Hoy went two- for- four at the plate as the Giants, with a 5-run rally in the 9ᵗʰ inning, went on to win 5-3. It was the first time two deaf mutes faced off against each other in a major league game; truly a "Groundbreaker."

122. Who was the first player to sign a contract to produce a baseball bat with his signature on it, and become the first professional athlete to endorse an athletic product?

All those accolades belong to John Peter "Honus Wagner, the Hall of Fame shortstop of the Pittsburgh Pirates. In September 1905, Wagner signed a contract with his good friend, Bud Hillerich, of J.F. Hillerich & Son to make, and endorse a bat, known since 1894 as the "Louisville Slugger", with Wagner's signature on it, and to be sold in stores, making "The Flying Dutchman" the first player to sign a contract to have a bat made with a player's signature on it, and to endorse an athletic product.

123. Who was the first player to have the term "Texas Leaguer" be applied to the way he stroked base hits?

As the story goes Oliver "Ollie" Pickering, a centerfielder, who made his major league debut with the Louisville Colonels on August 9, 1896, and had seven consecutive base hits be of the bloop variety, which may have reflected on his Texas League background, had that type of hit attributed to those hits that just fell in between the infield and outfield, and the term, "Texas Leaguer" became a part of the baseball lexicon.

124. Who was the first person to wear the uniforms of all four New York City teams?

Charles Dillon Stengel was born on July 30, 1890 in Kansas City, Missouri, and due to that birth place acquired the sobriquet "Casey". He started his major league career as a right-fielder, on September 17, 1912, with the Brooklyn Dodgers, and stayed with them through the 1917 season. From 1921 to 1923 he wore the uniform of the New York Giants.

In 1949 he joined the New York Yankees as their field manager and successfully stayed with them until 1960.

He joined the New York Mets in 1962 as their manager, and had a challenging four-year career in Queens with that new entry into the National League.

125. Who was the first, and only, player to play in the last game in New York Giants history, and in the first game in New York Mets history?

On September 29, 1957, Frank Thomas played first base for the Pittsburgh Pirates in their game against the New York Giants at the Polo Grounds.

On April 11, 1962, Thomas patrolled left field for the New York Mets at St. Louis, against the Cardinals, when the New York Mets made their debut in the National League.

126. Who was the first major league player to wear a batting helmet with ear flaps?

On June 26, 1966 Ron Santo, the Chicago Cubs third baseman, was hit in the face by a pitch from New York Mets right-hander Jack Fisher, and had his cheek bone fractured. After returning to play after two weeks Santo had a special batting helmet made with protective ear flaps to prevent a reoccurrence of that happening to himself or other players.

127. Who was the first player to have over 12,000 plate appearances with just one franchise?

Ty Cobb was the first player to exceed 12,000 plate appearances, when he came to the plate 12,101 times for the Detroit Tigers, over his 22-year career with them.

128. Who was the first National League player to have over 12,000 plate appearances for one franchise?

Willie Mays came to the plate 12,012 times while with the New York/San Francisco Giants during his 21-year career with them.

129. Who was the first player to hit a home run out of Pacific Bell Park and into McCovey Cove?

On Monday evening, May 1, 2000, before a crowd of 40,930, the long-awaited answer to the oft-wondered question was satisfied in the 6th inning when San Francisco Giants leftfielder, Barry Bonds powered a 3-run home run, his 11th of the season, off New York Mets southpaw Rich Rodriguez, deep to right field where it cleared the wall and fell into the Bay for the first splashdown into McCovey Cove in Pac-Bell Park history. The Giants went on to a 10-3 victory.

130. Who was the first player to win the All-Star game MVP award and the World Series MVP award in the same season?

The year was 2000, and the player was New York Yankees shortstop Derek Jeter, who won both awards for his outstanding play in the mid-summer event and the early Fall Classic.

131. What team was the first to wear uniforms for a baseball game?

The New York Knickerbocker Baseball Club instituted the wearing of uniforms in 1849. Their outfit consisted of white dress shirts, a bow tie, and dark blue trousers, topped off by a straw hat.

132. Who was the first player to be fined for swearing during a baseball game?

As the story goes James Whyte Davis, a fiery and extremely devoted man to the game of baseball, was fined by Alexander J. Cartwright, considered "The Father of Modern Baseball", and who was a member of the Knickerbocker Baseball Club, when he was named the umpire for the game played on June 19, 1846 at Elysian Field, Hoboken, New Jersey, in a game against the New York Nine. In those days a fined player was assessed a sum of 12 ½ cents for each infraction. The New York Nine came away with a crushing 23-1 win, and Davis a little lighter in the pocketbook.

133. Who was the first player to win three Most Valuable Player Awards?

He made his major league debut on May 1, 1925 as a catcher with the Philadelphia Athletics, but Jimmie "Double X" Foxx played a good part of his career, 1919 games, as a first baseman, and a power hitter extraordinaire.

His first MVP Award came with the Philadelphia Athletics, in 1932, after six seasons of batting over .300, when he led the American League in batting with 58 home runs, 151 runs scored, 169 runs batted in, 438 total bases and a slugging percentage of .749, falling just short of the batting championship by hitting .364 which was just under Red Sox 1B Dale Alexander's .367.

He came right back in 1933 to win back-to-back MVP's, by again leading the league in home runs with 48, runs batted in with 163, total bases with 403, a slugging percentage of .703, and yes, this time, the batting championship with a .356 average.

On December 10, 1935 he was traded to the Boston Red Sox in a four-player, plus cash, deal that brought him his third MVP Award in 1938. He led the American League in walks with 119, runs batted in with 175, total bases with 398, and in slugging with .704 percentage while racking up a .349 batting average, all the best in the league.

When old "Double X" finished his 20-year, Hall of Fame career with the Philadelphia Phillies on September 23, 1945 this 9-time All-Star had amassed 534 home runs, 2,646 hits, 1,751 runs scored, and 1,922 runs batted in, a .609 slugging percentage and a .325 batting average. "Double X" was a "Groundbreaker" who also did a lot of damage to pitcher's earned run averages.

134. Who were the first players to be recognized as being paid professionals?

I am not sure how much publicity was given to pitcher James Creighton and shortstop George Flanley, but it was reported that these two outstanding players of their time, received envelopes of cash "under the table" for their continued play with the Brooklyn Excelsior Club in 1860. Dickey Pearce was also thought to be one of the first to be paid to play, but records are not always accurate going back that far when it came to who was being paid to play.

135. Who was the first radio announcer to be asked to step down from the announcers' booth, and return to the mound to pitch for the team he was the announcer for?

Talk about being desperate for a starting pitcher, the St. Louis Browns called Dizzy Dean down from his announcer's booth to start on the mound for the Browns final game of the season, on Sunday, September 28, 1947, against the Chicago White Sox, at Sportsman's Park.

Now Dizzy had not pitched since his retirement in 1941, but that made no difference to Dean for he donned the uniform and started the game that afternoon.

He pitched four scoreless innings, giving up just three hits, walked one, and faced fourteen batters, while getting a single in his only plate appearance before he gave way to right-hander Glen Moulder, who went the final five innings giving up five earned runs on five hits, walked four and faced 22 batters in losing to southpaw Eddie Lopat, 5-2.

The 15,901 fans on hand were treated to the final appearance by the great Dizzy Dean whose stats on his last day read a batting average of 1,000 and an Era. of 0.00. That's a way to finally go out.

136. Who was the first player to retire from major league baseball on religious principles?

Allan "Red" Worthington, a born-again Christian, and a right-handed pitcher, made his major league debut with the New York Giants on July 6, 1953, and moved from the Giants over to the Boston Red Sox briefly, and then on to the Chicago White Sox in 1960.

While in Chicago, under owner Bill Veeck, Worthington thought the exploding Comiskey Park scoreboard installed by Veeck, was immoral because he learned that inside the bevy of lights was a clever sign-stealing scheme using an obscure flashing red light in the upper right hand corner of the scoreboard that was used to flash the type of pitch that was coming to White Sox batters.

Worthington told manager Al Lopez that it was cheating and it had to stop or he would quit the team, which he later did. He became the first player to quit a team due to his religious principles.

Worthington re-entered the majors in 1963 with the Cincinnati Reds and went on to complete his 14-season career with the Minnesota Twins on October 2, 1969 with a 75-82, 3.39 Era. record.

In 1961 major league baseball banned the use of electronic equipment to steal signs.

137. Who was the first player to have his bats custom-made?

He was born in Louisville, Kentucky in 1861, and this infielder made his debut with the Louisville Eclipse/Colonels on May 2, 1882. Pete "Gladiator" Browning was a well-built 180-pounder who could tear the cover off the ball, and showed his hitting prowess by batting well over .300 in his first seven seasons, once hitting .402, and was a three-time batting champion in his first nine seasons. Later in his career, in 1885, Pete switched over to patrolling left field and centerfield, but never took his eye off his batting.

The fans, who gave him the name "Louisville Slugger," was very particular about the bats he used. One day, in 1884, an amateur baseball player by the name of John "Bud" Hillerich, who worked at his family's wood working shop, and supplied bats to his teammates, saw Browning break his favorite bat and offered to make him a new one out of white ash. Browning accepted and became the very first player to have his bat custom-made. And as the story goes, Browning picked up three hits in his next game.

A new industry was born, and all these years later it is common practice employed by all hitters.

138. Who was the first major league player to be drafted into military service in World War II?

This Philadelphia Phillies right-hander toiled for a cellar-dwelling team from his debut on July 24, 1935 out in Forbes Field, Pittsburgh, in a relief role that saw his Phillies have annual losses of 91, 100, 92, 105, 106, and 103 during his initial stay with the team. From 1937 to the end of 1940 season Hugh Mulcahy had started 126 games for the Phillies and had lost 76 games while winning 40 with his team having a .250 batting average over that time, thus giving reason for the press, after seeing the box score read, "LP Mulcahy" giving him the sobriquet, "Losing Pitcher."

Granted he did lose 20 games in 1938 and 22 in 1940, but Mulcahy was a hard luck, workhorse of the Phillies staff.

He, like all adult males, was registered for the draft and he went from being shelled by National League batters to possibly being shelled by the Axis Powers when on March 8, 1941, nine months before Pearl Harbor, Hugh "Losing Pitcher" Mulcahy became the first major leaguer, not to be called on to start a game for the Philadelphia Phillies, but called on to protect his country, when the 27-year old right-hander was drafted, and sent to Camp Devens, Massachusetts for training. He served in the United States Army for 53 months seeing overseas duty in New Guinea and the Philippines before being discharged on August 5, 1945. He returned to the Phillies for the remainder of the '45 season and spent the 1946 season with them before finishing his career with the Pittsburgh Pirates on May 8, 1947.

139. Who were the first major league players to trade, not only their wives, but their children, and their pets as well?

It didn't really happen, did it? Yes, it did, and it happened in 1972, but wasn't announced until spring training in 1973. Two Yankee southpaw pitchers, Fritz Peterson and Mike Kekich had been inseparable friends since 1969. Their families, who lived in New Jersey, would go to the shore together, picnic together, and their children were very close. They even double dated, and on one occasion even joked about swapping wives.

Well it came to fruition, and the trade of the season took place with Fritz Peterson trading his wife Marilyn, his two kids, and their poodle, for Susanne Kekich, the two Kekich children, and a Bedington terrier. No mention of cash was involved, nor a child or pet to be named later. As Kekich stated after the announcement, "we didn't trade wives, we traded lives." Who was it said, "baseball is a funny game."?

140. Who was the first player to have participated in 10 no-hitters?

Fans would give their eye-teeth to be witness to a no-hitter, and those who have seen one never forget the thrill. Well here we have Dagoberto (Bert) "Campy" Campaneris who made his big league debut, as a shortstop, on July 23, 1964, with the Kansas City Athletics, and through his 19 seasons, with the Athletics in Kansas City and Oakland, the Texas Rangers, California Angels, and the New York Yankees, participated in being there for 10 no-hitters before July 4, 1983, at Yankee Stadium, when Yankees southpaw Dave Righetti pitched a no-hitter against the Boston Red Sox. Campy, playing third base for New York that day became witness to his 11th no-hitter before playing in his last game on October 1, 1983.

Campy had been there for his first no-hitter, on May 8, 1968, when Jim "Catfish" Hunter pitched his perfect game for Oakland, defeating Minnesota, 4-0; on August 13, 1969 when the Orioles' Jim Palmer no-hit Oakland, 8-0; on July 3, 1970, when California southpaw, Clyde Wright, no-hit Oakland, 4-0; Oakland southpaw Vida Blue no-hit the Twins on September 21, 1970; Jim Bibby no-hit Oakland for Texas, 6-0, on July 30, 1973; Cleveland's Dick Bosman no-hitting the Athletics on July 19, 1974, 4-0; Vida Blue, Glenn Abbott, Paul Lindblad, and Rollie Fingers combining for an Oakland, 5-0, no-hitter over California; the White Sox's John "Blue Moon" Odom and Francisco Barrios combined no-hitter on July 28, 1976 over Oakland, 2-1; and Jim Colburn's, 6-0, no-hitter for Kansas City over the Texas Rangers on May 14, 1977; and his 10th came on Bert Blyleven's no-hitter for Texas on September 22, 1977, a 6-0 win at California.

141. Who was the first major league player to request, and have granted, that his uniform number be the same as his favorite verse from the Bible?

In 1988 Harold Reynolds, the Seattle Mariners second baseman, because of his strong religious feelings, requested management to change his uniform number from 37 to 19.

142. Who was the first player to be a season-long holdout?

When Tom Lovett, a pitcher for the Brooklyn Bridegrooms, received his 1892 contract for $3,000 he declined to sign it because it was for less than he had made the year before.

His record in 1890 had been 30-11, and followed that in 1891 with a 23-19 season. He claimed he was being victimized by the league-wide salary cut imposed after both the Players League and the American Association had been dissolved. He did return the following year for an unknown salary, but ended that 1893 season with a 3-5, 6.56 Era. before joining the Boston Beaneaters in 1894 for his final season, where he went 8-6, with a 5.97 ERA before he was released by them on July 9, 1894.

143. Who was the first player to receive a $100,000 bonus?

On January 31, 1950 a 19-year old southpaw pitcher, Paul "Lefty" Pettit, out of Narbonne High School in Harbor City, California, was signed as an amateur free agent by the Pittsburgh Pirates to a $100,000 bonus to pitch for them. What is interesting was that a contract was originally signed for $85,000 with a movie producer who wanted to do a film on the southpaw high school phenom who had pitched 6 no-hitters, 3 in a row, while in high school.

The movie producer then turned around, and sold Pettit's contract to the Pirates.

On Friday, May 4, 1951, Pettit came on in relief, in his major league debut, in the bottom of the 8th inning, at the Polo Grounds, with Pittsburgh behind 5-1, to the New York Giants. He retired CF Bobby Thomson, 3B Hank Thompson, and catcher Ray Noble in order for an impressive rookie start. He finished that rookie season without a decision, pitching 2.2 innings with a 3.38 Era.

In 1953, in his second, and last season, he appeared in 10 games, starting 5, finishing 4, over 28 innings, and coming away with a 1-2, 7.71 Era. record, along with a .222 batting average, to end his major league career. The first major league "bonus baby", one that cost the Pirates a tidy $100,000 per major league win.

In today's world he would have spent some time in the minor leagues before being introduced to big league hitting.

144. Who was the first pitcher to pitch in, and win a game in, over 45 different ballparks?

This feat takes not only longevity, but ability, and Hall of Fame resident "Smiling Tim" Keefe qualifies. The right-hander not only won 342 games, to be 10th on the all-time victory list, but he did it in 47 different parks, parks from a bygone era, but they all count.

On August 6, 1880 he made his major league mound debut, at age 23, with the Troy Trojans where he led the National League in earned run average that rookie season with an unheard of .086 Era.

During his 14-season career, predominantly with the New York Giants, "Smiling Jim" first played, when with the Troy Trojans, in Haymakers' Grounds, and the Troy Ball Club Grounds, before moving to the Polo Grounds, Metropolitan Park, St. George Grounds and the rest to make up his 47 different parks where he came away with a "W" in his ever-growing victory column.

145. When was the first time that National League teams were not required to wear "clown costumes"?

This is stretching a point just a bit, but you will see the relevance to the question in the following explanation. In 1882 the National League assigned specific stocking colors to each team. White was assigned for Chicago, gray for Buffalo, brown for Worcester, red for Boston, navy blue for Cleveland, gold for Detroit, light blue for Providence, and green for Troy. They also assigned the jersey and cap colors, not by team, but by the player's position, rather than his team.

For the 1883 season the players were relieved to learn that they would not be required to wear uniforms that they referred to as "clown costumes" which displayed different color combinations for each position, and thus created some havoc among the players.

146. Who was the first batter to come to the plate to hit with a piano leg instead of a baseball bat?

Let me set the scene for this Sunday afternoon game in Tiger Stadium, on July 15, 1973. Forty-one thousand, four hundred eleven fans sat in awe as the California Angels right-hander, Nolan Ryan, was on the verge of pitching his second no-hitter of the season, leading the Detroit Tigers 1-0 going into the top of the 8th inning. The Angels exploded for 5 runs in that inning, and Ryan, who had struck out 17 batters in the game, came into the bottom of the 9th ahead 6-0.

He retired the leadoff batter CF Mickey Stanley on a ground out to SS Rudy Meoli, DH Gates Brown lined out to Meoli, and that brought up 1B Norm Cash, who had struck out twice previously.

Cash approached the plate swinging a piano leg, and was halted by plate umpire Ron Luciano, and was told he couldn't use that to hit, and to go back and get a regulation bat. Cash responded, "Why, I can't hit him anyway." Cash got his regular bat, and proved his remarks accurate as he popped up to Meoli to end the game and give Nolan Ryan his 11th win, and his second no-hitter of the season.

147. Who was the first player to fracture his leg upon hitting a walk-off home run?

You can't make this stuff up! This is a true story about a first baseman with the Los Angeles Angels, Kendry Morales, who came up in the bottom of the 10th inning, in a 1-1 tie against the Seattle Mariners, on Saturday, May 29, 2010, and faced right-hander Brandon League with 3B Maicer Izturis on third after doubling to right field, RF Bobby Abreu on second, after an intentional walk, and CF Reggie Willits who was on first due to an error by Seattle 2B Chone Figgins.

With the bases full, and the 39,382 fans chanting for a base hit of any kind, the Cuban-born slugger fulfilled their dreams by smashing a grand slam walk-off home run to deep center field to give the Angels a 5-1 victory. As Morales stepped on home plate he was mobbed by teammates who hoisted him in celebration, and in so doing he came down hard and fractured his leg. He may have become a "Groundbreaker" that day, but he also became a leg breaker in doing so.

148. Who is the first, and only known, player to have two different color eyes?

This may take the esoteric to the extreme, but by its unusualness it does make an interesting sidelight when a pitcher looks down to get the sign from his battery mate.

Right-hander Max Scherzer, formerly with the Arizona Diamondbacks, and currently with the Detroit Tigers, has a left iris that is brown, and a right one that is blue. It obviously doesn't affect his pitching ability for he's won 27 games in two seasons since coming over to the American League.

149. Who was the first full-bearded major league player in modern day baseball?

This is a typical "Cup of Coffee" story. This player had bounced around the minor leagues for a few years, including pitching for the bearded "House of David" team during the summer of 1934 until the right-hander was spotted pitching an exhibition game in Baltimore, by Albany, Georgia manager, Jim Cambria, who set up a tryout with Joe Cronin's 7th place Washington, pitching against the Senators' regulars. Seeing he had decent speed, a good curve ball, and change-up, Allen "Bullet Ben" Benson was signed as a free agent to a contract on August 13, 1934.

His major league debut came on Sunday, August 19, 1934, at Griffith

Stadium, against the Chicago White Sox right-hander Milt Gaston. "Bullet Ben" lasted until there were two out in the 8th inning when a blister developed, and he had to give way to Alex "Red" McColl who finished up, taking the loss as Chicago nosed out Washington, 9-8.

Benson's first start showed 39 batters faced over 7.2 innings pitched, giving up 7 earned runs, 5 walks and 4 strikeouts.

His second start, on Sunday, August 26th, he faced right-hander Jack Knott, of the St. Louis Browns, in Griffith Stadium, and lasted two innings as he faced just 14 batters giving up 10 hits, 7 runs, 6 earned, before giving way to Red McColl as the Brownies rolled to a 9-5 win. The following day "Bullet" Ben was released, but as he remarked, upon his release, "I was in the major leagues just long enough to have a cup of coffee."

He remains today as the first player in the 20th century to sport a full beard while playing. It would be 40 years later until another bearded player came on the scene.

150. Who was the first player to receive his league's MVP Award, League Championship Series MVP, and the World Series MVP all in the same year?

The 1979 season was quite a rewarding one for "Pops", the Pittsburgh Pirates first baseman, as Willie Stargell tied with fellow first baseman, Keith "Mex" Hernandez of the St. Louis Cardinals, as co-recipients of the National League's Most Valuable Player Award.

It didn't stop there for Willie as he helped take his Pirates to a three-game sweep of the Cincinnati Reds in the LCS by hitting two home runs, driving in six, and batting .455 in the series, and then went on to hit three home runs, driving in seven runs, and batting .400 in the World Series as Pittsburgh defeated the Baltimore Orioles in seven games to become World Champions and giving Willie the World Series MVP, his third award in 1979.

151. Who was the first African-American broadcaster in major league baseball history?

Bill White's successful career began when he made his major league debut on May 7, 1956, hitting a home run in his first major league at bat, with the New York Giants, and carried over with them to San Francisco in 1958. In 1959 this first baseman went to the St. Louis Cardinals till 1965, then on to the Philadelphia Phillies from 1966-68. In 1969 he came back to the Cardinals, playing his final game on September 22, 1969, showing a career .286 batting average, 202 home runs, and 810 runs batted in, seven Gold Gloves, and eight All-Star games.

On February 10, 1971 White was hired to do play-by-play for the New York Yankees, and joined Phil Rizzuto, and Frank Messer in the booth to become the first Afro-American to broadcast major league games. He left the booth with the Yankees and became the President of the National League from 1989 till 1994.

152. Who was the first player to turn an unassisted triple play, and also hit for the cycle?

On Friday, July 8, 1994 the Seattle Mariners brought rookie shortstop Alex Rodriguez into Fenway Park to make his major league debut, against the Red Sox. He would be a witness to history, performed for only the 10th time in major league history.

In the 6th inning, with Seattle up 2-0, 1B Mike Blowers opened up the inning by singling to centerfield off Red Sox southpaw Chris Nabholz. RF Keith Mitchell then walked, bringing up DH Marc Newfield. With the runners going with the pitch, Newfield laced a liner to SS John Valentin, who stepped on second to double off Blowers, then tagged Mitchell coming down from first for the unassisted triple play. The 33,355 in attendance were treated well with their Sox winning, 4-3, and Valentin hitting a solo home run in the 6th, and history made with the unassisted triple play, and watched A-Rod, who went 0 for 3 at the plate, make his major league debut.

Now for the second half of the story. That took place on Thursday, June 6, 1996, also at Fenway when a pair of Sox, White and Red, hooked up before 24,382. Chicago southpaw Joe Magrane was on the mound for the Pale Hose, and John Valentin liked his servings as he hit a two-run home run to deep left field, scoring 2B Jeff Frye in the 1st, tripled to center in the 3rd, singled to left, scoring CF Dwayne Hosey in the 4th, and completed the cycle with a double to left field in the 6th, all off the offerings of Magrane. Boston went on to a 7-4 win.

Valentin became a "Groundbreaker" that day by being the first to turn an unassisted triple play, and then hit for the cycle.

153. Who was the first major league baseball player to develop and market his own mobile game?

"Buster Bash" was a game developed and marketed by San Francisco Giants catcher Gerald "Buster" Posey, and launched in August 2012, for Apple mobile devices. It offers baseball fans a chance to hit home runs against a virtual pitcher.

154. Who was the first grandfather to hit a major league home run?

If there ever was a grandfather who could hit a home run or even get just a base hit, "Stan the Man" would be that person.

The "Donora Dandy" as I like to call him, came up in the first inning of a Tuesday night game in Busch Stadium on September 10, 1963, before a crowd of 13,883, and greeted Chicago Cubs right-hander Glen Hobbie with a one out, two-run home run, scoring SS Dick Groat, to send the Cardinals on their way to an 8-0 win. It had to make Musial the grandfather of the year for no other one had ever hit a major league home run claiming a grandchild.

155. Who was the first National League pitcher to win an All-Star Game, and a World Series game in the same season?

The 2012 season was quite an exciting one for San Francisco Giants fans, but also one of great accomplishment for their ace right-hander Matt Cain.

The string of his accomplishments started on June 13th when he threw the first perfect game in Giants history, and the 22nd in major league history, when he shut down the Houston Astros, 10-0, striking out 14, before 42,298 at AT&T Park.

He followed that up by being named the starting, and winning pitcher, in the 83rd All-Star Game on Tuesday night, July 10, 2012, at Kaufman Stadium, Kansas City, as the National League cruised to an 8-0 win.

Moving on to the post season the Giants met the Cincinnati Reds in the National League Division Series, and here Cain shined again when on Thursday, October 11, 2012 at the Great American Ball Park, he won the deciding Game 5, 6-4, sending the Giants into the NL Championship Series against the St. Louis Cardinals.

In a hard fought series Cain was called upon to pitch the 7th and deciding game on Monday night, October 22, 2012, before a crowd of 43,056 at AT&T Park and came through once again with a 9-0 shutout to send the Giants into the World Series.

The first two games of the World Series started in AT&T Park where the Giants took both games. Going to Comerica Park, Detroit, for the next three games, the Giants took Game 3 and on Sunday night, October 28, 2012 Matt Cain was selected to start, and close out, the series and he didn't disappoint by going seven innings, and leaving after seven innings with the game tied 3-3, and the Giants pulling out the game in the 10th inning 4-3, with right-handed reliever Santiago Casilla credited with the win and the Giants with the World Championship.

So Cain not only won the All-Star Game, and a World Series Game to be the first National Leaguer to do so, and also the deciding games of the NLDS and NLCS to boot.

156. Who was the first catcher to win the Rookie-of-the-Year and Most Valuable Player Awards, and a World Championship in his career?

When Johnny "Little General" Bench made his major league debut at age 19, as a catcher for the Cincinnati Reds, on August 28, 1967 he was tagged as a "can't miss."

The proof began the following year when Bench was named the National League Rookie of the Year with a .275 batting average, 15 home runs, and 82 runs driven in.

In 1970 he was named the MVP with a season .293 batting average, and a league leading 45 home runs and 148 runs driven in. He came back in 1972 to win his second MVP Award by leading the National League with 40 home runs, 125 runs driven in, 12 sacrifices, and 23 intentional walks, but with just a .270 batting average.

Then he, and the Big Red Machine, went on to win the 1975 World Series. The "Little General" led the way by being the first catcher to capture all three achievements in his career when it came to a close on September 29, 1983.

Thurman Munson, in 1977, after winning the World Series with the New York Yankees that year, became the second to do so, and Buster Posey rounded out the trio with the San Francisco Giants by winning both the MVP and the World Championship in 2012.

THE ROSTER OF GROUNDBREAKERS

B.

Jennings, Hughie, I-70
Jennings, Jason, A-202, F-53
Jensen, Jackie, I-29, N-63
Jeter, Derek, I-136, M-149, M-327, N-130
Jethroe, Sam, M-29
John, Tommy, I-49, J-6
Johnson, "Ban", N-58
Johnson, Davey, B-265, K-19, L-55
Johnson, Ken, A-56
Johnson, Lance, B-219, M-169
Johnson, Randy, A-110, A-147, A-151, A-168, A-212, I-161, M-40, M-42, M-109
Johnson, Walter, A-26, A-57, A-90, A-140, J-2, M-102, N-50
Johnston, Doc and Jimmy, G-32, I-46
Jones, Andruw, I-108, L-52, M-327, M-329
Jones, Charles "Bumpus", F-46
Jones, Charley, B-95
Jones, Chipper, I-120, M-51, M-329
Jones, Mack, L-7
Jones, "Sad Sam", A-198
Jones, "Toothpick Sam", A-4, A-5
Joss, Addie, A-206, J-41
Judge, Joe, B-277
Jumonville, George, B-275

K.

Kaat, Jim, C-66
Kamm, Willie, F-44
Kanehl, Rod, M-95
Kansas City Royals, M-7, M-232, M239, M-255
Kauff, Benny, D-37
Kavanagh, Marty, B-218
Keefe, "Smiling Tim", N-144
Kekich, Mike, N-139
Keller, Charlie, I-62
Kendall, Jason, C-13
Kennedy, Vern, M-211
Key, Jimmy, A-150
Killebrew, Harmon, B-315
Killian, "Twilight Ed", A-142
Kinder, Ellis, B-279
Kiner, Ralph, H-24, M-57
King, Hal, M-323

S.

CPSIA information can be obtained at www.ICGtesting.com
Printed in the USA
BVOW071228040613

322403BV00002B/79/P